T0299275

An Economic History of Nineteenth-Century Europe

Why did some countries and regions of Europe reach high levels of economic advancement in the nineteenth century, while others were left behind? This new transnational survey of the continent's economic development highlights the role of regional differences in shaping each country's economic path and outcome. Presenting a clear and cogent explanation of the historical causes of advancement and backwardness, Ivan Berend integrates social, political, institutional, and cultural factors as well as engaging in debates about the relative roles of knowledge, the state, and institutions. Featuring boxed essays on key personalities including Adam Smith, Friedrich List, Gustave Eiffel, and the Krupp family, as well as brief histories of innovations such as the steam engine, vaccinations, and the cooperative system, the book helps to explain the theories and macroeconomic trends that dominated the century and their impact on the subsequent development of the European economy right up to the present day.

IVAN T. BEREND is Distinguished Professor in the Department of History at the University of California, Los Angeles (UCLA). His publications include *An Economic History of Twentieth-Century Europe: Economic Regimes from Laissez-Faire to Globalization* (Cambridge, 2006) and *Europe since 1980* (Cambridge, 2010).

An Economic History of Nineteenth-Century Europe

Diversity and Industrialization

IVAN T. BEREND

CAMBRIDGE
UNIVERSITY PRESS

CAMBRIDGE
UNIVERSITY PRESS

University Printing House, Cambridge CB2 8BS, United Kingdom

One Liberty Plaza, 20th Floor, New York, NY 10006, USA

477 Williamstown Road, Port Melbourne, VIC 3207, Australia

314-321, 3rd Floor, Plot 3, Splendor Forum, Jasola District Centre, New Delhi - 110025, India

79 Anson Road, #06-04/06, Singapore 079906

Cambridge University Press is part of the University of Cambridge.

It furthers the University's mission by disseminating knowledge in the pursuit of education, learning and research at the highest international levels of excellence.

www.cambridge.org
Information on this title: www.cambridge.org/9781107689992

First published 2013

A catalogue record for this publication is available from the British Library

Library of Congress Cataloging in Publication data
Berend, T. Iván (Tibor Iván), 1930–
An economic history of nineteenth-century Europe : diversity and industrialization / Iván T. Berend.
p.   cm.
Includes bibliographical references and index.
ISBN 978-1-107-03070-1
1. Europe – Economic conditions – Regional disparities.   I. Title.
HC240.B3947   2012
330.94′028 – dc23   2012015392

ISBN 978-1-107-03070-1 Hardback
ISBN 978-1-107-68999-2 Paperback

I dedicate this work to the postwar generations of economic historians with whom I have had intellectual contact, been acquainted, and whom I have befriended, and, most of all, from whom I have learned immensely throughout my career:

György Ránki, lifelong friend and co-author

Derek Aldcroft, Paul Bairoch, Theo Barker, Luben Berov, Knut Borchardt, Jean Bouvier, V. I. Bovikin, Fernand Braudel, Rondo Cameron, Alfred Chandler, Carlo Cipolla, Nicholas Crafts, François Crouzet, Barry Eichengreen, Michael Flinn, Alexander Gerschenkron, Max Hartwell, Rita Hjerppe, Eric Hobsbawm, Michael Kaser, Arnošt Klima, Jürgen Kocka, Zbigniew Landau, David Landes, Angus Maddison, Peter Mathias, Herbert Matis, Alan Milward, Joel Mokyr, Giorgio Mori, Douglas North, Patrick O'Brien, Zsigmond Pál Pach, Michael Palairet, Sidney Pollard, Michael Postan, Barry Supple, Alice Teichova, Jerzi Tomaszewski, Gianni Toniolo, Gabriel Tortella, Clive Trebilcock, Jan de Vries, Herman Van der Wee, Anthony Wrigley, and Vera Zamani.

Contents

Boxes

Figures

Maps

Tables

Preface

In 2006, Cambridge University Press published my *An Economic History of Twentieth-Century Europe: Economic Regimes from Laissez-Faire to Globalization*. The book was met with an unexpected level of interest, and has been published in thirteen languages. This level of attention has encouraged me to go back to discover the deeper roots of Europe's contemporary economy – back to the nineteenth century, the period of the most dramatic discontinuity in European history. This earlier period is not unknown to me. I conducted research on the peripheral regions for about two decades, and published several related works with my late colleague and friend, György Ránki, in the 1970s and 1980s (Berend and Ránki, 1974, 1982, 1987). I am revisiting this topic after a quarter of a century.

Writing an economic history of an entire continent and over a long time period is a gargantuan task for any single person. My work, however, has benefited greatly from the extensive research and publications of hundreds of my American and European colleagues, whose works are broadly quoted in this book. Their works were mostly available in the outstanding Charles Young Research Library of UCLA.

I am extremely grateful to my anonymous reviewers for Cambridge University Press, who assisted me with their critical remarks and suggestions based on a previous version of this work. I am in debt to my commissioning editor, Michael Watson, with whom I have had an excellent work history for more than a decade preparing and publishing three books.

My intellectual home, the History Department of the University of California, Los Angeles, has provided a harmonious and inspiring environment for my work. As always, I am most grateful to my wife Kati, who has carried a heavy burden during the years of my long workdays, conjuring up – adequately to the topic – the workdays of early capitalism. She has greatly assisted me in conducting my library research and finalizing the manuscript with her invaluable critical mind and editorial talent.

Introduction

Nineteenth-century economic history is flourishing again. New generations of historians and economists have returned to discover its secrets. Since, as Benedetto Croce once noted ([1921] 1960), every history is contemporary because historians are most influenced by the present,[1] the ongoing integration of Europe and the advance of globalization during the recent decades have called attention to the historical roots and outcomes of similar processes in the past. Although "we cannot know everything that happened," and "there is a vast iceberg of the unknown that remains forever hidden" (Ged, 2004, 246), the generation of economic historians working today have made new calculations, applied new theories from other social sciences, especially economics, to history, dug out new sources, and discovered much more about the nineteenth century than did their predecessors one or two generations before. Additionally, the scope of historical interest is also significantly broadened. Virtually all of the specific areas of social sciences became and are part of history, thus society, behavioral patterns, psychological reactions, political choices, and the impact of the laws of economics on economic performance all require consideration and inclusion. This is the basis of ongoing debate over, and formidable challenges to, several previous interpretations.

This work delves deeply into these discussions. Based on my lifelong research on economic backwardness and peripheral economies, and a vast amount of information and evidence produced and accumulated by generations of historians, this book compiles and explains the historical material around a central hypothesis.

1

Content and comparative method: pan-European interconnections, major regional differences

The core idea of this book is that Europe's economy has developed in a closely interrelated environment, and that a single country or region's case cannot possibly be understood without those interconnections. Interrelated European development, however, did not produce a similar economic level throughout the continent. Huge regional differences remained characteristic. Some regions achieved high levels of industrialization and progress while others preserved various levels of backwardness.

Europe was a continent of independent nation-states; consequently, most of the economic history books, including several previous economic histories of Europe, have rigorously followed a country-by-country approach.[2] This tradition, however, has been strongly challenged in recent decades. Indeed, industrialization, the driving force of nineteenth-century economic development, and the rise of modern transportation and banking systems, were all transnational. The development of some countries often had a positive impact on others. Trade with Britain held advantages for, and had a stimulating effect on, its less industrialized neighbors. As Sidney Pollard maintains, Britain "was a major channel of transmission of the process of industrialization ... [which] equipped her rivals ... The benefits of the British connection for Germany [were] widely recognized ..." (Pollard, 1981, 183–4).

Ireland's or Denmark's ties to Britain; Hungary's ties to Austria and the Czech lands; Poland, Finland, and the Baltic countries' ties to the Russian Empire: all had a huge influence on these countries' development. Direct British, French, and German investments, and the enormous market that these countries provided (buying about 70 percent of all exported goods), often played a more important role in shaping the economies of Spain, Portugal, and Italy than did the policies and tariff systems of the latter's national governments. It was equally likely that the competition of the more developed neighbor had a negative economic impact on its less developed adjacent areas. Portugal, Romania, the borderlands of Austria-Hungary, and the entire Balkan area are compelling examples. Besides, despite the rise of sacrosanct nation-states in the nineteenth century, national units in Europe were of questionable importance in that period during which borders often changed dramatically.[3]

Technology and innovation, so characteristic of the period, extend across borders and are not contained by national boundaries. As Joseph Schumpeter stated more than seventy years ago: "A process such as railroadization or electrification transcends the boundaries of individual countries" (Schumpeter, 1939, 666). Forty years later S. Pollard concurred: "Advanced technology shifted constantly outwards . . . thus . . . driving the whole of Europe" (Pollard, 1981b, 38).

Economic assumptions and the institutions they generated also spread throughout the continent. The theories of Great Britain's Adam Smith and David Ricardo created the economic systems of most European countries.[4] Germany's Friedrich List became the prophet of protectionism throughout the less developed European regions. The free trade system, the gold standard, modern property rights, and a host of other new institutions spread throughout and conquered the continent. At the end of the century, all the countries of Europe had similar economic institutions and legal systems. They all had mixed banking and similarly functioning central banks. Europe had become "Europeanized."

Two clever metaphors illustrate this point quite well. François Crouzet likens European industrialization to "an epidemic [that] took little notice of national borders and crossed them with ease" (Crouzet, 2001, 120). Carlo Cipolla suggests looking at Europe from without. He proposes that a hypothetical "Asian historian" might look at World War I, which ended the "long" nineteenth-century history of Europe, as "the European Civil War" (Cipolla, 1994, 278).

Central to this book's hypothesis is the *comparative method*. Here, however, we must ask what kind of comparison? Hans-Gerhard Haupt and Jürgen Kocka have distinguished two basic types of comparative method, one that aims at "weighing contrasts . . . [and] differences between individual comparative cases," and the other that "focus[es] on . . . generalization and, thus, the understanding of general patterns" (Haupt and Kocka, 2009, 2).[5] This book offers the second type by differentiating various patterns of development and regional types of economic progress.

Comparison is a major source of new knowledge since it compares similarities and differences between countries, regions, or continents. It enables one to measure the roles of various growth factors by comparing their importance and effects in some areas and the lack of them in others. Why did certain factors assist economic development in some countries while they failed to have the same effect in another? Why was an institution efficient here but inefficient there? Why did certain regions follow paths to economic development that were different from those of others? Some new pan-European economic histories have already been published.[6] This book, however, represents a different type of comparative generalization, and discusses various types of paths of modern economic transformation based on strong empirical information in a consistent pan-European economic environment. It also calls attention to the Western European impact on economic transformation before and during a strongly Western European-based "British" Industrial Revolution. My findings demonstrate that a prevailing northwest European Enlightenment and technological change penetrated Europe over time, and pan-European integration became the driving force of transformation throughout the continent, although with rather different outcomes. This also clarifies that independent nation-states were not decisive factors of success and failure. While several independent nation-states failed, several (though not all) of the occupied and politically oppressed countries that had became parts of multinational empires had in fact profited from their positions of attachment to more – but also less – developed empires.

The main goal of this book is to present the distinct *regional differences* that characterized the economic paths and their outcomes in the inter-related continent during the century. In addition to the evidence-based description of these differences, it will proffer a complex explanation of their causes. "To take any unit disconnected from others... is in itself false," affirmed Lev Tolstoy in his astonishing discussion on history in *War and Peace*.[7] Following this advice, I reject the simplified, sometimes mono-causal argumentations that so often frequent the literature. They overemphasize one or two "main" causes, such as geopolitical factors occasionally combined with natural endowments, or the availability of free labor and capital, or the central role of certain institutions, or the prevalence or lack of certain "virtues" and values. Instead, I try to present the *complexity* of causes and their *combinations*.

I believe in path dependence in a complex way. Paths, however, are not determined strictly by the past. Besides the vertical connections in history, additional important effects and influences arise from the horizontal interrelationships among various regions. The more successful development paths have a demonstrational effect, attracting other regions to emulate that success. Successful development paths also initiate direct connections among regions, offering markets, capital investments, technology transfers, raw materials, and food resources that, in the long run, pave the way to changes in other regions.

Special attention is given here to *knowledge* that expands from one country or region to the other. The role of knowledge has recently received enormous attention in history literature.[8] This discovery is not new. Even the late eighteenth-century observers of the emerging British miracle recognized its central importance. The German Johann Gottfried Herder, in his *Journal Meiner Reise im Jahr 1769*, recognized that England "possessed a number of peculiar advantages," among them "its maritime position, its institutions, its freedom, its *Kopf*" (head, or mind). Emma Rothschild noted that "England's destiny, in the view of these foreign observers, [was] determined in substantial part by the *English Kopf*... a revolution which unfolded... in the minds of the people" (Rothschild, 2002, 31–3; italics added).

Knowledge revealed by science is applied to education; education is institutionalized by modern states and permeates new generations. Knowledge may challenge the legacy of the past and effect change and discontinuity. An important intention of this book is to present the interrelationship between the historical past, formed by long-standing and complex social-political and economic developments, and the prevailing situation in nineteenth-century Europe – hence the interrelationship between various paths of development that characterized different regions of an interrelated Europe. I discuss the features of the broad historical – social, political, institutional, and cultural – environment in separate chapters and sections of this book, introducing and describing the economic paths of various specific regions. Historical processes have an almost opaque complexity. Social, political, economic, and cultural spheres, and their embodiment in institutions, are closely and inseparably interrelated. They generate and influence each other.

The early dissolution or non-existence of serfdom in northwestern Europe during the late medieval and early modern periods fostered the development of urban settlement and self-government, liberated these societies from religious fundamentalism, and laid the foundation for the Renaissance, Reformation, scientific advancement, innovation, and education – most of which emerged in the region much earlier than in other parts of Europe. It was here that new institutions arose that facilitated the development of a market economy and modern companies. As a result, people gradually developed new values and attitudes toward work and business. They invested more labor input and turned to the market. This *Zeitgeist* prepared the ground for the rise of merchant capitalism and merchant empires, which in turn paved the way for industrial capitalism. The regions where these characteristics were strongest became the forerunners of transformation. Other areas, which shared similar qualities but developed and emphasized them less strongly, were able to follow relatively soon.

In contrast, industrial capitalism could not gain ground easily in regions where serfdom continued, aristocratic rule endured, obsolete institutions were preserved, social mobility was extremely circumscribed, and the mostly illiterate peasant masses were excluded from society. Similarly, industrialization could not permeate regions where a communal peasant society was preserved and egalitarian values dominated. Hence, social-political and economic institutional structures, coupled with the prevailing cultural values, created the appropriate historical environment for a society's modern economic transformation or lack thereof.

Interrelated Europe: four distinctive paths towards modern economic transformation

The closely interrelated European "cape of Asia," with its relatively small territory comprising 9.9 million square kilometers (3.9 million square miles), was hardly a homogeneous economic unit. Given the long-standing core–periphery relations[9] that had emerged during the early modern period, one can clearly differentiate among markedly *diverse regions* within Europe. This simple truth, however, requires some qualification. What does one mean by "region"? Disagreements about regions are many, for there are competing concepts of what a region actually entails.

Some authors, such as Anthony Wrigley and Sidney Pollard, prefer a *micro-regional approach to European history*.[10] This is absolutely legitimate since micro-regional differences in one single country are widespread and significant. Indeed these are sometimes as significant as macro-regional differences between core and periphery. However, within a macro-region hundreds of micro-regional differences would have to be distinguished and discussed and so I will not attempt to combine the two approaches in this book. I will, though, engage with the new economic geography which makes clear that backward and advanced regions within the same country cannot be separated. Advanced urban industry is built on "backward" agricultural regions behind it.

My book represents a rather different and consistent *macro-regional approach*. This is one of the most important novelties of this study. Macro-regions – with major differences in region formation – have been differentiated by several authors. In our *Industrialization and the European Periphery*, György Ránki and I discussed the special characteristics of three peripheries, the Scandinavian, Mediterranean, and Central and Eastern European, in the long nineteenth century (Berend and Ránki, 1982). Sidney Pollard in *Peaceful Conquest* differentiates between four, chronologically defined regions: "the first industrializer," Britain; the "early industrializer advanced western half of the continent;" the third wave of industrializer, "Inner Europe;" and, lastly, the fourth-wave industrializer peripheries, such as Scandinavia, the Mediterranean region, the entire Habsburg Empire, the Balkans, and Russia (Pollard, 1981). In their monumental *Power and Plenty*, Ronald Findlay and Kevin O'Rourke distinguish seven world zones, of which only two are European: the "Roman Catholic Western European" and the "Greek Orthodox Eastern European" regions. In this scheme, Mediterranean Europe, Poland, Hungary, and Croatia all belong to Western Europe (Findlay and O'Rourke, 2007).

The Cambridge Economic History of Modern Europe differentiates between advanced and less developed areas or countries, but, rather than making consistent regional distinctions, it employs a "counterpointing" method of noting differences within a unified European environment. At times it creates categories such as Northwestern European – including, among others, Britain, Norway, and Finland – Southern European – where France, Italy, Spain, Greece, and Portugal are together – and Central Eastern European – with Switzerland, Germany, Austria-Hungary, Romania, Serbia, and Bulgaria in one group – in various tables (see, e.g., Broadberry and O'Rourke, 2007, II, 70). These regions, however, reflect geographical units rather than relatively consistent economic regions.

The regional approach in this book offers a new type of comparative analysis. Regarding the advanced, industrialized West European region, it discusses the industrialization process by differentiating between three main variants: the exceptional British, followed by some others; industrialization based on agriculture and food processing; and industrialization based on the second Industrial Revolution, led by the chemical and electric industries from the late nineteenth century. Although "clear types" hardly exist, this distinction sheds light on major sub-regional differences.

The macro-regions, discussed in separate sections and chapters, are composed of countries and parts of countries that exhibited a relatively similar economic performance and reached a relatively similar economic level at the end of the period under review. Chapter 1 presents the rise of the pioneering early modern development of Northwestern Europe, crowned by the Industrial Revolution; Chapter 2 discusses the West European "core," including the Scandinavian periphery that successfully joined; and the focus of Chapter 3 is on the peripheries with their three different types and levels of relative backwardness. At the two ends of the spectrum, by 1913 the least industrialized regions reached only one-third to less than half of the per capita income level of the most industrialized ones. In the regions that followed the most successful path of modern transformation, 35–40 percent of the active population worked in industry, and 25–30 percent in agriculture, prior to World War I. Other regions, trapped in a dead-end trajectory, exhibited 75–80 percent agricultural employment and only 7–10 percent industrial employment. In the former regions life expectancy increased to fifty years; in the latter ones it was fifteen years less. In the former regions, illiteracy disappeared; in the latter, it characterized 70–75 percent of the population.[11]

Countries and regions that followed different paths achieved different levels of modern development. I differentiate between *four primary paths of European economic development that created distinctive regional types*, with different levels of economic advancement, in the "long" nineteenth century (see Map I.1). Each path and type was dominant in a geographical area, though almost none of them were homogeneous geographical units.

The *path of successful modernization and industrialization* predominated in Western Europe, albeit in three distinct ways. "Western Europe" in this sense did not comprise the Irish part of Great Britain and the eastern provinces of a united Germany, but it did include the northern parts of a united Italy and the western Austrian-Bohemian part of the Habsburg Empire. The quite homogeneous Scandinavian region, which exhibited backward peripheral economic characteristics until 1870, was able to join the West on the path of successful industrialization because of its non-peripheral social-political-institutional structures.

Vast regions, however, were unable to progress on the main path of successful industrialization and fell behind. Some of them, those that took *the second path*, were able to attain a certain level of modernization, but they did not become industrialized even though they had developed agricultural-industrial structures and had reached medium income levels compared with the rest of Europe. This development trend was most typical in Central Europe and the Baltic area, but Finland and Ireland also progressed in this way.

Some regions tardily took a *third path* to modern transformation around the turn of the century. Their transformations were very late and painfully partial. While modern transformation began during the last two decades before World War I, these regions were unable to eliminate their pre-industrial economy. The regions on this path remained almost entirely agricultural, only partially modernized, and preserved traditional institutions, illiteracy, and a low cultural level. However, some pockets of a modern economy emerged, which paved the way for future development. Russia, the Iberian peninsula, and southern Italy exhibited this development path in the most typical way.

The *fourth path* turned out to be a dead-end entirely. The regions that succumbed to this were characterized by a total lack of industrialization, with only a semblance of modernization in other sectors of the economy. These regions remained behind by a century, exhibiting the lowest income level in Europe, the most traditional demographic trends, and mass

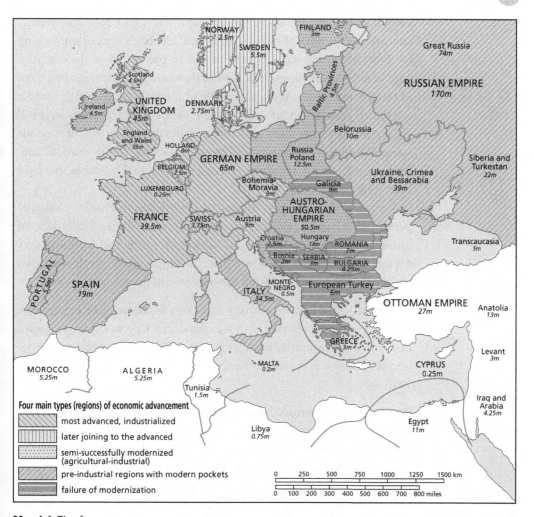

Map I.1 The four main types (regions) of economic advancement (McEvedy, 2002, 37)

illiteracy. This path was dominant in the Balkans and the easternmost and southernmost borderlands of the Habsburg Empire.

The different historical paths and outcomes, and the various development levels, are explained in the context of their past development and the nineteenth-century environment, the level and role of knowledge, culture, behavioral pattern, and the main characteristics of the social-political systems, state activities, and institution-building.

Debates and differences

Covering the economic history of an entire continent over a time-span of more than a century, I naturally confront myriad views and concepts.

I agree with many and disagree with not a few. This book consequently comprises a number of implicit and explicit debates. Since I am writing for a broader audience, I do not intend to present all of the extensive and, in many cases, unresolved debates that have emerged regarding most of the covered topics. At the given state of research, often a single, simple question is answered in three or four different ways.[12] In my narrative, I will present a view that in many cases incorporates the solid results of previous research, and will mention only some of the debates. In this introduction, however, allow me to review several major conceptual questions that have been subject to debate.

Various paths and regional disparities in nineteenth-century economic performance have caused economic *backwardness*. This is a highly debated historical question. In his seminal work from nearly half a century ago, Alexander Gerschenkron suggests that each European country is somewhat less developed as one goes from the west toward the east and south.

Few would disagree that Germany was more backward than France; that Austria was more backward than Germany; that Italy was more backward than any of the countries just mentioned. Similarly, few would deny England the position of the most advanced country of the time. (Gerschenkron, 1962, 44)

Based on Gerschenkron's theory that state intervention characterizes countries of severe backwardness, Sidney Pollard discusses in *Peaceful Conquest* (1981b) the separate national cases of the peripheries without classifying them as archetypes. Paraphrasing Lev Tolstoy's famous first sentence in *Anna Karenina* ("All happy families are alike, each unhappy family is unhappy in its own way."), Joel Mokyr expresses the same view: "all rich and successful economies are alike, every economic failure fails in its own way" (Mokyr, 2006, 12). In other words, one cannot generalize economic failures but must discuss each case separately. I disagree. Just as successful economies exhibit certain general patterns and have pursued certain paths to economic success, so too economic failures exhibit certain typical paths and patterns. My regionalization, as briefly discussed above, is thus rather different: based on consistent social-economic development levels, I form three different *types* of backward regions: a few Central European countries, the Baltic areas, Finland, and Ireland are semi-successful by reaching the agrarian-industrial structure and a medium income level within Europe; Russia, Spain, Portugal, and southern Italy remained pre-industrial, but with pockets of modernization; while the Balkan region, together with the borderlands of the Habsburg Empire, failed to modernize or industrialize.

Furthermore, Scandinavia, north Italy, and the Austrian-Czech provinces of the Habsburg Empire neared Western levels of development before World War I and thus, in my categorization, belong not to the peripheries (as according to Pollard) but to the West European macro-region. In this book, consequently, I will present different types and levels of backwardness. But what is the meaning of the term "backwardness"?

Backwardness is a relative concept, determined by comparing the economic performance of different countries or regions. Comparative backwardness of countries and regions is often measured by income or gross domestic product (GDP), either in official exchange rate parity or, more commonly, in purchasing power parity (PPP).[13] Income level alone, however, cannot directly reflect important social and cultural factors. This consideration has led to the introduction of the so-called "human development index," which, in addition to income level, includes literacy rate, enrollment in all levels of educational institutions, and life expectancy – thus measuring the quality of education and health conditions of a given country.[14] Addressing relative backwardness, I will discuss several other structural and qualitative factors of the economies of the various regions as well.[15] In this comparative economic history, I present the historical differences of various non-economic factors of backwardness, such as social, educational, and political conditions and the "social capability" to absorb new technology. On that basis, this book presents *various types of backwardness* and avoids commonly used euphemisms that, for instance, redefine south Italian backwardness as "difficult modernization" and present it as a mere cultural representation (Moe, 2002). My approach opposes the postmodern historiography that rejects making value judgments and prefers to speak about social-cultural differences, and, for example, replaces the concept of Balkan backwardness with the sanguine notion of a "different civilization."[16]

Backwardness is a harsh reality, and it is not the construct of bias or cultural prejudice. It not only indicates different consumption patterns, but also expresses radically different patterns of the quality and standard of living. Backwardness means having less food to eat and less clothing to wear, living in inferior or substandard housing, receiving less or lower-quality healthcare and education, and enjoying less entertainment and culture. "Perceptions" alone cannot explain away the fact that advanced countries and regions had two to three times more goods and services available for their population than did backward ones. "Different cultures" cannot justify the fact that in nineteenth-century Europe people in advanced regions had a life expectancy of fifty-five years, while those in backward regions had that of only thirty-five years.

Another major debate revolves around the *role of institutions* in economic development. Institutional economics and institutional economic history present institutions as the central determinant of economic performance. While I accept the major role of institutions, I nonetheless view them as only a part of the whole package of historical factors that influence economic performance. The amalgamation of rules and institutions is part of a historical legacy. History changed, over time, the behavioral culture and dominant value systems that were the sources of institution-building. This complexity will be presented as the cradle of certain paths of economic development.

Furthermore, institutions are mostly established by the state. The *role of the state* is, however, much broader than simply creating the legal and institutional "rules of the game." The state's modern financing and monetary policy, its building of infrastructure, its tariff and trade policy, its active role in industrial development are all equally important factors. Just as entrepreneurial states are crucial players in economic progress, the predatory state, in contrast, with its oppressive, kleptocratic, corrupt practices, is a central obstacle to economic advance. Therefore the same institution that worked well in certain regions would become inefficient in another. A dearth of certain institutions did not preclude progress and growth in some countries but very much did so in others.[17]

Resources were extremely abundant in Russia, in some ways similar to the case in Britain, but that did not make the country advanced. Protective tariffs in the eighteenth century elevated Britain to the top of the heap, but the same did not happen to Russia and Spain a century later. A centralized state was one of the advantages that Britain enjoyed, but it did not help Russia. The decisive role of Parliament after 1688 is believed to have been a major advantage for British economic development, but it caused chaos and backwardness in Poland. The patent system encouraged innovation in several Western countries, but its long absence did not hinder development in Switzerland. "Power," especially naval power, became an important contributing factor in British economic success and its accumulation of "plenty," but military might and triumphant expansion hardly engendered plenty in Russia.

One should also consider the role of geography and climatic impacts in influencing economic progress or failure. These aspects definitely had consequences from natural resources to attitudes and life-style. The northern and southern behavioral patterns are rather different and influence economic activities, and thus a geographic-climatic approach can bring new insights, but it requires, in many respects, very different types of analysis and so is beyond the scope of this work.

The discourse regarding *revolution in economic development* is another ongoing debate. The terms "agricultural revolution," "industrial revolution," "demographic revolution," "banking revolution," and "transportation revolution" (among others) have been broadly used in economic history,[18] but recently they have been strongly challenged. Several scholars in recent decades have questioned the existence of a revolution in economic development at all. They challenge the term because "the noun 'revolution' is apt . . . to suggest rapid change," as Wrigley affirmed in his Ellen McArthur lectures at Cambridge (Wrigley, 1988, 11). The British economy, Nicholas Crafts argues in his *British Economic Growth during the Industrial Revolution* (1985), enjoyed an increasing growth rate for decades before, and did not exhibit an immediate transformation of all of its industry in the period after, the so-called Industrial Revolution. Based on his own calculations, Crafts therefore rejected the concept of revolution.

Gregory Clark similarly rejected the concept of "agricultural revolution" and instead suggested a slow, steady increase of productivity (Clark, 1993). Other scholars prefer the term "agricultural transition." In his book *The Scientific Revolution*, Steven Shapin provocatively states, "There was no such thing as the Scientific Revolution, and this is a book about it" (1996, 1). Ten years later, the prestigious *Cambridge History of Science* intentionally avoided the term "Scientific Revolution." The main reason for denying the existence of the Scientific Revolution is that the development was not a "sudden radical change" but rather a gradual one.[19]

I employ the term revolution in this book. My approach is based on Thomas S. Kuhn's *change of paradigm* concept. Kuhn established the theory of the development of science in his famous work *The Structure of Scientific Revolutions* (1962). Scientific progress, he argued, is not a cumulative process. New scientific discoveries cannot fit into existing paradigms. The basic conceptual change, or change of paradigm, comprises the essence of a scientific revolution, *regardless* of the length of the changes (Kuhn, 1962).

In this sense, the nineteenth century was, indeed, a period of a dramatic and revolutionary paradigm change. The century was the setting for crucial (though not abrupt) transformations in agriculture, industry, demography, and scientific culture, and it thus represents a major revolutionary discontinuity in European history. By the end of the long nineteenth century, there were two to three times more goods and services, food, clothing, housing, schooling, healthcare, and entertainment available for the European population than there had been at the beginning of the century (though it was hardly distributed on an equal level), and the lifespan of the better educated was often extended by some ten to fifteen years. Consequently, I do not share the view that the term "revolution" is over-used or even abused (Mokyr, 2002).

As noted above, this book is a comparative economic history of nineteenth-century Europe. This simple sentence begs two additional questions. When did the nineteenth century begin? And what kind of economic history are we talking about?

The time-span

When did the nineteenth century begin, with its dramatic discontinuity and spectacular industrialization and urbanization? In 1801, according to the calendar? In 1789, when the French Revolution changed history? In 1769, when James Watt patented the first modern steam engine heralding a new industrial age? "Deep is the well of the past. Should we not call it bottomless?" quips Thomas Mann so memorably in *Joseph and his Brothers* (Mann, 2005, 1). Indeed, one may place the starting date of those monumental changes even farther back, at the discovery of America by Europeans and the beginning of the building of colonial and commercial empires that paved the way for industrial capitalism. One might choose as the starting point the victory of Protestantism, the scientific revolution from Galileo to Newton, and the emergence of the Enlightenment.

We could therefore date the beginning of the nineteenth century back to the early modern age between the sixteenth and eighteenth centuries. Where are we to find the fundamental roots of the process that culminated in industrialization, urbanization, and the other historic changes of the nineteenth century? When did these changes actually begin? Quoting again Lev Tolstoy: "there is and can be no beginning to any event, for one event always flows uninterruptedly from another."[20] When Jan de Vries challenged the narrow chronological approach to the Industrial Revolution, he spoke about the "early modernist revolt," arguing that the industrial transformation had been rooted in earlier centuries (de Vries and Van der Woude, 1997). Soon, however, he was challenged by Jan Luiten van Zanden, who went farther back and spoke of the "revolt of the medievalists," suggesting that the transformation had an even earlier start in the late Middle Ages (Van Zanden, 2002, 635).

There is no exact date one can designate as the genuine point of departure. The late medieval handicraft industrialists of Flanders and the Italian city-states, the long-distance traders connecting the two regions, the great Dutch shipbuilders, the moneylenders and the first bankers in north Italy, all belong to this story. Changes happened gradually and multiplied continually from the late medieval period, paving the way for a series of small and big "breakthroughs" occurring one after the other.

Chasing the "origins" of historical phenomena is a rather hopeless and even misleading enterprise, as Marc Bloch warns us. Although the origins of nineteenth-century industrial-economic transformations are deeply rooted in history, the century's "moment in time" started in the late eighteenth century and continued throughout the nineteenth up to World War I (Bloch, [1941] 1992). This book is about this period. Chapter 1, however, sums up the seventeenth- and eighteenth-century developments that constituted the immediate background of the dramatic changes that took place in the long nineteenth century.

What kind of economic history?

This question is legitimate since economic history has diverged into at least two distinct schools in the past few decades. First a new trend of cliometrics[21] emerged, and it then evolved into a new discipline: *historical economics*. *Economic history* is an empirical discipline, based on narrative descriptions of vast historical material. Gathering an endless quantity of sources, economic history interprets the economic processes as part of a complex fabric of history, inseparable from social, political, and cultural development. This interdisciplinary approach may lead to a better understanding of the complexity of economic development.[22]

The other school of economic history, the new *historical economics*, is a kind of applied economics and the application of formal economic methodology to historical questions that explains certain historical processes with economic concepts and models, and abundantly employs quantitative weaponry. Participants are "motivated by current debates among academic economists and policymakers rather than following agendas set by historians" (Hatton *et al.*, 2007, 1, 2). They use the mathematical formalism of economics and reject the narrative approach of traditional economic history. Sometimes the representatives of this school go so far as to declare the "end of economic history," as it has supposedly become an "integral part" of economics (Romer, 1994). Several economic historians share the view that economic history is "running the risk of losing its own identity" (Toniolo, 2004, 92).

Economic history and historical economics gradually separated from each other. Representatives of the classical school point to the limitations of applied models of economics and the mathematization of history research. First and foremost, they argue, quantification in history and applying economic modeling clearly lead to oversimplification.[23] In several cases economic phenomena are explained by other economic phenomena, such as prices, comparative advantages, fiscal and monetary institutions, labor and capital supply, etc. (Mokyr, 2005, 287). According to one legend concerning Albert Einstein, he wrote on the blackboard of his office at Princeton: "Not everything that counts can be counted, and not everything that can be counted counts." Or in short: "what counts can't be counted."[24]

Socio-political and cultural factors, and all of those other phenomena that are impossible to quantify or incorporate into a few factors of an economic model, are evidently marginalized in historical economics, or they appear only as decorative ornaments in the analysis. In many ways, however, it is precisely those qualitative features, those knowledge, social-cultural, and behavioral patterns and those historically determined characteristics that are the most profound factors influencing economic growth. Moreover, in most cases, one given effect may be the outcome of several causes. Another limitation of historical economics is rooted in the difficulties of calculating historical figures and statistics: the earlier the period, the more fictive the figures. Generalizing from haphazardly gathered facts may cause major misinterpretations.[25] The Nobel Laureate economist, Robert Solow, expressed his doubts:

As I inspect current work in economic history, I have the sinking feeling that a lot of it looks exactly like the same kind of economic analysis . . . the same integrals, the same regressions . . . Why should I believe, when it is applied to thin eighteenth century data, something that carries no conviction when it is done with more ample twentieth century data? (Solow, 2006, 243)

As presented in this book, economic history is an independent empirical *historical* discipline[26] that "follow[s] agendas set by historians."[27] However, I clearly recognize the significant findings and contributions of the new schools. They have challenged several old interpretations and have provoked inspiring debates. Applied economic theories, calculations and quantitative analyses, the creation of new databases on economic growth, demographics, and human development, and the school's achievements in countless other areas enrich our knowledge of the past.

Fortunately, one discerns a recent trend towards a new cooperation and an integration of the different schools. Leading economists, including the Nobel Laureate Kenneth Arrow, have published a whole compendium of studies with the telling title, *History Matters: Essays on Economic Growth, Technology, and Demographic Change*. They declare: "The discipline of economics has become more open to taking explicit account of the influence of the past . . . Past dependence describes processes in which the long-run character of the system depends critically on the history of the system." They add that even "historical 'accidents' cannot be ignored," and that "small historical events . . . can have large and persistent long-run implications" (Guinnane *et al.*, 2004, 1, 2, 4). Others have expressed skepticism that one single method "can cut through the fog of history and illuminate our economic past once and for all. [We need] many approaches, including traditional ones . . . none are powerful enough to warrant scorning the others" (Hohenberg, 2008, 342). Institutionalist historians of economics have "expanded" and refined their one-sided approach to institutions by incorporating the historical background that led to new attitudes and institutions.[28] Major attempts have been made to present complex interpretations of the Industrial Revolution and the historical roots and cultural trends that led to it (Mokyr, 1999, 2002). These are positive signs of a new cooperation. Gianni Toniolo underscored the need for cooperation: "Good economic history may be found in sophisticated cliometrics as well as in refined anecdotal story telling . . . It is the combination of state-of-the-art applied economics with archival research and broad historical knowledge that provides the deepest understanding of past economic events" (Toniolo, 2004, 292). Mokyr and Voth second this appeal in one of the most important volumes that historical economists have produced: "A closer collaboration between those who want to discern general laws and those who have studied the historical facts and data closely may have a high payoff" in discovering the "far greater riches" of economic history (Mokyr and Voth, 2010, 42). In my book, I seek to coordinate, confront, and incorporate the findings of historical economics into my information- and data-based history analysis.

Notes

1. François Crouzet documented the conceptual changes of French historiography, influenced by the given state of the French economy after World War II. The "retardation-stagnation" concept, and then its revision, and the "revision of revisionism" were all "influenced by the economic and political state of France at the time they were writing" (Crouzet, 2003, 215, 230).

2. Some well-known works include Milward and Saul (1973, 1977), Trebilcock (1981), Cipolla (1973). I also published an economic history of nineteenth-century Europe with G. Ránki in Hungarian (Berend and Ránki, 1987) that was a "hybrid" – a combination of five country and four regional chapters.

3. Some nation-states of the late nineteenth century did not exist as united and independent units until the second half or the second third of the century.

Before becoming an independent state, Norway enjoyed two different statuses in the nineteenth century: a union with Denmark from 1536 to 1814, followed by a union with Sweden from 1814 to 1905, at which time Norway declared independence. Ireland, on the other hand, became part of the United Kingdom in 1801, and declared independence from Britain and signed the Anglo-Irish Treaty only after World War I. The status of the Low Countries dramatically changed several times in the early modern centuries, and again in the early nineteenth century – with Belgium becoming an independent country in 1830. Switzerland preserved its ancient confederation of thirteen small sovereign states and a few associated republics until 1798. The *Tagsatzung*, the Swiss confederate governing body, had little power over the independent *Orte* (states). Finally, in 1847, a short civil war left the Separatist League defeated, and the federal constitution of 1848 created a unified Switzerland and a national market, while preserving considerable autonomy for the cantons. It was only around the last third of the century that Germany and Italy were established as united, independent states. Alsace-Lorraine went from being part of France to being part of Germany, and Germany took Schleswig-Holstein from Denmark in the second half of the century. Finland was not yet an independent country, being an integral part of Sweden. In 1809, Finland was conquered and became part of the Russian Empire, though it gained the status of an autonomous grand duchy. Russia also annexed the entire Baltic region and two-thirds of tri-partitioned Poland. The economic trends of those conquered regions, however, were quite different from those of Russia proper. The Balkans, which belonged to the Ottoman Empire for half a millennium, for the most part became independent in the 1870s, but the newly created states changed borders upon gaining independence. After the Treaty of San Stefano (March 1878), Great Bulgaria included Macedonia, but the territory was reduced to half the size after the Treaty of Berlin in July of the same year.

4. Even in far-away early nineteenth-century Russia, the national poet Alexander Pushkin mentions Adam Smith in *Eugene Onegin*: "He cursed out Homer and Theocritus / But read Adam Smith instead, / And was a profound economist" (Douglas and Frazier, 1992).

5. Comparative history has deep roots in Germany where *Allgemeine Wirtschafts-geschichte* and *vergleichende Geschichte* were broadly practiced. In 1928, Marc Bloch's famous study in *Revue Synthèse* established his *méthode historique comparative*. With György Ránki, I published a study on our comparative concept in the *Mélanges en l'honneur de Fernand Braudel* in 1973 (Berend and Ránki, 1973). Hartmut Kaelble distinguishes four types of comparative studies: besides the classical *histoire comparée*, he speaks also about "transfer" comparison, when representation of one culture appears in another by the transmission of concept; "entangled, or shared history" of entirely different

cultures; and "histoire croisée," a combination of comparative and transfer analysis (Kaelble, 2009).

6. Sydney Pollard's *Peaceful Conquest* (1981) was a pioneering, but somewhat inconsistent attempt, since he combined a regional approach to Western Europe with a country-by-country discussion of the peripheries. François Crouzet's masterful pan-European economic history (Crouzet, 2001) covered an entire millennium and discussed the nineteenth century in one chapter. Most recently the two volumes of the *Cambridge Economic History of Modern Europe* (1700–1870, and 1870 to the present) (Broadberry and O'Rourke, 2010) has offered an "explicit pan-European approach, with the material organized by topic rather than by country" (xiii). This work, "a new comparative economic history" as they call it, was an enterprise of leading representatives of the new *historical economics* school and was "motivated by questions being posed by economists that are less nation-specific" (Hatton *et al.*, 2007, 2). Consequently, it is not a broad, empirically based comparison, presenting generalized patterns or types of development, but uses a counterpointing method to, as Haupt and Kocka phrased it, weigh "contrasts . . . [and] differences between individual comparative cases."

7. This part of the novel is published in Gardiner (1959, 179).

8. This was certainly inspired by the present experience of "knowledge-based economy." One of the best examples is Mokyr (2002).

9. The history of this concept goes back to Rosa Luxemburg's agrarian "third person" as a crucial market for the rich countries (Luxemburg, [1913] 1975), to Nikolai Bukharin's country and metropolis metaphor (Bukharin [1915] 1966), to "industrial Europe A" and "agrarian Europe B" in Francis Delaisi's (1929) categorization, and most of all to Raúl Prebisch's theoretical works (1981). He used the center–periphery terminology for the first time in his lecture series in 1944, describing it as a "single system, hegemonically organized." From that time on a huge literature covered this topic. One of the most widespread popularizations was achieved by Immanuel Wallerstein (1974). See an excellent theoretical handling of the history of the concept in Love (1996).

10. "It is inexact to talk of England and the Continent rather than, say, of Lancashire and the Valley of the Sambre-Meuse. Each country was made up only by a number of regional economies" (Wrigley, 1962, 16). Pollard similarly stated: "Industrialization in Britain was by no means a . . . unitary, still less a nationwide process . . . Large parts of France and Germany were . . . indistinguishable from similar areas in the periphery" (Pollard, 1981b, 3, 191). François Crouzet speaks about "Industries concentrated along two major axes: one extended from the Scottish Lowlands to Lombardy . . . The second from Paris and the English Channel to Saxony, Bohemia, Silesia . . . Around the crossing of these

two axes was the most industrialized, populous and urbanized part of the Continent, a number of neighboring but distinct regions in northeastern France, the Low Countries, and the Rhineland, with the Ruhr district as the most powerful" (Crouzet, 1991, 120–1).

11. According to Jaime Reis, "no precise, generally accepted definition of the periphery exists;" however, he speaks about a "consensus" on the main "ingredients," such as late start of development, long-surviving agricultural structures and dominant agricultural exports to the markets of the core, and weak, late start of industrialization and urbanization. "Geographically, [the peripheries] lay on the rim of Europe . . . [and] the most important of their common characteristics . . . was their relative poverty." He did not mention the generally accepted per capita income level, mentioned above (Reis, 2000, 17).

12. To the most evident question, "was there a British Industrial Revolution?" one may find the following contradictory answers in the economic history literature: (1) "yes, it was an Industrial Revolution and it was British"; (2) "there was no such thing as an Industrial Revolution"; (3) "there was an Industrial Revolution, but it was not British and it emerged as an all-West European phenomenon"; (4) "'Industrial Revolution' is an inappropriate term because it was not only industrial but a much broader phenomenon, incorporating agriculture, and it was the crowning of a process spanning several hundred years."

13. Comparing income levels based on official currency exchange rates is misleading because price levels vary between countries. The PPP index eliminates the price differences by calculating the purchasing power of the different currencies. Identical goods are calculated on the same price expressed in the same currency. One of the popular PPP indexes is the so-called Big Mac Index, which is based on the price of a Big Mac in the different countries as the basis of purchasing power parity.

14. This index, introduced by the United Nations Development Program, has been in regular use by it since 1990.

15. Among others, the structure of employment and the various sectors' contribution to GDP, the structure of foreign trade, dependence on capital and technology imports, share of modern sectors, and the level of the development of infrastructure, etc.

16. According to Maria Todorova, the concept of Balkan backwardness is the product of a "frozen" Western image of the Balkans as a region "of industrial backwardness, primitive social relations and institutions, irrational and superstitious cultures, and tribal barbarity . . . [These negative views served the] positive and self-congratulatory image of the European and the West" (Todorova, 1997, 7, 188). Hence, rather than suffering from backwardness, the Balkans, she argues, simply comprise a different civilization: "Value judgments

on entire civilizations and cultures are, indeed, often biased and questionable. When discussing different cultures, values and behavioral patterns, I do not judge them or attempt to rank them as superior or inferior. It is a matter of opinion, for example, whether individualism or collectivism has a 'higher' value. I evaluate social-cultural differences for their economic *impact*. Some value systems and certain social behavioral patterns are stimulating, while others hinder the rise of industrial capitalism."

17. Everybody agrees on the importance of education in modern economic growth. Britain, however, had a relatively backward educational system and was at least a century behind Prussia. Yet it still became the pioneer of transformation.

18. Since the economist Arnold Toynbee's famous lecture series in 1884, when he introduced the terms "agricultural revolution" and "industrial revolution," these expressions have become used widely. Thomas S. Ashton's *The Industrial Revolution, 1760–1830*, first published in 1948, made "revolution" a household term. Adolphe Landry, the French demographer, coined the term "demographic revolution" in his influential *La révolution démographique* in 1934. In his lecture series in 1948 and his book published in 1950, Herbert Butterfield (1962) described the period of scientific development between Copernicus and Newton (the second half of the sixteenth century and most of the seventeenth century) as the "Scientific Revolution."

19. Another and more important argument maintained that there has not been a unitary set of approaches to the natural world that could be considered directly analogous to modern twentieth- and twenty-first-century science. "Natural philosophy," as early physics was called, did not use mathematical formulas, and "natural history," which was the forerunner of biology, had a theological orientation.

    The editors of the *European Review* devoted the greater part of the October 2007 issue of the journal to a debate of this question (Yerxa, 2007; Harrison, 2007; Shea, 2007; Heilbron, 2007; Cohen, 2007; Rabb, 2007). Abstract definitions of revolution, state Smelser and Baltes (2001), "vary widely." Is a revolution a "traumatic readjustment," a "complete and forcible overthrow" of an existing regime, a "radical and pervasive change," a "revolutionary outcome of successful changes over time," or a "totality of changes in the economic organization"? The answer: "Scholars never achieved consensus" (Smelser and Baltes, 2001, 13311).

20. This part of the novel is published in Gardiner (1959).

21. Cliometrics was a response to the mathematization of economics after World War II – especially after the start of the publication of the journal *Econometrica* in 1954, which generated a new scholarly culture in economics and a sea-change in economic history.

22. Jürgen Kocka argues for such an interdisciplinary cooperation (Kocka, 2010).

23. Gregory Clark boldly declares: "the rococo establishments of economic theory help little in understanding the pressing question that an ordinary person asks" (Clark, 2007, 372).

24. The original source, however, may be Cameron (1963). The *British Journal of Political Science* cited the latter, even more apt, version in 1976.

25. Examples are numerous. Gregory Clark in his otherwise excellent *A Farewell to Alms* (2007) calculates productivity improvement between the birth of Christ and the Industrial Revolution. We certainly cannot take his figure of a 24 percent increase as a convincing result. In his *Contours of the World Economy* (2007), the remarkable Angus Maddison, who has produced most of the applied historical statistics in recent decades, arrived at an estimate of $400 (in 1990 price level) as the subsistence minimum of GDP per capita in the year 1000. He concludes that by 1820 the average West European's real income had tripled. Jan de Vries does not accept this and suggests $700 for AD 1000. In this case, there would be no economic growth at all by 1820. (See de Vries, 2009.)

26. Leandro Prados de la Escosura notes the contradiction that "economic history is more present than ever in social sciences journals" while "its size as an independent field [is] shrinking" (Prados de la Escosura, 2007). "Economic history," Lance Davis observes, "has largely been taken over by economists, and they don't much care what anybody else says . . . " (in Lyons *et al.*, 2009, 227). Many economic historians defend their field as an independent historical discipline and not as applied economics. They insist, as Lars Magnusson has stressed, that economic history is not a "specialized sub-discipline of economics," and they long for the "return to what was worthwhile in the 'old' program of economic history" (Magnusson, 2005, 929).

27. This kind of economic history, as John Kenneth Galbraith put it, presents the lessons of economics: "it has long been my feeling that the lessons of economics that reside in economic history . . . provide an interesting and even fascinating window on economic knowledge" (Galbraith, 1961, 4).

28. Douglas C. North, who established the theory of the role of institutions in economic history, realizes that economics "neglects to explore the context within which choice occurs" and he speaks about "dominant beliefs," guided by "human perceptions," that are the outcome of a "cumulative learning process of generations." Thus, "cultural heritage will determine the success or lack of success of the actors" and the institutions they established (North, 2005, viii, ix, 2, 6, 11, 18).

Part I
Gradual revolution

CHAPTER 1

From merchant to industrial capitalism in Northwestern Europe

The global environment: Europe, the Islamic world, and China

Modern economic development – the rise of industrial capitalism – was a European phenomenon, but it was not coded in the "genes" of Europe. In the previous millennium, Europe was not the center of the world. In productive agriculture, science, and international trade, the Islamic world and China were actually ahead of Europe. The Islamic world, however, began to decline between the sixteenth and seventeenth centuries, and it reached the stage of ultimate decline at the turn of the eighteenth century. Three "gunpowder empires" – the Ottoman, Safavid, and Mughal empires – emerged from the mid-sixteenth century on, and they ruled the vast region from India to North Africa and the Balkans. After their early "golden ages," these empires became agricultural military-patronage states that no longer availed themselves of markets and declined as prominent mercantile states.

Recent studies have rejected the traditional view on Asian stagnation and argued that there were basic similarities with Europe until 1800. Bin R. Wong maintains that "China and Europe shared important similarities of preindustrial economic expansion based on Smithian dynamics" (Wong, 1998, 278). Kenneth Pomeranz's highly debated work, *The Great Divergence: China, Europe, and the Making of the Modern World Economy* (2000), states that genuine differences between the Eurasian West and East were not significant. The Chinese Lower Yangzi Delta could potentially have generated a development trend of modern industrialization similar to that in Europe. Agriculture was more developed, and more labor- and land-intensive than it was in Northwestern Europe. Transportation was compatible because of coastal shipping and the efficient inland canal and waterway system. In addition to intensive rice and cash crop cultivation, proto-industry was advanced and widespread, especially the cotton, silk, pottery, and tobacco industries. China had less restricted trade and a stronger market economy than did the more mercantilist Europe before the British Industrial Revolution. China and Europe thus exhibited surprising similarities between 1500 and 1800. At the turn of the nine-teenth century, however, Asia encountered ecological limitations, such as deforestation, and declining marginal labor productivity. China was unable to compete with Britain's advantage of "coal and colonies." At that point Asian and European development decisively diverted from each other.

Although this new concept attracted tremendous interest, questions soon arose regarding the solidity of the research and argumentation. A broader comparison proved that there were genuine differences between Asia and Europe, and major advantages for Northern Europe from the 1500s. As P. Vries has argued, the entrepreneurial and innovative eco-nomic culture and the positive role of the state in Europe, compared with that in Asia's unified agrarian empire, played a decisive role. Instead of "coal and colonies," it was the scientific revolution (with roots in the late Middle Ages), the creation of universities (the nests of rational thinking, the growing interest in nature, and experimental observation), and the resulting Reformation and Enlightenment that ultimately distinguished Europe from China. Social order was conservatively frozen in China, while it was radically modernized in Northwestern Europe; this modernization provided Europe with additional major advantages (Vries, 2001).

Although Chinese and south Indian peasant incomes were on a par with English agricultural wages in the eighteenth century, the quantitative analysis of S. Broadberry and B. Gupta (2006) established that the differ-ence between grain and silver wages totally alters this equation. Although grain wages were comparable, silver wages were substantially higher in Northwestern Europe, a fact that reflected the high productivity in the tradable sectors. Higher grain and low silver wage levels characterized the less developed regions. The exact same situation existed in periph-eral Europe, which exhibited the agricultural characteristics of the Asian regions, as well as a low level of urbanization. The prosperous parts of Asia, the authors concluded, resembled the stagnating southern, central, and eastern parts of Europe rather than the northwest. The "great diver-gence" was well under way for centuries prior to 1800 (Broadberry and Gupta, 2006, 2, 3, 5).[1]

Altogether, I agree with Geoffrey C. Gunn who states in his book on the Eurasian exchange in the early modern centuries: "The roots of the divergence on the road to modernity between Europe and China . . . strike back to the early discoveries, the Columbian exchange, the rise of print media, the Copernican revolution, and the Enlightenment in general" (Gunn, 2003, 278).

Northwestern merchant capitalism and colonialism

In late medieval times Mediterranean Europe was the powerhouse of the old continent. Among the richest and most advanced areas of Europe towered northern Italy, Flanders, and in a certain sense, Spain – the main beneficiary of the sixteenth- and seventeenth-century inflow of more than 36 million pounds of silver and nearly 400,000 pounds of gold. Northern Italy and Flanders played central roles in long-distance trade, early banking, and craftsmanship, and they became the prime forces behind an early European expansion. By 1600, however, as a result of the destruction by floods of a great area of land during the geo-historical catastrophe in the Mediterranean known as the "Little Ice Age" between the turn of the thirteenth and the mid-fifteenth century (Tabak, 2008), as well as a series of devastating wars, the economic power of Venice, Genoa, and Flanders was virtually gone. A new center of power began to emerge in Northwestern Europe.

European colonization of the New World and other continents signaled a new age that began with perilous adventures of courageous sailors, ruthless conquistadors, and stalwart settlers. The Portuguese and the Spanish crossed the Atlantic Ocean and reached the Americas in the fifteenth century and the Indian Ocean in the sixteenth century. The Dutch and the English assumed the leading role in the seventeenth century, joined by the French, Swedes, and Danes in the eighteenth. The triumph of Europe was based, as Fernand Braudel (1979) put it, on the multitude of ships, ports, and shipyards. Adds Carlo Cipolla: "It was the gun-carrying ocean-going sailing ship developed by Atlantic Europe during the fifteenth, sixteenth, and seventeenth centuries that made the European saga possible" (Cipolla, 1994a, 212).[2]

By the end of the eighteenth century, most of the major overseas centers were established; the "white colonies" were settled and governed by the new rising powers. The interconnected "Anglo-world," that is, European settlements on almost every other continent, assisted European expansion (Belich, 2009, 9, 23). In 1500, Europe controlled 7 percent of the world's land; by 1800, 35 percent. Only the interior of Africa and the Australian desert remained unexplored. At the end of the eighteenth century, the population of Spanish America was five times that of Anglo-America, but, during the long nineteenth century, Anglo-America became twice the size of Spanish America. The Dutch and English commercial empires of Northwestern Europe became the basis of commercial growth and a "Smithian" market-led expansion linked to their exploitation of resources. As a consequence, "the Northwestern littoral was the only region able to escape from prolonged economic stagnation" (Ormrod, 2003, 335, 339, 343, 345, 350).

The highly debated question of the role of empires and colonization, including a number of calculations of the income generated from colonies that at times led to the conclusion that "empire did not pay," is an independent study of its own. From Eric Hobsbawm to Ronald Findlay to Kevin O'Rourke, a long series of inquiries have focused on the central role of colonial and informal empire:

Purely domestic accounts of the "Rise of the West," emphasizing Western institutions, cultural attributes, or endowments, are hopelessly inadequate, since they ignore the vast web of interrelationship between Western Europe and the rest of the world that . . . was crucially important for the breakthrough to modern economic growth. (Findlay and O'Rourke, 2007, xx)

Geography also played a role. Both the Low Countries and Britain enjoyed easy access to the Atlantic trade route, and no part of either country was very far from the ocean. Both regions capitalized on this advantage by building canals (mostly in the seventeenth and eighteenth centuries) and creating the most extensive water transportation systems in the world. In the eighteenth century, each kilometer of navigable Dutch river and canal served seven square kilometers of land area. It was easy to reach the oceans from any part of the country or to deliver goods to the German territories by boat. This transportation network density was not surpassed even by the railroads.

As part of an island located in the middle of the international trade routes, and with no part of the country located further than seventy miles from the ocean, England also had a huge navigable river and canal network. The pioneering Exeter canal (1564) was only the first of many, and by 1815 each kilometer of the nearly 7,000-kilometer canal and navigable river network served no more than thirty-three square kilometers of land (Mathias, 1969, 110–12). By the beginning of the nineteenth century, the cost of water transportation in the northwestern region of Europe dropped to one-quarter of the cost of ground transportation. Such cheap mass transportation gave the region a unique advantage.

Northwestern Europe had even greater advantages. Slow but gradual development in the late Middle Ages had unmistakably transformed this part of Europe. In the Low Countries, feudal class structures either did not exist at all or had been abolished very early, from the thirteenth century on in Flanders and Brabant. "Serfdom, where it had existed at all, had by 1500 ceased to [exist]...in the 'maritime provinces'...[A] basically free peasantry...functioned in a relatively individualistic society" (Vries, 2001, 75).[3] By the early 1500s, the Low Countries had a remarkably modern society and economy. Wage labor was dominant at a time when it was only marginal across the continent.

Urbanization began uniquely early, in the eleventh century in the southern provinces of the Low Countries and the thirteenth in the northern provinces. Unparalleled transformations took place between 1300 and 1500. The northern Low Countries suffered from the typical drawbacks of a periphery, with considerable impediments to settling and farming. To attract new settlers ready to reclaim the land, dig peat, and cultivate the soil, the authorities sanctioned mass private ownership – affecting no less than two-thirds of peasant land. By the mid-fourteenth century cultivation was predominant. The urban population already made up one-quarter of the population in the fourteenth century, only to rise to 45 percent in the United Provinces by 1500. The urban elite attained political dominance in the six *hoofdsteden* (capital cities) and the twelve smaller townships, and the new *Staten* (estates) in 1572 allotted eighteen votes for the towns and only one for the nobility. More efficient institutions were created. The urban elites in certain regions began buying land and soon owned a third of it. "[The] adaptation of an urban-bourgeois practice to the larger stage of the territorial state is often seen as a key Dutch innovation" (Vries, 2001, 109).

In the fifteenth century, less than one-quarter of the population worked in agriculture, and that sector contributed less than one-fifth of the income level of the region. The industrial population reached 38 percent, and its contribution to the GDP was 39 percent. Trade and transportation employed 22 percent of the population and produced 30 percent of the GDP. In most parts of Europe, several centuries would have to pass before such a socio-economic level could be reached (Van Zanden, 2002, 634).

Small wonder that this region experienced the earliest "bourgeois revolution" in Europe, which cleared the way for social-institutional transformations by removing the remnants of feudal obstacles. The Netherlands achieved independence as a result of the Eighty Years War with Spain (1568–1648); the war ravaged the southern provinces, but it led to the formation of the Republic of the United Provinces – a de facto state since the end of the sixteenth century, and a de jure independent one after 1648. The Dutch Revolt was an early bourgeois revolution that further transformed society by introducing constitutional rule, free markets for land and labor, modern property rights, and relative religious freedom.[4]

Historical trends in the United Provinces established social and property relations that were very different from those in other parts of Europe. Judicious property rights were granted, and taxation was based on expenditure and not on income, strengthening modern attitudes toward thrift and investment. These social transformations laid the groundwork for a new ethic, well-embodied in Protestantism. Opposed to the dogmatic Catholicism of their Habsburg and Spanish enemies, the United Provinces grounded their identity in Protestantism.[5] A radical Anabaptist legacy, with its stance on the separation of church and state, coupled with Calvinist anxieties, stemming from faith in predestination that was thought to determine one's worldly success as a sign of heavenly salvation, both contributed to the creation of an ethos of hard work, thrift, self-discipline, and a rejection of luxury as sin. Puritan Calvinist thinking fundamentally created a new way of thinking and a new way of life. (See Map 1.1.)[6]

The Protestant Reformation had an additional impact on Dutch prosperity: it endowed the northern Low Countries with an enormous flood of immigrants. More than 10 percent of the population of the southern Low Countries moved to the north, comprising at least 125,000 people, mostly skilled workers, merchants, and Jews fleeing from Spanish-Catholic repression. The inflow of human capital – the immigrants made up half of Amsterdam's population– played an important role in raising prosperity.

The Low Countries evolved into Europe's most democratic and tolerant region that was grounded on and governed by a constitution. Provincial charters in Flanders and Brabant, *les Joyeuses Entrées*, had to be respected by the sovereign as early as the fourteenth century. The region became a flourishing center of arts and sciences at that time, reflecting rising prosperity. Together with Britain, a few Swiss cantons, and the German free cities, the Low Countries (including the United Provinces) developed a new social pattern fundamentally different from that in other parts of the continent: prestige and autonomy for merchants and financiers, and free rein for economic and technological innovation.

This modern social-political framework and fiscal system were based on taxation and financing procedures that were an offshoot of the earlier Italian financial revolution in the Low Countries from the fourteenth century on. The property tax on land and houses was a fixed percentage of the assessed value. The excise tax (previously called "urban taxation") on the sale of wine, beer, meat, grain, soap, cloth, and later several other consumption goods, provided two-thirds of the state's tax income. Inheritance and stamp taxes, and tolls for using canals, bridges, ports, and roads,

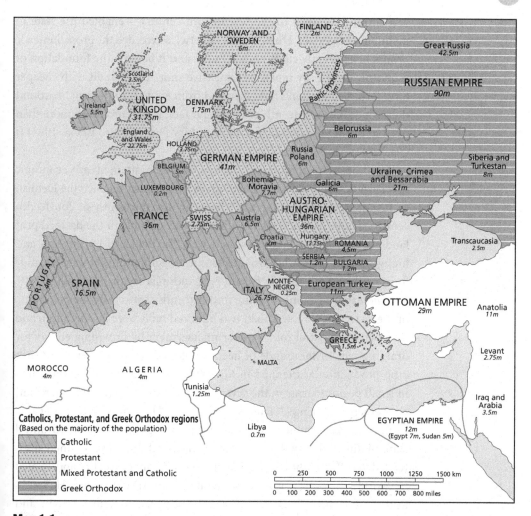

Map 1.1

Catholic, Protestant, and Greek Orthodox regions of Europe (according to the majority of the population, 1870) (McEvedy, 2002, 47)

provided additional state revenue. Beginning in the 1720s, the Low Countries also collected wealth taxes. Some elements of a taxation system had existed in European urban settlements before, but the United Provinces transformed the modern state when it "nationalized" the old provincial system by creating a uniform taxation policy.

A need for revenue for an almost permanent state of war led to the introduction of a public debt system to finance state expenditures. Based on the earlier practices of Venice and Florence, and later Flanders and Brabant from the thirteenth century on, the state consolidated public debt with short-term (*obligation*) promissory notes and issued long-term (*lijfrenten*) self-amortizing life annuity bonds. The growth of savings – Amsterdam merchants increased their savings by nearly 13 percent per year around the turn of the seventeenth century – enabled the state to maintain a huge debt. Dutch public debt twice exceeded the gross domestic product in the early eighteenth century, and it became the foundation of economic growth by replacing expensive short-term credit with cheaper long-term debt. Issuing rates dropped from 8.3 to 6.25 percent at around the turn of the seventeenth century, and Dutch debt increased more than fivefold during the first half of that century (Vries, 2001, 105–6, 109–11; Gelderblom and Jonker, 2011, 1, 7, 10).

Treading such a unique path, the Low Countries attained early economic specialization. The importation of grain from France enabled the Flemish to begin producing butter and cheese in the thirteenth or fourteenth century. Grain production was practically impossible in the drained peat lands of the United Provinces, and was thus replaced by imports and highly specialized, market-oriented domestic agriculture between the mid-fourteenth and mid-fifteenth century. Windmills began to be built in 1407 and increased in number in the mid-fifteenth century. By the beginning of the sixteenth, no fewer than two hundred mills were in operation, and they played a central role in water management by providing energy for draining tens of thousands of hectares of land. Dairy farming and cash crop production accelerated in the sixteenth century and predominated in small peasant farms in the seventeenth. Moreover, a flexible merchant class emerged during Holland's Golden Age. The United Provinces came to the fore as a country of trade and shipping, based on an advanced shipbuilding industry that produced a thousand ships a year – their ships (called *fluyts*) were the best-designed cargo ships in the world – and created the world's strongest navy and merchant marine. At 20,000 units, Holland's fleet was four times larger than that of its nearest competitor, Britain, and thirty times larger than France's. The Netherlands emerged as the world's strongest maritime power. In the late seventeenth century, the Dutch merchant fleet's carrying capacity, 568,000 metric tons, was almost equal to the combined capacity of the British, French, Spanish, Portuguese, and Italian merchant fleets.

In 1602, the Dutch Vereenigde Oostindische Compagnie (United East India, or Dutch East India Company) was founded,[7] and it secured a monopoly of Asian colonial trade. At the end of the century, it was the wealthiest company in the world, with 150 merchant ships, 50,000 employees, 40 warships, and a private army of 10,000 soldiers.

Dutch middlemen became the masters of Baltic, Russian, and distant overseas trade. Shipping and long-distance trade promoted the growth of domestic agriculture and a handicrafts industry. Bruges emerged as a main transit center in the fourteenth and fifteenth centuries and Antwerp in the fifteenth and sixteenth; Amsterdam would appropriate that role in the seventeenth century. The southern regions had traditionally served as the primary dyeing and processing centers of the Low Countries, but Dutch artisans soon began processing and reselling various kinds of imported goods: they wove raw silk, refined sugar, and cut and wrapped tobacco. From imported copper, Amsterdam's and Rotterdam's foundries manufactured guns.[8] Heat-intensive industries, including brewing, salt-refining, distilling, bleaching, textile-dyeing and printing, and brick- and tile-making, sprang forth in the fourteenth century – a period when cheese and herring became export items, and half the beer production and 30 percent of textile output was exported. Holland was also a high wage country in the fourteenth century. Silver wages surpassed the wages in Flanders, London, Florence, and Paris by 20 to 50 percent until the fifteenth century. Cultivation restrictions inspired peasants to turn to cottage industry, which became even more pronounced when urban merchants bought huge plots of land. Household industrial activities were a recurrent theme of Dutch seventeenth-century genre painting, such as Quirijn van Brekelenkam's *The Spinner* and Nicolaes Maes' *The Lacemaker*.

"The jump-start of the Holland economy in the late middle ages was built on the foundations laid down in the high Middle Ages and . . . makes it a clear case of path-dependent development" (Van Bavel and Van Zanden, 2004, 505, 509, 518–21, 528–9). Indeed, the bonanza of the northern Low Countries was essentially the high point of a continuing process of late medieval northern Italian and Flemish economic development. The Netherlands acquired most of its wealth through being a trade and service intermediary – a point of continuity with its late medieval economy (Van der Wee, 1999). E. A. Wrigley emphasizes that the Dutch economy became an "advanced organic economy" with foremost pre-industrial traits (Wrigley, 1988, 18, 34).[9]

François Crouzet summed up this concept in the following way: "Holland was an entrepôt, like Venice had been . . . was more imitation and transfer than mutation . . . Eighteenth century [Netherlands] was rather the zenith of old-regime economies than the dawn of a new era" (Crouzet, 2001, 74, 97).[10]

Colonial conquest reached "its height during the second half of the seventeenth century and the first quarter of the eighteenth" (Israel, 1995, 936), and it generated massive international trade. Originally, the United Provinces imported non-bulk, high unit value goods from the Indies and the Levant, but, already by the seventeenth century, it dominated the bulk trade of grain and herring from the Baltic region and the North Sea as well. First Antwerp and then Amsterdam emerged as the most important international trade centers that routinely dictated market prices, and they became the homes of the first stock exchanges.[11] The Dutch Golden Age became the cradle of modern European transformation, and the Netherlands became "the first area of Western Europe to escape the Malthusian checks . . . The first country to achieve sustained economic growth . . . " (North and Thomas, 1973, 132, 145).

Merchant capitalism emerged in Britain as well, but only in a partly parallel way. Britain was far behind the United Provinces during the Dutch Golden Age of the sixteenth and seventeenth centuries, and its social-property relations differed markedly. Although Britain pursued the Dutch path to development, it was in Britain that the world witnessed a real discontinuity between the past and the dawn of a new age. The British appropriated from the Dutch and the French exclusive rights in the slave trade to Spanish America during the first half of the eighteenth century, and by the 1780s they "were well on their way to controlling the lion's share of non-European resources and markets" (Esteban, 2004, 47). Britain invested one-third to one-half of its enormous profits from the slave trade in its home industry, and its empire-generated income covered more than half its domestic fixed capital formation. Exploited and looted Indian wealth helped pay down Britain's foreign debt. Overseas demand became as important a driving force as the domestic environment. Between 1700 and 1770, between half and nearly three-quarters of additional British industrial production was exported. Eighteenth-century British growth was export-led (Esteban, 2004, 58–64).

Britain had several unique advantages, among them its geographical location that protected it from foreign attack. The early start of the enclosure system[12] created a special agricultural and social environment in a much different way than it did in Holland: the system eliminated the peasant economy in half of the country by the mid-eighteenth century, when the rapidly capitalizing system of big estates predominated. By 1790, freeholders cultivated only 20 percent of the land, while 80 percent was in the hands of modernizing capitalist big estates.

The enclosure system led to the creation of more efficiently sized estates: by the mid-nineteenth century, the size of the average estate was 100 acres, more than three times larger than in France. The expansion of arable land was combined with the introduction of crop rotation, borrowed from the Flemish "intensive husbandry" that had eliminated fallow land, and the Dutch "extensive husbandry" that had helped maintain huge grasslands. During the first two-thirds of the eighteenth century, a large part of the land that had been previously cultivated by small estates was appropriated as pastureland in the newly enlarged big estates. The price paid for this technical improvement was social decline and poverty. Smallholders lost their land, millions of people were uprooted, and the condition of laborers declined. A large part of the countryside was depopulated.

On the other hand, agricultural productivity increased threefold between 1700 and 1850. As agriculture was and remained the largest sector of the economy until 1840, this growth of output was the real driving force of the British economy. "The key feature of the British economy was its (virtually) complete conversion to capitalist farming" (Crafts and Harley, 2004, 104, 107).[13] At the same time, a multitude of people, without means of subsistence and uprooted from agriculture, migrated to the growing urban centers and provided an unlimited labor force for industry.

The number of small towns with 5,000–10,000 inhabitants doubled in Britain between 1600 and 1750, while that number declined on the continent. In addition to London (the largest city in Europe), several new cities emerged around 1800 to become some of the largest in the country, including Manchester, Liverpool, Birmingham, Leeds, and Sheffield. Throughout the eighteenth century, 70 percent of Europe's urban development took place in Britain (Wrigley, 1988, 13, 15).

During the early modern centuries in Britain, the old feudal institutions of serfdom were gradually replaced by free labor. The elimination of serfdom, as well as the burgeoning production and trade of wool in the fourteenth century, led to gradual industrial development. A flourishing woolen industry emerged in Stroud, Chipping Camden, Colchester, Coventry, Norwich, and other townships. The amount of woolen fabric exported surpassed that of raw wool as early as the mid-fifteenth century. One century later, wool represented 80 percent of British exports, while only 6 percent of it was raw wool. By the end of the seventeenth century, processed wool made up less than half of British exports.

Britain's real industrial breakthrough began in the mid-sixteenth century, with the development of iron, lead, and other manufacturing sectors. Blast furnaces produced 5,000 tons of iron per year in 1550, but only half a century later production topped 18,000 tons. In 1790, per capita iron output reached 15 kilograms, a level not attained in continental Europe until around 1870. Cotton consumption was also unparalleled; its 2 kilograms per capita was achieved on the continent only in 1885. England pioneered a new energy source: coal – "the soul of all English industries."[14] The amount mined in Britain jumped from 210,000 tons in 1550 to 1.5 million tons in 1630, and then to 2.5–3.0 million tons by 1700. This quantity was between three and three and a half times the heating equivalent of Dutch peat production. By 1800, Britain produced no less than 15 million tons a year. "Well before ... the industrial revolution, the dependence of the

English economy on organic raw materials had been significantly reduced, and as a result constraints upon growth were eased" (Wrigley, 1988, 55, 57). As Wrigley observes, Britain's apparently unlimited coal resources, and their early extraction, enabled the country to advance from a high-level organic economy to a mineral-based energy economy.[15] Britain had overcome the built-in limitations to growth. The more advanced Dutch economy, which had attained an income level that was 50 percent higher than Britain's, was unable to enter the age of industrialization in the late seventeenth century. It was left to Britain to pioneer industrialization in the eighteenth century.

To run such a powerful centralized state, Britain emulated and reinvented the modern Dutch fiscal system. In 1688, Parliament took control of state finances, but the state finances had been gradually modernized since the Civil War. Excise consumer taxes and direct taxation (poll tax, property tax) provided huge revenues for the state. In 1799, William Pitt introduced the first income tax.[16] To finance a series of wars, Britain also adopted the Dutch public debt system. When William of Orange was elevated to the English throne in 1689, he "introduced the well-tried financial techniques" of the Dutch Republic. This act was linked to the issuing of Parliament-guaranteed securities (Treasury Orders), which had begun to be traded in the 1660s. The establishment of the Bank of England was a significant turning point, and public debt financing reached its height during the Napoleonic wars. Debts comprised only 6 percent of the GDP in 1690; by 1815, however, it was 220 percent. In 1677, the Exchequer introduced annuities as the first instrument of long-term investment. From the end of the seventeenth century on, a major innovation – long-term borrowing from the Bank of England – covered debt financing. Tax revenues made up less than 4 percent of GDP in the mid-seventeenth century, but this share increased to nearly 11 percent by 1739 and to more than 18 percent by 1815. Unlike Holland, England developed a vigorous secondary market for public debt that sharply increased liquidity. After the Glorious Revolution, it was England's strong centralized state, as well as Parliament's right to control spending, that made its commitment to service its debt at all credible. Fragmented and absolutist states could not do the same. Fiscal centralization, however, was a century-long process that was completed during the Napoleonic wars (Capie, 2001, 26, 28, 38; Gelderblom and Jonker, 2004, 642; Stasavage, 2003; Dincecco, 2009, 70–80). A financial revolution was a major prerequisite for economic greatness. According to Richard Sylla, "past and current differences in development... can be explained by... the spread of modern financial systems" (Sylla, 2002, 280).

Figure 1.1
Carrying capacity
of merchant
fleets,
1570–1780
(tons) (Maddison,
2001, 77)

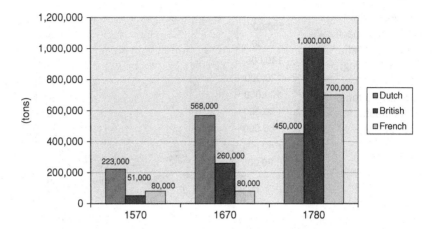

No doubt, the sound financial system was the basis for Britain's superior naval strength. The Royal Navy safeguarded the lucrative imperial commercial network. A new naval strategy of permanent active service (a continuing standing armed force) in both war and peace, and the establishment of naval bases in Gibraltar, Port Mahon, Jamaica, and Antigua in the early eighteenth century, required massive state expenditures (Baugh, 2004, 245, 255).

Like Holland, England also developed a modern society and a genuine market economy, and it evolved into a merchant and maritime power. Also like Holland, England dominated emergent "modern trade." Both countries initially based their economies on a modern division of labor and then switched to increased commodity production for a permanently expanding buyer's market. English merchants transported vast quantities of goods of mass consumption. A triangular Atlantic trade emerged: the merchants shipped textile and other manufactured products from Europe to Africa; they bought and transported slaves to the overseas colonies; and they sent sugar, rum, coffee, cotton, indigo, and other items as cargo back to Europe. "British manufacturing, American agriculture, and the African slave trade were all deeply interrelated" (Findlay and O'Rourke, 2007: 342).

By 1780, the British merchant fleet, with its million-ton capacity, became more than twice as large as the Dutch fleet, and nearly the same size as the Spanish, Portuguese, Italian, Norwegian, Swedish, and Danish fleets combined. By 1850, the carrying capacity of the British fleet surpassed 4 million tons – nearly one-third of the world's fleets' total shipping capacity. (See Figures 1.1 and 1.2.)

The rise of Northwestern Europe exhibited both continuity and discontinuity in European development. While the Netherlands continued and

Figure 1.2
Carrying capacity
of British and
world shipping,
1670–1913
(thousand tons)
(Maddison,
2001, 95)

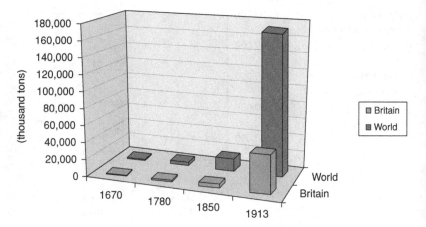

fortified Flanders' late medieval path to development, Britain appropriated the economic innovations of the Low Countries and amplified them. As Amsterdam had replaced Antwerp, London now replaced Amsterdam. Britain continued and expanded upon the Flemish and Dutch agricultural revolution.[17] Based on this inheritance and the spectacular rise of industry, Britain's development led to a dramatic discontinuity and opened a new chapter in economic history.

All the gradual but revolutionary socio-economic transformations in the early modern period affected the customs and habits of the emerging new societies in Northwestern Europe. The increasingly affluent upper and middle classes, the upwardly mobile peasant families working in proto-industrial enterprises, and even the lower wage-earning workers were able to consume much more than they had ever before. Proto-industrial peasants increased labor input by using female and child labor in family businesses to boost income and consumption even more. Adopting the Japanese concept of "industrious revolution," Jan de Vries documented the impact of the "structure and behavior of the households" that had reallocated their productive resources and expanded both supply and demand on the market. "Parisian" fashions transformed customary attire[18] – improvements augmented by rapidly spreading colonial luxuries, coffee, tea, sugar, cocoa, and distilled spirits. European watch production jumped from a few thousand to 400,000 in one year in the late seventeenth century, with fully 38 percent of inventories being sold to poorer families. Expensive furniture, tapestries, and tiles adorned more and more homes; in the Netherlands in the 1660s, 3 million paintings, produced by some 700–800 painters, lined the walls of private homes.

Towards the end of the eighteenth century, Dutch consumption was two to four times greater than the European average, and British consumption surpassed it several times. As abbé G. Raynal described it in 1770, the "taste for luxuries and commodities has induced a love of work, which is today the principal force of states" (Rothschild, 2002, 31). Such a high level of consumption sharply stimulated demand for extensive economic growth, provided an increasingly sophisticated consumer market, and set "the stage for the Industrial Revolution" (Vries, 2008, 3, 9, 10, 55, 71, 134, 139, 161, 180).

These socio-economic transformations also generated new ideas. A new value system began to take root – one that was strengthened and institutionalized by Henry VIII's Act of Supremacy establishing the English monarch as the head of the Church of England, which paved the way for a Reformation from above. The Protestant ethic, the notion of thrift and hard work, coupled with the elevated social status of traders and merchants, assured British society's increasingly favorable attitude toward business and wealth. As it had previously done in Holland, religious tolerance led to rising immigration from the continent. The first wave arrived from the southern Low Countries beginning in 1550; the second comprised French Huguenots after the revocation of the Edict of Nantes in 1685. Immigrants made up roughly 40 percent of the populations of Sandwich and Norwich, and they contributed to the growth of market gardening and the cloth, leather, furniture, and iron industries in eastern England (Goose and Lun, 2005).

Aside from the Netherlands and Britain, no other country in the world had such a free, self-organizing society. Large groups of people founded clubs and associations to initiate and promote artistic, scholarly, technological, and economic progress by offering a host of awards and bonuses; this created open fora on burning scientific and practical questions. The socio-political transformation created an educational boom that was unique at that time in Europe. In merchant societies as early as that of Renaissance Florence, the sons of the commercial classes studied mathematics. "Basic mathematical skills diffused earlier than literacy. Around the mid-seventeenth century, in Western Europe it reached about 70 percent, and by 1800, 80–90 percent. The skill of calculations was a basic human capital in the period of rising capitalism" (A'Hearn et al., 2009, 785, 804). By the late seventeenth century, 75–85 percent of the upper and middle classes were also literate, while literacy among the working classes reached 35–40 percent. At the end of the eighteenth century, 54 percent of newlyweds were literate. As literacy reports and marriage documents attest, no fewer than 68 percent of grooms and 52 percent of brides were literate by 1839 (Hartwell, 1971, 237–9).[19] Numeracy and literacy provided an exceptional advantage for the Northwestern countries. Hungary, for example, could claim only a 30 percent numeracy rate in the mid-seventeenth century and a 65 percent rate by the mid-eighteenth; Serbia's was 55 percent in 1800, and literacy in Eastern Europe at the turn of the nineteenth century was only 10 percent.

Hundreds of years of gradual transformations were the historical foundation of the Glorious Revolution of 1688, which led to the establishment of the world's first parliamentary system and constitutional monarchy. A modern, business-friendly legal system was introduced that guaranteed property rights. Max Hartwell underlined the central and unique role of English law: "Perhaps the most distinctive and unique national characteristic that distinguished England from Continental countries in the eighteenth century... was English law" (Hartwell, 1971, 252).[20] Government institutions definitely played an important role in shaping the country's modern economic transformation. But there is no evidence that, as Douglas North and Barry Weingast suggest in their pathbreaking study, the Glorious Revolution and its constitutional commitments, particularly regarding property rights, were the *real* turning point that sparked the Industrial Revolution. Institutions are the "rules of the game... the humanly devised constraints that shape human interaction" (North and Weingast, 1989; North, 1990, 3). Institutions are not exogenous factors, and they are shaped by socio-economic developments. As North himself later asserted, revising his previous position, institutions are shaped by "human evolution" and "cumulative learning," that is, by culture (North, 2005).[21]

The United Provinces reached their zenith by the 1650s and 1660s, but started declining afterwards. More than a century later, the Dutch East India Company – the engine and symbol of Dutch supremacy – went bankrupt. The processing and shipbuilding industries waned, agriculture was hit by natural disasters, and cattle herds were decimated by epidemics. After 1720, urban decay followed. The Netherlands' advanced organic economy exhausted its potential for the time being and proved incapable of advancing further or competing with Britain's expanding, innovative mineral-based economy.

The rival great powers, Britain and France, aptly exploited this situation, and they did their best to impede Dutch economic growth. Military power had played a key role in Dutch economic advances from the sixteenth century on. During the seventeenth and eighteenth centuries, however, the Netherlands suffered several military defeats. At the same time, a series of successful British wars against Spain, the United Provinces, and France strongly contributed to Britain's ascendancy. The defeat of the legendary Spanish Armada in 1588, and the eruption of three Anglo-Dutch wars up through the the mid-1670s, eroded Holland's control of the waters and established Britain as the most powerful world power. The Fourth Anglo-Dutch War in 1780–3 demonstrated Britain's overwhelming military strength. During the one and a half centuries between 1670 and 1810, the size of the British navy grew by three times, and the number of British troops jumped from 15,000 to 250,000. Faltering Dutch naval power was effectively eliminated in a final confrontation with the nearly eight times as large British navy. The United Provinces were powerless to defend their merchant fleet and colonies and lost a third of their fleet and their trade monopoly in East India to Britain.

From the late seventeenth century to the early eighteenth century, Britain fought several wars with France and had clearly emerged as the world's dominant super power. British military victories over a two hundred year time-span had eliminated its main rivals and established its leading position in the world. Expanded sea and military power represented the real comparative advantage of a modernizing Britain.

However, France – the model state of absolutism in the seventeenth and eighteenth centuries – also emerged as a powerful European country. Its population was 19.3 million in 1715 and 26.6 million in 1788, surpassing Britain's by 2.7 and 2.8 times respectively. Per capita national income was higher in France than in Britain and France was more powerful during the eighteenth century. Under the seventy-two-year rule of the *Roi Soleil*, Louis XIV, France also possessed the strongest military force and became one of the largest colonial powers. The Thirty Years War between 1618 and 1648, and a victorious war against the United Provinces between 1672 and 1678, elevated France to its leading position on the continent.

Together with Britain, France was the pioneer of modern colonialism and dynamic expansion. The founding of the French Indian Company in 1664 to promote trade with India, and the establishment of the Pondicherry and Chandernagore trading posts in 1671 and 1688, signaled this development. In the course of the first half of the eighteenth century, French colonial trade – based on French rural industries including cotton, wool, and sugar – quadrupled. France's Indian trade increased tenfold and made a 25 percent profit.

France emerged as the third European power to compete for primacy, and in the eighteenth century, it significantly bolstered its leading position in world trade. In 1715, the French share in international trade hardly amounted to half of Britain's; by the mid-1780s, however, the value of French trade had surpassed that of Britain.

Absolutist France established its economy through strong state interventionism, and, along with Britain, became one of the pioneers of mercantilism. Jean-Baptiste Colbert, the powerful minister of Louis XIV, introduced strict state regulations. The government administered a number of foreign trade companies, supervised the construction of ports and roads, and established preeminent state-owned manufacturing firms. In the eighteenth century, Lyon, one of the largest cities on the continent, emerged as the center of the silk industry. At the same time, Paris, with its large population and booming markets, emerged as one of the most prominent hubs of artisan work: in the early 1790s, no fewer than 350,000 Parisians worked in handicrafts.

At the beginning of the eighteenth century, the province of Languedoc became the world's largest textile center – producing high-quality, expensive woolen broadcloth that was sold on France's Mediterranean trade routes. Coal production increased eightfold to nearly 500,000 tons during the eighteenth century. The French iron industry, employing the old charcoal technology used in blast furnaces in the big estates, produced more iron than did Britain: 132,000 tons in the 1790s. The royal cannon factory in the Loire Valley was an important player in the iron industry, its output increasing more than threefold in the second half of the century. Fifty years after the invention of coke smelting in Britain, the Frenchman Ignace Wendel built the world's most modern blast furnace in Le Creusot. This was representative of the situation generally. Along with original French innovations, Alan S. Milward and S. B. Saul report, "most of the British innovations in textile manufacture were adopted in France in considerably less than a decade" (Milward and Saul, 1973, 97). On average, French industrial output increased 1 percent per annum during the eighteenth century.

Nevertheless, France preserved its feudal institutions and landownership until the end of the century. Political and economic freedoms were sharply restricted in the absolute state, and noble society stubbornly retained its anti-capitalist prejudices. The *ancien régime* also perpetuated the country's huge income disparities. Before the French Revolution, the upper 10% of the population garnered 50% of the income, while the lower 70% earned only 25%. As Jean-Laurent Rosenthal has shown, the cost of France's randomly defined property rights was very high, for they prevented investments from becoming productive assets. In sharp contrast to agriculture in the Netherlands and Britain, French agriculture remained hopelessly behind. Land reclamation through drainage, irrigation, and canal building was a rare occurrence on French farms. "Between 1650 and 1789," Rosenthal noted, "little was accomplished" in France.[22]

French crop cultivation mostly preserved the medieval three-field rotation system. Large fields were left fallow, plowing was superficial (no deeper than the topsoil), and grain was harvested with sickles. Crop yields remained traditionally low, with seed-to-crop ratios hovering between 1:3 and 1:7, depending on the soil and weather. Productivity stagnated. Feudal rents, including payments to the Catholic Church, consumed roughly one-third of the peasants' income. Population growth languished and reflected medieval norms: prior to the Revolution, the birth rate of 25–36 per 1,000 was more than offset by a death rate of 30–35 per 1,000. As a large country with relatively less coastline, and despite its extensive road construction over the century, France lacked the dense waterway system and shipping capability that had characterized the Netherlands and Britain. The dearth of cheap, rapid mass transportation was also a primary obstacle to modernization.

French feudal institutions prevented the development of modern state financing. Despite its much larger population and income, France lacked the modern taxation and debt financing systems that were found in the Low Countries and Britain. Tax revenues dwindled thanks to a patchwork of personal and regional privileges and the absence of a national tax-collecting body. In the early eighteenth century, the proportion of French tax revenues amounted to 9.4% of GDP; by 1788 it had declined to 6.8%, barely more than half that of Britain. In 1715, France's share of taxes from its commodity output was 11%, compared with 17% in Britain; by 1785, the French share declined to 10%, while the British increased to 22%. With its "privilege shaped" society and its obsolete institutional system, France was unable to generate higher state revenues and lacked an efficient debt financing system. "France remained shackled by macroeconomic institutions and policies that failed to provide the requisite revenue" (White, 2001, 96).

True, with lavish royal sponsorship, science and culture continued to flourish in France. But the French lost their military supremacy to Britain during the Seven Years War (1756–63). The absolute state remained incorrigibly frozen in its *ancien régime*; hence, only "the Revolution [could bring] France into the modern world" (Rosenthal, 1992, 173). Manorial dues and various state-chartered monopolies were all eliminated, and freedom of enterprise and a modern legal system were introduced. The Napoleonic Codes made property sacred. Social transformations that had been gradually gaining ground were now institutionalized. The Dutch, British, and French rivalry for economic primacy – and, indeed, that of Europe generally – strongly contributed to the rise of Northwestern Europe, but it ended with a clear victory for Britain.

New science and values

The rise of Northwestern Europe during the seventeenth and eighteenth centuries was also driven by a revolution in science and philosophy, which evolved into a new *Zeitgeist*. This development had roots in several West European countries, including the Netherlands, England, France, Germany, Italy, and Switzerland, and it goes back to at least the Renaissance. Universities became hotbeds of rational thinking and the cultivation of mathematics and philosophy. The flow of ideas hardly respected national borders and crossed them with ease. A new conception of human society and the universe, a new value system, and a new way of thinking began to spread throughout the West. Increasing numbers embraced the belief that reason and experience can reveal the laws of nature and facilitate the just reorganization of society. Secularized science and political theory replaced religion and thus became the basis for the most fundamental intellectual transformation of the modern world. The relationship between the church and the state disintegrated – culminating in the Treaty of Westphalia (1648), which made the state the most sacrosanct institution.

This process of radically changing ways of thinking, together with the spread of a commercial spirit that gradually appeared in Europe's late medieval centers, was closely connected with the Renaissance. The reclaiming of ancient arts and scholarship was a tacit challenge to medieval religious bigotry. Men looked for God in themselves, became fascinated with the human body, and began to establish a new materialistic and rationalistic society. Renaissance individualism and *joie de vivre* created an intellectual ferment that became a forerunner of the Reformation (Parker, 1984).

The Reformation of the sixteenth century represented the "triumph of the commercial spirit over the traditional social ethics of Christendom . . . [T]rade and tolerance flourished together" (Tawney, 1954, 17, 75). The Reformation paved the way for the scientific revolution – a "twin advance," Herbert Butterfield observed, "of scientific conceptualization and factual discovery" (Shea, 2007, 459). The titans and trailblazers of this scientific and ideological cataclysm between the mid-sixteenth and seventeenth centuries – Copernicus, Pascal, Kepler, Galileo, Descartes, and Newton – effectively revolutionized human awareness. An entirely new comprehension came to light in astronomy, physics, and anatomy. The invention of new instruments such as the telescope and the microscope assured a deeper understanding of nature. The proliferation of scientific societies under royal patronage in the 1660s, including the Royal Society, the Académie Royale des Sciences, and others, engendered a "monumental change in the realm of learning," a "seismic shift in understanding of the natural world" that led to the "crucial transition in the formation of the modern world" (Harrison, 2007, 446, 450).

The Renaissance prepared the ground for the Protestant Reformation in Germany, Switzerland, the Netherlands, and Britain, which in turn paved the way for the scientific revolution, which in sequence ushered in the Enlightenment. The four countries swept up into Protestantism were united in their commitment to change and modernization. This centuries-long process was genuinely West European in origin. The forerunners of the new trend included Joost Lips (Justus Lipsius) in Leiden (Leuven) and Antwerp, whose translations of the classics induced a fundamental change in the European worldview, and René Descartes, who presented the first modern concept of the universe operating under mathematical laws in his *Discours de la méthode* published in 1637. Descartes and his disciple Benedict (Baruch) Spinoza emerged as the philosophers of rationalism and natural law. Spinoza developed the concept of social contract, majority rule, and individual freedom, and rejected religion as the product of human fear of the unknown forces of nature. The pioneering ten-volume work of Bernard Picard and Jean-Frédéric Bernard, published between 1723 and 1743, promoted greater tolerance when it elaborately depicted the religions of the world as essentially equal curiosities, with none apportioned higher value over others (Hunt *et al.*, 2010).[23]

The philosophy of the Enlightenment emerging from Holland paved the way for a revolution of thought in Britain. Isaac Newton, the son of an illiterate English farmer, published *Philosophiae naturalis principia mathematica* in London in 1687, the "capstone of the Scientific Revolution of the sixteenth and seventeenth centuries and . . . often said to be the greatest work of science ever published" (Dobbs and Jacob, 1995, 10). In this and in his next three works of the early eighteenth century, Newton utilized rigorous experimentation and scholarly methodology to explain the laws of the physical world. He presented a "grand unified vision of the universe . . . [and] provided a rational mechanics for the operations of machines on earth" (Dobbs and Jacob, 1995, 38, 44).

The Newtonian concept of the universe was one of a secure and harmonious system, and it presented science as a prime mover of human progress. A wide array of lectures and publications, including Voltaire's, popularized Newton's theories and gave rise to a number of practical works on applied mechanics and machine building. The Newtonian scientific *Weltanschauung* transformed the way people thought about nature and society. It was the foundation not only of Enlightenment scholarship, but of civil engineering as well.

Most of all, the scientific revolution turned people's interest from metaphysical issues to physical problems, and to the utilitarian opportunities of applied science. Important links developed between renowned philosopher-scientists and humble instrument makers. As A. E. Musson and Eric Robinson have shown, mathematics became a practical tool for artisans in the early seventeenth century. Traders, merchants, seamen, and carpenters developed it to a greater degree than did academics. A number of inexpensive textbooks became available, widening access further. Gresham's College in London encouraged collaboration between scholars and artisans. The newly founded Royal Society "was actively concerned with the practical applications of natural philosophy," and its members sought to improve "mechanic arts" such as building, metal smithing, shipbuilding, and agriculture. Inexpensive textbooks were published in Antwerp in Dutch, French, English, and German beginning in the sixteenth century. Many artisans bought Francis Walkinghame's bestselling textbook *The Tutor's Assistant* (published later in the eighteenth century), which appeared in eighteen editions of 5,000–10,000 copies each (Musson and Robinson, 1969, 12–25). The *Dictionnaire universel des arts et des sciences* was first released in 1690, the *Lexicon technicum* in 1704. A flourishing encyclopedic culture emerged, embodied in Diderot's *Encyclopédie*. Among its 72,000 entries, a plethora of precise technological descriptions facilitated everyday industrial practice: 33 pages on masonry, 44 on glass, and 25 on paper making (Mokyr, 2002, 68–9).[24] The new *Weltanschauung* became increasingly accessible and served as a guiding compass for thousands of entrepreneurs.

Besides Newton, Thomas Hobbes is preeminent among seventeenth-century pioneers of thought as the first plebeian English philosopher and the founder of modern political philosophy. In *Leviathan* (1651), Hobbes challenged basic feudal concepts, such as the ancient bonds of loyalty to sovereigns, and replaced them with the notion of individualism: "The condition of man . . . is a . . . condition of war everyone against everyone . . . everyone is governed by his own reason and every man has a right . . . of doing anything he likes" (Hobbes, [1651] 1956, 122–3).

John Locke, the most popular philosopher of the late seventeenth century (the age of the "Glorious Revolution" in Britain), went even further. His *Two Treatises on Government* posited the central role of laws as the most important "guarantor of freedom," and called for a social contract between kings and commoners that limited governmental power and made it constitutional: "All men by nature are equal . . . [and] born . . . with a title to perfect freedom and an uncontrolled enjoyment of all the rights and privileges of the law of Nature . . . It is evident that absolute monarchy . . . is indeed inconsistent with civil society, and can be no form of civil government" (Locke, [1690] 1947, 801). Locke also propagated the separation and mutual limitation of legislative and executive powers. He became one of the most influential apostles of the modern *Rechtsstaat* and parliamentary system.

Among the giants of the English Enlightenment, Francis Bacon deserves singular standing. This statesman and scholar envisioned the creation of "Salomon's House," an imagined research university for basic and applied science, and called for the establishment of a Ministry of Science and Technology. Having coined in his *Meditations* the slogan that "knowledge is power," Bacon became the "father of scientific method" by advocating observation, categorization, classification, measurement, and most particularly, experimentation. Joel Mokyr (2002) labeled this scientific branch of the Enlightenment as the "industrial Enlightenment." It created an experimental method to tackle practical problems, a scientific mentality and culture that encouraged applied science, and a utilitarian approach "at the service of commercial and manufacturing interest."

It is well known that science did not play a direct role in the Industrial Revolution. Mokyr found the spread of "useful knowledge, the beliefs people hold about their physical milieu," and scientific methods, i.e. the "industrial Enlightenment," as the determinant intellectual development that "bridge[d] the Scientific and the Industrial Revolution." Although it may be an exaggeration to suggest that useful knowledge "affected the world more than all other social and political changes taken together," there is no doubt that it was an organic part of a complex package of social, intellectual, cultural, political, and economic factors that transformed the world in the nineteenth century (Mokyr, 2002, 35–7, 39, 297; 2005, 287, 290).

Special attention should be given to the rise of a modern political economy, which emerged in the second half of the eighteenth century with the work of François Quesnay, Richard Cantillon, Anne-Robert-Jacques Turgot, Sir James Stuart, and Adam Smith. The field incorporated ideology, scientific theory, and practical policy proposals.[25] Turgot and Smith were especially influential. Anne-Robert-Jacques Turgot, the baron de l'Aulne, became the *intendant* of the *généralité* of Limoges in 1761. As a follower of the physiocrats, who believed that agriculture was the only source of wealth, and as an administrator of an impoverished province, Turgot became a pioneer of modern economics. In 1759, in his *Elegy to*

Gournay (his mentor), Turgot harshly attacked the mercantilist regulation of industry and maintained that commercial transactions were by nature reciprocal: it made no sense, he insisted, to attempt to sell without also buying. In various writings,[26] he strongly advocated free trade. The government, he argued, should always protect the natural liberty of the buyer to buy and the seller to sell. He acknowledged the importance of a division of labor, the necessity of savings and capital accumulation, and the role of supply and demand as a regulator of prices. Turgot recognized self-interest as the prime mover of the market, and affirmed that individual interest in the free market must always coincide with the general interest.

Box 1.1   Adam Smith: the birth of modern economics

One genius did not create modern economics, a novel scholarly discipline that played a monumental role in nineteenth-century economic development. Its origins are rooted in the rise of a new *Zeitgeist*, based on the scientific revolution that took place over a period of two to three hundred years. Astronomy, physics, and biology presented a natural law of harmony in nature, the order of the universe, the self-perpetuating harmonious work of the human body, and the Newtonian discovery of the laws of physics. Once the world was created, Newton argued, it operated with its own rules in integrated harmony without further outside intervention. It was only a short step to excluding God from the natural harmony of the universe, from human biology, and from the worldly functioning of humankind.

The British and French *philosophes* of the Enlightenment took this step: they applied the scientific worldview to human society, and maintained that harmony, and an ideal society, could be created through human action. History, they reasoned, is progress.

Though the conditions of harmony are natural, it can be achieved only through an understanding of the laws of nature and by working in accordance with them. Ignorance and deceit have kept man in bondage for thousands of years. It is only now that he can free himself by his knowledge of natural law. (Heimann, 1964, 50)

These ideas were soon applied to the economic faculties of human society. Economics was not born as Pallas Athena, burst forth fully armed from Zeus' forehead. The first important steps were taken by the French school of physiocrats. They turned against the predominant mercantilism of their day, and rejected the concept that wealth is created by trade, by exporting more than one imports (through state intervention and tariffs) to enable one to accumulate gold. Applying natural law, the physiocrats maintained that nature, land, and natural resources – transformed by human labor – are the sources of wealth. The economic society reproduces wealth via production and exchange in harmonious cycles. The eighteenth-century French physician François Quesnay, a proponent of the Enlightenment, emerged as one of the first economists with his famous *Tableau économique* (1758), which presented the self-perpetuating process of the creation of wealth with agriculture, without outside force and interference. The French statesman Anne-Robert-Jacques Turgot, associated with the school of physiocrats, abolished mercantilist policy, including internal tariffs, and introduced free trade during his short time in office in the 1760s.

Adam Smith, the son of a customs comptroller in the town of Kirkcaldy, Scotland, entered Glasgow University at the age of fourteen and enthusiastically studied mathematics and natural philosophy (science). He was appointed Chair of Logic and Rhetoric at Glasgow in 1751, and became the Professor of Moral Philosophy a year later. Teaching this subject led him to publish his *Theory of Moral Sentiments* in 1759. This was the first part of a planned comprehensive treatise, a kind of philosophical history that would include literature, theory, and the history of law and government. The latter portion would explore problems of the economy as well.

In 1764, Smith resigned his position and accepted an invitation from France to be the tutor of the young Duke of Buccleuch. During his stay, he met with Quesnay, who was working on a new version of his *Tableau*, and with Turgot, who was writing his *Reflections*. Smith also had contact with contemporary British thinkers such as David Hume, and was familiar with Petty's economic theories positing that land and labor together created the value of goods. Richard Cantillon, the pathbreaking Irish economic theorist living in France, presented a new theory on price and output and the proliferation of revenue in his *Essai sur la nature du commerce en général* (1732), which was translated into English in the 1750s. Mercier de la Rivièra's and Ferdinando Galiani's theoretical works and anti-tariff polemics were also at hand.

But it was Smith's *An Inquiry into the Nature and Causes of the Wealth of Nations* (1776) that established the independent discipline of economics. *The Wealth of Nations* was based on the description and analysis of the existing economic system. As Skinner put it, "What Smith had produced was a model of conceptualized reality, which is essentially descriptive, and which was further illuminated by an analytical system which was so organized as to meet the requirement of the Newtonian model" (Skinner, 2001, 14193).

Smith did not intend to establish a new discipline, but his thorough analysis elucidated most of the central problems of economics. His monumental thousand-page book was the very first of its kind, in sharp contrast with the booklets and essays of most other theorists, and it changed the scholarly landscape. Smith developed the first growth theory based on his concept that the division of labor is central to increasing productivity. For Smith, economic growth results from expanding markets, which intensifies the division of labor and leads to rising productivity, profits, savings, investments, and wages. His pathbreaking theories on the cost of production, value, and prices created a solid foundation of economics. Smith established the basis of the theory of factors of production, land, labor, and capital, and the categories of return, rent, wage, and profit. His theory created the ideology of laissez-faire economics, for free trade is a prerequisite for developing the division of labor and free competition – the essence of a well-functioning economy. Economic freedom is the proper environment for individual activity, and self-interested profit-seeking leads to public good. His famous words, "it is not from the benevolence of the butcher, brewer, and baker, that we expect our dinner, but from their regard for their own interest," reflect the essence of his theory: self-interest serves the public good in a preordained economic harmony, regulated by the "invisible hand" of the free market.

His disciples, however, including the modern neo-liberal school, often oversimplified Smithian economics. Himself a realist, Smith calculated the negative effects of self-interest and the market. Uncontrolled self-interest leads to monopolies, which, for Smith, are baneful and destructive. He called for guaranteed but controlled free competition. Private and public interests, he insisted, are harmonious only when there is free competition. Outside intervention against ever-present monopolistic tendencies is thus necessary. He warned against businesses cooperating among themselves, and thus argued that the interest of labor requires regulation of work conditions. He was aware that markets can produce socially undesirable outcomes and thus necessitated outside intervention. Contrary to others' subsequent simplifications, Smith maintained that public investment is needed in areas such as public utilities, transportation, and universal education, which cannot attract private capital. "Adam Smith was not a doctrinaire advocate of laissez-faire. He saw a wide and elastic range of activity for government, and was prepared to extend it even further if government ... showed itself entitled to wider responsibilities" (Wood, 1984, 164).

Smith's economics was a product of his age, the beginning of the Industrial Revolution, and was unable to foresee the change of the economic system. He believed in private ownership and management, but had strong reservations about corporations (joint-stock companies). He failed to take into account the role of technology in economic growth. But he fostered the birth of classical economics, which became a forceful factor in economic development.

Based on Heimann (1964), Skinner (2001), and Wood (1984).

Turgot's ideas predated those of Adam Smith, who began his career as one of Britain's moral philosophers. In 1776, he published *Wealth of Nations*, a thousand-page treatise that became "the crowning peak of the early development of economic theory" (Heimann, 1964, 63–4). In Smith's view, the economy was a part of the natural world, and economics a part of natural philosophy. The preordained harmony of the market, governed by an "invisible hand" of market forces, rules Smith's economic world in the same way that a preordained harmony rules Newton's universe. This divine harmony of the market invariably resulted in both private advantage and public good. Human intervention (such as tariffs), Smith suggested, only served to block this harmony and was thus harmful; the only good policy, therefore, is allowing the "natural progress of opulence" (Schabas, 2005, 3). Trade and exchange were natural characteristics of human beings, and market capitalism a genuine product of human nature.[27] Smith formulated his free trade theory as a natural law that applied universally across the globe, even though his ideas were based on British experience and interests.

In the Smithian universe, the laws of supply and demand together with the "infallible panacea" of the price mechanism under competitive conditions created a self-regulated market where savings from the proceeds of production naturally turned into purchasing power. Specialization and the division of labor are the primary instruments for increasing productivity and economic growth both in the factory and in the international arena. Smith's *Wealth of Nations* reverberated across the globe. Between 1776 and 1810, twenty-six translations were published, among them six French editions appearing in four different translations.[28]

Based on Smith's economic theory, David Ricardo established the theory of comparative advantage: free trade, he posited, is advantageous for both parties, since each party sells what it can most efficiently produce and buys what it cannot. Trade between industrial and agrarian countries, therefore, is not a zero-sum game in which one party wins and the other loses.

John Stuart Mill introduced the notion of unrestricted private property and the free market being the sole basis of freedom and human rights. In *On Liberty* (1859), Mill relates: "It was once held to be the duty of governments . . . to fix prices, and regulate the process of manufacture. But it is now recognized . . . [that it is much better to leave] the producers and sellers perfectly free . . . Restrictions . . . are . . . evils . . . "(Mill, [1859] 1946, 695, 698). This perfectly corresponded with the principle of individual liberty. In this way, a laissez-faire economy, personal liberty, and democracy were seen as prerequisites for one another. The idea that "almost everything which the State did in the eighteenth century . . . was, or seemed, injurious or unsuccessful . . . [and] that wealth, commerce, and machinery were the children of free competition" (Keynes, 1927, 13–14) pervaded Europe.

These innovations of British philosophy had a strong impact on the French Enlightenment. François-Marie Arouet, who in 1722 adopted the name Voltaire, traveled to England and lived there for three years. He was impressed by the intellectual freedoms the British enjoyed and was inspired by the teachings of Locke and Newton. In *English Letters* (1734), he exudes admiration for Britain and bemoans the rather different French intellectual environment. Through his poems, novels, essays, and pamphlets, Voltaire became one of the most powerful proponents of both natural law, "the instinct which makes us feel justice," and tolerance, since "intolerance is absurd and barbaric, it is the right of the tiger" (Voltaire, 1946, 833, 841). He therefore passionately called for an intellectual revolt against an antiquated church and state.

The French Enlightenment showcased the wit, sarcasm, and lucidity of a legion of writers and philosophers. Charles-Louis de Secondat, baron de Montesquieu, idealized the British parliamentary system and attacked absolute power. Political liberty, he insisted, cannot exist "when the legislative and executive powers are united in the same person or in the same body . . . [T]here is no liberty if the judiciary power [is] not separated from the legislative and executive" (Montesquieu, [1748] 1946, 936, 938). Here, the ideas of a revolutionary social and political system were clearly germinating. The Geneva-born Jean-Jacques Rousseau, who moved to Paris in the mid-eighteenth century, expressed the aura of revolution most eloquently. The very first sentence of his *Social Contract* reads like a declaration of war against the *ancien régime*: "Man is born free and everywhere he is in chains." Whereas every philosopher before him had appealed to elites, Rousseau addressed the masses. He defined an entirely new concept of legitimate power: "Each, while uniting himself with all, may still obey himself alone, and remain as free as before... [Only the] State that is governed by laws... [and] the public interest... [has a] legitimate government" (Rousseau, [1762] 1946, 957, 965).

The Enlightenment was a fundamentally West European phenomenon. One of its greatest representatives in the German principalities was Immanuel Kant, professor at Königsberg University. In his 1784 essay, *Beantwortung der Frage: Was ist Aufklärung?* (Answering the Question: What is Enlightenment?), Kant declared that enlightened mankind was beginning to emerge from its self-incurred immaturity. Jacob Talmon goes so far as to suggest that "Kant and his followers are said to have carried out in the sphere of thought a revolution no less significant than the French Revolution" (Talmon, 1967, 82).

The leading and most celebrated philosopher of the post-Kantian generation, Georg Wilhelm Friedrich Hegel, was mesmerized by Napoleon. On the very day Napoleon entered Jena in 1806, Hegel enthusiastically wrote in a letter: "I saw the Emperor – this world-soul – riding out of the city on reconnaissance."[29] Hegel eagerly welcomed the arrival of the new world order, the end of history embodied in the *Weltseele* (Absolute Spirit) and "Reason" of Napoleon, "who... reaches out over the world and masters it" (Hegel, [1806] 2005, October 13, 1806).

Major intellects such as Cesare Beccaria of Italy, Gaspar Melchor de Jovellanos of Spain, Moses Mendelssohn and Jacob Mauvillon of Germany, Benjamin Constant of Lausanne, and Adam Weishaupt, the founder of the Order of Illuminati, were contemporaries and/or adherents of the Enlightenment. The ideas they espoused were not obscure or inconsequential in the western half of Europe. The new and liberating values of the Enlightenment held tremendous appeal for the elite and the educated throughout the region. "The religion of liberty took hold on the European continent... England, France, and Germany exemplified the evolution of the religion of liberty in Europe" (Mosse, 1988, 119, 130).

This "religion" made liberalism the dominant political trend in the nineteenth century. It was genuinely cosmopolitan and internationalist and it guaranteed individual freedoms under the law. The essential tenets of this secular religion included equality, freedom of belief, the inviolability of private property, and popular sovereignty in both government and civil society. The ideal of liberty incorporated the separation of church and state, the Protestant work ethic, and a new middle-class morality that rejected extravagance. It included as well a belief in the importance of education as a builder of character, and also argued for the respectability of business and business-related occupations. Romanticism, an artistic and intellectual current, became the most influential propagator of liberty, personal freedom, the brotherhood of people, and a yearning for change. The values of the Enlightenment had become institutionalized by newly created legal systems and were now the norms of a modern society.

Demography, agriculture, and industry

During this period Northwestern Europe underwent an immense agricultural revolution. Like that of the chicken or the egg, the question of whether the new agrarian system was a cause or a consequence of economic and demographic changes in the region is one that is endlessly debated. Europe did manage, however, to avoid the "trap" described by the eighteenth-century scholar and clergyman Thomas Malthus, in *An Essay on the Principles of Population* (1798). Malthus found that food production in pre-modern societies increased only arithmetically, while population growth grew geometrically. For centuries crop production created no more than a 20–25 percent marketable (or taxable) surplus – exactly the amount that was taken by the landlords, the church, and the state. The only way to increase output was to expand the area under cultivation, but this required the use of more marginal and less fertile land, which decreased productivity. This Malthusian Trap, with certain fluctuations, led in the long run to stagnant demographic and economic growth, because any population increase resulted in declining living standards, which in turn would restrict population growth.

Northwestern Europe avoided this vicious circle, however, thanks to the combined efforts of Holland and Britain. The answer to the Malthusian Trap was to improve technology, as this was the only way to increase production to feed a growing population. It has also been demonstrated that more affluent families had more surviving children; hence, the growing wealth of Northwest European societies clearly contributed to population growth.[30]

The Low Countries played a pioneering role in the agricultural revolution. Its technological base was partly connected to an early expertise in hydraulic management, land drainage, and irrigation, which enabled it to reclaim large areas of new land. Leading hydraulic engineers honed their skills mastering a challenging Dutch environment, using windmills as power sources for pumps to control water flow in canals. Traditional grain production was replaced by productive and specialized agriculture. Farmers kept livestock in stables and began feeding them forage crops that were byproducts of the crop-rotation system, rather than letting them graze in pastures. In this fashion, they could avoid slaughtering a great part of their stock in winter and springtime, a necessity that for centuries had prevented augmentation of their stock. Consequently, milk production from Dutch cows increased by three to four times during the second half of the eighteenth century. Farmers began specializing in meat, milk, butter, and cheese production. Dutch agriculture also switched from cereal production to horticulture, vegetable cultivation, and, in time, labor-intensive industrial crops such as hops, hemp, flax, madder, and flowers.

The Dutch were among the first to use manure to enrich the soil, which the penning of cattle had made possible. In contrast, most European countries at that time dried the manure to use for heating. Land improvement in Holland led to the highest yields in the sixteenth and seventeenth centuries, two to three times higher than anywhere else in Europe. Indeed, Holland was then "the only part of Europe which had, thus far, experienced a true agricultural revolution" (Israel, 1995, 111–12). "The province of Holland . . . is a richer country than England," observed Adam Smith in 1776.

Britain's agrarian advances were the direct result of the Flemish and Dutch agricultural revolutions. The British borrowed methods of soil reclamation, such as drainage and canalization, from the Dutch, and employed the Dutch hydro-engineer Cornelius Vermuyden, to successfully attain higher yields. By that point Britain was more than ready for a breakthrough: a long process of replacing feudal with capitalist landownership, and serfdom with tenant farming and yeomanry, assured increasing development between the fourteenth and seventeenth centuries. Its enclosure system created a new class of wage earners, and its emerging market system led to a more advanced division of labor.

The key to modernization was the enclosure system, the last stage of which was seen in the eighteenth century.[31] "[T]he principal landowners of the village petitioned Parliament for a bill to enclose their village. Unanimity of the owners was not required." If 75–80 percent of the owners were in favor, the bill passed (Allen, 1994, 98, 115). More than 5,200 acts enclosed 6.8 million acres of common pastureland. Improvement and expansion of land soon followed. The arable pasture and meadowland increased from 21 million acres in 1700 to 36.6 million by 1850. This was accompanied by dynamic technological innovations, which proliferated with the help of accessible publications.[32] Among them, the modern crop-rotation system merits attention. The old method of preventing soil depletion through two- or three-crop rotations meant that half or a third of arable land remained fallow at any given time. Modern scientific crop rotation – the so-called Townshend four-crop rotation (wheat, turnips, barley, and clover) – decreased fallow land dramatically. The more sophisticated Norfolk system successfully used seventeen kinds of rotating crops to preserve and even enrich the soil, thanks to the nitrogen-fixing mechanism of legumes. This single innovation increased the area of cultivated land by at least a third. By 1850, the yield of wheat in Britain was more than twice that on the continent. Indeed, this higher productivity was true for both land and labor.[33] The average British farmer was able to feed two and a half families in the seventeenth and eighteenth centuries. Marketable surplus products increased from 20–25 percent of the harvest to 40–50 percent. Herds multiplied during the seventeenth century, with the average size of sheep flocks on farms in the Oxfordshire region increasing more than fourfold (Jones, 1967). Britain's horse population rose from roughly 1.3 million in 1811 to nearly 3.3 million by 1901. According to E. A. Wrigley's estimations, output per worker in British agriculture generally increased by 60–100 percent between 1600 and 1800. England's ability to feed its population doubled during this period – in sharp contrast to France, where agricultural productivity grew by only 20 percent.

A great part of Britain's growing population was now employed outside agriculture, and its agricultural labor force eventually stagnated – totaling 1.5 million in both 1700 and 1851. The quality of the labor force improved as the number of working women and boys dropped, while employment of adult males rose by a third. Of the adult male workforce, 61.2% was employed in agriculture in 1700, which decreased to 40.8% in 1800 and 28.6% in 1840. Instead, an increasing number of workers were employed in industry – jumping from 18.5% in 1700 to 47.3% in 1840 (Crafts, 1994, 45; Allen, 1994, 107).[34] This was paralleled by a rise in industrial investment in the country, surpassing agricultural investment by 1820.

Britain's unique agricultural history paved the way for industrialization. Cheap and sufficient food supplies enabled the country to build a manufacturing base quite early at the local level and were a key factor in Britain's rapid urbanization between the sixteenth and eighteenth centuries – a period that witnessed a doubling of the number of British towns, while urbanization on the continent declined.

The Dutch Golden Age in the sixteenth and seventeenth centuries, and, more importantly, the British rise to prosperity and power during the seventeenth and eighteenth centuries, went hand in hand with demographic change. The "demographic revolution," as the French demographer Adolphe Landry called it (Landry, 1934), led to a population growth that was unparalleled in history. According to Angus Maddison's calculations (2001), the demographic changes shown in Table 1.1 took place between 1500 and 1820.

Table 1.1 The population of Western Europe, Britain, and the Netherlands, 1500–1820 (thousands)[a]

	1500	%	1600	%	1700	%	1820	%
Holland	950	100	1,500	157	1,900	200	2,355	248
Britain	3,942	100	6,170	157	8,565	217	21,226	538
Western Europe[b]	52,376	100	66,108	126	70,995	136	109,307	209

Source: Maddison (2001, 232).

[a] According to Roger Mols' evaluation, of Europe's inhabitants from roughly 82 million in 1500 to approximately 105 million by 1600 and more than 120 million by 1700. However, from the eighteenth century on, and particularly from the 1740s on, an unprecedented population explosion took place: the number of people increased from 120–140 million to 180–190 million, i.e. the growth rate doubled in half a century (Mols, 1974).

[b] Western Europe excluding Britain and the Netherlands.

Figure 1.3
Population growth in Western Europe, 1500–1820 (million) (Maddison, 2001, 232)

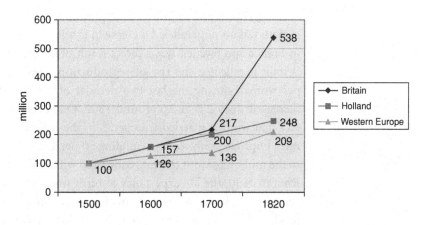

During the sixteenth century, the population of the Netherlands and Britain increased somewhat faster than did that of the rest of Western Europe, but that differential became much more pronounced by 1700: Western Europe's population increased by 36 percent, while the Netherlands' and Britain's more than doubled. Holland's population growth did level off in the eighteenth century, but this was by no means the case with Britain: its population increased by two and a half times in the eighteenth century, compared with a 54 percent rise in Western Europe; and Britain's total was five times higher than in 1500, while Western Europe's was only twice as large. (See Figure 1.3.)

For centuries, high birth rates had always been offset by high death rates. Famine, wars, and disease (including smallpox, plague, and cholera) regularly decimated the population, assuring that growth rates remained low – about 0.5 percent annually.[35] Another factor of slow population growth was an extremely high infant mortality rate. Until the eighteenth century, roughly half of the newborns died each year. Even in the first half of the eighteenth century, nearly every fifth infant died in the first year of life in England.

This situation changed dramatically in the Netherlands and Britain, primarily owing to a significant increase in the food supply. In addition, the advanced European countries slowly began to control the spread of a number of contagious diseases. Edward Jenner, a British general practitioner in Berkeley, Gloucestershire, developed a vaccine for smallpox in 1796 – ridding society of the horror of smallpox pandemics, which for centuries had wiped out a third of those contracting the disease. Civil initiatives were launched to improve healthcare and develop vaccines – a drive that was institutionalized with the founding of the National Vaccination Establishment in 1808.

After 1750, however, the most important factor in Britain's population growth was an unparalleled increase in fertility. While population growth in France and Sweden was a direct result of declining mortality rates, in Britain it reflected the rise of reproduction rates: between 1.9 and 2.2 per woman during the last two decades of the seventeenth century, it increased from 2.8 to 3.0 around 1800. One explanation for this is the fact that women married younger.[36] In the meantime, British mortality rates improved only slowly – totaling 30 per 1,000 in England and Wales in the mid-eighteenth century, compared with a birth rate of 35 per 1,000. Even in 1830, the life expectancy at birth was a little less than forty-one years in Britain, an increase of only four years since 1700. However, better food supplies and higher income levels had a positive impact on birth rates, and population growth began to take off throughout the country. This necessitated the creation of jobs and the employment of more people outside agriculture, and it assured a larger labor force for an increasingly dynamic economy.[37]

Proto-industrialization[38] also developed in this period. For centuries, the main forms of industrial activities were performed either in peasant homes or by strictly regulated urban guilds. The peasant cottage industry was self-sufficient and produced everything the family needed, from clothing to tools. However, this cottage industry became the springboard of market-oriented manufacturing from the fifteenth century on, especially in areas with limited agricultural prospects and/or poor soil quality.

Proto-industry produced goods not only for local markets, but also for world markets in need of mass-produced, specialized products. This became a major source of supplemental income. J. L. Van Zanden concludes that the rural structure in the Netherlands was "characterized by small holdings that were generally too small to maintain a household... [I]n large parts of the countryside agriculture was only of secondary importance." Rather, herring fishing, peat cutting, spinning, and cloth making, he notes, were often the "most important means of livelihood" (Van Zanden, 1993, 33; 2001, 88).

Proto-industry developed in various ways during the early modern centuries. One way was the *Kaufsystem*, in which self-trained peasant artisans produced their own raw materials from their land and processed them with their own tools. Where the guild system was weak or non-existent, independent urban artisans broadened the artisan industry's domain. They sold low-quality products to their community, often to merchants at the local marketplace.[39]

Another form of proto-industry, called the putting-out, or *Verlag*, system, became more important and pervasive.[40] An urban phenomenon that dated back to the fourteenth century in Flanders and Brabant, it spread to rural areas in the eighteenth. Peasant households and the traditional cottage industry became part of a larger organization led by a merchant-industrialist, who bought raw materials and distributed them among the peasants. Family members, in most cases women and children, processed or produced some kind of unfinished product or a part of a product, and then passed it on to other cottage industries, which finished the job. Weavers continued the work of spinners, and dyers continued the work of weavers. The merchant-industrialist, the key figure in the putting-out system, paid for the piecework, quite often completing production in his factory, and sold the product. Entrepreneurs regularly organized hundreds or even thousands of peasant home workers, devised a division of labor among them, supplied them with raw materials, collected their products, and sold them, often to foreign markets.

Franklin Mendels argued that the putting-out system was "the first phase of industrialization." The system produced an army of industrial workers and provided capital for merchant-industrialists, who occasionally became factory owners and "captains of industry." In most cases, however, cottage industry did not play this role, for it was highly seasonal, fluctuated according to the demands of agricultural work, and was unable to sustain permanent production. Moreover, this peasant activity exhibited the traditional behavior of non-market-oriented self-sufficient households: unlimited self-exploitation in bad times, but refraining from doing additional work for higher income during good harvests and price rises. In other words, the putting-out system was not a gateway to a higher stage of industrialization. The Industrial Revolution mostly eliminated proto-industry (Schlumbohm, 1983; Medick, 1976; Jeannin, 1980). Still, proto-industry did increase family income and consumption, and the "industrious revolution" that it represented created the market and the demand-side incentive for further industrial development.

The merchant-led putting-out, or *Verlag*, system triggered a boom in industrial activity that led to the rise of the factory system, a major British invention during the eighteenth century. In the putting-out system, the final phase of production at times took place in a factory building, where hundreds and sometimes thousands of laborers worked under one roof. Before the mid-eighteenth century, factories with several hundred workers were already in operation.[41]

The factory, however, was not simply a larger workplace; it was also a new form of organization. Merchant entrepreneurs organized production in a new system: each worker performed only a single element of the operation. One group of workers produced one set of parts, another group a second set of parts, while a third group assembled the complete product. The industrial division of labor, Adam Smith enthusiastically noted, increased productivity. At the same time, it enabled unskilled laborers to be trained on the job.

At the turn of the nineteenth century, factories employed large numbers of underpaid, unskilled women and child laborers. During this period factory workers labored from dawn to dusk in substandard conditions and under strict regimentation, and endured an average 60–76 hour work-week by 1840. The mistreatment of workers and particularly of child laborers sparked immediate social outrage and several state inquiries.[42]

Erecting factories made it possible to control workers, and later to introduce modern management and quality control. A successful proto-industry combined with the factory system made Britain the "industrial workshop of the world" in the eighteenth century. Another important advantage was the factories' ability to accommodate modern machinery that required large, centralized layouts, and to use the same power source for several machines.

Industrialists were able to take full advantage of large factories when high wages engendered labor-saving investment in machinery. "England stood apart from the rest of the world in having high relative wages" (Allen, 2009a, 904). Nominal wages in London increased by nearly five times between 1575 and 1825, while they stagnated in Antwerp, Vienna, and northern Italy. Wages remained at around subsistence level in the

European and other peripheries, but they surpassed it in London by five to six times. Wages relative to the cost of capital in 1730 were 0.8 in France and 1.3 in England, and the gap would significantly increase by 1830. Real wages in England were roughly 50 percent higher than anywhere else in Europe at the dawn of the Industrial Revolution. In the large French and especially Indian textile industries, maintaining cheap labor did not encourage investment in machinery. In contrast, "the Industrial Revolution," Robert Allen correctly notes, "was the consequence of the high-wage economy" in Britain (Allen, 2009a, 911, 923: 2004, 19–20).

Britain gradually became the world's leading exporter of industrial products thanks to successful proto-industrialization. The woolen industry in the Cotswolds, Oxfordshire, East Anglia, and other regions played a unique and important role in the British economy much earlier than it did elsewhere. Already in 1700, more than 80% of British exports were manufactured goods. In the mid-eighteenth century, 85% of British imports consisted of raw materials and food (Crafts, 1985: 62, 143). Between 1700 and 1750, the value of British overseas exports doubled. At the same time, Britain duplicated the Dutch practice of re-exporting goods. It processed and re-exported sugar, tobacco, cotton, and indigo, which had been imported from its colonies in North America, Asia, and Africa. In 1750, one-quarter of its overseas exports consisted of re-exported goods – roughly 80% of which went to continental Europe. Until the early 1770s, its most important export items were woolen goods (more than 57% in 1700, and still more than 42% in 1772), other textiles (3% in 1700 and 13% in 1772), and iron (less than 2% in 1700, but 8% in 1772) (Mathias, 1969, 96–7).

In the meantime, practically all of the rest of Europe endured continual stagnation. Per capita income increased only about 0.04–0.08% per annum in Europe between 1500 and 1800.[43] However, Northwestern Europe was much more dynamic. Labor productivity in British agriculture increased by two and a half times between 1600 and 1800, and its output grew by 70–75% in the eighteenth century. A gradual growth of industry also contributed to an increase in productivity.

Table 1.2 clearly reflects the economic dynamism of early modern Northwestern Europe. In 1500, Italy, Spain, and Portugal had a higher per capita GDP level than did Northwestern Europe. The Dutch success dominated the sixteenth and seventeenth centuries, with a near trebling (267%) of their income. Britain was unable to match this achievement (attaining a 184% rise), but it had a much better performance record than any other European country. Its dynamism markedly

Table 1.2 GDP per capita between 1500 and 1820 (in 1990 Geary Khamis dollars)

Country	1500	1700	1820	1820 (as % of 1500)	1820 (as % of 1700)
Holland	754	2,010	1,821	242	91
Britain	762	1,405	2,121	278	151
France	727	986	1,230	169	125
Mediterranean[a]	810	951	1,047	124	110

Source: Maddison (2001, 90).

Note: [a] Includes Italy, Spain, and Portugal.

Figure 1.4 Per capita GDP in the Mediterranean and northern Europe, 1500–1820 (in 1990 dollars) (Maddison, 2001, 90)

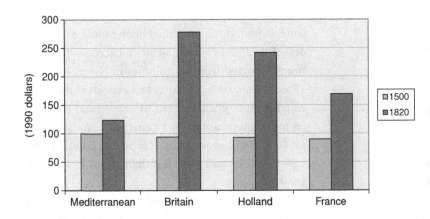

increased in the eighteenth century. While the Netherlands' income declined 9% from its 1700 level, Britain raised its income by more than 50% – to double that of France. The Mediterranean countries, meanwhile, continued to stagnate (10% increase of per capita GDP). (See Figure 1.4.)

Britain's mastery in world trade, its immense colonial monopoly, its progress in proto-industrialization and the factory system, and its substantial population growth and wage hikes opened the gates to a revolutionary transformation – traditionally called the British Industrial Revolution. The process that started in the 1770s–1780s and continued through the 1820s led to the greatest discontinuity in modern history.

The Industrial Revolution

Coming on the heels of all these developments, a slew of technological innovations "suddenly" appeared, one after the other, in late eighteenth-century Britain. The invention of the flying shuttle in 1733 by John Kay was but one of a series of inventions that increased the productivity of weaving by 30–50 percent and triggered a demand for thread. In 1760, the Society of Arts offered an award for the creation of a more productive spinning machine. Four years later, and after several unsuccessful attempts, the weaver and carpenter James Hargreaves created the eight-spindle spinning jenny, which raised productivity eight to ten times. One worker could now operate two machines by hand in a traditional family workshop. A few years later (1769), Richard Arkwright, a hairdresser, patented a spinning water frame that utilized water power to move a hundred spindles. Arkwright also revamped the carding machine, patented by Lewis Paul in 1742, to better prepare cotton for his machine. In 1785, Samuel Crompton combined Hargreaves' jenny and Arkwright's frame into his spinning "mule," which produced fine thread and could be powered by a steam engine. Richard Roberts' self-acting mule (with its improved version in 1830) was yet another innovation of this groundbreaking technology. Productivity consequently skyrocketed: while it had previously taken 50,000 hours to spin 100 pounds of cotton, this was now reduced by the self-acting mule to 135 hours (Chapman, 1972; Mokyr, 1990: 99).

The mechanization of spinning raised productivity to such a degree that weaving began experiencing bottlenecks. To solve this problem, a clergyman named Edmund Cartwright invented mechanized weaving and patented the power loom in 1787. Thomas Johnson's dandy loom accelerated weaving further in 1805. In 1783, James Bell patented the roller printer machine, which did the work of forty hand-block printers and increased productivity by forty times. The process of whitening yarn required it to sit for weeks or months under the sun, until Claude Louis Berthollet, a French chemist and an inspector of the Gobelins tapestry factory, began in 1784 to use chlorine as bleach. Charles Tennant improved this process in 1799 by adding slaked lime to the chlorine and producing bleaching powder, thereby shortening the bleaching process to a few hours. Copper cylinders mechanized the printing of colored patterns by a rolling process that was invented by Thomas Bell in 1783. The working hours for producing cotton yarn dropped to 6 percent of what was required for Indian hand-spinning. As a result, the piece price of cotton had dropped by two-thirds by 1841.

In addition to cotton bleaching, the French contribution to the textile revolution was especially important in mechanizing the silk, woolen, and linen industries. The mechanization of weaving silk or worsted (from combed wool) was the brainchild of Jean-Marie Jacquard, who used coded punch cards to control the pattern in his loom in 1801. French ingenuity in using interchangeable parts in musket production, sugar refining, and other domains was put into practice and improved on in Britain. This was also the case with Philippe de Girard's 1810 invention of the wet spinning of flax, which made the mechanization of linen spinning possible; or with N. L. Robert's invention, the continuous paper-sheet maker; or with N. Appert's important innovations in food canning. The Frenchman Josué Heilmann's 1845 patent of a wool-combing machine led to a breakthrough in mechanizing the least mechanized branch of the textile industry. Christine MacLeod goes so far as to state that the mechanization of Britain's cotton industry was an offshoot of Western European technological development, since "Britain was able to draw on a reservoir of technique accumulated across the whole of Europe . . . The British Industrial Revolution was ultimately a European achievement." In her view, only the rise of the coal industry was a genuinely British invention (MacLeod, 2004, 115, 120, 126).

The fact that many important inventors were amateurs, and not engineers, has suggested to some that there was virtually no connection between science and industry in the Industrial Revolution. Technological inventions, it has been pointed out, were mostly the products of uneducated empiricists. Several authors have posited that education was not important at this stage of industrial development.[44] According to the traditional view, only the second Industrial Revolution during the second half of the century, which revolutionized the steel industry and created modern chemistry and electricity, was actually based on science. It was at that time that the "regular flow of ideas between laboratories and firms set in" (Postan, 1967, 154). A. E. Musson and Eric Robinson have challenged this traditional view and have stressed "how fruitful [the] collaboration between science and technology [was] during the Industrial Revolution," which "was not simply a product of illiterate craftsmen, devoid of scientific training" (Musson and Robinson, 1969, 7).

To be self-taught in technological matters was not an uncommon occurrence in Britain because of the myriad popular publications and public lectures in London coffee shops. In the 1780s, the Chapter Coffee House began a lecture series on mathematics, while the Marine, Button's, and Bedford coffee houses held talks on "experimental philosophy." Towering figures of the Industrial Revolution, such as James Watt and Josiah Wedgwood, regularly attended such lectures. Even members of the Royal Society were intrigued by the practical applications of "natural philosophy," as physics was called at that time. "Intelligent empiricism and applied science" were inseparable. Current research has produced a wealth of information on how science and Newtonian physics impacted on everyday, practical experiments (Jacob and Stewart, 2004).

Several private arts and science associations, such as the Dublin Society, the Manchester Literary and Philosophical Society, the Birmingham Lunar Society, and the Society of Arts in London, offered awards for innovative technological solutions to practical industrial problems. Prizes were awarded for improvements in tanning procedures and for innovations in the chemical and agricultural fields. Artisans, tradesmen, and instrument makers were regularly made members of the Mathematical Society, which lent out books and instruments such as air pumps, telescopes, and microscopes (Musson and Robinson, 1969, 31, 53–4, 58–9). Most of these associations were gathering places for scientists, engineers, and mechanics, who exchanged ideas in organized discussions. Joel Mokyr stresses the role of the "penetration of 'scientific method' into technological research: accurate measurement, controlled experiment, insistence on reproducibility and systematic reporting of materials and methods... [and the] applications of mathematics... in mechanical engineering... Mathematics was needed in measurement, civil engineering, ballistics, optics, navigation, and hydraulic systems" (Mokyr, 1994, 36; 1990, 75). Scholars, engineers, technicians, skilled workers, and interested amateurs flocked to these associations to apprise themselves of the latest developments in technology.

Britain held a tremendous advantage in its skilled labor force before the Industrial Revolution, thanks to its long-standing industrial climb. Its advanced and pervasive cottage industry was one of the "training camps" of a large army of wage laborers. The other main source was the urban guilds, which produced hundreds of thousands of highly skilled workers. At the beginning of the eighteenth century, roughly 300,000–460,000 apprentices received advanced, state-of-the-art technical training in metallurgy, textiles, mining, and instrument and glass making, and they applied that knowledge throughout the country (Epstein, 2008, 161–5).[45] A vast supplemental source of mostly unskilled laborers came from Ireland, representing approximately 9 percent of the 6.8 million workforce in 1841 (Mokyr, 1999, 91).

Britain's cutting-edge clock-making and shipping industries, its production of highly developed naval instruments, and the continuing collaboration of scientists, engineers, and businessmen, all pointed to a British environment that was highly suitable for technological and industrial progress. It was often pointed out at the time that Britain's technological advantage was owing to an ability not to invent new technology, but to improve on the existing one.[46]

This fact demonstrates the truly pan-European nature of the Industrial Revolution, particularly if one considers its historical development and its wide circle of European sources – determining a pattern of theoretical inventions leading to practical innovations.[47] This is aptly demonstrated by the history of the hallmark invention of the British Industrial Revolution, the steam engine. Its discovery would have been possible without an understanding of atmospheric pressure or vacuity, for it had been common knowledge for centuries that air had no weight. But the Italian Evangelista Toricelli found that the opposite was in fact true, and he measured atmospheric pressure using a barometer in 1643. A few years later, the German Otto von Guericke, later the mayor of Magdeburg, proved that vacuity was a genuine phenomenon when he created a vacuum with an air pump in 1657. The fact that a vacuum could be repeatedly created led to the realization that it could be a source of power. In 1679, Denis Papin, a French Huguenot collaborating with Christiaan Huygens and Gottfried Leibniz in Paris, invented a steam digester (high-pressure cooker) with a steam-release valve. His prototype machine in 1691 became the model for the piston-and-cylinder steam engine. On that basis, the military engineer Thomas Savery, conducting experiments at Hampton Court for King William III and the Royal Society, constructed and patented a "fire engine," the first steam engine, in 1698. In the early eighteenth century, the blacksmith Thomas Newcomen improved Savery's steam engine and repeatedly created a vacuum by condensation. And unlike Savery's, Newcomen's engine was safe. The early steam engines were able to pump water from mines, but they were unable to work continuously. This problem was solved when James Watt separated the condenser from the piston cylinder, enabling the latter to stay hot continuously. After several additional improvements, Watt created the efficient steam engine. In 1802, after the expiration of Watt's patent, another Englishman, Richard Trevithick, constructed the high-pressure compound engine, which, with a few more improvements, became twice as fuel-efficient as Watt's engine. It took from the mid-seventeenth to the early nineteenth century, and required the consecutive contributions of a host of Italian, German, French, and British trailblazers, for the modern steam engine to be fully realized.

Although French science was more theoretically oriented, its practical applicability was incentivized during the Napoleonic years. France established the first institute for advanced engineering, the École des Ponts et Chaussées, in 1747, followed by a number of higher learning science and technology institutes. During the revolutionary and Napoleonic years, the entire system was reorganized and new institutions established.[48] Condorcet advocated the teaching of mathematics and physics in his report to the Committee of Public Instruction in 1792, asserting that students of science would "see the coming of an epoch when the practical usefulness of their application will reach greater dimensions than were ever hoped for" (Cameron, 1966, 38). In 1794, the Committee of Public Instruction founded the École Centrale des Travaux Publics (renamed École Polytechnique the following year), a model institution for the entire continent. These technical schools trained students from all over Europe – among them the Germans Alexander Humboldt and Justus Liebig, scholars of central importance in the second Industrial Revolution. One-fourth of the student body of the École Centrale was from other European countries. Between 1825 and 1875, the École des Ponts et Chaussées had more than three hundred foreign students.

Box 1.2   James Watt and the mother of all inventions: the steam engine

Legend has it that, when James Watt was a young boy, he was sitting in his mother's kitchen watching steam rise from the top of their tea kettle when he got his big idea. Not exactly. The steam engine has a long history. Thomas Savery, a highly trained military engineer reportedly influenced by Denis Papin's pressure cooker, patented "The Miner's Friend," the first fire pump engine in 1698. There are stories that the engine exploded when it was exhibited in the presence of King William III at Hampton Court. The Savery engine was designed to pump water out of mines. Fourteen years later, in 1712, Thomas Newcomen, a blacksmith, patented his fire machine. Watt was not even born at that time. The Newcomen machine, though an improved version, was still a pump engine, incapable of continuous movement and extremely ineffective because of its tremendous loss of steam and thus its huge consumption of coal. Nevertheless, his engines were used in mines for sixty years. By 1775, some 130 Newcomen engines were in operation in Britain.

James Watt was the inventor of, if not the steam engine, then the first modern, efficient steam engine – the new power source of the Industrial Revolution and the nineteenth-century economy. As were many leading contributors to the rise of the modern economy, Watt was a Scotsman, born in 1736, at the outset of the Industrial Revolution. The young James learned much about instruments and machines from his father, a carpenter who worked in shipbuilding, and he decided to learn instrument making. At the age of eighteen, he went to Glasgow, but was advised to go to London to learn the skill as an apprentice. John Morgan accepted him and, recognizing his talent, taught him in a year, instead of the official seven-year apprenticeship period. In 1756, Watt went back to Glasgow and set up a shop at the university as "Mathematical-Instrument Maker of the University."

In 1763, Professor John Anderson commissioned Watt to investigate the cause of the severe steam loss and high coal consumption of the university's Newcomen model. Watt began working on the problem, scrutinized the workings of the machine, and, at the age of twenty-nine, while (as he described it) walking across the Glasgow green on a Saturday afternoon in 1765, he suddenly found the solution. On Monday, he ran to his shop and began building a model of the first modern steam engine. He had realized that the main source of energy loss was the alternate heating and cooling of the cylinder of the Newcomen engine. The cooled cylinder had to reheat again, which hindered continuous operation and caused a tremendous loss of energy. His idea was to make the condensation of the steam separately in a condensing vessel that was kept cool, while the cylinder was kept hot all the time, avoiding the cyclical cooling and reheating process. While a vacuum was pulling the cylinder down, valves permitted the steam to go into a separate condenser. In 1769, Watt patented the separate condensing chamber.

His revolutionary idea, however, was not sufficient. It took six months for Watt to build a model machine, and eleven years before a functional machine was ready. The first two experiments failed, with steam escaping from the engine. As one of the early chroniclers of the story of the steam engine, Andrew Carnegie, observed, Watt the mechanic was almost as important as Watt the inventor (Carnegie, 1905). Dozens of "minor" problems had to be solved, among them an appropriate isolation of the cylinder, oil lubrication, etc. In 1775, Watt proved the engine's viability. It was much better than the Newcomen, but Watt was not yet satisfied with the result. He continued his research. It took another fifteen years before the Watt engine was actually ready. In 1781 and 1782, Watt replaced the reciprocal engine motion with rotating motion, and then with a double-acting engine. The rotary engine (one wheel rotating around the other), called "sun and planet motion," increased efficiency since it admitted the steam alternately into both ends of the cylinder. In 1788, Watt invented the centrifugal governor that automatically regulated the speed of the engine, thus inventing the principal of servo-mechanism (later so crucial for automation).

Genius that he was, James Watt the inventor and mechanic was still not enough to spread word of this miraculous machine. Watt the businessman was also needed. And he sought, indeed, collaborating entrepreneurs with large capital resources. First, he found John Roebuck, a mine owner, and then Matthew Boulton, a venture capitalist who had an engineering factory in Birmingham. Boulton wanted to secure a longer monopoly period, and Watt arranged that the patent be extended until 1800. At last Boulton & Watt Co. began producing steam engines. Eventually, this company produced every steam engine operating in Britain before 1800. In that year, 321 engines were in operation with 5,210 horsepower capacity. Most were in new industries, such as cotton, which installed fifty-four engines with 1,382 horsepower. Fifty-four steam engines were in use in Manchester, Birmingham, and Leeds.

Measuring the capacity of the steam engine by horsepower was also Watt's invention. In 1782, a sawmill ordered an engine from the company to replace twelve horses. According to the precise data that the mill provided, a horse could lift 33,000 pounds the distance of one foot in one minute. Watt calculated the capacity of the engine accordingly, and called the unit horsepower.

For a century, James Watt's steam engine served as the main energy source and the engine of mechanization of industry and transportation. This invention became the mother of Europe's industrialization during the nineteenth century.

Based on Carnegie (1905), Marsden (2004), and Hills (1993).

The direct connection between technological training and the Industrial Revolution is well illustrated by the fact that Joseph M. Jacquard, the inventor of the silk loom, Joseph-Eugène Schneider, the manager of the Creusot factory, and Jacques Peugeot, the founder of a leading car factory, were all students who received a specialized scientific education that stressed practical application. As the prospectus of the École Centrale des Arts et Manufactures (established in 1828–9) specified, its mandate was "the training of civil engineers, factory managers, industrialists."

French science was indeed the best in the world around the turn of the nineteenth century. Thanks to another French invention, the specialized scientific journals such as the *Annales de chimie* (1789), *Journal des mines* (1794), and *Journal de l'École Polytechnique* (1795), French scientific and technical know-how spread rapidly across the continent. French educational textbooks were translated and used in institutions all over Europe. When Justus Liebig returned to Germany from France in 1826, he established the first modern laboratory in Germany (in the town of Giessen).

Belgium established its own Corps des Ponts et Chaussées and École des Mines de Liège. The Paris Polytechnique became the model for similar institutions in Prague in 1806, in Vienna in 1815, and in Stockholm in 1825.[49] Denmark would soon follow in 1829, and Liège and Ghent in 1835. A number of German Technische Hochschulen were established in the 1820s and 1830s, and Zurich's Eidgenössische Technische Hochschule opened its doors in 1848 (Cameron, 1966, 37–45).

One invention precipitated the need for another, and this succession of inventions characterized the entire age. Technical breakthroughs revolutionized the cotton industry, and they enabled countries to mechanize their factories without having to make prohibitively large investments.[50] In Britain, the leader of merchant capitalism, the bulk of the capital it generated filled the pockets of its wealthiest families. During the Industrial Revolution, those in the top 10 percent income band acquired 45 percent of the country's revenue. This enabled many to amass considerable savings and make crucial investments: the rate of investment compared with the Gross National Product was only 4 percent in 1700, but it doubled by 1801 and trebled by 1831 (Crafts, 1985, 73–4). And investment, including the buying of raw materials and the hiring of workers, was possible primarily because of family savings. Such investments were often bolstered by loans and investments by extended family members. In addition to this, the early British banking system (discussed in Chapter 4) offered ample credit opportunities. Shedding their role as deposit and loan institutions, several banks began acting like "venture capitalists" in the late eighteenth century and became "investment vehicles for wealthy people" – mostly insiders, closely connected to the bank. Borrowing two hundred and fifty times a median salary was quite common. At the turn of the nineteenth century, moreover, "some of the county banks were investing aggressively in speculative new technologies" (Brunt, 2006, 75, 86, 98).[51]

As Larry Neal has convincingly argued, Britain profited from the dramatic changes in international capital transactions, which "occurred precisely during and because of the Napoleonic Wars." The international capital market played a much larger role in financing the British Industrial Revolution than has been previously considered. During those years, astute merchants and rentiers liquidated their continental assets and placed them "in secure and liquid British government securities." Neal pinpointed "an economically logical link between the French Revolution and the British industrial revolution" (Neal, 1990, 218, 222).

This "logical link" was not only financial connections, however. Britain also enjoyed the unique advantage of facing scarce competition during the Industrial Revolution, because continental Europe was preoccupied with the French Revolution and the Napoleonic wars for a quarter of a century.

Britain's Industrial Revolution was best exemplified by its cotton textile industry. In 1760, Britain imported 2.5 million pounds of raw cotton; by 1787, it was 22 million, and by the 1840s, it was 366 million. Raw cotton at that time represented nearly one-fifth of British imports. This would soon change. By 1845, there were 17.5 million spindles and 250,000 mechanized power looms in operation in the British textile industry. The cotton industry stood at the center of the Industrial Revolution and became the most dynamic sector of the economy. During the first half of the eighteenth century, the cotton industry grew by 1.37% per year; between 1770 and 1780, however, yearly growth jumped to 6.2%, and then to 12.76% the following decade. Though it would settle back to the 5–6% level between 1790 and 1830, its impact on the British economy was unmistakable. Exports skyrocketed. Between 1700 and 1800, the value of British exports increased by six times, and, by 1830, 50% of those exports were cotton. Nothing better illustrated the one-sided structure of the British economy.[52]

Mechanized textile factories also dramatically cut the price of merchandise. The price of one pound of cotton yarn dropped from 10.11 shillings in 1784 to 0.11 shillings in 1832, one-twentieth of the price before mechanization. Britain supplied the entire world with cotton products, and the volume of its exports was one-and-a-third times greater than its home consumption.

The hallmark of the new technology, however, was the steam engine. Wind and water power had been widely used for centuries in cottage industries, and they continued to be used in eighteenth-century British factories. But these sources of energy were not readily available in every location. This impelled the most enterprising Englishmen to find a way to extract energy from the country's abundant coal reserves. The continual forward strides from Savery's "fire engine" in 1698 to Watt's steam engine in 1765 illustrate this process well. The story of the steam engine, however, did not end in 1765.[53] The Boulton and Watt steam-engine factory was an enormous success, and it retained a patented monopoly of the engine until 1800. By that juncture, the factory had already produced 2,500 steam engines. Watt's engine used 7.5 pounds of coal per horsepower hour, but this fell to 2.5 pounds by the mid-nineteenth century – a fragment compared with the 30 pounds that Newcomen's engine consumed. In David Landes' estimation, 496 factories and mines in Britain used steam engines with nearly 10,000 horsepower capacity in 1800. By 1815 that capacity increased to 210,000 and by 1850, the combined horsepower of stationary and mobile steam engines was 1.3 million.

The development of the steam engine hastened the modernization of the textile industry, and was crucial to the transformation of the iron industry. The smelting and refining of iron was not nearly as important an industry in Britain as textiles, but it nevertheless led to a new spate of technological innovations. Iron had been produced in ancient China and then in medieval Europe. Smelters and smiths had traditionally used charcoal and later coal, but they lacked the technology to produce pure metal. Several industries had utilized coke in the seventeenth century, but the iron industry could not find a way to do so. This would change in 1709, when Abraham Darby substituted charcoal with coal in a blast furnace. But it took several more decades to improve the process.

Important innovations quickly followed: the invention of the cast-iron blowing cylinder in the 1760s, its combined application with the rotating steam engine in 1776, and their integration with preheated air discovered by James Beaumont Neilson in 1829. These improvements decreased coal and coke consumption by up to two-thirds and increased furnace output. Coke replaced charcoal in Britain in the 1780s when the building of charcoal-heated furnaces finally halted. In 1788, 53 coke-heated furnaces produced 79 percent of the country's iron; by 1806, 195 furnaces produced 97 percent.

The 1780s saw another major breakthrough for the iron industry. In 1775, an ironmaster named Henry Cort bought a forge and iron mill in Portsmouth harbor. Two of his patented inventions, the steam-powered rolling process in 1783 and the puddling furnace in 1784, radically transformed the process of iron making. The use of grooved rollers to finish the iron replaced slow and labor-intensive hammering, while the combination of puddling and rolling to decarbonize pig iron and produce wrought iron in one step, and using coal for it, decreased coal consumption to one-third per one ton of crude iron. By 1820, 8,200 of Cort's furnaces were already in operation. In the 1830s, Joseph Hall, a puddler, substituted sand with his patented "bulldog," roasted tap cinder that decreased waste to 8 percent. He established his own iron works at Tipton. During the 1830s, several cost-reducing methods were introduced that decreased the cost of production by two-thirds. In 1839, an engineer, James Nasmyth, invented the steam hammer and established his own foundry. The series of inventions during the Industrial Revolution established the modern iron industry in Britain.

The advance of the steam engine and of modern iron technology increased the demand for coal. The existence of coal fields had been known in Britain since the fifteenth century, and use of coal for heating was a common practice in such a wood-deficient country. Extraction was relatively easy because reserves in Leicestershire were buried only 100 feet deep. Using traditional coal mining technology, Britain's production totaled 3 million tons in 1760 and 15 million by 1800, but it jumped to 44 million tons by 1850 – a time when Britain produced roughly 80 percent of the world's coal output. Anthony Wrigley rightly considers the rise of a coal-based economy in Britain as the most momentous transformation in British history, an energy revolution that replaced a thousand-year organic economic regime with a mineral-based economy (Wrigley, 1988).

As David Landes observed in *The Unbound Prometheus*, the long line of inventions that mutually reinforced one another

may be subsumed under three principles: the substitution of machines – rapid, regular, precise, tireless – for human skill and effort; the substitution of inanimate for animate sources of power, in particular, the introduction of engines for converting heat into work, thereby opening to man a new and almost unlimited supply of energy; the use of new . . . raw materials, in particular, the substitution of mineral for vegetable or animal substances. These improvements constitute the Industrial Revolution. (Landes, [1969] 1995, 41)

The birth of the modern textile and iron industries, along with the enormous increase of coal production, led to a huge expansion of newly mechanized industries in Britain. Industrial output rose by 23% in the first decade of the nineteenth century, by nearly 39% in the second decade, and by 47% during the 1830s. A new age of industrial capitalism had begun.

Recent calculations of British economic growth demonstrate that industry had relatively high growth rates prior to the Industrial Revolution, and that technological change did not transform all of British industry overnight. Based on these new figures, a number of economic historians have challenged the concept of a sudden break with the past, or Walt W. Rostow's use of the metaphor "take-off" in describing these events. According to some, even the term "revolution" is questionable. "The phrase 'Industrial Revolution' can undoubtedly be extremely misleading . . . a 'cataclysmic' interpretation of economic change in the late eighteenth century is inappropriate" (Crafts, 1985, 6).

Phyllis Dean and W. A. Cole's study (1962) maintained that annual real industrial output in Britain increased by 0.6% between 1760 and 1780, but jumped by 3.4% and 4.4% during 1780–1801 and 1801–31 respectively. According to the more recent calculations of Nicholas Crafts

(1995), annual industrial output increased by 1.5% from 1760 to 1780, and then accelerated to 2.1% and 3.0% during 1780–1801 and 1801–31 respectively. New calculations have also reduced the difference between the pre-industrial decades and the period of the Industrial Revolution; rather than 2.1%, the growth per annum during 1780–1801 was actually only 1.3%, and rather than 3.1%, there was less than 2.0% growth per annum between 1801 and 1831. Discontinuity was therefore much less drastic than historians had previously thought. A sustained growth of commodity output and growth in GNP of more than 2.0% per year would not be achieved until 1820. Hence, modern economic growth took place over a longer period of time.

Regardless of whether the length of the process and the rate of growth it generated were unique or not, the consequences of the decades between the 1770s and 1830s were unquestionably revolutionary. The rupture with the past is clear if one compares general average economic growth with the growth rates of the leading sectors of the Industrial Revolution – cotton textiles, iron, and coal – that experienced extremely rapid growth rates of 7%, 3%, and 2.5% per annum respectively. The country's average growth rate was slower because new sectors were relatively small, and several other branches of industry still clung to old technology.[54]

The other decisive fact is that the British Industrial Revolution was the first economic phenomenon in history to generate permanent, sustained growth. Annual industrial growth fluctuated at around 3%, and GDP increased between 2.0% and 2.5% per year during the entire nineteenth century. Neither the yearly industrial growth rate nor the increase of the GDP declined below 2.0% until the early twentieth century. More importantly, technological revolution never stopped after that time.

Only a few sectors of British industry – textiles, iron, and coal – changed radically. These dynamic sectors, however, represented only 10–13% of industrial output, while 86.8% of industry stayed stuck in proto-industrial conditions for a few more decades. The steam engine and the steam-powered mechanization of industry remained isolated in cotton, iron, and a very few other industrial sectors. In 1851, more than 80% of British industry did not employ any workers at all or employed fewer than five. "In most industries there was no technical revolution in the century before 1850 . . . there had been no widespread introduction of steam-powered mechanization and the factory system" (Musson, 1982, 252–3).

In other words, British industry remained mostly traditional until the mid-nineteenth century, and small-scale, non-mechanized workshops, without real productivity growth, employed roughly 60% of the industrial

Figure 1.5
Employment structure in Britain, 1700–1840 (percentage employed in industry, agriculture, and other) (Crafts, 1994, 45; Allen, 1994, 107)

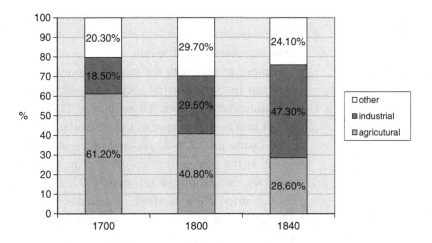

population. Moreover, statistical records for 1841 clearly show that a great part of the active population, 3.4 million people, still worked in agriculture. Traditional construction and clothing industries employed nearly 1.3 million workers, while the textile industry employed 1.5 million; coal mining was well behind, with only 200,000 workers, and the iron industry had considerably fewer. Nevertheless, the Industrial Revolution generated unique historical structural changes in Britain; in 1760, 53% of the male workforce was employed in agriculture, but this had dropped to 29% by 1841. (See Figure 1.5.)

Moreover, Britain's technological breakthroughs, it is important to note, did not remain isolated episodes. So-called mini industrial revolutions had taken place several times during previous centuries, but they had failed to generate momentum for further change. In contrast, the major innovations in Britain after 1750 were followed by series of secondary and tertiary micro-innovations that made the process ongoing. "What ultimately matters is the irreversibility of the events" (Mokyr, 1999, 127). Although a general breakthrough did not take place until the mid-nineteenth century, other industries did take initial steps toward modernization. Nicolas Leblanc's invention of a soda-making process in 1787, and the aforementioned chlorine bleaching process, were the first steps toward a modern chemical industry. In 1798, the controlled burning of gas created gas lighting, which became an international enterprise.[55] Gas lighting was the first "network technology," to be used on streets, in factories, and even in homes by the 1820s. Machine-tool making was established as well and played a central role in the mechanization of industry. The ceramic industry made significant leaps, with the emergence of Dutch Delft tin-and-enamel ware and German Meissen chinaware. In 1759, Josiah Wedgwood established an earthenware factory in Britain. And continental glass and paper industries made important breakthroughs.

In another break with the past, the dominant rule of the Malthusian constraint in pre-industrial society was eliminated in Britain. A huge population increase from 5.9 million in 1751 to 14.9 million in 1841 did not lead to the collapse of living standards, but only to a leveling of them. Taking the 1878–82 real wage level as equal to 100, in 1770–2 it was 95, at the turn of the century 103, in 1818–22, 111 (Mokyr, 1999 quotes the calculations of Feinstein, 1972, 120). Moreover, for the first time in history, living standards increased at least by 50–80 percent along with population growth during the coming decades, particularly after 1840.

Capital accumulation also did not increase quickly. The ratio of investments to national income remained virtually unchanged at around 8% between 1770 and 1810 and increased to roughly 10% from the 1810s to the 1850s. Similarly, capital stocks and total factor productivity grew by 1.5% and 0.7% per annum, respectively, during the first three decades of the nineteenth century, and they increased to 2% and 1% during the second three decades. "Thus, the acceleration in economic growth in the Industrial Revolution was modest, agricultural productivity advance played a major part in the development process" (Crafts et al., 1991, 141).

Mechanized heavy industry was established in Britain only during the later decades of the century, in connection with railroad construction and, as it is often called, the second Industrial Revolution. In 1841, "revolutionized industry" employed only 19% of the labor force, while agriculture employed 28.5% and small-scale manufacturing employed nearly 34%. Still, in 1870, nearly one-third of the steam power used in industry was concentrated in the textile industry. Between 1780 and 1831, the cotton industry achieved 7.3% annual growth and the iron industry 4.8%, but most of the other industries such as wool (1.4%), copper (1.5%), leather (0.8%), and paper (2.8%) remained far behind. Gross national product, which had increased by 0.69% per year between 1700 and 1760 and then stagnated between 1760 and 1780, rose on average 1.32% per annum between 1780 and 1801 and 1.97% per annum between 1801 and 1831. On a per capita basis, the real growth difference appeared only between 1801 and 1831 (0.52% per year), while during the last four decades of the eighteenth century it was either slower or more or less the same as during the first six decades of the century (Crafts, 1985, 23, 45).

The Industrial Revolution did not affect most British industries during the seven decades between 1760 and 1831, but those decades witnessed a great discontinuity both in industry and in human history. Industrial breakthroughs were in many ways an evolutionary process, but the few leading sectors of those decades had a determinant role in influencing all other industries and the economy generally. This limited transformation, with its backward and forward linkages, ultimately resulted in a real revolution. Nothing remained the same after the turn of the nineteenth century. Transformation in one area of Britain invariably spread to others, and eventually to all of Europe. Innovations from the Netherlands, France, and particularly Britain spread throughout Northwestern Europe and, after some delay, to other regions as well.

Conclusion

The reasons behind the British Industrial Revolution are extremely complex. The classic economic histories on the topic, such as Toynbee, Ashton, Mantoux, Dean, Cole, Mathias, and even the recent work of Allen, all provide a domestic, British explanation. The Industrial Revolution was long considered to be an abrupt cataclysm and a singularly British phenomenon ("British exceptionalism") that served as a model to be emulated first by Western Europe and then by the whole world. The British Industrial Revolution, however, was not a *deus ex machina*, but rather the outcome of six hundred long years of gradual progress and change inside Europe, especially the two to three centuries of development in Northwest Europe during the early modern period. Industrialization is a complex civilizing process, "a phenomenon which exists only on a certain level in the cultural, economic, social . . . evolution of man" (Zamorski, 1998, 36). Socio-economic and cultural developments occurred in a very symbiotic way, inspiring and engendering one another.

The most crucial cultural-institutional transformations were broad European processes, hammered out by the consecutive chain of intellectual revolutions represented by the Renaissance, Reformation, scientific revolution, Enlightenment, and Romanticism – leading to the rise of a new secularized value system and the accumulation of extensive knowledge on nature and the environment. All of these were expansive European developments originating from north Italy, the Low Countries, Britain, and France with deep roots in and influences on Germany, Switzerland, and Scandinavia. From the late eighteenth century and during the nineteenth, a *common West European Zeitgeist* emerged. Rousseau's "société des peuples de l'Europe" was based on complementary West European trade, customs, civil laws, religion, literature, and a mutual balance of power. Voltaire's "la société d'esprit" emphasized the similarity of Western ideas that had permeated society. Auguste Comte's "Grande République Occidentale" envisioned cooperation between France, Italy, Germany, Britain, and Spain. Giuseppe Mazzini's "Giovane Europa" movement in the mid-nineteenth century was predicated on his "Europa dei popoli," a *European* people uniting nations and humankind (Bettin Lattes and Recchi, 2005, 42–6). This was a long-standing gradual revolution. "Non-economic institutions and social attitudes are, of course, not exogenous factors; they are often outcomes of previous socio-economic changes that accumulated and ignited modifications in thinking and attitudes" (Supple, 2007).

In the 1770s–1780s, a startling number of technical inventions began to transform Britain's key industries. The process that commenced had already been dubbed by some contemporaries as the Industrial Revolution. It took place in Britain, but the road that led to it was a fundamentally West European phenomenon – one that took several centuries, from the high and late Middle Ages through the early modern period to the late eighteenth century. Its trajectory crossed the north Italian city-states, flourishing Flanders, and Brabant, where embryonic capitalism was born and the first merchant and banking activities predominated.

Although these early outgrowths of a new system did not endure, their seeds spread widely over the continent and were sown in Northwestern Europe. They attained their apogee in Holland. Unheard-of social and economic innovations characterized the Dutch merchant empire – from religious and political freedom, urbanization, revolutionized agriculture, and widespread proto-industry, to modern banking and state finances. Its grandeur, however, would prove transitory, for Holland was limited by its type of development and its organic economy. Defeated militarily by its French and British rivals, it was unable to cross the Rubicon toward modern industrialization.

Still, the historical march continued. England had already exhibited many similarities to the Dutch Republic during its early modern development. It prevailed in naval and military power, modernized its agriculture to attain the highest efficiency and liberate a great part of its labor force, and became the dominant merchant and colonial empire of the world. England adopted the most important innovations that the continent – from Venice to Antwerp to Amsterdam – had produced, and was able to polish and perfect them in London, Manchester, and Liverpool.

The expansion of urbanization, free-wage labor, productive agriculture, free thinking, and industrial activity fundamentally transformed the country's mode of consumption that cast all existing production arrangements in turmoil. Internal and colonial trade, massive domestic and imperial resources, accumulated capital in the hands of merchants and, thanks to high wages, certain segments of the working population, effectively created a supply and demand incentive for the modernizing British economy.

On these grounds, an exceptionally positioned Britain, with its central geopolitical location, its ability to transport inexpensively, and its endowment of new energy sources, was able – at least in certain branches of the economy – to effect dramatic change through the mechanization of industry in concentrated workplaces, the factories. With the world's strongest navy, and a secure position on a safe island, Britain was able to defend its interests in the integrated world economy. By adopting the earlier achievements of continental Europe and improving on them with myriad new inventions, Britain emerged as the center of the European and world economy at the turn of the nineteenth century.

Notes

1. Robert Brenner and Philip Huang had already reached the same conclusion and spoke about "involutionary, stagnant" Asian and "revolutionary" European development since 1500 (Brenner and Isett, 2002; Huang, 2002).
2. The cost of a 74-gun ship was £50,000 in the later years of the eighteenth century, ten times more than the cost of an early factory in Britain.
3. One of the main reasons for the rise of the free peasantry might be the importance of reclaimed land that had been colonized; the colonists became virtual owners of their land. Land reclamation had a long history: Flemings and Zealanders started to reclaim land in the eleventh and twelfth centuries, and Holland and Friesland started in the thirteenth century. The Dutch nobility and the Benedictine abbeys were weak, and thus owned only 20–25 percent of the land.
4. This process was abetted by the regional, decentralized structure of the Low Countries in which provinces preserved a large amount of autonomy. Catholics had strictly limited rights. They could live in the United Provinces, but they were not allowed to organize religious services and could not be appointed to public functions.
5. During the Spanish offensive and the bloody rule of the Duke of Alba (who arrived in the provinces in 1567), William of Orange, the leader of the Dutch resistance, declared himself a Calvinist in 1573.

6. The religious ideology of Protestantism was only *one* element of a complex historical phenomenon and should therefore not be overemphasized. Several Catholic countries and regions, the southern Low Countries, later Belgium, northern Italy, the Rhineland, and France attained similar development standards.

7. The founding capital was 6.4 million guilders. The company issued stocks and for two centuries paid an 18 percent dividend.

8. At the height of Dutch power in 1650, the value of re-exported goods out of the total of Dutch exports reached 60 million guilders, i.e. half of total Dutch exports (Maddison, 2001, 81).

9. Cheap and abundant energy from fossil fuels and three thousand windmills gave Holland a strong comparative advantage in proto-industry.

10. Van der Wee's, Wrigley's, and Crouzet's evaluations strongly contrast with the statement that Holland became "the first modern economy" (Vries and Van der Woude, 1997).

11. The new Beurs was built and opened in Antwerp in 1531, and became the model for the London (end of the sixteenth century) and Amsterdam (early seventeenth century) stock exchanges.

12. Before they were enclosed, common or open fields impeded improvement in the agricultural system. Land was badly cultivated, regularly flooded, and quickly exhausted by repeatedly planted crops. "The open-field system was doomed, therefore, to disappear" (Mantoux, 1928, 170).

13. Besides climatic and natural endowments, some old, and very many new, technologies such as hollow drainage, correcting the acidity of the soil, cultivating turnips, and seed drilling resulted in high yields (Brunt, 2004, 194, 215–16).

14. In Europe, only the Low Countries and Britain used fossil fuels rather than wood in the early modern period. Coal, however, was a much more valuable and efficient heating material than was the peat used in the northern Low Countries. Half a ton of coal produced the same amount of heat as one ton of peat. In the southern Low Countries, the expansion of the Liège and Hainault mines paralleled the English trend at the end of the sixteenth century.

15. Water, wind, and animals were still important modes of energy supply. In the Netherlands, fuel accounted for 70 percent of the total energy consumption of 17,800 kcal per day and per person in 1700. In Britain, fuel accounted for 68 percent, and it increased to 83 percent by 1800. In late eighteenth-century France and mid-nineteenth-century Italy, half of their much lower energy consumption totals were still being met with animal, human, water, and wind energy.

16. Although the tax was repealed at the end of the Napoleonic wars, it was reintroduced in 1842.

17. The Dutch contribution to British economic development was manifold and very direct. In the early stage of its transformation, England – at a later time the world's leading capital exporter – imported capital from the Netherlands, receiving no less than half of all Dutch capital exports. In 1780, Dutch financiers held 80 percent of English overseas debts.

18. The value of wardrobes in probate inventories increased even in poor households, from 7.5 to 16 percent of total value between 1700 and 1789. Expenditure on clothing more than doubled, even in wage-earning families.

19. Dame schools provided elementary education in most of the villages. Sunday schools, schools for industry, and other primary schools also existed, and they trained children during the early modern centuries.

20. In most European countries, noble privileges denied mortgage lenders the right to the very land for which they extended credit, and thus did much to impede mortgage crediting. In England, however, the mortgage creditor had more control over the property than did the legal owner.

21. A strong critical analysis regarding the one-sided institutional explanation can be found in Clark (2007) and Ogilvie (2007). Furthermore, a unified common law system predated modernization by centuries and was followed by commercial, maritime, and mercantile laws.

22. Wetland drainage was ultimately a "national failure." "Indeed, the pre-Revolutionary expansion of the irrigated area represents only 16 percent of what was actually planned before 1789 and built before 1860" (Rosenthal, 1992, 43–4, 110).

23. Although this book did not "change Europe," as the title of Hunt *et al.* (2010). suggests, it was definitely part of a long chain of transformative events.

24. Mokyr's list also contains the *Encyclopaedia Britannica* (1771), the *Allgemeines Lexicon* (1721), the *Oekonomische-Technologische Encylopedie* in 221 volumes (1796), the *Brockhaus Encyclopedia* (1809), and the *Dictionary of Arts, Manufactures and Mines* (1839).

25. In 1756 François Quesnay, the founder of the physiocratic sect, published his first economic essay; two years later his *Tableau économique* appeared. In 1755 Richard Cantillon's *Essay on the Nature of Commerce in General . . .* was published. A few years earlier David Hume had issued his penetrating essay on some leading economic topics, *An Enquiry Concerning the Principles of Morals* (1751). In 1766 Turgot committed to paper his *Réflexions sur la formation et la distribution des richesses*, and in the following year Sir James Stuart published his *Inquiry into the Principles of Political Economy*. Finally, in 1776, as a culmination of this burst of creative activity, there came the work which borrowed from, synthesized, and in many respects surpassed these earlier writings: Adam Smith's *Inquiry into the Nature and Causes of the Wealth of Nations* (Winch, 1973, 511–12).

26. *Lettres sur la liberté du commerce des grains, Letters to the Abbé Terray on the Duty of Iron,* and the 53-page *Réflexions sur la formation et la distribution des richesses.*

27. Karl Polanyi criticized the Smithian view, which was later called the Economic Man: "In retrospect it can be said that no misreading of the past ever proved more prophetic of the future." Polanyi rejected the genuine capitalist character of man, and "the habit of looking at the last ten thousand year[s] . . . as a mere prelude to the true history of our civilization." He maintained that never before have history and society been subordinated to the market as had occurred in the laissez-faire system (Polanyi, 1964, 43, 45).

28. A telling episode is that Napoleon, before being deported to St. Helena, took a number of books from the palace of Rambuillet, among them the 1802 five-volume French translation of Smith's *Wealth of Nations* (Cohen and Federico, 2001).

29. Letter to Friedrich Niethammer.

30. Gregory Clark made this generalization based on the case of 645 men living in Suffolk. On that basis he generalized this phenomenon from the eleventh century in Britain (Clark, 2007). Nevertheless, in his co-authored study he discovered that in wealthy families with a larger number of children, the children progressively lost their status from generation to generation, and exhibited a "considerable net downward mobility in the population" (Clark and Hamilton, 2006, 732).

31. By 1550 45% of the land was enclosed and by 1760, 75%. An additional 19% was enclosed as a result of parliamentary stipulations between 1760 and 1914 (Simson, 2004, 81).

32. Among the pioneers of agricultural literature was John Dorne, a Dutch bookseller who established his headquarters in Oxford as early as 1520. John Fitzherbert's *Boke of Husbondrye* came out in 1523. During the seventeenth century, a number of landowner-writers, the best known being Viscount Charles "Turnip" Townshend and the gentleman-farmer and propagandist Jethro Tull, shared their experiences with modern rotation and new crops (Erle, 1925). Hugh Platt and Walter Blith publicized the potential of manuring land and drainage, which had a large impact on modern farming.

33. In 1851, if British agricultural productivity = 100, Holland totaled 54%, France 44%, and Germany 42% (Simson, 2004, 71).

34. In 1700, the Dutch agricultural population of 40% was by far the lowest in the world, and much lower than that in Britain. By 1820, reflecting the Dutch stagnation, the number in Britain did not decline further, but rather increased to 43%. Industrial employment during the same period declined from 33 to 26% (Maddison, 2001, 95).

35. London's situation was characteristic: plague hit the city in 1592, 1603, 1625, 1630, 1636, and 1665. In 1665 16 percent of the city's population died.

36. Populations in Northwest Europe practiced "preventive birth control" in early modern times by delaying marriages (or not marrying at all). The average age at marriage was 26.1 years in the first two decades of the eighteenth century, but it dropped to 23.2 between 1825 and 1849 (Schofield, 1994, 67, 74).

37. A recent demographic interpretation of the origins of the British Industrial Revolution is based on "natural selection." Britain's demographic development and income distribution between 1250 and 1800 led to a higher rate of childbirth and longer lifetimes among the wealthier families; this gradually changed human nature, causing people to select mates from the more economically successful, harder working, and more rational layer of society. These people, in turn, passed their values down to younger generations, making the Industrial Revolution possible (Clark, 2007). The "survival of the richest" explanation, however, is not without flaws. One flaw is that it does not explain why northern Italy, Flanders, Spain, or the Netherlands (the richest countries of medieval and early modern Europe, and countries that excelled in "natural selection") did not become the cradle of the Industrial Revolution. (See also note 30.)

38. The term and concept of proto-industrialization – the industrialization process prior to the Industrial Revolution – was introduced by Mendels (1972).

39. A unique institution in Yorkshire based on an independent artisan proto-industry (mainly specializing in woolens) led to the formation of cooperative firms, or company mills. Organized under a trust deed, ten to fifty artisans created a de facto joint-stock company. As a factory inspector described in 1843, "The history of Joint Stock Company Woolen Mills exhibits a singular instance of energy amongst the smaller capitalists of the manufacturing districts... The clothiers of certain country districts... put their heads together and subsequently their purses... Partnerships are drawn, land is bought, a mill erected and machinery put up" (Hudson, 1983, 134).

40. Some experts introduced a stage theory within the proto-industry, maintaining that the *Kaufsystem* was the first and the *Verlag* the second stage that led to the factory system (Kriedte *et al.*, 1981).

41. The Crowley Ironworks in Stourbridge employed 800 workers in one factory building as early as 1682. Thomas Lombe's silk mill in Derby employed 300 workers in a five-story building in 1718.

42. The Lords' Committee investigated child labor in 1818, and Sadler's Committee dramatized the brutality of factory life and called for a ten-hour workday in 1832. Dr. Charles Turner Thackrah's 1831 book focused on the impact of factory work on health and longevity. Though the Factory Act introduced certain regulations in 1833, the situation did not change very much. During

his stay in Manchester between 1842 and 1844, Friedrich Engels, comrade-in-arms of Karl Marx, published his classic book on *The Condition of the Working Class in England* (Engels, [1844] 1975).

43. Income levels increased by 30–60%, i.e. 0.27–0.31% growth per annum, while the population increased by an annual 0.23%.

44. Max Hartwell lists a number of "historians who argue that education was unimportant for the industrial revolution" (Hartwell, 1971, 233–4). They include N. Smelser, P. Deane, C. Cipolla, and S. Pollard. Hartwell quotes Eric Hobsbawm as stating in 1969: "Britain could even manage to do without a system of state elementary education until 1870, of state secondary education until after 1902" (Hobsbawm, 1969).

45. The historical role of the guild system, denounced as a symbol of conservatism and anti-innovation since Turgot and Adam Smith, has been re-evaluated on the basis of its providing a huge army of skilled workers and technicians for the Industrial Revolution.

46. A Swiss calico printer's oft-quoted statement from 1766: "[The English] cannot boast of many inventions but only of having perfected the inventions of others . . . for a thing to be perfect it must be invented in France and worked out in England" (Wadsworth and Mann, 1931, 413).

47. The distinction between invention (a science-based idea) and innovation (the successful commercialization of the invention in a new science- or technology-based product) has been rephrased in various ways. Joel Mokyr distinguishes between *macro-inventions* and *micro-inventions* as follows: a macro-invention is predicated on "a radical new idea . . . emerg[ing] more or less ab nihilo," while micro-inventions are "small, incremental steps that improve, adapt, and streamline existing techniques already in use . . . " (Mokyr, 1990, 13). Others differentiate between first, second, and third inventions.

48. The Collège Royal and Le Jardin du Roy (which became Le Muséum National d'Histoire Naturelle in 1793) offered instruction from an outstanding faculty, including Lamarck. The Observatoire (which became Le Bureau des Longitudes) was also a teaching institution with world-famous mathematicians such as Lagrange and Laplace. A special institution, the École des Mines, trained mining engineers. Both the Conservatoire des Arts et Métiers and the École Normale Supérieure had large student bodies. The latter institution opened with 1,400 students.

49. After the French Marshal Bernadotte became the king of Sweden, he invited the founder of the École Centrale, Theodore Olivier, to reorganize Swedish technical and military education in 1821.

50. The early machinery, mostly wooden and built by one person, was not expensive. In 1795, a spinning jenny cost £6 and a mule cost £30; in 1811 a hand loom cost £5 and a smaller steam engine cost £150–200 (Crouzet, 1972).

51. Brunt compares the risky lending activity of these banks to the 1988 situation when venture capitalists, on average, lent one hundred and twenty-five times a median salary (p. 86)

52. In 1772, cotton products represented only somewhat more than 2% of the value of total exports. The export of woolen fabric dropped from 57% in 1700 to 14% by 1850, and iron and steel represented only somewhat more than 12% of the exports

53. Watt had several consecutive innovations, among them using John Wilkinson's technology to build large cylinders with tightly fitting pistons. Further modifications included the rotary motion engine, which Watt produced in 1781. New improvements and patents in 1782 and 1784 led to a highly improved steam engine – five times more efficient than the Newcomen steam engine.

54. J. H. Clapham clearly stated decades ago that until 1850, not a single branch of British industry experienced a complete revolution in technology (Clapham, 1930).

55. The Belgian Jean-Pierre Minkelers, the German J. G. Pickel, and two Frenchmen, Philippe Lebon and Aimé Argand, did important preliminary work on gas lighting. However, its actual invention took place in Britain when William Murdock used coal gas rather than gas produced from wood.

Part II

Successful industrial transformation of the West

CHAPTER 2

Knowledge and the entrepreneurial state

The spread of the new *Zeitgeist*

The barriers to spreading the new *Zeitgeist* were considerable in most of continental Europe because the *ancien régime* had survived the eighteenth century and remained in place during the first half of the nineteenth. With the defeat of Napoleon, the new *Zeitgeist*, too, had met its Waterloo. In countries adjacent to France, which Napoleon had occupied and reorganized/modernized, the new ideas and institutions were considered "French" and thus antithetical. Because modernization had been imposed with foreign bayonets, it was invariably met with resistance and began to be discarded by post-Napoleonic regimes. One particularly curious example was Italy's annulment of Napoleon's policy of compulsory universal vaccination after its liberation from France.

The Bourbon restoration rushed to destroy what remained of the Revolution and the Napoleonic era in France. Nevertheless, the period following the Congress of Vienna (1815), though it was dominated by the conservative, monarchist Holy Alliance, and though it had restored several major elements of the *ancien régime*, proved unable to erase the Revolution's impact. Strong administrative and institutional continuity was characteristic in many states in Italy. The Napoleonic tradition was retained in the duchy of Parma. In Piedmont, "French-inspired institutions" survived and, moreover, after the unification of Italy, were extended "to the whole country" (Cohen and Federico, 2001, 70). The Habsburgs preserved the administrative institutions in reoccupied Lombardy-Venetia, as did even the Papal State. Social and economic reforms introduced during the "French Decade" remained mostly intact in the Kingdom of Naples. Prussia also borrowed from Napoleon, especially from his Concordat with Rome that had introduced state control over the church and led to "major enduring changes . . . in the south and west of Germany" (John, 2000, 85).

"As the 1820 and 1830 revolutions show clearly," the editors of *Napoleon's Legacy* conclude, "it was not feasible simply to return to the old order" (Laven and Riall, 2000, 15). A few years of revolutionary French rule exerted a long-term positive influence on the continent because of the legalized institutions of the revolutionary state. The Napoleonic Codes were the first codification of a comprehensive modern legal order[1] that established the "rules of the game" in West European economy and society. Property was deemed sacred and free, defended by law, and business was unfettered from regulation. After an initial period of steadfast rejection of French ideas and institutions, the Napoleonic Codes became the basis of nineteenth-century law throughout Europe. The secular state was also an important legacy of the Revolution and its Napoleonic realization, but it took the entire century for it truly to permeate West European society.

The Enlightenment held tremendous appeal throughout the region, and its ideals crossed borders and converted large parts of the elite and the educated with ease. A major consequence of this fact was absolutism's replacement by constitutional and parliamentary regimes in most countries. Representative assemblies were elected, citizens' armies were constituted, strong centralized executive powers, backed by professional bureaucracies, were created, and elaborate state institutional structures were gradually established to form the modern entrepreneurial state. Indeed, the ideals and values of the Enlightenment even influenced the contemporary despots and absolute monarchs who had governed their empires with an iron fist and suppressed any revolutionary opposition to the *ancien régime*. While refusing to allow their people to do anything, these paternalistic dictators desired to do something for their people. The enlightened absolute rulers of Prussia and Austria, Frederick the Great, and Maria Theresa and her son Joseph II, began to modernize their empires in step with the new liberal ideas. Frederick and even Catherine the Great of Russia had often corresponded with Voltaire. Catherine the Great had also read Montesquieu and invited Diderot to Russia. Hence, significant reforms and major institutions were introduced in Prussia and Austria as a result of the towering influence of the new *Zeitgeist*s over Europe.

The Prussian king realized that the country's military was endangered without a modern transformation and liberation of the serfs. Prussia's military defeat by France was a wake-up call: two modernizers in the leadership, Baron Heinrich F. K. Stein and Prince Karl August Hardenberg, abolished serfdom in 1807 and regulated peasant landownership in 1811. At the same time, Maria Theresa and Joseph II introduced major reforms in the Habsburg Empire. Among them was the introduction of a customs union of the Hereditary Lands entailing the western provinces of the empire in 1770, which preceded the German Zollverein by more than sixty years. All internal custom barriers were abolished. The freedom to establish companies was also granted in most of the country's industrial branches (in the cotton industry, for instance, in 1773). In 1774, the empress declared, "The education of the youth is the foundation of the true welfare of the nation." She introduced mandatory education and ordered schools to be built in every village providing the foundation of a modern education system.

Joseph II liberated the serfs and gave them the freedom to move, marry, and engage in various trades. Noble land was taxed and the peasants' feudal fees had to be paid in cash, but they were not to exceed approximately 17 percent of the value of their production. The Edict of Tolerance in 1781 limited the power of the Catholic Church, closed its monasteries, and granted almost equal status to Protestants. It also had a spillover effect. Tolerance opened the "free market of opinions" and accepted atheism (Chadwick, 1975, 21, 27). Additional reforms followed in 1836: several feudal fees were abolished, and the peasants were allowed to inherit and sell land. However, the final abolition of serfdom and noble privileges took place only with a new wave of European revolutions in 1848. All these reforms and institutional changes made labor and capital more mobile and paved the way for economic expansion.

The ideals of the early nineteenth century permeated influential circles on the continent. New urban, bourgeois middle-class elites gradually emerged. Merchants, industrialists, bankers, managers of companies, professionals, teachers, medical doctors, engineers, freelancers, artists, and writers comprised this social stratum. Among them were high-ranking white-collar employees of private companies and the state bureaucracy. A new stratum of society that rose in social status through higher education (what the Germans call *Bildungsbürgertum*) became an important part of the new elite. In the mid-nineteenth century these represented some 5–15 percent of the societies of Western Europe (Kocka and Breuilly, 1988, 13). As heterogeneous as they were, they shared common interests and attitudes. The Smithian ideal that profit-motivated entrepreneurial selfishness is ethical since it serves all society became a broadly shared concept that the middle class happily internalized. The new elite fought the same enemies in the form of the *ancien régime* and its social pillars. They were primarily urban in nature, were highly critical of the aristocracy and absolutism, and exhibited similar cultural traits. "Europe developed a new society of trade and industry" and this society was convinced that obsolete laws which hampered progress could be changed (Chadwick, 1975, 26). This increasingly mobile and urban society began to emerge in the late eighteenth century, and it gained considerable momentum in the early nineteenth. However, modern bourgeois society particularly advanced in continental Western Europe from the 1840s to the 1870s, and at that time became the champion of liberalism. Aristocratic values, which prevailed only in the most backward of societies, were rendered obsolete and were replaced in the West by the cult of work, business, and thrift. Failure was viewed as a personal shortcoming. The ethos of capitalism took off before the term even became widely used in Europe.

The educated elite, most of the professionals, the emerging modern bourgeoisie and middle class, and a large number of political leaders all embraced the new ideals of liberalism. As the French republican politician Léon Gambetta maintained, the "new social stratum is liberal, republican, and anti-clerical; it provides the basis for the new order" (McLeod, 2000, 94, 101). Church attendance sharply declined after the 1848 revolutions in France and Germany. In the latter country, the ratio of Protestant pastors to the Protestant population was 1:3,000 in 1800, but by 1890 it was 1:9,593. Friedrich Nietzsche noted in 1886 that the "German Protestants in the middle classes, especially in the great industrial centers of trade and commerce, and the great majority of industrious scholars and the whole university population" are indifferent to religion (quoted by McLeod, 2000, 100–1).

The reasons for this were complex.[2] The gradual progression of urban and modern economic development was an important factor. National euphoria and ardent nationalism became a substitute religion and contributed to declining religious involvement. Modern materialist science played an important role as well. Herschel and Laplace developed theories regarding the origins of the planets and stars. The new discoveries in chemistry by Liebig and others, and in electricity by Volta, Galvani, and Maxwell, dramatically expanded knowledge about nature. Paleontologists discovered the origins of the globe. As the French biologist Lamarck remarked, "How little the idea of those who attribute to the globe an existence of six thousand and a few hundred years duration" (Stromberg, 1990, 118). Expeditions across the world led to scientific breakthroughs in various fields of scholarship, which helped undermine, and in some ways also substitute, religious belief.

In this respect, Darwin played the most important role. His landmark 1859 study, *On the Origin of Species*, became "the most important book of the century." With the book Darwin "took [his] place along with Galileo and Newton . . . [as] those who have altered the entire mentality of civilization" (Stromberg, 1990, 123). Darwin and the scientific advances strongly influenced philosophy as well. As the outstanding twentieth-century biologist Julian Huxley concluded, "Newton's great generalization of gravitational attraction made... [it] necessary to dispense with the idea of God guiding the stars... Darwin's equally great generalization of natural selection made... [it] necessary to dispense with the idea of God guiding the evolutionary course of life" (quoted by Stromberg, 1990, 127).

Political and social thought, economic theory, and modern philosophy evinced and disseminated the new way of thinking. When political liberalism, the standard bearer of the Enlightenment and the French Revolution, turned against the *ancien régime* and conservatism, it also turned against the church as its main representative. The state in the *ancien régime* was a confessional state, and religion governed private and public life. The struggle against the *ancien régime*, its remnants, or its restoration was necessarily a struggle against the church.

Liberal politics dominated the mid-century years between 1848 and 1870.[3] Even *il*liberal Germany became, after its unification, one of the main antagonists of the Catholic Church. "Across Europe, the emergence of constitutional and democratic nation states was accompanied by intense conflict between Catholics and anticlerical forces over the place of religion in modern polity" (Clark and Kaiser, 2003, 59, 1). The campaign for the secularization of the state became a pan-West European phenomenon from the mid-nineteenth century on. A unified Germany enacted a series of laws designed to neutralize Catholicism as a political force. Secularization was pervasive in practically all areas of social life and the public sphere.

The confrontations intensified because of the Catholic Church's attempt to maintain and even strengthen its position in European social and political life. A strong centralization or "Romanization" of the clergy and the church went hand in hand with the formation of Catholic political parties which played a central role in the political life of Germany, Belgium, and other Western countries. The papacy fought a bitter war to regain its upper hand – mounting bloody retaliation against the Rome revolution in 1848, and fighting against Italian unification. Its provocative declaration of papal infallibility in 1870 elicited an angry response throughout Europe.

The illiberal German state of Otto von Bismarck launched the *Kulturkampf* against what Hans-Ulrich Wehler described as the "irrationality of the Vatican, the traditional straitjacket of reactionary" policy of the Catholic Church. This was, in reality, not a "cultural war," but a secularization campaign. Wehler speaks, however, about a "first Kulturkampf" in the 1830s, when the Prussian state imposed strict restrictions to counter efforts to reestablish the "papal dictatorial" regime of Leo XIII, Pius VIII, and Gregor XVI between 1813 and 1846. The papacy's attack against the liberal July revolution was also rebuffed (Wehler, 1995–2005, Vol. II, 471, 473).

Bismarck introduced a series of laws and institutional changes between 1872 and 1876 in his typical authoritarian manner, but he did so with the help of the German liberals, among them his Minister of Culture, Albert Falk. These strict measures, Wehler suggests, "were inspired partly by etatist, partly by liberal" ideas. They abolished the Ministry of Culture's *Katholische Abteilung*, removed schools from the church's jurisdiction, certified civil marriage and funerals, and even "nationalized" Catholic charities. The state began to regulate theology departments in the country's universities, and it made the clergy state employees. In the end, Bismarck's "charismatic system of rule" broke the power of the Catholic Church in Germany (Wehler, 1995–2005, Vol. III, 893–7).

Most of the other European states, practically the entire "common European political-cultural place" (Clark and Kaiser, 2003, 3), launched a *Kulturkampf* during the 1860 to 1880s. Thousands of German workers participated in the *Klostersturm*, an attack against the Dominican Moabit monastery in 1869. The Congress of Journalists in Vienna that same year demanded the closing of all Catholic orders and the expulsion of the Jesuits. In Belgium the *Kulturkampf* was dubbed the "school war" in 1879–84; violent confrontations commenced in the Netherlands, and demonstrations were staged in Spain in 1878. A protest movement in Italy initiated a campaign for the victims of the church and erected a statue for Giordano Bruno on Campo di Fiori, the spot where he was burned at the stake in the pope's presence in 1600. Switzerland embarked on one of the most drastic *Kulturkampfs* in Europe, especially in the Berne Jura and Geneva cantons. In 1867 and 1868, Berne drastically cut the number of religious holy days and expelled the religious orders from schools. When a Catholic bishop dismissed and excommunicated an anti-infallibility parish priest in Solothurn Canton in 1872, the canton's government annulled the decree.[4] The canton then appointed its own "state priests" and disbanded any parochial council that refused to accept them (Clark and Kaiser, 2003, 103, 109–13, 124, 130–1, 255–67).

The prevailing secularization campaigns in Western Europe were accompanied by an intellectual movement at the universities that spread to the press and to the populace at large. The ideas of the Enlightenment, which had started out as the ideas of a few, now became the beliefs of the many. The process of secularization, which at first brought about the "dissociation of church and state [and] then separated religion from society," did not happen all at once but was rather a gradual process (Rémond, 1999, 127). At the final stage, for instance in France in 1905, the parliament enacted a law proclaiming that the Republic neither recognized churches nor paid ministers their salaries; separation was an accomplished fact and religion was now a strictly private matter.

In the changing public spirit, civil organizations played an important role. They were varied and numerous, and included reading clubs, debating clubs, and singing and literary societies throughout Western Europe. In the Netherlands, the Society for Public Welfare was a nationwide organization with local branches. In Germany and Austria, urban societies held various cultural and leisure activities and organized political civil associations. In Austria alone, 2,234 associations were in operation in 1856, and no fewer than 85,000 by 1910. These self-organized associations were often considered to be the main network for transmitting new ideas and values. Freemasonry, for example, attracted a significant part of the elite.[5] The movement spread throughout Europe, to Switzerland, Germany, Italy, and even to the oppressive regimes of the peripheral countries. It formed a micro-society based on the Enlightenment ideals of equality and elected self-government, thus establishing a norm for the entire society. The lodges were strongly anti-clerical and anti-religious during the nineteenth century. The Belgian and French Freemasons deleted all reference to the "supreme architect" from their statutes in the 1870s. The lodges became gathering places for advocates of a secular society and organizing hubs of election campaigns. It was no accident that Pope Pius IX lambasted them as an enemy of the church and the "Synagogue of Satan."[6]

The power of ideas was enormous. As Isaiah Berlin astutely noted, "philosophical concepts nurtured in the stillness of a professor's study could destroy a civilization" (Berlin, 2000, ix). Those professors' studies were increasingly accessible in Germany, and universities such as Göttingen and Königsberg emerged as cradles of the new thinking. The genie was out of the bottle the minute the Enlightenment began, and nothing anyone did in nineteenth-century Europe could put it back in again. Educated people discovered and read Diderot's Encyclopedia. Personal correspondences did much to circulate new ideas and ways of thinking. Voltaire alone sent about ten thousand letters.

More importantly, this was the age when journals were published and publishing houses printed and sold books. Innovations in printing from the invention of the revolving cylinder in 1812 (quickly followed by the rotary press) to the development of the steam-powered mechanical press in the 1830s, to the linotype machine and the monotype in the 1880s – drastically reduced the cost of printing. Prior to 1810, approximately 1,000 titles (not copies) were published each year in France; by 1815, the number was more than 3,300; by 1830 it was in excess of 6,700; and by 1875, it topped 14,000.[7] Personal reading habits were transformed. Rather than reading and rereading a few books, educated people began reading several books at a time, and constantly looked for new titles. Reading out loud at home for the family and in coffee houses was common practice. Reading and lending libraries opened throughout Europe.[8]

Newspapers and magazines inundated the continent. Their numbers started skyrocketing during the eighteenth century. As the French *Revue encyclopédique* reported, in 1828 the number of journals and reviews reached 483 in Britain, 490 in France, 593 in the German states, 150 in the Low Countries, 80 each in Denmark and Austria and 30 in Switzerland. In the last quarter of the century, the mass popular press and mail-order journals attained a circulation of hundreds of thousands of copies in Western Europe (Sassoon, 2006, 321, 709). Reading became fashionable and proliferated through the influence of salons and middle-class gatherings – and with it spread the new *Zeitgeist*.

One of the most important propagators of these ideas was a new and extremely popular revolutionary ideological and artistic wave that swept through Europe, Romanticism. It started in Britain and France nearly half a century before the French Revolution, but it gained new impetus during the nineteenth century on the continent, especially in Germany. "Man wished to be free from restrictions imposed by religious traditions, political absolutism and a hierarchical social system in order to express and determine himself and create the kind of order in which he wished to live" (Talmon, 1967, 136). Isaiah Berlin equated the magnitude of Romanticism with the most important historical events of the age: it was "no less far-reaching," he affirmed, than the British Industrial Revolution and the French Revolution (Berlin, 1999, xiii). Romanticism passionately called for the freedom of man to create his own values (Berlin, 2000, 9–10). This message was popularized by poets, writers, composers, and painters. In 1804, the 34-year-old Ludwig van Beethoven sensed both instinctively and intellectually the dawn of a heroic new age, and he expressed his sentiment with an emotionally robust and violently revolutionary musical piece, Symphony No. 3, the "Eroica," which he originally planned to name "Bonaparte Symphony."

Romantic artists became national heroes who addressed not only the small educated elite, but the nation as a whole and humankind in general. The art of the century became pan-European. At the time of the Industrial Revolution, one of the leading British painters, Joshua Reynolds, spoke in one of his lectures about various *European* schools of painting "giving a general view of human life." He denounced "the minute particularities of a nation differing in several respects from the rest of mankind"

(Reynolds, [1771] 1987, 17, 23).[9] Tomasso Minardi identified an emerging international style in 1834 (Minardi, [1834] 1987, 175). Théophile Thoré in the mid-century spoke of "a new, truly human art expressing a new society." He celebrated triumphant Romanticism as "the end of the old . . . superstitions. There is but one race, and but one people; there is but one religion and but one symbol: Humanity!" (Thoré, [1857] 1987, 360).

The old Johann Wolfgang Goethe coined the term *Weltliteratur* in 1827, maintaining that world poetry and literature are the universal possessions of humankind, and that national literature had become meaningless (Eckermann, [1835] 2006). Indeed, art on the continent was fundamentally pan-European in the nineteenth century.[10] The European art world was able to mobilize the masses and indoctrinate them with the new values and ideals. Nineteenth-century novels, operas, symphonies, and the newly invented Romantic musical genres such as symphonic poems and program music, which contained literary and philosophical messages, became effective promoters of the new *Zeitgeist*.

The defeat of Napoleon, the Congress of Vienna in 1815, and the restoration of the *ancien régime* temporarily halted the spread of these new changes across Europe, but did so only fleetingly. The entire period between 1815 and 1848, in spite of the harsh repression, censorship, and subjugation of Metternich's police state, was an age of riots, revolts, and liberalism. To quote Eric Hobsbawm, Europe experienced an "age of revolutions" between the end of the eighteenth and the middle of the nineteenth century. The restoration policy completely collapsed in France in 1830, and a slew of revolutions swept through Europe in "the Spring of Nations" in 1848.[11] Although several were militarily suppressed at the end of the day the revolts were able to remove the *anciens régimes* from Western Europe.

Liberalism became the dominant ideological and political orientation, comprising the core ideas of the Enlightenment and the French Revolution. This triumphant ideology influenced state policy, institution-building, private behavior, and business prospects. William Parker has rightly argued that "an economic historian must bring 'ideology' back on centre stage" (Parker, 1991, 86). The essence of the French Constitution of 1793 and the "Declaration of the Rights of Man and of Citizens" became common values in Western Europe. Civil liberties, institutionalized property rights, individual freedom, tolerance, equality under the law, free markets, limited government, and the secular state were embodied in the new values. The common cultural space of Western Europe was cross-fertilized by the new *Zeitgeist*. The bourgeois middle class gradually became the dominant social and political force. This new cultural-social-institutional development spearheaded an economic transformation based on the Northwest

European pattern. It is more than symbolic, however, that 1848 was also the year of the *Communist Manifesto* of Karl Marx and Friedrich Engels. The old conflicts between conservatives and liberals had been largely resolved, leading to new confrontations and new rebellions.

The social and economic transformations in Northwest Europe during the early modern period now began to spread across the continent. The southern Low Countries (later Belgium), an early economic leader in the late medieval and early modern centuries, reemerged. Serfdom had never really existed or had disappeared very early in the mountainous areas that later became Switzerland, the Vorarlberg part of Austria, and parts of Scandinavia. Based on traditional proto-industrialization, Flanders, northern Italy, several German city-states, and other areas became cradles of early merchant capitalism beginning in the late Middle Ages and laid the groundwork for the modern transformation.

It is my contention that the nineteenth-century economic transformation was deeply rooted in West European history; hence, the countries of Western Europe duplicated the earlier Northwestern transformation relatively easily. I do not agree with the wonderfully phrased idea that "*Capitalism* came into human history with an English accent... This meant that the market economy retained a bit of foreignness for those for whom English and, by extension, capitalism are second languages" (Appleby, 2010, 21; italics added).

Capitalism had a long history in several West European countries. The impact of Britain's *industrialization*, however, was undoubtedly tremendous. Emulating Britain's institutions and legal system became synonymous with economic success. Other countries viewed Britain in the eighteenth and especially the nineteenth century with respect and fear of its economic superiority and growing military might. All sought to duplicate the British paradigm. This was, however, not a question of will, but of the *social capability* of a given country to reform its institutions, and the acceptance of capitalism among its populace. These social and cultural factors were prerequisites to economic change. Although, in a certain respect, institutions and ideologies were exogenous factors vis-à-vis the economy, they were embedded in the social fabric of the pioneering countries.

The French Revolution transformed the western part of the continent in a dramatic way, along the lines of the earlier Flemish, Dutch, and British development. Western Europe was, indeed, eager to emulate the transformation that had begun in the northwest. The engine of successful adjustment here was the social, cultural, and institutional systems, which were markedly similar on the entire western half of the continent.

In most of Western Europe, the feudal system was preserved until the end of the eighteenth century. However, social changes gradually set the stage for a modern transformation. In France, land was in the hands of the nobles. The personally free *censitaire* peasants paid rent to the nobles and became virtual rather than legal owners of the land. In some parts of the country, noble estates represented only 9% of the land, although in others this figure was as high as 99%. Church land also varied between 1% and 20%. According to some calculations, land rented to peasants comprised 22–70% of the French countryside. Feudal fees consumed roughly 30–40% of peasant incomes. Alexis de Tocqueville correctly characterized the situation; although the feudal system, he noted, did not exist as a political institution, it remained the basis of the French economy.

Despite the gradual loosening of the feudal regime, it took the French Revolution of 1789 to eliminate feudalism once and for all. The modernized state now became the central player: it abolished all noble privileges as well as all remnants of the feudal legal system of the *ancien régime*, and it established the social and political basis for a modern transformation. The abrogation of local tariffs, the consolidation of a national market, the nationalization and selling off of a great part of noble lands, and the introduction of modern institutions such as private ownership and personal freedom all radically altered the social-political landscape.

The French Revolution, with its dramatic, romanticized display of valor, became the eternal model for those seeking fundamental change. The immediate impact of the Revolution was quite negative and resulted in significant economic decline. "Not only France but the whole continent lost the war" (Crouzet, 2001, 122). But its abolition of feudal institutions spread to its neighboring regions, the "Frenchified" border areas of Germany (as Clive Trebilcock called the Ruhr- and Rhineland), and the southern Low Countries that later became Belgium. Napoleon's conquests led to the destruction of feudal institutions, and their replacement by revolutionary ones, in Spain, the southern Low Countries, Italy, and a part of Germany.

Based on the earlier development of the constitutional monarchy, the nineteenth century saw the rise of the *Rechtsstaat* ("the state of law"), a legal and political system in which the power of the government is based on and limited by the rule of law, replacing the power of individuals. The emergence of democratic political systems was not far behind. As Alexis de Tocqueville recognized, "the arrival of democracy in Europe was an inevitable development" (Winks and Kaiser, 2004, 182).

Religious tolerance, the secularization of the state, and a gradual democratization led to the emancipation of religious minorities: Catholics in Protestant countries, Protestants in Catholic countries, and Jews throughout Western and Central Europe. Religious hostility, and the expulsion of Huguenots and Jews, had been natural byproducts of previous centuries. Now, there was a slow and gradual turn towards inclusion. True, the 1787 Edict of Toleration in France had already granted equal status to Protestants. But the real milestone of emancipation was the French Revolution, which granted citizenship and equal rights to everyone.

Emancipation progressed gradually in Europe. Britain did not officially recognize the Jewish religion, and officially considered a synagogue to be an illegal establishment until 1847; but in 1858, it recognized the right of Jews to sit in Parliament. A decade and a half later, Britain elected Europe's first, and for a long time only, Jewish Prime Minister, Benjamin Disraeli. Karl August Hardenberg emancipated the Jews in Prussia in March 1812, but this did not happen in other German states; ultimately, it took the German unification of 1871 to finalize the emancipation process. Likewise, the French occupation emancipated Italian Jewry in 1797, but the final step was made only after Italy's unification beginning in the 1870s (Liedtke and Wendehorst, 1999). The emancipation of various religious minorities provided equal opportunities to the most business-oriented elements, who, because of their minority status, had for centuries found their only career possibilities in the business world, and were thus more mobile and entrepreneurial than were most of the local peoples in the countries in which they lived.

However, democracy was far from an accomplished fact. There were no immediate or simple breakthroughs toward democracy. In the Netherlands, the voting population doubled by 1887 and again by 1896, but voting rights still remained the privilege of 700,000 men alone. Belgium first enacted universal male suffrage in 1893. It had intended to introduce genuine universal suffrage in 1913, but did so only after World War I. Unified Italy had a parliamentary monarch, but only 2 percent of the population had voting rights. That was somewhat enlarged in 1880, but universal male suffrage was introduced only in 1912. The British House of Lords retained its veto rights over Parliament as late as 1911. The German chancellor answered to the emperor and not to Parliament. The old aristocracy still held enormous power in Britain and continued to dominate modern Germany and Austria.[12]

The French Revolution challenged the ruling elites in most countries in Europe and served as either a harbinger of additional reforms, or, more likely, a warning to avoid them. In Germany, the uprooting of the past was much less radical, more restrained, and infinitely more controversial than it was in France. The creation of a national market was hindered by the loose alliance of 350 German states, principalities, and independent cities. The situation improved somewhat after the Congress of Vienna in 1815, which established the confederation of 39 sovereign German states. The next step was the gradual formation of a German common market – first by eliminating internal tariffs within Prussia in 1818, then by enacting a series of agreements with other German states in 1821 to 1833, when several states joined the customs union.[13] The foundation of the Zollverein, a general customs union, culminated the process in 1834, and paved the way for the political unification of Germany in 1871. Germany also adopted Montesquieu's principle and separated legislative, executive, and judicial power. However, all three branches of government, along with the army, remained in the hands of the Prussian nobility, the Junker class.

The uprooting of feudal institutions was also slow and gradual, with major regional differences among the German states. The western German states, adjacent to France and in several ways similar to it, liberated their serfs as early as the 1790s. Prussia acknowledged the need for reform only after its defeats by Napoleon at Jena and Auerstädt in 1806. Larger than the other German states and with 10.3 million inhabitants, only 2.3 million fewer than the other German states combined, Prussia emerged as Germany's leading state. There, liberation went hand in hand with the expropriation of peasant land: Prussia's *Bauernlegen* granted the peasants ownership of land, but it also incorporated a million hectares of peasant land in the landlords' big estates.[14] During the first decades of the nineteenth century, a great part of the peasantry lost their land entirely and became free laborers. By 1867, roughly half of the peasants were landless. In the meantime, the aristocratic owners of the large estates amassed even more land and accumulated even more capital to hire wage laborers and buy machinery. The Prussian reform thus played a vital role in the modern capitalist transformation of the former noble estates. Germany continued to bear the heavy burden of the *ancien régime*, but the reforms created most of the institutions for modern transformation. Following the British path now became possible.

In the western hereditary provinces of the Habsburg Empire, the social, political, and institutional preconditions for modernization were also created by reforms from above, even though they were slower and more gradual: it took more than three-quarters of a century, from the 1770s to

1848, to create them. Multiparty free elections, however, proliferated and male suffrage was gradually introduced.[15] The region also saw its legislative, executive, and judicial branches separated and it began to be governed by the rule of law. Vestiges of feudal inequality, however, survived for a long time. The peasantry remained a politically unrepresented, unequal, and uninfluential part of society, and the former noble elite preserved much of its dominance. Still, democracy was slowly becoming the norm in Western Europe.

Science into education

The socio-political transformation of Western Europe also led to a historic breakthrough in education. This was probably one of the central factors in the rise of the West. Since the Reformation and the Enlightenment, the promoters of the new *Zeitgeist* took a special interest in education. The emerging social and economic system in the nineteenth century required a certain minimum standard of general education and training if the masses were to satisfy the basic technical demands of modern industry. It also required the requisite training of scientists, engineers, and medical doctors, as well as the administrators and skilled employees of business. It would be a mistake to assume, however, that modern education was a mere response to the challenges of the Industrial Revolution. It actually predated it, and in a certain sense was a prerequisite for it. The northwestern region of Europe pioneered the modern transformation partly because it, and not other regions, had attained a higher level of education long before industrialization.

In Britain between the mid-sixteenth and mid-seventeenth centuries, a major pedagogical breakthrough raised the educational level of the country. By 1660, half of the young population was already literate, and between a tenth and an eighth of those in the relevant age group attended secondary schools. (Numeracy was much higher during the early modern centuries.) Of those between the ages of eighteen and twenty-four, 2.5 percent were enrolled in universities. Yet Britain paradoxically did not become a pioneer of modern education. It restricted child labor in industry and enabled the enrollment of working-class children in schools only with the factory laws of the 1830s and 1840s. Free and compulsory education became universal only after the educational law of 1870.[16] At the same time, secondary schooling continued to be the domain of high-priced or charitable institutions, at the apex of which were the "public" schools, in reality expensive private boarding schools, which catered to a small minority of the well-educated, wealthy and established classes. Even in 1900, only one in seventy children of secondary-school age attended school. The Balfour Act in 1902 changed this situation only slightly, when it ordered the local authorities to provide secondary and technical education to all children up to the age of fourteen.

The turn of the nineteenth century was the real turning point in European education. Two central figures of the Enlightenment and Romanticism, the French Jean-Jacques Rousseau and the German Johann Gottlieb Herder, popularized the idea of mass education. Their influence was decisive, especially with the rise of nations and nationalism, as education played a key role in national indoctrination. Napoleon centralized the national school system when modernizing his administration. Model institutes were established, such as Johann Pestalozzi's school in Yverdon, Switzerland. And Rousseau's emphasis on early education was actualized by Friedrich Froebel's kindergarten. A new and transformative approach to education was in the making.

From the Netherlands and Britain to Germany and Scandinavia, Protestantism was a primary player in promoting literacy. Advocating personal contact with God, Protestants introduced vernacular languages into the church, fostered the reading of the Bible, and regularly translated scripture into local dialects. The rise of capitalism was facilitated by the educational requirements of religious practices. National rivalries and national leaders also played a role. A good example of the former is the devoutly Catholic Habsburg queen, Maria Theresa, who, emulating her rival, the Prussian king, issued her *Ratio educationis* in 1774, while the German Wilhelm von Humboldt best exemplified the genius as political leader.

Nineteenth-century education was revolutionized in Lutheran Germany, which became the model for several European countries. Lutheranism was adopted as the state religion in seventeenth-century Germany, which pursued the educational goals established by Martin Luther. The Prussian educational order of 1763 introduced public elementary education a century before the advent of industrialization. The real breakthrough occurred during the Napoleonic wars, when Germany surpassed all others in the education revolution.[17] In the mid-nineteenth century, illiteracy among Germans declined to 20 percent, that being mostly the elderly population. As Hans-Ulrich Wehler noted, it was more than ironic that England, with its pronounced liberal political culture, possessed a relatively non-democratic and, in terms of basic education, underdeveloped school system, while conservative, authoritarian Germany heralded an open, democratic, and comprehensive school system that was an object of admiration for the French and British alike (Wehler, 1995–2005, Vol. II, 478).

One of the greatest scholars and liberal statesmen of the time, Wilhelm von Humboldt, introduced groundbreaking educational reforms during his short tenure as Minister of Public Instruction in 1809–10. He initiated the best type of secondary education, the eight-year gymnasium. Based on the eighteenth-century French model of the École Polytechnique and other specialized higher educational institutions, the German education administration promoted the establishment of a number of *Technische Hochschulen*, a unique institution offering higher technological education. Between 1820 and 1830, several *polytechniques* were founded in Dresden, Stuttgart, Munich, Darmstadt, and Hanover, providing training in mining, veterinary education, engineering, and other fields (Wehler, 1995–2005, Vol. II, 485–91, 499).

Humboldt effectuated a radically new type of university education, the combination of teaching and research, a system that spontaneously emerged at Göttingen University by the late eighteenth century. Duplicating the Göttingen model, Humboldt established the University of Berlin in 1810 as a modern research university. Tirelessly promoted by the Prussian government, the new system spread throughout the country. New universities were established in Breslau and Halle in the following decades, and soon twenty universities transformed German higher education to become the forerunner in establishing research laboratories and specialized institutes (Wehler, 1995–2005, Vol. II, 505–6).[18]

The founding of the École Polytechnique de Paris in 1795 became a model for similar-type institutions throughout Europe: Christian Willenberg's college of engineering in Prague, established in 1707, was revamped as the Prague Polytechnique in 1806; Vienna (1815), Karlsruhe (1825), and London (1834) also established *polytechniques*. Other countries, however, emulated the German school system.

Schools proliferated widely in France: while 50% of French army recruits signed with a cross in 1835, only 20% did four decades later. Between 1837 and 1877, the number of schools and teachers in France increased by 36% and 85%, respectively, and the number of students nearly doubled from 2.7 million to 4.6 million. The latter number represented 74% of French children between the ages of five and fifteen. Free and compulsory elementary education, however, was introduced in France only in 1881 and 1886. Italy introduced mandatory elementary education in 1859, though it was not strictly enforced; it also established a chain of technical high schools and became second behind Germany in that area, and spent 0.5–2% of its GDP on education. In 1913, an average French person between the ages of fifteen and sixty-four had spent 7 years in school; this figure was 8.4 years in Germany, 8.8 years in Britain, and 6.4 years in the Netherlands. By the mid-nineteenth century, illiteracy had declined to 20% in Prussia, 20% in Scotland, to less than 30% in the Netherlands and Switzerland, and to 30–33% (that being mostly the elderly) in Britain, but it remained roughly 40–45% in France, Belgium, and the Austrian-Bohemian half of the Habsburg Empire. By the end of the century, illiteracy had virtually disappeared, dwindling to 1–3%, in the West and in Scandinavia. These average figures, however, conceal a much higher schooling for males, the critical workforce of the age. Discrimination against girls at all education levels continued to characterize most of Europe until the end of the century.

The new education systems, the rapid growth of journals and dailies, and the flourishing literature of the century all facilitated the expansion of modern knowledge and culture. The centuries-long development of science and secular enlightenment permeated the schools, providing people easy access to science-based practical knowledge, and influencing their daily lives. Economic historians who searched for an explanation for the historical discontinuity of the revolutionary economic transformation often found it in natural endowment, the geopolitical standing of certain countries that gave them a comparative advantage, as well as those countries' legal and institutional systems. Even those who tried explaining these events with economic laws and models increasingly accepted the role of culture and knowledge. Joel Mokyr probably went too far when he stated that useful knowledge "affected the world more than all other social and political changes taken together" (Mokyr, 2002, 297). Without any doubt, however, social and political changes *together* with the dissemination of knowledge (initially theoretical, later practical), in a historically developed cultural environment, were what ultimately transformed Europe.

The entrepreneurial state, promoter of trade and industry

The rising modern, secular, and mostly liberal nation-states became effective representatives of the new societies, and they were crucial to forming, and then modernizing and industrializing, their countries. What happened in the Low Countries and Britain was no longer a distant miracle for Western Europe. If nothing else, the outbreak of wars that included nearly all the West European countries made them appreciate the necessity of modernization to keep pace with more advanced and industrialized rivals. In more than a century and a half between 1650 and 1815, the crucial period of the beginning of Europe's transformation, wars raged 60 percent of the time. "[A s]trong state . . . based on a large and successful navy and military, and extensive control over foreign trade and shipping," were the lessons to be drawn from Britain's rise to world dominance (Engerman, 2004, 269). The British state demonstrated how to use its navy effectively by establishing naval bases throughout the world, from Gibraltar and Malta to Aden and Singapore.

The almost permanent warfare demanded centralized and interventionist power. The rivalry between England and the Netherlands, which consequently led to the decline of the latter, was another important lesson. One of the primary reasons that the Netherlands lost its previous standing was that the Dutch Republic was not a centralized power, and had eventually proved to be an "anti-state" that worked mightily in England's and France's favor (Ormrod, 2003, 351). Any state seeking to increase its military strength had to become an interventionist state, one that actively contributed to economic development.

Thanks to Alexander Gerschenkron's influential work, it was commonly accepted by historians during the 1950s and 1960s that state involvement in the economy was strictly the domain of backward countries,[19] for only they had to substitute the genuine prerequisites of industrialization, particularly capital accumulation. "Moderately backward" countries, such as mid-nineteenth-century Germany and continental Western Europe, had their banks create the prerequisite of capital accumulation. In countries of more considerable backwardness (Russia and the Balkans), a more aggressive substitution of the missing prerequisites of industrialization was needed; here the state played a key role.

The continental practice of industrial investments through banking was a special means of industrialization in the underdeveloped countries . . . The role the state played in Russia's industrialization clearly distinguishes that process from the analogous ones in Germany and Austria. (Gerschenkron, 1962, 14, 19)

The degree of backwardness of the underdeveloped areas is the most dominant factor determining the nature of the substitutions that have taken place. (Gerschenkron, 1970, 103)

This theory is more than debatable.[20] Decisive state intervention was not solely linked to backwardness or capital substitution. The state throughout nineteenth-century Western Europe, including Britain, played a crucial role. For one, state power, navies, and armies heralded the expansion of international power, colonization, and trade. As Eric Hobsbawm demonstrates in *Industry and Empire*, the British state was an important factor in the genesis of the Industrial Revolution. It was "willing to wage wars and colonize for the benefit of British manufacturers... [it] was prepared to subordinate all foreign policy to economic ends" (Hobsbawm, 1969, 49). Patrick O'Brien has stressed the role of the Royal Navy, which "protected Britain's growing share in international trade and profits... destroyed and degraded competitors" (O'Brien, 2000, 7). R. Findlay and K. O'Rourke have convincingly returned to the idea of war and "power" as determinants of trade and wealth ("plenty"). Britain, they concluded, successfully used "Power in order to secure Plenty" (Findlay and O'Rourke, 2007, 351).

Warfare required rock-solid finances and vast state revenue. "Europe's most powerful states... founded... large standing armies or navies and sometimes both. They did so through a combination of taxation, wartime borrowing, and an ever growing public debt" (Bogart et al., 2010, 77). Public finances in the *ancien régime* were chaotic and characterized by huge deficits and a lack of sufficient income; the state thus often defaulted on its obligations and consequently lacked credibility that it would repay its debts, which increased the cost of capital and consumed the countries' resources. The Dutch Republic and Britain invented modern *public finance* in the pre-industrial period. They were followed by virtually every West European country during the nineteenth century. The principal solution was the formation of the parliamentarian, multiparty system that created constitutional checks on fiscal and budgetary policy and thereby assured credibility. This made borrowing easier and cheaper and enabled the state to invest in infrastructure (Stasavage, 2003). The fiscal champions introduced modern direct taxation on real estate and income, roughly equal to 10% of the GDP, which comprised 20–40% of state revenues by 1870 (Bogart et al., 2010, 82). The often-heard idea that small government and low taxes created modern Britain was a myth: military expenditures topped 83% of government expenditures and 16% of the GDP, an amount higher than private capital accumulation. Taxes were twice as high in Britain as they were in most continental countries, including the centralized absolutist states of France and Spain. British taxation incorporated one-fifth of the national income, compared with 10–13% in the continental absolute states (O'Brien, 2002).

For a country to put its fiscal household in order, it needed a modern taxation system that evenly distributed the tax burden and abolished feudal privileges, and it needed to control spending and balance its income with expenditures. Financial stability, along with public state investment, made it possible to replace the tariff-based system with a free trade one. Fiscal stability thus contributed to the increase of exports. What's more, it created the appropriate environment for private business. In the case of the German states, modern state finance was accompanied by a falling interest rate between 1820 and 1840. State-imposed financial stability generated a "positive response of private capital supply... [it] encouraged capitalists to invest more in real assets and, hence, in the promotion of economic growth" (Pierenkemper and Tilly, 2004, 38). As I will argue in Part III, the lack of stable public finances and the permanence of huge deficits, which in the worst cases led to state bankruptcies, virtually crippled several peripheral countries.

One of the primary functions of state activity was indirect intervention in destroying the old, that is, creating the institutional framework for a modern economy by abolishing feudal institutions and establishing the legal and institutional base for industrialization.[21] The role of the state, therefore, was not exclusively connected to backwardness; it was a major factor in the economic success of the most developed countries as well. In his study "The State and the Industrial Revolution," Barry Supple (1973) clearly recognizes the widespread role of state intervention *throughout* Europe. Besides the role of the armed forces, warfare, and colonization,[22] Supple underscores the importance of indirect state activities in creating *laws and institutions.* The entire modern legal and institutional system was the work of the state.

New institution-building was part of that transformation. Political, social, and economic institutions have played an important role in generating economic performance. In recent decades, economists and economic historians have embraced an institutional interpretation of economic history.[23] Institutions are "the rule of the game in a society... the humanly devised constraints that shape human action" (North, 1990, 3). "Institutions shed light on why some countries are rich and others poor" (Greif, 2006, 3–4). The first sentence of the chapter on "State and Private Institutions" of the new *Cambridge Economic History of Modern Europe* boldly declares: "Economic growth depends upon institutions (rules that constrain human behavior and their enforcement mechanism)" (Bogart *et al.*, 2010, 71). According to D. North and B. Weingast, the Glorious Revolution of 1688 and the institutional system that was created afterwards, especially that of property rights, created Britain's economic success (North and Weingast, 1989). This concept, however, has been strongly criticized as "truncated in chronology, narrow in conception, and insular in focus" (O'Brien, 2002, 245). In O'Brien's view, the Glorious Revolution was not the key turning point "as a discontinuity in the development of private property... and the diffusion and integration of free market."

Rather, that development has had a much longer history and was connected to the period after the Civil War, when modern state finance gradually emerged.

The institutional interpretation of economic history as the single most important factor is one-sided and unavoidably simplistic.[24] The strong entrepreneurial state, which was the product of a centuries-long historical development and influenced by a host of cultural and ideological factors, underwent a gradual social-economic transformation that led to the creation of new "rules of the game." The most legitimate question to ask thus is: "what caused institutions?" (Ogilvie, 2007, 651).

Path-dependent and culturally inspired institutions, or the lack of them, indeed play an important role in economic performance (both success and failure), but one cannot point to them alone, especially not as *the* determinants of economic development. Institutions often serve the interest of a certain layer of society and not society as such; the same institution may have a different impact in a different social-cultural environment, since it and other factors are interdependent on one another. The best institutions that work in a given social-cultural environment often do not work in a clientalist or corrupt society. Successful countries sometimes had a mix of efficient and inefficient institutions; moreover, evaluating the efficiency of institutions is often highly subjective, as one tends to hold up institutions in successful countries as the ideal without considering the endless interrelated social, cultural, and political factors. Consequently, institutions are only part of a much larger cultural-ideological-behavioral package, and only part of the state's much broader interventionist activities in economic affairs.[25] Jean-Laurent Rosenthal added an important critical consideration to the debate: formal institutions are not always better and more efficient than informal ones, which are based on social customs and contracts that – as was the case in China – worked as well as formal institutions in Europe, and, indeed, had entirely substituted them (Rosenthal and Wong, 2011).

Modern institutions served partly to generate better economic performance and higher state revenue. This required abundant sources of income, for the state made a flourishing economy and huge business tax base "mandatory." Prevailing in wars during the eighteenth and nineteenth centuries was impossible without strong shipbuilding, construction, communications, and armament industries. Besides institution-building, ultimately the key to the success of the entrepreneurial state was its use of its revenue to build infrastructure and support private export activity and industrialization.

Indeed, it was in both the state's and the ruling elite's interest to build infrastructure; this was at least as important as having viable institutions, as were various policies that had, deliberately or not, a major impact on the economy. *Mercantilism* dominated Western state policy during the eighteenth century and a great part of the nineteenth. In the mercantilist mindset, a nation's wealth is accumulated from the inflow of gold from exports. Hence, a country should always defend its market against imports, halt the outflow of gold, and increase exports by any means possible. High protective tariffs helped achieve these goals. In the literature of economic history, the role of Colbert's mercantilist policy in France's development, and Maria Theresa's "kameralism" in Austria's, is commonplace. Besides protective tariffs, both Colbert and Maria Theresa made state investments in industry. Colbert's interventionism included the building of sugar refineries, and the husband of the Habsburg queen himself owned industrial firms.

Britain, however, was no less protectionist than France. Protectionist measures in the seventeenth century, such as the Navigation Act of 1651 and a revised version of 1660 that banned the anchoring of foreign ships in British ports, became a primary arsenal of state intervention in economic affairs. The Staple Act restricted Europe's exports to the colonies by way of foreign ships. The Corn Law, first introduced in 1804 and then strengthened between 1815 and 1846, imposed tariffs on imported corn. "Merchants and businessmen turned to government for help in the opening up of markets and the breaking down of local monopolies; they also sought naval and military support for trade" (Morgan, 2002, 165). Protectionist measures bolstered the country's economic power. The state also encouraged export activity by controlling the quality of exported goods, paying export subsidies, and issuing tariff rebates for imported goods that assisted export production.

Frederick the Great's Prussia exhibited one of the most telling examples of state interventionism. His mid- to late eighteenth-century state-initiated industrialization and state-owned industry served the Prussian military and was the origin of German industrialization in Silesia. The Prussian state played a direct entrepreneurial and managerial role. It created the Silesian putting-out textile industry by offering free looms to immigrants, and it established the first mechanized mill to weave worsted.[26] The state also invested in low-profit pursuits that were not attractive to private investors, subsidizing the construction of canals, roads, and railroads, and the creation of public utilities, educational systems, and health services.

The state played an important role in the economic transformation throughout Europe, and did so by assuring fiscal stability, passing requisite legislation, building institutions and modern infrastructure, defending domestic markets, and strengthening strategic sectors. Currency manipulation, tax and tariff policies, and the signing of trade-enhancing international agreements were also important functions of state activity. It is widely accepted that the state played an important role in Italian industrialization. Zamagni argues that the state in Italy ranked alongside those of Japan and Germany as among the most interventionist of the advanced countries (Zamagni, 1993). Some Italian historians speak about "state capitalism," and "political capitalism" which "supported industry through protection, purchases of its output, and the occasional bail-out of ailing companies" (Cohen and Federico, 2001, 63–4). "The state's varied role in industrialization must be seen not as the product of unique, national histories, but as part of a *European-wide phenomenon*" (Supple, 1973, 353; italics added).

Ever since laissez-faire ideologues, from the French Turgot to Adam Smith[27] and John Stuart Mill, first denounced mercantilist state intervention, it has been negatively evaluated in the economics and economic history literature. True, the mercantilist theory on the origins of wealth via the amassing of gold was plainly wrong. Nevertheless, the policies mercantilists employed to achieve this goal played a most positive role in economic advancement and industrialization. Indeed, the recent literature of economic history has rehabilitated mercantilism. "It was the mercantilist state which decisively shifted the balance of power and influence towards London . . . The Dutch state was unable to respond appropriately to the aggressive mercantilist challenges of her neighbors" (Ormrod, 2003, 337, 350). In other words, laissez-faire *and free trade policy*, initiated by the strongest powers in the mid-nineteenth century, were, paradoxically enough, the *child of state intervention*.

The mercantilist and *kameralist* policy of France, Prussia, and Austria applied all sorts of state intervention, including state investments in industry, such as shipbuilding in the early nineteenth century in the southern Low Countries and the creation of Prussian state-owned iron works in Silesia. The expansion of the north Italian "military-industrial complex" was a "direct result of . . . government support" (Cohen and Federico, 2001, 23). Most importantly, strong state intervention helped build vital infrastructure throughout Europe: national transportation networks, roads, canals, and railroads. In some cases, as with the Belgian and Prussian networks, state-ownership was used; others, such as France, combined private and public enterprise. The state usually took responsibility for its railroad infrastructure by donating land and building bridges, tunnels, etc. Several states made investment in the railroads especially attractive by guaranteeing a 4–5 percent interest for investors.

The nineteenth century was the cradle of a "free trade episode," as Karl Polanyi (1964) called the short-lived system, but the state as the defender of the domestic market dominated virtually the entire century. When one considers that free trade as a full-fledged economic theory prevailed only in 1848 with the publication of John Stuart Mill's *Principles of Political Economy*, and in practical terms only after 1860 when the French–British trade agreement initiated the basic free trade system, it becomes clear that free trade was but a brief episode in the nineteenth century. From the 1870s on, a host of countries returned to protectionism: Germany in 1879 and in 1902, France in 1880, 1892, and 1910, Sweden in 1888 and 1892, Austria in 1906, and Italy in 1878 and 1887.[28] As Paul Bairoch has argued, protectionism bolstered economic growth in the late nineteenth century (Bairoch, 1989). Kevin O'Rourke's new calculations have also demonstrated that "the data are far more comfortable with the hypothesis that tariffs boosted late nineteenth century growth" (O'Rourke, 2000, 468).[29] Aside from Britain, only some of the small and strongly export-oriented countries – the Netherlands, Denmark, Belgium, and in a much lesser extent Switzerland – remained more or less liberal. Beginning in the 1870s and throughout the early 1900s, free trade or low tariff regimes remained intact only in four or five European countries. State power, in various ways and forms, was a genuine weapon in Europe's modern economic transformation and industrialization.

*

The mid-nineteenth century was a turning point in the modernization and industrialization of Western Europe. It was symbolized by two major exhibitions: London in 1851 and Paris in 1855. London's Great Exhibition in the 563 by 138 meter iron and glass Crystal Palace in Hyde Park displayed the most modern technology of the age, including steam engines, steam-powered tractors, threshers, and locomotives. Altogether there were 13,000 exhibits – listed in a 116 page catalogue – admired by 6.2 million spectators. This was a world sensation that was extensively reported on and widely celebrated. (See Box 2.1.) Four years later, the Exposition Universel in Paris unveiled the latest in industrial, cultural, and social progress. The Exposition featured exhibits from thirty-four countries in the Palais de l'Industrie. It was a "mass display of consumer goods and the machines that produced them" (Eisenman, 1994, 221). In other pavilions, the fine arts exhibition represented the post-Romantic generation, reflecting a new realistic modernity, personified by Jean-François Millet ("The Sower"), Gustave Courbet ("The Stonebreakers"), and Honoré Daumier ("The Third Class") – revealing the pain and virtue of work and the nobility of poverty. This truly marked the beginning of a new age.

Box 2.1   The Crystal Palace exhibition in London, 1851

On May 1, 1851, Queen Victoria opened the exhibition of the century. The "Hallelujah Chorus" from Handel's *Messiah* was performed, and the Archbishop of Canterbury prayed for its success. The monumental iron and glass building erected in Hyde Park to host the international event symbolized modernity and modern political transparency. Leading the world, Britain was entering a new industrial age.

During the half-century between 1770 and 1830, France contributed scientific theories to the British Industrial Revolution. The idea of an industrial exhibition was also a French initiative. As early as September 1798, a state-sponsored exhibition was opened on the Champs de Mars in Paris, in the temporary "Temple of Industry" building, with 110 exhibitors from the Paris region. In his opening speech, Minister François de Neufchâteau celebrated the event as "not merely an episode in the struggle against English industry, but also the first stone in a mighty edifice which time alone can complete." Paris hosted a second national industrial exhibition in 1801, and the eleventh national industrial exhibition celebrated France's economic advance with more than 4,500 exhibitors in 1849. The French example was then followed by Germany, Switzerland, Sweden, Spain, and even Russia, mostly during the 1820s.

However, the idea of exhibitions was slow to emerge in Britain, where modern mechanized industry had been born. The British Museum was founded in 1753, the National Gallery in 1824, and London Zoo, patronized by the Zoological Society, in 1828. The Adelaide Gallery, founded in 1832, exhibited working machines and models. When the Society of Arts organized an industrial exhibition in 1761 and a second one in its own building in December 1844, the very few exhibitors and the mere 150 visitors signaled a palpable lack of interest. The French challenge, however, led to the foundation of a Royal Commission to prepare an international exhibition, the first of its kind in the world. With 2.4 million inhabitants, London was at that time the largest city in the world.

The first planning meeting, presided over by Prince Albert, was held in Buckingham Palace in June 1849. Hyde Park, a royal deer-hunting park until the late eighteenth century, was selected as the site for the planned exhibition. An international competition attracted 245 proposals for the exhibition building. In the end, the pioneering proposal of Joseph Paxton, "a translucent iron and glass structure, with an internal area of 19 acres (eight hectares)," was accepted. The enormous 900,000 square foot greenhouse, with 293,655 glass panels, 330 standardized iron columns, and 250,000 sash bars, and using 3,800 tons of cast iron, 700 tons of wrought iron, and 40 kilometers of rainwater gutters, was completed in nine months. An article in the satirical magazine *Punch* nicknamed it the Crystal Palace. Half of the enormous floor space was reserved for British and colonial exhibitors, the other half for more than 6,500 overseas participants. Among others, the French received 50,000 square feet of exhibition space, the Americans 40,000 square feet, and the Belgians 15,000 square feet.

A hundred thousand exhibits from twenty-eight nations evinced the opening of a new age, as well as the might of Britain, the glorious expansion of its colonial empire, and the country's industrial hegemony. Raw materials, machinery, and industrial products, including ordinary household products, represented the opening age of industrialization. Next to the exhibition, on the grounds of a cavalry barracks, model cottages for working-class families showed how industrialization improved the quality of life. The exhibition was a smashing international success. Half of London's population visited the Crystal Palace. Even the working class was able to afford it on so-called "shilling days." During its 141-day run, more than 6 million visitors – among them 27,000 French, 12,000 Germans, 5,000 Americans, and 3,800 Belgians – marveled at the miracles of industrialization.

The exhibition expressed "a passionate national pride," the greatness of the empire and the Victorian age, and, as several commentators suggested, "a point of social contact and reconciliation between the classes," "an island of social understanding." In his opening speech, Prince Albert addressed the idea of "peace and harmony through industrial progress." Most of all, the exhibition, Eric Hobsbawm (1996, 32–3) noted, heralded "the triumphant world of capitalism . . . The era of its global victory was initiated and punctuated by giant new rituals of self-congratulation . . . [The Crystal Palace erected] a princely monument to wealth and technical progress . . . "

Based on Gold and Gold (2005, 49–70).

Notes

1. The *Code civil* (1805), *Code de procédure civil* (1806), *Code de commerce* (1807), *Code d'instruction criminelle* (1808), and the *Code penal* (1810) became the backbone of European legal systems. Before that, ancient Roman law and – after Constantine's conversion that made Christianity the state religion in 380 – its merger with the church ecclesiastic laws (the canon law) created a comprehensive legal system in Europe. In medieval and even in early modern times canon law offered guidelines and rules not only for the church, but also for public and even private life, including economic activities of merchants and moneylenders.

2. "Where did the Protestant Ethic come from? . . . Can we analyze economic development as if this institutional norm were a given . . . ? Or was it itself the product of contextual changes in society and the economy? . . . Protestantism stimulated capitalism, or capitalism stimulated Protestantism . . . We have to take into account [the possibility of] a prior history . . . producing more liberal and flexible institutions and outlooks" (Supple, 2007, 10).

3. In various West European countries, liberal rule prevailed during parts of the nineteenth century. In Belgium, the new state established a liberal regime in 1830, and liberals dominated elections until the 1880s. France had a liberal regime during the 1860s and 1870s, in the period of the Third Republic. Switzerland experienced a liberal era between 1848 and World War I. The German liberals were the weakest in the western half of the continent, with a brief ascendancy in 1848.

4. When the ultraconservative Gaspard Mermillod was appointed apostolic vicar in 1873, the government in Geneva expelled him from Switzerland.

5. The first Freemason lodges were established in eighteenth-century Britain, France, and the Netherlands. At the time of the Revolution, the lodges attracted 100,000 members in France.

6. Pope Leo XIII denounced Freemasonry in his encyclical *Humanum genus* in 1884. The Catholic Church organized an anti-Masonic congress in Trent in 1896, condemning the "satanic cult" in the lodges (Clark and Kaiser, 2003, 213, 217, 74).

7. In Britain, publication of titles increased from 4,600 to 18,000 between the first years of the century and 1860–70. Germany published some 13,000 titles by 1845.

8. For example, Paris had eighteen libraries in 1784. By 1800, 390 lending libraries operated in Britain, 122 of them located in London. At that time, there was at least one *Lesegesellschaft* (reading club) in every German city; a decade later there were twenty-seven in Berlin and sixteen in Dresden (Sassoon, 2006, 48–51, 69).

9. Surprisingly enough, he rejected the Flemish school that followed a "narrow principle" and focused on locality.

10. Hippolyte Taine spoke of the "philosophical poetry of France, Germany and England [and listed the] great modern writers, from Chateaubriand to Balzac, from Goethe to Heine, from Cowper to Byron, and from Alfieri to Leopardi...Music left its natal countries and diffused itself over all Europe" (Taine, [1865] 1987, 379–80).

11. It began in Sicily in January, but the central event that ignited a European chain reaction was the February Revolution in France that disbanded the constitutional monarchy. Revolutions followed in March in Vienna, Milan, and Budapest. The "march of Christiansborg" led to the introduction of a constitutional monarchy in Denmark. In May, the All-German National Assembly convened in Frankfurt. In November, Rome revolted.

12. Three-quarters of the members of the upper house, and one-quarter of the lower chamber, were noblemen (Tipton and Aldrich, 1987, 102, 76).

13. Anhalt, Mecklenburg, Hesse-Darmstadt, Saxony, and Thüringen.

14. Emancipated peasants had to compensate the landlords with one-third to one-half of their parcels. Their financial burdens also increased significantly. According to some calculations, 37–74 percent of the peasants' monetary income was paid as compensation to landlords.

15. Until World War I, suffrage for the entire population was not achieved. Half of the populace, the women, continued to be excluded.

16. The low quality of primary school education offered a "low return," and its importance lagged far behind intergenerational occupational training (Long, 2006, 1050).

17. In Germany by 1816, 20,345 elementary schools were in operation with 1.2 million students representing 60 percent of the school-age generation. By 1846, more than 24,000 schools registered 2.4 million students, twice the number compared with a generation before.

18. One of the first was the chemical research laboratory of Justus Liebig, who had studied in France prior to introducing the new system in Giessen in 1826. Franz Neumann at the Königsberg University established at that time completely new research seminars, in the early 1830s.

19. Gerschenkron (1962) argued that the historical path of advanced countries created certain preconditions for industrialization. Among those "prerequisites" was the rate of capital formation; cultural and technology-related factors were also important. In Britain, these preconditions genuinely developed over time. Moving from the west to the east and south on the European continent, countries represented various increasing levels of backwardness. According to Gerschenkron, the prerequisites for industrial transformation did not emerge spontaneously except in Britain.

20. Richard Sylla and Gianni Toniolo edited a volume with contributions from leading economic historians, who were "members of Alexander Gerschenkron's Economic History Workshop at Harvard" (xi) in the 1960s, to examine, reinstate, but mostly revise Gerschenkron's concept of the nineteenth-century pattern of industrialization (Sylla and Toniolo, 1991).

21. Alexander Eckstein speaks of four types of European state interventions: the creation of the societal infrastructure; direct forms of assistance such as tariffs and concessions; the founding of state enterprises; and ultimately, state economic planning (Eckstein, 1958).

22. Powerful advanced states often forced latecomer countries and peripheral regions to introduce laissez-faire systems in much the same way as Britain forced free trade policy on China after the Opium War. The Treaty of Nanking limited Chinese tariffs to 5 percent in 1842.

23. England's exceptional success, Gregory Clark maintains, has been one-sidedly attributed to its institutions. "Not coal, not colonies, not the Protestant Reformation, not the Enlightenment, but the accidents of institutional stability" are supposedly responsible for it (Clark, 2007, 11).

24. Gregory Clark goes so far as to state that the institutional explanation "exerts its powerful hold over the economics profession in part because of the limited historical knowledge of most economists" (Clark, 2007, 211).

25. In addition to the basic state-institutional framework created mostly in the nineteenth century and discussed in this chapter, I will explore the role of institutions in several chapters of this narrative in relation to infrastructure, banking, mining, industry, etc., in the context of several other factors of economic development.

26. Malapane Hütte was established in 1753. The government's iron works in Königshütte and the Gleiwitz foundry in 1802, the armament factories in Spandau and Potsdam, and the lead works in Friedrichsgrube that installed the first British steam engine in Germany – all these signaled the beginning of Prussia's war-oriented industrialization. During the last two decades of the eighteenth century, Silesia's industrial labor force and mining output increased fivefold. A state industrial and mining agency, headed by von Heinitz, and the special commissioner for Silesia, Graf von Reden, made successful efforts to duplicate the British Industrial Revolution.

27. Smith, however, was much more nuanced in his argumentation than was laissez-faire literature after him. The "duty of the sovereign or commonwealth," he suggests in *The Wealth of Nations*, "is that of erecting and maintaining those public institutions and those public works, which . . . [are] of such a nature that the profit could never repay the expense to any individual . . . and which it therefore cannot be expected that any individuals should erect or

maintain" (Smith, [1776] 1976, Book V, Chapter I, Part III, quoted by Supple, 1973).

28. The United States, an important partner of Europe, rose to an advanced economic level using protective tariffs, which were first introduced in 1890, when the McKinley tariff set import duties at an average rate of 50 percent. Seven years later, the Dingly tariff increased it to 57 percent.

29. It pays to note that the same institution, the protective tariff system, had the opposite outcome in the interwar decades.

CHAPTER 3

Agriculture, transportation, and communication

The agricultural revolution

During the long nineteenth century, most European countries duplicated in varying degrees the earlier social and agricultural transformations of the Northwest. In the early nineteenth century, Dutch and British yields of the four main types of grain were twice as high as they were in continental Western Europe.[1]

As had happened in the Northwest, revolutionary reforms replaced feudal institutions with modern ones on the continent. Serf labor was supplanted by free farmers or/and mobile wage labor. In the southern Low Countries (later Belgium), all seigniorial claims and obligations were abolished without payment in 1793. When the region became part of France in 1795, the government confiscated church lands and sold them to private farmers. Indeed, the Revolution created an owner-entrepreneur farmer economy in France: of the country's 3.8 million peasants, 68 percent had become independent farmers by 1851. The French reclaimed previously uncultivated land such as marshes, and built drainage systems that made cultivable vast swaths of river valleys and coastal regions.

The French occupation of northern Italy during the Napoleonic era abolished the last remnants of feudal rights; the sale of communal and church land increased the number of peasant proprietors, in some regions by 20 percent. Uniquely, Lombardy inherited from earlier periods (as had Belgium and the Netherlands) a highly developed capitalistic agriculture with an efficient irrigation system and specialized agricultural production. The advanced agronomy "was the work of many generations . . . and represented the gradual adaptation . . . [to] geography and climate" (Greenfield, 1965, 32).[2] Similarly, the fertile soil of the plain was the result of generations of labor building up a thin layer of cultivable soil and "sloping" the field to keep the water moving without washing the soil away. In the higher elevations of the Alpine region, the abundance of rich, fertile lands for grazing led to the development of animal husbandry. In lower elevations on the hills, farmers produced mulberries, grapes, and wheat, and in the "exuberant fertile" plain area, they cultivated forage crops, rice, flax, and grain.

An early crop rotation system kept the land fertile. In the rotation with rice, farmers improved the land by adding manure six times in a nine-year cycle; in the rotation without rice, they did so four times in a six-year cycle (Greenfield, 1965, 21). Specialized agriculture was combined with food processing, especially cheese production. Parmesan cheese output trebled from the mid-eighteenth century to the 1830s. The large mulberry plantations provided a solid base for a flourishing silk industry.

Northern Italian agriculture was further modernized between the second half of the 1880s and World War I. This resulted in an annual 1.4 percent agricultural growth in the Po Valley. According to new calculations, Italian agricultural output nearly doubled during the half-century before the war. In 1910 the Po Valley produced 31 percent of Italy's agricultural output with only 13 percent of its arable land, as its productivity level was three times higher than the rest of the country's.

Cultivating fallow land also helped develop the production of potato and corn (maize) crops that came from America.[3] Corn and potatoes produced more calories per land unit than did grain. As wheat prices were twice as high as those for corn, the peasants, Fernand Braudel (1979) related, began eating their corn and selling their wheat. Potatoes became even more important than corn. The yield from the same amount of land could feed twice as many people as could wheat. Small wonder that potatoes became the staple diet in poorer areas, such as in certain regions of France. In Flanders, potatoes replaced 40 percent of wheat consumption.

Both peasant farms and capitalist big estates adopted modern rotation systems in place of the traditional three-year rotation, and they radically decreased fallow land by alternating their planting of legumes, turnips, and clover with grain. These methods improved the soil without leaving it fallow. The cultivated land of the continent had increased by 38 percent, from 110 million to 151.8 million hectares, between 1800 and 1910. Altogether, 3.5 million hectares were irrigated by 1900. The new rotation system also produced fodder and helped introduce stall-feeding animal husbandry instead of grazing. Animals now survived the winter and early spring; prior to this, a great part of the stock had to be slaughtered because of a lack of grazing possibilities. Consequently cattle and pig stocks roughly doubled in the second half of the century.

The period also saw the introduction of various mostly science-based innovations. One was animal breeding. The British breeder Robert Bakewell founded the science of animal breeding in the late eighteenth century by "breeding the best with the best." Gregor Johann Mendel, an Austrian monk, built upon Charles Darwin's theory of evolution to provide a scientific basis for new and improved agriculture and animal husbandry. Selective line breeding and cross-breeding of livestock effected vast improvements. In 1780, the development of artificial insemination led to both an increase of animal stocks and a refinement of animal types. New breeds of cattle produced a better quality and increased quantity of milk and meat. Improved pig stocks produced a leaner meat (bacon and ham). A number of associations and research institutions promoted modern animal husbandry in the latter part of the nineteenth century.[4] At the same time, plant breeding, an applied academic science, also contributed to increasing yields (Wieland, 2006).

The appearance of new inventions emblematic of the nineteenth century – advanced tools such as cast-iron moldboard plows, horse-driven drills, reapers, cultivators, and grain- and grass cutters – increased labor productivity five- to tenfold. The milking machine became available in the 1870s, the corn picker in 1900. Full mechanization, however, was characterized by one agricultural activity alone: the use of steam threshers. These had come to the fore in the early decades of the century, but they became popular only with the production of portable models that enabled rapid adoption after the middle of the century. Still, the main power source of the century, the steam engine, was not broadly applicable to agriculture.[5] It wasn't until the invention of the combustion engine that a new wave of mechanization took hold. The revolutionary tractor contributed to an increase of productivity and output at the turn of the century, but its proliferation in Europe occurred only after World War I.

The introduction of new animal husbandry helped raise production. Stabling animals made it possible to collect manure and use it, on average, at least every fourth year to improve soil quality. More advanced countries began importing nitrates from Chile and guano from Peru; this had an important impact on British and German agriculture. The most revolutionary innovations, however, came by way of the modern science-based chemical industry. The German Justus von Liebig was the founder of organic chemistry in the 1830s; his 1840 work *Chemistry and its Application to Agriculture and Physiology* became the foundation of scientific agriculture.

Laboratories and factories began producing organic substances based on von Liebig's discoveries. The commercial production of phosphate took off in 1840, followed by that of potash, artificial nitrogen fertilizer, and ammonium sulfate. West European agriculture began using artificial fertilizers around 1880 and increased their use more than fivefold by 1913. Pest control chemicals appeared in the first half of the nineteenth century, and were crucial in combating vine parasites such as peronosphora (that attacks the leaves).

An additional aspect of the agricultural revolution was increasing specialization, which ended the planting of a great variety of crops on each individual estate or in each regional unit. Specialized, highly productive agriculture and animal husbandry, in combination with food processing, led to an agricultural revolution that served as the starting point for industrialization in several countries.

But an agricultural revolution in this complex sense was characteristic of only the most advanced regions. The structure of landownership was different in Britain and Austria-Bohemia, where the agricultural system was uniquely based on the modern capitalist big estates,[6] from that in most of continental Western Europe, where peasant farms predominated. Nevertheless, the modernization of agriculture was commonplace throughout the entire western half of the continent.[7] The facts clearly show that all types of farming resulted in highly revolutionized, modern agriculture.

On the continent, some of the peasant plots were small subsistence farms that were unable to market their products. In a number of regions, however, even very small farms were specialized and market-oriented. In certain areas agricultural production was combined with food processing, in others not at all. In various ways and forms, West European agriculture was revolutionized, with increased productivity and the liberation of a great part of its labor force. This transformation became the solid basis for industrialization.

The agricultural revolution began to transform Flemish, Dutch, and later British agriculture from the late Middle Ages on, and particularly during the eighteenth century. Building on the Flemish and Dutch achievements, Britain became the crib of the eighteenth-century agricultural revolution, but it gradually renounced self-sufficiency in agricultural production, especially during the second half of the nineteenth century. Cultivation in the country declined: in 1867, 54 percent of British land remained pastureland; by 1913, the figure was 69 percent. However, even meat (including bacon and ham), butter, cheese, and eggs were mostly imported during the second half of the century.

Britain switched to the fifth gear of industrialization and gradually opened its markets to food, while covering its consumption by dramatically increasing its share of imports. While its population roughly quadrupled,

Britain's agricultural production, calculated in constant prices, increased only by 56 percent between 1781–90 and 1905–14. The most important step toward promoting food imports was the repeal of the Corn Laws in 1846, which made food imports duty-free. Parliament also abolished the restrictions imposed by the Navigation Act against delivery of goods to the country in foreign ships.

Consequently, wheat and wheat-flour imports increased fifty times, and barley and oats imports twenty-two times, in nineteenth-century Britain. Meat imports grew twelvefold, while sugar, tobacco, coffee, and tea imports doubled. Between 1855–9 and 1900–9, British imports increased by 337 percent, while the share of textiles and other industrial raw materials and goods shrank to 40 percent of imports. In 1800, half of the country's population was employed in agriculture; by 1841, the number declined to 35 percent, and by 1911 it fell to an unparalleled 9 percent.

The Netherlands, the initiator of the agricultural revolution, continued its economic advance by augmenting its arable land mass during the nineteenth century. Between 1833 and 1911, state companies were established to dig canals and reclaimed 370,000 hectares of previously uncultivable marshlands, with an additional 100,000 hectares salvaged from the ocean. The state parceled out the newly acquired land rather equitably. In contrast to Britain, big estates did not exist in the country; moreover, mini-estates of 1–5 hectares, and small estates of 5–10 hectares, grew by 75,000 and 34,000 hectares, respectively. Uniquely, the Dutch mini-estates were the only ones in Europe to engage in specialized and market-oriented production. Although the proportion of those working in agriculture decreased from 45 percent to 28 percent between 1846 and 1906, the absolute numbers increased by one-third, from 394,000 to 528,000, in the latter six decades of the century, when the country's population doubled from 3.1 million to 6.2 million.

The new agricultural prosperity in the Netherlands was based on changes in the British customs policy and the introduction of the free trade system. Once that door opened for Dutch exports, the Netherlands' farmers rapidly adjusted to the new market opportunities. Increasing numbers specialized and developed intensive animal husbandry. Their cattle and pig stocks increased by 50 percent and 448 percent, respectively. More importantly, (as will be discussed in Chapter 5), they methodically combined animal husbandry with food processing.

Although no other countries on the continent attained the advanced level of the Netherlands, some in the West did engage in specialized agriculture, mostly in Denmark, Switzerland, northern Italy, and in the western provinces of the Habsburg Empire. These parts of Europe showed significant similarities to the Netherlands with their highly specialized agricultural production and its combination with food processing. Switzerland and Austria-Bohemia, at the eastern edge of the West European region, also began their economic modernization with specialized agriculture.[8] Until the nineteenth century, Swiss agriculture remained traditionally self-sufficient on both the local and regional level.[9] The nineteenth century, however, radically changed Swiss agriculture. The state abolished the country's restrictive community structures and plot-system, and it privatized pastureland during the 1860s and 1870s. Subsistence farming was replaced by a market and trade economy. Three-rotation was halted in favor of modern crop rotation, but the grain economy soon declined substantially and gave way to specialized fodder, root vegetables, and potato production, as well as a cattle and milk economy. The area sown with cereal crops decreased to one-third between 1850 and 1913. Cattle stocks, on the other hand, increased by nearly 50 percent, and milk production doubled between 1866 and 1911. Having been self-sufficient in food until the mid-nineteenth century, Switzerland began importing various food products; measured in calories, only half of Swiss food consumption was supplied by domestic agriculture immediately before World War I (Walter, 1991, 92–4). Its specialized cattle and milk economy, however, served an innovative and highly developed food-processing and export industry.

In contrast to the Netherlands and Britain, the French and German social and political environment, with its ever enduring serfdom, noble privileges, landed estates, and feudal institutions, froze agriculture in its medieval mode for a long time. Despite the country's traditional features, feudal fees in France were mostly paid in the form of money. The French *censitaire* peasants, comprising in various regions 22–70 percent of the entire peasantry, became renters of the noble lands. The church remained a big landowner, in certain regions possessing 20 percent of the land, while in others only 1 percent. Loosening feudal ties, nevertheless, did not lighten the crippling impact of the peasants' burdens. Peasants paid 30–40 percent of their income to the landlords, the church, and the state. Cultivation remained backward, and two- and three-rotation systems predominated, resulting in a high percentage of fallow land. The primary crop continued to be grain, which produced a yield five to six times that of the seeds. Besides grain, only vineyards were significant; other kinds of specialized cash crops or garden production did not exist.

The revolutionary abolition of feudal fees, the enactment of modern property rights, and the nationalization and parceling out of a significant part of the noble estates created a real turning point. The smallholder independent peasants became the central figures of the French village and the vehicle for modernization. The system of inheritance and the very slow migration from the countryside significantly increased the peasant population from 9 million to 15 million between 1815 and 1881. Consequently, peasant plots were split up and shrunk. Fernand Braudel and Ernest Labrousse observe that the average size of the peasant estates was 3.5 hectares. By the 1860s, small peasant farms comprising 1–10 hectares made up 28 percent of the land, while those comprising 10–40 hectares made up 32 percent. Well-to-do peasants with more than 40 hectares owned roughly 40 percent of the land. New research suggests greater similarities in the rural structures and market-oriented farming of France and Britain than was traditionally believed (Broad, 2009).

The modern rotation system, however, only slowly and gradually replaced traditional cultivation. This process went hand in hand with the decline and final disappearance of the *métayage* or sharecropping system, which continued to exist after the Revolution and posed significant obstacles to innovation and change. Consequently, the proportion of fallow land decreased from one-third to one-quarter of total land mass during the first half of the century, and practically disappeared by the century's end. In the mid-nineteenth century, three-quarters of the cultivated land was used for grain. Yields increased by 30 percent in the first half, and another one-third during the next third of the century. Mechanization of French agriculture made some progress.[10]

The most important advance towards introducing specialization and diminishing the grain economy was the development of grape production and a wine economy. As J. C. Toutain (1961) aptly put it, France's nineteenth century was "the century of grapes." In addition to the Bordeaux wine region, which had already flourished in the eighteenth century, the Burgundy and Champagne vineyards rose in importance in the nineteenth century. Wine production increased from 25 to 60 million hectoliters[11] between the 1780s and the 1870s. Specialization also characterized the densely populated Alsace-Lorraine region (seventy people per square kilometer of land), where wine, tobacco, fruit, and hemp production had a value per hectare that was two to three times higher than grain. Agricultural output was also combined with processing. Between the 1820s and 1860s, French agriculture reached an impressive 2.3 percent annual growth rate (Lévy-Leboyer, 1968).

In the mid-nineteenth century, however, a series of pestilences, including oidium (mildew) and fungal epidemics, began to hit the wine economy. In a fifteen-year period during the 1860s and 1870s, a mysterious pestilence plagued the Rhone Valley, gradually spreading and destroying 40 percent of French vineyards. The culprit was vine blight or phylloxera, which attacks the roots of the grapevine. Wine production was cut in half, to 30.7 million hectoliters, by 1885–94. Recovery came only at the turn of the century, with the importation of immune genera of grapes from the United States. Output gradually, though not entirely, recovered and reached 52.8 million hectoliters by 1905–14.

Another element of agricultural specialization was the introduction of a sugar economy. Sugar beet output increased by nearly five times between 1835–44 and 1875–84 and then stagnated, while sugar production rose from 26,000 to 706,000 tonnes[12] between 1835–44 and 1905–14. Agriculture remained an important sector in the French economy, employing more than 40 percent of the active population.[13]

The united German Reich[14] exhibited a wide range of different agricultural systems.[15] The western parts of Germany exhibited similarities with successfully industrializing Western Europe. The serfs were liberated in the 1790s, while Prussia – after its defeat by Napoleon at Jena – introduced reforms from above and liberated the peasants in the early nineteenth century. This happened nearly half a century later in Bavaria. In the western regions, in Hanover, Westphalia, Schleswig-Holstein, Baden, Hessen and Württemberg, 92 percent of the land belonged to peasant farms.

Agricultural modernization received a strong impetus in the first half of the century. Following the English pattern, various agricultural societies were founded whose publications taught modern cultivation methods. A number of model farms were also established, such as Caspar Voght's estate near Hamburg and Albrecht Thaer's in Möglin. Modern six-, nine-, and twelve-rotation systems replaced the traditional three rotations, and fallow land decreased from 40 percent to 7 percent of the arable land by mid-century, while cultivated land almost doubled in the German states. Although grain was produced on 60 percent of the land, the most important new development was the introduction of more intensive cultures. Potato and sugar beet production expanded. The former was produced mostly on peasant farms, where efficient production was possible. The area reserved for potato cultivation increased from 0.3 million to 1.4 million hectares between 1800 and 1850. Sugar beet production characterized the big and factory estates.

Agriculture retained its important role in the nineteenth-century economic modernization of France and Germany. The value of output increased rapidly, though, in a characteristic way, its share of national revenue decreased sharply. (See Table 3.1.)

In certain respects, the western half of the Habsburg Empire, the Austrian and Czech lands, revealed certain similarities to the previously discussed transformation, though on a somewhat smaller scale. These areas

Table 3.1   The role of agriculture in the French and German economies

Years	France		Germany	
	Agricultural output (in constant prices)	Agriculture's contribution to GNP (%)	Agricultural output (in constant prices)	Agriculture's contribution to GNP (%)
1781–90	4,411	50	–	–
1845–54	7,212	–	4,402	32[a]
1875–84	7,705	42	6,898	–
1905–14	10,266	35	11,241	18

Source: Mitchell (1973, 766, 811).
Note: [a] In 1861–5.

represented a transitory stage between the West and the East. In the westernmost Vorarlberg area, which enjoyed a free peasantry, Alpine animal husbandry was close to the Swiss type. Still, the grip of Austrian and Czech feudal institutions was not loosened until the first half of the nineteenth century, and they were abolished only by the 1848 revolution. Huge aristocratic estates survived, however, not unlike those in Eastern Europe. Princes Schwarzenberg and Lichtenstein, and the Stahremberg, Windischgrätz, Esterházy, and Lobkowitz families all owned enormous estates that endured as symbols of the *ancien régime.* No less than 30–40 percent of Austrian-Czech land remained in the hands of the aristocracy.

On the other hand, a significant number of serfs were liberated without land or with only tiny parcels. During the second half of the century, 30 percent of the Austrian and 36 percent of the Czech agrarian population became wage laborers. These liberated peasants had to pay compensation to the surviving big estates – payments totaling 450 million gold crowns. Mortgage credits also became available from the emerging modern banking system from the 1850s on; the more than sixfold increase in credit was a huge boost for modernization.

Modern capitalist big estates gradually emerged. Mechanization began in the mid-nineteenth century. By 1902, half of the Czech estates used machines. A modern rotation system also spread rapidly: 22 percent of the Czech land was left fallow in 1848, but by 1908 only 1 percent remained so. In Upper Austria, fallow land decreased from 14 percent to 9 percent. In

Austria-Bohemia, the use of phosphorous fertilizer reached only one-third of the German and one-fifth of the British levels, but it was three times greater than Hungarian usage. In the western hereditary provinces of the Habsburg Empire, grain output doubled between 1789 and 1913, but it was only enough to keep pace with population growth as per capita output rose by only 10 percent during that period. Agricultural productivity increased by only 50 percent in Austria and the Czech lands, while it trebled in Germany. Agriculture was thus on a higher level than in the neighboring East, but it remained less developed than in the West. The division of labor in the Habsburg lands led to some agricultural specialization in Austria-Bohemia, while Hungary supplied grain for the western provinces of the empire.

Cultivated land increased by almost 20 percent in four West European countries during the second half of the century, but it decreased in Britain and France. Labor input generally decreased. What made the real difference was the impressive growth of labor productivity. Agriculture became even more intensive in the second half of the century.[16] Because of technological development, agricultural productivity, that is, the value of output per agricultural worker, increased by 50 percent during the last third of the century (North, 2000, 135, 216–20).

The total factor productivity of ten European countries jumped by 30–40 percent between 1870 and 1913 (i.e. by 0.7 percent per year), in part as the result of market integration and technical improvement. Between 1870 and World War I, West European agricultural growth slowed somewhat to an annual 0.9 percent, but some countries, such as Germany, Denmark, and Italy, boasted a 1–1.5 percent growth rate (Broadberry *et al.*, 2010, 65–7). This was a relatively good performance in a period of a major grain crisis in Europe, and was reflective of the fact that the Western countries found a way to adjust and restructure their agriculture by shifting to more efficient sectors and producing at more competitive prices.

The role of agriculture in modern economic transformation

It is a common assumption in economic history literature that efficient agriculture provides the basis for industrialization. Simon Kuznetz has underscored agriculture's product contribution, its supply of food and raw material. Agriculture always produces raw materials for processing, and in some cases becomes the basis for industrialization via the dominant role of food processing in industrial development. In addition to supplying the population and certain industries with raw materials, agriculture provides export goods that play an important role in the so-called follower countries, the latecomers to industrialization. "The contribution of agriculture to exports assumes strategic importance," Kuznetz notes, "and it is exceedingly important for follower nations to trade with the more advanced countries" (Kuznetz, 1963, 39–61).

Agriculture has also played an important role as a large market for industrial products, both consumer and investment goods. Increased iron production in Britain before the railway age was a consequence of agricultural demand. Agriculture thus provided an important stimulus for the iron industry, an important sector of the Industrial Revolution. The more affluent agricultural populace provided a market for industrial consumer goods, including textiles.[17] Besides product and market contribution, agriculture has also supported factors of production, that is, capital and labor for industry. The more efficient the agriculture, the greater its potential for capital accumulation, which materializes as direct investment in other sectors and/or in bank accounts. At the beginning of industrialization in Britain, industry required a very low level of capital investment. Agriculture required nine times more capital per worker than did industry at the turn of the nineteenth century. The sale of a farm with one worker, Paul Bairoch concluded, would produce enough capital to employ eight workers in industry. Agriculture has consequently also provided "a large part of the capital and entrepreneurs" for the early stage of industrialization (Bairoch, 1973, 480–98).

Finally, an increase in agricultural productivity frees a large part of its workforce to migrate to the cities and become laborers in industry and construction. Economic history literature often argues that Britain's pioneering role in industrialization was partly connected to the early stages of enclosure that made available a labor force for industry.

Giovanni Federico speaks, albeit somewhat skeptically, about the "three-pronged role" of agriculture in nineteenth-century economic growth. He concedes that it is highly questionable, but argues that so far no alternative theoretical framework has emerged.[18]

Sectoral interrelations in the economy go beyond industrialization. The marketing and exporting activity of agriculture also contributes to infrastructure development, providing incentives for building modern transportation systems. The nineteenth century is often and rightly called the century of industrialization, but agriculture remained, to varying degrees, one of the prime movers of the modern transformation of Europe. Productivity levels and agricultural growth were high before and during industrialization, and agriculture's contribution to economic growth continued to be an important factor even in Britain.

Erik Thorbecke has emphasized the interdependence of agriculture and industry: both sectors must perform in an interdependent way, with neither leading nor lagging (Thorbecke, 1969, 4). A. J. Coale and E. M. Hoover have called attention to a backward agricultural system's "blocking" or limiting role in economic development as indirect proof of agriculture's importance: "If one sector limited the growth of the other, it is more likely to be a case of agricultural growth limiting non-agricultural than vice versa" (Coale and Hoover, 1958, 139). Western Europe was able to duplicate the agricultural revolution initiated by the Northwest. A modernized and more productive agriculture provided a broad foundation for the industrial breakthrough in continental Western Europe.

Transportation: canals and roads

The integration of markets and the spectacular rise of the Northwest inspired Western Europe to emulate the advanced countries and expand the construction of modern transportation. Road construction, which had been fervently pursued in eighteenth- and nineteenth-century France, was far from sufficient. According to some estimates, France's investment in canal and road construction quadrupled between 1800 and 1850, and it could boast a 35,000 kilometer road network by the mid-nineteenth century. Nevertheless, transportation remained slow and expensive. Canal building was an obvious solution, but it was neither easy nor sufficient in large countries and regions.

As Alexander Gerschenkron recognized, several countries and regions needed substitute factors to replace the missing advantages of the Northwest. Waterway and road construction escalated until the 1830s–1840s. In large land-locked countries, however, it could not offer a real solution. From the second third of the nineteenth century on, the western half of the continent began extensive railroad construction to create a modern transportation and communication system.

The superiority of navies and merchant fleets played a central role in the rise of the Northwest in the early modern centuries. Trade and shipping were a significant factor in Europe's advance,[19] but they became even more important in the nineteenth century. Intercontinental trade had a slow 1 percent annual growth rate before 1800, compared with the roughly 3.5 percent annual growth after the Napoleonic wars. The value of British merchandise exports increased thirty-five times between 1820 and 1913, French exports twenty-three times, and Swiss and Belgian exports fifty-five times.[20] During the nearly half-century between 1870 and 1914, the value of the merchandise exports of Western Europe increased by almost

Figure 3.1

Europe's share in worldwide manufactured goods exports, 1876/80–1913 (percent) (Lamartine-Yates, 1959, 226–32)

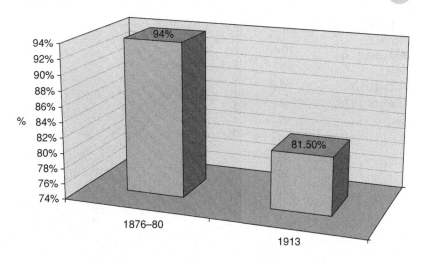

four times. European trade represented 68 percent and 64 percent of the world's exports in 1870 and 1913, respectively (based on Maddison, 2001, 361–2). (See Figure 3.1.) Intercontinental trade rose from 4 million tons in 1800 to 27 million in 1873, and to 63 million by 1900. By 1914, the volume of goods transported by ships increased twenty- to twenty-five-fold (Woodruff, 1973, 696–7).

This expansion of international trade played a tremendously important role in West European modernization. Cheap ocean transport carrying inexpensive bulky goods overseas and raw materials from the colonies to Europe was essential for rapid economic growth. The Industrial Revolution, specifically the invention of the steam engine and the steam ship, revolutionized water transportation. The technological development of steamers continually advanced between 1770 and 1820,[21] but the real breakthrough was Robert Fulton's steamship in 1807. The propulsion system was discovered in 1808–9,[22] and shipping safety was enhanced by the invention of modern lighthouse technology by the French physicist Augustin Fresnel in 1822.[23] In 1819, the *Savannah* was the first steamboat to cross the Atlantic Ocean. The slew of inventions continued: the patent for a screw propeller turned a new page, but the first ship to carry this technology, the *Archimedes*, appeared only in 1840. New technological innovations – the turbine-propelled ship, the paddle wheel, and the screw-propeller and twin-screw-propeller systems – modernized shipping further in the last decades of the century. At the same time, iron and then steel ships replaced the wooden boat. The first iron steamship operated on the River Thames in 1821. Giant ships soon began looming on the oceans: the *Great Western* (1,340 tons) in 1838, followed by the *Great*

Figure 3.2
Declining
transportation
costs,
1820–1910
(Bairoch, 1976,
36)

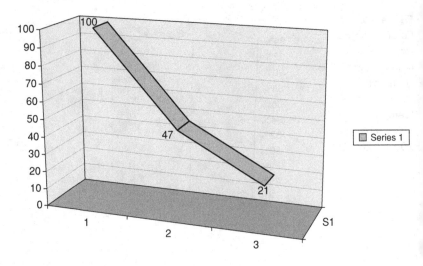

Eastern (nearly 19,000 tons) in 1854–7. By the late nineteenth century, ships employed up to 28,000 horsepower and vastly larger engines.

Yet another page in shipping technology was turned with the construction by the Copenhagen Burmeister & Wain Shipyard of the world's first ship propelled by a diesel internal combustion engine, the Selandia, in 1912. Germany then built diesel-engine U-boats just prior to the outbreak of World War I.

It took several decades before the more efficient steamships with their lower coal consumption would become competitive in the 1850s. Steamboats represented only 15 percent of the shipping capacity in 1850. During the first decades of their existence, steamships consumed vast quantities of coal, which mandated huge space outlays for coal storage, and left little room for transported goods.[24] After 1850, however, more sophisticated steam engines consumed half the coal that was previously needed. By 1880, steamships attained more than 40 percent of the carrying capacity of sailboats; by 1914, sailboats amounted to but one-tenth of shipping capacity.

Modern technology drastically cut the cost of water transportation. (See Figure 3.2.) The cost of transporting cotton from India to Britain dropped by a third. The least expensive price for a passenger to travel from Europe to the United States in 1825 was $100; by the 1880s, it had plummeted to $8. Before this sharp decline in transportation prices, merchants transported only high-value goods, which represented 58 percent of European imports from America and Asia. From the mid-century on, cheap high-quantity products such as grain and coal comprised the bulk of transported goods. Without this change, a modern economy could not emerge. (See Table 3.2.)

Table 3.2 Transportation costs
in constant prices

Year	1820 = 100
1820	100
1860	46
1910	21

Source: Bairoch (1976, 36).

The explosion of shipping signaled a real transportation revolution. In 1800, the world's shipping capacity was 4 million tons; by 1840, it had grown to 9 million tons, and by 1914, 33 million tons. Britain monopolized the shipbuilding industry and produced two-thirds of newly built vessels during the last third of the nineteenth century. Its shipping carrying capacity expanded from 1 million tons in 1780 to 11 million tons before World War I, comprising one-third of the world's total. Shipping was and remained a European privilege. In the mid-nineteenth century, 54 percent of the world's shipping capacity was in European hands; by World War I, it had grown to 79 percent.[25]

Major international *canal building* and the creation of a suitable communication system boosted the efficiency of water transportation. Canal building dramatically shortened water routes connecting continents and linked land-locked regions to the seas. By constructing the 163 kilometer Suez canal in 1869, the French developer Ferdinand de Lesseps shortened the distance to India by nearly a third. The success of the enterprise encouraged others to build canals. Among them, the 6.3 kilometer Corinth canal, completed by the Hungarian István Türr by 1893, reduced the route through the Mediterranean by 400 kilometers. The dream of connecting the Atlantic and Pacific oceans had a long history.[26] After many failed efforts and thorny diplomatic arrangements, the 77 kilometer Panama canal was opened in 1914.

Still, ocean transportation could not have expanded so dramatically if there had not been a revolution in the delivery systems on land, which made inexpensive *inland* mass transportation of goods to ports possible. A dense water transportation network was created in Northwestern Europe during the seventeenth and eighteenth centuries. Every country in the region attempted to use and, if necessary, regulate its natural waterways and make its rivers navigable. Some of Europe's rivers were easily navigable or did

Map 3.1 The Belgian waterways form a national network (Kunz and Armstrong, 1995, 37)

not pose insurmountable challenges,[27] but most required reconstructing banks, deepening river beds, and eliminating reefs and bottom-rocks. River regulation was often connected to canal construction. In Western Europe, a boom in the latter characterized the early modern and nineteenth centuries. Belgium, for example, built the second most developed waterway system[28] in Europe after that of the Netherlands; each kilometer of its waterways served 14 square kilometers of land. This was twice as much as in the Netherlands, but less than half of Britain's landed area per unit of canals. Extensive canal building distinguished the entire continent.[29]

The importance of canals, however, was mostly local or regional, and not national or international, in nature. Perhaps only Britain, the Netherlands, and Belgium had national networks of canals and navigable rivers (Map 3.1). In general, European canal transportation entailed mostly short-distance deliveries of 15–30 kilometers (Turnbull 1987, 537–60). The only exceptions were when inland waterways led to the sea and connected to coastal shipping. If inland and coastal navigation created an integrated system of "canals and rivers . . . [it became] part of a more truly national or even international system of transport" (Armstrong, 1995, 310). The Northwestern European countries had this type of integrated

Map 3.2 The mid-Swedish waterways with local importance (Kunz and Armstrong, 1995, 91)

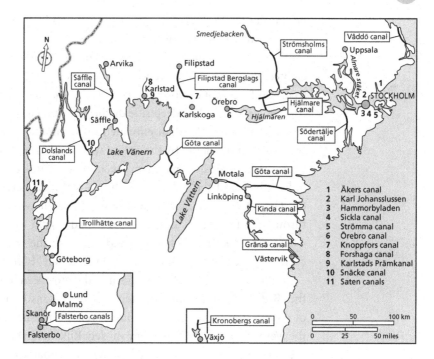

inland and ocean waterway system. In most of the other countries of Europe, such as in mid-Sweden, northern France, western Germany, and northern Italy, waterways were of local or regional importance (Map 3.2).

The water transportation system, however, did not replace, but was dependent upon, a dense network of surface roads. Traditional road transportation was indispensable for reaching the canals, especially in relatively land-locked countries. Britain launched an expensive road construction program in 1705, when Parliament enacted a law to establish trusts and build a toll-road system, the turnpike roads. Extensive construction took place during the next three decades, with a yearly investment of £1.5 million. In 1770, 24,000 kilometers of turnpike roads connected cities in England and Wales, and 35,000 kilometers by 1835. By the early twentieth century, 370,000 kilometers of first-class roads were already in operation.[30]

In contrast with the British private toll-road system, France established a central civilian authority, the Corps des Ponts et Chausses, in 1716. It opened a special school for the training of road and bridge engineers in 1747,[31] and built 130 cable bridges in the 1830s and 1840s. At that time, France could boast the largest road network in Europe: the 33,000 kilometer *routes royales*, completed in 1824. Local and regional roads spanned similar distances and made the network markedly denser. Travelling now became a great deal faster: a trip from Paris to Lyon, which took four to five days in 1816, took only two days in 1848.

New road construction technologies began to be introduced in the late eighteenth century. The French engineer Pierre Trésaguet built modern roads on large stone sub-bases, covered by a layer of gravel and smooth surface, and framed by deep side ditches for drainage. In Britain Thomas Telford and John McAdam emulated his technique and developed road construction further.[32] By the end of the nineteenth century, most European roads used the "macadam" technology. Until the 1830s, however, only France and the Netherlands had a real road network, followed by the German Rhine region. In time, a similar network was introduced throughout Europe.[33] "In general, the road system was most satisfactory where industrialization had proceeded fastest; the road map of Europe corresponded to that of the industrial revolution" (Girard, 1965, 220).

In the latter part of the century, the northern countries adopted the British organizational system of road construction, while most of the others followed the centralized French pattern. In the Netherlands, the Vereeniging van Opzichters va den Rijkswaterstaat (1894) oversaw the maintenance of the 2,300 kilometers of primary roads and the nearly 30,000 kilometers of secondary and tertiary roads.

Road (and later railroad) construction often required extensive *tunnel building*. One of the modern forerunners of European tunnel construction was the Bridgewater canal tunnel, built in Manchester in 1761. From the mid-nineteenth century on, major Alpine tunnels, among them the St. Gotthard and Simplon tunnels, were constructed.[34]

By the early twentieth century, a vast road network of 1.6 million kilometers existed in Europe, which effectively connected local communities to water and rail transport. In the early twentieth century, the Permanent International Association of Roads Congress was established in Paris; by 1913, fifty nations had become members in an effort to standardize road construction and maintenance systems. However, road transportation began to lose its importance when the railroads took over. From the 1860s on, roads supplied mostly short-distance transportation and transportation to the railroads and ports.

Railroads

No network of waterways or roads could provide the cheap mass transportation that the transforming economies and increasing populations of nineteenth-century Europe demanded. Hence a new invention, the railroad, became the cornerstone of the modern inland transportation system, and the nineteenth century unquestionably became the age of the railroads. This development was pan-European: the railroads connected national to international networks and formed a united European transportation system. The history of the railway age commenced in 1825, when the world's first steam railway, the Stockton–Darlington Railroad Company, using George Stephenson's locomotive, began regular service.[35] In 1830, the Liverpool–Manchester line was launched.

The British railways quickly set the international standard.[36] Stephenson's first locomotive pulled thirty-four wagons and transported goods and passengers at a "speed" of 4 miles per hour. His subsequent "Rocket" carried 13 ton loads and covered 12 miles (20 kilometers) per hour. Transportation fees soon dropped from 18 to 8 shillings per ton. Manufacturers transporting goods from ports to factories saved £20,000 in the first six months. From that time on, a railroad mania reigned. Between 1830 and 1841, the British Parliament approved the construction of more than 2,000 kilometers of rail-lines.[37] Between 1830 and 1850, Britain built nearly 10,000 kilometers of railroads. At the same time, continual improvements were made to the steam locomotive which guaranteed faster and safer service – innovations such as the railway switch, patented in 1832, and the Morse telegraph lines, introduced on the Paris–Rouen line in 1845. By 1870, 21,558 kilometers of railroad were in operation in Britain, by far the largest network in Europe. By 1910, the length of the British railroads was 32,182 kilometers.

The new transportation network transformed life as Europeans knew it. In 1870, 336 million passengers traveled, and 235 million tons of goods were transported by train; by 1912, the number jumped to 1.3 billion people and 520 million tons. The cost of inland transportation was cut in half between 1820 and 1860. In England in 1865, the cost (per ton) of transporting minerals on rail-lines was 16 percent that of canals and 2 percent that of roads. By 1910, general transportation costs were cut in half yet again, to merely one-fifth of what they were a hundred years earlier.

Throughout the 1830s, the railroad became the symbol of modernity and for the boom erupting across the continent. The best artists of the age painted railroads: in 1844, Joseph Turner's *Rain, Steam, and Speed: The Great Western Railway* celebrated the small yet robust engine, speeding across a bridge in a golden landscape, as an agent of modernity. Thirty years later, the train was still immortalized as the symbol of modernity. Claude Monet's *Arrival of the Normandy Train: Gare Saint-Lazare* depicted the profound impression the locomotive made on consecutive generations of the century. The prosaic railroad inspired Romantic poets as well.[38]

Politicians such as the Italian Camillo Cavour and the Hungarian István Széchenyi drafted plans for their countries' railroad networks. Kings considered the railroads as symbols of their power. Even the most backward of kingdoms, Naples and Russia, pushed to develop their railways. Five years after the launching of the world's first railroad, locomotives started running between Naples and Portici, followed six years later by those between St. Petersburg and Tsarskoie Selo. Both lines connected the rulers' winter and summer palaces.

Early and mid-twentieth-century economic history literature has credited railroads with having integrated national markets, with initiating industrialization with its backward and forward linkages, with contributing to the development of the mining, engineering, and construction industries, and with abetting the transformation of peasants into wage workers. Alexander Gerschenkron challenged this view when analyzing Italian railroads: the railroads, he concluded, did not play a role in unifying Italian markets, and they were built too early to influence domestic industrial production (Gerschenkron, 1962).

The real challenge to the conventional wisdom, however, was issued by Robert Fogel in 1964. His counter-factual analysis concluded that railroads accrued limited social savings in the United States, only about 4 percent of GDP per year through the end of the century (Fogel, 1964). Patrick O'Brien has also asserted that the railroads' impact on social savings in England was less significant than generally thought. Savings from rail transport in mid-1860s England were about 4 percent of the national income, though they increased to 11 percent by 1890 because of more efficient technology and a larger network. Savings in other countries were also about 4–5 percent of GDP (O'Brien, 1983, 10).[39]

Evaluating the role of railroads by social savings, I would suggest, is hardly appropriate. True, an annual 4–5 percent share of GDP is hardly insignificant, especially given the fact that it became much larger at the end of the century. Nevertheless, national savings were only a part of the railroads' impact on economic development. The non-quantifiable effects were probably more important. Besides offering cheap mass transportation, the railroads transformed the entire economy. First, they changed the capital markets and the corporate organizational system. Their construction was extremely capital-intensive,[40] and Britain's old financial mechanisms were unable to finance it. New forms of corporations were needed, and the stocks of the 200 railroad companies (in 1843) became the "prima donna" of the stock exchange (Dyos and Aldcroft, 1974, 202). Railroads throughout Europe greatly contributed to the legalization and development of the joint-stock corporate system.

Construction and operation also created a huge labor market. According to certain estimates in the 1860s, roughly 2 million people worked on railroad construction, and tens of thousands were employed in operations (Schram, 1997, 154). For hundreds of thousands of peasants, railroad construction embodied their transition from peasant-agricultural to urban-industrial work. A well-known and oft-mentioned effect of railroad building was its backward and forward linkages. Railroads provided a huge market and ample incentives for the mining (coal and iron ore), iron, steel, engineering, and construction industries. In Western Europe, railroads often initiated industrialization. In the middle of the nineteenth century, they consumed 2–4 percent of coal output and 15–25 percent of iron and steel, and they comprised one-fifth of engineering activity. In some cases, such as north Italy, one-third of the steel output was consumed by railroads in the 1910s.

Still, railroads had an even more far-reaching impact on the economy. They connected inland areas to waterways and thus revolutionized landlocked countries lacking large waterway networks. Railroads were the first transportation system that connected all countries on the continent with each other. They were able to cross the Alps and other high mountain ranges, and they linked otherwise isolated regions to an all-European network. One should add that railroads unified the European market, connecting, for instance, Italian silk producers with the French silk industry, and the Hungarian grain economy with Austro-Bohemian industrial zones. By linking the rapidly industrializing West with the latecomer and less developed peripheral regions, railroads stimulated the export of primary goods and facilitated the modernization of the peripheries. They were also a powerful force in the "Europeanization" of Europe. Lastly, railroads played an important political[41] role in modernizing warfare, which was the primary motivation of a number of governments for constructing rail lines.[42] A lack of railroads led to Russia's humiliating defeat in the Crimean War.

Partly because of their strategic importance and partly because of the huge investment requirements, railroads were mostly state-owned or were nationalized, such as in Germany in 1879 and Italy in 1905. The stark exception to this rule was Britain. In some cases, private railroads operated in a mixed state–private system. Both state assistance and regulation were prevalent throughout the continent. State subsidies, guaranteed interest rates, and an almost military-like organization characterized their operation. A feverish construction of railroads took off throughout the continent in the mid-nineteenth century. The first French steam railroad connected St. Étienne with Lyon in 1831. Six years later, the festive opening of Gare

Saint-Lazare marked the real starting point of the French railroad age. The railroad law in 1842 marked the beginning of state involvement, for the state owned the land and built the rails that were rented out to private companies running the railroads. The law projected the construction of 6,320 kilometers of lines by 1857.[43]

Another important institution, state-guaranteed interest rates, sparked a huge railroad boom by eliminating risk and assuring a fixed profit. The Freycinet Plan of 1878, which invested 5 billion francs in transportation, created an additional incentive to build local lines.[44] By 1890, the French had a more than 33,000 kilometer-long railroad network carrying two-thirds of the country's cargo; by the outbreak of World War I, the network had expanded to 40,484 kilometers. Between 1880 and 1913, France invested more than 3.7 million francs in its railroads.

The railroad revolution in Germany was even more successful. The state assumed responsibility for developing the country's rail infrastructure and devised its first plans to that effect in the 1830s. Prussia introduced the system of guaranteed interest rates for invested capital in 1842. The first railroad line, the Ludwigsbahn, which connected Nuremberg and Fürth, was opened in 1834. Between 1837 and 1839, the first long-distance line linked Leipzig with Dresden. The state built a total of 5,856 kilometers of lines in the 1840s. Until 1850, half of railroad investment was financed by states. The system of guaranteed interest rates gave a tremendous impetus for additional construction, which soon proliferated across the country. By 1870, an 18,876 kilometer network was already in operation – a network that was officially nationalized in 1879.

After German unification in 1871, an unprecedented railroad boom led to the construction of 10,000 kilometers of lines in every decade. More than 48,000 kilometers were built between 1870 and 1913, and the length of the network ultimately reached 63,378 kilometers. Railroads absorbed 15–25 percent of investments; from the 1870s on, they became the driving force of German economic development. Berlin in the north and Cologne in the west emerged as the predominant railroad centers. The quantity of goods transported by rail increased from 3 million tons in 1860 to 63 million by 1910, while the cost of transportation decreased by 80 percent.

Western Europe's most developed railroad system was built in Belgium. After the country secured political independence, it put 334 kilometers of lines into operation. By 1910, however, it had 4,679 kilometers. One kilometer of railroad served only 6.3 square kilometers – the best railroad density in Europe. Northern Italy also made progress in emulating the West. Construction there began in the 1840s. The Milan–Monza,

Padua–Mestre, and Turin–Trofarello lines were followed by trans-Alpine lines such as the Semmering Line (1854) and the Brenner Line (1867).[45] Before the unification of Italy, only Piedmont had an accomplished network system. In Habsburg Lombardy and Venice, 1,800 kilometers were in operation. After unification, a dense northern network was created: by 1912, 7,225 kilometers of railroad were built in a region of 102,000 square kilometers. A number of main lines connected the southern parts of the country as well. Altogether a railroad system of 19,000 kilometers modernized the country's transportation systems, which comprised somewhat more than half the density in Belgium, France, and Western Europe.[46]

As far as railroads were concerned, the Habsburg Monarchy could boast a unified system. In this respect, agricultural-industrial Hungary was equal to the industrialized western half of the Monarchy, with both possessing a Western-type railroad network and density.[47] A network of 6,430 kilometers provided modern transportation in 1867; by 1873, the network had grown to 15,597 kilometers. A radical nationalization policy created a state railroad system beginning in 1880. Prior to World War I, 44,748 kilometers of lines were in operation connecting the empire to German, Swiss, Romanian, and Russian railroads. One kilometer of railroad line served an area of 13.5 square kilometers; hence, the network was nearly as developed as in the western parts of Europe.

Western Europe constructed the world's densest railroad network. There had already existed 38,000 kilometers of lines in 1860, and roughly 62,000 kilometers were completed by 1870. But the most exuberant railroad boom took place during the half-century prior to World War I, when the length of railroads nearly trebled. Western Europe attained a density of 1 kilometer of railroad for 10.14 square kilometers and 90.2 kilometers per 100,000 inhabitants. The railways transported 8.18 tons of goods per 100,000 inhabitants in each year, and an average inhabitant traveled twenty-two times annually. (See Tables 3.3 and 3.4.)

By building dense railroad networks, all of the large and partly landlocked countries of Western Europe, particularly France and Germany, secured fast and cheap transportation capabilities that were required for modern economic transformation. Without the railroads, no European region would have been able to pursue the Industrial Revolution. The railroads led the way for industrialization. (See Figure 3.3.)

The railway, based on steam-engine technology, was the child of the first Industrial Revolution. Steam locomotives were overwhelmingly predominant until World War I. However, railroad technology began to transform around the turn of the century thanks to the second Industrial Revolution. Two groundbreaking inventions, electric power generation combined

Table 3.3 The development of the European railroads

Year	Europe (km of lines)	% (1910=100)	Western Europe (km of lines)	% of Western Europe (1910=100)	Western Europe as % of total European
1830	165	0.0005	165	0.001	100
1870	104,900	29	90,000[a]	61	86
1910	362,700	100	147,000	100	41

Source: Wojtinsky (1927, 34–5).
Note: [a] 1880.

Table 3.4 Level of railway development in Western Europe in 1911

Country	Land area per 1 km railroad (in km²)	Length of railroads per 100,000 inhabitants (in km)	Weight of goods delivered per 100,000 inhabitants (tons)	No. of railway journeys per inhabitant
Britain	10.14	71.3	11.62	28.6
Germany	8.72	95.5	9.50	25.3
France	13.20	103.7	3.09	12.6
Belgium	6.30	63.0	10.89	26.8
Netherlands	10.34	54.5	2.63	7.7
Switzerland	9.12	120.8	4.84	31.0
West European average	10.14	90.2	8.18	21.9

Source: Berend and Ránki (1982, 100).

with electric engineering, and the combustion engine, began to transform Europe's railroads. The first electric train was exhibited at the Berlin Fair in 1879; two years later, the first electrified railroad line began operation in Germany. Before World War I, the German Rudolph Diesel provided another epoch-making technological transformation: the first

Figure 3.3
Length of
railroads in
Western Europe,
1830–1910
(thousand
kilometers)
(Wojtinsky, 1927,
34–5)

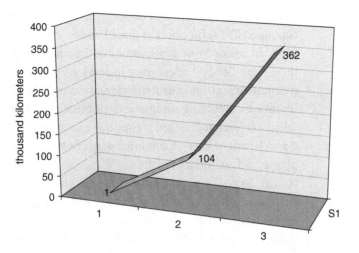

Diesel-locomotive entered service in Sweden in 1913. The dawn of a new railroad age had occurred.

Communication and postal service

In an increasingly interrelated world, with international traffic between continents and a Europe that was intricately interconnected, it became crucially important to have an internationally organized communication system. An optical telegraph system began functioning in France in 1793, with a 3,000-mile network in operation by 1842.[48] The electric telegraph made it possible to create the first international communications network, for it was the first technology capable of sending messages across continents and hemispheres.[49] In 1850, the Anglo-French Telegraph Company laid the first cable under the English Channel,[50] and by 1914, a 516,000 kilometer cable system connected the world's continents. The telegraph networks also established fast inland communication. France, for example, which had begun building its network in 1844, was able to connect all sectors of the country with a 10,000 kilometer network by 1855. By 1881, the network's length topped 88,000 kilometers. In 1913, 256 million telegrams were sent in Western Europe. Building on Heinrich Hertz's discovery of electromagnetic radiation or radio waves, the Italian Guglielmo Marconi sent the first wireless telegraph signal over the open seas in 1897. From that time on, both transoceanic ships and transcontinental trains were in telegraph contact.

In 1876, while working to improve the telegraph in the United States, Edinburgh-born Alexander Graham Bell invented that daringly revolutionary device, the telephone. Europe's first telephone exchange opened in the summer of 1879 in London. The first telephone directory in 1880 contained 250 subscribers in three London exchanges. Between 1880 and 1883, all major West European cities installed telephone networks, and there were 260,000 telephones in service by 1885.[51] This new communication system remained rudimentary until World War I, though new inventions, including automatic circuit changers (1886) and an automatic telephone exchange (1891), continued to improve it. By 1910, between 2 and 10 out of every 1,000 inhabitants in Western Europe owned a telephone, and one-quarter of the world's telephones could be found in Europe (Calvo, 2006). In 1914, 4 out of every 100 inhabitants had a telephone in Scandinavia and nearly 2 in Britain and France (Wallsten, 2005, 706). In 1913, more than 5 billion telephone calls were made in Europe alone (based on Foreman-Peck and Millward, 1994, 109, quoted by Broadberry and O'Rourke, 2010, 80).

Equally important was the birth of an international *postal service*. Some form of postal service had long existed, such as the French and British royal postal services, which began operation in 1477 and 1516 respectively. These institutions did not serve the public. Private mail service, however, was legalized in France and Britain in the seventeenth century.[52] The postal service became a state monopoly in France and Prussia, which was the model followed by most European countries. Britain pioneered the modern, international postal service.[53] In the mid-1830s, Rowland Hill proposed setting uniform rates for delivery without regard to distance, to be based on weight and paid for by the senders. He "invented" the stamp as well. These reforms appeared in Britain in 1840 and set the international standard: Switzerland incorporated it in 1843, France, Belgium, and Bavaria in 1849. Regional postal unions were established from 1850 on. An international postal service began to be organized in 1863; twenty European countries, the United States, and Egypt enacted an agreement to that effect in 1874; and the General (later renamed Universal) Postal Union began functioning in 1875. Three years later, an international money order service was introduced, and nineteen countries signed the parcel-post agreement in 1885. From the 1870s onward, telegraph and telephone services were incorporated into postal services throughout Europe.

Notes

1. The ratio of yields to seeds in Britain and the Netherlands was 11.3:1, compared with only 5.6:1 in Western Europe and Scandinavia. However, all of Western Europe needed only one acre of land to feed one consumer, compared with

three acres in Eastern Europe between the fifteenth and seventeenth centuries (Maczak, 1967, 28).

2. The irrigation system – the great arterial canals that supplemented the lake-fed rivers – had existed in this region since medieval times. One fifth of Lombardy inherited an advanced and well-kept irrigation system.

3. Corn had appeared in sixteenth-century Spain, the Po Valley in Italy, and around Toulouse in France, but it generally began to be used in Europe in the late seventeenth and eighteenth century. The potato, though in evidence in some parts of Europe by the sixteenth century, became a staple in Europe around the turn of the nineteenth century.

4. The British National Pig Breeders' Association of 1884 and the Institute of Animal Husbandry at the Catholic University of Louvain (established by the Belgian veterinarian Leopold Frateur) clearly illustrate this development.

5. Steam plows, for example, were used in advanced big estates from Britain to Germany, but they were very difficult to move and could be used only in large areas of land. Hence, they were unsuitable for peasant farms and therefore had no broad-based application. Steam tractors, which appeared as early as 1868, were even less suitable. The five-ton machines were used mostly for road hauling.

6. In Britain, some 36,000 landowner families, with landed estates of between 100 and 3,000 acres, and 1,700 proprietors with more than 3,000 acres, owned 81 percent of all land.

7. Marxist literature since Lenin has differentiated between the so-called Prussian and American paths to agricultural development, maintaining the superiority of the American farmer-types over the transformed former feudal big estates in Europe. The so-called Prussian type of development, I would argue, led to a lower level of modernization only on the peripheries of Europe. The relative backwardness of this type of agricultural transformation was caused by the belatedness and partiality of complex socio-economic and political transformations and not by the structure of landownership.

8. Animal stocks increased significantly; the number of cattle doubled and pig stocks trebled between 1850 and 1910. More importantly, the specialization of agriculture benefited food processing between the 1870s and 1910s. Output of sugar beet, produced by big estates for sugar refineries, trebled between the 1870s and 1910s. Export-oriented sugar refineries as well as a huge modern beer industry led the Czech and Austrian export sectors.

9. In the lowlands, cereal crops were produced and the traditional three-crop rotation system predominated. At higher elevations, the *Hirtenland*, a long tradition of Alpine grazing and cereal production held sway. In 1805, above Interlaken, a shepherd's festival celebrated the traditional Alpine life.

10. In 1900, 30,000 steam threshers were in use, each servicing 156 hectares. More than 52,000 steam sowing machines were also in operation, each servicing nearly 500 hectares. The mechanization of other activities was less successful.

11. One hectoliter (hl) is equal to 21.9 UK and 26.4 US gallons.

12. One tonne is 1,000 kilograms or 2,204.6 pounds.

13. While the country's working population increased by less than 50 percent, its agricultural population, in absolute numbers, almost stagnated: 8.3 million in 1851, and 8.6 million in 1911.

14. The unification of Germany, comprising 350 independent units in 1806 and 39 sovereign units after 1815, was not accomplished until 1871.

15. The peasants in the eastern provinces of Prussia declined into a "second serf-dom" during the early modern centuries, while the situation in the Rhineland was similar to that in France. East of the River Elbe, the German territories exhibited similarities to the nearby agrarian-industrial region of Central Europe and the Baltic area. Evaluating the evidence of these differences, Nikolas Wolf aptly entitled his study "Was Germany Ever United?" (Wolf, 2009, 846).

16. Yields significantly increased – in the case of the potato, by 90 percent. The sugar content of sugar beets was only 6 percent in the 1830s, but it reached 17 percent before World War I. Meat production increased two and a half times, and milk output doubled.

17. According to some estimates, the annual consumption of raw cotton in the first half of the eighteenth century increased from 90 to 200 grams per capita in England, and from 50 to 180 grams during the second half of the century in France.

18. The agricultural sector must (1) provide goods to feed the population and earn foreign currency ("product" role); (2) furnish a huge market to purchase manufactured goods both for consumption and for investment ("market" role); and (3) supply manpower and capital to industry and services ("factor" role). These "roles" are related to each other in the framework of the "trade" balance between agriculture and the rest of the economy (Federico, 2005, 223, 231).

19. "The success of the European Industrial Revolution is intimately connected with trade and overseas expansion ... By the mid-eighteenth century, there was a well-developed international trading system that linked almost all the continents through trade" (Findlay and O'Rourke, 2007, 364, 365).

20. The even more slowly developing Austria and northern Italy increased their combined exports by seventeen times.

21. The very first experimental steamship used a far from efficient Newcomen steam engine in 1736. More than four decades later, in 1776, the rotating paddles steamship was successfully introduced.

22. The propulsion machine produces thrusts to push an object forward. It may drive a paddle wheel or a propeller.

23. His lens captured 83 percent of the light, and a rotating round beam created a flashing effect visible for more than 30 kilometers.

24. The 1,400 ton *America* consumed 60 tons of coal per day. The 1,139 ton *Britannia*, built in 1840, required 38 tons of coal per day and was able to carry 225 tons of goods. The 4,556 ton *Bothnia*, which began service in 1874, was able to carry 3,000 tons of goods.

25. The United States also became part of the water transportation revolution. However, only 6 percent of the world's total shipping capacity belonged to countries outside Europe.

26. The Panama railway established transportation connections in 1855. In 1880, Lesseps was commissioned to build the canal, but the enterprise failed in 1893 after several years of difficult work and thousands of deaths (caused by malaria). John F. Stevens, the American new chief engineer, dropped Lesseps' sea-level project and planned to build the canal with locks.

27. The Thames, Severn, and Trent in Britain, and the Rhine in Germany are examples.

28. By 1830, the country had 1,600 kilometers of navigable waterways, of which 450 kilometers were canals linking the Meuse to the Scheldt. In the mid-century, Liège was linked to Maastricht.

29. Canals connected Rotterdam to the North Sea in 1872; the 98 kilometer German Kaiser-Wilhelm (or Kiel) canal connected the North Sea to the Baltic. After the canal was lengthened and deepened in 1905, it became available for ocean-bound ships as well. It reduced the route by 250 nautical miles and connected the Baltic region to the world. Prussia and later Germany also built a dense network of canals. The Oder–Spree canal (1669) and the Plauen and Finow canals (1745) linked Upper Silesia with Hamburg and the Elbe with the Oder. The Bromberg canal (1774) linked the Oder with the Vistula, and the Klodnitz canal connected the Upper Silesian coal fields with the Oder. Prussia built nearly 800 kilometers of waterways (600 kilometers were improved riverways) by the mid-1830s. Canals connected Berlin with several rivers, and a dense canal network was constructed around the River Rhine. The 349 kilometer Rhine–Rhône canal (completed in 1833), the Rhine–Herne (1914), the Datteln–Hamm, and the Dortmund–Ems (1899) canals connected all the major cities and linked them with the Baltic and North seas.

    France initiated extensive canal building beginning in the seventeenth century, when the Briare canal (1642) and Orléans canal (1692) connected the Loire and Seine rivers, and the 360-kilometer canal du Midi (built between 1667 and 1694) connected the Mediterranean Sea with the Atlantic Ocean. The Burgundy canal (242 kilometers) and the eighteenth-century canal du

Centre (1783–1802), with its 118 kilometer French section, created waterways between the English Channel and the Mediterranean. The Saint-Quentin canal (1810) and the Oise canal (1836) connected Paris with the northern coal fields. The "Canal Monsieur," which connected the Rhône to the Rhine (1832), guaranteed Alsace's coal supply. In 1820, F. L. Becquey, director-general of the Ponts et Chaussées, completed a plan for a 10,000 kilometer canal system, of which some 3,000 kilometers were completed in later decades. The canals and navigable rivers established an impressive waterway system in France (Pollard, 1981, 127).

In the Habsburg Empire, the River Danube offered virtually the only major natural waterway. Work on regulating the river was conducted for several decades from the 1830s–1840s on. In the early nineteenth century, Emperor Franz's advisors proposed making massive public investments in road and canal construction, but were unable to do so. The builders of the first canals were landed aristocrats, who also owned mines and huge forests. Prince Schwarzenberg, who owned the largest estates in Bohemia, in 1788 built a canal from his forests in Český Krumlov to float timber, and the Wiener Neustadt Coal Company did so to deliver coal to Vienna. The first cargo arrived in 1803.

The first steamship appeared on the Danube in 1817, but the turning point was the founding of the Danube Steamship Company by the British John Andrews and Joseph Pritchard in 1829. The company soon owned 51 steamships and 200 river barges. In 1851, the company transported 216 tons of goods. Nevertheless, between 1870 and 1875, a new river bed had to be built next to Vienna. The dangerous Iron Gate blocked the way towards the Black Sea and required major work to open it. Several more decades were needed to complete it. Finally, one of the most important European waterways was created by making the Danube accessible to traffic from the Black Sea to Vienna and Ulm between 1830 and 1895.

30. There were forty-two regular service routes in existence by 1797. It took forty-three hours to travel from London to Edinburgh. Regular stagecoach service began as early as 1640, and mail-coaches ran between London and Bristol beginning in 1784. In the early nineteenth century, regular carriage connections were established on surface roads between London and Manchester.

31. In the first years of the nineteenth century, more than 500 engineers oversaw the road works. In 1841, nearly 700 engineers, 3,000 foremen, and 15,000 permanent work forces built, improved, and maintained the national road system.

32. Strong and long-lasting roads were created on a base of large stones, crushed stone bound with gravel covered by cobblestones and built in a slightly convex shape for rapid drainage of the road surface.

33. Roads connected Berlin and Breslau, Vienna and Prague. In the latter case, the coach trip took twenty-eight hours in 1807. The Habsburg Empire under Emperor Joseph II initiated an impressive construction program beginning in 1792, and linked Vienna via the Semmering Pass to the Adriatic ports. By 1818, in the Bohemian province alone, a 1,755 kilometer road network assured faster transportation. Regular express carriages operated between Vienna and Prague, and Vienna and Trieste. By 1885, a network encompassing more than 61,000 kilometers of roads served north Italy, i.e. nearly 5 kilometers per 1,000 inhabitants (Schram, 1997, 97).

34. The Mont Cenis tunnel (1857–71) was 13.6 kilometers long, the St. Gotthard (railroad) tunnel (1872–82) 15 kilometers, and the Simplon tunnel (1898–1906) 20 kilometers.

35. Rail transportation had a long prehistory. In sixteenth-century Britain men or animal power transported coal from mines on wooden rails. Cast-iron rails were produced in England in 1767. The first rails were fragile and not strong enough for transporting heavy loads, but 1816 saw the advent of wrought-iron rails; later, in the 1860s, steel rails were employed. By that time, several hundred kilometers of railroads were used in the British mining industry. Early experiments worked on replacing animal power with steam engines. The first steam-engine locomotive was used in a mine in Wales in 1804, but failed after a few experiments. The narrow-gauge Middleton Railway used a steam locomotive, the *Salamanca*, successfully in 1812. The first passenger road locomotive was patented in 1821. At the beginning, there was a plan to move trains by cables, pulled by stationary locomotives.

36. A huge majority of countries followed the 4ft $8\frac{1}{2}$ inch (143.6 centimeter) gauge pattern.

37. The London–Birmingham, London–Southampton, and London–Bristol lines began service.

38. In the 1840s, when the first 40 kilometer line was opened in Hungary, the celebrated poet, Sándor Petőfi, welcomed it as the messenger of an interconnected European civilization. "Railroads by the hundreds, by the score!/Keep building more and more!/Cover the world with railways/As the earth covered with veins./They are the veins of the earth,/Civilization pulsing through their girth" (Petőfi, 1985, 701).

39. "Social savings were large only where there was no good system of inland waterways, as in Spain" (Broadberry *et al.*, 2010, 79–80).

40. The cost of construction of one mile was £40,000, and it required an investment totaling £250 million by 1850.

41. The railroads, argued Friedrich List, together with the customs union, would pave the way for the political unification of Germany. He drafted the first plans for the German railroad network in 1833.

42. Railroads as instruments of war were first demonstrated in Europe in the Italian wars of unification, in the war between Piedmont and Austria in 1849. A decade later, Austrian troops were transported from Vienna to Lombardy and Venetia. Even with chaotic, inexperienced organization and long waits, the troops arrived in two weeks, four or five times faster than with traditional means of transportation (Schram, 1997, 18–19).

43. By 1847, with an investment of 1.5 billion francs, a 1,600 kilometer railroad connected Paris with Lille, Rouen, and Tours. The Paris–Marseille and the Paris–Strasbourg lines followed in 1853.

44. The Péreire brothers established the Compagnie du Chemin de Fer du Nord in 1845, the Argenteuil railroad in 1851, and the Auteuil line in 1852. Six main lines, centered in Paris, were planned with a dense spider-web design. From that time, until 1890, a feverish construction boom led to the building of 1,000 kilometers of lines per year. During those decades, railroad investments became the most important investment activity in the country.

45. Foreign investment in Italian railroads increased from the 1850s on. At the end of the decade, French investment totaled 300 million francs ($60 million), and it increased to $350 million by 1900, and $500 million by 1913. French financial groups invested in the Venice–Milan and Bologna lines. By the mid-1880s, 60 percent of the 2.2 billion franc railroad investment was financed by France, mostly by the Rothschilds. British investment trailed the French, with a total of roughly $100 million by 1913.

46. Sixty percent of railroad investment was financed by French capital. South Italy represented a different level of railroadization. Until unification, there were practically no railroads in the south; by the outbreak of World War I, however, more than 6,000 kilometers connected various parts of the country.

47. The first line in the Habsburg Empire was built as early as 1832, the horse-driven 53 kilometer Linz–Budweis line. The construction of the Vienna–Bochnia (Galicia) line began in 1836, and the Vienna–Brno line started operation in 1839. By 1854, the length of the mostly state-owned railroads in the Habsburg Empire topped 2,617 kilometers. That year, the Monarchy returned to the private system, introducing a 5 percent guaranteed interest rate for invested capital and triggering a huge railway boom.

48. Visual signaling stations, run by the War Department, monitored signals by telescope.

49. The principle of electronic communication by wire was devised by a British inventor, William Sturgeon, in 1825. Five years later, an American, Joseph Henry, solved the problem of sending long-distance messages. The practical solution was created by another American, Samuel F. B. Morse, who established the signal transmission by his code in 1835. It took another nine years before it would become usable.

50. Within two years Britain and Ireland, London and Paris were connected, and the following year connections were established between Britain and the Netherlands. In 1858, the first transatlantic cable was laid, but it failed. A working connection was established only in 1865–6, when the SS *Great Eastern* laid down cables. Cables connected Britain with India in 1870, and London with Hong Kong in 1872. They reached Latin America in 1874.

51. Some countries such as Belgium (1895) created a national public system; in others, such as Norway, local municipalities established local systems. In most countries, the international Bell Company established and operated the telephone system, but local companies began to compete in short order. In Sweden, Lars Magnus Ericsson began producing telephone sets, and he founded the Allmänna Telefonaktiebolag in 1883.

52. In 1680, William Dockwra established his London Penny Post service with four (for business centers six to eight) daily deliveries. The Taxis family ran a private postal service in German and Austrian states for three centuries.

53. Britain established the General Post Office in 1660 and introduced stagecoach service between cities in 1784. By 1830, when passenger trains began carrying mail, next-day delivery became commonplace in many parts of Britain.

CHAPTER 4

The organization of business and finance

Three consecutive banking revolutions

The Dutch and British economic transformations were mostly financed by huge family fortunes, accrued from the profits of proto-industrial, trade, and colonial ventures. Investment demand was relatively modest because of the scale of the economy and the type of technology. Relatively small amounts were invested in fixed assets at the beginning of industrialization, and most of that amount (according to some estimates, six-sevenths to seven-eighths of investments) was spent on material stocks. Kinship connections and partnerships frequently sufficed to mobilize additional financial sources. As large joint-stock enterprises did not exist, industrialists mostly required short-term credits or working capital for purchasing raw materials and hiring labor.

A modern banking system emerged in Scotland and England in the eighteenth century. This *first British banking revolution* transformed medieval and early modern finance, which was partly usury, into modern banking. This momentous change, however, was built on several preliminary stages.[1] Although modern finance had gradually replaced medieval moneylending during the early modern period in Europe, modern banking emerged in Britain. British banks connected rich agricultural regions with industrializing towns and linked savers with investors. Legislation creating the modern institutional framework greatly contributed to the modern banking system. Britain played a pioneering role in this process. The Usury Laws of 1714 to 1832 permitting 5 percent maximum interest abolished medieval usury lending. The elimination in 1826, 1833, and 1844 of previous bans on joint-stock companies, and the creation of limited liability companies in 1858 and 1862, paved the way for large-scale banking.

At the core of the new system was the central bank. The Bank of England, established in 1694, gradually became a modern central bank that sold government bonds, served as a government clearing house, and functioned as the banker of the London banks. Laws regulated the main activities of national banks. The British Banking Act of 1844 reorganized the still private Bank of England, splitting it into two departments, one for the issuing of banknotes, the other for banking activity. The Bank of Scotland was chartered in 1695, and the Royal Bank of Scotland in 1727. Earlier forms of banking had issued banknotes as the principal form of credit. From the creation of the modern central banks, however, the state forbade the issuing of banknotes by other banks. Issuing became strictly the task of the central bank during the nineteenth century. After 1826, the Bank of England, a London bank until that time, established branches in the provinces, the first in Manchester. Central banks had immense assets, totaling one-fourth to one-half of all bank assets in Western Europe.

The Bank of England introduced a number of services that had not been offered by the previously predominant Exchange Bank of Amsterdam (established in 1609). In addition to money transfers between accounts, discounting bills before final payment assisted capital market transactions. International payment by bills and multilateral settlements made foreign trade easier. During the Napoleonic wars, a massive capital flight from occupied Europe to England permanently made London (instead of Amsterdam) the new financial capital of Europe (Grafe *et al.*, 2010, 190–4).

The first banking revolution around the turn of the nineteenth century made banknotes common in Europe. Until the mid-eighteenth century, the predominant form of money was commodity money, gold and silver. Banknotes were used only locally and sporadically. During the latter part of the eighteenth century and in the nineteenth, modern banks created money by issuing banknotes.[2] Goldsmith bankers in London used deposit receipts that were payable on demand and thus similar in value to money. In everyday transactions, Scottish banks generalized the use of notes, followed by the English country banks. An important innovation was the introduction of small £1 notes. The system soon spread to the continent, where issuing was more restricted and monopolized (Cameron, 1967, 314–15).

Beyond the central bank, several private London banks comprised the second most important group of financial institutions. Private banking was the original mode of early modern finance and characterized the first stage of the British banking revolution.[3] In London, the number of private bankers, who discounted bills of exchange and provided short-term loans, rose from fewer than thirty in 1750 to seventy in 1800. The third pillar of finance was the provincial banks – the first established in Bristol in 1716, followed by some 650 others across the country by 1810.[4]

Country bankers established agencies in London to keep in contact with the Bank of England and the London banks. The Bank of England, which gradually became a modern central bank and the lender of last resort with huge gold reserves, formed a vast, loosely connected network with the private London banks and the country bankers (Mathias, 1969, 167–73). Rather than receiving deposits and making loans, some English county banks acted as high-risk venture-capital firms, "investing aggressively in speculative new technologies. The English financial market was even more sophisticated than we had previously thought" (Brunt, 2006, 76, 98–9).[5]

The Rothschild family opened a new chapter in European banking. In 1811, Mayer Amschel Rothschild emerged in Frankfurt as the most prominent banker of the age.[6] The London branch of the Rothschild house, headed by Rothschild's son, Nathan Mayer, became one of the pillars of the British banking system. During the Napoleonic wars the British government entrusted the Rothschilds with managing its payments to its continental allies. In this way, Rothschild established contacts with almost every European ruler. Mayer Amschel placed his other sons in key European capitals – Jacob in Paris, Solomon in Vienna, and Karl in Naples – to expand the Rothschild franchise. The Rothschilds thus became the most influential banking network throughout Europe, "exporting" the basic features of British banking to the continent. The rise of the Rothschild banking empire was a unique phenomenon, but a similar pattern was repeated several times in the early stage of modern banking.[7]

Displaced merchant elites played a central role in laying a foundation for a Europe-wide banking network. The flight and expulsion of these elites has had a very long history.[8] International merchant networks of various diasporas were already well established in the seventeenth and eighteenth centuries. Indian merchants and bankers from Shikarpur and Hyderabad in Sind created a worldwide network in the eighteenth and nineteenth centuries, and Greeks from the Black Sea area built up a trade network to Livorno, Marseille, and London (Marcovits, 2000; Kardasis, 2001). The kin-based Julfan Armenian and Multani Indian networks, and the more flexible Sephardic Jewish network, extended from the Indian Ocean to the Mediterranean and Northwestern Europe. "Armenian mercantile settlements... [existed in] three... Muslim empires... as well as... the British, Dutch, Portuguese, French, and Spanish [empires]... [These] socially bounded mercantile communit[ies] shar[ed] the same codes of conduct and commercial law." The Sephardic Jewish network procured several centers including Lisbon, Amsterdam, Livorno, Hamburg, London, and Istanbul (Aslanian, 2011, 234, 225). Given the close connection between trade and banking, these networks invariably played an important role in the emerging European banking system. "These cosmopolitan entrepreneurs... were in direct contact with the international financial and trading networks... in Western Europe" (Baghdiantz McCabe *et al.*, 2005, 162–3). "From the time of Henry VIII... England benefited from receiving numbers of the most skilled and adept of these religious minorities who had been persecuted in their homelands" (Neal, 1990, 10–12). The very first merchant bankers in Germany were immigrant Dutch, Italian, and Portuguese merchants. In the early seventeenth century, sixteen of the top twenty merchant banker families in Cologne and Hamburg were Dutch. At the same time, Huguenots monopolized the British–French financial nexus.

From its inception, banking has always been a transnational business. Mobile, cosmopolitan minority groups held genuine advantages in that early stage of banking. Daniel Chirot has suggested that it was their own identities and cultures that were the basis of their success in the transnational networks: "Their 'Greekness,' 'Jewishness,' 'Armenianness'... meant an entry ticket to an international business network, because the diaspora entrepreneurs were always more loyal to international capital than to the nation in which they lived" (Chirot, 1997, 13).

The most innovative banking was found in Scotland. At the beginning of the nineteenth century, eighteen note-issuing banks operated there, pumping new money into the economy without a huge depository reserve. Another forty independent banks created a dense network of financial institutions; four hundred branches served the population, that is, one branch for every 7,200 inhabitants, twice as many branches per inhabitant as in England. A major innovation was the introduction of savings banks,[9] along with mutual credit societies and specialized mortgage credit banks. Bank density, that is, the number of bank offices per inhabitant, was rather high in Britain.[10]

The innovation of Scottish banking was also seen in its introduction of a new, modern lending system. Traditional English and Dutch lending was for a period of ninety days and was based on the security of goods. In contrast, Scottish banks began lending for unspecified periods with no tangible securities. The so-called "running cash" credit, invented by the Royal Bank of Scotland, lent money against the signatures of the borrower and two guarantors. The Royal Bank also began an extensive deposit operation by accepting small deposits of £10 and paying six-month interest rates of 5 percent (later lowered to 3 percent). Personal or inheritable bonds made it possible to establish private businesses with little means.[11] In the 1820s, the most important new development was the emergence of *joint-stock banking*. This type of bank had already existed in

Scotland, but it was now legalized and gradually became fully accepted in England. No fewer than a hundred joint-stock banks were established in Britain between the mid-1820s and the mid-1830s, which made deposit banking a common phenomenon. This new development ended the era of pre-modern financing. Several leading private banks changed into joint-stock companies, including Barclays in 1862 and Lloyds in 1865.

Near the turn of the nineteenth century, Scottish and English banking underwent a revolutionary transformation and pioneered modern financing. British banking, however, mostly remained a traditional banking business. "A very stable, very efficient instrument for short-term accommodation without being an important instrument for financing investments" (Mathias, 1969, 353). The turn of the nineteenth century thus became the period of the *first banking revolution*: the time when modern merchant banking gradually replaced the medieval moneylending and court financing, the Medicis, Fuggers, and court Jews.[12] However, the "court Jews did not completely disappear from the royal entourage of European monarchies until the dynasties themselves were eliminated by the First World War" (Chapman, 2006, 37).[13] The role of the diaspora bankers, however, began to decline after 1880, as their old-style intermediary positions, personal connections, and corrupt business practices became obsolete in a rapidly transforming Europe (Pepelasis Minoglou, 2002).

Most of the merchant bankers did not specialize in banking, but rather combined trade and banking. This was also a remnant of the past and a quite natural occurrence, as trade was based on credit. The most important banking activities, mostly combined with trade, were brokerage and clearing, that is, the buying and selling of commodities and securities, and the transfer of payments on the clients' behalf. Prominent merchants established accepting houses around 1825, providing guarantees for three- to six-month loans. They were intermediaries who took on the credit risk. These commercial banks were also active in check-clearing, which made it possible to write and cash checks for customers of other banks and countries.

Some of these private merchant banks, however, began to specialize. Rothschild pioneered this by dealing only with finances, bills, bonds, and bullion. Until the mid-nineteenth century, private merchant banks, *maisons de Haute Banque*, dominated the Paris financial market. Several of them, such as the Mallet (1723), Delessert (1776), and Périer (1792), were founded in the eighteenth century. In the first two decades of the nineteenth century, several new banks began operation, including the Lefebvre, Carrette, and others, a number of them former tax collectors with close connections to the state.[14]

Several chartered banks in Rouen (1817), Nantes (1818), and Bordeaux (1818) issued notes for the *départements* in which they were located. This practice was restricted from the 1830s on, when the Banque de France was granted a monopoly on note issuing. Consequently, it gradually absorbed the départemental banks and established its own branch networks. The modern credit system still did not exist in the countryside, and private moneylending with usury interest continued to hold sway there. After the 1848 revolution, a *comptoirs d'escompte* bank was founded in virtually every important French city. Until 1850, joint-stock banks were still a rarity. The French banking system was based on the English model and clearly distinguished between deposit (commercial) banks, which specialized in short-term loans and the management of customers' portfolios, and the merchant banks, which supplied credit to industry and commerce (Caron, 1979, 53).

However, unlike the British system, French banking adopted an interim step towards modern banking. Thus, from the 1830s on, *sociétés commandites* became the most common type of French company. The Code de Commerce distinguished three types of business organizations: sandwiched between simple partnerships and the corporations (*sociétés anonymes*) were the *sociétés commandites*. These were limited partnerships where active partners assumed unlimited liability and were a type of corporation that did not require government authorization. A simple partnership was not sufficient for big businesses like banks and railroads, while the *sociétés anonymes* had to be chartered by the state and were strictly limited to insurance and canal and railroad building (between 1826 and 1837, only 137 *sociétés anonymes* (joint-stock companies) obtained state authorization). The *commandite* thus provided the perfect interim substitute for the joint-stock organization, which was only legalized much later, and thus from the 1830s became the most common type of company in France, with 1,100 operating in the country.[15]

Joint-stock companies were legalized in England before the mid-nineteenth century and required only state registration, not authorization. This would happen in France in 1863 and 1867, in the North German Federation in 1870, in Belgium in 1873, in Italy in 1883, and in Sweden in 1895 (Cameron, 1966, 26–8). In 1820–1, 330 private banks operated in Prussia, but their number increased to 642 by 1861.[16] Bank density increased from one per 33,000 inhabitants to one per 29,000 during these four decades. In 1848, the Schaffhausensche Bankverein in Cologne created the large Kreditbank, and others were established outside Prussia during the 1850s, such as the Bank für Handel und Industrie zu Darmstadt (or Darmstädter Bank) in 1853. Since Prussia continued to ban joint-stock companies, the so-called *Kommandit-gesellschaft auf Aktien* type banks, similar to the French *commandites*, were established. One of the first was the Disconto-Gesellschaft of Berlin in 1851. During the 1850s, eight *Kommandit* banks began operation. In the mid-1860s, however, the state ended its restrictions on joint-stock banks, thus creating new opportunities for German banking (Tilly, 1967).[17]

In continental Western Europe, where industrialization began to take off in the mid- to late nineteenth century, family wealth and short-term credit were rarely enough to finance the economy. Because of the growth of the capital-intensive iron, steel, chemical, and electric industries, and the extensive construction of railroads, technological development required huge investments from the mid-nineteenth century on. Industrialists needed long-term credits for these ventures,[18] and West European countries needed new and efficient capital sources to finance industrialization. British banks were not up to the task of fulfilling these requirements.

Concurrent with the railroad age was a *second banking revolution* – this time in the western half of the continent. A new type of banking was invented in Belgium. The Société Générale was established by the royal decree of William I, king of the United Kingdom of the Netherlands, in 1822. As the decree's title explicitly suggested, the goal of the Algemene Nederlandsche Maatschappij ter Begunstiging van de Volksvlijt was to "promote trade and industry." At the beginning, the bank sought to increase its resources by issuing shares, selling crown lands obtained from the king, and collecting deposits. The last option became increasingly viable when the bank took over the Brussels and Ghent savings banks. A new and innovative banking policy was initiated mostly after 1830, when Belgium won independence. Between 1830 and 1840, industrial loans and shares gradually increased, and they "took the Société Générale along very innovative paths that helped it to develop into the world's first successful modern investment bank" (Van der Wee and Verbreyt, 1997, 43).

Ferdinand de Meeûs, the bank's talented and daring governor, predicted the railroad construction boom and began to invest heavily in the transportation, coal, iron, and engineering industries, mostly in the Charleroi, Centre, Borinage, and Liège areas.[19] To ensure their success, the Société Générale insisted on converting the industrial firms from family businesses to joint-stock companies. This signified a historic turning point in modern banking. While preserving traditional banking services, the new system activated funds in private accounts and, by the issuing of shares, supplied vast sums for investment, founded industrial companies, and provided long-term industrial credits.

This new type of banking appeared on the continent in 1852, when Emile and Isaac Péreire, strongly influenced by the Saint-Simonian concept of merging banking and industry, founded the Société Générale du Crédit Mobilier in France – and in the process transformed the entire French banking system. The new joint-stock banks owned large assets and invested in railroads and the iron industry. The Péreire brothers embodied the connection between investment banking and railroad construction.[20] If the private merchant banks were already operating on a Europe-wide basis, the Crédit Mobilier type of bank was classically an all-European bank, investing throughout the continent.

During the same decade, three other important banking institutions set up shop in France: the Crédit Industriel Commercial, the Société Générale, and the Crédit Lyonnais. A merger including the Rothschilds' and other private banks established the Banque de Paris et des Pays-Bas, or Paribas (1872), a *banque d'affaires*, or specialized investment bank. The big banks rushed to open a large network of branches: 64 were already in operation in various cities and townships in 1870, but 1,519 branches functioned by 1912.[21]

The modern French banking institutions amassed tremendous amounts of money. The sums deposited increased from 550 million francs in 1875 to 5,681 million by World War I. Liquid savings in the form of banknotes, deposits, and current accounts topped 25 billion francs, 65 percent of GDP, and became a decisive factor in economic development. Banking activity created an abundance of capital and significantly increased investment. Roughly 20–25 percent of bank assets were invested abroad.[22]

The new type of banking did not eliminate the old private merchant banks. The latter adjusted to the new requirements and worked in tandem with the new Crédit Mobilier type of banks. The number of private banks in London even increased – totaling 93 in 1885 and 139 by 1914. One-quarter to one-half of them were merchant banks, but the most important ones were transformed into joint-stock companies and went far beyond traditional short-term lending. The Rothschilds, Erlangers, Bleichröders, and Bethmanns became involved in railroad and industrial investment. The Frankfurt Boerse, which dealt exclusively with public loans until 1820, gradually turned to company shares as well.[23]

From the 1860s and 1870s on, a *third wave of the banking revolution* materialized, this time in Germany. Alexander Gerschenkron's classic theory of "substitution" posits that, in cases of moderate backwardness, modest capital accumulation was no longer sufficient for the industrialization process during the second Industrial Revolution. To substitute genuine capital accumulation, the banks played a key role in industrial business.

The Belgian–French Crédit Mobilier type banks had already done so, but the German type of banks went much further and turned a new page in modern banking.[24] Unlike the Crédit Mobilier type of banks, the German mixed banks combined traditional banking activities with industrial investment, not only investing in industry, but also permanently maintaining industrial shares in their portfolios. The Société Générale and Crédit Mobilier type of banks did not merely provide long-term credits for industrial firms; they established the companies themselves. However, they also engaged in stock speculation. Bank profits from industrial investments accrued from the difference between the value of industrial shares at the time a certain firm was established and the firm's assets' highly increased value a few years later. At that time the bank sold the shares and pocketed the difference.

The German universal banks, first the joint-stock Schaffhausensche Bankverein (1848) and then the Darmstädter Bank für Handel und Gewerbe (1853), the Berliner Handelsgesellschaft, and the Disconto-Gesellschaft (both in 1856), concentrated on industrial pursuits. During the 1870s, the Deutsche Bank and the Dresdner Bank did so as well. The four giant mixed "D-banks," unlike the Crédit Mobilier banks, did not seek to acquire the profits from the increase in the price of the shares between the foundation of a company and a few years later when the shares were sold, but kept the shares of the joint-stock industrial firms in their portfolios and built huge industrial empires.

The new type of banking predominated from 1870 on. This occurred partly because all previous restrictions on the formation of joint-stock companies had been eliminated and partly because the 1873 financial crisis (see below) had destroyed a large number of private and even joint-stock banks and created an opening for new institutions. There were 2,100 joint-stock companies operating in Germany in 1886; by 1912, there were 5,400, with triple the capital value at 18 billion marks. The banks' managers sat on the directorial boards of leading industrial companies. After the turn of the century, the top officers of the sixteen largest German banks were on the boards of 437 industrial firms, effectively ensuring that the banks dictated industrial policy. German-type banks did very much the same in other countries of the Western European and Scandinavian regions.[25]

The new German type of bank oversaw the merging of the coal and iron industries, and supervised industrial activity, transportation, and marketing. The banks organized the backward and forward linkages between their own coal mines and iron works, and managed a wide array of industrial, service, and transportation companies. This was possible because a large number of industrial firms were owned by the same banks.[26] A vast and continually growing industrial sector merged with the banks, and it was the latter that had the greater financial strength, 20 percent above the value of industrial wealth. Between 1860 and 1913, the assets of the agricultural, industrial, transportation, and construction sectors topped 1,260 million marks, while the assets of German financial institutions were nearly three times more; by 1913, the assets of the agrarian-industrial and related sectors were 8,170 million marks, but the financial sector's were roughly ten times as much (Tilly, 1991b, 91).

Rudolf Hilferding called the new combination of banking and industrial capital (monopolies) *financial capital*. His influential *Das Finanzkapital* (1910) became the foundation of social democratic reform. Financial capital, he suggested, ended the separation of industrial, mercantile, and banking capital, and replaced competition with monopolies that put firm controls over social production. "Financial capital," that is, the fusion of banking and industrial capital, "is the highest stage of concentration of economic and political power in the hands of the capitalist oligarchy" (Hilferding, [1910] 1981, 370).[27]

The German banks were uniquely decisive in the creation of the new electric industry. The Berliner Handelsgesellschaft, along with Carl Fürstenberg and Emil Rathenau, established the Edison Gesellschaft für angeweldte Electrizität and its reorganized form, the Allgemeine Electrizitäts Gesellschaft (AEG). The Darmstädter and Dresdner banks founded the Union Electrizitäts Gesellschaft. The ties between the Deutsche Bank and the Siemens Company were also molded by personal connections, since Georg Siemens was one of the founders of the bank. In the early twentieth century, fourteen members of the board of the Deutsche Bank, ten directors of the Berliner Handelsgesellschaft, eight from the Darmstädter Bank, and six from both the Disconto-Gesellschaft and the Dresdner Bank sat on the boards of electric companies. Indeed, no fewer than 105 bank directors were to do so between 1897 and 1902 (Broder, 1991, 475, 477–8).[28] The merging of banking and industrial capital, however, was not a one-way street. The owners of industrial empires also secured a place in the big banks, assuring the complete conglomeration of banking and industry.[29]

The banking revolutions in Britain, Belgium, France, and Germany led to the creation of the modern banking system throughout Europe.[30] The second half of the nineteenth century was the time when modern *central banks*, usually called national banks, appeared across the continent. The forerunners of these banks had already existed, sometimes as early as the late seventeenth century, but they were then only one of many banking institutions. Since the British Banking Act of 1844, however, modern central banks were established throughout Europe. They were often private banks and acted as banks do generally, but they acquired a number of special functions. In time, these gradually crystallized as the government banks monopolized note issuing and took responsibility for monetary management to maintain the convertibility of the national currency and to control inflation. As central banks were the largest financial institutions until the late nineteenth century, they became the banks of last resort in a financial crisis – the bankers of commercial banks and the proxies for micro-crisis management.[31] But the central banks were *primus inter pares* and did not take on the supervisory and regulatory functions that would prevail in the postwar decades of the twentieth century.

Central banks with these powers became the primary players in the second half of the nineteenth century. Traditional seventeenth-century institutions, such as the Bank of England and Banque de France, acquired that capacity around the middle of the nineteenth century. The history of the Banque de France is quite typical.[32] A number of newly established central banks, such as the Swiss National Bank (founded in 1906), were created to play such an important role from the beginning. Led by the central banks, a modern banking system emerged throughout Europe. The Swiss banking system[33] became strong only between 1850 and 1870, when 248 new banks opened their doors, among them the Schweizerische Credit Anstalt in Zurich in 1856. It was completed during the second half of the nineteenth century, when a large network of cantonal banks was established in a country with a traditionally high savings rate. By law, cantonal banks had to be partly – at least one-third – owned by the cantons.

In the Austrian-Czech provinces of the Habsburg Empire, the banking system arrived on the scene at the beginning of the nineteenth century. Modeled after the French system, the Österreichische National Bank was founded in 1816 as an issuing central bank.[34] The emergence of the new Crédit Mobilier type banks prompted the Austrian Rothschilds to enter modern banking. The Austrian government, and particularly its Minister of Finance, Karl Ludwig Bruck, strongly encouraged this outcome. As a result, the Rothschilds established the Österreichische Credit-Anstalt für Handel und Gewerbe in 1855 as a prototype of the new mobile and universal bank.[35] Already 19 joint-stock banks were in operation in Vienna in 1866, and their number increased to 72 by 1873. A modern capital market was established, with 780 joint-stock banks, with assets of 19,946 million krowns, operating in the Austrian-Czech provinces prior to World War I.[36]

The Austrian banking system closely emulated the German pattern and built large industrial empires. Linked to the Crédit Mobilier, the

Credit-Anstalt and the Wiener Bankverein kept in their portfolios a huge share of the Austrian-Czech coal, iron, steel, engineering, paper, textile, chemical, and glass industries. The Vienna Länder Bank and the Anglo Österreichische Bank secured leading positions in the new chemical and electrical industries.

The three waves of the banking revolution between the late eighteenth and late nineteenth century established modern banking, which not only provided credit but also created the capital to invest in and purchase large sectors of the modern economy and to industrialize Western Europe and Scandinavia. Banks were elevated to a central role in the economic modernization of Europe.

The insurance industry

The revolution in modern banking soon affected the insurance industry. Bankers sought to gain control of the liquid assets of others, and they found that the best way to do so was by way of insurance. The modern insurance industry appeared on the scene in the nineteenth century, at the same time as banking.[37] As it did in several other areas, Britain played a pioneering role in insurance.[38] The industry expanded its initial coverage of fire, marine, and livestock insurance to also offer life, burglary, liability, and accident insurance. The French mathematician Blaise Pascal's discovery of probability calculation in the mid-seventeenth century, and the rapidly developing field of statistical analysis in the nineteenth, provided a solid mathematical base for insurance. Insurance companies were established throughout Western Europe between the mid-eighteenth and the mid-nineteenth century.[39]

At the same time, *reinsurance* became increasingly common throughout Europe beginning in the mid-nineteenth century.[40] This development put the insurance industry on a more solid footing. It became an organic part of the business community, reducing risk, mitigating losses, and enhancing the social welfare of Western Europe and Scandinavia's populace.

Business organization, joint-stock companies, and the stock exchange

Concurrent with railroad construction and the banking revolution, an organizational and corporate upheaval also transformed the industrial sector. Until the 1830s and 1840s, private companies during the Industrial Revolution were genuinely small-scale, family-owned enterprises.

They simply could not adjust to the modern transformation of the economy. New organizational arrangements and managerial skills were sorely needed, and they would soon materialize. The mindset of the late eighteenth century had preserved the mentality of the guilds and handicraftsmen, and thus rejected the employment of trained managers. "Management was a function of direct involvement by ownership... [and the] system of large-scale management was to be avoided at all costs because managers... were not to be trusted" (Pollard, 1965, 23, 111). This attitude was fully shared by Adam Smith, who insisted that the only acceptable manager of a firm is its owner.[41]

These beliefs began to change, however, during the half-century epoch of the Industrial Revolution. The specter of big banking, mining, and railroad companies, and the increasing scale of industrial enterprises, demanded organizational and managerial expertise. The owners of expanding companies began to employ salaried staff and professional managers. Modern forms of business organization and management gradually emerged. The proliferation of joint-stock, corporate companies and stock exchanges transformed the institutional infrastructure of modern business in the late nineteenth century. As was noted earlier, joint-stock companies had already existed in the early modern centuries.[42] After the crash of the British South Sea Company in 1720, however, the British Parliament banned the selling of shares. This prohibition would last for a long time. Orthodox views on speculation and profiteering would continue to hold sway until the Industrial Revolution and beyond. "Buying and selling shares... was an activity commonly perceived to be fraught with dangers for the morality of the individual... Speculation was perceived to be a godless activity" (Taylor, 2006, 57–8). It slowly became clear, however, that certain industries required a larger scale of investment than family businesses could muster. Parliament repealed the "South Sea Bubble Act" (1720) a century later, and, between 1824 and 1844, passed a series of laws regulating the return of joint-stock companies.

The organization of businesses was rather rigid in Britain until 1844. The most common interpretation of its strict restrictions has been the low capital requirements of its early businesses, which had mostly been family firms molded on traditional values and family hierarchies. Co-partnerships became prevalent in the seventeenth and eighteenth centuries, mostly in canal building, banking, maritime insurance, and the coal industry. The common law framework regulated the business of non-independent legal entities. On the continent, limited partnerships, made legal by Napoleon's Code de Commerce, allowed the participation of silent investors who did not partake in a business's operation. This particularly enabled aristocrats to invest in certain businesses. Certain capital-intensive sectors, however, remained outside the sphere of common law. In shipownership and mining, joint-stock businesses, whose shares were freely transferable, were allowed to function without government regulation, and they were not stigmatized as unincorporated companies.

Still, the realities of business soon demanded the advantages of the joint-stock company. In 1779, the English Linen Company petitioned Parliament to grant it a charter of incorporation, arguing that such a structure had already been established in Switzerland and other countries.[43] Legislation in Britain between 1844 and 1856 made state-chartered privileges a freely available right. These changes culminated in the introduction of limited liability in 1855–6 (Taylor, 2006, 135). The more advanced form of corporation made the companies independent legal institutions, allowed the free transfer of interest, limited the shareholders' liability, and established a hierarchical managerial structure. The corporate form began to predominate in the later period of industrialization. It did so because the legal advantages of a joint-stock system fused with the financial benefits: the ability to raise money by selling shares and the division of profits among shareholders. Business was freed from the medieval straitjacket of legal restrictions.

This legal and institutional change was fundamentally important in the rise of industrial capitalism. Harris has compared its importance to the invention of the steam engine (Harris, 2000, 23). The formation of joint-stock companies became routine after the passing of Gladstone's Company Law in 1844, and it was strengthened by new regulations in 1856. But Britain did not truly embrace the institution until the railroad boom and the rise of modern banking made it absolutely clear that modern business required a more advanced structure. In 1810, 60 joint-stock companies existed in Britain; by 1834, 216 did, mostly in shipping and canal, turnpike, and railroad building. No fewer than 1,000 joint-stock companies registered in a three-month period in 1845. Between 1844 and 1854, 4,400 joint-stock companies were fully or provisionally registered. The earlier religious and moral taboos were replaced by secular business considerations. "Once associated with corruption and degeneracy . . . [s]peculation was now portrayed as essential to the economic health of the nation" (Taylor, 2006, 158).[44]

Previously banned in most of Europe, joint-stock companies now became the leading regulated business institutions from the 1860s–1870s on. At that time the pillar of modern business regulation, the *corporate accounting system*, was already at hand; Napoleon's Code de Commerce had created this internationally accepted form of corporate accounting in

1809. The law required businesses to make balance sheets, register profits and losses, and later, in the 1860s, to provide semiannual accounts. Several other countries similarly enacted commerce codes: the Netherlands in 1811, Sweden in 1848, and Italy in 1882. Prussia already had one in 1794. Modern legislation adopted most of the Western legal-institutional structure.[45]

The proliferation of joint-stock companies went hand in hand with the rise of a marketplace for shares, the *stock exchanges*. These, too, had a long history. Commercial capitalism in the Low Countries had already required an institution for dealing with bonds and notes, although not stocks. This led to the opening of the predecessor of the Amsterdam Stock Exchange in 1531. The London Stock Exchange opened in the first years of the Industrial Revolution in 1773, and soon it became the model institution, garnering security, bond, share, notes, and Treasury bills. Virtually all of the European countries followed. The modern Frankfurt Stock Exchange[46] emerged as the aggregate of twenty-nine German stock exchanges following the Stock Exchange Act of 1896 (Taylor, 2006; Harris, 2000).

The modern *organization of industrial companies* was an automatic response to technological challenges, and its first step, Alfred Chandler suggests, was the enlargement of firms. Large companies required vertical integration to minimize costs and dependence on other companies. For a secure and undisturbed flow of goods, many large processing firms preferred a "backward" integration to incorporate raw material extraction into the same company's framework. In various new industries, where distribution had not yet been established, new forms of credit arrangements were introduced to promote marketing. Installment, service, and eventually repair also became part of producers' undertakings. These led to a "forward" integration of transportation and distribution networks, retail chains, and service branches. The modern industrial enterprise integrated mass production with mass distribution "within a single business firm." Integration proceeded mostly with mergers of existing companies. Beginning in the 1890s in the United States, a "merger mania" permeated the economy and led to an impressive increase of company size (Chandler, 1977, 285).

This growth of firms led to changes in managerial structure as well. Family management could no longer handle the more complex companies. Salaried managers at all levels signaled the rise of the managerial firm. Chandler speaks of a "three-pronged investment" – first in production facilities to exploit the advantage of scale and scope; then in a marketing and distributive network to keep pace with mass production;

and finally in management to administer the expanded, complex business ventures (Chandler, 1990, 8). The managerial firm employed new, scientific methods of management to adapt procedure to the requirements of mass production. Two pathbreaking American innovations transformed modern industry: Henry Ford's assembly line and Frederick W. Taylor's scientific management.[47]

In Chandler's reading, the rise of the managerial firm is a general "organizational response to fundamental changes in the process of production and distribution" (Chandler, 1977, 376). According to his "stage theory," the "entrepreneurial firm" represents a higher stage than that of the family firm, and the "managerial firm," which may reach the internationalized level of a multinational company, is the highest stage of firm development (Chandler, 1977, 498). On this conceptual basis, Chandler faults Britain and Western Europe for not having adopted three-pronged-investment, as had the United States.

This was not exactly the case. Europe generally did not follow the American approach to business management at the turn of the century, but it did develop its own response to technological challenges (Berend, 2006a). A different pattern of market forces, policy concerns, and cultural traditions led to a different organizational and managerial response to the technological challenges of the century (Wilson, 1995; Alford, 1977; Hannah, 1991; Scranton, 1991).[48]

Distribution networks were highly developed in the relatively smaller countries of Europe, with a legacy of early merchant capitalism. In France, where a dense commercial network existed before the rise of big companies, entrepreneurs were hardly motivated to integrate production and marketing (Fridenson, 1997, 214).

In several other countries, especially Italy and France, small firms were part of a long tradition and played an important role in the modern economy. This attribute might not be considered "backward."[49] In reality, smaller markets and larger income disparities limited opportunities and precluded the need for creating integrated companies. Britain had continued to preserve its preponderantly (77 percent) privately owned company structure as late as 1914. The country did not require organizational and managerial modernization and the formation of entrepreneurial and managerial firms. The existence of a huge imperial market and the predominance of exports made it unnecessary. Britain exported close to 45 percent of its industrial output and had "a highly developed distribution and mercantile network for both domestic and overseas trade," including a widespread foreign agency network (Wilson, 1995, 88, 120). British companies established overseas branches, or "freestanding companies," as Mira Wilkins (1988) described these early forerunners of multinationals.[50]

European traditions and practices created an alternative type of business organization, the *cartelization* of the economy, from the late nineteenth century on. The role of cartels predominated in Germany, Switzerland, and Austria-Hungary. What turn-of-the-century Marxist literature has called "monopoly capitalism," that is, the widespread development of cartels and trusts that administered entire industrial sectors, was an effective way to regulate output and distribution without merging various enterprises into a single gigantic company. In Europe, the strong entrepreneurial class, in some cases in alliance with the traditional noble-bureaucratic-military elite, was able to determine government policy.[51] Anti-cartel legislation was not introduced in Europe until World War I.

In 1905, more than 350 cartels were in operation in Germany, coordinating output and markets, and often establishing joint marketing networks in the coal, steel, and chemical industries. The coal cartel controlled 74 percent of coal output, the iron and cement cartels 50 percent, and the paper cartel controlled 90 percent. They divided up markets, including export markets and raw material resources, among their member companies, and they fixed prices and severely restricted competition.[52] "Cartelization did . . . inhibit horizontal merger activity as a means of concentrating production, largely because the security afforded by cartels provided little incentive to acquire competitors" (Wilson, 1995, 72).

As the nineteenth-century European economy was genuinely intra-European, the cartels inevitably became so as well. Cartel cooperation existed between the Belgian Solvay, the Dutch AKU, and the British chemical firms. Under the leadership of Dutch Philips, the Deutsch-Englisch-Norwegische (DEN) international nitrogen cartel and the Phoebus international incandescent lamp cartel were pan-European in nature (Schröter, 1997, 193). The international incandescent lamp cartel established a joint marketing office, the Verkaufsstelle der Vereinigten Glühlampenfabriken, in 1903.

This idiosyncratic European alternative to the American multidivision managerial firm is also connected to the special banking system on the continent, as I have discussed above. In the central and north Italian parts of Western Europe, German-type banks played a central role in facilitating economic cooperation. The merging of banks and industrial monopolies in the late nineteenth century, what was called "finance capital," rendered the American type of backward and forward integration and complex multidivision companies unnecessary. This phenomenon was certainly the most widespread in Germany, where the banks became the primary investors in industry.[53] As Knut Borchardt has noted, the big German banks were the decision-making and organizational centers of the German economy (Borchardt, 1973, 183).

Cultural factors also hindered any meaningful introduction of scientific management and rational procedure into European industry. In most countries of Europe, Taylorism was considered inhumane and counterproductive. The tradition of feudal paternalism permeated the capitalist industrial system, and it preserved a sense of managerial responsibility for the workers' welfare. Owners sought to win the loyalty of their workforce in this manner. This attitude animated British policy during the Industrial Revolution and the de-urbanization of industry. Newly created company towns were accompanied by entrepreneurial community-building activities. Companies regularly offered their workers housing and schooling; some sold them food at wholesale prices. Several factory towns, such as the Mona Mine, provided stable employment.[54]

The welfare-oriented labor policy of Robert Owen while he was a manager in Manchester and New Lanark was certainly unique, but it was so influential that the latter location became a well-known British tourist attraction. It helped establish an outlook that placed value on winning worker cooperation. More than half a century later, London's gas industry continued to act in a similar manner: in a conflict with the unions, it offered profit-sharing in the late 1880s. The large gas companies, match manufacturers, and port transportation firms were the first to provide pensions, sick pay, accident benefits, and recreational and sport facilities in the late nineteenth century. In the British confectionery trade, Quaker employers encouraged cooperation between management and workers through the policies they adopted, a stance that presaged "welfarism." British entrepreneurs believed that such measures generated greater loyalty and higher quality work from their workforce.

Similar measures were initiated in Germany at the end of the nineteenth century. Socialist ideas, represented by social democratic parties and union organizations, also became part of the new European value system. Although they were not able to directly influence government policies before World War I, they did have a significant impact in an indirect way. Fighting against the socialist movement, Chancellor Bismarck of Germany attempted to take the wind out of the socialists' sails when he introduced major socialist programs such as the world's first compulsory national health insurance in 1883, industrial accident insurance in 1884, and old age and invalidity pension insurance in 1889. The German social initiative was immediately emulated in the Scandinavian countries.[55]

Western Europe did not follow the American business pattern, and its economic system exhibited the embryonic beginnings of a welfare orientation. Its labor productivity, however, fell increasingly behind that of America. In seven West European countries, one worker produced an average of $1.88 GDP per hour in 1870 and $3.51 in 1913. Although this represented an 87% increase, it was still behind the 127% increase of American productivity. In 1879, Western Europe reached 80% of the American productivity level of $2.26 GDP per hour; by 1913, however, the American level of $5.12 was 46% higher than the European one (based on Maddison, 1995, 249).

In any case, the American multidivision, integrated managerial giants began operating in Europe around the turn of the twentieth century. Many European companies began multinational operations almost as soon as they were established. In several small countries on the continent, such as Holland, Belgium, Switzerland, Sweden, Norway, and Denmark, modern integrated giant firms could not find a large enough market domestically. As they grew, they had to operate internationally.[56] Large, multidivision managerial companies emerged in France around the turn of the twentieth century.[57] Altogether, however, only a few firms "had really moved into managerial capitalism" (Fridenson, 1997, 213). The merger activity in Britain before World War I absorbed nearly two thousand firms, and it led to the rise of a few giants such as Metropolitan-Vickers Electrical and others. In 1919, the ten largest firms in each of its eleven industrial branches produced more than 43 percent of industrial output (Wilson, 1995, 144–5, 167).

As many as 88 percent of the largest one hundred German industrial corporations had vertical integration, forward or backward, at the beginning of the twentieth century. A major investor abroad and a leader in some of the newest branches of industry, Germany operated 153 foreign production subsidiaries in the chemical industry alone by 1914. Altogether 336 German-owned companies operated abroad, nearly half of them production units, and roughly 12 percent in the banking and insurance industries. Many German companies were already global players prior to World War I.[58] In the modern sectors, international market activity became crucial for nearly all of Europe.

Notes

1. Larry Neal, in his *The Rise of Financial Capitalism*, speaks of the "first financial revolution" in sixteenth-century Europe (Neal, 1990, 3). He challenged the long-established concept that the inflow of gold and silver from Latin America

caused the so-called price revolution that doubled the price levels in that century. Instead, he argues, government policies and grandiose military goals played a central role in the rise of financial markets or financial capitalism by directing the outcome of goods and factor-of-production markets. James Tracy speaks of a financial revolution in the 1540s Habsburg Netherlands (Tracy, 1985), while Herman Van der Wee puts it in late sixteenth-century Antwerp, where the negotiability of the foreign bill of exchange was invented (Van der Wee, 1977).

2. The Swedish Riksbank at first issued notes after its establishment, but it soon ended this policy.

3. Bankers such as the Hoares and Childs emerged from goldsmith business. A Quaker family, the Barclays established their bank in 1690. The son of a German emigrant from Bremen, Francis Baring, a cloth merchant, founded a trading company in the eighteenth century and merged it with banking in the 1820–1830s.

4. The Fosters, merchants and millers in Cambridge, entered banking in 1804; the Lloyds in Birmingham came from the iron trade and the Smiths from the hosiery trade, while most of the Cornish bankers came from mining; fifty brewers also became bankers in Hertfordshire and Essex.

5. Praed & Co. financed James Watt and the Cornish copper mines. Lending often went to "insiders."

6. Until 1810, he was an antique and coin dealer who operated as a commodity trader and was involved in the exchange business. He became the financial agent of the Landgraf, later Electoral Prince, of Hessen-Kassel, and soon started providing state loans to other countries, Denmark first among them.

7. Ralph Erlanger, a Frankfurt employee of Rothschild during the Napoleonic wars, copied the Rothschild pattern and formed his own independent banking house, dispatching his three sons to London, Paris, and Vienna. Modern merchant banking became a pan-European phenomenon, and diaspora merchants became diaspora bankers.

8. This began at the end of the fifteenth century with the expulsion of the Sephardic Jews from Granada, and continued with the persecution of Ashkenazi Jews in Central Europe in the sixteenth century, the displacement of Moors from Valencia, and the expulsion of the Huguenots from France in the seventeenth century.

9. The Ruthwell Savings Bank (1810) and the Edinburgh Bank of Savings (1813) were among the first.

10. Every county had at least one of the banks or branches: in the West Midlands bank density reached 1 per 12,000 inhabitants, in London 1 per 17,000, and in England and Wales generally 1 per 21,000.

11. Checks also proliferated, based on deposits during the 1830s, and the Scottish banks popularized checking by introducing printed checks (Cameron, 1967). Checks spread slowly on the continent but were not legalized until 1860.

12. Early banking in modern times, however, preserved several transitional elements from the past, one being the medieval "court Jew," a moneylender characterized by his close contact with courts or governments. The story of Jewish banker Bleichröder's close relationship with Bismarck in the 1860s clearly demonstrates the existence of a modernized "court Jew" system in the nineteenth century.

13. Joseph Süss Oppenheimer, a merchant who ran a money-exchange business in Frankfurt, became the court Jew of Württemberg in the seventeenth century. The Bethmann brothers financed the Habsburgs in the late eighteenth century. The permanent warfare of this period created such positions for wealthy merchants and moneylenders. Samson Wertheimer financed wars against the Ottoman Empire and France in the seventeenth century, and Feidel David became the financier of the Landgraf of Hessen-Kassel (North, 2000, 159–62). The Greek Rallis brothers from the island of Chios started their own firm, expanded it to Syria, Constantinople, Malta, and then to Livorno and London. The Armenian Toumantiantz brothers, originally from Baku, expanded operations to Odessa, Moscow, Vienna, and then to Paris (Baghdiantz McCabe *et al.*, 2005). In several cases, seventeenth-century court Jews became nineteenth-century court bankers. This institution was rooted in the church's prohibition of usury, i.e. medieval moneylending. Jews filled the "lücken Positionen," as Karl Marx called the intermediary positions in medieval and early modern societies. Consequently, a great many of the early nineteenth-century merchants and government bankers were Jewish. They formed an international network and enjoyed the advantage of using an international contact language, Yiddish. They built and maintained personal contacts with governments and dynasties, and remained the chief financiers of modern states. The Gebruder Bethmann Bank provided the first Imperial Austrian Loan in 1778, and continued with another eighty-two state loans until 1819.

14. The Bischoffsheim-Goldschmidt house, the Hentsch-Lütscher house, the Kohn-Reinach house, the Erlangers, Betzold, and other houses, were all preoccupied with brokerage activities. They contributed to proprietary trading, financial operations, and the issuing of securities, and they sold them to wealthy investors (Bonin, 2007).

15. Similarly, in north Italy, the *società in accomandita* type of stock company provided significant amounts of money to their shareholders and contributed to industrial financing. By 1845, of twenty-seven stock companies in Milan, only eight were genuine limited companies that financed only insurance,

navigation, and railways. The Cassa di Risparmio, the Savings Bank, provided long-term credits and mortgages for agriculture and real estate. By mid-century, Lombardy and Venetia had twenty-two savings banks. Numerous private banks, about thirty in Milan in the 1830s, financed commercial activities (Greenfield, 1965, 131, 137).

16. A huge network of merchant banking houses operated in Germany: the Behrens, Oppenheimer, and Heckscher in Hamburg, Erichthal in Augsburg, Seehandlung and Benecke Brothers in Berlin, and Bethmann in Frankfurt. Frankfurt had no fewer than forty-five bankers in 1790. Salomon Oppenheim founded a company in 1789 in Bonn, moved to Cologne, and became connected with the Rothschilds through marriage in 1834. The German banking network gradually expanded in the first half of the century. Until the 1830s, banknote circulation was unimportant. The first modern bank of issue, the Bayerische Hypotheken- und Wechselbank, was founded in 1835, followed by a second branch in Leipzig in 1838 (later the Bank of Saxony), and the Prussian Bank in 1846. In 1856, Prussia chartered seven new issuing banks.

17. In Vienna, the Austrian National Bank, established in 1816, opened branches in Prague (1847) and Pest (1851). In addition, savings banks or cooperatives began working mostly in the countryside. The Erste Österreichische Sparkasse (1819), Prague (1836), Kronstädter (1836), and Pest (1836) savings banks were forced into the straitjacket of non-profit, philanthropic institutions until the 1860s. The first commercial and mortgage banks in the Habsburg Empire followed beginning in the 1840s. One of the leading financiers was the Greek banker Georg Simon Sina.

18. The size of an average textile firm in the decades of the first Industrial Revolution was 93 persons in linen, 125 in silk, and 176 in cotton. The "industrialist par excellence," as F. Crouzet put it (1985, 17), was the cotton spinner industrialist who ran a single unit with one proprietor or two or three partners (Clapham, 1930, 196; Berg, 1994, 126). A few decades later, on the wave of the second Industrial Revolution, large companies sprung up: the Krupp works in Essen employed close to 12,000 workers, and Schneider in France had 12,500 in the early 1870s (Hobsbawm, [1975] (1996, 213).

19. The bank established specialized subsidiaries to finance various sectors of the economy, such as foreign trade, coal, and other industries. Between 1835 and 1840, the bank's industrial portfolio grew from 5.7 million to 38.6 million francs. Of that amount, transportation represented 36 percent, metal industry and coal mining nearly 57 percent. The success of the Société Générale led to the establishment of the Banque de Belgique in 1835, which had the same goals and pursued the same activities. This institution, however, went bankrupt after seven years of operation.

20. Their first significant endeavors between 1835 and 1852 were closely connected to the construction of the French railroad system. Later they built railroads in Switzerland, Spain, and Russia as well.

21. In the early twentieth century, several new big banks, such as the Banque Nationale pour le Commerce et l'Industrie (1901) and the Banque de l'Union Parisienne (1904), began operations.

22. With several international partners, the French banks had immense endeavors in the Ottoman Empire, Austria-Hungary, Romania, and Russia. French banks provided roughly two-thirds of Russian state loans (Bonin, 1991, 75).

23. The first shares that appeared on the stock exchange were the Österreichische Nationalbank's in 1820, but it took another sixteen years until more shares, those of the Bayerische Hypoteken- und Wechselbank, were traded (Heyn, 1981).

24. Hubert Bonin speaks of two banking revolutions. The first, the emergence of the private and local banks, took place approximately from 1750 to 1840; a second revolution, characterized by the founding of the Crédit Mobilier *and* the German universal investment type banks, was completed at the beginning of the 1870s (Bonin, 1991, 72).

25. The Basel Bank was involved in the Swiss Walter Boveri Company, and the Credit Suisse and the Stockholm Enskilda Bank established electric companies. In 1895, a Swiss Electrobank was established in Zurich for the electric industry.

26. In Europe at the turn of the century, the banks' activities replaced the so-called "merger mania" in the United States, which created backward and forward linkages between raw material extraction, industrial production, transportation, marketing, and services, in the framework of a single giant, multifunctional company.

27. While the Dresdner Bank possessed the largest industrial empire, and all the leading German banks held huge assets in various industries, some special orientation had also become characteristic; the Berliner Handelsgesellschaft focused on the coal industry, the Darmstädter Bank on the railroads, and the Deutsche Bank dominated the electric industry.

28. The British and French banks did not invest in the new industries, nor did the Paribas, the Société Générale, or the Rothschilds own shares of electric companies. "Faced with the appearance of a new technology whose industrial consequences were uncertain, complex, and costly . . . the British and French were more cautious, hesitant, and reticent" (Broder, 1991, 471).

29. The industrial giants also gained influence in banking. As will be discussed later, German industry attained a unique level of capital concentration: 550 large industrial companies employed 1.3 million workers before World War I. The Gelsenkirchen coal mining company employed 37,000 workers and bought up a great part of the iron and steel industry in Lotharingen

and Luxembourg. The Krupp empire, with its nearly 69,000 workers, and the Thyssen conglomerate dominated the Ruhr areas; Rochling did so in the Saar region; and Henckel-Donnersmark controlled the industry of Upper Silesia.

30. Italy presents an outstanding example of the role of foreign banking. Before the unification of the country, Italy had a weak, backward banking sector. Prior to the early 1870s, six banks had the right to issue banknotes. In addition to those, four other institutions provided agricultural credits, and altogether 123 local savings banks served a small segment of the population. From the 1860s on, however, French banks entered Italy and financed 60 percent of total railroad investment. They also entered the local banking business. During the 1860s, the Banca di Credito Italiano in Turin, the Banco del Commercio dell'Industria in Florence, and especially the Società Generale di Credit Mobiliare in Milan, with a combined capital of roughly 100 million lire, followed the French pattern and turned towards industry. During the 1870s, 143 joint-stock banks were established, and their capital totaled 792 million lire. However, several of them, including the issuing bank, collapsed in the mid-1890s. Italian banking virtually disappeared.

The severe banking crisis in the 1870s led to a dramatic turning point. The Berliner Handelsgesellschaft, the Bleichröder Bank, and the leading D-banks entered the scene and established the two largest, modern, mixed Italian banks, the Banca Commerciale Italiana and the Credito Italiano. German investment and the introduction of German-type banking opened the floodgates. Two other modern banks were founded with Italian capital, the Banco di Roma and the Società Bancaria Italiana. In 1895, in place of the six issuing banks, the Banca d'Italia became a modern central bank instead. Between 1896 and 1914, half a billion lira investments strengthened the banking system. Mostly with German contributions and following in the footsteps of German banking traditions, modern Italian banking radically contributed to a dramatic change in the north Italian economy and to the beginning of industrialization. Through the new investment banks, German capital invested in the Italian electric and chemical industries.

Foreign investment played the key role in Italian economic development before unification, but even in the decade after the Risorgimento, foreign loans and investment provided capital that equaled half the amount of domestic accumulation. Foreign investment contributed to the late start of the Italian economic boom, but it sharply declined from the 1890s on, and had to be replaced by domestic financial sources.

31. One of the first rescue actions of the Bank of England was to save Baring Brothers in 1890. The Banque de France and the Banca d'Italia played similar roles in the latter decades of the century.

32. In 1796, a group of bankers founded the Caisse des Comptes Courants, a special bank for Paris banks. In 1800, it was reorganized as the Banque de France with the right to issue notes in the Paris region. This right, however, was also granted to nine provincial banks throughout the country, from Nantes and Bordeaux to Lyon and Marseilles. The sole right to issue notes in the country was granted to the Banque de France only in 1848, when the nine provincial banks became branches of the central bank. From that time on, the central bank established a dense network of its own branches, altogether 411 throughout the country by 1900.

33. The St. Gallen and Geneva banks in Switzerland opened for business in the mid- and late eighteenth century. The Pictet Bank and Cie Bank became modern commercial banks in the early nineteenth century, investing in railroads and industry.

34. In addition to wealthy private banks, Vienna's Rothschild, Simon Sina, Arnstein and Eskeles, Wodianer, and Königswarter banks were involved in issuing state and agricultural credits. The Rothschild and Sina houses began investing in railroads and industry in the mid-1830s. One hundred and twenty-four savings banks were also in operation during the first two quarters of the century. Although a few new banks were established in the 1850s, "a complex, modern credit market for companies, industry, agriculture and construction, was not yet created" (Baltzarek, 2005, 24–5).

35. The Credit-Anstalt soon became the leading Central European banking institution, with branches in Prague, Pest, Brünn, Kronstadt, Lemberg, and Trieste.

36. The ten largest banks in Vienna monopolized 67 percent of the capital assets of joint-stock banking and owned 53 percent of total joint-stock capital in the Monarchy's western provinces. Banking in Prague was also expanded; the most significant step was the foundation of the Živnostenská Banka pro Čechy a Moravu in 1868. In 1890, the capital assets of the Viennese banks were nine times larger than those of Prague; by 1913, they were four times larger.

37. Insurance in an embryonic form has had a long history. Village communities and urban guilds offered an organized form of social "insurance," and, in the early modern centuries, civil organizations such as friendly societies and burial clubs provided "insurance" for their members. At that time, the forerunners of the insurance companies also appeared in London, providing fire insurance after the great fire and livestock insurance in the countryside.

38. In the early eighteenth century, the first corporate maritime insurance institutions, Royal Exchange Assurance and London Assurance, began operation. In 1793, the Friendly Society Act regulated civil organizations as well. Maritime insurance acquired an important underwriter in the coffeehouse of Edward Lloyd; the Society of Lloyd's, incorporated in 1871, became a leading provider of modern insurance.

39. Prudential, the Universal Railway Casualty Compensation Co., the Accidental Death Insurance Co., the Farmers' and Gardeners' Hailstorm Insurance
Co., and the Farmers' and Grazers' Cattle Insurance Co. followed Lloyd's and
other early institutions in Britain in the 1840s. The Société Anonyme des
Assurances Générales in Paris (1818) combined, for the first time, maritime,
fire, and life insurance in one single company in the 1840s, and the Compagnie Française du Phénix (1820) introduced employee pension and protection plans in France in 1844. By 1848, thirty joint-stock insurance companies
operated in France. Cantonal fire insurance became compulsory in Switzerland in 1805, but the first modern insurance companies were established
only after the devastating 1861 Glarus fire that caused damages totaling 8
million Swiss francs. In that year, however, the Helvetia Fire and St. Gallen
insurance companies began operation. Following the late eighteenth-century
Mecklenburg Hail Insurance Association and livestock insurance institutions,
Allianz AG, one of the largest insurance companies of Germany, was founded
in 1890. The Försäkringsaktiebolaget Skandia began as a small fire and life
insurance company in 1855 and offered most other types of insurance by 1890.
In 1800, when the life insurance industry was in its infancy, the entire amount
of insurance extended in both Britain and France was only $1.6 million. By
1875, however, the assets of the life insurance industry in Britain, France, and
Germany topped $2,461 million; by 1900, it was $6,530 million.

40. Corporate fire reinsurance had already existed earlier, but institutionalized
insurance-for-insurance-companies emerged mostly during the 1860s. Probably the Cologne Reinsurance company was the first in Europe, established
in 1842, after the devastating Hamburg fire. In the 1860s, however, the Compagnie Française de Réassurances, the Magdeburg, and the Zurich-based Swiss
Re (1863) were also founded. The first reinsurance company opened its doors
in Britain in 1867 (Pearson, 2001).

41. Directors acting as managers of other people's money "cannot well be expected,
that they should watch over it with the same anxious vigilance with which the
partners in a private copartnery frequently watch over their own . . . Negligence
and profusion . . . must always prevail . . . in the management of the affairs of
such a company" (Smith, quoted by Pollard, 1965, 12).

42. These establishments, such as the Portuguese, Dutch, British, Danish Asiatic, and French East Indian Companies, were independent legal entities that
owned property and were subject to litigation. They were enormous enterprises with lucrative state monopolies, high value shares, and huge dividends.
However, virtually all of these state-awarded monopolies, including banking
and maritime insurance monopolies, disappeared by 1800–30.

43. "Establishing a manufactory, for making and printing cotton and linen cloths
upon a more extensive plan than has hitherto been practiced . . . cannot be

established ... without a very large capital or joint stock" (quoted from the Commons' Journal 1779 by Harris, 2000, 174).

44. In France, joint-stock companies required royal charters. After 1816, joint-stock insurance companies proliferated throughout the country. By 1848, thirty were already in operation. But the country did not enact legislation making joint-stock companies free entities until 1867. The Danish Supreme Court accepted limited liability and recognized joint-stock companies as legal entities in 1827, but the government codified the institution only in 1917. Hamburg and Bremen were the first to embrace the principle of unfettered creation of limited liability companies and required only their registration. However, joint-stock companies were restricted until 1869, when the North German Confederation enacted the law of free incorporation. After the crisis of the mid-1870s, the German parliament introduced restrictions in 1884 by raising the minimum size of shares and requiring the disclosure of financial information. From the late 1880s on, however, such overregulation became a burden, prompting the government to introduce a new organizational form, the Gesellschaft mit beschränkter Haftung (GmbH), a company with limited liability. Other countries soon followed. The British Parliament passed the Company Act of 1900 imposing restrictions and demanding financial transparency, but it soon allowed the creation of limited liability companies (Lamoreaux, 2009, 26–7).

45. However, after the stock exchange crisis of 1873, new legislation placed heavier taxation on joint-stock companies (1874), twice as much as for privately owned firms, and imposed stricter state control of the stock exchange (1875).

46. This evolved from a sixteenth-century annual fair and the regular meetings of its participating merchants. The institution became regulated in 1682 and began its bond business in 1779.

47. In Ford's system, "the various parts needed for assembly were moved from one workstation to another in a constant flow throughout the workday. The Ford assembly line reduced the time required for chassis assembly from twelve to less than two hours" (Singer, 1998, 242). Taylor studied time and motion in the workplace, measuring each movement and reorganizing the work in a more rational and efficient way. His *Principles of Scientific Management*, published in 1911, influenced the organization of labor the world over. Another American expert, Charles Bedaux, invented a variant of Taylor's methods, "based on the increasing division of tasks, the separation of skilled from unskilled labour, the mechanization of skilled tasks ... designed to achieve economies of scale through mass production of standardized products" (Eden, 2000, 330).

48. Sidney Pollard also rejects the general validity of the managerial firm. "It may well be doubted ... if the American organizational model, even if appropriate for a large, fairly homogenous and rapidly expanding home market, should

have been the pattern adopted for a smaller, more diversified and fairly stable home market coupled to a highly volatile and unpredictable export market" (Pollard, 1994, 71).

49. During the last third of the twentieth century, small firms have reemerged as important players in most modern sectors. As Naomi Lamoreaux, Daniel Raff, and Peter Temin have demonstrated, the role of large multidivisional enterprises began to decline during the last third of the twentieth century – even in America (Lamoreaux *et al.*, 2003).

50. Freestanding enterprises were special firms designed "to obtain capital by bringing together profitable... operations overseas." They were "set up in one country for the purpose of doing business outside that country" (Wilkins, 1988, 262; Wilkins and Schröter, 1998, 3). In the period between the 1880s and World War I, forty-six British, Belgian, French, Swiss, and German companies established and registered freestanding companies in Italy, and their nominal capital totaled 360 million lire during the prewar years. Similar business activities took place in Russia as well.

51. In the United States, the Sherman Anti-trust Act of 1890 banned the creation of monopolies, and the Standard Oil Trust was broken into several independent companies. Anti-trust legislation pushed firms to merge and create multidivision companies.

52. The German type of cartelization was also predominant in Austria-Hungary. In 1900, fifty-six Austro-Hungarian cartels existed in the Habsburg Empire, and they controlled most of its leading industrial sectors (Berend and Ránki, 1955, 89).

53. The Dresdner Bank controlled the largest industrial empire, while the Schaffhausensche Bankverein acquired a large share of the industrial complex of the Rhineland. Representatives of the Deutsche Bank retained a major share in the electric industry. The banks played the primary role in the "marriage of coal and iron" in the Ruhrgebiet and Rhineland.

54. "In some industries, as in the Cornish tin-mines, in the dockyards, and in some South Wales ironworks, medical assistance was commonly provided... service was usually accompanied by the support of sick clubs and by pension" (Pollard, 1996, 202). "No matter how detached the entrepreneur community-builder was from his workers as persons... the very fact of having to cater for a broad range of their needs forced on him some modicum of understanding of the humanity of his hands" (Pollard, 1965, 206).

55. Denmark introduced a non-contributory pension system in 1891 and several other welfare steps followed. Denmark, Norway, and Sweden all introduced various kinds of health and pension insurance plans. Indeed, Scandinavia pioneered the modern welfare state (Kudrle and Marmor, 1981, 140).

56. In tiny Switzerland, 23 companies owned 25 foreign subsidiaries, mostly in textiles, as early as 1870. In 1900, 98 multinational companies operated 144 subsidiaries abroad. Before World War I, Swiss companies retained 265 foreign subsidiaries. There were a number of modern multinational companies in Belgium, such as Cockerill, Gaevert (which later merged with Agfa), Petrofina, Solvay, and others. In Holland, there were Unilever, Royal Dutch Shell, and Philips (Schröter, 1997, 180–1; Jones and Schröter, 1993, 52–3, 101–3).

57. Forges et Aciéries de Marine-Homécourt and Schneider in the steel industry, Compagnie Française Thomson-Houston in electrical engineering, Peugeot and Renault in the car industry.

58. These included Siemens and the Allgemeine Elektrizitäts-Gesellschaft (AEG), I. G. Farben and Bayer in the chemical industry, as well as Linde, Zeiss, Bosch, and Metallgesellschaft. "More than any other new industry before, the German electric engineering industry developed into a multinational business from the very beginning" (Wengenroth, 1997, 151; Kocka, 1980, 79–88; Jones and Schröter, 1993, 29).

CHAPTER 5

Three versions of successful industrialization

Long-surviving proto-industry

Although Western Europe shared several socio-political and cultural characteristics with the Northwest, it took some time before socio-political reforms, state-sponsored infrastructure building, and an agricultural revolution would lay the groundwork for its own industrial transformation. The Industrial Revolution did not generate immediate economic change even in Britain, where most industrial branches remained in a pre-industrial revolutionary state until the mid-nineteenth century. After the landmark invention of the steam engine, it would take between one-half and three-quarters of a century before new energy sources would begin to proliferate in that pioneering country. As late as 1870, 29 percent of steam-power capacity was still concentrated in the textile industry. Traditional handicrafts continued to predominate in most other sectors until the mid-nineteenth century. "The typical British worker in the mid-nineteenth century was not a machine operator in a factory, but still a traditional craftsman or labourer" (quoted in Crafts, 1985, from Musson, 1978, 252–3, 141). In 1841, when the major portion of the British workforce was for the first time in industrial employment, the "revolutionized" industries employed only 19 percent of the country's workers.[1]

Continental Western Europe lagged far behind. Traditional French iron, gun, and tapestry manufacturing remained non-mechanized. The putting-out system, based on France's traditional cottage industry, predominated in the countryside, including the famous Alsace textile and Lyon silk industries. Only 10 percent of Alsace's spindles were modern self-actor spindles in 1856, and the 110,000 hand-weaving machines of Lyon's silk industry were twice the number of its modern mechanized weaving machines until the third quarter of the nineteenth century. The proto-industrial complex in the Languedoc area, the largest concentration of textile production in pre-industrial France and most likely in all of continental Europe during the seventeenth and eighteenth centuries,[2] was based on the *Kauf* and *Verlag* systems. In addition, hundreds of independent artisans were also working for urban merchants. The Industrial Revolution in Britain, however, ended this prominence; French proto-industry turned out to be a cul-de-sac. "Languedoc's situation of primacy in France's textile industry had been lost decisively by the turn of the century, and by 1810, Languedoc . . . [had] begun a permanent decline" (Thomson, 1983, 88–9). Moreover, the former textile center began supplying wine to Paris in the nineteenth century. A significant part of proto-industry was not transformed into mechanized modern industry, but died out during the years of the Industrial Revolution. In France, however, the handicraft industry played an important role in its gradual industrial progress: "artisan production . . . allowed for steady increase in per capita output without . . . the factory system" (Berg *et al.*, 1983, 34).

Modern steam engines, however, were slowly introduced in France. A total of only 625 were in operation there prior to 1830, and, even by 1845, the country's waterpower capacity still surpassed that of its steam engines by two and a half times. The iron industry employed eighteenth-century technology and wood-heating until 1815, but charcoal-heating was still four times more prevalent than coke-heating in 1840, when 421 iron works used charcoal but only 41 used coke. The achievements of the British Industrial Revolution appeared on French soil, but they remained diffused and erratic until the mid-century. Industrialization was stimulated by railroad construction and the Crédit Mobilier banks from that time on.

New research suggests that industrialization had begun in the western regions of Germany prior to the Industrial Revolution. There were important advances in the eighteenth century, when export-oriented rural textile and iron industries in Krefeld, Elberfeld, Barmen, Zwickau, and the Aachen-Stollberger region generated capital accumulation. In 1800, approximately 900,000 cottage workers held contracts in the putting-out system in Germany.[3] This cottage industry was combined with early, non-mechanized factories built by Huguenot immigrants: roughly 1,000 factories with some 100,000 workers operated in the territory of the old empire, producing typical luxury products such as china, tapestry, glass, and sugar, together with woolen, silk, and cotton goods. In the silk industry, large cottage industry-based factories produced 90 percent of the country's output. This well-developed proto-industry, however, faced stiff competition from mechanized industry during the second quarter of the nineteenth century. The new railroads transported modern imported mass products to several parts of the country, which led to the decline of German proto-industry (North, 2000, 147–9, 223).

Except for the southern Low Countries (Belgium), and despite initial steps taken in France and a few other countries, most of continental Europe enviously eyed the British miracle but was unable to duplicate it at the turn of the century. Domestic obstacles actually increased during the revolutionary and Napoleonic wars. The continental blockade generally hindered the spread of new technology until 1815. Britain also tried to uphold its monopoly position by banning exports of new machinery and prohibiting the migration of skilled workers. The latter restriction was abolished in 1825, but that on the export of machinery was not lifted until 1842. Much of the continent remained frozen at its earlier stage of development. In other words, the proto-industrial age was preserved during at least the first half of the nineteenth century. Industry progressed somewhat, but it basically remained within the framework of a traditional putting-out, proto-industrial system.

Switzerland had one of the strongest and longest cottage industry traditions.[4] Linen, lace, and calico printing had all collapsed, however, by around the 1820s owing to international competition in the new industrial age. Still, the Swiss cotton industry was able to transform itself after the Napoleonic wars, once British competition had destroyed a great part of it. Manual and mechanized production were commensurate in 1820, but 150 large factories, each with 4,000 mechanized spindles, were at that time already in operation. Their size continued to increase and their output doubled between 1840 and 1870. The trademark export-oriented watch-making industry remained a putting-out cottage industry until the last third of the nineteenth century.[5] Watch-making employed 35,000 workers in 1870, but three-quarters of them continued to work at home. Swiss watch-making was transformed into a modern factory-based industry only in the last third of the nineteenth century. By 1905, nearly 39,000 workers produced watches in factories, while only 13,000 worked at home.

The traditional Swiss silk industry was already flourishing in the eighteenth century, but the big producers such as Seidenhöfe, Muralt an der Siehl, and the Schwarzenbach group operated within the putting-out framework. In the strong Swiss textile industry, only 1,000 workers were employed in factories, but 158,000 worked in the cottage industry in 1800. The first fully mechanized textile factory was opened in Wil in 1830. In 1850, 130,000 employees worked in the cottage industry and 143,000 in small-scale industries, but only 42,000 were employed in mechanized factories.

North Italy was an economic powerhouse during the early modern centuries.[6] However, the Italian silk fabric industry, which had predominated in Europe, steadily lost ground to French and British competitors, and Italy was gradually reduced to being a silk-thread producer for France. In the first half of the nineteenth century, Lombard and Venetian silk output increased by three times. According to some estimates, north Italy was the largest raw silk producer in Europe in the mid-century. Moreover, other branches of the textile industry, such as wool, cotton, linen, and hemp, also emerged. In the newly created cotton industry, twenty-two large spinning factories were in operation in the 1840s. As weaving and spinning had been traditional industries in north Italy, they continued to be cottage industries at this time. A part of industrial production, however, was concentrated in big factories employing hundreds of workers.

Food processing was also part of Italy's industrial heritage. Butter, parmesan and gorgonzola cheese, and clotted milk in Lombardy were already being exported as early as the 1830s. The country's strongest base for industry was its flourishing agriculture.[7] The new wave of industrial development was connected to its strong northern middle class, partly a landowning bourgeoisie, which accumulated large amounts of capital by renting out land and investing the proceeds. Unlike the rest of the peninsula, the industrial regions in Piedmont, Lombardy, and Liguria were commensurate to the developed parts of Western Europe.

An interesting example of proto-industrial development during the British Industrial Revolution was the relatively rapid industrial growth in Austria-Bohemia, the western provinces of the Habsburg Empire. An export-oriented textile industry began operation at the turn of the nineteenth century, employing 579,000 people in 1798. The cotton industry utilized 435,000 spindles in 1828 and 1 million by 1841. The initial isolated appearance of textile machines notwithstanding, hand spinning continued to predominate in the Habsburg Empire until the 1840s.[8]

In the Czech lands, the eastern German territories, Hungary, and Russia, feudal landlords owning large estates played an important role in the development of industry. The mining, lumber, and iron industries were important players in manorial proto-industry, using feudal serfs to extract and process their own raw materials, and paying wages to skilled workers. The manorial proto-industry was built upon the peasant cottage industry, and the putting-out system was combined with centralized factory work.[9] Austrian merchants established several textile factories derived from the Bohemian cottage industry; the Linz textile factory, for instance, employed 16,000 spinners who worked at home. According to Arnošt Klíma, approximately one-quarter to one-half of the villagers in Bohemia worked in the putting-out system, and 80 percent did so in the northern mountainous regions.[10] Until the 1830s, proto-industrialization was successfully adopted only in the Czech lands. During the 1840s, the mechanization of the Czech linen industry began. Proto-industrial textile and iron industries produced 33 and 13 percent of Czech industrial production respectively as late as 1880, when modern mechanized textile, iron, and other industries first predominated. Proto-industry's longevity is demonstrated by the fact that, even in the early twentieth century, "home workers" made up almost 40 percent of the textile industry's workforce. In Western Europe, proto-industry was preserved until the mid-nineteenth century.

Frank Mendels considered proto-industry to be the first phase of a linear development of industrialization, "paving the way for factory production and wage labour at a later date. Thus rural domestic industry...constituted the first phase of the industrialization process, which...created the conditions for industrialization proper" (Mendels, 1972, 241; Berg *at al.*, 1983, 16–17). In reality, however, proto-industry was not the anteroom of the Industrial Revolution. In most cases, it declined in importance and ultimately disappeared because of the competition of mechanized industry.

Some areas of Western Europe took their first steps in following Britain at almost the same time as the British Industrial Revolution, but the transformation gained momentum only from the mid-century on, and in some cases in the 1860s–1870s. It was not until World War I, however, that Western Europe, including the western provinces of Austria-Hungary and north Italy, successfully industrialized.

Most of the economic history literature maintains that the British Industrial Revolution was duplicated by countries on the continent. According to Sidney Pollard,

the process started in Britain and the industrialization of Europe took place on the British model; it was...[on] the Continent...a purely and deliberately imitative process...Even after the 1860s, when technological and organizational innovations came increasingly from other advanced countries...it was still a development from the base of the British model. (Pollard, 1981b, v)

Two decades later, François Crouzet reiterated the same idea:

In Britain...revolutionary process had started...The rest of Western Europe...was ready to follow after a short lag...Industrialization of the Continent was an imitative process by businessmen, and sometimes by governments, of the new technology and forms of organization that the pioneer country had created. (Crouzet, 2001, 97, 116)

However, the theory of the "imitative" character of continental industrialization explains only a very small part of the story. There is no doubt that Britain played an inspirational role for certain countries on the continent; a few countries followed Britain's development closely, and several reproduced certain elements of the British model. But imitating the British Industrial Revolution was only one of a number of variants of continental industrialization. When the continent finally began to industrialize, a new generation of inventions revolutionized technology further and created new branches of industry. This process, called the *second Industrial Revolution*, was led by the science-based steel, chemical, electric, and car industries. Thus, the industrialization of the continent was not just a belated imitation of the British pattern, but also the initiator of a new surge of technological and industrial change. The industrialization of Western Europe, therefore, exhibited different patterns and paradigms and did not follow a single imitative road, though the end result, the emergence of modern industrial capitalism and the rise of the standard of living, was everywhere the same.

It is important to differentiate between *three distinct* though often composite *variants of Western industrialization*. The *first* was the close and relatively early imitation of the British pattern, that is, establishing mechanized textile, coal, and iron industries by adopting British technology. This pattern was most apparent in Belgium, the first industrialized nation on the continent, where modern industry was based on coal and iron, and partially on textiles. This pattern was also discernible in the early industrialization in France and Switzerland, where textiles played a leading role in the transformation. Parts of this model were also seen in the Austrian-Bohemian industrialization after 1880, when export-oriented textiles became the leading sector of industry.

The *second variant* of industrialization was launched by the second Industrial Revolution. The most typical examples of this pattern were the western provinces of Germany, but it is also seen in the later period of French, Swiss, and north Italian industrialization. However, all of Western Europe exhibited aspects of this type of industrialization after the 1860s–1870s, including Britain and Belgium, when the second Industrial Revolution created new technology. Scandinavia also fell into this category after the 1870s.

The *third variant* represented an alternative road towards the highly modernized, advanced economy, based on the most productive, specialized agriculture that organically integrated with export-oriented food processing. This type was later combined with import-substituting industrialization to establish consumer goods industries producing for the domestic market and replacing imports at around the turn of the twentieth century. Some elements of science-based industries also appeared in the early twentieth century in those countries that experienced this type of modernization. This model was classically seen in the Netherlands and Denmark, but elements of it also appeared in Switzerland and Austria-Bohemia during the first stage of their mechanized industrial transformation between 1840 and 1880. Differentiating between three types of industrialization, however, is an abstraction, since entirely "pure types" did not exist; hence, much of the region experienced a *mixed* industrialization pattern. A chronological point has to be added here: some countries followed a certain type of industrialization in the early period of their transformation, but turned to another pattern upon entering a second stage.

Industrial development on the continent was rather gradual and in many cases did not undergo any dramatic turning points.[11] This was true even for Britain, where growth rates were equally rapid before, during, and after the Industrial Revolution, and whose industry was completely transformed during the second half of the nineteenth century (Crafts et al., 1988). Germany had quite consistent growth after 1840. Railroad construction grew 20% per year in the 1840s, while iron and coal increased output by 4.0% and 4.5% per annum. During the 1850s, coal output increased by 9% and iron by 30% per year (Tilly, 1991a, 106). Industrial development continued and did not slacken after 1873, when the so-called *Gründerzeit* ended.

Gradualism characterized the Austrian-Bohemian industrialization. The confusing debate about an abrupt beginning or "take-off" is quite instructive.[12]

French studies have traditionally rejected the existence of any take-off period in the country. Indeed, between 1826–46 and 1900–13, France's annual industrial growth rate did not reveal any major fluctuations or sudden discontinuities. From decade to decade it varied between 1.3–1.8% and 2.0–2.6%; investment levels remained stable between 6% and 8% of GDP; and annual GDP growth stayed at an even 1.6–2.0%, lowering only slightly to 0.8% and 1.3% between the mid-1820s and the mid-1840s and during the 1880s. François Crouzet characterized the French industrialization process as a "connected series of rises and declines" (Crouzet, 2001, 73). Most countries experienced a longer and more gradual stop-and-go process. The outcome was, however, similar in many ways. Western Europe became highly industrialized: France increased its industrial output tenfold during the long nineteenth century; Germany achieved this somewhat later, but it took only some sixty years to do so.

Table 5.1 The development of the British textile industry between 1830 and 1913

Year	Number of spindles (1913=100)	Cotton yarn (1913=100)	Cotton goods (1913=100)	Woolen goods (1913=100)
1830	18^a	11	9	23
1860	56	50^b	45^b	48^b
1913	100	100	100	100

Sources: Based on Mitchell (1975, 306) and Hoffman (1955).
Notes:
[a] 1834.
[b] 1870.

Fully industrialized Britain

The Industrial Revolution created a whole new blueprint for economic development. British textile, coal, and iron industries entered a new era at around the turn of the nineteenth century. During the post-Industrial Revolution decades, those industrial sectors that were early leaders continued their remarkable progress. The textile industry rose to new heights and retained its unchallenged monopoly until 1870–80. Cotton consumption increased more than eightfold, and woolen output expanded fivefold. The number of spindles in the cotton industry grew three and a half times between 1815–24 and 1865–74. During the entire post-Industrial Revolution period between 1830 and 1913, the number of cotton spindles increased by five and a half times and the production of cotton threads and cotton goods tenfold. The share of textiles in industrial exports, however, declined from 67 percent in 1830 to 44 percent by the turn of the century. But textiles remained the single most important export item, and the quantity of exports was much higher than ever before. (See Table 5.1.)

The output of other leading sectors of the Industrial Revolution, coal and iron, had also multiplied, partly because of extensive railroad construction and a huge increase in shipping. Britain emerged as the pioneer of the railroad age. After the opening of the Liverpool–Manchester line in 1830, it had roughly 10,000 kilometers in operation by 1850 and 23,441 (with Ireland 38,000) kilometers by 1912, delivering 520 million tons of goods and servicing 1.3 million passengers a year. At the same time, shipping saw an immense expansion. In the 1820s, the capacity of newly built, first-registered steamships was 3,000 tons per year. By the turn of the century, it had increased by eighty-six times to 258,600 tons.

The consumption of coal and iron skyrocketed. In the closing years of the Industrial Revolution, annual British coal output totaled 22–23 million tons. This figure more than quadrupled by the late 1860s, and rose to 275.4 million tons by the early 1910s. In 1870, Britain produced more than 68 percent of Europe's coal output, and its share in 1913 was still 50 percent – representing one-quarter of the world output. Pig iron output grew fourteenfold between the early 1830s and 1910–13.

The age of transportation revolution thus had a decisive impact on British industry. In the mid-nineteenth century, railroads consumed only 2 percent of coal output, but one-quarter of the iron, and they employed one-fifth of the country's engineering production. The continental railroad boom, especially during its first decades, also opened an enormous market for British coal, iron, and engineering products. Altogether, the leading sectors of the Industrial Revolution accelerated their spectacular development after the 1830s. The predominant position of the traditional branches is clearly seen in the fact that coal, iron, steel, cotton, and woolens together provided 65 percent of British exports in 1851 and 51 percent by 1913.

Britain's non-revolutionized industrial sectors, which comprised more than 86 percent of its total industrial output at the end of eighteenth century, also gained new momentum and became rapidly mechanized. Fixed domestic capital formation, which had totaled £2.75 million per annum between 1791 and 1800, increased to £11.50 million between 1821 and 1830 and nearly doubled to £20.7 million between 1851 and 1860. On average, industrial growth was 2.2 percent between 1760 and 1830, and rose to 3.1 percent per year between 1830 and 1873. During the last quarter of the century, economic growth continued to be as rapid as it had been between 1800 and 1830. It was only during the decade and a half prior to World War I that the growth rate dropped back to the pace of the Industrial Revolution period.

The industrialization process thus culminated during the post-Industrial Revolution decades. All of British industry became mechanized, and the capacity of the industrial machinery increased from 620,000 to 13.7 million horsepower between 1840 and 1900. Industrial employment trebled, and output increased fivefold during those decades. The growth of the value of exports was twice as fast after, than it was during, the Industrial Revolution. Between 1800 and 1913, the value of exports increased thirtyfold from 10 percent to 40 percent of GDP.[13]

During the second half of the nineteenth century, a new factor accelerated British industrial development: the impact of the second Industrial Revolution. The new driving force of development was not only the expansion of the leading branches of the Industrial Revolution, not only the mechanization of other sectors of the economy with steam energy, but also the adoption of new technology and new industrial sectors. I will discuss this new trend later in the chapter.

British decline after 1870?

The pioneer of industrialization, Britain achieved spectacular industrial growth between 1780–90 and 1905–13; the value of its industrial output increased by more than 25 times. In the 1870s, Britain alone produced one-third of the world's industrial production. While Britain's industrial output continued to increase rapidly, by 2.2 percent per annum between 1873 and 1899 and 1.4–1.6 percent between 1899 and 1913, other Western countries also shifted into fifth gear, the United States first among them. As a consequence, Britain gradually lost its industrial monopoly. In 1913, it produced only one-seventh of the world's industrial output, while the United States supplied one-third of it.

A portion of the economic history literature suggests that late Victorian and Edwardian Britain was an economic failure that experienced relative decline beginning in the last third of the nineteenth century. This issue was debated throughout the entire twentieth century, but particularly from the 1960s on. The advocates of the concept of decline first employed a well-known social-psychological argument. They blamed the British entrepreneurs, who had lost "drive and dynamism," were entrenched in "conservatism" and "indifference," and who proved unable to respond to the challenges of changed conditions. "[That by] the late nineteenth century British entrepreneurs, taken as a whole, were less dynamic, less adaptable and less efficient than their counterparts abroad or their forerunners at home is now a commonplace" (Aldcroft and Richardson, 1969, 113). David Landes took a more general approach and put the blame on the spoiled "*third generation*" of the British upper middle class, which, having grown up in affluence and dwindled in decadence, "worked at play and played at work" (Landes, [1969] 1995, 336).[14] Prominent voices of turn-of-the-century Europe have ardently argued this well-known "third generation syndrome." A strong and energetic first generation of founders was followed by a second generation that retained its legacy; but the third generation, having grown up spoiled in an affluent environment, neglected and even ruined its inherited businesses, and squandered its wealth, by turning to the arts. Two Nobel laureate writers have brilliantly described this syndrome.[15]

The third generation syndrome has also been transformed into a Toynbee- or Spengler-type "rise and fall of civilizations" saga. James Foreman-Peck described the atmosphere of Britain in the 1980s that had prompted historians to search for the historical roots of Britain's contemporary failings. They found them in the "not quite matching" analogy of the "tale of Roman imperial degeneration over a millennium ... [that] tell[s] the story of continuous British economic decadence over a century or more" (Foreman-Peck, 1999, 135).

Most historians, however, have maintained that the decline was a relative phenomenon: the rise of continental Europe (and especially the United States) led to strong competition that eliminated Britain's export monopoly. Although British exports to Europe more than doubled between the 1850s and 1910s, Britain's imports from Europe increased by roughly ten times.[16]

Another oft-mentioned cause of relative decline was the massive export of capital. Britain invested more abroad than it did at home from the 1870s on. Investments abroad consumed roughly 30 percent of British capital formation during the 1850s–1870s, but more than half of it was spent during the 1880s–1910s. This proportion of foreign investment was several times higher than that of rival Germany, which invested only 9 percent of its accumulated capital abroad before World War I.

Further, the strength and legacy of the old leading sectors and technology of the first Industrial Revolution, which had established Britain's primacy, is often described as the obstacle to continued dynamic growth and the cause of diminished productivity. The advantage became a handicap, which hindered a flexible adjustment to the most modern technology. Nicolas Crafts affirms C. K. Harley's and D. N. McCloskey's observation that Britain had effectively exploited its comparative advantage in the old sectors until the war, but adds that

the legacy of the early start was that the economy was "overcommitted" and ... [the] rapid transfer of resources to the new industries [was slow] ... [T]he early start had produced an entrepreneurial psychology and an institutional structure which retarded structural change ... Britain's early start in industrialization adversely affected later growth performance. (Crafts, 1985, 157–8)

As a result, Britain, the technology leader in the late eighteenth and early nineteenth century, lost the international technological race in the second half of the century.

David Landes, James Foreman-Peck, and others discuss in detail Britain's subordinate role in the chemical, electric, and car industries. In these most modern technology branches, Britain turned to technology transfer and became a "latecomer," "a colony of the United States and Germany" (Foreman-Peck, 1999, 120).

Several authors have connected the decline to the growing relative backwardness of the British educational system, which gradually lagged behind the highly modernized systems in the United States and continental Europe, particularly Germany. From the second Industrial Revolution on, countries with top-notch technical training and research universities toppled Britain from its leading position. Between 1900 and 1915, British scientists were awarded 8 percent of Nobel prizes, in sharp contrast to Germany's 29 percent. However, the average length of schooling was still highest in Britain (7.28 years) in 1913, ahead of Germany (6.94) and the United States (6.93) (Crafts, 1997, 15–20, 30–5).

Whatever the motivations, adhering to the old sectors proved to be an obstacle during the new technological revolution, which rendered the earlier technology and leading sectors obsolete. While Britain was relishing the comparative advantage of its old leading sectors that seemed oblivious to change, its competitors, with no commitment to the past, were building up their industries by focusing on those of new technology. In many ways, some argue, this was the consequence of an "institutional sclerosis." Obsolete regulations will at times inhibit new technology, just as the infamous "Red Flag Act" delayed the age of the automobile.

Mancur Olson's 1982 work *The Rise and Decline of Nations* provided a new twist to this debate. Olson argues that the long period of political stability in Britain had had a negative effect on its economic growth, for it embedded social rigidity, strengthened the position of special interest groups, and allowed the lobbies of various producers to enforce inefficient redistribution. Institutional sclerosis slowed technological progress down and created inefficiency (Olson, 1982). For many, Britain serves as the most instructive example of institutional sclerosis.[17]

All of these arguments contain elements of truth. No one can deny that new frontrunners emerged at around the turn of the twentieth century. The United States and Germany took the lead in industry during the decades of the second Industrial Revolution. However, those historians who reject the concept of British failure and decline rightly point to Britain's financial strength, particularly its extraordinarily high revenues from foreign markets and investments. Having lost its monopoly as the technological leader, Britain nevertheless remained a strong competitor. During the first half of the nineteenth century, it procured fifty-two major

Table 5.2 The share of new technology
industries in total
manufacturing output (percent)

Year	Britain	Others	Total
1800	6–10	0	–
1860	60–70	18–24	29–36
1900	68–78	49–57	52–61
1913	72–80	55–65	60–65

Source: Bairoch (1991, 5).

technological inventions, compared with twenty-nine on the rest of the
continent. Continental Europe's number would nearly double to forty-
seven in the second half of the century, but Britain could still boast of
thirty-one major inventions during that period.

Britain's technological monopoly was not ordained by God to last forever. Still, it remained a major player and proved quite resilient in the
development of new industries and technologies. British trade in high-
tech products before World War I reflected an enormous export surplus. In electric prime movers and machinery, British exports surpassed
imports by 1.7 times; in total exports of electrical goods, by 3.4 times;
and in chemicals, including medicines, by 1.7 times. Britain exported
nearly three times more machine tools than it imported. The balance
was negative only in typewriters, watches, and automobiles (Foreman-
Peck, 1999, 117). Britain's share of the world's manufactured exports in
1913, at almost 31%, was higher than Germany's at 27%, the United
States' 13%, and France's 12%. Compared with the advanced Western countries, Britain's share of new technology industries remained
very high, significantly higher than the Western average before the war.
(See Table 5.2.)

The oft-mentioned "parasitic" deformation of profiting from foreign
loans and investments is also questionable if one considers that the
employment-to-population ratio in Britain was 44%, which was surpassed
only by a handful of countries. Though it decreased by 10% between 1870
and 1913, the annual number of hours worked per person in Britain still
remained 2,624 hours, the highest in the world – higher than in the United
States and Germany, and equaled only by Switzerland. Britain did not
become parasitic before the war.

Table 5.3   Comparative labor productivity, 1869–70 and 1909–11 (Britain = 100)

	1869–70			1909–11		
	Britain	**Germany**	**USA**	**Britain**	**Germany**	**USA**
Agriculture	100	55.7	86.9	100	67.3	103.2
Industry	100	91.7	153.6	100	127.7	193.2
Services	100	62.8	85.9	100	73.4	107.4
Aggregate	100	59.5	89.8	100	75.5	117.7

Source: Broadberry (2006, 20).

Additional evidence is found in the fact that Britain continued to increase its industrial productivity: output per hour in the country rose by 60% between 1870 and 1913 to $4.4 (in 1990 dollars). This figure was one of the highest in Europe – 54% higher than France's labor productivity, 36% higher than Switzerland's, and 11% higher than Holland's. According to new estimates, German industrial productivity was only 4.7% higher than Britain's in 1907; hence, "manufacturing labor productivity was broadly equal in Britain and Germany" (Broadberry and Burhop, 2008, 932, 934).[18] Only the productivity levels in the United States and Australia proved higher than Britain's. The British also had the highest agricultural and aggregate labor productivity in Europe, though it remained behind the United States. (See Table 5.3.)

Different statistics will lead one to draw different conclusions. New direct estimates of British real income, instead of appraisals regarding long time periods, revise the picture quite significantly. Angus Maddison's (1995) long-term estimates depicted a continual decline of Britain's GDP compared with that of the United States: Britain stood at 128% of the American GDP in 1872, but dropped to 111% in 1891, and then to 95% in 1905. Britain's output per worker was 96% of the United States' in 1872, but only 86% by 1905. Recent direct estimates, however, reveal a more stable relation: the British GDP was 85% of the American in 1872, 82% in 1891, and 82% in 1905. The direct estimate, moreover, suggests a British rebound: 63% of the American GDP in 1872, and 75% by 1905. Britain kept pace with the United States. "In this reading of the evidence, the United Kingdom performed strongly during the Victorian era" (Ward and Devereux, 2003, 840, 842).

Indeed, the British GDP per head of population was only 5% below the American level, and at least 20–30% above that of the West European countries before World War I. The British income level was by far the highest, its ships transported most of the world's trade, and its foreign investments surpassed those of all other leading countries combined (Floud, 1994, 1).[19] Considering all these facts, it would be strange to speak about "failure" and decline, even in relative terms.

Western Europe, however, made tremendous progress and began to catch up with Britain, whose industrial superiority began to diminish; in the modern industrial sectors, Germany definitely surpassed it. Non-residential investment represented less than 7 percent of GDP in Britain, while it exceeded 10 percent in France and the United States, and reached nearly 13 percent in Germany between 1870 and 1913. In 1883, the number of British patents was roughly equal to those of France and Germany combined; in 1913, however, the number of French and German patents was together almost twice as many as the British. Germany and the United States undoubtedly attained superior industrial performance.

In most parameters, however, Britain was surpassed by only a few *non-European* countries between 1870 and 1913. Regarding the per capita real GDP, Britain was second in the world behind Australia in 1870; by 1913, it was fourth behind Australia, the United States, and New Zealand. Considering the Human Development Index,[20] Britain's position declined from second to fourth place as well, behind Australia, New Zealand, and the United States.

Those who reject the "British decline" theory, as Sidney Pollard does, point to the fact that, despite failure in certain areas, British performance "was much better among services and among consumer goods, and . . . the older staples" (Pollard, 1994, 89). For his part, Donald McCloskey has noted that Britain reached economic maturity earlier than any other country (McCloskey, 1972). These views make an important point. Speaking of a so-called relative industrial decline is, I would submit, indeed misleading. Because of its successful early industrialization, Britain entered a higher stage of structural renewal than did all of its rivals. During the decades of industrialization in Western Europe, Britain's economic performance shifted to *services*, a phenomenon that characterized the advanced world only half a century later. This aspect, surprisingly enough, had been neglected in the debate. Between 1860 and 1911, the fastest growing branch of the British economy was banking and insurance, which saw a three- to fivefold higher annual growth than did industry. While growth in labor input was minimal in industry after 1860, mostly about

Table 5.4 Employment share of services
(transport, communication,
distribution, finances, and
other) in total (percent)

Country	1870	1910
Britain	30.4	40.0
Germany	17.9	23.3
USA	22.9	34.3

Source: Broadberry (2006, 42).

0.8–1.2 percent per year, it was 3–5 percent in financial services. Transport, communications, distribution, and professional services also increased their labor forces at faster rates than did industry; indeed, Britain's shipping service was the world leader (Feinstein, 1972, 50, 53). In the second half of the nineteenth century, investment in infrastructure increased from 36 percent to 44 percent, and half the growth of Britain's national income was produced by services (Lee, 1994, 143). Service employment significantly increased in Britain and reached the highest level compared with its most advanced rival countries. (See Table 5.4.)

Contemporary observers, who were raised in an intellectual environment that equated services with pre-industrial backwardness and accepted Adam Smith's distinction between productive industry and unproductive services,[21] probably viewed the shift from industry to services as decadent. Post-World War II economics, however, considered the "service revolution," the structural change that shifted dramatically towards services, as the most modern trend of economic development. Britain indeed started this transformation earlier than any other country. This new and most modern development in Britain put the very relative industrial "decline" in an entirely different context. The relatively shrinking industrial and ever expanding service sectors presaged the twentieth-century Western economic sectoral model.

In the footsteps of Britain

The successful industrialization of continental Western Europe began by implementing the achievements of the British Industrial Revolution. The

creation of modern, mechanized textile and iron industries, and the introduction of the steam engine and the railroads, reflected Britain's immediate impact on Western Europe at the beginning of its transformation. The
southern Low Countries (later Belgium) were the first to follow Britain.
The rich coal and iron resources in the Liège region, the export-oriented
cottage industry that ranked among the world's best, the legions of skilled
workers, and a highly developed water transportation system (on par with
Britain's) all served as an excellent basis for duplicating Britain's Industrial
Revolution. The troubled history of the area, the devastating Eighty Years
War spanning from the late sixteenth to the mid-seventeenth century, and
the successive rule of Spain, Austria, France, and Holland, had, surprisingly enough, some positive consequences. The southern Low Countries
became part of huge empires and were linked to vast colonial markets,
which enabled them to initiate extensive export activities that contributed
to their recovery. The revolutionary French army also abolished outdated
medieval institutions and social barriers. In the long run, all this helped
the region jump on the bandwagon of the British Industrial Revolution
before any other.

Flanders had one of Europe's most flourishing woolen and linen proto-
industries in the early modern period. Already in the eighteenth century,
the woolen proto-industry served as the basis for opening mechanized
finishing factories in Verviers. Although the rural linen industry began
to decline in the mid-nineteenth century, the cotton industry around
Ghent was gradually mechanized in the early years of the century. The
capital city of Flanders had only 55,000 inhabitants at the end of the
eighteenth century. Rising from the city's traditional handicraft industry,
Liévin Bauwens, the scion of several generations of local tanners, emerged
as one of the first modern textile magnates.[22] Three engineering firms produced textile machinery for the more than thirty textile factories by 1815.
When Napoleon banned textile imports from England, the Ghent textile
industry promptly filled the vacuum by rapidly integrating the spinning,
weaving, bleaching, and printing processes (Dhondt, [1955] 1969, 19–27).
Textiles became a dynamic sector of early Belgian industrialization.

A British immigrant named William Cockerill moved to Belgium at the
age of thirty-eight with two of his sons, settled in the Liège region, and
became one of the founding fathers of the Belgian industry. With a Verviers
entrepreneur, Jean-François Simonis, he founded five mechanized wool-
spinning factories in the 1790s. Textiles remained a rapidly growing industry until World War I, with an annual 3 percent growth between 1830 and
1913.[23] Textiles and clothing employed nearly 25 percent of the country's
industrial labor force. The per capita consumption of cotton before the

war, however, was only 6.6 kilograms, compared with Britain's 16 kilos. Antwerp emerged as a center of processing imported colonial goods and grain, as well as shipbuilding and repair.

Textiles, however, was not the leading sector of Belgian industrialization. From the mid-eighteenth century on, the coal and iron industry predominated. Coal output in Borinage increased from a few thousand tons in the mid-eighteenth century to 750,000 tons by 1806. At the end of the Napoleonic wars, 400 coal mines produced a million tons a year, and roughly one-third of the country's machine capacity was concentrated in coal mining. In 1720, production of the Newcomen steam engine, the very first in continental Europe, began in the Liège region. The mines of the Charleroi region adopted the Newcomen engine in 1727. By 1846, Borinage itself produced 2 million tons of coal. Coal output skyrocketed in the later decades, totaling 25.5 million tons and employing 100,000 workers by 1910.

At the same time, the iron industry also rose to prominence, partly as a result of the huge quantities of high quality coal, which was suitable for coking. The traditional Belgian iron industry duplicated the British transformation in the eighteenth century; Belgian manufacturers began using coal and charcoal in place of wood. As early as 1803–4, Belgium built continental Europe's first modern blast furnaces, and by 1831, nine modern blast furnaces, employing British technology, were in operation. Belgium profited from its proximity to Britain. Several British technicians and entrepreneurs settled in the country: Bonehill, Roger, Bridger, Weller, and Thomas from London, Canterbury, and Dublin contributed to the development of Belgium's modern iron industry, with Charleroi as its center. Paul Huart-Chapel was one of the pioneers who introduced modern puddle technology and coke-heating in 1824. His giant iron works, with eight blast furnaces, became the largest iron producer on the continent.

After having started in textiles in 1799, William Cockerill opened an engineering factory in 1807–8 and produced textile machinery, continental Europe's first wool carding and spinning machines. His son John was the first to build steam engines in 1813. He soon delved into coal mining and pig iron processing, using the puddling process, and he built the first modern blast furnaces and the first iron ships and locomotives. Belgium began producing all this machinery for export.

By 1850, with more than 200,000 tons of output, the Belgian iron industry was the most developed in continental Europe. Moreover, iron output nearly trebled by 1870–4. Steel production began near Liège in 1865. Producing 2.2 million tons of iron and 2.3 million tons of steel in 1910–13, Belgium emerged as one of the leading manufacturers in this highly export-oriented industry. Belgian industry preserved the practices of the first Industrial Revolution and did not become a pioneer of the second.

France was also among the very first followers of Britain. "The impulse for revolutionary change," François Crouzet observed, "came from outside, from Britain." The Industrial Revolution was thus "an imported 'transplant' or an imitation" in France (Crouzet, 1996, 37). With a flourishing cottage and putting-out industry in the eighteenth century, France was one of the first countries to begin mechanizing its industry. The centralized state possessed a well-organized industrial spying apparatus to discover and smuggle new methods and machinery from the industrial zones of Britain. It also paid subsidies, salaries, and pensions to British experts and professionals, about two hundred of whom moved to France (Harris, 1998). British technicians and entrepreneurs, who migrated to France in the last years of the *ancien régime*, served as the missionaries of the new technology on the continent.[24]

According to some scholars, French industrialization enjoyed a rapid and vibrant take-off between 1760 and 1790. However, during the quarter-century of war and revolution between 1790 and 1815, the process slowed down considerably. After the end of the Napoleonic wars, France gradually regained its industrial dynamism, led, as in Britain, by the textile industry. Its first hub of textile production, Normandy, was fully mechanized in the early nineteenth century. In the mid-century, Alsace would replace Normandy as the leading textile center, with a stock of spindles increasing from 70,000 to 500,000 between 1818 and 1828. No fewer than 50,000 spindles were in operation in some of its largest factories. A third textile center would later emerge in the north around Lille and Roubaix. Indeed, the textile industry was heavily concentrated in the north in the mid-1860s: 80% of Waterloo's active industrial population worked in textiles, 65% of Roubaix's, and 50% of Marcq's. By 1845, France had as many spindles as all other continental countries combined. Nevertheless, the cotton industry never played as central a role in France as it did in Britain. In 1845–54, France consumed only 22% of the cotton, and operated only 21% of the spindles, that Britain did; on a per capita basis, its consumption was one-third that of Britain. French exports of cotton products totaled only 7% of Britain's.

Britain enjoyed a huge advantage in basic industries that produced semi-finished goods like cotton yarn and pig iron. Unable to compete in these areas, France began specializing in labor-intensive consumer goods and luxury silk products. The country retained and even strengthened its leading role in the silk industry, producing 20% of Europe's silk output.

Lyon remained the silk-production center until the last third of the century, although it was still dominated by small-scale manufacturing and handicrafts. Mechanized industry, however, continued to develop, with 20% of the city's population operating 110,000 hand looms and 60,000 mechanized looms in the 1860s. At that time only 12% of French exports were cotton goods, and 25% were silk. Moreover, unlike in Britain, the woolen industry did not decline, but was combined with luxury designer clothing. Until 1840, specialized textiles and clothing remained the leading industrial sector in France, producing 30% of total industrial output, and surpassing the production value of the iron industry by five times.

After the Napoleonic wars, several thousand skilled workers moved from Britain to France. The immigration of entrepreneurs also continued.[25] Aaron Manby and Daniel Wilson established a large iron and engineering firm near Paris in 1822 and took over Le Creusot in 1826. The skilled British immigrant workers served mainly as foremen and instructors of French workers. Their role was decisive.

France was one of the few countries on the continent that had a strong scientific base, actually stronger than that of eighteenth-century Britain. The French contribution to scientific and practical innovations was an important factor in the first Industrial Revolution. Nicolas Leblanc was one of the pioneers of the chemical industry, producing soda in 1791. French innovators and engineers, graduates of the École Polytechnique, École Centrale des Arts et Manufactures, and the Écoles des Arts et Métiers, made France self-sufficient in the production of various kinds of machinery by the middle of the nineteenth century. In their Chaillot iron works, Constantin and Auguste Périer began operating one of the continent's first Watt steam engines in 1781.[26] All these achievements at around the turn of the century, however, represented only the very first steps of industrialization, but they established the foundation of an industrial economy. A new wave of industrial development gained momentum from the 1820s on, and achieved a significant breakthrough beginning in the 1850s.

Steam engines proliferated: 6,800 were in operation in France by 1850, more than in any other country on the continent. By the 1860s, French industry could claim a machine capacity of 8,950 horsepower per annum. However, the conversion to coal and steam engines was not completed until the end of the 1860s, and water power continued to supply twice as much energy as the steam engine until that time. The development of the mechanized cotton industry rapidly gained momentum. The number of spindles increased by 80 percent and output doubled between 1830 and

1860. More importantly, the silk industry increased its production even faster, and the French iron industry soon adopted British technology. Le Creusot's blast furnace was the first in the country to use coke in 1782. The first foundry at Saint-Chamond employing British technology for refining cast iron began operations in 1820. Pétin and Gaudet introduced the steam hammer in 1841. Over the next few years, 117 blast furnaces adopted Scottish 'hot blast' technology, using steam engines as blowers. In the iron industry, the use of steam power replaced water power between 1830 and 1860. French pig iron production was significant: the country produced twice as much as Belgium, but only a quarter of Britain's output. Until 1860, the French iron industry combined old and new technology. As late as that year, twice as many iron works used charcoal as used coke, and traditional charcoal-heated furnaces produced more than one-third of the iron. The French iron industry was revitalized from the mid-nineteenth century on. Between 1851 and 1865, it constructed 562 new blast furnaces, and its capacity increased nearly tenfold.

The shortage of coal was one of the weaknesses of early French industrialization. The country did not have abundant coal reserves, and the quality of its coal was inferior and not suitable for coking. Extraction was also more difficult and expensive. In the 1820s, only one-fifth of the coal consumed in the country was produced domestically.[27] In 1913, France produced only 6.4 percent of Europe's coal output, while Britain and Germany together supplied nearly three-quarters. Domestic production did not surpass 40 percent of the country's consumption during the 1850s and 1860s. Altogether, however, industrial production increased fivefold between 1781–9 and 1865–74. Until the 1870s, France, *mutatis mutandis*, followed the British pattern of industrialization, with textiles, coal, and iron playing the leading roles. All in all, France made impressive economic progress.

France's agricultural population continued to rise until 1820, when it totaled 57% of the country's population, but it then declined to 48% by 1856–72. On the other hand, the percentages of the labor force in industry, transport, and commerce, which had virtually stagnated between the turn of the eighteenth and the turn of the nineteenth century, increased significantly from 29% to 42% between 1790–1820 and 1856–72.[28] Nonetheless, France remained far behind Britain and did not complete industrialization. Less than one-third of its population lived in urban settlements in 1870, and only 29% of its male labor force worked in industry, which produced 36% of the country's income, hardly more than agriculture (34%). France was the second industrial power in the world, but it was not fully industrialized.

Table 5.5   Coal output in Western Europe, 1820s–1910s, in million metric tons

Years	Germany	Belgium	Britain	France	Austria	Total	% of 1825–9 total)
1825–9	1.6	2.3	22.3	1.5	0.2	27.9	100
1870–4	41.4	14.7	123.2	15.4	9.2	203.9	728
1910–13	247.5	24.8	275.4	39.9	41.1	628.7	2,253

Source: Mitchell (1973, 770).

Table 5.6   Pig iron output in Western Europe, 1820s–1910s, in thousand tons

Years	Germany	Belgium	Britain	France	Austria	Total	% of 1825–9 total
1825–9	90	–	669	212	73	1,044	100
1870–4	1,579	594	6,480	1,211	305	10,515[a]	1,007
1910–13	14,836	2,171	9,792	4,664	1,655	34,151[a]	3,271

Source: Mitchell (1973, 773).
Note: [a] With Sweden and north Italy.

A new stage of French industrialization that followed was connected to the second Industrial Revolution (discussed later in this chapter).

To a lesser extent, the first steps of duplicating the British pattern were made in several other parts of Western Europe. (See Tables 5.5–5.8.) This region exhibited rather mixed types of industrialization. An alternative approach is apparent in Switzerland, Denmark, and Austria-Bohemia, where specialized agriculture-based food processing at least temporarily played an important supplementary role, though some scattered elements of British industrialization also appeared. The first British spinning machine began to operate, initially with water power, in Josef Leitenberger's factory in the Czech lands in 1801. The Briton John Thornton established a modern mechanized textile firm in Pottendorf, with more than 18,000 spindles, in 1805.[29] By 1840, when France and Germany attained a total steam engine capacity (including locomotives and

Table 5.7 Raw cotton consumption in Western Europe, 1825–34 to 1905–13, in thousand metric tons

Years	Austria	France	Germany	Italy	Britain	Total	% of 1825–34 total
1825–34	6.8	33.5	3.9	–	105.6	149.8	100
1875–84	67.1	99.5	134.3	30.7	475.8	807.4	539
1905–13	191.4	231.1	435.4	186.0	868.8	1,912.7	1,277

Source: Mitchell (1973, 780).

Table 5.8 Indicators of the development of the iron and textile industries

Countries	Iron production per capita (kg)			Cotton consumption per capita (kg)		
	1830	1860	1910	1830	1860	1910
Western world	6.0	19.9	100.4	0.7	2.5	6.3
European average	6.3	22.0	79.5	0.7	2.5	5.4
Britain	29.0	131.7	212.1	4.7	15.1	19.0
Austria[a]	3.1	8.9	40.6	0.2	1.2	3.8
Belgium	24.2	69.4	242.9	0.7	2.9	9.2
France	6.9	25.7	103.3	0.9	2.5	6.0
Germany	4.0	15.0	198.7	0.1	1.5	6.8
Italy[b]	0.7	1.1	7.9	0.1	0.4	5.5
Netherlands	–	–	–	0.6	0.8	4.6
Switzerland	2.9	5.6	5.1	1.9	5.6	6.3

Source: Bairoch (1991, 8).
Notes:
[a] Austria-Hungary (Hungary had a minimal share in iron, and almost nothing in cotton).
[b] Italy total: in iron the south had virtually no share, in cotton an extremely limited one.

steamships) of 90,000 and 40,000 horsepower respectively, the Habsburg Empire (according to the highest estimates) could claim only 20,000.

In many ways, Switzerland was also a follower of the British pattern. Based on its strong cottage industry tradition, the Swiss textile industry developed early and rose to be one of the continent's leading textile centers.

In 1801, the first mechanized spinning mill began operation in St. Gallen.[30] The Swiss introduced virtually every innovation in the textile sector during the first half of the nineteenth century, and 72 percent of their exports were textile products by 1840. In this respect, Switzerland was emulating the British model. Indeed, textiles remained the country's leading sector until the end of the century, though it was soon joined by the clothing industry, which gradually rose to equal strength and merged with the textile sector. In 1800, the proportion of textiles and clothing was 7:1; by 1850, it was 3:1; and by 1910, 1:1. Still, textiles remained the leading export sector: in 1840, 72% of textile production was exported; by 1887, 58%; and by 1912–13, 45%.

In addition, the Swiss engineering industry continued to resemble the British model. Production of textile machinery and steam engines continued to predominate until the 1890s. The country's long-standing watch-making proto-industry enabled Switzerland to dominate the world's watch market. It produced one million watches in 1850, mostly in the Geneva and Jura regions. The industry's traditional cottage character proved to be stunningly permanent. As late as 1880, the country's watch industry employed 120,000 cottage-industry workers. However, 1880 was also the first year that the number of modern factory workers exceeded cottage employees (130,000). The watch-making industry was highly export-oriented and sold more than 90 percent of its output abroad – providing, along with textiles, 60 percent of Swiss exports in the mid-nineteenth century (Fritzsche, 1991, 136, 139).

Beginning in the last decades of the century, Austria-Bohemia turned to the British road more consistently when its textile, iron, and steel industries became its leading sectors. Switzerland, on the other hand, joined other Western European countries to lead the second Industrial Revolution.

Although the German states remained predominantly agricultural during the first half of the nineteenth century, and though 60–70 percent of its active population continued to work in agriculture in 1840, they began a gradual process of industrialization. In many ways, the process was imitative, following the British pattern. The development of a mechanized textile industry was one of their main achievements. Saxony had a strong tradition of putting-out textiles, but it rapidly adopted the jenny in the early years of the nineteenth century.[31] Cotton, however, was not the largest branch of the textile industry; until 1860 it represented only 30 percent of total output while the traditional linen industry produced more than 20 percent. The woolen industry also remained strong. Textiles played only a secondary role in Germany during the first phase of industrialization, unlike in Britain and some other western regions.

Figure 5.1
Increase in coal
output in Western
Europe, 1825/9–
1910/13 (tons)
(Mitchell, 1973)

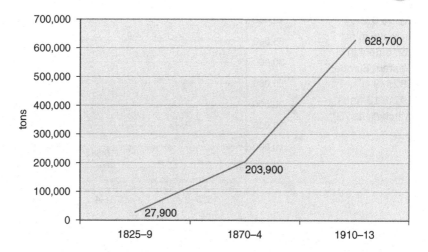

Like England and Belgium, but unlike France and Switzerland, Germany's plentiful supply of high-quality coal and iron elevated its coal and iron industries to become leading branches of its economy at the beginning of industrialization. The Ruhr region had certain industrial traditions since medieval times. By 1850, 12,000 miners produced 1.5 million tons of coal. The mining of coking coal and steel casting in the Bochum Basin assured that it would gradually become a powerful industrial region. Indeed, the area emerged as Europe's most modern industrial center after the Napoleonic wars.[32] (See Figure 5.1.)

The first blast furnace in Upper Silesia signaled the beginning of the iron industry in 1753. Prussia brought in new British technology as early as 1802, when the state-owned Kungshütte and then Gleiwitz mines introduced coke-heating and the steam engine. With the contribution of British experts, the continent's largest and most modern iron industry was born.[33]

In this first period, in conjunction with the Prussian military and the armaments industry, and as required by agriculture and textiles, the Germans built a relatively strong engineering industry on the basis of iron and coal, which employed nearly 9 percent of their industrial labor force in the 1850s.

The unification of the Prussian markets in 1818, and of all the German markets by the Zollverein in 1834, was an important factor in the development of the iron, coal, and engineering industries around the mid-nineteenth century. The Prussian state launched a well-organized industrialization drive, which was based on the railroads. The German railroads more than tripled in size between 1850 and 1870, and they became the prime mover of industrialization. In that period, coal output

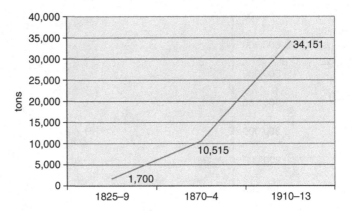

increased fivefold to 26.4 million tons and the capacity of mining machinery topped more than 200,000 horsepower. German iron production, however, approximated only 80 percent of the French and hardly a fifth of the British. (See Figure 5.2.) In any case, industrialization continuously progressed before German unification.

From the 1870s on, Germany embarked on its own unique path to industrialization. This was based on what were Europe's most advanced technological research facilities and educational system, which greatly contributed to the second Industrial Revolution. From this point on, Germany enjoyed Europe's greatest industrial prosperity.

Until the 1870s, only initial, tentative steps characterized the industrial development of north Italy and the western Austrian-Czech provinces of the Habsburg Empire. North Italy's long urban tradition and city-states, along with its advanced agriculture, good waterways and roads, made it one of the most advanced regions in the Habsburg Empire: annual per capita income in Lombardy increased from $346 to $597 (in 1990 Geary Khamis dollars) between 1836 and 1857, above the Austrian norm. But industrialization did not really begin there except in silk production. The empire's policy of increasing import tariffs by one-third and reducing export duties by two-thirds encouraged silk manufacturing in the 1820s. Silk provided half of the exports in the early decades of the century, and jumped to 90 percent in the 1840s–1850s (Pichler, 2001, 36–7, 40–4, 54). According to the estimates of Gianni Toniolo, Vera Zamagni, and Nicolas Crafts, per capita income in Lombardy, Piedmont, and Liguria was only half that of Britain, but only 10–15 percent lower than that of France and of Germany in 1870.[34]

In 1870, per capita income in the Austrian-Czech provinces was roughly the same as in north Italy. The pattern of industrial development that took place during the last third of the century, however, was more traditionally based on Britain's. The mechanization and modernization of Austrian-Czech industry primarily in the 1880s opened a new chapter of rapid industrial development of the easternmost part of Western Europe. The textile, iron, steel, and engineering industries were now predominating.[35]

Between 1880 and 1913, Austrian-Bohemian textile production more than doubled (230%), food processing increased by more than two and a half times (269%), metal making by more than nine times (932%), and machine building by nearly ten times (1,981%). Nevertheless, Austria-Bohemia remained behind its western counterparts. Crude iron production per head totaled only one-quarter of the German total and 30% of the British. Coal and iron consumption per head was not even a third of the German level. The most substantial industrial production in the western provinces of the empire was in the Czech lands, which had 60% of its textile spindles, 90% of it sugar production, and 57% of its iron output. While only a third of the labor force was engaged in machine building, the factories in the Czech lands employed more than 52% of the industry's workforce in the early twentieth century.

Industrialization thus followed the British paradigm in several countries. But imitating the British Industrial Revolution went only so far. The great boom of continental industrialization began during the second half of the nineteenth century, in several cases starting in the 1860s–1870s, and they followed separate, independent roads. One of the alternative models was the rise of export-oriented food processing.

Specialized agriculture combined with food processing

The Netherlands was one of the pioneers of the agricultural revolution and had developed a highly specialized agriculture during the early modern period. New agrarian prosperity, however, was seen in the first half of the nineteenth century, thanks to Britain's revised customs policy and the introduction of a free trade system. Vast markets were opened to Dutch agricultural exports. Seizing the opportunity, Dutch farmers specialized their production further, particularly with intensive animal husbandry. Cattle stock increased by 50 percent, and pig stock by 448 percent. Cattle exports jumped from 1,000 to 143,000 animals between 1870 and 1913 and sheep exports from 42,000 to 261,000 over a twenty-year period in the mid-nineteenth century. Exports of improved types of animals doubled again between 1890 and 1914.

Based on a highly developed and specialized agriculture, food processing became the starting point of Dutch industrialization. Butter and cheese production and exports grew extremely rapidly. In a single decade in the 1830s, butter and cheese exports increased by two and three times respectively. Butter output grew by nearly eight times between 1846 and 1914. Around the turn of the century, sixty-three factories produced these new products. The country exported 900,000 tons of cheese, of which 70 percent was produced in modern factories, and the Netherlands became the world's largest cheese exporter before World War I. Half of its butter and cheese exports were sold to British markets, and most of the rest to German markets.

Milk processing went far beyond modernizing traditional butter and cheese production, expanding to new areas such as canned condensed milk and milk powder. At this point, the importance of inventions deserves special attention. The modern food processing industry was also based on a number of innovations that went back to the turn of the century. French inventors played the leading role at the beginning. Nicolas Appert won Napoleon's prize for food preserving in 1810.[36] The French scientist Louis Pasteur opened a new chapter in 1862 by demonstrating how pasteurization through the application of heat could protect wine, beer, and milk from destructive pathogenic microorganisms in food. The mass production and transportation of various food products, especially milk, wine, and beer, now became possible.[37]

The Dutch food processing industry pioneered potato processing and produced potato flour, glucose, and potato spirits. Another new and promising discovery was the production of margarine from various vegetable oils. This established a whole new industrial branch, with twenty-eight factories producing margarine before World War I. Most of the new processing sectors targeted the British market.

Traditional local beer brewing was replaced by the importation of the new lager beer procedure, the "Bavarian beer," during the 1860s. Several Dutch entrepreneurs established modern breweries based on German technology in the 1870s. In 1864, the 22-year-old Gerard Adrian Heineken bought an old brewery in Amsterdam. By 1869, he had changed the old "workingman's" ale to "gentleman's" lager beer and increased output by five times between 1880 and 1914. Heineken beer won the gold medal at the Paris Exhibition in 1889 and began to be exported on the world market.

The Dutch food processing industry continued to process colonial goods, imported from the Dutch colonies. Sugar cane imports from Java increased by about seven times to 1.5 million tons between 1870 and the 1910s. Half of Amsterdam's industrial output was produced by sugar refineries. From the 1870s on, however, the Dutch introduced sugar beets, which increased production from 732,000 tons to 1.9 million tons between 1870 and 1913. Twenty-seven factories produced chocolate from imported cacao beans in the early nineteenth century, and further expanded when the Van Houtten factory invented cacao powder. From imported tobacco, the celebrated Dutch cigar industry also produced for export. The Dutch food processing industry employed 11 percent of the industrial workforce in the mid-nineteenth century, and 16 percent by 1910. During the second half of the century, the cooperative movement also worked in food processing.[38]

During the half-century before World War I, the Netherlands became fully industrialized. It did not follow the British pattern. Agriculture and food processing remained strong, even dominant, until the end of the period. During the last decades of the century, however, an additional import substituting process emerged, the production of industrial consumer goods for the domestic market to replace imports.

In 1860, agriculture still employed 38 percent of the Netherlands' labor force, compared with 29 percent in industry. The latter consisted mostly of employment in small-scale industry. Around the turn of the century, however, the country pushed on with industrialization to accommodate rising demand from the population. Instead of squandering its export-generated income on purchasing consumer goods from Britain, it invested that money into its textile industry, which produced for the domestic market alone. By 1910, Holland substituted textile imports with its own domestic production.[39]

The Netherlands did not have the necessary natural resources, coal and iron, which had been decisive factors in industrialization until the last decades of the century. It also lacked the natural environment for hydroelectric power generation. The only option was exploiting its human resources. The country began developing the most modern sectors and jumped on the bandwagon of the second Industrial Revolution. In 1891, two engineers established a small bulb factory, the Philips Company, in Eindhoven. Within twenty years, the factory employed 2,500 workers, produced 6.4 million bulbs, and emerged as the third biggest electric factory in Europe. Dutch experts had recognized the importance of oil early on and drilled exploratory wells in Sumatra in 1884. Striking oil, they established the Royal Dutch Company which began deliveries to Europe in the early 1890s. The Royal Dutch and the British Shell companies grew to become giant oil conglomerates which discovered reserves in the Far East, Russia, and Romania and controlled most of the world's oil fields. The Dutch and British companies merged and became Europe's largest oil company with a 70 percent share in European oil imports. That tiny but capital-rich country, Holland, established multinational companies in the most modern sectors of the newly emerging economy.

From the 1880s on, Dutch shipbuilding was also revitalized, with a production capacity of 4,000 tons per annum, which increased to 71,000 tons by 1913. In 1900, the industry produced one-quarter of the country's GDP, and Dutch industry as a whole provided for 70 percent of the domestic consumption of clothing, textiles, construction materials, and other branches.

Although Denmark was the only other country that followed the Dutch model of industrialization (as discussed in Chapter 6), several European countries exhibited elements of this model at certain points in their industrialization. Nineteenth-century Switzerland was one of them. Feudalism had long disappeared in its mountainous cantons, and its free peasants were market-oriented early on. Comprising 70 percent of the country's landed area, its mountainous regions, with their lush fields, were especially suited for animal husbandry and the milk economy. Local conditions genuinely excluded the possibility of a single-crop economy, and the majority of farms combined animal husbandry with grain cultivation. The latter, however, was soon eliminated.

Switzerland joined the Netherlands and Britain in introducing modern crop-rotation systems. The Ökonomische Gesellschaft (Economic Society) in Berne, established in 1758, assisted the production of fodder, clover, sainfoin, and lucerne. Potatoes, root vegetables, and sugar beets also became part of the rotation system.[40] Until the 1850s–1880s, agriculture and animal husbandry remained the leading sectors of the Swiss economy, producing roughly 40 percent of the GDP, on a par with industry. But agriculture gradually lost its position around the turn of the century, and it produced no more than a quarter of the GDP by 1910. Still, agricultural ventures were combined with food processing, and together they became important factors in industrialization. One of Switzerland's traditional leading branches was the milk and cheese industry, which had existed for several centuries. While grain prices declined by 30 percent in the first quarter of the century, the price of animal products increased by 40 percent and milk prices doubled – as did Swiss milk production. Land allotted for crops consequently decreased to one-third of the country's total between 1850 and 1910. Specialization also proliferated. In 1802 and 1815, the Talkäserei Hofwil and Kiesen factories were the first Swiss endeavors in modern food processing. By the end of the century, 2,600 cheese factories operated in the country.

Still, milk processing was much more developed than butter and cheese production. In 1866, proprietors founded in Zug the first Anglo-Swiss condensed milk factory, which merged with Nestlé around the turn of the century to become the largest food processing company in the country. In 1888, there were thirteen milk processing factories unconnected to the butter and cheese sector; by 1901, there were twenty-two.

The Swiss food industry was the most innovative in the world. Highly trained chemists and pharmacists created a number of new branches of food processing. Several small companies produced chocolate, first as a medical experiment in 1803; then, Philippe Suchard in Neuchâtel opened the first modern chocolate factory in 1826. The industry advanced with a series of inventions by chocolatiers: Charles-Amédée Kohler invented and produced hazelnut chocolate in his factory in 1828, and François-Louis Cailler introduced the chocolate bar in 1849. Theodor Tobler opened a factory in Berne in 1869 and produced the famous "Toblerone." The export-oriented chocolate industry, however, expanded from the 1870s on, when the pharmacist Rudolph Lindt invented soft fondant chocolate, and Daniel Peter, a third-generation chocolatier of the Sprüngli family, invented milk chocolate. The Lindt and Sprüngli factories merged in 1899 and became one of the leaders of the industry. By 1901, twenty-two factories produced and exported Swiss chocolate, increasing exports eightfold.

One of the pioneers of the industry was Henri Nestlé.[41] After a series of successful experiments in his Vevey factory, Nestlé began producing a children's formula by powdering milk and adding wheat flour and sugar. Production of the formula commenced in 1868, and it became an instant success. During the first seven years, Nestlé sold more than one million tins in eighteen different countries.

Moreover, new branches of food production were introduced in Switzerland, such as the "Bircher-muesli" cereal, produced by Maximilian O. Bircher-Benner in 1900, and Ovomaltine, manufactured by Albert Wander in 1904. Swiss entrepreneurs also invented *fast food*: Julius Maggi produced in his Kemptthal factory the first instant soup in 1886, followed by various kinds of soups in cubes or bags, and even beef cubes in 1908. The Knorr factory in Thayingen introduced the bouillon cube and various instant spices in 1907. Having comprised only 2 percent of Swiss exports in the mid-nineteenth century, modern food processing increased its share to 15 percent and emerged as the country's third most important export sector before the war (Pfiffner, 1991, 128–30).

Export-oriented food processing represented the real beginning of industrialization in Austria-Bohemia. The early textile proto-industry, which had begun developing in the late eighteenth century, and the traditional manorial iron and glass industries declined because of competition from mechanized industries in the West. Taking their place was

Table 5.9 Sugar beet production in Western Europe, 1865–74 to 1905–14, in million quintals

Years	Austria	France	Germany	Italy	Total	% of total
1865–74	21.9	77.4	25.2	–	124.5	100
1885–94	45.4	63.0	95.1	0.07	203.6	164
1905–14	64.3	78.8	160.9	14.6	318.6	256

Source: Mitchell (1973, 256).

mechanized big industry when modern industrialization took off between 1860 and 1880, mostly driven by the rise of the sugar and beer industries. Food processing in the Netherlands, Denmark, and Switzerland was based on highly specialized agriculture, the marked decline or complete cessation of grain production and its replacement by imports, and the development of intensive animal husbandry. The Habsburg Empire, however, remained a self-sufficient economic unit. The division of labor was not an international or inter-European process, but a development within the empire. From the eighteenth century on, Austria-Bohemia became the industrial core of the entire empire, while Hungary and some other eastern and southern provinces became the breadbaskets.[42] Based on this traditional division of labor, Austria turned to animal husbandry,[43] and Bohemia-Moravia to sugar beet and barley production, both of which nearly trebled to more than 64 million quintals between the 1870s and World War I. Specialized agriculture in the western provinces served as the base for food processing.

Sugar-beet refining was a nineteenth-century innovation[44] that flourished during the Napoleonic wars but collapsed when cane sugar imports resumed after the lifting of the continental blockade. But as French and German technology began expanding in the 1830s and 1840s, the sugar-beet industry recovered. The first sugar factory began production in the Czech lands in Dobrovicé in 1830. In 1837, the Belgian Florentin Robert moved to the Czech lands and established the first modern, mechanized sugar factory in Zidlochovice. By the early 1860s, 130 sugar refineries operated in Austria-Bohemia and produced 80,000 tons of raw sugar. Austrian entrepreneurs opened more than a dozen sugar factories even in Hungary. (See Table 5.9.)

The booming sugar industry initiated new inventions of international importance: the French Mathieu de Dombasle developed a new and more efficient diffusion technology that replaced mills and presses and transformed the industry. Julius Robert, son of the pioneer Belgian-Czech industrialist Florentin, was the first to employ it (Baxa and Bruhns, 1967). In a single decade, a hundred large sugar factories were established in the Czech lands, and their output exploded from 80,000 tons in 1848 to 1.8 million tons by 1913 – 60 percent of which was exported. The sugar industry remained the leading export sector of Bohemia-Moravia, where 82 percent of the empire's sugar industry was located until the war. The empire became the world's third largest sugar producer.

Next to the sugar industry, modern brewing[45] became the second leading industrial branch of Austria-Bohemia. Gabriel Sedlmayer from Munich and Anton Dreher from Vienna introduced the lager method in the 1830s. The old Klein-Schwechat beerhouse near Vienna, which had operated since the early seventeenth century, now became one of the first hubs of modern lager beer production. Within a decade, the Bavarian brewer Josef Groll began production of the golden Pilsner beer in the Bohemian Plzen, using locally grown barley and hops and the soft water of the Radbuza River. The beer was stored ("lagered") for three weeks in cool caves cut in sandstone rocks. The production of the world's most popular and widespread lager beer began in 1842. Budweis became a second center of the rising Czech beer industry. In Lower Austria and Bohemia, some one thousand large modern breweries produced 20 million hectoliters of beer by 1913. Beer exports, though only 10 percent of the value of sugar exports, were nonetheless important for Austrian-Bohemian industrialization. Food processing produced 11 percent of industrial production in 1865, but its output increased threefold by 1880. It employed a third of the industrial labor force and a quarter of the horsepower capacity of mechanized industry, and it produced 35 percent of Austria-Bohemia's industrial output.

For the Netherlands and Denmark, the modern food economy, combined with processing, was the sole road for modernization. Switzerland and the Austrian-Czech provinces of Austria-Hungary began industrialization with this model, but turned to other industries at a later stage of industrialization and developed new industrial export sectors. Switzerland embraced the achievements of the second Industrial Revolution and developed modern chemical, engineering, and electric industries. Austria-Bohemia returned to the British model after 1880 and developed its textile, iron-steel, and engineering industries.

The second Industrial Revolution

Though it started somewhat earlier, the successful industrialization of continental Western Europe really took off when a new wave of technological development commenced from the 1860s on. What happened between the 1860s and World War I, what has been dubbed the second Industrial Revolution, was probably "history's most remarkable discontinuity," much more so than the first Industrial Revolution a century before. Vaclav Smil speaks of the birth of a new civilization, brought about by four types of fundamental advances:

1. "Formation, diffusion, and standardization of electric systems;"
2. "Invention and adoption of internal combustion engines;"
3. "Introducing new, high performance materials and new chemical syntheses;"
4. "Birth of a new information age." (Smil, 2005, 29)

Myriad innovations, mostly from several continental European countries, came out in clusters. Signaling a transition from the first to the second Industrial Revolution, a number of important inventions established the modern steel industry. Steel had been in the picture before,[46] but its production from iron was a long and extremely expensive process that was carried out on a small scale by artisans using traditional pre-revolutionary methods. Consequently, it was rarely produced. Instead of refining pig iron with heat at its periphery, as was traditionally done, Henry Bessemer introduced a new method: blowing compressed air to the bottom of the furnace through the molten metal.[47] This removed carbon and other impurities from the molten pig iron and effected the decarburization of 3–5 tons of iron in 10–20 minutes, in stark contrast to the previous procedure's 24 hours. The cost of production plummeted and steel was made available in huge quantities. Steel was a higher-quality version of iron since its lower carbon content made it more pliable and much less breakable than the more rigid iron. The Bessemer method, however, required non-phosphoric hematite iron ore.

At the same time, the pathbreaking Siemens–Martin procedure for steel production was the product of two inventions from France and Germany. The Siemens brothers, Frederick and Wilhelm (William), built a new regenerative furnace in the 1850s that used waste gases of oxidation and was able to function with low-quality coal, saving fuel but generating higher temperatures. But the Siemens furnace did not become common until two French brothers, Emile and Pierre Martin, introduced the use of scrap iron for decarburization in 1865. The Siemens–Martin procedure complemented the Bessemer process and became the standard technology from the 1870s on.

Box 5.1 The architect of the industrial age: Gustave Eiffel

With its strong historicism, Romanticism, the elemental cultural movement at the dawn of the nineteenth century, embraced "neo" styles in architecture. The reinvention of neo-classicism, neo-gothicism, neo-renaissance, and eclecticism (a mixture of several historical styles) prevailed in a flourishing urban architecture, in newly erected public buildings, museums, opera houses, churches, and government centers. The turn to the past, however, was soon counterbalanced by the force of the present, the Industrial Revolution.

The new technologies produced by the economic transformation offered bold new opportunities for architecture. Behind the innovations were the modern iron and steel industries, which created new materials that were used in new, hitherto undreamed-of structures. Steel became the principal material in the mid-1870s. Masonry and brick buildings were suddenly relegated to the past; engineers replaced master builders, carpenters, and traditional architects. Iron beams and pillars, the steel skeletons of buildings, were quickly followed by reinforced concrete structures and steel-and-concrete frames. The new architecture was the product of the Industrial Revolution, and it further fostered the economic transformation. Iron and steel beams first appeared in factory buildings and on railroad bridges.

The symbolic embodiment of this architectural revolution was the Eiffel Tower. The young Gustave Eiffel was rejected by the renowned Ecole Polytechnique, and instead attended and graduated from the Ecole Centrale des Arts et Manufactures in 1855. The new materials were already in use by a few pioneer architects at that time. An early pathbreaker was Henri Labrouste, whose cast-iron Bibliothèque St.-Geneviève was among the first applications of the new technology. Standing on sixteen slender cast-iron columns and semi-circular cast-iron arches behind a neo-classical façade, the building became an instant sensation in 1850. Labrouste created another masterpiece four years later with his Bibliothèque Nationale, a reading-room featuring nine iron domes and encircled with windows and iron shelves.

Iron and steel architecture soon prevailed in bridge building. In 1850, the 500-meter Britannia Bridge across the Menai Straits in Wales, designed by Robert Stephenson, was at the time the longest iron-chain suspension bridge. From then on, hundreds of iron bridges were built for the rapidly expanding railroads. As with the railway, the iron bridge was a product of the Industrial Revolution. And this was the field that Gustave Eiffel soon entered, working as a young project manager at a railway bridge construction company. He made his name as a "bridge man" with the Saint-Jean Bridge in Bordeaux in 1859, the Rouzat Viaduct in 1869, and particularly with his spectacular design for the 165 meter Garabit Viaduct with its 122 meter high arch, built without scaffolding over the River Thuyère in 1883.

It is small wonder that his blueprint was selected out of seven hundred applications to build the symbol of the Paris Universal Exhibition in 1889. The 320 meter tall structure, the tallest building in the world during the entire nineteenth century – only overtaken forty years later by the Empire State Building – was an amazing novelty. The tower was built from 12,000 pre-formed steel pieces, using 7 million rivets. Its enormous square base, 125 meters on each side, could weather the strongest storm. Along with another innovation, the elevator, the Eiffel Tower heralded the future, the cities of skyscrapers.

The tower was planned as a temporary structure for the exhibition, and most Parisians did not even like it. Contemporary legend has it that the writer Guy de Maupassant ate dinner every evening on the restaurant level of the tower, the only place, he quipped, where he could not see the tower itself. The "Colossus of Iron" survived, however, and became the beloved symbol of Paris and France.

Eiffel's name remained connected with the revolutionary transformation of the nineteenth century. He built the steel structure of Le Bon Marché, the pioneering Paris department store and icon of the new consumer culture. He designed railroad stations the world over, including the Santiago de Chile and the Budapest West-Railway Station.

The new structures and materials were most successfully employed by the Chicago School of Architecture. The pathbreaking Rookery (1879), Tacoma (1886), and Schiller buildings (the early 1890s) were harbingers of the new urban landscape.

Based on Ragon (1988) and Blanc *et al.* (1993).

The revolutionary transformation of the iron and steel industries was accomplished at the end of the same decade. Two Englishmen, Sidney G. Thomas[48] and his cousin Sidney Gilchrist, solved the problem of how to use phosphorous iron ore that had previously not been suitable for steel making. By adding limestone into the molten iron, they made phosphorous ore suitable for use. The three inventions that established the modern steel industry lowered the cost of crude steel by 80–90 percent between the mid-1860s and the 1890s.[49]

In this same period, a number of inventions transformed several heretofore untouched branches of industry and created whole new industries. These inventions and innovations were developed in scientific laboratories and were the products of meticulous research and experimentation. All of the new industries were based in science.[50] An army of scientists at universities and industrial laboratories continuously engaged in pathbreaking research. Invention and innovation themselves became industrialized. The age of congenial amateurs working at their kitchen tables was over.

A chemical revolution was launched, based on the chemical know-how and theoretical research of the late eighteenth century, among others by Lavoisier, Scheele, and Priestley. France's Augustin Jean Fresnel discovered a new ammonia-soda technique in 1811; unaware of this breakthrough, Belgium's Ernest Solvay reinvented the process and established factories in Charleroi in 1861 and Nancy, France in 1874.

A number of landmark discoveries in the 1820s paved the way for the modern chemical industry. Michael Faraday's discovery of benzene and liquefying gases such as chlorine, and Friedrich Wöhler's experiments converting ammonium cyanide into synthesized urea (the first organic compound), were the first steps. During the 1850s and 1860s, artificial dyestuffs were discovered. Although the Germans would ultimately dominate the field, its development was due to contributions from throughout Western Europe. It was British and French inventions that led to its emergence. William Perkins accidentally invented aniline purple in 1856, and Emanuel Verguin aniline red. A new era in the chemical industry had begun, and its theoretical roots ran deep. France's all-round genius, Louis Pasteur, discovered, among various other things, the existence of mirror-image molecules in carbon compounds. This drew the attention of legions of chemists, especially in the laboratory of Justus Liebig at the University of Giessen.[51] Analyzing oil isolated from coal tar, Liebig discovered the benzene in which one hydrogen atom was replaced by an amino. It was called aniline, and it reacted with nitric acid to form different colors of dyes. Friedrich August Kekulé[52] described the model of carbon in 1857–8, proving that carbon has the capacity to link up in chains of any length. Kekulé's ring theory for the structure of benzene contributed to the establishment of Germany's world-renowned chemical industry (Datta, 2005; Schiemenz, 1993). A long line of inventions led to the electrolytic methods of preparing chlorine and caustics gained ground in the 1890s.

Applied chemistry transformed old industrial branches and created new ones. One of the biggest new success stories in the chemical industry was the mass production of pharmaceuticals, replacing the meager creation of medicines by individual physicians and pharmacists. The isolation from plants and purification of medicinal compounds such as quinine and morphine, and the production of antiseptics such as phenol and bromines and anesthetics such as chloroform, transformed the entire medical field. Based on extensive research, the pharmaceutical industry also produced new vaccines such as those for tetanus and diphtheria and synthetic chemicals that were able selectively to kill parasites, bacteria, and other microbes. One of the most successful pharmaceutical products was an acetylsalicylic acid called aspirin.[53] Continually improved over time, it was one of the most successful medicines in history (Mann and Plummer, 1991).

Metallurgy, paper, cement, rubber, and several other industries were also revolutionized by applied chemistry. Aluminum was identified early and Robert Bunsen separated it from bauxite (named after the south French Les Baux district) electrolytically in 1854. The American Charles Martin Hall and the Frenchman Paul Héroult simultaneously invented the Hall–Héroult aluminum production process in 1886, creating new prospects for metallurgy and the large-scale smelting of aluminum. The German F. G. Keller was the first to use wood to make pulp and paper in the 1840s, and others improved the procedure with sulfite pulping at the turn of the century. Paper making became a largely chemical process. Beginning in the 1860s, silica-soda-lime glass was invented with the use of sodium carbonate and calcium oxide. The production of cheap, modern glass with chemical procedures would rejuvenate ancient glass making at the end of the nineteenth century.

Artificial fertilizers were also crucial new products of the chemical revolution. In 1835, James Murray treated phosphate rocks with sulfuric acid and created superphosphate. A new industry did not emerge, however, until Justus Liebig published a pathbreaking book on artificial fertilizers in 1840. The Swede Alfred Nobel invented treated nitroglycerin, the most effective and controllable explosive in 1866, which markedly improved the process of mining and tunnel building. The first artificial materials, synthetic plastic (1869) and bakelite (1907), opened whole new fields for the chemical industry.

The other landmark invention of the second Industrial Revolution was the *combustion engine*, which led to the rise of the auto industry.[54] After a full decade of work, the German Nicolaus August Otto[55] produced the first practical four-stroke engine in 1876. Gottlieb Daimler, technical director of the Deutz Gasmotorfabrik (co-owned by Nicolaus Otto), took the next decisive step in 1887 when he constructed the first petrol-driven car together with another German inventor, Karl Benz. Another invention in the 1860s, the process of oil refining, provided suitable fuel for the engine. Around 1900, several micro-innovations led to further perfections.[56]

When Rudolf Diesel[57] filed for a patent in 1894, he launched the Diesel engine on its historical course. Diesel had invented internal combustion, the combustion within the cylinder that thus created compression-induced combustion (that is, ignition) without a spark. This highly efficient engine was widely used for cars, ships, railway locomotives, and electric and water plants.

Concurrent with the birth of the modern chemical and automobile industries, the third landmark invention that transformed the industrial landscape was *electric power generation*, which enabled the widespread use of electricity in transportation, metallurgy, chemical, and other industries, and the illumination of entire cities. This fundamental scientific discovery was rooted in the early nineteenth century.[58] By the 1870s, thermodynamics was already a mature science. A completely new power source, electric power, became available and gradually ended the age of the steam engine. Electric power was clean and could be used much more flexibly, and it could mechanize domains for which the steam engine was simply not practical, such as households and offices.

At first there was no solution to the problem of transporting electricity even over short distances, for the power of transported electricity invariably dissipated. Discovering how to transform low voltage into high voltage and back again was the achievement of three engineers of the Hungarian Ganz factory: the Croat-American Nikola Tesla and the German Siemens brothers. In so doing they made the transportation of electricity possible from the 1880s on. Transformers were the key to such transport, as well as to electricity's unlimited application on any scale by reducing voltage for low-voltage circuits.

The construction of hydroelectric power stations began in Europe in 1881, when the Siemens brothers built the Godalming power station in Britain. The light bulb was invented in the 1880s, and several micro-inventions improved it and made it more affordable; by 1900, the price of a doubly efficient bulb was 20 percent less than for a bulb two decades before.[59]

In 1879, the Siemens brothers delivered the first electric locomotive in Berlin, and the first electric tram began operation in that city in 1884. The London tram network expanded to 3,533 kilometers by 1906, and the Paris network was 2,000 kilometers long by 1912. The Paris electric metro network was opened in 1900, and the inner circle of the London subway was electrified in 1905.

Energy-deficient countries such as Italy, Norway, Sweden, and Switzerland rushed to tap their abundant water power resources and to build power stations. The Swiss Brown Boveri Company, founded in 1890 in Baden, became Europe's leading turbine producer for electric power generation and erected efficient electric transformation networks throughout Europe. Countries lacking sufficient coal resources suddenly became rich in electrical power.

Throughout the second Industrial Revolution, noteworthy inventions transformed several other branches of industry and everyday life. Shipbuilding advanced to a new stage, as large, propeller-driven iron and steel vessels loomed on the seas. Europe's armies began employing Hiram Maxim's machine-gun, which made them seemingly invincible in the myriad colonial wars they fought. New technology facilitated the mechanization of processes that had not been mechanized before. The sewing machine, the shoe-sewing machine, the typewriter, the lino-type printing press (1890), the photo camera (between 1826 and 1889), the motion picture (1894), the gramophone (1877), the first adding and listing device (1884), and the Hollerith punch card (1889) all quickly became mainstream in everyday life.

From the 1870s on, the second Industrial Revolution provided an enormous boost to industrialization in practically all of Western Europe and Scandinavia. Latecomer countries such as Germany, Sweden, and Norway, together with northern Italy, began industrialization on a new technological basis and built new industrial branches in the steel, chemical, and electric industries. Those like Belgium and France that industrialized by following the British pattern in the early nineteenth century now turned to new technologies and new branches of industry – as did Britain itself.

With the emergence of the modern steel industry, Britain regenerated its iron and steel sector and again predominated by introducing new technology. Applying Bessemer technology in 1858 and the Siemens–Martin process in 1869, Britain produced 44 percent of its steel using Siemens–Martin furnaces by 1879, and nearly 80 percent by 1913. In the latter period, Germany produced only half of its steel output with that process, and France only slightly more than a quarter. Britain remained the last word in steel technology,[60] and it produced more than France, Belgium, and Sweden put together – though at that time Britain supplied only 12 percent of the world's steel. (See Table 5.10.)

Britain's rivals made much greater progress, however.[61] Germany produced 0.69 million tons in 1880 but totaled 17.32 million tons by 1913,

Table 5.10 Steel output in Western Europe, 1870s–1910s, in million tons

Years	Germany	Belgium	Britain	France	Austria	Total	% of 1875–9 total
1875–9	–	0.09	0.90	0.26	–	1.25	100
1885–9	1.65	0.21	2.86	0.54	0.34	6.14[a]	491
1910–13	16.24	2.28	6.93	4.09	2.45	33.59[a]	2,687

Source: Mitchell (1973, 775).
Note: [a] With north Italy and Sweden.

which was 23 percent of the world's steel output. In that year, British production was only 44 percent of that of Germany. The loss of British predominance in the steel industry has been the subject of intense debate in the field. For a long time, there was a search for scapegoats, for those "responsible" for the relative decline.[62] Countries with the best educational systems, especially with the best technological education, gained the advantage. Britain was not one of those countries. Both French and particularly German higher education and science were superior.[63]

German industry embraced the relatively new joint-stock enterprise more than did any other country. From the 1880s on, four-fifths of its largest industrial firms were joint-stock companies. Gigantic industrial behemoths now emerged. The size of German industrial factories was the largest in Europe. Between 1880 and 1913, the market share of its top ten producers jumped from 24 percent to 53 percent.[64] Continental Western Europe, especially Germany,[65] took over, and Britain lost supremacy in its trademark iron and coal industries.

Germany benefited greatly from industrialization in the coal and steel sectors. By 1913, its iron, steel, and metal industries became its strongest branches: some 2 million workers produced a sixth of the country's industrial output. German coal resources were virtually unlimited. Before the war, Germany produced six times more coal than France, and was behind Britain by only 10 percent.[66] Its mammoth coal mining companies continually expanded and established horizontal and vertical syndicates. Coal, iron, construction, chemical, and electrical industries were consolidated in single giant companies.

In the 1870s, Dortmund emerged as a mass producer of iron. Entrepreneurial geniuses like August Josef Thyssen established rapidly expanding steel works in Dinslaken and elsewhere. Three generations of the Krupp family, Friedrich, his son Alfred, and grandson Fritz, created one of the world's most important industrial giants. Duisburg, Gelsenkirchen, Essen, Oberhausen, and several other industrial centers mushroomed one after the other. Its outstanding location, extensive railroads, unique water transport capabilities, and rich coal and iron reserves made the Ruhr area the industrial heartland of Europe.

Box 5.2　The Industrial Revolution and industrialized war – the Krupps of Germany

In the early summer of 1912, the Krupp city of Essen celebrated the hundredth anniversary of the founding of the "Fried. Krupp" Company. Kaiser Wilhelm II and his wife, the Chancellor von Bethmann-Hollweg, Admiral Alfred von Tirpitz, and the entire Generalstab participated. Wilhelm II ended his brief speech with the rallying cry, "Das Haus und die Firma Krupp: hurrah, hurrah, hurrah!" (Manchester, 1968, 266). A feudal tournament was planned for the festivities' third day, complete with the Krupps donning medieval garments. Krupp executives would follow as vassals and the workers as serfs (though 14 million marks were distributed as gifts for the employees). However, an explosion in one of the Krupps' mines, killing 110 miners, put a damper on this very curious ending.

At the time of the celebration, the Krupp empire employed 82,500 workers (jumping to 150,000 during the Great War). It had eighty factories in Essen, eight giant steel works, a shipyard in Kiel, and coal and iron ore mines throughout the country, producing 2 million tons of coal, 0.8 million tons of coke, 100,000 tons of iron ore, and 800,000 tons of pig iron. It controlled a great part of Australia's metal industry, and owned mines as far away as India and New Caledonia. The company produced the world's largest and most destructive cannon of the time: the "Big Bertha" (named after Bertha Krupp), a 94 ton steel colossus and mobile howitzer, which was successfully fired in a public demonstration by 200 artillerymen in March 1914. This monster weapon would soon bombard Paris, devastate Liège, Namur, and Antwerp, and kill tens of thousands at Verdun. The Krupp family was the wealthiest in Germany – well ahead of Baron Goldschmidt-Rothschild, who was only number three.

Four generations of Krupps were decisive players in Europe's Industrial Revolution, particularly in equipping the continent for its first industrialized war, World War I. The family's history goes back to the sixteenth century, when Arndt Krupp, probably from a Dutch immigrant family, registered as a merchant in Essen. They owned a large store at the Flax Market, and soon added a butcher shop and a paint and clothing department. The widow of Jodocus Krupp, Helene Amalie, bought four coal mines and the iron works of Gutehoffnungshütte at the turn of the nineteenth century. She appointed her nineteen-year-old grandson, Friedrich, to be the firm's manager. In 1811, Friedrich Krupp founded Gusstahlfabrik Fried. Krupp, a cast-iron works producing "English" cast steel. By the time he died in 1826, however, the firm was bankrupt. The family lost even their Flax Market home and had to move to a small wooden cottage next to the factory. Friedrich's oldest son, Alfred, then fourteen years old, dropped out of school. Although he was a twelfth-generation Krupp in Essen, the real Krupp story begins with him.

Alfred began working as his mother's manager at the bankrupt firm with five employees. He learned by doing and taught himself. He later stated, "I myself acted as clerk, letter writer, cashier, smith, smelter, coke pounder, night watchman at the converting furnace" (Manchester, 1968, 43–4). He became a master smith and produced first-class crucible steel within four years. The firm became solvent again and began to expand. Employees had to adhere to military discipline and take an oath of loyalty. When his brothers joined the business, Alfred trained new workers and traveled throughout the country to drum up business. He stayed in England for five months to learn and steal secrets. By 1840, he had ninety-nine employees and took out loans for investment.

The first breakthrough was connected with the railway boom. The factory produced steel rails, axles, springs, and particularly steel wheels (a major Krupp invention patented in 1853). The company displayed the new product at the Münchener Industrieaustellung in 1854, whereupon it supplied thousands of wheels to the Köln-Mindener railroad and the Bayerische Staatsbahn. It produced 20,000–25,000 pieces per year during the 1850s, and 32,000 in the 1880s (Gall, 2000, 87).

Alfred Krupp, however, was obsessed with producing new steel weaponry and always dreamed of building "monster cannons." In the age of bronze cannons, he strived to assemble superior steel ones. After conducting his first experiment in 1836, he ardently sought out military orders. They began to arrive in 1844, and he delivered the first cannon in 1847. At the London Crystal Palace exhibition, Alfred displayed a massive steel ingot and his glittering six-pounder steel cannon. Queen Victoria stopped to take a look at it, which became a sensation in the London journals. Alfred donated the cannon to the Prussian emperor and exhibited it in the Potsdam Palace. In those years, he cultivated a close personal connection with the crown prince, soon the soldier king, Wilhelm II, who several times visited the factory in Essen. Wilhelm decorated Alfred with the Roter Adler Orden, fourth class. Other honors would follow, including one from Napoleon III after the 1854 Paris world exhibition, where Krupp exhibited his new cast-steel twelve-pounder gun. Krupp sold cannons to Russia, Belgium, Spain, Austria, Romania, England, and Switzerland.

The real breakthrough was connected with Chancellor Bismarck's wars for German unification against Denmark (1864), Austria (1866), and France (1870–1). As Bismarck declared, he had united Germany with "iron and blood." John Maynard Keynes later paraphrased it, "by coal and iron." Krupp delivered both. Military orders flooded the company. His revolutionary rear-loading steel cannons had twice the range of the old-fashioned front-loaded bronze cannons of Germany's adversaries. New types grew larger and larger, including four-pounders, six-pounders, and twenty-four-pounders. On January 5, 1871, a staff-officer reported to Bismarck: "'Marshal von Moltke wishes you to know that the big Krupp cannons are now in position and ready to fire.' 'God be thanked,' murmur[ed] the Iron Chancellor . . . 'Then let them begin'" (Mason, 1984, 51). His cannons destroyed 1,400 buildings in Paris and led to victory in Sedan and Metz. Krupp's business flourished. The "Cannon King," as he was lauded in the Berlin papers, demolished the old Krupp factory building and built modern new structures. He owned fifty coal mines in the Ruhr area, bought iron-ore mines in Spain, introduced the Bessemer and then the Siemens–Martin procedure, and sold his products throughout the world. By the end of the unification wars in 1871, the Essen complex had 10,000 employees. Around the end of the 1870s, 25,000 Krupp "cannons were pointing at each other" in Europe (Manchester, 1968, 167).

Alfred also built his own monumental castle, Villa Hügel, with 216 rooms in two buildings, with a "Kaiser's apartment," where he (and then his son) hosted the emperor, the Russian tsar, the Portuguese king, Emperor Franz Joseph of Austria, and the Prince of Wales, later King Edward VII. When this business and industrial-technical genius died at the age of seventy-five in 1887, his industrial empire boasted 20,000 employees.

Alfred Krupp was also the forerunner of an industrial welfare policy geared to block the spread of social democracy, a decade before Bismarck's welfare legislations. With 50,000 inhabitants in 1870, Essen became one of the largest company towns in the world, with low-rent factory housing, a factory health service, and schooling. The company built playgrounds, a large chain of stores (including the Konsum Anstalt), a non-profit retail outlet, and a bread factory, and it established a charity fund and a life insurance institute.

The Krupp empire continued to expand under the leadership of Alfred's son, Fritz, who reorganized and modernized his factories, built new electric and coking plants, signed contracts with Rudolf Diesel and Hiram Maxim, and manufactured steel Diesel engines and machine-guns. In his enlarged empire, Fritz employed 43,000 workers and tripled his income by the end of the century.

A series of homosexual sex scandals in Berlin and Capri, however, destroyed his life. Even the emperor was unable to squelch the scandal, and Fritz Krupp committed suicide in 1902, leaving two teenage daughters. The family empire was transformed into a joint-stock company (corporation), with Alfred Hugenberg as head of the board. But this reorganization was merely a façade, for 99.99 percent of the shares remained in the hands of young Bertha Krupp. Four years later, when Bertha turned twenty, the Kaiser himself arranged her wedding to one of his diplomats, Gustav von Bohlen und Halbach. He became Krupp von Bohlen und Halbach after the marriage and gradually took over the empire. The dynasty continued: Bertha delivered her first son, Alfried, in 1907, and altogether had two daughters and six sons. The Krupps played a central role in transforming pre-Industrial Revolution conflicts into a new, mechanized type of warfare.

Based on Manchester (1968), Gall (2000), and Mason (1984).

The German engineering industry also gained international importance. Linked with the railroad boom, a number of major engineering factories were established in the mid-nineteenth century.[67] Iron processing and engineering employed more than 15 percent of Germany's industrial labor force.

From the 1860s on, the German organic chemical industry dominated the world market. In the 1870s, leading German companies, such as Badische Anilin, Höchst, and AGFA, controlled half the world market, and their share increased to an unheard of 90 percent by the turn of the century. Second behind Germany, the Swiss organic chemical industry produced only one-fifth of German dyestuff output in 1895, but Swiss production was equal to that of all other countries combined.[68] In the rising chemical industry, Germany and Switzerland were indisputably the world leaders.[69]

With its pioneering role in the steel, chemical, automobile, and electrical industries, Germany became the strongest industrial power in Europe before World War I. While industry employed 25% of its labor force in the mid-nineteenth century, it employed 38% in 1910–13. Producing only

22% of GDP in the early 1850s, German industry produced 45% of GDP before the war.

Western Europe underwent radical change in the second half of the nineteenth century. French industry clearly reflected this. Growth of its initial leading sectors, such as cotton and coal, slowed down significantly: the growth of the cotton industry dropped from 4.63% per annum between 1830 and 1860 to 1.5% between 1860 and 1880, and then down to 1.2% between 1880 and 1913. Coal output decreased from a rapid growth of nearly 4.9% each year between 1830 and 1860 to 3.2% between 1860 and 1892, and 2.0% between 1892 and 1913. Production of consumer goods from the 1870s on never attained the dynamic growth of the earlier periods.

On the other hand, new sectors based on the new technological revolution rose sharply. Investment goods production, with less than 1% growth per annum before the 1870s, increased by 3% per year at around the turn of the century and by 2% until the war. The chemical industry saw 5.1% annual growth and increased its output fivefold; engineering had the fastest growth of all, with 5.7% per annum, and it increased its production by more then six times.[70]

Britain's electric industry made impressive gains in electric power generation, producing more electricity than France and Sweden combined in 1907, but totaling only 45 percent of Germany's output. Indeed, British output dropped to less than a third of that of Germany by 1913. Austria[71] and Switzerland both built their first hydroelectric power stations in 1886. Switzerland progressed faster and more successfully. By 1913, thirty-two stations were in operation in the country, totaling 100,000 horsepower capacity.

North Italy closely followed. Its water resources in the Alps compensated for its lack of coal. The building of its first electric power station in 1883, a few months after the first one was built in the United States, signaled the change; forty-two would follow by 1909. In 1913, Italy produced 2,200 million kilowatts in electric energy, which met half the energy needs of Italian industry. Electricity would provide new impetus for industrial progress in northern Italy. Beginning in the 1890s, north Italian industrialization took off in the most modern sectors created by the second Industrial Revolution (Toniolo, 1990). Direct foreign investment played an important part in this process. Although the amount invested was only one-seventh of the total capital of joint-stock companies, it was concentrated in the modern sectors (Hertner, 1981). With the exception of shipbuilding, machinery production increased nearly fourfold in this period. German-type investment banks established a strong foothold in the electric industry. Other modern branches, such as the automobile

(FIAT) and office machine industries (Olivetti), also emerged. According to Fenoaltea's estimates, industrial growth in north Italy, though slow during the 1860s, became increasingly rapid after 1870. Taking 1890's output as 100, industrial production was 52 in 1860, 57 in 1871, 70 in 1880, and 175 by 1913. Industrial growth rose an unprecedented 7.87% annually between 1896 and 1908 (Fenoaltea, 1983; 2003a, 698). Italian economic growth generally (2.16% per annum) was three times faster than that in Britain, and faster than in France, Germany, and the United States, between 1900 and 1913. Industrial development made impressive progress in the north, centered on the so-called industrial triangle of Genoa–Turin–Milan, where modern engineering sectors gained ground.[72] Half of Italy's industrial employment, 58% of its factories, and 61% of the capacity of its machines was concentrated in that region. The Italian north was industrialized with half of its active population employed in industry. Per capita income level in the north surpassed that in the south by 62% (and the Italian average by 21%). *Average* Italian statistical figures had no real meaning in the long nineteenth century (Zamagni, 1978, 71–2, 158, 160–1, 164–5).[73]

West European countries with large coal resources also turned to electric energy production.[74] France entered the new technological age by hosting the Exhibition of Electricity in Paris, the "*capitale électrique*" in 1891. Extensive construction more than trebled the capacity of its hydroelectric power stations to 500,000 kW between the turn of the century and the war. The steam engine rapidly lost its predominance; in 1900, electric machines totaled only 7 percent of the capacity of France's steam power machines, but by World War I they totaled 22 percent. Based on power stations in the Alps, proprietors established an aluminum industry in the Grenoble region that produced 16 percent of the world's aluminum output. Electric energy production in France was roughly equal to that of Italy and somewhat less than that of Britain, but it was only one-quarter of Germany's.

Germany, indeed, became the leading force in electrification. The Siemens Company merged with Schuckert in 1903 to become one of the world's leading builders of hydroelectric power stations.[75] By 1913, it produced 8,010 million kW – as much as Britain, France, Italy, and Sweden combined.

Siemens also entered the new telephone business and built telephone exchanges with 10,000 lines. Emil Rathenau's AEG, established in 1887, pioneered the mass production of electric household appliances. Electrical engineering became one of Germany's export sectors.

Car manufacturing, the industry of the twentieth century, was born in Germany. Most of the industry's important inventions originated there.

Figure 5.3
Western Europe
catching up with
Britain: British
and continental
Western
European GDP
per capita
compared,
1820–1913
(Maddison,
2001, 85)

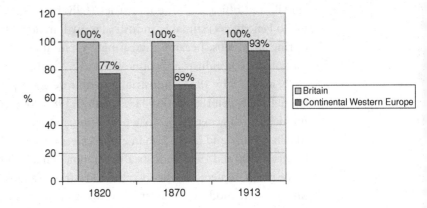

In 1901, the country manufactured 900 cars; by 1913, that number had risen to 20,000. France would emerge, however, as Europe's leading car manufacturer (and second to the United States), though none of the important inventions came from there. France's formidable engineering industry, its pervasive production of bicycles,[76] and the most widely used road networks in Europe literally paved the way for the new industry. In 1913, France produced 45,000 cars, one-quarter by the Peugeot and Renault factories.

A number of other countries also entered the car age. In 1899, Giovanni Agnelli, a former cavalry officer, established the Fabbrica Italiana di Automobil Torino (FIAT), which with 50 workers produced a hundred cars in a year. In 1914, FIAT manufactured 4,000 cars with 4,000 employees. Britain's Frederick Simms purchased the Daimler patent from Germany and opened the first British car factory in 1893. The industry developed thanks to the Locomotives Highway Act of 1896, which lifted the strict restrictions of the Red Flag Act. Britain soon became Europe's second largest car manufacturer behind France.

Continental Western Europe's successful transformation meant that it would inevitably catch up with Britain. A number of calculations demonstrate this process during the nineteenth century. According to Paul Bairoch, continental Western Europe attained 61% of Britain's per capita GNP in 1800, and 80% sixty years later. According to Angus Maddison's calculations, the gap began narrowing between 1870 and 1913. Six West European countries achieved 67% of the British per capita GDP in 1870, and 76% by 1913. (See Figure 5.3.) Nicholas Crafts' evaluation for four countries, including northern Italy, also reveals the narrowing gap: between 1870 and 1910, these West European countries advanced from 58.7% to 66.3% of the British level. (See Table 5.11.)

Table 5.11 Continental Western Europe catching up with Britain

	1820		1870		1913	
	GDP/ capita	Western Europe as % of Britain	GDP/ capita	Western Europe as % of Britain	GDP/ capita	Western Europe as % of Britain
Western Europe	1,321	77	2,202	69	4,567	93
Britain	1,707		3,191		4,921	

Source: Based on Maddison (2001, 85).

Notes

1. "Revolutionized" industry employed 30 percent of the workforce in only a few regions, including Lancashire, Cheshire, Central, and Fife. It was less than 10 percent in most regions, such as southern England and the Scottish Highlands, and only 19 percent in London (Crafts, 1985, 4–5).

2. An admirable road system, navigable rivers (the Rhône and the Garonne), and the port of Marseille offered Languedoc proto-industry an excellent transportation network for connecting to foreign markets. The industry in the principal towns of Carcassonne and Clermont-de-Lodève enjoyed steady expansion and prosperity until 1750. The total labor force of Clermont in 1732 was 5,649. In addition, fifty-six villages and towns spun, wove, and carded for the urban center in 1754. Carcassonne employed cottage workers in eighty-one villages.

3. In the 1780s, the Calwer Zeughandlundskompanie had a network of 5,000 workers in the cottage industry.

4. The villages of this overwhelmingly mountainous country used their labor force extensively for industrial activities. Around the turn of the nineteenth century, lace making, linen, cotton, calico printing, and watch making comprised the leading industrial sectors. Linen production in the Schaffhausen and St. Gallen areas, and lace making in Neuchâtel, thrived in the eighteenth and early nineteenth centuries. Some merchant-industrialist families employed 500–600 cottage workers. In 1800, 10,000–12,000 workers were engaged in calico printing at home, although the first centralized factory, Fabrique-Neuve of Cortaillod, was also opened.

5. A product of peasant work at home, watches had been produced in Geneva since 1550 and in Neuchâtel since 1680. Roughly a hundred small parts of the mechanical watch were produced by the traditional putting-out system, and final assembly was carried out in the merchant-industrialist's factory. The world's first clock shop was opened near Schaffhausen in 1760. In 1790, Switzerland exported 60,000 watches annually. The first modern watch factory was established in Geneva in 1840.

6. Until the mid-seventeenth century, "the changes in British industry between 1540 and 1640 . . . seem almost primitive compared to the panorama of technological sophistication of Venetian industries . . . when Venice excelled in the international market through her luxury products" (Poni and Mori, 1996, 161). The world's largest silk industry emerged in Genoa, Bologna, Milan, and Venice and employed some 100,000 people in the late sixteenth century.

7. As Kent Greenfield put it, this was "a direct and necessary consequence of the extension of sericulture. Meanwhile the second stage of manufacture, object of an industry independent of agriculture . . . had made great progress [in the 1850s]" (Greenfield, 1965, 85).

8. Some of the largest industrial enterprises, such as the Linz woolen factory (established by a merchant in 1672), combined the traditional cottage industry with a large centralized factory; local agents of the company provided wool and collected the yarn from thousands of home spinners, while the final finishing process was performed in the centralized factory.

9. Among the first "industrialists" was Franz Stephan von Lotharingen, the husband of Empress Maria Theresa, who founded a majolica factory on his Holić estate in 1742, a cotton factory on his Šaštin estate, and the Zbiroh iron foundries. Franz Stephan invited Belgian textile workers and British metal experts to run profitable enterprises. Count Johann Wallenstein began exploiting the raw material resources of his large estate. He embarked on silver mining in 1704, founded a gun factory that supplied weaponry for the army in 1712, established a woolen mill in Horni Litvinov in 1715, and opened a coal mine four years later. Several aristocrats became early textile manufacturers, including Count Bolza in Kosmonosy-Jusefuv Dul and Count Heinrich Haugwitz (the nephew of the empress's chief minister) in Namesti in 1795.

10. The woolen industry was not mechanized. In 1841, only 40 out of 3,000 looms were mechanized in the large Liberec textile center. In the Brno center, guilds performed five-sixths of the woolen production in 1850.

11. A debate raged during the post-World War II period that sought to clarify whether modern industrialization was the result of a breakthrough caused by a sudden "*big spurt*" or "*take-off*," as Alexander Gerschenkron and Walt W. Rostow called the turning point towards industrial maturity (Gerschenkron,

1957; Rostow, 1960). New research and calculations have modified this picture significantly.

12. Jaroslav Purš' (1960) widely rejected view placed this period on a par with the British Industrial Revolution. Richard Rudolph (1976) speaks of a continuous process from the early modern centuries onward; John Komlos (1983) opts for 1825–30; Herbert Matis (1972) prefers the years of the 1830s–1840s; Nachum Gross (1966) maintains that growth rates were the highest between 1865 and 1885 (4.1 percent) but slowed down afterwards (to 3.4 percent); Eduard März (1968) maintains that the upswings of the 1850s and the 1867–73 period represented only "false starts," and that the actual take-off occurred only after 1895 (Rudolph, 1976, 50–5, 84).

13. Between 1800 and 1834, the average annual value of British exports was £38–40 million, but before World War I it reached £455 million.

14. A complex compendium of studies on the decline of Britain after 1870 was published by Dormois and Dintenfass (1999).

15. The German Thomas Mann, in his family saga *Buddenbrooks* (1901), subtitled "Decline of a Family," presents the three-generation saga of a wealthy Lübeck merchant's family that suffered continuous economic and spiritual decline. The British John Galsworthy's trilogy, the *Forsyte Saga* (1906–21), presents the upper-middle-class Forsytes, with the dominant, possessive instinct of Soames, the shrewd, strong Old Jolyon, and the freethinking and artistic Young Jolyon, who renounced the commercial world of the Forsytes for painting.

16. Trade was balanced during the 1870s, but Britain's deficits rose afterwards. In the early 1910s, the value of British exports to Europe was £65.8 million, which was far behind the £98.9 million of imports coming from the continent.

17. As a negative argumentation, Olson associated the post-World War II Japanese and German economic successes with a positive outcome of the war, the total destruction of existing institutions.

18. German productivity was much higher in the chemical (26.6%), iron, and steel industries (37.8%), but it was 16.4% lower in the textile and clothing industries, almost 22% lower in coal mining, and 33% lower in the food and beverage industries.

19. Sidney Pollard investigated *Britain's Prime and Britain's Decline* in more than 300 pages and also concluded: "there was nothing like a failure along the whole front, a lack of ability to compete ... [Britain was able to] build up its science and technology teaching and research ... before the war ... [and] in the years to 1913 the British economy was ... the most productive in Europe ... the economy was fundamentally sound" (Pollard, 1989, 266, 270–1).

20. The Human Development Index combines per capita GDP, longevity, and education to reflect human well-being in a more complex way.

21. Adam Smith stated in *The Wealth of Nations*: "Thus the labour of a manufac-
    turer adds, generally to the value of the materials which he works upon . . . The
    labour of a menial servant, on the contrary, adds to the value nothing . . . "
    (Smith, [1776] 1976, 430, quoted by Lee, 1994, 117).

22. Bauwens was sent to Britain to learn modern tanning techniques but returned
    to open a mechanized cotton-spinning factory. At the end of 1798, he bought
    modern textile machinery, the first mule-jennies, which had been smuggled
    out of England. He established cotton-spinning and weaving factories, and
    began building machinery, including mule-jennies. He also introduced the
    first fly shuttle in Flanders and a steam engine in his brother-in-law's factory.
    Bauwens' brothers-in-law, mostly scions of merchant families, also became
    textile industrialists.

23. The number of cotton spindles increased from 200,000 in 1834 to 1.5 million
    by 1913.

24. John Holker brought the drawing of the newly invented spinning jenny to
    France in 1771; James Milne of Lancashire built the first water-frames and
    mechanized seventeen French factories after 1785. The jenny appeared in
    Normandy and Picardie in France as early as the beginning of the 1770s. The
    cotton factory of the Herzogs in Orléans, as well as a few large firms with
    10,000 spindles each, introduced the modern factory system in France by the
    time of the French Revolution.

25. James Jackson, Job Dickson, John Heathcote, Isaac Holden, and others
    founded textile companies, imported machines, and produced steam engines,
    locomotives, and other new technologies. Their numbers were, of course,
    limited: five of twenty-four steam-engine manufacturers were British before
    1830.

26. There were already 200 steam engines operating in France in 1810 and 625
    by 1830 – some of them home-made, with 10,000 horsepower capacity. The
    number of modern, mechanized cotton mills increased from 37 in 1799 to
    266 by 1810. In 1807, 15 firms produced spinning machines in Paris.

27. Coal output increased from 0.8 to 12.7 million tons between 1811 and 1865–9,
    matching Belgium's output but way behind Britain's 105 million tons.

28. This is based on Wayne Snyder's (2006) meticulous on-the-ground historical
    research of the occupational structure of the country, which covered several
    regions and produced a sample of 1.5 percent of France's population.

29. In one of Brno's textile mills, the first imported British steam engine was put
    into operation in 1816. The German Heinrich Luz from Württemberg settled
    in Brno and established a machinery workshop in 1821. By 1841, Luz built
    roughly one-third of the steam engines produced in Austria-Bohemia.

30. In 1820, Escher Wiss opened a textile machinery factory that expanded from
    the domestic market into exports. In 1853, twelve large textile factories, with

more than 10,000 spindles each, owned 39 percent of the country's spindles. Cotton weaving was introduced in 1825, and 3,000 mechanical looms were in operation by 1850. By 1867, their numbers increased to 13,000,

31. By 1840, 626,000 cotton spindles were in operation, and more than 2.2 million by 1860. In the mid-century, 789,000 workers, about one-fifth of the total industrial labor force, were employed in the textile industry.

32. In 1788, only 3,200 workers were employed in Prussian coal mining. In 1801, however, the first steam engine was employed in the project of deepening the Ruhr mines. Including also the traditional Silesian and Saar coal fields, coal mining's output totaled 1.8 million tons of anthracite and 0.5 million tons of lignite.

33. Until 1834, modern coke-heated furnaces produced only 5 percent of German iron output. Even in the middle of the century, only 39 furnaces out of 220 used coke. But by 1856, 56 percent of the output was produced by modern methods. Iron production totaled 110,000 tons in 1830, and 529,000 tons by 1860.

34. The textile industry in Piedmont and Lombardy in the mid-nineteenth century comprised 60 factories and 200,000 spindles, but the number increased to 745,000 spindles by 1876. Coal imports increased from 0.3 million to 2.0 million tons over a twenty-year period, clearly signaling the beginning of industrial progress in north Italy.

35. In 1880 1.6 million cotton spindles were in operation, and 4.9 million by 1914. One-quarter of the horsepower capacity of the machines worked in textiles. Before the war, 41 percent of Austrian-Bohemian industrial output was produced by the textile industry. Austria-Bohemia's 6.2 kg cotton consumption per inhabitant surpassed that of France (5.4 kg), came close to that of Belgium and Germany (6.6 and 6.8 kg), but remained far behind that of Britain (16 kg). Industrial production in Austria-Bohemia increased more than four times between 1880 and 1913. The iron and engineering industry produced nearly one-fifth of its total industrial output. Machine building saw important progress even before 1870, when the empire became self-sufficient in locomotive production and established engineering hubs in Prague and Vienna. The value of the output of the machine-building industry totaled 60 million crowns in 1870, but it rose to 630,000 million by 1912 (measured in constant prices). Compared with total industrial growth, machine building became one of the most dynamic sectors of Austrian industry: total annual industrial growth was 2.4 percent between 1882–94 and 1908–12, but machine building's was roughly three times faster (7.1 percent per annum).

36. Appert conserved all kinds of foods by sealing them in glass jars and boiling them in water. His book on *L'art de conserver les substances animals et végétales*

led to a series of innovations, including a French patent for preserving food in tin cans. Such processing began in Britain two years later, when Bryan Donkin and John Hall bought the patent and produced canned food for the navy.

37. Transporting food, however, was a major problem that was solved by ice-cooling train cargo. The French ship *Frigorifique* crossed the Atlantic Ocean in 1876 carrying meat that was artificially refrigerated by three methyl-ether refrigerating machines invented by the French engineer Charles Tellier. The real solution, however, came with Ferdinand Carré's patent (1860) of aqua-ammonia absorption refrigeration of at −27 to −30° Celsius, which was first employed by the French ship *Paraguay*. The journal *Ice and Refrigeration* popularized these solutions in 1891.

38. The cooperative idea had deep roots in Europe since Robert Owen's initiative and Britain's retail Cooperative Society (1844), Cooperative Wholesale Society (1864), and Cooperative Union (1869). The number of cooperatives surpassed 18,000 in 1910, and nearly 30,000 additional credit cooperatives facilitated agricultural financing in Europe. Dutch potato producers established cooperative potato starch production in 1898.

39. The first mechanized textile company was established in 1830, but fewer than 56,000 spindles operated in the cotton industry in 1860. By 1910, their number was 487,000, and the consumption of cotton jumped from 70,000 to 2.1 million tons.

40. The society engaged in extensive activities, offered prizes, initiated international correspondence, and published papers concerning the rural economy. By 1773, it had published and translated twenty-five volumes into French.

41. The German-born pharmacist Heinrich Nestle moved to Switzerland in 1839 at the age of twenty-five and changed his name to the French-sounding Henri Nestlé.

42. Between 1850 and 1913, Hungarian deliveries to the western provinces of the empire increased twelvefold.

43. Austria-Bohemia's cattle stock increased from 5,126 to 9,160 head, and its pig stock from 2,156 to 6,431.

44. The invention of German chemist Andreas Marggraf, it was first put to use by his student Franz Carl Achard, who selected the white Silesian beet and established the world first sugar-beet factory in 1801.

45. Although beer had been produced for centuries, and Britain had long had a highly developed beer brewing industry, the modern beer industry was born in the nineteenth century when dark and often low-quality warm- and top-fermented ales were replaced by cold- and bottom-fermented "lager" beer. In 1876, pasteurization stabilized the lager beers.

46. Frenchman René Réaumur recognized in 1722 that steel was an intermediate product between cast and wrought iron. More than half a century later, the

Swede Tobern Bergman realized that the reason for the differences between the three types of iron was their carbon content (which he called plumbago) (Mokyr, 1990, 169).

47. Bessemer founded a company in Sheffield, which became the center of the world's steel industry.

48. Thomas, a clerk in a police court, was probably the last amateur inventor of the British Industrial Revolution.

49. From the mid-nineteenth century on, massive railroad construction revolutionized several new sectors in the iron, steel, and engineering industries. One should not forget that, between 1850 and 1910, more than 165,000 kilometers of railroad lines were built in Western Europe and Scandinavia. The railroads were a significant factor in the onset of the new technological age and the industrialization boom after the mid-nineteenth century.

50. "Change was built into the system . . . [A]round the turn of the century [new inventions introduced new industries such as] electric power and motors; organic chemistry and synthetics; the internal-combustion engine and automotive devices; precision manufacture and assembly-line production – a cluster of innovations that have earned the name of the Second Industrial Revolution" (Landes, [1969], 1995, 235).

51. Liebig, the German founder of organic chemistry, himself studied in Paris and learned from leading French scholars. He copied the laboratory system in Paris.

52. Kekulé was a German architect, who accidentally met Liebig and enrolled in the university to learn chemistry from him. In 1890, a "Benzolfest" honored Kekulé in the town hall of Berlin in the presence of the Kaiser.

53. Carl Duisburg reorganized Friedrich Bayer's small German dye factory, which had been established in 1863. In a new research laboratory in Eberfeld, a young chemist, Felix Hoffman, successfully refined salicylic acid in 1899 and eliminated its dangerous side-effect of destroying prostaglandins, a protective organism produced in the stomach. In just three years, 160 reviews and studies on aspirin were published.

54. Steam-engine road vehicles, experimented with in the late eighteenth century, did not work. The Belgian Jean-Etienne Lenoir's experimental engine fueled by a mixture of gas and air in 1859 was a curiosity. In 1862, the French Alphonse Beau de Rochas described an efficient four-stroke engine and patented it, but his model was never developed.

55. Otto was one of the rapidly disappearing amateur inventors, a traveling salesman without technical education, who put his mark on the second Industrial Revolution.

56. One of them was the injection of gasoline through a carburetor into the engine (patented in 1887 by Wilhelm Maybach).

57. Rudolf Diesel, born in Paris to an immigrant German family, was sent back to Augsburg to relatives during the Franco-Prussian War and studied at Munich Polytechnic.

58. The chemical battery of Volta (1800), the electric circuit of Ohm (1827), and the electromagnetic induction of Faraday (1831) gradually led to various applications and the founding of a number of new industries.

59. By 1903, nearly all of the cities in Britain with more than 100,000 inhabitants had an electric energy supply, though only 6–7 percent of the urban population used electric lighting. In 1906, 3,000 communities got electric energy in France.

60. In 1879, British output of more than 1 million tons surpassed the combined German, French, and Belgian output of 922,000 tons, producing more than half of the total output of the leading producers. By 1910–13, Britain further increased its steel output by nearly seven times and produced 7.66 million tons.

61. The United States increased production from 1.25 million to 31.3 million tons between 1880 and 1913, by the latter date producing 42 percent of the world's output.

62. In reality, as Peter Temin (1966) has explained, the demand for steel in the emerging American and German economies, combined with protective tariffs in those countries and an approximate equalization of resource costs in the major steel-making countries, naturally decreased British predominance. The domestic industries of Britain's rapidly industrializing rivals met most of the extra demand.

63. Between 1850 and 1914, of the 248 owner-manager entrepreneurs in the heavy industries in Westphalia, 82 percent had some higher education and 71 percent had received diplomas. The nine-year-long education of the science schools and the eight-years of the "real" gymnasiums produced well-trained industrialists and managers (Pierenkemper, 1979, 51).

64. In the new electrotechnical industry, the two giants, AEG and Siemens, monopolized half the market. By 1907, cartels controlled and regulated one-quarter of industrial production (Tilly, 1991, 112).

65. France also emerged as a major power in the modern iron and steel industry. The new Thomas procedure was crucial to France's development of its iron and steel industry, for it enabled it to use its low-quality phosphorous iron ore. The steel industry's output nearly trebled between 1880 and 1913 with 3.1 percent annual growth.

66. Between 1870 and 1913, anthracite output rose from 26.4 million to 190.1 million tons per year, and lignite extraction from 1.8 million to 872 million tons.

67. The factories of August Borsig, Josef Anton Maffei, and Emil Kessler began producing for the railroads. Iron processing and engineering employed 600,000 workers in 1875, and 1.9 million by 1913.

68. Sixty-five percent of Germany's chlorine output was electrolytic by the early twentieth century, while Britain's remained at 18 percent. Britain's early advances with the Leblanc procedure proved to be an obstacle to change when the old technology was preserved for too long.

69. Friedrich Bayer opened a small dye factory in 1863 but almost went bankrupt in 1884. He then employed a young chemist, Carl Duisburg, who invented synthetic dyes and, more importantly, as head of the research and patent department, began the production of pharmaceuticals. Under Duisburg's managerial leadership, Bayer became a research pioneer. In 1890, Duisburg built laboratories in Eberfeld, specializing in pharmaceutical research. Similarly, in Switzerland, Alexandre Clavich's small textile dyeing factory was transformed in 1884 into what would later become the giant CIBA, one of the world's leading pharmaceutical companies; 20 percent of the firm's employees were engineers, technicians, and researchers. In the same decade, J. R. Geigy's chemical firm and Alfred Kern and Eduard Sandos' pharmaceutical company made Swiss industry a European leader.

70. The capacity of power machines in industry was 178,000 horsepower in 1860, but 3.6 million by 1913.

71. "In 1883, a euphoric Vienna opened its Electric Exhibition when Crown Prince Rudolf coined the idea of a sea of light which would spread from Austria across the whole world... [In reality the opposite happened, and] foreign companies were playing a dominant role in the electrification of the country" (Sandgruber, 1994, 231–2). Six power stations were in operation in Austria by 1890, but, even in 1900, three times more Viennese households were powered by gas supply than by electricity. The latter represented only 3 percent of households. By 1914, however, 358 power stations supplied electricity for most of the bigger cities. The power plants produced 370,000 kW of electric energy before the war.

72. The dense network of northern urban settlements became the hub of modern industrialization. Before World War I, 45 percent of Italy's population lived in the north. The population density (153 people for each square kilometer) and the decline of illiteracy (falling from 54 percent to 19 percent between 1871 and 1911) made the area similar to Western Europe.

73. The central parts of the country remained somewhat behind. But the south did not follow the modern transformation of the north and represented a different level and path of modernization, as will be discussed in Chapter 10.

74. Britain produced 2,500 million, France 1,800 million, and Germany a whopping 8,010 million kilowatt hours before World War I.

75. The company had 57,000 employees in Germany and another 24,000 abroad. It began actively building power stations. The country produced 960 million kW in 1900, but it built hundreds of new stations in 1911 alone, and put 110 new stations into operation.

76. The Peugeot bicycle factory was among the first that turned to auto production.

CHAPTER 6

The miracle of knowledge and the state: Scandinavia

The economic situation in the periphery: Scandinavia until 1870

There was no economic transformation in Scandinavia until the last third of the nineteenth century. The region exhibited classic peripheral economic characteristics. Karl-Gustaf Hildebrand commented that Sweden is "a peripheral country that builds on her natural assets, exporting . . . forests and minerals, semi manufactures or simple and easily made products" (Hildebrand, 1992, 11, 13). Indeed, until 1870, the Scandinavian region experienced typical slow, pre-industrial economic growth. During the half-century between 1820 and 1870, its per capita GDP increased by only 18% compared with Western Europe's 54% growth. Per capita income in the three Scandinavian countries was only 63% that of Western Europe. Until 1870, Sweden had a typical one-dimensional agricultural character, with 72% of its active population working in agriculture and forestry, and only 15% in industry. Norway was similar, with 60% of employment in agriculture, forestry, and fisheries, and 16% in industry.

Agriculture was somewhat modernized and benefited from what Lars Magnusson (2000) suggests was an agricultural revolution.[1] The traditional agricultural sector, however, was not an important factor in Norwegian and Swedish development. This was a consequence of the natural environment of these sparsely populated Nordic countries. Sweden had only twelve inhabitants per thousand square kilometers in the last third of the century, and Norway had only seven. Only 8% of the land in Sweden was cultivable. Although roughly two-thirds of the population worked in the primary sector, their contribution to the national income was limited – only 39% in Sweden and 45% in Norway in 1865.

About 55% of the workforce of more densely populated Denmark (with seventy-one inhabitants per thousand square kilometers) was engaged in agriculture in the 1860s–1870s, and two-thirds of those who worked in industry were employed in small-scale, handicraft shops. Scandinavian labor productivity in the 1860s was only 49% of Britain's, 72% of Switzerland's, and 80% of Germany's.

The export structure of Sweden remained traditional until the 1880s; unprocessed food and raw materials (grain, iron ore, wood) represented 67% of the total. Sweden in the seventeenth and mid-eighteenth centuries produced one-third of Europe's iron, exported 60% of its iron output, and was Europe's leading iron producer and exporter.[2] Peasants worked in the more than three hundred iron estates owned by landed aristocrats and town merchants at the end of the seventeenth century. The Swedish proto-industrial iron sector practically collapsed during the first Industrial Revolution.[3] The other leading export sector of Sweden, the timber and wood industry, was not mechanized until 1849, when the first steam engine was put into operation. However, iron and wood exports made a merchant class significantly wealthy and added to the country's capital accumulation.

In Norway, 45,000 workers were employed in industry at the end of the 1880s, one-third of them in lumbering. The leading export item of the country was fish, comprising 47% and 35% of total exports in 1866 and 1880 respectively. Denmark remained an agricultural exporter during the entire second half of the nineteenth century: roughly 80% of Danish exports consisted of food products in the mid-nineteenth century, and 90% did at the turn of the twentieth. Until 1870, Denmark exported mostly grain and livestock. In the late 1870s, the country halted grain production and turned to processing animal products and milk. The demand for industrial products was met either by imports or by small-scale handicraft production.[4]

The Scandinavian countries thus exhibited classic peripheral characteristics: their predominant agricultural and raw material production, exporting sectors, lack of processing, and moderate level of income. Compared with other peripheral regions, Scandinavia was somewhat behind the Mediterranean countries and roughly on a similar plane with Central Europe until 1860–70.

Modern society without a developed economy

Scandinavia belatedly jumped on the industrialization bandwagon in the last third of the nineteenth century, and was uniquely successful in catching up with the West in a relatively short time. This process was not fully accomplished by World War I, but was completed during the interwar period. What made the Scandinavians so exceptional? What drove their spectacular rise?

A part of the answer is the region's virtually unlimited export capabilities. The Scandinavian countries were simply in the best place at the best time. They were close to the world's largest markets, Britain and Western Europe, and had the tremendous advantage of cheap water transportation to deliver their products. They also had the exact natural resources and export items that were needed in the industrialization age, and were thus assured huge markets in the rapidly industrializing and transforming West. Scandinavia's wood,[5] iron ore, meat, and milk products easily found their way to British and West European consumers. Two-thirds of British wood imports came from America in 1870, but only 13% did so in 1913, when Sweden and Norway took the lead, delivering 83% of British wood imports (Schlote, 1952).

For its part, Denmark targeted the British "breakfast table" with its butter, bacon, and eggs. In constant prices, the value of its butter exports increased by 336% between 1875 and 1910. The three above-mentioned items comprised nearly 40% of Danish exports before World War I, and close to 60% of those exports were sold in Britain (Bjerke and Ussing, 1958).

The international market created the demand that propelled the Scandinavian economies forward, especially during the first decades of its transformation. But the unprecedented trade boom during the second half of the nineteenth century provided export opportunities for every agricultural and raw material-producing peripheral country. Spain had valuable mineral resources, Russia had unlimited timber. Most traditional agrarian-peasant peripheral societies, however, were unable to generate a catching-up process from increased exports. What made the difference in the Scandinavian case? The answer is the successful, though gradual, socio-political and institutional change, the radical reforms that abolished the *ancien régime* and cleared the way for modern social transformation. Reforms here were more radical and consistent than in Prussia or Austria, let alone Russia. In contrast to its peripheral economic traits, Scandinavia, by the nineteenth century, was not peripheral from a social, political, cultural, or educational perspective. Scandinavia's social, institutional, and educational systems, its predominant values, and its political and military power were all rather similar to those of the European core in the early modern period.

The two Scandinavian kingdoms, Denmark and Sweden, were military great powers in the early modern centuries. From the late Middle Ages on, Norway had been united with Denmark, and Finland was part of Sweden.[6]

Scandinavia established itself militarily as an important and independent power.

Swedish military power, however, met its Waterloo at Poltava. Unlike in Britain, the Swedish Age of Empire ended abruptly. This, however, turned out to be an advantage. The Swedish state turned inward. Instead of trying to become a great conquering power, it began building a great society grounded in economic strength and institutional reform. Rather than using the power of the state against its rivals, it targeted ancient institutions and obsolete laws within the country in order to peacefully transform society and create a plentiful economy. Unlike the peripheral regions, Scandinavia became both socially and politically a free society, and it was deeply imbued by a puritan Protestant ethic (Samuelson, 1968).

Both Denmark and Sweden were absolute monarchies in the seventeenth century. Swedish history depicts the half-century following the Great Nordic War in the early 1700s as "the Age of Freedom," for the Swedes established a genuine parliamentary system after adopting their constitution in 1720 – one of the first parliamentary systems in Europe.[7] The roots of this breakthrough, however, were much deeper, for they went back to the revolt against the Kalmarunion in the 1430s, which elevated the peasantry to a unique central position with representation (along with the burghers) in the Riksdag (Parliament) (Emilsson, 2005).[8] The building of democratic institutions began, and a series of reforms followed during the next two centuries. Laws guaranteed the freedom of the press as early as 1776, and the equality of women and freedom of religion in 1860. The *produktplakat*, the Swedish Navigation Act, was gradually abolished by the middle of the nineteenth century, and Sweden turned to free trade. The Act of Unity and Security granted power to the parliament and stripped the nobles of their exclusive right to hold office. In 1810, the new constitution abolished the nobility entirely. The iron industrialists, the wealthy urban elite, and the rising entrepreneurial bourgeoisie gained political power. Swedish peasants became free tenants during the Age of Empire (1600–1720), and their position was significantly strengthened by subsequent legislation.[9] The enclosure decrees were enacted at virtually the same time as the British enclosure law. In 1823, the state forests were privatized. Noble holdings decreased from 72 to 33 percent of the Sweden's landed area during the years of *reduktionen*, further expanding the crown lands.[10] The latter were then parceled out to tenant peasants, who became freeholders; as a result, 90 percent of the land was owned by freeholders. Small independent holdings, the *hemmeansklyvning*, were established, and the peasantry became an important economic and political factor in Sweden – quite unlike anywhere else in the European periphery. The freeholders, the Fourth Estate, won parliamentary representation.

Like Sweden, Denmark eliminated the *ancien régime* with a series of reforms. The absolute ruler, Christian V, eroded the aristocracy's power during the last third of the seventeenth century. In the eighteenth century, 80 percent of the land belonged to the large and medium-sized estates, to which the serfs paid feudal fees. But the state liberated the serfs in 1788, a year before the French Revolution. It offered various benefits to the big landowners for selling their estates, among them tax exemptions if they sold their lands to the tenants. By 1830, the peasant tenants became freeholders. By the mid-nineteenth century, Danish agriculture was based on small peasant farms, with 80 percent of peasants owning small parcels of land. The Great Village Commission drafted these reforms; as in Sweden, it enclosed the communal fields, strengthening the free peasant holdings. The reforms culminated with the constitution of 1849, which introduced modern democratic political institutions and political structures.

As in Holland, serfdom did not exist in Norway, and unlike the southern or eastern European peripheries, the peasantry gained political power in that country. The landowning nobility was virtually non-existent. In its place, freeholders, tenant farmers, free fishing communities, and urban elements with trade and industrial privileges comprised Norwegian society. Norway's parliament would abolish those privileges and guarantee the freedom of trade and industry, which was a prerequisite of modern society.

Concurrent with this gradual but radical transformation, Norwegians naturally turned to puritan Protestantism, which strengthened the ethical values pervasive in their free society, and compounded their ethics of hard work and thrift. Protestantism was also an important factor behind Norway's modern educational system. Education predated industrialization in Scandinavia, as it did in the Netherlands and Britain. At the end of the eighteenth century, agrarian Denmark became one of the first countries to make primary education mandatory. Norway, with its premodern economy, would do the same in 1827, and Sweden would follow in 1842 – long before either France or Britain. Mass education was thus pervasive in Scandinavia before the mid-nineteenth century. Consequently, illiteracy dropped to roughly 10 percent in Sweden and less than 30 percent in Denmark and Norway – far lower than in several Western European countries, and in sharp contrast to the mostly illiterate peripheries. Enlightened state policy abolished the *ancien régime* and its medieval remnants, and replaced them with socio-political institutions that were suitable for a modern economic transformation.[11]

After achieving this peaceful reform, Scandinavia turned to economic change. It did so, however, not by following the British path, but in its

Table 6.1   The population of Scandinavia (millions)

	1800	1850	1880	1910
Sweden	2.4	3.5	4.6	5.5
Denmark	0.9	1.4	2.0	2.7
Norway	0.9	1.4	2.0	2.4
Total	4.2	6.3	8.6	10.6

Sources: Cipolla (1973, 747) and Lafferty (1971).

own innovative way. During the second half of the nineteenth century, the region's interventionist, regulatory states played a crucial role in this process by creating efficient institutions for modernization. L. Magnusson begins his economic history of Sweden by suggesting that the "view that capitalism is something imposed by government and other centres of power, is not without foundation... This process is usually driven by a vigorous government that attempts to gain benefit for itself – but... [its actions] are as essential to the new capitalist actors as the very air they breathe" (Magnusson, 2000, 1).

Rapid modernization and industrialization

Scandinavia experienced rapid population growth, as shown in Table 6.1. Denmark's population increased from 900,000 to 2.7 million between 1800 and 1910, with half of the population working in agriculture, even at the end of the century. The country carried out one of the most flexible adjustments to the changing European environment. Like their Dutch counterparts, Danish farmers turned to intensive, specialized production and sold a large part of their output abroad, mostly in Britain. When grain prices significantly increased during the first half of the century, especially during the second quarter, Danish grain production and exports predominated – doubling between 1830 and 1860, with nearly a third of output sold to foreign markets.

From the mid-1870s on, however, cheap overseas grain flooded the European markets. As a result of inexpensive water transport and a surfeit of cheap American grain, the world's grain market dramatically changed. World grain prices dropped 30–35 percent by the early 1880s.[12]

Unlike their Central and East European counterparts (as will be discussed in Chapter 11), Danish farmers adjusted to the new situation, cut grain production, and turned to animal husbandry and the raising of livestock. Denmark began importing grain, and pigs were now its main export item, sold to German markets. When import restrictions and tariff increases in Germany closed this door not long afterwards, Danish farmers were again able to make quick adjustments. Cattle, a traditional export item of the country, now became the new core of the economy. Related to this development, fodder production also steeply increased.[13] Cattle exports doubled, and pig exports increased sevenfold.[14]

Improvements in types of cattle, and the proliferation of the world-famous Holstein, increased output. Milk production per cow doubled between 1870 and 1910. The increase in productivity was indeed impressive: while cultivated land mass increased by less than 50% and labor input by 10%, Danish agriculture raised its output by 140% and its exports (in constant prices) by 336% between 1870 and 1914.

Embracing a unique path to development, Denmark, along with the Netherlands, remained agricultural during most of the long nineteenth century and preserved its agricultural export character. Combining export-oriented, specialized agricultural production with food processing, however, elevated the country to one of the highest economic and income levels in Europe. Because of its high productivity, Denmark no longer needed a large part of its agricultural population.

As the Dutch combined specialized agriculture with food processing, Denmark began processing milk and meat. Between 1871 and 1914, milk output increased by three and a half times, butter output by four times, and bacon production by five and a half times. The food processing industry was export-oriented; the country exported 80% of its butter output. Exports increased by 4–5% per year and 90% of them consisted of agricultural and food products at the turn of the century. Quite uniquely, however, 80% of the exports were processed foods, including butter (47%) and bacon (26%). The value of exports increased from 150 million to 500 million crowns between 1870 and World War I, when the export branches produced 28% of the country's GDP. Half of the exports ended up on British breakfast tables.

This unprecedented flexibility – non-existent in peripheral agricultural countries – was partly the consequence of a deeply rooted solidarity in Danish villages, which led to common efforts to organize the community to solve problems, and to provide the most up-to-date education to every farmer. Ordinary Sunday and summer schools, established in the early nineteenth century, conveyed information about the newest developments in technology.[15] Danish agrarian society was also better organized than anywhere else in the world. It began a grassroots cooperative movement,[16] establishing the first cooperative in Hjedding in 1882. By 1888 244 dairy cooperatives were in operation in the country, and 1,500 by the beginning of World War I.

Box 6.1   **"What is outwardly lost must be inwardly won": the Danish Cooperative Movement**

The last third of the nineteenth century could have been a devastating disaster for Denmark. The country fought two wars against Prussia in 1848 and 1864, and, in the end, lost Schleswig-Holstein to the German Federation. The loss was devastating and was soon followed by a severe depression and grain crisis in the late nineteenth century. The inflow of cheap overseas grain hit the grain producers of Europe hard, for they could not compete. Denmark was a grain producing and exporting country. It could have easily been paralyzed by the war and the depression. But the exact opposite happened.

The Danish poet Hans Peter Holst expressed the common sentiment: "For every loss a replacement will be come upon, what is outwardly lost must be inwardly won." Denmark took its destiny into its own hands. A combined peasant and intellectual movement transformed the country and restructured its economy with an unparalleled collective effort. Unlike traditional Russian and South Slav peasant communities that retained long-established ways of life, the Danish collective movement was innovative and looked for the most effective responses to their historical challenges.

One of the explanations for the Danish peasants' modern, innovative reaction is their tradition of education and self-organization. The Kongeligt Dansk Landhusholdningsselskab (Farm Household Society) began work in 1769, and the Landøkonomisk Konsulentvirksomhed (Agronomic Consultancy Service) had great influence over the entire country. Nikolaj Frederik Severin Grundtvig, a Renaissance man, philosopher, historian, writer, and pastor, was the inspiration behind the founding of a network of practically oriented folk high schools in the 1830s. The Association of Friends of Peasants and the then unique peasant political party Venstre became major organizational forces.

Grudtvig delighted that Denmark had "ennobled its peasantry" and prophesied that it was entering an "Age of Peasants." At the same time that self-organization developed, government statutes of 1831 and 1834 established the Advisory Class Councils. These regional councils represented various layers of society, including the peasantry, and became the cradle of decentralized democratic government. Emerging from this social-educational backdrop was the Danish cooperative movement.

The cooperative idea was born in Britain but was exemplified in Denmark because of the Danes' strong feelings of solidarity, community cohesion, and recognition of mutual self-interest. The first consumer cooperative, the Thisted Kjøbstads Arbeider Foreng, was opened on the west coast of Jutland in 1866 by Hans Christan, a local priest in Thisted, and Doctor F. F. Ulrik, an admirer of the cooperative idea. Characteristically enough, the cooperative opened a library and a reading room, established unemployment and healthcare funds, and created a colony garden for its members to grow their own vegetables. By 1890 540 cooperatives were already in operation. The Association of Danish Consumers Cooperatives was established in 1896 to create a joint purchasing organization.

While consumer cooperatives sought to lower the prices of the community's purchases, the cooperative idea spread throughout the agricultural productive sector as a means of improving performance. Once the first cooperative dairy was founded in the village of Hjedding in 1882, the idea began to proliferate. Within five years, the first cooperative bacon factory was opened. This was followed by cooperative slaughterhouses, as well as breeding and exporting, egg-packing, egg-exporting, feedstuff-producing, machine-sharing, butter-exporting, cattle- and poultry-producing and exporting, and ultimately banking- and insurance-selling cooperatives. A widespread network of self-organization began to operate. A typical cooperative institution was the machine station, embodying the joint-ownership of expensive farm machinery. What individual peasant farms were unable to do, the cooperative organization could easily accomplish by buying modern machinery and establishing food processing factories. Control associations assisted farmers in calculating the output and fat content of their milk, and offered the peasants regular advice and consultations. Sixty-five consultant associations were up and running by 1900. Danish peasant society developed a booming export business based on cooperative food processing and export industry.

The response to the challenges of military defeat, territorial losses, and the shattering grain crisis was fast and deliberate. The Danes succeeded dramatically in structurally changing their economy, and began to focus on animal husbandry and food processing. The cooperative movement was a crucial factor in this process, and it was a decisive player in the national economy.

Based on Jensen (1982), Jensen (1945), Holm (1888) and Ravnholt (1945). I also broadly used my student Thomas Ribbs' research paper (2009).

In the cooperatives, the farmers were able to invest together and build processing factories. The Danish cooperative movement became the primary agent of food processing. In the early twentieth century, 80 percent of Danish farms sold their milk to cooperatives for processing, quality control, and butter production. Cooperatives were also established for an array of enterprises: bacon factories, slaughterhouses, butter exporting, egg exporting, manure purchasing, and horse breeding.[17] Soon a national network was created, and a Central Cooperative Committee elected. Farmers also established joint-stock companies to run schools, including People's High Schools and agricultural schools. The central organizations created a domestic retail network, a Cooperative Bank, and even a Danish Sanatorium Society (Hartel and Faber, 1918).

The country's enormous milk industry attracted talented engineers and inventors. L. C. Nielsen, the builder of a machine factory, invented the milk separator in 1878, which mechanized butter and dairy production.[18] The cooperative food processing industry continually expanded. In the 1870s, more than 10,000 tons of butter were exported per annum; just before World War I, this reached 100,000 tons.

Denmark also took part in the century's brewing revolution.[19] Modern bottom-fermented lager beer production began to edge out home brewing in the second half of the nineteenth century. The first lager beer appeared in Denmark in 1847, but it did not spread widely until the late 1870s or early 1880s. Technological innovations, mechanical cooling, new malting processes, pasteurization, and bottling were all introduced from the 1870s on.[20] The Carlsberg Company controlled half the markets beginning in the 1880s. But a new company, Tuborg, established in 1873 with only a 9 percent market share, came close to equaling Carlsberg in size by the early twentieth century. Unlike most of the other food processing branches, beer production served the domestic market until World War I (Wilson and Gourvish, 1998).

Other industrial sectors were nearly embryonic. Until the 1870s, modern factories produced only one-third of Denmark's industrial output, and handicraft industries two-thirds. Between 1872 and 1913, however, industrial output increased sevenfold. In a single decade at the end of the nineteenth century, 1,700 new mechanized factories were established and the number of workers doubled. Modern, mechanized industry was an exception in 1855, but the proportion of handicraft and big industry became balanced by 1900. Industrialization grounded on import substitution took off from the 1850s on, as it had done in the Netherlands. But, also like the Netherlands, Denmark was hampered by its lack of coal and iron. The textile industry however, continually developed, for the domestic market, and it soon represented 20 percent of industrial output. Another 20 percent was produced by engineering. Before World War I, Denmark made significant progress in import substitution and was able to cover more than 70 percent of domestic consumption of industrial goods with domestic products. Industry and agriculture's contribution to the national economy became more or less balanced.

The two other Scandinavian countries, Sweden and Norway, did not follow the Danish road. Agriculture was not a leading sector in either of these Nordic countries. However, Swedish agriculture increased production by 256 percent between the 1860s and 1910s by introducing the potato and concentrating on meat and dairy. The country imported more and more wheat and rye, but exported oats, meat, and butter. Until the turn of the century, food exports and imports remained balanced. Sweden became a net food importer only in the early twentieth century. Norway had to import a great part of its food consumption. Potato output more than doubled between 1835 and 1910, and animal husbandry and the milk economy also made substantial progress. But grain imports trebled, as grain production was virtually non-existent in the country. Most of the rural population focused on woodcutting and fishing. By the mid-nineteenth century, fishing became the leading export sector, producing 47 percent of Norwegian exports. This role gradually declined: by 1900, the fishing industry, and the fish processing that was built upon it (sardines and herring), comprised one-quarter of all exports.

Sweden and Norway remained primary-product producers (including fishery and forestry) until the 1860s, but agriculture was not a key factor in their modern economic transformation. They found their own way towards industrialization. Despite their late start, they were able to exploit their "human capital" and profit from their geopolitical proximity to Britain and access to cheap water transportation. All the Scandinavian countries became free traders (though Sweden would soon turn to protectionism), and they guardedly maintained their links to the British market. The potential of ocean transportation was a tremendous advantage for the Scandinavian countries, and they were quick to exploit it. The region emerged as one of the leading shipping powers.[21] The Norwegian merchant fleet, which had increased capacity sixfold in a sixty-year period, became the world's third largest fleet, its shipping services generating 45 percent of the country's export revenue. Norwegian shipping capacity surpassed that of the French, German, and Dutch fleets by the 1880s. Sweden added a capacity of 0.9 million tons, and Denmark 0.5 million.

Transoceanic shipping, however, offered limited possibilities without a modern inland transportation network. Cheap mass transportation

Table 6.2   Railway development in Scandinavia, 1911

	Land area per km of railroad (in km^2)	Length of railroads per 100,000 inhabitants (km)	Weight of goods delivered per 100,000 inhabitants	No. of railway journeys per inhabitant
Sweden	32.32	252.5	6.89	10.9
Denmark	10.37	133.9	2.66	11.0
Norway	105.44	129.0	2.42	6.0
Scandinavian average	48.55	180.9	4.09	8.8

Source: Berend and Ránki (1982, 100).

systems had to be created. Until the mid-nineteenth century, inexpensive products such as wood and iron ore were transported only during the winter, when the heavy items could be hauled on the snow. Year-long transportation was achieved partly with canals,[22] but primarily with railroads during the second half (mostly the last third) of the nineteenth century – financed in part by foreign investment. As elsewhere in Europe, modern transport was furnished by railroads. Until 1860, only 600 kilometers of railroad lines traversed the three countries. The first line in Norway, the Oslo–Eidsvoll railroad, did not open until 1854.[23] Unlike the small Danish peninsula and the narrow swath of Norway, both with excellent water transport potential, Sweden desperately needed railroads. It did little to build them until 1860; over the next fifty years, however, its rail network increased to 14,400 kilometers. Railroads connected wooded areas and the northern iron reserves to its industrial centers and ports in Luleå and Narvik. But railroad density in large and sparsely populated Norway and Sweden could not match that of Western Europe. The Scandinavian railroads delivered half the weight of goods per inhabitant, and Scandinavians took less than half as many journeys per year, as in the West. In this respect, Scandinavia remained far behind. (See Table 6.2.)

Although human capital and excellent geopolitical advantages prepared the way for modernization, these previously poor peasant countries lacked sufficient accumulated capital for investment. A domestic merchant class, made affluent by exports over the previous centuries, were important investors in industry. But the West offered not only unlimited markets, but also investment capital. The Swedish state turned to Western financial markets for loans and used them for railroad construction. Several towns contracted foreign loans as well. French and British capital invested in the large wood-exporting companies and the logging industry. In the first stage of modernization, capital inflow was an important factor in Sweden: during the 1880s, it comprised some 45 percent of domestic capital accumulation.[24] "Whether directly or indirectly, the influx of foreign capital was one of the main prerequisites for the expansion of the Swedish economy throughout practically the whole period, ending with the outbreak of the First World War" (Heckscher, 1954, 247–8). As the domestic economy gained strength, foreign capital gradually lost importance. Between 1900 and 1910, it decreased to 16 percent of domestic capital formation.

Foreign capital inflow played an even bigger role in Norway. Since industrial progress was closely connected with electric power generation, and since electric industries had large investment requirements, direct foreign investment was crucial. Until the end of the nineteenth century, 50% of the capital invested in the electric industry came from abroad. It totaled 80% in Norway's mining and chemical industries, and comprised 39% of all industrial investment. After the turn of the century, however, domestic capital formation became paramount. Between 1894 and 1914, foreign capital inflow decreased to one-third of domestic accumulation and a mere 5% of GDP. In 1906, the government banned the foreign ownership of hydroelectric power stations. If foreign capital played an important role at the beginning of the *Gründerzeit*, domestic accumulation and investments gradually predominated at around the turn of the century.

This was partly a consequence of the creation of the modern banking system. Backward, entirely agricultural Sweden established Europe's first national bank in 1668,[25] but the Sveriges Riksbank became a real central bank with issuing monopoly only in 1897. The Scandinavian banking system was thus a relatively late development. The first Danish bank was established in 1846, but the first modern Crédit Mobilier type, the Privatbanken, opened only in 1857. Its services immediately included crediting and investments. Moreover, following the German model, the bank built a huge industrial empire in the sugar, distillery, and beer industries. Government legislation in 1851 made the founding of the Kreditforeninger association possible. There were eighteen commercial banks in Denmark in 1870[26] and thirty in Sweden in 1860. Scottish-type banks were opened in 1864, all chartered "enskilda banks" with unlimited liability, and all note-issuing. Twelve enskilda banks, as well as the first joint-stock banks, were established in 1864–5.[27] One of the most innovative banking institutions was A. O. Wallenberg's Stockholm Enskilda Bank (1856), which functioned as a quasi-central bank until 1897 (Samuelson, 1958; Lundström, 1991).

The creation of modern transportation and financial systems made exploiting the region's geological potential possible. Denmark had rich soil, Sweden and Norway unlimited woods, high-quality iron ore, and a large variety of several other ores such as bauxite. Of great importance, the region's abundant waterways made the production of cheap electric energy possible in countries lacking coal reserves. This paved the way for successful industrialization during the last third of the nineteenth century.

New power resources significantly contributed to the development of the Scandinavian region. Norway and Sweden were among Europe's early electrifiers.[28] Scandinavia profited mightily from the second Industrial Revolution, and it developed the most modern industrial sectors of the turn-of-the-century period. Lumber stood as the point of departure for Norway and Sweden, though less so in Norway. These large countries were covered by immense forests and had long traditions in lumbering and wood exports. Swedish industrial growth gradually accelerated in the nineteenth century – growing 11–20% per decade between 1810 and 1840, 25–34% per decade between 1840 and 1880, and 54–78% per decade from 1880 on. Iron ore and timber production predominated until 1880,[29] when the metal, pulp and paper, and engineering industries took over. Similarly, before 1880, consumer good industries, especially the cotton and woolen industries, produced two-thirds to three-quarters of the region's industrial output; but after 1880, half and ultimately two-thirds of its output was produced by the investment-goods industries (Schön, 1988; Gustafsson, 1991, 210–12).

In the 1870s and 1880s, pulp, paper, steel, and engineering became the dominant sectors of Swedish industry.[30] Europe's paper consumption increased markedly from the 1860s on. Research continually expanded in Sweden's developing chemical industry, which discovered methods for producing pulp by using chemicals to break down wood fibers.[31] Four mechanical paper factories operated in Norway in 1872, but fifty did by 1890. In 1870, 99% of wood was exported in unprocessed form, but only 34% was by 1910. On the other hand, the share of pulp and paper combined increased to more than 65% of exports.

Sweden surpassed Norway and developed the world's most modern pulp and paper industry. At the end of the nineteenth century, mechanical and chemical pulp production was roughly similar in size; by the 1910s, however, two-thirds of pulp was produced by the superior chemical procedure. At that time only about a quarter of exported wood was unprocessed. The pulp and paper industry became the most dynamic leading sector of Swedish industry: output increased by more than 6% per annum between the 1860s and 1895, and it grew yearly by 11% between 1895 and 1914. Pulp

Figure 6.1 Wood, pulp, and paper exports as share of total Swedish exports, 1881/5–1911/13 (Fridlizius, 1963)

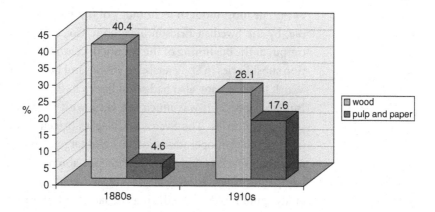

output increased twelvefold between 1892 and 1913, and three-quarters of it was exported. Between 1880 and 1913, paper production grew tenfold. (See Figure 6.1.)

A special use of wood was in the modern match industry, which later became a Swedish monopoly. Matches were invented in the 1830s, but their toxic phosphorus chemicals posed significant risks for workers in match factories. A safer match was invented in the 1840s, and Sweden became one of its leading producers.[32] The Jönköpings Tändsticksfabrik, established in 1848, became a joint-stock company in 1857.[33] The Vulcan Match factory began operation in the 1870s and led the industry during the 1890s. Both firms merged (along with a third competitor) in 1903 to form the Jönköpings & Vulcan Co., which purchased large tracts of Swedish forests. At that time it became a multinational company, with subsidiaries and distribution networks in Britain and other countries.[34]

In addition to wood, Sweden also had some of the highest-quality iron ores, which it processed into iron during the early modern period. The Industrial Revolution in Britain, with its unbeatably cheap products, undermined Sweden's traditional iron industry. The introduction of the Bessemer and Siemens–Martin procedures changed the situation dramatically. Swedish iron output increased by 50% between the 1880s and the 1910s, and steel production more than doubled to comprise 10% of Swedish exports. The iron and steel industry became the country's leading export sector: 80% of domestic production was exported during the last decades of the nineteenth century, and 66% before World War I.

Connected to the paper, iron, and steel industries, the Swedish engineering industry made spectacular progress. Engineering employed 11% of the industrial labor force in 1869, and 19% before the war. At the same time, engineering's share in industrial production jumped from 8% to

14%. The most modern technology of the age was represented, for example, by the Swedish Ericson Telephone Co., which exported 95% of its output at the beginning of the twentieth century, and established production subsidiaries in St. Petersburg, Russia and Beeston in Britain. By World War I, the company also had subsidiaries in Paris, Vienna, Budapest, and Buffalo, USA. This was much the same with Electrolux, which operated in four countries. The Svenska Kullagerfabriken (SKF), a roller-bearing producer, began operations in 1907 and targeted the British, French, and American markets with four subsidiaries abroad. The first multinational companies appeared in Scandinavia. Swedish industrial growth was generally quite rapid: 5.1% during the last third of a century before World War I, with engineering, pulp, and paper attaining a 10.4% annual increase (Gustafsson, 1991, 218, 220).

At the same time, import substitution also played a role in industrial development. Textile production increased by three and a half times between 1890 and 1910, raising its share of domestic consumption from 60% to 80%. In all, Swedish industry more than trebled its labor force, and increased its gross value of production by more than three times, between the 1870s and the war.

Norway was at a disadvantage when it came to the traditional sectors of industrialization. The country's standing, however, changed when electric power generation became possible.[35] Abundant and inexpensive new energy sources enabled it to establish its chemical industry, including the production of artificial fertilizers. Another factor was the inventiveness of Kristian Birkeland, a Norwegian physicist who used electric-arc to nitrogen fixation to produce nitric acid and, as an end product, norgesalpeter (calcium nitrate), a successful artificial fertilizer. The country established electric metallurgy, bauxite, aluminum, and electrotechnical industries partly with British, French, and Swedish investment.[36] Nearly 40% of Norway's joint-stock companies, employing 15% of the labor force, were in foreign hands. Unlike Sweden, however, Norwegian industrialization was less successful prior to World War I. In 1910, more than 43% of the active population still worked in agriculture, forestry, and fishing, and only 25% in industry. But services became the leading sector here before they did so in any other European country. Norway's commercial fleet's shipping services produced huge revenues, comprised half of the country's GDP, and employed more than 30% of its workforce before the war.

An economically backward region until the 1860s, Scandinavia was the only industrial and modernization success story outside the West European core before World War I. (See Table 6.3.) Before the war, only Scandinavia provided a viable model for catching up with the West. Between 1850 and 1870, the per capita income of the Scandinavian

Table 6.3 Per capita industrialization index of Scandinavia, 1800–1913 (Britain in 1800 = 100)

	1800	1860	1913	1800 = 100
Denmark	8	10	33	413
Norway	9	11	31	344
Sweden	8	15	67	838
Advanced West	8	16	55	688
European average	8	17	45	563
Scandinavian average	8.3	12.0	43.7	527
Scandinavia as % of the West	103	75	79	–

Source: Bairoch (1991, 3).

Table 6.4 The catching-up process in Scandinavia: GDP per capita (in 1990 Geary Khamis dollars)

Year	Scandinavia	% of Britain	% of continental West Europe
1850	1,356	57	79
1870	1,642	50	75
1913	3,108	62	81

Source: Maddison (1995).

Note: According to Paul Bairoch, Scandinavia's GNP totaled only 60% of Western Europe's in 1860, but increased to 95% by 1910. According to Angus Maddison's calculations (1995), the three Scandinavian countries' GDP was 75% of the average GDP of six continental West European countries in 1870, but 81% by 1913. In 1870, Scandinavia's GDP was only 50% that of Britain, but 62% by 1913.

countries grew more slowly than it did in Britain or in continental Western Europe, but this dramatically changed after 1870. The GDP of the three Scandinavian countries, only 45% of that of Britain in the mid-nineteenth century, rose to 60% by 1913, and was 80% of continental Western Europe's. (See Table 6.4.) Between 1820 and 1913, the Western and Scandinavian regions both achieved a spectacular transformation

Table 6.5 GDP of twelve countries of Western Europe and Scandinavia (million 1990 Geary Khamis dollars)

	Western Europe	Scandinavia
1820	132,629	100
1870	303,101	229
1900	550,612	415
1913	732,332	552

Source: Maddison (1995, 211).

and increased their gross domestic product by five and a half times. (See Table 6.5.)

Notes

1. Grain output increased by 75 percent between 1720 and 1815, though there were decades of decline during this period. This led not only to an end of grain imports, but also to the creation of export surpluses. Agriculture increased faster than the population did, and per capita production rose by 0.4–0.6 percent per year. The last (mostly localized) famine to hit the country was in the 1860s (Magnusson, 2000, 3–5).

2. Output totaled 42,000 tons during the 1740s, but it stagnated during the following half-century. Iron ore mining was relatively easy in opencast mines, which remained shallow. Primitive furnaces produced iron, though the smelting process was improved in the seventeenth century by adopting the bigger German and French types of furnaces.

3. Russia, in 1760, and Britain, in 1795, attained the Swedish level of iron production and then outstripped it significantly.

4. Mechanization proliferated very slowly; in 1855, the production of the small-scale handicraft industry was valued at 56 million crowns, while mechanized factories produced goods valued at only 18 million crowns.

5. The quantity of Swedish wood exports increased by 566 percent between mid-century and the early 1870s.

6. The Swedish *Stormaktstiden*, the Age of Empire between 1600 and 1720, was a period of wars: warfare raged during seventy-five of these years. The country played a decisive role in the devastating Thirty Years War; its troops

invaded a large part of Russia and even Central Europe. Its natural borders were established during its two wars against Denmark in the mid-seventeenth century and although it lost Finland to Russia in 1809, Sweden established the dual kingdom with Norway in 1814, which existed until 1905.

7. The crowning achievement of the reform, the constitution of 1865, transformed the assembly of the four estates and established a modern bicameral parliament.

8. The Kalmarunion (1397), a union of the three Scandinavian countries under one monarch, led to Danish domination and generated two Swedish revolts in 1434 and 1436. The Swedish peasant armies pushed the Danes out of Sweden. From that time onward, the peasantry became the decisive player in Sweden.

9. The Field Consolidation Act of 1749, the Surveying Act of 1783, the enclosure decrees of 1803 and 1807, and the Redistribution Act of 1827.

10. When Scandinavia became Protestant, the land of the Catholic Church was expropriated and transformed into crown lands, comprising one-third of the region's landed area in the early sixteenth century.

11. Sandberg described the interesting and unique Scandinavian situation as "impoverished but sophisticated," i.e. economically backward but endowed with "a strikingly large stock of human and institutional capital" (Sandberg, 1979, 225).

12. The large number of immigrants and the unlimited amount of virgin land on the American frontier led to a trebling of cultivated land and a quadrupling of the number of farms in the United States during the second half of the nineteenth century. Between 1850 and 1878–82, the combined yearly wheat production of the United States, Canada, Argentina, and Australia increased from 3.1 million to 14.3 million metric tons. In a single decade between 1870–4 and 1880–4, the quantity of exported American grain increased threefold. American grain was cheaper than the cost of production in several European grain-producing countries.

13. It was insignificant in 1870; only 5,000–6,000 hectares were used for its production. By the beginning of World War I, farmers produced fodder on 300,000 hectares. The number of cattle more than doubled between 1871 and 1914, from 1.2 million to 2.5 million. Pigs also increased from 442,000 to 2.5 million.

14. Poultry farming, insignificant in the early 1870s, also increased by leaps and bounds, and the poultry stock rose from 5.9 million in 1893 to 15.1 million by 1914.

15. By the early twentieth century, eighty schools trained 7,000 farmers on a regular basis.

16. A group of farmers gathered in the Ølgod parish in the winter of 1881–2 to discuss joint action to develop their milk business. They commissioned one of the participants, Jacob Stilling-Andersen, who had been trained in

dairy farming at the Tune Agricultural School, to establish a communal dairy factory. This was the first cooperative in Denmark.

17. All worked independently in provincial regions; each member had a single vote, although each was paid according to the number of cows and amount of milk delivered to the cooperative.

18. The inventions of W. Lefeldt, C. Leutschy, and Carl Gustav De Laval in Sweden produced different kinds of centrifugal cream separators more or less at the same time.

19. Traditional home beer production took place throughout the history of Europe. Until the mid-nineteenth century, traditional home brewing methods produced the "hvidtol" in Denmark.

20. Output increased from 130,000 hectoliters in 1870 to 1 million hectoliters by 1905, but only 51 hectoliters were exported.

21. Norway had a shipping capacity of 300,000 tons (sailboat fleet) in 1850, but the capacity of its fleet totaled 1.8 million tons by 1914. Only 12 percent of shipping capacity was composed of steamships prior to 1890, but it rose to around 60 percent by 1910.

22. In Sweden, the 190 kilometer Göta canal, opened in 1868, made inland navigation between Göteborg and Stockholm possible, and it connected the Göta River to the waterways. Extensive construction created a dense Swedish canal network. At the end of the nineteenth century, one kilometer of waterway on average served 66 square kilometers of land – twice as much as in Britain. Denmark built several small waterways, the Øarnas, Köpenhams, and Thyboron canals.

23. With its scarce population, large distances, and extremely mountainous terrain, Norway was not an ideal country for railroads. Construction was very expensive and not profitable. The railroad network increased only modestly, from 400 kilometers in 1870 to 3,100 in the 1910s.

24. According to some estimates, Sweden contracted 1.5 billion crowns ($400 million) during and after the 1880s. Roughly 60–65% of it was French capital. About 10% of the foreign capital inflow went to the credit industry, but only 5% of industry was in foreign hands.

25. Moreover, Johan Palmstruch founded the first private bank, the Stockholm Banco, and issued banknotes in 1656. This bank, however, was also a pioneer in financial fraud: it printed many more notes than its silver reserve warranted, and was unable to exchange the notes for silver coins in 1667. The bank collapsed, and Palmstruch was sentenced to life imprisonment.

26. The newly established Landmandsbanken and Handelsbanken followed during the 1870s. Only 8 banks existed in Denmark in 1855, but 36 did by 1875, and 140 by 1914. The value of deposits increased from 51 million krona in 1857 to 208 million in 1877, and 910 million by 1914.

27. In 1874, 35 commercial banks, 300 savings banks, and 40 mortgage banks operated in Sweden. A number of leading institutions, such as the Svenska Handelsbanken, Skandinaviska Kreditbanken, the Stockholm Enskilda Bank, and the Göteborg Bank, controlled half of the country's banking capital, which rapidly increased from 206 million krona in 1860 to 3,230 million by 1913.

28. Twenty-three power stations with 150,000 horsepower capacity existed in 1900, and 123 stations with 920,000 horsepower capacity in 1914. They served as the basis for the establishment of electric, steel, aluminum, and chemical industries. The Swedish hydroelectric industry produced 1,230 million kilowatt hours of electric energy before the war.

29. During the first wave of industrial development, mechanized textile factories predominated, attaining a 4.4 percent annual growth rate. The sawmill industry boasted a 5 percent annual growth rate. Iron and steel output doubled between 1825 and 1855.

30. In the early 1870s, 2.3 million square meters of wood were exported; this increased to 5.2 million by the end of the century. Wood output in Norway, though it was much less predominant, nonetheless increased by 600,000 square meters between 1850 and 1870 and comprised 42 percent of exports. It declined, however, from that time on, and it made up only 13 percent of exports by 1910.

31. The French scientist René de Réaumur was the first to make paper from wood in the eighteenth century. The German Friedrich Gotlob Keller, who transformed wood to pulp by mechanical grinding and patented the procedure in 1845, effectively established modern mechanized paper production. His procedure, however, soon lost its importance.

32. The real breakthrough, the invention of non-poisonous matches with the use of sesqui-sulfide of phosphorus, occurred only during the 1870s–1880s. The market for matches dramatically expanded at that time as cigarette smoking rapidly proliferated around the turn of the century.

33. This emerged from the proto-industrial cottage industry, and employed 1,300 cottage workers, and only 850 factory workers, as late as 1875.

34. Before World War I, a young managing director, Ivar Kreuger, took over the company. His name became known worldwide during the interwar period.

35. There were already 23 hydroelectric power stations producing 110,000 kW of electric energy by 1900; by 1914, 123 stations increased capacity by more than six times.

36. A professor at the University of Christiania (Oslo), together with an engineer, Samuel Eyde, and financed by the Swedish Wallenbergs, built a hydroelectric power station in Notodden and opened a factory.

CHAPTER 7

Demographic revolution, transformation of life, and standard of living

The key players in the economic transformation in the nineteenth century, as always, were the people – illiterates and the highly educated, males and females, country folk and urbanites, peasants, workers, entrepreneurs, researchers, inventors, doctors, bankers, and government administrators. Demographic changes are themselves important factors in the complex history of the nineteenth century, for Europe's population, for the first time ever in human history, doubled, tripled, and quadrupled in a single century.

The effect of the demographic revolution, however, was not only a much larger European population, but also significantly lengthened life-spans, a healthier population, and decidedly more modern marriage customs, family structures, and even dietary habits. Residential patterns also changed, as a great part of the population moved to rapidly growing cities. The urban explosion had terribly negative side-effects in the first decades, but conditions then improved; the urban settlements were modernized, with better housing, running water, an electric infrastructure, and public transportation. Although industrialization and urbanization uprooted millions of people and led to social upheaval and deteriorating living conditions, the standard of living began to improve from the mid-nineteenth century on. Income differentials were high and even increased for a while. But practically the entire population ultimately enjoyed a higher standard of living around the turn of the twentieth century, and their lives were significantly transformed for the better.

Demographic revolution

Continental Western Europe shared basic socio-political and institutional similarities with the pioneering countries of modern capitalism in Northwestern Europe, and it rapidly adjusted to the developments in that region. This is true for the population explosion that erupted in the Northwest in the eighteenth century. This development, however, began somewhat later in other countries, and it gained full momentum in the nineteenth century. The population of the western half of the continent stagnated between 1300 and 1500, and then increased very slowly, with an annual average of 0.16 percent between 1500 and 1700. As historical statisticians have suggested, the population of Europe was only slightly greater in the seventeenth century than it was in the thirteenth. According to Roger Mols (1974), Europe's population was 82 million in 1500, 105 million in 1600, and 120 million in 1700.

The turn-of-the-nineteenth-century British scholar Thomas R. Malthus analyzed the slow population growth between the eleventh and seventeenth centuries. In his view, the exponential growth (or geometric progression) of the population was in sharp contrast to the linear growth (or arithmetic progression) of agricultural production. The "Malthusian check" occurs when population growth is greater than agricultural production. This cycle of food crises was reproduced frequently and stunted population growth. Fernand Braudel (1979) has listed seventy-three famines in France between the tenth and seventeenth centuries, and sixteen famines in the eighteenth century.[1]

When Malthus published his study, the centuries-long phenomenon that he described and believed to be an eternal truth had just changed in Western Europe. This distinguished professor of history was remarkably ahistorical when he failed to account for the dramatic transformation taking place before his very eyes. A tremendous upheaval had occurred from the second half of the eighteenth century on, first in Northwestern Europe, including his home country. Reflecting the change was a profound shift in European demographic history. Britain and the Netherlands more than doubled their population (by 13.1 million); Western Europe as a whole experienced 0.41 percent population growth per year, in the place of a stagnating 0.16 percent. (See Table 7.1).

A sparsely populated Europe became a relatively densely populated continent. At the end of the eighteenth century, there were between sixty and eighty people per square kilometer in Northwestern Europe, and nineteen per square kilometer in Europe as a whole, which made the region "probably the most highly populated part of the whole world" in 1800 (Armengaud, 1973, 28). In comparison, there were only fourteen inhabitants per square kilometer in Asia.

The miracle of population growth continued in Western Europe during the nineteenth century. The population of the Northwest more than doubled (222.6%) during the first half of the century, though the less

Table 7.1 Population of Western Europe, 1700–1820 (in thousands)

Region	1700	1820	1820 as percent of 1700
Netherlands and Britain	10,465	23,581	225.3
Other West Europe	42,171	64,783	153.6
Total Europe	**126,810**	**224,068**	**176.7**

Source: Based on Maddison (2001, 241).

developed regions experienced slower growth (142.5%). Britain's population more than quadrupled during the century, from 10.5 million in 1801 to 45.6 million in 1913. The population of the Netherlands nearly trebled (from 2.1 to 6.2 million) during this same period. The dimensions of West European population growth were striking: from 45.1 million in 1800, the population totaled 100.4 million in 1850, and 162 million in 1910. The population increased by 223% during the first half of the century, and 360% by 1910 (Cipolla, 1973, 747–8). Such an increase in a single century is unparalleled in history. As the demographic revolution spread throughout Europe, the continent's proportion of the world population rose from 21% to 28% between 1800 and 1913. Its population density also rapidly increased, though it would vary from region to region. There were, on average, 223 inhabitants per square kilometer in England, Belgium, and the Netherlands, and 95 in France, Switzerland, Germany, and Austria before World War I.

Centuries of stagnation were replaced by rapid and continuous population growth. What did Malthus miss in his analysis? What were the causes of these dramatic changes? Initially, birth rates increased significantly, especially in Britain; but ultimately the most important factor was a sharp decline of mortality, especially infant mortality. For centuries, very high death rates (35–36 per 1,000), with some fluctuations, remained constant. Britain's death rates in the mid-eighteenth century were still 30 per 1,000, but they dropped to 26–27 per 1,000 at around 1800, and to 15.1 per 1,000 by 1905–9. Dutch death rates also declined to 26 per 1,000 in the 1850s and to 15 per 1,000 by 1901–10. In the second quarter of the eighteenth century, 195 of every 1,000 newborns died in the first year of their lives in Britain. But the number dropped to 144 in the first quarter of the nineteenth century, and to 127 during the first decade of the twentieth. Infant

Figure 7.1
Changing birth
and death rates
in Europe,
1800–1913
(Glass and
Grebenik, 1965,
83, 97)

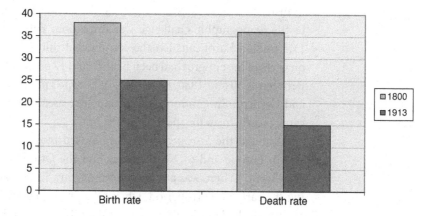

mortality began to decrease in several other countries as well – dropping in France, for example, from 191 to 132 per 1,000.

Death rates were also cut in half in the West to 14–16 per 1,000. While the average adult life-span did not markedly change, the life expectancy of infants rose to a dramatic degree. Most historical demographic studies maintain that life expectancy was virtually constant between 1000 and 1820 – immovably fixed at 25–26 years.[2] This remained the case in India, China, and Africa until 1900. In Western Europe, however, a demographic shift began to be seen in 1820: in that year, life expectancy rose a full decade to 36 years and then jumped to 46 years by 1900–13. In the Netherlands, Britain, Switzerland, and France, it rose even further to 50–52 years.

For centuries, high birth rates of 36–40 per 1,000 accompanied very high death rates throughout Europe. Birth and death rates continually counterbalanced each other and caused only moderate population growth. This suddenly changed in the nineteenth century. Although both birth and death rates began declining in the rapidly industrializing West, the decline of the death rates far exceeded the decline of birth rates. In France, the birth rate decreased from 36–37 per 1,000 at the end of the eighteenth century to 20 per 1,000 before World War I. It dropped to 25 per 1,000 in Britain, and to 23 per 1,000 in Belgium. Most of the Western countries saw 20–26 births per 1,000 at that time. (See Figure 7.1.) The larger decline of death rates was the cause of the rapid population growth. The nineteenth century became a period of massive population explosion. This meant many more available hands in the fields and workshops, and many more mouths to feed and bodies to clothe. This development became one of the most important driving forces of the economic transformation in the century.

With its still relatively backward economy, Western Europe was unable to absorb its spectacularly growing population until the 1860s. There was not enough land to support the rural population, and not enough new industrial and service jobs to take up the slack. The only viable solution to the demographic challenge was migration. Between 1800 and 1880, 11.5 million Europeans left the continent. Until 1850, more than three-quarters of the émigrés had been British, and 17 percent had been German. Between 1850 and 1880, 82 percent of Europe's migrants were still British and German. Emigration dramatically increased after that period, but it came mostly from the peripheral regions.

Although the European migrants moved mostly overseas, migration within Europe and to North Africa and the Ottoman Empire was also significant.[3] There was a long pattern of intra-European migration during the early modern period, when religious intolerance and destructive warfare pushed people to other countries. The Spanish Jews moved to the Netherlands, the French Huguenots moved to the Netherlands and Germany, the Walloons migrated from the war-ridden southern Low Countries to Scandinavia. Hungary invited German peasants to settle in deserted areas when the Ottoman occupation of the country's mid-section ended. Settlers were offered feudal fee holidays for years in the seventeenth century. Serbs moved north when the Ottomans occupied their country, and settled in the border zone of the Habsburg Empire as free peasant-soldiers.

Migration became more common in the nineteenth century. Approximately 4 million German peasants moved to Russia to obtain free land in Siberia, and millions of Jews left Russia and the Polish territories for Central Europe and countries overseas after a wave of government-organized pogroms. Of the 5–6 million intra-European migrants, only a few thousand entrepreneurs made the risky move to another country to try their luck and profit from their skills. Even Britain was not an exception. Eric Hobsbawm noted that "dynamic entrepreneurs of Edwardian Britain were, more often than not, foreigners or minority groups" (Hobsbawm, 1969, 169). Aside from hundreds of entrepreneurs, those engineers[4] and skilled workers who migrated were also of tremendous value to the so-called latecomer countries.[5]

The causes of the population explosion

What caused the population explosion in Western Europe? A fundamental factor was a significant improvement in health. This was partly the result of the eradication of medieval killer diseases. The plague, smallpox, cholera, and other contagious diseases had decimated the populations of Europe during the Middle Ages.[6] The plague died out thanks to Western Europe's control of its ports and inspection of migrants from disease-ridden regions outside Europe. Other common medieval diseases, however, lingered much longer. Major outbreaks of smallpox dramatically raised the death toll in several parts of Europe in the eighteenth century, killing between 25 and 50 percent of its victims. Cholera struck Europe in the 1820s, 1830s, and three times between 1848 and 1872. The cholera epidemic of 1830 killed half of those who contracted it – a catastrophe that was repeated only a few years later.

Box 7.1 The "pan-European" invention of vaccination

One of the most important factors behind the demographic revolution of the nineteenth century was the invention of vaccines. The elimination of medieval diseases contributed to the complex phenomenon of demographic changes and the rapid population growth that transformed Europe. The demographic revolution was a pan-European phenomenon, as was the invention of vaccines. Three giant personalities, a Briton, a Frenchman, and a German (and quite a few others beside them), played central roles in this development.

The breakthrough emerged in the British countryside. At the age of fourteen, Edward Jenner became an apprentice to the resident surgeon in Chipping Sodbury, and was then trained by a London surgeon to practice medicine in Berkeley, Gloucestershire. Jenner was a man of curiosity and a keen observer of nature. He became a fellow of the Royal Society in 1789, based on his observations on the predatory conduct of the cuckoo bird. He had heard legends of the rarity of milkmaids contracting smallpox and began to study the problem. He made some interesting observations in 1778, and again in 1798, when smallpox returned to Berkeley. He realized that peasant women who milked cows and had contracted so-called cowpox, a mild infection stemming from a common bovine illness, developed immunity against the deadly smallpox. Like all of his contemporaries, Jenner knew nothing of microbes or viruses. Nonetheless, he inoculated his subjects with secretions from a cowpox rash to prevent smallpox. He called the procedure vaccination, using the Latin word for cow (vacca). The experiment succeeded. A relatively harmless microbe, the cowpox virus, stimulated the human body to produce antibodies against smallpox. Jenner published his *Inquiry into the Causes and Effects of the Variolae Vaccination*, which became a world sensation. Within three years, 100,000 people had been vaccinated in Britain.*

The scientific basis for vaccination that paved the way for the discovery of additional vaccines was discovered much later, through the work of France's Louis Pasteur. Born into a peasant family – his father, a veteran of the Napoleonic wars, trained and worked as a tanner – Louis was the first in his family to go to high school, and then to the École Normale in Paris. He became a research chemist. He learned of Jenner's discovery and assumed that other vaccines must also exist. His primary tool was the microscope, and his watershed discovery was the existence of microorganisms in the air that cause disease. In so doing, he established the scientific basis for additional research. Pasteur was the founder of microbiology and the germ theory of diseases.

He, of course, was not a lone researcher, though he worked with very few assistants, mostly with Charles Chamberland and Pierre P. E. Roux. He also utilized his rivals' findings, among them those of Antoine Béchamp and Henri Toussaint. In the 1860s, he discovered a procedure to preserve wine, beer, and milk; the process, "pasteurization," was named after him. Pasteur determined that microorganisms in wine, beer, and milk led to their souring and deterioration. Before bottling, he briefly heated wine to 60 degrees Celsius, and milk to much higher temperatures, to kill the microorganisms and preserve the products.

In 1867, public funds were used to build Pasteur a laboratory, which became known as the Pasteur Institute. He began working there on vaccinations. In 1880, using fourteen-day-old, and thus weakened, bacteria in an experiment, Pasteur quite accidentally discovered (as so often happens) that weakened microbes and viruses are the best way to stimulate the body to produce antibodies and provide immunity. In 1881, he produced a vaccine against anthrax, which was pervasive among cows and other animals, using weakened anthrax organisms. An experiment with fifty sheep was a great success. He was equally successful with silkworm disease. Five years later, he discovered the vaccine against rabies, and, before he could undergo human experiments, was compelled to use it in an emergency case on a young boy who had been bitten by an infected dog. It worked. These pathbreaking discoveries had a tremendous impact on the economy, animal husbandry, food and beverage processing, and, most of all, on human mortality rates.

Just as he was inspired by Jenner, Pasteur had a similar effect on other scholars. Among them was the British Joseph Lister, a surgeon in Edinburgh and Glasgow. He grappled with an egregious 50 percent death rate among patients undergoing operations in hospitals. Pasteur's discovery of the existence of airborne microbes led Lister to identify the cause of sepsis. By spraying carbolic acid into wounds and using post-operative carbolic acid dressing on surgical incisions, he was able to prevent sepsis.

Another of Pasteur's cohorts, the German medical doctor Robert Koch, studied the cause of disease and identified various microbes that caused anthrax in 1875 (prior to Pasteur's discovery of the vaccine). In 1882, Koch's hypothesis established the methodology for further research and experiment. Most importantly, he discovered the bacteria that caused one of the greatest killers of the age, tuberculosis. A premature announcement in 1890, however, almost destroyed his career, because he was at that time using too high a dose of the vaccine and killed most of his patients. He solved the problem, however, after 1900. Henceforth, Koch made enormous progress: he began using dyes to stain invisible microbes, and had a tremendous breakthrough in discovering the cause of cholera. By 1900, after twenty-one years of research, Koch had identified twenty-one disease-causing organisms.

Paul Ehrlich, a younger German co-researcher who had begun his work at Koch's institute, went on to discover the causes of, and develop vaccines for, diphtheria and malaria, and he began to tackle syphilis, the sexually transmitted mass killer of the age. He successfully developed an arsenic-based drug arsphenamine (commercially named Salvarsan 606), which was first administered to patients in 1911.

Together with several others, Jenner, Pasteur, and Koch changed the history of healthcare, and were important players in the nineteenth-century transformation.

Based on Allen (2007), Debré (2000) and Brock (1999).
* During the Franco-Prussian War of 1870, smallpox infected many people in both armies. Of the Prussians who contracted the disease only 5.4 percent died because all conscripts were vaccinated. The death toll among the French soldiers was 19 percent because vaccination was not compulsory in France.

The historic turning point occurred when Dr. Edward Jenner, an ingenious Gloucestershire physician, invented a cowpox virus vaccine that stimulated the production of antibodies and created strong and long-lasting immunity. The British government institutionalized vaccination and provided free vaccines in 1840. Mandatory universal smallpox vaccination was introduced in 1853, which successfully eradicated the disease.

The most important breakthrough was the discovery of the germ theory of diseases, developed by the Frenchman Louis Pasteur and the German Robert Koch, the founders of bacteriology. The two demonstrated that organisms cause diseases (the Koch postulate), and that immunization, using weakened bacteria, could prevent them. Appointed to the Imperial Health Office in Berlin in 1880, Koch isolated several bacteria, among them tuberculosis, the cause of one in seven deaths that century. Medieval diseases were eradicated as a result of these theoretical discoveries, as well as the isolation of various bacteria, among them the vibrio cholera bacterium. New vaccines and practical health regulations began to be introduced in the mid-nineteenth century.

The discovery and application of antiseptic procedures, the sterilization of surgical instruments, and the emphasis on hygiene in hospitals also dramatically decreased death rates.[7] In the 1840s, infectious disease caused a third of the deaths in Europe, and, when combined with respiratory diseases, half of the deaths. Between 1848–72 and 1901–10, deaths caused by infectious diseases in Britain decreased by 60 percent, and deaths by respiratory diseases by 16 percent. Appreciating just how much the lack of sanitation caused illnesses was a major factor. This was clearly seen in maternal mortality. In 1847, the Hungarian-born Viennese Ignáz Fülöp Semmelweiss discovered the cause of puerperal (or childbed) fever, which on average killed every third mother giving birth in hospitals. Semmelweiss reported that washing hands and meticulously disinfecting facilities decreased infection and reduced the death rate to one in a hundred. All these discoveries spread like wildfire across the continent: Napoleon ordered compulsory vaccination against smallpox in all the conquered countries. The first step toward state-regulated sanitation in the Habsburg Empire was the *Normativum Sanitatis* issued by Maria Theresa (Berend and Ránki, 1982, 53).

Technical improvements in tools were also a factor. In the first half of the eighteenth century, the German-born (and Dutch resident) Gabriel Fahrenheit and the Swedish Anders Celsius invented various types of modern thermometers. In 1816, the French René Laënnec invented the stethoscope, which was developed further by Arthur Leared's binaural stethoscope in 1851, and then replaced by the version used today developed by George Cammann. The German Carl Friedrich Zeiss, who opened a small workshop in Jena in 1846, produced the first modern optical microscope.[8] This modern and incomparably better magnifying tool became the prized instrument of Pasteur and Koch and aided them immensely in diagnosis and research.

Improving health naturally increased life expectancy. But the most important factor in ridding Europe of the Malthusian check and in generating a rapid increase of its population was the agricultural revolution and the enormous increase in food production. The significance of food supply, Paul Bairoch (1973a) notes, is demonstrated in the fact that Britain's population doubled in a seventy-year period between the middle of the eighteenth and the middle of the nineteenth century, an increase which had previously taken sixteen centuries to occur. In 1780–90, the average height of men from France and Austria was 160 centimeters, but by 1900, it had increased to 167 centimeters (Mironov and A'Hearn, 2008, 912).[9]

During the nineteenth century, the earlier achievements of the Flemish, Dutch, and British agricultural revolutions spread throughout the European continent, and they were the most decisive factor in ending famine, strengthening the population's resistance to disease, and contributing to a heretofore unheard-of population growth. It indeed seems "beyond doubt that the increase in food resources . . . in the first half of the century was a vital factor in sustaining, if not initiating, the demographic revolution" (Bairoch, 1973a).

Changing family functions and female labor

One consequence of the demographic and economic changes was the transformation of the basic unit of society, the family. The nineteenth century witnessed the disappearance of the traditional family structure. In his six-volume classic work, *L'organisation de la famille*, Frédéric Le Play (1871) described the gradual disappearance of the three-generation *famille souche* or stem family, and the rise of the two-generation nuclear family. This transformation started much earlier in the most advanced Western countries. According to M. Mitterauer and R. Sieder (1982), the mean household size was around five in Britain in the seventeenth and eighteenth centuries, and three in Amsterdam in 1755. "The mean size of co-resident groups remained remarkably constant at about 4.75 persons per household across Northwestern Europe from the seventeenth to the early twentieth century" (Seccombe, 1992, 236).

This new structure became characteristic of Western Europe during the nineteenth century. The gradual dissolution of the stem family led to comprehensive social change. One element was the gradual liberation of women from a subordinated status in the family. "Marriage lost its character as a property transaction . . . Parental and community influence . . . declined" (Seccombe, 1992, 235). The increasing independence of women, who began working outside the household, undermined old patriarchal relations. Female employment was pervasive: in Britain, more than 40% of women were employed outside their homes; they comprised some 30% of the workforce between 1850 and 1870, and they made up 34% of British workers in 1880. This was more or less characteristic of Western Europe in general, though the proportion was higher in Norway and Denmark (40% and 50% in non-agricultural employment respectively) and substantially lower in Germany and Sweden (18%). Women comprised 40% of the workforce in France in the middle of the nineteenth century, but their share decreased to 36% by 1910.

The proportion of female employment in Western Europe generally remained roughly 30% in 1910. This slight decline was caused by the spread of a new social norm in the better-off strata of society. Hygiene in the home, nutrition, and children's health became newly recognized values and social standards. It became fashionable to leave a job before one's marriage and become a housewife. Being the only breadwinner became a source of male pride, and having a working wife a source of shame. This new attitude gradually predominated in Britain, the Netherlands, and other affluent societies. In the first decade of the twentieth century, four out of five middle-class women in the Netherlands left their jobs before getting married. The lower strata of society could not afford to do the same, and 35–45% of women who married unskilled workers continued working themselves. Nevertheless, as "social classes competitively emulate the social strata above them . . . , being a housewife became over time the dominant choice among the lower classes as well" (Van Poppel *et al.*, 2009, 100–1, 118). The withdrawal of married women from the workforce slowly began in the early twentieth century. At the same time, women remained second-class citizens: they did not have political rights, were excluded from parliamentary electorates, and were paid far less than men. In the early nineteenth century, Britain's female workers earned one-third to one-half of a male worker's salary.

The function of the family dramatically changed as well. At the same time that large numbers of women began working outside the home, Europe's modernizing states began assuming several traditional family functions. Before the eighteenth century, servants and apprentices had belonged to the family and were under its "surrogate parental supervision." The head of the household was even legally responsible for their actions. But one of the first changes was to end this arrangement (Kussmaul, 1994, 2). The traditional three-generation family (and even the early nuclear family) with servants and apprentices was a basic work organization unit and a protector of its members, exacting revenge for harm done to members of the family. The family also educated and socialized its children. The modern two-generation family, however, lost most of these functions when they were shifted to the public sphere. Work was organized outside the families, protection was provided by public law enforcement, and children were educated in schools and workshops. The family, a "rigidly hierarchical institution . . . , [gradually became] a partnership of individuals . . . [with] greater independence and the right to live their own lives" (Mitterauer and Sieder, 1982, 88).

Urbanization

The modern economic transformation went hand in hand with urbanization. A new type of settlement, the industrial city, emerged, at times out of small villages that had expanded their populations. New industrial suburbs mushroomed around old capital cities. Urbanization was probably the most important life-style change in the nineteenth century. Millions of peasants abandoned their villages and descended on industrial centers seeking jobs and new opportunities.

Urbanization was a momentous and punishing process. Manchester, a medieval township and marketplace with 2,000 inhabitants, became a center for the wool, cotton, and silk proto-industries during the early modern centuries. Nicknamed "Cottonopolis," it contained 10,000 inhabitants already in the early eighteenth century. Manchester emerged as the heartland of the British Industrial Revolution and the rising textile industry in the late eighteenth century. A whole network of industrial satellite settlements (Blackburn, Bolton, Burnley, Oldham, Wigan, Rochdale, Salford, and others) sprang up around it and in some cases incorporated into it: prior to World War I, greater Manchester was a city of half a million inhabitants.

Another type of urban development was embodied by the German Ruhrgebiet, a 4,500-kilometer agricultural area encompassing three rivers. In the nineteenth century, a number of walled medieval settlements (such as Dortmund, Essen, Duisburg, Bochum, Gelsenkirchen, and Oberhausen), each with a few thousand inhabitants, gradually combined to form an enormous polycentric urban-industrial agglomeration – the home of some of the world's largest industrial companies (including Krupp and Thyssen). Essen alone had grown to a population of nearly 600,000, and Ruhrgebiet as a whole contained more than 3 million residents around World War I.

The rise of Budapest is characteristic of a third type of urban development. It was made up of a medieval capital city (Buda) and three connected settlements with 150,000 inhabitants in 1848. The three townships united in 1873 to create Budapest, already the center of the growing flour mill industry. Rapid, American-type, urban growth culminated with the expansion of a ring of satellite industrial suburbs (such as Kispest, Ujpest, Pesterzsébet, Csepel, and Budaörs) at the turn of the twentieth century. The suburbs' population increased tenfold by World War I. Budapest grew to a population of one million and comprised 54 percent of the Hungarian industrial workforce – the eighth largest industrial city in prewar Europe.[10]

The number of urban inhabitants increased by 1–2% per annum during the nineteenth century, and did so with increasing urgency. In 1860, 100–120 million Europeans were living in some seventy major cities in an entirely new human environment. A total of 11 million were living in the 35 largest European cities, most of them in Western Europe, in 1850, and the urban population more than trebled to 34 million by 1910. In that year, 75% of Britain's population, 57% of Belgium's, 53% of the Netherlands', and 49% of Germany's was concentrated in cities.

One-third to one-half of the population of Western Europe had been uprooted from their rural villages and relocated in an alien urban environment, where they worked twelve hours a day in dreary, oppressive factories. The change was dramatic. As the poet William Blake ruminated, "And was Jerusalem builded here,/Among the dark Satanic Mills?" In his fictitious "Coketown," which probably reflected Manchester which he visited in 1839, Charles Dickens in *Hard Times* painted this urban environment in dismally dark colors, and sarcastically refuted Jeremy Bentham's and John Stuart Mill's "utilitarian" optimism over improving the human condition in Victorian England.

This cataclysmic change itself created a social earthquake. As Karl Polanyi explains:

Social calamity is primarily a cultural not an economic phenomenon that can be measured by income figures... the disintegration of the cultural environment of the victim is then the cause of the degradation... its lies in the lethal injury of the institutions in which his social existence is embodied... [It] happen[s] to people in the midst of violent externally introduced... change... though their standard of life... may have been improved. (Polanyi, 1964, 157–9)

The standard of living and the diet revolution

Although wages slowly increased, the standard of living did not improve for the first two or three generations of the nineteenth century, or it did so extremely moderately. For one thing, housing and sanitary conditions could not improve at the same rate as urbanization progressed. As the young Friedrich Engels dramatically described in 1844, based on his own experience in Britain, the living conditions in urban housing were inhumane and grueling. Quite often ten to twelve laborers, who worked at different times, were jammed in one room, often sharing the same bed in rotating shifts. Many lived in crowded attics and cellars. In the worst workers' slum in Manchester, one hundred houses shared a single common "toilet," a large hole in the corner of the yard. Even in 1907, only one-third of the city's toilets were water closets, with sewage running directly into the river that supplied the city's drinking water. Not surprisingly, a calamitous cholera outbreak decimated the population in 1832. Twenty percent of the inhabitants of Liverpool lived in cellars in 1840, and 10 percent of Berlin's did so as late as 1880. Death rates were 25 percent higher among people who lived directly under roofs or in cellars. In Glasgow in 1911, the mortality rate was twice as high for people who lived in one-room dwellings as it was for those living in two to four rooms. Until the 1870s, running water and appropriate sewage systems were mostly lacking. Only 15 percent of German cities had running water in 1870. The conditions of urban Europe hardly improved until the 1870s, and generally did so only in the 1880s and 1890s. Until then, the urban environment was a web of sicknesses, especially respiratory and digestive diseases, such as tuberculosis and diarrhea. Demographers speak of an "urban penalty" in the period of early urbanization. Infant mortality was about 50 percent higher in the ten largest cities in Germany in the 1870s than it was in the countryside. In Britain, where improvement had already begun in the 1840s, the infant mortality rate was only 15 percent higher in the big cities at that time. By 1900, the gap narrowed throughout Western Europe to 10–15 percent (Leonard and Ljungberg, 2010, 118–22).

Box 7.2 The misery of the working class and the birth of welfare institutions

The Industrial Revolution and the industrialization of Western Europe created a rapidly growing class of industrial workers, which gradually became the majority of the working population. For the first time, the industrial workers amassed in newly built or expanded cities, living in miserable slums under abominable housing and working conditions. The first generations of laborers worked ten to twelve hours daily, including the pervasive and severely under-paid female and child workforce. Industrial accidents were commonplace, such as the mine catastrophe in Ferndale (Wales) that killed 178 miners in 1867, or the one in Mons, Belgium that left 110 dead in 1875. Workers were regularly dismissed if they were injured or once they turned fifty, and were left to decline into abject poverty. In *Oliver Twist* (1838), Charles Dickens, himself having been a child laborer, painted a dramatic picture of the workhouses to which the Poor Law sent tens of thousands of destitute paupers, as well as the horrific slums, crime, and poverty that engulfed this young working class.

In 1844, 24-year-old Friedrich Engels, a scion of a well-to-do German entrepreneurial family, published *The Condition of the Working Class in England* based on his experiences during his stay in Manchester. He paints a grim picture of the big new industrial cities, where the mortality rate was four times higher than in the surrounding countryside (Engels, [1844] 1975).

Although working conditions and workers' living standards improved during the last third of the nineteenth century, the great majority of workers continued to live at the edge of poverty. At a British Industrial Remuneration Conference in 1885, a speaker noted:

Two millions of skilled workers ... are living habitually in a state of ease ... of the modest sort ... The other five million include the labourers and less skilled workers, male and female, whose maximum wages only suffice for the necessities and barest decencies of existence, and for whom therefore any mischance means penury, passing swiftly into pauperism. (quoted in Hobsbawm, 1996, 228)

After a period of spontaneous riots from the 1810s to the 1840s, and of short-lived relief organizations such as the Chartist movement, an array of workers' self-defense groups, trade union organizations, powerful party organizations, and the socialist movement grew during the last third of the century.

The Paris Commune, the first workers' revolution, signaled a turning point in 1871, though it was suppressed in a bloodbath. Marxist socialist parties were founded in Germany in 1875, in Denmark in 1876–8, in Belgium in 1885, in Sweden in 1887, and in several other Western countries at the turn of the century. The socialist parties achieved their first electoral successes at the same time that democratizing societies first allowed universal male suffrage. The German socialists won 20% of the votes in 1890, and nearly 35% in 1912. The Danish socialists won nearly 20% and 30% in 1901 and 1913, respectively. The socialists in Finland scored the most dramatic victory at the beginning of World War I, winning 47% of the vote.

German Chancellor Bismarck's attempt to strangle socialism failed miserably. His anti-socialist legislation, which banned and suppressed the socialist movement, proved highly counterproductive and resulted only in strengthening the socialist party. Bismarck changed tactics between 1883 and 1889 and attacked from the other side: he sought to take the wind out of the socialist sails by stealing their programs and introducing welfare institutions, such as accident and health insurance and a general pension scheme for aged and invalid workers.

The Vatican joined the battle against socialism. In a quite unprecedented manner, Pope Leo XIII delivered his encyclical on the Condition of Labor, the *Rerum Novarum*, in 1891. Though explicitly condemning the socialist solution, the Pope's description of the workers' conditions was not so very different from that of Engels.

Some opportune remedy must be found quickly for the misery and wretchedness pressing so unjustly on the majority of the working class... [The] working men... isolated and helpless, to the hardheartedness of employers... a small number of very rich men have been able to lay upon the teeming masses of the labouring poor a yoke little better than that of slavery itself. (*Rerum Novarum*, 1891)

The Scandinavian countries followed the German initiatives, though they had taken their own first steps even before Bismarck. The Commission on Workers' Conditions functioned in Denmark and proposed a mostly state-funded but voluntary pension system in 1878. In the end, both Denmark and Sweden made the first significant steps towards a universal, basically tax-financed, welfare system. Unlike in Germany, where measures targeted the "class enemy," the Scandinavian system covered all of society. It did so because it acknowledged that solidarity was a deeply rooted cultural value, and because the agrarian-farmer middle class, especially after the agricultural crisis of the 1870s–1880s, demanded it. A special characteristic of these systems was the use of taxes instead of the insured's personal contributions to finance the program. Sweden introduced the first compulsory and universal pension system in the world in 1913. As Peter Baldwin maintains, "It embodied a solidarity of the entire community, including all citizens regardless of class, frequently offering them equal flat-rate benefits and relying heavily on tax-financing to distribute burdens by the ability to shoulder them" (Baldwin, 1990, 60).

France introduced welfare programs, such as pension plans, in 1910, and Britain institutionalized a national insurance system, old-age pensions on a non-contributory basis, and unemployment benefits in 1911. Austria established insurance for occupational injuries in 1887, and health insurance in 1888; the Netherlands introduced insurance for occupational injuries in 1901, and a pension system in 1913. Finland, Italy, and Norway followed with partial insurance schemes. The seeds of the welfare state were sown.

Based on Hobsbawm 1969, [1975] 1996), Sassoon (1996), Baldwin (1990), and *Rerum Novarum* (1891).

As several observers described it, an emerging working class was "dehumanized into slum dwellers" during the first half of the nineteenth century. Social conditions became a "veritable abyss of human degradation." The "avalanche of social dislocation . . . [and human] catastrophe was the accompaniment of a vast movement of economic improvement" (Polanyi, 1964, 39–40).

In the 1950s and 1960s, a highly political debate sought to clarify the consequences of the Industrial Revolution and early industrialization for the living standards of the population. "Optimists" and "pessimists" held diametrically opposing views on this issue (Hartwell, 1971; Hobsbawm, 1964). The debate was resumed in the 1980s, and has continued since. Peter Lindert and Jeffrey Williamson (1983) revisited the controversy and concluded that English real wages increased by 50 percent between 1780 and 1830, and then doubled by 1851. But other analyses have drawn different conclusions. Feinstein (1972) estimates a 20 percent increase between 1820 and 1850, and an additional 9 percent between 1850 and 1870. Studies reviewing the wages of construction workers suggest that wages declined in most of Northern and Western Europe during the last decades of the eighteenth century and the Napoleonic wars, and then recovered in varying degrees after 1820 (Pamuk and Van Zanden, 2010, 224). Anthropometric studies came to the same conclusions: the average height of British soldiers decreased by 2 centimeters during the last four decades of the eighteenth century, and began to increase only after 1860 (Komlos, 1998). At the end of the day, "it is clear that improvements in standard of living were limited until 1870" (Pamuk and Van Zanden, 2010, 219). Industrialization negatively impacted three generations of Western Europeans until economic development began to improve the living standards and quality of life of those that followed.

Particularly in the last third of the nineteenth century, improvement was significant in all respects. Government legislation improved conditions in both factories and housing and restricted the length of workdays. The British Parliament set the stage when it limited workdays to nine hours in 1873, but France would follow only in 1904 with a ten-hour workday. Several countries prohibited the employment of women at night or in mines. Germany introduced a six-week maternity leave. Child labor was restricted, and the employment of children under twelve was banned in most countries by 1900.

The central water supply gradually expanded from the 1860s–1870s on (though water purification would take longer), and sewage systems and water closets were installed in one or two decades. In addition to improving sanitation systems, a general awareness of cleanliness and personal hygiene proliferated, first among the middle class. Together with the proliferation of families with a single male breadwinner and the gradual withdrawal of women from the workforce, home cleanliness and the breastfeeding of babies radically changed living conditions and sharply cut infant mortality.

A public health infrastructure, such as pest control, water purification, the disposal of urban waste, improved medical procedures, and the building of hospital networks, increased life expectancy by decades in the most advanced Western regions during the nineteenth century (Suchit, 2001, 735, 737).

The quality of life in the overcrowded industrial cities and most urban settlements began significantly improving during the last third of the century. Governments took action to ameliorate the conditions in housing. The 1868 Health Reform Act in Britain closed cellar dwellings, opened public baths, and eradicated slums – a gradual process that was completed before World War I with the construction of council houses. Along with running water and water closets, gas and later electric lighting began to proliferate. Gas lighting was introduced in Brno in 1847, and its Municipal Theater was lit by electric lamps in 1882.

Box 7.3 The Bon Marché department store: the retail trade revolution

The industrialization of Europe went hand in hand with rapid urbanization. London and Paris increased their populations sevenfold before World War I to 7.2 and 2.9 million, respectively. Two million people lived in Berlin, and between 0.5 and 1.0 million resided in Hamburg, Munich, and Cologne. Manchester, Glasgow, Liverpool, Marseille, and Lyon each had a population of 700,000–800,000. The transformation of the economy, the urbanized settlement structure, and the rise of living standards, especially for the growing middle class, soon generated new consumption habits, the mania for "shopping," and a revolution in retail trade.

In the 1830s–1840s, new types of stores appeared. These were bigger establishments dependent on large turnover which they achieved by selling at lower prices. One of them, the Ville de Paris, employed 150 people. They introduced fixed prices, exchanged goods, and reimbursed shoppers for returned products. The Petit Saint-Thomas featured catalogues, discount prices, and sales in the 1840s. Specialized chain stores proliferated. Marks and Spencer in Britain had 286 stores, employed 68,000 workers, and served 13 million shoppers by 1903. The real milestone of the retail revolution, however, was the birth of the department stores, the "cathedrals of consumption" (Crossick and Jaumain, 1999).

Just as the railway inspired the best painters of the age, Turner and Monet, the department store captured the imagination of one of the greatest writers of the age, Emile Zola. After visiting the Bon Marché department store, he wrote *Au bonheur des dames* (*The Ladies' Paradise*) in 1883 about an imaginary department store with 39 departments and 800 employees. Zola celebrated as symbols of modernity the soaring consumerism and the advance of modern businesses, which vanquished the outmoded small shops. He called his novel "a poem of modern activity."

The allure of the department store is even more apparent in mass culture. Around the turn of the century, several musicals and plays in Britain featured department stores as their settings or topics. These included *The Girl from Kay's*, *The Working Life of a Shop Assistant*, *The Shop Girl and her Master*, and the one-act *Selfrich's Annual Sale*. In the mid-1890s, H. J. W. Dam wrote the extremely popular musical comedy, *The Shop Girl*. In one song, the shop girl glorifies the department store:

When I came to the shop some years ago
I was terribly shy and simple . . .
But soon I learnt with a customer's aid
How men make up to a sweet little maid;
And another lesson I've learnt since then
How a dear little maid "makes up" for men.
A touch of rouge that is just a touch
And black in the eye, but not too much;
And a look that makes the Johnnies stop
I learnt that all in the shop, shop, shop!

(Rappaport, 1999, 195)

One of the first "cathedrals of consumption" in Europe was the Bon Marché in Paris. This opened as a modest store in the 1830s, and had four departments and twelve employees in 1852, when Aristide Boucicaut became one of its co-proprietors. Boucicaut had been an employee, later department chief, of the Petit Saint-Thomas. Paying 50,000 francs of his own or borrowed funds, he became co-owner, and then, in 1863, the store's sole owner. The business quickly expanded. Sales volume increased by leaps and bounds, and the workforce grew to an astounding 1,788 people in the late 1870s. Boucicaut erected a large new building, spanning an entire block, on nearly 53,000 square meters. This was the first building in Europe specifically built for a store. The foundation cornerstone was laid down in 1869. Paris's top architects, L. A. Boileau and Gustave Eiffel, built something like a genuine cathedral, using thin iron pillars and glass skylights to create an enormous open space to exhibit goods. A sensation at the time, the *grand magasin* served as the model for department stores appearing throughout Europe. Bon Marché employed 3,173 people when it opened its new building in 1877, and 7,000 prior to World War I.

Bon Marché opened more and more new departments: thirty-six in the 1880s, and fifty-two by 1912, selling clothing, children's wear, furniture, rugs, perfume, camping wares, travel goods, stationery and toys, shoes, kitchen wares, leather products, and Chinese and Japanese specialties. On a good day, 10,000–20,000 shoppers visited the store, and far larger numbers on special sale days. "By 1914, then, there was little in the way of consumer goods that one could not buy at the Bon Marché" (Miller, 1981, 52).

The store invariably needed more space, and it added a new annex in 1899 and another major extension in 1912 (connected by underground passage). This shopper's paradise was not only enormous in size, but also a pioneer of customer service. Its doors were open from 7:30 a.m. to 9:00 p.m. in summertime, and from 8:00 a.m. to 8:00 p.m. in wintertime. Interpreters roamed through the store looking for foreign customers to assist. The store mailed out 1.5 million illustrated catalogs in 1894, a quarter of a million being sent abroad. It had introduced mail order service as early as the 1860s: 150 horses and 80 wagons delivered goods to shoppers' homes at the end of the century, reaching 600 suburbs, towns and villages by 1912.

Bon Marché developed its own production sectors making clothing and lingerie, partly by relying on the old putting-out system with small workshops, but also by opening its own factory inside the store. The latter employed 600 workers by the 1890s. The store developed a paternalistic policy towards its workers and created its own welfare institutions to attract and maintain its staff. It provided housing on the top floor of the store's new building for single employees. It gave free meals to every employee twice a day in four large dining rooms. It offered free German and English courses in the evenings and sent the best students to London for six months, all expenses paid. Invited lecturers covered a variety of subjects, doctors provided free consultations, and music and fencing courses were readily available for all employees. Bon Marché saw itself as a *grande famille*.

Based on Miller (1981) and Crossick and Jaumain (1999).

Retail chains and department stores vastly improved services, and public transportation networks were built, at around the turn of the century. Trams, buses, and (in some cities) subways enabled the population to commute faster and more easily. In Paris, buses replaced the horse-driven omnibus and transported more than 200 million passengers in 1913. Taxi cabs appeared in Berlin in 1900 and on London's streets in 1904. London built the world's first subway network in the late nineteenth century, and electric cars replaced steam locomotives at the turn of the century. A short subway line was opened in Budapest in 1896, and construction of six subway lines (the "Metro") began in Paris three years later. Theaters, universities, and cultural centers began to germinate in the former industrial slum-cities.

Real wages also increased. The Human Development Index, which appraises income, longevity, and educational levels, rose by 20–30 percent in Western Europe in the half-century between 1820 and 1870. The region as a whole virtually attained the British level between 1870 and 1913, though it had been 25–30 percent behind a third of a century before. Two factors were crucial to increasing living standards: a significantly improved transportation system, which cut the cost of food and other consumer goods, and a rise in agricultural productivity (barring the grain crisis), which lowered prices further. Nutrition improved in Europe after 1870.

All this helped bring about a genuine *diet revolution*. A modernized diet improved the quality of life for a significant part of Europe's population. The diet revolution did not happen all at once, but, as with the modern transformation generally, began in the mid-eighteenth century and gradually spread throughout the nineteenth, with a turning point occurring between 1850 and 1880. The first and most important element was the end of starvation. In the 1840s, starvation was rampant not only in peripheral Ireland, but also in Europe's first industrializing country, Belgium. This plight recurred, with less frequency, until 1860. Starvation basically disappeared in Western Europe during the second half of the century. Calorie intake from the late eighteenth to the mid-nineteenth century varied between 1,800 and 2,500 a day. The latter figure reflected the national average in Belgium, but Swedish rural laborers also had similar levels: some 2,000–2,700 calories a day, 10 percent of which consisted of animal products (Essemyr, 1992, 266–7).

Calorie intake significantly increased between the 1890s and the 1910s, when it totaled 3,100–3,560 calories a day in Belgium. Middle-class consumption was around 3,500–3,600 calories a day between the mid-nineteenth century and World War I. Compared with the first half of the century, calorie intake increased by more than 50 percent.

In addition to intake, the composition of calories was also important; in worker and peasant families, most of the calories came from bread and potatoes. These two items provided 69% of the calories consumed at the beginning of this period. Animal products, including meat, eggs, butter, milk, fish, and cheese, accounted for only 16% of consumed food, and did not exceed 2–4% in some periods. It wasn't until the 1890s that a more balanced diet emerged, with the proportion of animal products comprising 25% and soon 35% of consumption (Scholliers, 1992, 75, 83). The Belgian figures reflect the West European trend.

Diets dominated by bread and potatoes gradually disappeared during the latter decades of the nineteenth century. The first scientific study on nutrition was published in the Netherlands in 1847 by Jan Mulder, a professor of chemistry at Utrecht University. Mulder warned against the overconsumption of potatoes, and recommended an increase in protein-rich food for children. He emphasized the importance of diet and rejected the view that laborers are "lazy," as the proprietor classes often asserted at that time. "The lack of vigour is . . . due to a diet solely based on potatoes which lacks sufficient albumen" (Hartog, 1992, 57).

The medieval two-meal system, with warm meals of equivalent status at 9 or 10 a.m. and 4 or 5 p.m., was the norm throughout Europe and remained so until the eighteenth century. The English "leisured society" retained this custom in the eighteenth century in the form of a late, hearty breakfast and a dinner at around 3 or 4 p.m. in the countryside and as late as 6 p.m. in cities, with some snacks at midday and a light cold supper at around 9 or 10 in the evening. The two-meal system, however, began to change among the upper classes in the eighteenth century, with the introduction of the three-meal system.

The two former meals moved forward in time during the day so the first came to be eaten at midday, and the new element, breakfast, had a menu that differed from that of the midday and evening meals and became organized around the new warm drinks, tea and coffee. (Kisbán, 1992, 207)

The two systems existed concurrently for quite a while, and the traditional one endured among peasants and workers for much of the nineteenth century. But the three-meal system, with a greater variety of food and higher proportion of animal products, gradually became the norm at the time of industrialization and urbanization.

Living standards improved for the entire population of Western Europe, but income inequality was pronounced. Having risen during the first period of industrialization, income inequality began to decrease in the late nineteenth century. Income differentials in real terms nearly doubled between 1759 and 1802, partly due to rapid population growth that pushed wages down. The cost of living, however, declined for the poor population: if the 1770 level was equal to 100, it increased to 150 in 1802, but declined to 122 by 1910. At the same time, the cost of living for affluent households remained virtually unchanged throughout the century. The nominal share of the wealth for the bottom 40% of the population increased from 9% in 1802 to more than 16% by 1911, while the top 5% of the population received 35% in 1802 and less than 20% by 1911 (Hoffman *et al.*, 2002, 342–3). Conditions in Italy reflected the decrease of inequality after 1880: the Gini index[11] declined from 0.448 to 0.397 by 1901 (Rossi *et al.*, 2001, 916). In the wealthiest countries, however, inequality again increased from the turn of the century on. The Netherlands, Britain, and Italy were the least egalitarian countries in 1913, but income inequality increased in France, Belgium, and Germany as well. Denmark and Norway were the exceptions. In most of Scandinavia, inequality continued to decrease (Leonard and Ljungberg, 2010, 127).

Notes

1. Famine decimated Silesia in 1730, Saxony in 1771–2, and Bavaria in 1816–17. The tragic connection of famine to death toll is well demonstrated by a calamity in Finland in 1696–7: one-quarter to one-third of the Finnish population perished (Braudel, 1979).

2. According to Angus Maddison (2001), life expectancy was 24 years in ancient Roman Egypt, 24.3 years in England between 1301 and 1425, and 24.8 years in France between 1740 and 1751.

3. "From the Napoleonic era to the Great War, tens of thousands of people . . . crossed the sea from north to south to settle in North Africa, Egypt, and the Levant." In 1847, 69,000 inhabitants of Algiers' population of 100,000 were Europeans and 15 percent of the residents of Tunisia's capital city were immigrants. About 2 million Muslims were forced out of Europe and fled to the Ottoman Empire in the nineteenth century (Clancy-Smith, 2011, 3, 5, 13, 99).

4. Entrepreneurs such as the de Besches and the Momma-Reenstierna families, and Louis De Geer, one of the leading entrepreneur iron manufacturers in the most traditional Swedish industry in the seventeenth century, moved to Sweden from Liège. The German Heinrich Nestle moved to Switzerland; the Belgian Florentin Robert and the Bavarian Josef Groll played important roles in the Czech lands; Abraham Ganz and Karl Haggenmacher migrated from Switzerland to Hungary; and Anton Dreher, the owner of the Schwechat Beer Factory, established the Hungarian branch of his family. Expatriate French

engineers supervised railroad construction throughout Europe, including Belgium, Switzerland, and the Netherlands, and built harbors and docks for half of the European seaports. In 1849, 2,500 French engineers worked in the Habsburg Empire (Cameron, 1966, 46, 72, 77).

5. As John Macgregor, Secretary of the Board of Trade in Britain, stated in 1840: "We find in France that the principal foremen at Ruen and in the cotton factories are from Lancashire; you find it in Belgium, in Holland and in the neighborhood of Liège... [and in Vienna] the directors and foremen [are] chiefly Englishmen or Scotsmen, from the... manufactories of Glasgow and Manchester" (quoted by Clapham, 1930, 491).

6. In France, the last outbreak of the plague – "imported" from Syria by a ship that arrived in Marseille – killed 32 percent of the population of Provence in 1720–1. The plague still appeared in the Balkans in 1828–9 and 1841.

7. During the Franco-Prussian War of 1870, 13,000 amputations, performed by French army surgeons, led to 10,000 deaths.

8. In 1857, the compound microscope signaled further development. Joining forces with Ernst Abbe, a lecturer at the University of Jena, in 1872, Zeiss used modern optical theory to construct the seventeen objectives microscope imaging system.

9. Anthropometric evidence proved that people's average height grew significantly over time and that they were taller in wealthier countries with abundant food supplies: about 172 centimeters in Sweden, 166 centimeters in Britain, but only 161–162 centimeters in more backward regions (A'Hearn, 2003, 370).

10. Medieval Brno in the Czech lands also emerged as a proto-industrial center. Thirty-two independent industrial settlements sprang up around the walled-fortified town in the early nineteenth century, and became part of the city in 1850. By 1902, 4,000 modern textile, engineering, and electric engineering companies operated in the city, which had 200,000 inhabitants by 1914.

11. The index from 0 to 1 reveals income inequality ranging from 0, when every person has an equal income, to 1, when one person acquires the entire income of a country.

CHAPTER 8

The Europeanization of Europe

Colonial Western Europe in the globalizing world

Europe began to build global empires beginning in the early modern period. The Iberian countries were the first to do so, and were followed by the Northwest European countries in the seventeenth century. As the etymology of the word suggests, colonialism was the migration of European settlers to colonies in foreign territories abroad. Between the sixteenth and twentieth centuries, roughly 60 million Europeans established European "colonies" in America, Africa, and Asia. Modern colonialism, however, was launched by conquest or coerced agreements along with external control and rule. European powers controlled more than a third of the world by 1800. Nevertheless, the nineteenth century became the real culmination of the "age of empire," as Eric Hobsbawm called that process between 1875 and 1914 (Hobsbawm, 1989).

The period following France's defeat in the Napoleonic wars has been often dubbed the *Pax Britannica*, when Britain emerged as an unchallenged superpower and began to conquer or at least control most of the world. By that time Britain had already possessed a large empire, which included North America, Australia, and major trading positions in India. The nineteenth century, however, was Britain's imperial century.[1] Britain's initial goal was to build an informal empire (Gallagher and Robinson, 1953), but, amidst a wild and desperate race for colonies after the 1870s, it "formalized" its empire to ward off any outside attempts to take it over. Imperial rule was also crucial for preventing the local elites in its colonies from seizing control of their plantation economies (Frieden, 1994). John A. Hobson, a British economist, drew attention to this phenomenon in his influential work, *Imperialism. A Study*, in 1902.[2] "Imperialism is the natural product of the economic pressure of a sudden advance of capitalism which cannot find occupation at home and needs foreign markets for goods and for investments" (Hobson, 1902, 85).

From the 1880s on, when a single generation expanded Britain's colonial empire by a third, the revenue from British foreign investments doubled. Hobson also analyzed the various indirect benefits of colonization. Still, Britain tried to rationalize its imperial possessions by establishing indirect rule through collaboration with local elites. The largest part of the world's map consequently became pink, the color of the British Empire, which ruled lands spanning nearly 26 million square kilometers with some 400–420 million inhabitants before World War I. The former white colonies had already either been lost and become independent, as had the United States, or were self-governed dominions like Canada, Australia, New Zealand, and South Africa. A large "informal empire" expanded the British sphere of interest and was controlled and institutionalized by imposed agreements, such as the Treaty of Nanjing with China in the early 1840s, at the end of the first Opium War.

France was the second largest colonial empire. Although it had lost several colonial possessions from the seventeenth century in its rivalry with Britain, France went on to establish a second empire, beginning with the invasion of Algeria in 1830 and nearly two decades of war there.[3] France ruled a territory spanning more than 12 million square kilometers. In 1898, an attempted French invasion in eastern Africa led to the Fashoda conflict between Britain and France, but it was peacefully settled. From then on, the two colonial giants divided the world between them and forged an alliance.

Other Western European countries also belonged to the envied club of colonial powers. The Netherlands was one of the earliest colonizers, with large possessions in the East Indies, the West Indies islands, the plantation colonies on the northeastern coast of South America, and the Gold Coast of Africa.[4] In Java and its surrounding islands, the Netherlands' empire comprised 35 million inhabitants. Belgium owned the Congo, which was eighty times larger than Belgium itself, and was actually the private property of King Leopold II. In the 1880s, Germany occupied Togo and Cameroon – their territory was five times larger than Germany itself – proving that even a dilatory colonizer could create an empire. Italy also sought to become a colonial power by occupying Somalia and Libya, but was defeated in Ethiopia. The pioneers of colonization, Spain and Portugal, had lost a great part of their empires, but still held vast tracts of colonial land. Portugal owned more than 10 million square kilometers of colonial property in Africa and Asia at the end of the Napoleonic wars, and was able to keep most of it during the entire century. Spain, however, lost the remnants[5] of its Latin American empire (Cuba, Puerto Rico, and the Spanish East Indies) to the United States after the Spanish–American War at the end of the century.

Various ambitions motivated colonial expansion or imperialism. In Hobson's view, Britain sought to ensure for itself a market for its goods and revenue for investment, for underconsumption precluded it from fully exploiting its economic potential. Trade with its colonies was indeed an important factor in Britain. Between 1892 and 1896, 33.2 percent of British exports went to its colonies, and 22.5 percent of the country's food and materials were imported from its empire. In the case of the Netherlands, however, exports to its colonies did not play an important role, as they comprised only 5 percent of total exports. But imported goods from its colonies, mostly for processing by its domestic industry, made up nearly 15 percent of Holland's imports. Similar ambitions included the creation of plantation economies in sub-tropical and tropical regions, specializing in sugar, coffee, and tea production, and the extraction of raw materials, such as silver, diamonds, copper, and oil.

Foreman-Peck, however, insists that colonies had a relative lack of economic importance. British colonial trade was dominated by trade with India; the French by trade with Algeria and Tunisia; and the Dutch by trade with the East Indies. Thus, other colonial possessions did not hold much economic importance. Colonial expenditures had in the meantime risen and at times exceeded revenue.[6] Germany and Italy, the latecomers to colonialism, garnered no profit at all, for they had launched risky adventures and bloody wars to *build* their colonial empires. At first glance, however, it is more surprising that France, the second largest colonial power, had relatively little economic interest in its colonies, which had received less than 10 percent of its exports and supplied 10 percent of its imports. "Theories that link colonization with the economic necessities of the capitalism of the time are on thin ground because the trade involved was so small" (Foreman-Peck, 1983, 115, 117).

Patrick O'Brien has similarly questioned the role of colonies in the advance of the colonial powers. Colonial investment (20 percent of the total in the case of Britain), he argues, did not secure higher returns than did investment elsewhere. Britain's market and resources would have made just as much money as its Indian colony, as was surely the case with the United States. In the end, the empire was subsidized by British taxpayers (O'Brien, 2004b, 166, 169–70, 189). O'Brien and Prados de la Escosura second this argument. They do not question the significance of colonies during the mercantilist era, when imperialism "helped to place . . . Western Europe upon a path that by 1914 provided [its] population with markedly higher standard of living than the rest of the world . . . Over time Europeans had made gains from imperialism . . . and [they] would have been poorer" without it (O'Brien and Prados de la Escosura, 1998, 3, 5). Nevertheless, they reject the view that colonialism was "the engine of economic progress." Economic connections with the rest of the world economy were "immeasurably more important than the links with empires." Indeed, "in a free trade world . . . at best empires had become economically irrelevant for the long run development of Europe." They note, however, that, despite this fact, "paradoxically, empires were growing" (O'Brien and Prados de la Escosura, 1998, 11, 19–20)

These arguments definitely have some quantitative basis, for revenue from colonial trade, according to their estimates, probably totaled only 2 percent of the colonial empires' GNP. So why did colonization reach its culmination, in this case, after 1870, when it was already "irrelevant"? Was it only the power of inertia? Was it the fact that, having benefited from them so much before, European nations failed to realize that colonies had lost their importance? This may very well have been the case, since inertia is a tremendous force in life and politics. The vested interest in colonies, however, was more complex than simply a higher return on investments and trade benefits. The British expansion was generated by a "particular type of economic development, centered upon finance and commercial services, which was set in train at the close of the seventeenth century and survived to the end of empire and indeed beyond" (Cain and Hopkins, 2001, 648). John Hobson offered another explanation a hundred years earlier: what was probably bad for taxpayers was extremely lucrative for some business interests.

Although the new Imperialism has been bad business for the nation, it has been good business for certain classes and certain trades within the nation. The vast expenditure on armaments, the costly wars . . . though fraught with great injury to the nation, have served well the present business interest of certain industries and professions. (Hobson, 1902, 51–2)

More importantly, Hobson also shed light on the complex motivations of expansionism and empire-building. Along with economic aspirations, he noted, there was a "passage from nationalism to a spurious colonialism . . . [and] imperialism" (Hobson, 1902, 4). French colonialism mostly originated from nationalism – an effort to redeem France and reestablish the *gloire*, particularly after the Napoleonic wars, the substantial loss of possessions to Britain, and the humiliation of the country's defeat by Germany in 1871 (Bouvier and Girault, 1976). It was even more so in the cases of Italy and Germany, latecomers in the European rivalry. They saw themselves as second-rate powers without colonial possessions. No one expressed this better than Heinrich von Treitschke, a leading historian, ideologue, and member of parliament, in late nineteenth-century Germany:

Every virile people have established colonial power... All great nations in the fullness of their strength have desired to set their mark upon barbarian lands and those who fail to participate in this great rivalry will play a pitiable role in time to come. The colonizing impulse has become a vital question for every great nation. (Treitschke, [1898] 1916, 115–16)

Social motivations also contributed. In the late nineteenth century, rising social tensions and polarization, and in some countries strong socialist mass movements, prodded politicians to forge national unity by channeling rage toward foreign rivals, emphasizing the need for internal social unity and fighting for colonies to redeem the nation. This is what motivated Chancellor Bismarck in Germany, and it was expressed most powerfully by Enrico Corradini, the intellectual leader of the Associazione Nazionalista Italiana (the Italian Nationalist Party) at its first congress in Florence in 1910.[7] As he put it, "syndicalism, nationalism and imperialism represent the rebirth of the valor of collective existence." Italy had to fight for its place as a proletarian nation and to secure colonies and raw materials through the "sacred mission of imperialism" in order to rise into the ranks of industrialized nations. "Imperialism as a natural and positive manifestation of nationalism... would lead to national rebirth and the advancement of civilization" (Marsella, 2004, 208–9).

A combination of economic, political, and social motivations thus led to the apex of colonization around the turn of the century. Europe's technological superiority and military power, the invention of the machine-gun, its advanced, rapid transportation and communications systems, and even the progress of its pharmaceutical industry (especially in the case of quinine) made the European conquest of tropical environments possible. At World War I, *half the landed surface of the globe, and one-third of its population*, was under colonial rule.

The European idea and national integration

Europe became the center of an interconnected world. Based on its Christian cultural heritage and the philosophy of the Enlightenment, the idea of an integrated Europe emerged. Both Jean-Jacques Rousseau and Jeremy Bentham called for a joint European parliament and army. Their aim was a political unification that would produce, as a byproduct, economic integration as well.

The American War of Independence and the establishment of the United States had genuinely inspired many Europeans. The source of optimism was George Washington himself. When the American Constitution was ratified, he wrote to the French general, Marquis de Lafayette, "I see the human race united like a huge family . . . we have made a sowing of liberty which will . . . spring up across the whole world. One day, on the model of the United States of America, a United States of Europe will come into being" (quoted by Fontaine, 2001, 1).

There were a great variety of supporters of a united Europe, all with vastly different perspectives. The German philosopher Friedrich Nietzsche called for European unity against "mad nationalism," annulled his Prussian citizenship in 1869 and moved to Switzerland, and boldly defined himself as a European. The French writer Victor Hugo argued for European unification and, at a peace conference in 1869, addressed the audience as "fellow citizens of the United States of Europe." In the late 1860s, a journal was published with the title of *The United States of Europe*.[8]

Nevertheless, the nineteenth century was the age of the birth of nation-states and the integration of national units. This often started in the economic realm before becoming a political reality. The nation-states emerging during the eighteenth century and the first half of the nineteenth began to integrate their national economies by eliminating internal tariffs. At that time, 1,800 customs frontiers existed within Germany alone. This was not necessarily caused by the lack of a united German state, for even within Prussia, there were sixty different customs and excise rates separating its various provinces. In France, on the River Rhône between Châlons and Arles, thirty tolls disconnected local markets (Pollard, 1981b, 18–19). But the French Revolution abolished all internal tolls in the country, followed by Prussia in 1818. Slightly more than one and a half decades later, the German Zollverein eliminated all internal tariffs within the German states. The Habsburg Empire gradually did the same between 1775 and 1851. The Swiss cantons formed a united federal unit in 1848.[9] These movements were closely connected to the rise of nation-states and the building of empires. Having been abolished within the state, tariffs were now shifted from provinces and cities to the national borders with other nation-states. The process of economic integration proved increasingly attractive. Integrating national markets induced leaders to move beyond their national borders. This was clearly illustrated by the proposed Franco-Belgian union, the Dutch–Belgian union, and the establishment of the Latin Monetary Union of Belgium, France, Italy, and Switzerland in 1865, which introduced a common bimetallic system and the mutual use of each country's currency. The Northern Monetary Union of the Scandinavian countries followed in 1873, with a common gold standard and circulation of each country's currency.

The most important step towards internationalization was the gradual introduction of the free trade system and the gold standard, with its stable exchange rates among national currencies. Both were major breakthroughs that superseded mercantilist protectionism and bimetal or paper money systems, which had prevailed during the previous century and had economically isolated each European country.

The theory of laissez-faire, or a self-regulating market economy, gradually emerged in Britain.[10] Since Britain was the economic leader and the primary import and export power in the world, it had a crucial interest in abolishing all obstacles to international trade and in creating an internationalized free market with an international monetary system, which would assure its smooth functioning. After several early attempts in the eighteenth century,[11] Britain began to gradually and unilaterally advance towards free trade in the 1840s. However, tariffs had not been merely a defensive shield against foreign competition, but were also one of the primary income sources of the state budget. Eliminating tariffs thus required finding substitute income for the government, which was not achieved until the 1840s.[12]

The severe Irish famines during this period led to the annulment of the Corn Laws, which had served entrenched agricultural interests, in 1846 and again in 1849. In that latter year, another major obstacle, the Navigation Law, was repealed. It took another quarter of a century and a series of Gladstone's balanced budgets for wood, sugar, and other items to become duty free in the 1860s. The free trade policy became fully institutionalized in Britain, and it was soon emulated in Western Europe. As Charles Kindleberger has pointed out, European governments turned to free trade between 1820 and 1870 for mostly ideological reasons (Kindleberger, 1975). Belgium repealed its Corn Law in 1873, and Austria, Spain, the Netherlands, and the Scandinavian countries liberalized their trade policies in the 1850s and 1860s. As a result, average tariffs dropped markedly.

Laissez-faire as a broader European system took hold during the second half of the nineteenth century. This was a gradual process. By the end of the 1850s, tariffs were low for food and raw materials, but they remained high for iron, steel and textiles. Overall tariff levels by 1859 were 16% in Britain, 12% in France, 7% in the German Zollverein, 3% in Belgium, and hardly more than 1% in the Netherlands (Lampe, 2009, 1014–15). The celebrated Cobden–Chevalier Treaty between Britain and

France in 1860 is still considered a major turning point.[13] This landmark treaty, with its most-favored-nation clause that made all bilateral tariff reductions automatically valid for any third partner in trade agreements with other countries, became the vehicle for the internationalization of free trade. Indeed, some fifty bilateral trade agreements followed.[14] By the mid-1870s, tariffs in continental Europe declined on average to 9–12%. Britain, the Low Countries, Germany, Sweden, Norway, and Switzerland became virtually tariff free, with a maximum 2–5% *ad valorem* tariff for manufactured goods.

This policy, however, was also imposed on some weak peripheral countries. Britain dictated free trade for the Ottoman Empire, and Austria-Hungary forced the Treaty of Passarowitz, made in 1718 between the Habsburg and Ottoman empires, onto the newly independent Balkan countries in the 1870s.[15] Overall, Europe gradually embraced free trade and low tariffs during the second half of the century.

This development was greatly facilitated by the emergence of a *multilateral payment* network. Though roughly 70 percent of trade transactions remained bilateral until World War I, at least 20–25 percent became multilateral. This encouraged international trade because countries could offset any trade deficit with one partner with a trade surplus with another. As a result, a much smaller amount of gold (and/or hard currency) was needed for balanced trade. In this way, another major obstacle to international trade – the lack of sufficient gold (and hard currency) reserves – was eliminated. Previously, many countries had to restrict trade to maintain their gold reserves.

Gradually, an international financial center emerged as well. In a limited way, Amsterdam had become the "financial center of the world" during the seventeenth and eighteenth centuries, but London replaced it as the new center of a global financial transaction network in the nineteenth century. Europe's economic integration took a major step forward. The crowning achievement toward a laissez-faire system, however, was the introduction of the *gold standard*. Until the 1870s, most European countries had a bimetallic system (as did France), a silver standard (Holland, Scandinavia, and the German states), or inconvertible paper money (Russia, Greece, and Italy). The pioneer of the gold standard, again, was Britain, which gradually adopted it beginning in the late eighteenth century, and fully implemented it in 1821. Other European countries would do so much later.[16] Western Europe was governed by the gold standard by the late 1870s, and all of Europe fell into line by the 1890s, when Austria and Russia followed suit. Each currency had a fixed gold content and was thus easily exchangeable. Although exchange rates fluctuated according to supply and demand, they remained surprisingly stable during these decades. The British pound sterling, unchanged in value between 1821 and 1914, was practically equal to gold and became the international currency. By the dawn of the twentieth century, a self-regulated, laissez-faire market predominated throughout Europe.

The one and a half decades prior to World War I, however, marked both the zenith and the beginning of the end of this short-lived system. Together with the rise of Britain's modern free trade economy, a countertheory of modern protectionism was born. A decade after Adam Smith's *Wealth of Nations*, Alexander Hamilton called on the US Congress to protect the infant American industry from competition from the advanced countries. Germany became the cradle of the new protectionism. Johann Gottlieb Fichte and Friedrich List had invented the theory of the protective defense of nascent industries a few years before John Stuart Mill published his laissez-faire classic, the *Principles of Political Economy* (1848).

Just as free trade had predominated side by side with free trade theory, now modern protectionism prevailed hand in hand with protectionist doctrine.[17] The dissolution of laissez-faire began mostly during the 1870s, when the grain crisis hit several countries on the continent. At the same time, an ambitious Germany scrambled to catch up with its Western counterparts. The backward, agrarian countries of South, Central, and Eastern Europe could only dream about industrializing with the Western model of free competition, and thus all sought to defend themselves from Western encroachments. Germany introduced moderate tariffs on both agricultural and industrial products in 1879, and then increased them in 1885 and 1888. By 1902, a new general tariff set very high levels of protection for finished manufactured and agricultural products, while semi-finished manufacturing had only low tariffs and raw materials remained duty free.

At around the turn of the century, the dual interests of a declining agriculture, which had been strongly hit by overseas competition since the 1870s, and growing industry made protective tariffs popular all over Europe.[18] Denmark raised its industrial tariffs to about 15–20%. In Italy, tariffs were 40% for wheat and 18% for industry; in Sweden, they were 28% for wheat and 20% for industry. Small wonder that the struggling peripheral countries rushed to impose their own tariffs.[19] Ultimately, the average tariff comprised 28% of the value of imported goods. Imports of certain goods, such as industrial products for railroads, were banned in a number of countries to stimulate domestic production. By 1913, France, Italy, and Sweden had imposed a nearly 20% *ad valorem* duty, while Spain's was more than 40% – assuring that tariff barriers totaled 20–40% of the value of imported goods. By World War I, only Britain, Holland, and, in some respects, Denmark retained free trade systems (Kenwood and Lougheed, 1971, 83–5). Tariffs had a positive impact on economic growth, which increased significantly in several countries during the high-tariff years. Denmark's annual growth rate of 1.2% between 1875–9 and 1880–4 nearly doubled to 2.1% between 1905–9 and 1910–14. In the same period, Germany's growth rate increased from 0.1% to 1.2%, Italy's from 0.5% to 2.3%, and Sweden's from 0.7% to 1.5%. "The data are far more comfortable with the hypothesis that tariffs boosted late nineteenth century growth" (O'Rourke, 2000, 464, 468).

Karl Polanyi has viewed this trend as a self-defense mechanism against laissez-faire: "By the end of the Depression [of 1873]," he observed, "Germany had surrounded herself with protective tariffs ... [and] set up an all-round social insurance system" (Polanyi, 1964, 216). O'Rourke and Williamson concur: "Rising tariffs during the last third of the century were mainly defensive responses to the competitive winds of market integration as transport cost declined" (O'Rourke and Williamson, 2001, 17).

Indeed, transportation costs in the early nineteenth century had created much greater "trade barriers" than tariffs did. The collapse of freight rates during the second half of the century was an important globalizing factor for free trade. With the proliferation of a modern network of steamships and railroads, freight rates dropped dramatically and continued to do so by 1.5 percent per annum for half a century between the 1840s–1870s and World War I. Transportation costs ultimately declined by 45 percent before the war.

Europeanization advanced by leaps and bounds. A number of important steps were taken in this direction with *internationalization agreements*. Europe's rivers were designated as international waterways, including the Rhine in 1831, and tolls were eliminated in 1868.[20] Railroad construction, a distinctly national project (albeit financed internationally), almost immediately became the subject of international cooperation and Europe-wide regulation. First, most countries accepted the British gauge system that consolidated national railroads into a European network. Next, Prussia's railroad administration, the Verein Preussischer Eisenbahnen Verwaltungen (established in the mid-nineteenth century), rapidly expanded by adding lines of neighboring countries. By 1879, it comprised 110 railroad administrations from Germany, Austria-Hungary, Luxembourg, and the Netherlands. Then, the European Time-Table Conference began regulating international trains in 1891.[21] Railroads became not only the real infrastructure of European integration, but also an engine for establishing European cooperation and regulation agreements.

Several international organizations were founded during the 1860s and 1870s promoting cooperation among states: the International Telegraph Union in 1865, the International Signals Code in 1871, the Universal Postal Union in 1874, and the International Meteorological Organization in 1878. Agreements on an international metric system, patents, copyrights, and other standardizations contributed as well to the internationalization and organized regulation of the national economies, as did a host of international conferences and understandings on fishing, health, labor, and other issues. Major attempts were made to establish the international rules for war, and twelve countries signed the Geneva Convention in 1864. The International Red Cross was founded in 1876. There were also endeavors to establish an international court of justice.[22] The countries of the world agreed on fixing an internationally accepted Prime Meridian (line of longitude) whose longitude is zero and whose location is arbitrary. London (Greenwich) beat all competition for the honor in 1851, which the International Meridian Conference of twenty-five countries ratified in Washington in 1884. International time zones were fixed accordingly. Internationalization was clearly in the air during the last third of the nineteenth century – so much so that serious, though unsuccessful, attempts were made to establish an international language.[23]

A pan-European identity was plainly apparent among the emerging working class – at least among its left-wing movements, as the founding of the International Workingmen's Association (The First International) in 1864 so aptly demonstrated. "The workers have no country," the Communist Manifesto boldly declared in 1848. Socialism would only come about, Marx and Engels prophesied in *The German Ideology* (1847), "as the common action of the leading nations."[24] The ascendancy of the Second International in the late 1880s and 1890s, comprising Europe's Social Democratic parties, and the designation of May 1 as a pan-European labor day, certainly signaled a rising internationalism. But it soon became clear that nationalism had also pervaded the workers' movement.

Prior to World War I, some 200 international organizations were in operation, holding 1,443 conferences and assemblies between 1900 and 1914 – almost five times the number in previous decades combined. Although some of the organizations and agreements were international in nature, most were preponderantly European with the extensive participation of all the countries on the continent.

Institutionalized economic integration and trade

For decades, economic historians have tended to use the term "internationalization" when analyzing the nineteenth century, especially its last third. A kind of proto-internationalization of the European economy was already characteristic of the late medieval and early modern periods, when long-distance trade extended over land. This trend continued in different forms during the nineteenth century. O'Rourke and Williamson (2001) suggest that history's "first globalization"[25] had gradually taken place after the first Industrial Revolution and had prevailed during the half-century before World War I. The first globalization has become the most commonly used term to describe the developments of this period.[26] But did Europe really become part of a globalized world economy before the war? In reaching their conclusions, O'Rourke and Williamson focus not on the extent of world trade or the opening of trade routes as the essence of globalization, but on the convergence of commodity prices. The nineteenth century witnessed a "big bang" of globalization when basic goods such as wheat and textiles dominated international trade. This occurred partly because international freight rates had collapsed and the resulting price convergence had created a genuine world market. Between 1870 and 1912, the difference between wheat prices in Liverpool and Chicago dropped from 57.6% to 15.6%, and that between meat prices in the United States and Britain fell from 92.5% to 17.9%.[27] The price differential between American and European manufactures decreased by 17%, and the prices became virtually equal (O'Rourke and Williamson, 2001; Findlay and O'Rourke, 2007, 404–5).

Even so, the world economy was not yet global in the nineteenth century. China and the non-European peripheries played only a complementary role. Jan de Vries has amply demonstrated that European–Asian trade had only marginal importance at that time. European companies maintained a monopoly over trade and would only countenance "oligopolistic competition" with each other. Patrick O'Brien maintains that intra-European trade had met the needs of Europe until World War I, and prefers, therefore, to speak of a *globalizing* (but not yet globalized) world economy. This approach is more realistic. Indeed, the division of labor preserved its traditional character of exchanging primary goods with processed or manufactured products. The interaction was still dominated by trade, and multinational companies and their subsidiaries were relatively rare. The world economy was not yet over-financed with free-flowing, uncontrolled capital that had no regard for national borders.

What instead took place on the European continent during the nineteenth century was actually Europeanization. The countries on the continent became interconnected with one another as a result of the increasing globalization of the world economy.

Both migration and railroad construction throughout Europe were important factors in the integration and internationalization of Europe.

Table 8.1 Value of world exports (million 1990 dollars)

Year	Million $	1820 = 100	1870 = 100
1820	7,255	100	12
1870	56,247	775	100
1900	139,671	1,925	248
1913	236,330	3,257	420

Source: Based on Maddison (1995, 239).

Table 8.2 Europe's share in world trade, 1876/80–1913 (US $ billion)

	1876–80				1913			
	Primary products		Manufactures		Primary products		Manufactures	
	Imports	Exports	Imports	Exports	Imports	Exports	Imports	Exports
World	4.6	3.7	2.5	2.3	13.7	12.2	7.4	6.9
Europe	3.7	1.7	1.0	2.2	10.2	5.6	3.5	5.7
%	80	46	41	94	74	46	48	82

Source: Based on Lamartine Yates (1959, 226–32).
Note: All figures are rounded.

But the prime mover of Europeanization was global trade, which shifted into high gear. During the rise of commercial capitalism in the early modern period, world trade increased an average of 1.0% per annum; but after the Napoleonic wars, it jumped to 3.5% per year. Angus Maddison (1995) has estimated that the value of world trade at constant prices increased by nearly 33 times between 1820 and 1913 (see Table 8.1).

Europe stood at the center of world trade. It bought more than 80% of the primary products sold on the world market in the 1870s, and it continued to dominate (with a slightly less 74.3%) in 1913. At the same time, Europe exported 94.1% of the manufactured goods sold on the world market in the 1870s, and a preponderant 81.5% in 1913 (see Table 8.2).

Figure 8.1
Europe's share of
imports of
primary products
worldwide,
1876–80
(percent)
(Lamartine-Yates,
1959, 226–32)

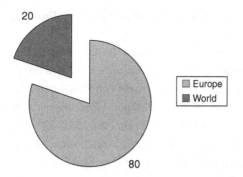

Europe's dominance of world trade is simply staggering, particularly in imports of primary products and exports of manufactured goods. Of the world's total imports of primary products, 69% went to Britain and continental Western Europe in 1876–80, and 62% did so in 1913. At the same time, Britain and continental Western Europe produced 85% of the world's total manufacturing exports in 1876–80, and 73% in 1913. One can certainly speak of a *European world economy* during this period. (See Figure 8.1.)

The importance of trade in nineteenth-century Europe increased dramatically. Paul Bairoch (1976a) estimates the value of the continent's exports at 4% of aggregate GNP in 1830, and 14% by 1913. A great proportion of Western manufactured goods and Eastern primary products were sold on export markets. The importance of raw material imports is clearly indicated by the sharp rise of unprocessed cotton, coal, coke, and petroleum imports.[28] Between 1872 and 1913, the value of per capita food imports to Western Europe increased (in constant prices) by 2.3 times (Mitchell, 1973, Appendix). The amount of mostly agricultural products coming from the Mediterranean and Central and Eastern Europe to the West during this same period had increased (in declining current prices) by 3.3 times.

Britain had been virtually self-sufficient in food and all important raw materials during the eighteenth century, and had imported only $118 million worth of goods in 1800. By the beginning of World War I, however, the country had retained self-sufficiency in coal alone; imports now provided 80% of the country's wheat and 40% of its meat, and their value ($3,767 million) had increased thirty-two times compared with 1800. Between 1880 and 1884, the value of imports totaled 36% of Britain's national income. A similar, though not quite so extreme, development was seen throughout Western Europe. The import figures for France and Germany most closely resembled the British reality.[29] France's imports increased sevenfold and Germany's fourfold between the early nineteenth century and World War I.

The division of labor between the advanced, industrializing regions and the less developed, agricultural ones remained surprisingly stable during the four decades preceding World War I: 64% of world trade comprised raw materials and foodstuffs in 1876–80, and this remained almost unchanged (63%) before the war (Kuznets, 1966, 33). Although the modern international trade system had incorporated most of the world at around the end of the century, the importance of Asia, Africa, Latin America, and East Indies in world trade was stagnant and limited, comprising only 24% of the total in the late 1870s, and 25% by 1913. Most of the expanding world trade, therefore, remained intra-European trade: 67% in 1876–80, and 62% before the war (Woodruff, 1982).[30]

European production of several import items increased significantly in the nineteenth century: 76% of Britain's sugar imports had originated from the British West Indies in 1831, but only 3% by 1913; instead, 56% of imported sugar now came from within Europe. Likewise, 83% of British meat imports had come from the United States in 1870, but only 17% in 1913; now, the proportion of British meat imports from inside Europe rose from virtually zero to 23%. Two-thirds of British wood imports came from America in 1870, but only 13% in 1913, with Scandinavia now supplying 83% of the total (Maizels, 1969; Schlote, 1952). Intra-European trade met the sharply rising demand for food and raw materials in the industrializing western regions, with Europe's eastern and southern peripheries providing the bulk of western imports. The Italian Camillo Cavour clearly recognized the tremendous potential of trade for the less developed peripheries when he declared in 1845:

The commercial revolution which is now taking place in England . . . will have a mighty impact on the Continent. By opening up the richest market in the world to foodstuffs, it will encourage their production, the principal aim . . . of all agricultural industry which everywhere is the most important. The need to provide for regular foreign demand will arouse the energy of these agricultural industries. (quoted in Mori, 1975, 91)

Indeed, exports from the European peripheries rose faster than those from the core. The annual growth of exports from the peripheral regions, including latecomer Scandinavia, increased by an average of 3.2% between 1860 and 1910, compared with 2.8% for Europe as a whole. The four Nordic countries led the peripheries with a 4.4% annual growth. In the 1880s, even Sweden's exports had a strong agricultural component (24%), though 43% of its exports were raw materials. While Spain, Russia, and the Nordic countries had sizeable raw material exports, most of the eastern and southern regions remained almost entirely food exporters. Greece supplied mostly agricultural products: 75% of its exports in 1887, and 78% in 1912. The five leading export items, all agricultural products, comprised between three-quarters and four-fifths of Balkan exports throughout this period. Nine of ten leading export items from mid-nineteenth-century Spain were agricultural products.

The peripheral regions of Europe contributed 16–17% of European trade in 1860, and 26% by 1910. A part of the peripheries' trade, however, was not intra-European in the proper sense of the term, but intra-imperial. The Habsburg Empire became a free trade zone in 1851, which created a huge and growing market for agricultural and raw material "exports" from the eastern half of the empire to the rapidly industrializing Austrian-Bohemian provinces. The Russian Empire became a free trade zone in 1860 and provided an enormous market for Finland, Poland, and the Baltic region, the more developed parts of the empire. And Ireland also found a valuable niche for its exports in British markets, even though it suffered enormously from the overwhelming competition of British industry.

In a paradoxical way, and in contrast to most of the national (and nationalistic) narratives of the peripheral countries, the politically subordinated and often oppressed minority nations of the various European empires[31] profited economically from the creation of large imperial markets. This became especially important at the beginning of the advanced stage of their modernization at around the end of the century, when protectionism returned to peripheral Europe. The protected market of Austria-Hungary, for example, not only expanded the grain market for Hungary, but effected a 30 percent increase in wheat prices at a time when those prices were declining by 30 percent on world markets. Industrial development in Ireland, Finland, Hungary, Poland, and the Baltic regions was actually a consequence of those imperial markets (as discussed in Chapter 11).

At this point, however, an important problem requires further clarification. The division of labor between the advanced and less developed regions is not as simple as the exchange of primary products, food, and raw materials for manufactured goods. Sidney Pollard (1981b) has correctly called attention to this mistaken overgeneralization. The advanced, industrialized countries also exported raw materials and unfinished products. Besides coal, Britain's main export items to Western Europe were cotton yarn, pig iron, and bar iron – all semi-finished products. During the first half of the century, the less industrialized regions of Western Europe bought British coal and semi-finished products and processed them in their own factories.[32]

Hence, trade patterns were strongly influenced by the Ricardian comparative advantage on the one hand, and (as Heckscher, [1919] 1949 and Ohlin 1966 emphasize)[33] the scarcity of certain goods on the other. Coal and semi-finished iron and cotton products were produced so cheaply in Britain that no other country could compete. Moreover, Britain was able to retain its comparative advantage until World War I. The West European countries, therefore, had to find niches in which they had a better chance of gaining a comparative advantage, and they found them, among others, in finished textile goods, which included the combining of the textile and clothing industries. On the other hand, several countries had to buy coal and iron because they did not have those natural resources.

Dependency theories maintain that trade between the advanced-industrialized and less developed countries is an uneven exchange. Processed goods, consisting of higher labor content, are more valuable than unprocessed goods; thus their exchange is inherently exploitative. Accordingly, uneven trade continuously reproduces underdevelopment (Love, 1996). Dependency theories' rejection of Ricardo's theory of comparative advantage – that both parties gain from trade since they are selling what they can produce in the most efficient way and buying what they cannot – is well substantiated. Mutual gain was not a rule of the game in a number of cases.

However, the opposite of what Ricardo hypothesized is also not a general rule and is often not true. Trade with more developed countries is often advantageous for less developed regions because it incentivizes them to find strong complementary economic areas to develop, and facilitates the spread of modern technology. Import-substituting or economic nationalism, which calls for high protective tariffs against goods from the more advanced countries, may help undeveloped countries advance industrially, but it also encourages them to develop the very sectors that their more advanced rivals had long since established – thus reinforcing areas of weakness, and not comparative strength. Trade between the advanced and less developed countries is thus neither mutually advantageous nor inherently unequal, with all the advantages going to the advanced countries and all the disadvantages to the less developed. In reality, both outcomes are possible – depending on the backward region's internal conditions, the role of the state in institution- and infrastructure-building, the level of education, and the prevalence or lack of a societal will to exploit potential advantages.

Box 8.1 The prophet of protectionism: Friedrich List

The latecomer and somewhat backward peripheral countries did not welcome, or became disappointed with, laissez-faire free competition. The prevalent assumption was that laissez-faire benefited the most advanced countries and harmed the less developed. This idea emerged almost simultaneously with the concept of free trade. It is difficult to single out particular advocates, as there were so many. However, the German Georg Friedrich List was the most renowned economist who clearly and convincingly conceptualized an alternative policy. The son of a tanner, List, a genuine talent, was self-educated, but became professor at Tübingen University in 1817. He influenced most governments' economic policies with his 1841 book, *Das nationale System der politischen Ökonomie*. The book was an immense success. In the first few months after publication, three editions and several translations appeared.

Sharply dissenting from British classical economics, List placed the nation at the center of his argumentation. He criticized Adam Smith's "boundless cosmopolitanism" because "between each individual and entire humanity... stands THE NATION... It is the task of the national economy to accomplish the economical development of the nation, and prepare it for admission into the universal society of the future" (List, [1841] 1947, 286–7).

A German romantic nationalist, List was the main advocate of the economic unification of Germany into a customs union, the Zollverein, and the creation of a unified railroad system. Moreover, he argued that German unification "cannot be considered complete so long as it does not extend over the whole coast... including Holland and Denmark... [incorporating these countries] to the German Bund, and consequently into the German nationality" (List, [1841] 1947, 288). Paradoxically, however, he was branded a *Heimatlose* (stateless person), imprisoned, and expelled from Germany in 1825 because of his liberal views. List became an American citizen and returned to Germany as an American consul in 1832. He wrote his celebrated book in France. He clearly recognized that England

maintains and extends its industrial and commercial supremacy by the freest possible trade... [It preserves its supremacy by inventing] a policy which aimed, and still aims, at obtaining a monopoly in manufactures and trade, and at checking the progress of less advanced nations ... For many nations ... [however,] the import of foreign manufactures can no longer benefit their powers of production. Such nations suffer many serious evils if they do not foster their own manufactures. (List, [1841] 1947, 274, 278–9)

List developed a theory of economic stages through which all nations progress: savage, pastoral, agricultural, agricultural-manufacturing, agricultural-manufacturing-commercial. The transition from the agricultural to the manufacturing stage, he asserted, would take place under free trade only if it simultaneously occurred in all nations. Because of special, advantageous circumstances, however, some nations held huge advantages and acquired industrial monopolies; the less advanced nations were unable to reach the manufacturing level without the help of "educational" tariffs, that is, until they reached the advanced level of industrialization. At the beginning of the transition period from the agricultural stage, importing foreign industrial goods is as important as exporting agricultural products and raw materials. However, it is imperative that home industries gradually advance, in line with imports, and eventually supply a greater part of the domestic market. Lastly, the nation must reach the stage where industrial exports predominate, accompanied by imports of agricultural goods and raw materials. The transition has to be promoted by protective tariffs against the competition of the more advanced nations.

The tariff system, as a means of advancing the economic development of the nation by regulation of foreign trade, must constantly follow the principle of national industrial education ... [until the nation reaches the level of industrial maturity and richness.] A nation is rich and powerful in the proportion in which it exports manufactures, imports raw materials, and consumes tropical products. (List, [1841] 1947, 276–7)

At that level of advancement, List suggested, the country could return to free trade. His *National System of Political Economy* became the bible of latecomer and peripheral countries, which applied his theory and introduced protectionism from the 1870s–1880s on. Friedrich List, however, could not enjoy his success. Because of personal troubles and financial difficulties, he committed suicide in 1846, at the age of fifty-seven.

Based on List ([1841] 1947).

Trade became the primary engine of economic development for nineteenth-century Europe, and the prime mover of the economic integration and Europeanization of the continent. It also accelerated the catching-up process of certain regions that had relative institutional and infrastructural development and a social inclination to profit from trade connections abroad – regions such as Scandinavia and parts of Central Europe. On the other hand, most of the Mediterranean region and Eastern Europe lagged further behind at the end of the century than they did at the beginning of it.

The West as a source of finance: capital flow into Europe

All the main factors of economic modernization and integration were linked with investment, both capital formation and capital inflow. Capital accumulation, facilitated by a modern banking system, took off from the 1830s–1840s on. The fixed annual domestic capital formation in Britain was £3.68 million, but it increased to £31.38 million in 1821–30 and £57.99 million in 1851–60. Capital formation was low, about 5–8% of national income, prior to the railroad age in the West, but it rose to 10–12% afterwards. Britain achieved a 10% level in the 1840s. Germany's capital formation totaled 12% of its GDP in the 1860s–1870s, and rose to 14–15% after the turn of the century.

During the first Industrial Revolution, at least two-thirds of domestic investment in Britain was financed from domestic savings. Profits from colonial trade comprised one-third of investments, and those from peripheral trade 15%. Beginning in the 1870s, the most developed countries of Western Europe attained a significant surplus of accumulated capital. Germany invested 7% of its GDP into its economy in the mid-nineteenth century, and raised it to 18% after the turn of the century. While its net national income increased fivefold, investment grew tenfold between 1850 and 1913.

Investors searched for the most lucrative investments, and often found them abroad. While interest rates in Britain were 3.18% in the early years of the twentieth century, foreign loans often charged 5.39% interest. In most cases, investors in railroads were guaranteed a 5% interest rate. Opening mines and oil fields, and investing in the railroads, in the less developed peripheries served the raw material needs of the rapidly industrializing countries. Foreign investment thus became highly attractive in the West. Investing abroad was also politically important for Western countries, for it served expansionist and military goals as well. The building of alliances

Figure 8.2
Capital exports
worldwide,
1825–1913
(million dollars)
(Kuznets, 1966,
324)

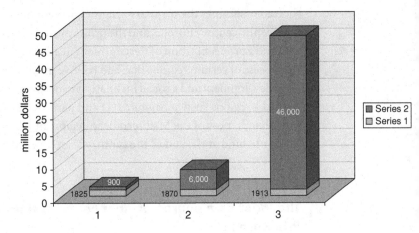

and the strengthening of the economic and military infrastructure of allies became an important consideration.

Foreign loans and capital investment began to increase after the Napoleonic wars. Joining the traditional British,[34] Dutch, and French capital exporters, Germany, Belgium, Switzerland, Austria-Bohemia, and the Scandinavian countries began engaging in these endeavors during the last third of the nineteenth century. Britain lent out 43% of the world's total capital exports of $46 billion in 1913, France 20%, Germany 13%, and the small West European countries a combined 13–14%.[35] (See Figure 8.2.)

Between 1870 and 1913, Britain exported 40% of its capital accumulation, France 25%, and Germany 10%. Prior to World War I, exported capital comprised 7–8% of Britain's GDP. Foreign investment in 1870 made up 7% of the world's aggregate GDP, and totaled 20% of a significantly expanded global GDP before the war.

A considerable part of exported capital was invested in railroad construction, which absorbed 40% of Britain's and 15% of France's capital exports. Half of French exported capital, however, was state and municipal loans earmarked for peripheral countries and used primarily for railroad construction. Investment in mining and industry made up 12% of Britain's and 10% of France's exported capital.

A large part of capital exports targeted colonies and regions of spheres of interest on various continents,[36] but 26% did go to the less developed regions of Europe. (See Figure 8.3.) The European creditor and investor countries changed over time. In 1830, Britain provided 64% of all European investment, but only 5% by 1914. In the latter period, nearly half of Britain's exported capital went to its overseas empire. French capital exports were almost entirely European (93%) in 1850. By 1914, however,

Figure 8.3
Receivers of foreign investments between 1870 and 1913 (percent) (Kenwood and Lougheed, 1971, 43; Woodruff, 1982, 253)

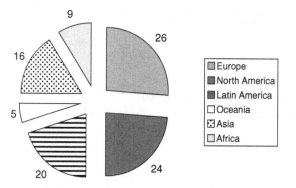

27% of French capital exports went to Russia in order to strengthen an ally in preparation for war against Germany. Another 33% of exported French capital was channeled to other peripheral regions of Europe. Germany lacked a colonial empire, but attempted to build a strong sphere of influence inside Europe by investing in peripheral European countries – a policy Hannah Arendt described as continental imperialism (Arendt, 1966). Prior to the war, 29% of German capital exports went to Russia and the Balkans, 15% to Spain and Portugal, and 23% to Austria-Hungary.

The Austrian-Bohemian part of the Habsburg Empire, a capital importer until the turn of the century, also became an exporter of capital, mostly to Hungary and to the Monarchy's backward eastern and southern provinces. Capital imports to, and capital exports from, Austria-Bohemia became balanced at around the turn of the century. Moreover, roughly one-third of capital investment made in Hungary, and up to 40 percent in certain modern sectors in the country, came from the western provinces of the empire. Most of the investments in Bosnia-Herzegovina originated from Vienna. During the last third of the century, the European peripheral regions became important recipients of exported capital from the West.

Did a European business cycle exist?

Economic development is not a linear progression. Rather, it is cyclical, with periods of rapid growth invariably followed by periods of slow development or near stagnation, or even recession and decline. In earlier times climatic cycles had spawned agricultural catastrophes. The first such report came from the Bible, when Joseph interpreted Pharaoh's dream and forecasted seven lean years to follow seven fruitful ones.[37] Long-term economic development was also interrupted by wars and pestilences. Demographic shocks also contributed.

Table 8.3 European capital export, 1825–1913

Year	Million dollars	1870 = 100
1825	900	15
1850	2,000	33
1870	6,000	100
1900	24,000	400
1913	46,000	767

Source: Kuznets (1966, 324).

Table 8.4 Share of capital exports by exporting countries in 1914

Exporting country	% of total
Britain	43
France	20
Germany	13
USA	7
Belgium, the Netherlands, and Switzerland	12
Others	5
Total	100

Source: Woodruff (1973, 707).

The modern market economy generates a cyclical phenomenon of a different sort, one that is inherent in the market system. In 1815, the Swiss Jean-Charles-Léonard Simonde de Sismondi called attention to the combined impact of limitless competition and mass poverty: while the first generates "overproduction," the second causes "underconsumption." As a result, recessions recur on a regular basis. Thomas Tooke was the first to identify price fluctuations in 1823, and John Wade maintained in 1833 that commercial cycles oscillate in five- to seven-year waves. Hyde Clarke noted five years later that periods of commercial distress recur in cycles of between ten and fifty-four years.

Lee Craig and C. García-Iglesias (2010) have listed dozens of economic crises after the Napoleonic wars.[38] Analysts cannot agree on the causes of these events, however. Still, in the mid-nineteenth century the French scholar Clément Juglar offered a consistent, market-related explanation for the cycle phenomenon, now called the Juglar cycle (Juglar, 1862; Besomi, 2009). In his view, millions of economic actors, entrepreneurs, and managers make independent decisions regarding investment and output. In a period of prosperity, they easily overestimate the market's potential. When they can easily sell their products, they have no qualms about investing to increase production. These overestimates and overinvestments can lead to overproduction. Goods pile high in storage, and companies are forced to lower their prices to sell off stock. They also halt or decrease production, lay off a part of their labor force, and sometimes lose liquidity or cannot pay back loans and end in bankruptcy. Increasing joblessness further shrinks the market. Juglar also speaks about an "excès de speculation" and an "extravagant application du capital flottant." Price increases generate "exaggerated extension," and an "abuse of credit" leads to excessive expenses. Credit gets out of hand, and the "speculation spiral" gradually destabilizes the entire system.

Recessions can spread internationally because the markets for goods and money are international. The free trade system and the gold standard increased the likelihood of such an outcome. Exports also decrease, as does the availability of capital imports from abroad. Like contagious diseases, bank failures spread to other banks and countries. The interconnected market economies can all suffer the same recession, though they would do so to different degrees. Clément Juglar also maintained that market mechanisms would automatically solve the crises. The decrease in prices and output would invariably lead to the sale of accumulated stocks and a renewed balance of supply and demand. The seven- to eleven-year cycle, Juglar suggested, would gradually lead to a return of new prosperity.

In the late nineteenth century, analysts identified another type of economic cycle, one consisting of prolonged, twenty- to twenty-five-year fluctuations of both upward swings and slumping (or stagnating) decline.[39] The Russian Nikolai Kondratiev described in detail what is now known as Kondratiev cycles from the turn of the nineteenth century to his time of writing in 1922. The long cycles are basically generated by major technological change. As Joseph Schumpeter (1939) observed, a "whole set of technological changes" rendered the old leading sectors obsolete and fostered the gradual rise of modern sectors based on the new technology. This transformation or "structural crisis," he added, may manifest as a Kondratiev downturn characterized by slow growth or stagnation, and is then followed by an inevitable upturn and rapid economic growth based on the new technology. The first cycle Kondratiev identified commenced with the Industrial Revolution, and the last one he described began in the 1890s, with its upward swing reaching its zenith during the war and creating the Belle Époque (Kondratiev, [1922] 1984; Barnett, 1998). The literature from the 1960s–1980s mostly agrees that the 1860s was a boom period that was followed by a recession between 1873 and 1878. Several authors speak of a "Great Depression" from 1873 to the mid-1890s, followed by great prosperity until the war. In the 1870s, a major grain crisis hit several countries, and a banking crisis led to the collapse of several banks across the continent. Nevertheless, precise calculations belie the notion that there had been a general "Great Depression" in Europe (Lewis, 1978; Saul, 1969).

A recent study, however, largely rejects any regularity in business cycles and argues that "empirical regularities that look like cycles result from behavioral responses to random exogenous impulses." It also suggests that "it is not possible to consider European economies as a homogeneous whole, affected by symmetric shocks and with perfect timing" while "country-specific shocks became more frequent" (Flandreau et al., 2010, 88, 101, 102). While rejecting the concept of regular cycles, the authors do not deny the existence of "bank panics," "bubbles," or speculative booms that led to economic collapse, nor question the fact that the market is anything but perfect. This has created some confusion or uncertainty. Another study also maintains that "there was something like a European-wide recession roughly twice every decade," and it presents findings, based on industrial statistical series on output, that show that several countries did experience seven- to ten-year cycles that closely corresponded to international developments and correlated with the Juglar cycles (A'Hearn and Woitek, 2001).

Nineteenth-century economic development definitely exhibited some kind of cyclical development, with slumps and rapid growth, and medium- and long-term fluctuations. Some kind of cyclicality clearly existed in nineteenth-century European development, albeit not with the punctuality of German trains, and certainly not with the excesses of the twentieth century. In the latter, an interwar depression was followed after World War II by the most prosperous quarter of a century in history, only to lead to a new depression from the 1970s on.

Notes

1. Sierra Leone became part of the empire in 1808, followed by Java, Singapore, Malacca, and Burma in the 1810s and 1820s. In 1840, the Treaty of Waitangi legalized British rule in New Zealand. Britain occupied the valley of the Indus River between Sindh and Kashmir between 1840 and 1850, and took possession of Assam and Lower Burma during the 1850s. In 1857, Queen Victoria was crowned empress of India. In the 1880s, Beludjistan and Upper Burma, Malaysia, North Borneo, and New Guinea were incorporated into the colonial empire. Although David Livingstone had discovered inner Africa, the Zambezi, and Nyassaland in the 1850s, the real colonial invasion did not occur until the 1870s. The colonization of Sierra Leone, the Gold Coast (Ghana), Gambia, Bechuanaland, Zanzibar, and Nigeria, and the occupation of Egypt and Rhodesia, took place at the turn of the century – followed by the second Boer War, which further enlarged Britain's African colonies. Tibet joined the British sphere of interest in the early twentieth century. All these conquests were milestones of aggressive British empire-building in Asia and Africa.

2. Colonialism and imperialism became a central question for turn-of-the-century socialist movements and ideology. Marxist theoreticians profited most from the non-Marxist J. A. Hobson. In her *Accumulation of Capital* in 1913, Rosa Luxemburg argued that capitalism needs a "third person" besides the bourgeoisie and proletariat to attain its "surplus value" – a non-capitalist sector that included, as it was later called, the Third World (Luxemburg, [1913] 1975, 299). Karl Kautsky, the leading theorist of the German Social Democratic Party, had a totally different interpretation in his 1914 work, *Der Imperialismus*. In his view, capitalism needs huge "agrarian areas" in order to expand. But imperialism, he insisted, is only a policy choice (as child labor and long workdays had been in the early stage of capitalism), and it could be replaced by other policies. Capitalism, therefore, could exist without colonies, and colonial conflicts might be superseded by international cooperation in a future stage of capitalism, what he called *ultra-imperialism* (Kautsky, 1914, 921). The Russian Bolshevik theorist Nikolai Bukharin, in his *Imperialism and World Economy* in 1915, introduced the popular concept of the internationalized capitalist world system, where the traditional metropolis–village dichotomy became worldwide in a coherent system, with the advanced countries playing the role of metropolis and the world's agrarian regions playing the villages (Bukharin, [1915] 1966, 21). In 1917, Vladimir I. Lenin popularized the concept of "Imperialism as the last stage of capitalist development," in which the world is divided by the leading imperialist powers who turn against each other to redistribute their possessions (Lenin, [1917] 1974).

3. The French occupied Saigon in Vietnam in 1859, and continued advancing towards the areas of Cochin China, Tonkin, and Laos. Between the 1860s and the 1890s, France colonized French Indochina. From the 1880s to the 1910s, Benin, Chad, French Guinea, Senegal, Tunisia, Somalia, the Ivory Coast, Dahomey, and Morocco (in 1912) became part of a French African empire that was bigger than Europe itself.

4. Although it had lost several of its possessions to Britain, Holland remained a major colonial power. Dutch colonies incorporated the East Indies, Java, the West Indies' islands, Suriname, and the new possessions in northern Sumatra (Aceh), West Papua, and Bali.

5. Spain's 400-year-old empire was mostly lost between 1810 and 1825, and was replaced by several independent states in South and Central America.

6. In the case of France, expenditures exceeded profits by 108 million francs in 1898. Germany spent 1,002 million marks on its colonies but had only a 972 million mark total trade turnover between 1894 and 1913. Italy's colonial expenditures also surpassed its volume of trade.

7. Corradini rejected the socialist idea of class struggle within the nation. In its place, he promoted the notion of an international conflict between the "bourgeois and proletarian nations."

8. Sidney Pollard reminds us that Pareto, the great economist, declared at the Peace Congress of 1889 in Rome that economic integration would later lead to political integration, and that the Political Science Congress of 1900 might once more revive the concept of a United States of Europe (Pollard, 1981a, 55).

9. Russia scaled down the tariffs between Russia and Finland in 1859. Poland was also exempt from the Russian protective tariffs of 1877.

10. Adam Smith became the prophet of this idea, and his modern economics became the apotheosis of international financial theory, irrespective of national frameworks. David Ricardo went further by introducing the theory of comparative advantage, maintaining that free trade is advantageous for both advanced and less advanced countries, since it is not a zero sum game. Both parties gain from it by selling products that they can produce in the most efficient way and buying others that are more difficult for them to produce.

11. The Methuen Agreement with Portugal in 1703 and the Eden Treaty with France in 1786.

12. In 1842, Britain's Prime Minister Sir Robert Peel produced a balanced budget without large tariff revenues. Having disposed of a major obstacle, he was now able to reduce import duties for 750 articles and export duties on British manufactured products. Peel made further radical tariff reductions in 1845.

13. Markus Lampe argues that the Cobden–Chevalier Treaty was not a break-through, but a "tailor-made liberalization for their exports that would not have been implemented unilaterally by the other party" (Lampe, 2009, 1017).

14. Among them the French–Italian in 1863, the French–Swedish, French–Norwegian, and French–Spanish in 1865, the French–Austrian and French–Portuguese in 1867, the British–Italian in 1863, and the British–Austrian in 1865.

15. This early eighteenth-century treaty imposed a maximum 3 percent duty for imported goods from the Habsburg Empire. Serbia, whose foreign trade was overwhelmingly linked to the Dual Monarchy (88 percent and 57 percent of exports and imports respectively), had to retain the century-and-a-half-old tariffs until 1880. Bulgaria was required to use the 8 percent Ottoman tariffs, forced on Constantinople in 1860–2. Paragraph 8 of the Treaty of Berlin (1878), which ratified Bulgarian independence, imposed the old Ottoman tariffs on Bulgaria. It would have to wait until 1894 to introduce its own trade policy.

16. France initiated a meeting of the franc-using Latin Monetary Union (France, Belgium, Switzerland, and Italy) in 1865, which reached an agreement on a joint currency policy. Two years later, the European Monetary Congress in Paris advocated the introduction of the gold standard. United Germany then introduced its new currency, the mark, based on gold. Holland and the Scandinavian countries followed suit over the next two years, and the Latin Monetary Union joined in 1878.

17. America took a first step in this new direction. Following Hamilton's advice, the United States introduced moderate protective tariffs as early as 1816, and significantly strengthened them with successive tariff acts in 1824, 1862, and 1864. Most important of all, however, were the McKinley Act of 1890 and the Dingley Tariff Act of 1897. These measures increased tariffs to 57 percent of the value of imported goods. In other words, the early twentieth century was characterized by high protectionism in the United States.

18. Italy introduced effective protection in 1878 and again in 1887, and Switzer-land in 1884 and particularly in 1906. France's Méline Tariff of 1892 granted protection for agriculture and industry, but the 1910 tariffs targeted the most modern industrial products and increased tariffs for chemical, rubber, and electrical manufacturing. Sweden reintroduced agricultural tariffs in 1888 and increased industrial tariffs in 1892. Austria-Hungary took its first steps in the late nineteenth century, and the empire became fully protectionist with the introduction of the 1906 tariffs.

19. Spain had implemented agricultural protectionism since 1820, intensified it in 1834, and then forbade the import of certain goods altogether. The regime of the 1868 constitution turned to free trade, but the restoration of

1873 restored protectionism as well. Russia emerged as the most protectionist country in Europe. In order to defend its infant industry from competition, it imposed tariffs as early as 1868, and then increased them in 1891, 1893, and 1900. For poor peripheral countries, tariff *revenues* also remained crucially important. In Spain, for example, tariff revenues comprised 10 percent of state income, for which the government was unable to find a substitute. For peripheral countries, in other words, protectionism was closely connected to the exigencies of the budget.

20. The same thing happened with the Elbe in the 1860s, the Danube in 1856, and the Po in 1849.

21. The International Sleeping Car Company also "Europeanized" rail travel. Based on a Swiss initiative, a series of conferences were held in 1874 that led to two intergovernmental agreements that created uniform legal and technical conditions for railroad connections among the Central European countries. France, Germany, Italy, and Austria-Hungary accepted common regulations regarding the use and exchange of carriages. In 1887, the Technical Unity of Rail Transport was established, with the participation of France, Germany, Italy, Austria-Hungary, and Switzerland.

22. The statute of the International Criminal Court was written in 1872; the Institute of International Law (1873) and International Union of Criminal Law (1889) were established.

23. In the 1880s, an artificial Volapük (world speak) immediately faltered. Dr. Ludowik Łazara Zamenhof, a medical doctor born in multilingual Białistok in Russian-Poland, created a more successfully constructed language, Esperanto. He published its first grammar book, *Lingvo Internacia*, in Warsaw in 1887. Although the first Esperanto world conference was held in France in 1905, Esperanto also failed to gain ground.

24. Socialism might not win in a single country, and "local communism" would be destroyed by its connection to the world system (Marx and Engels, [1847] 1970).

25. "First" distinguishes this period from the contemporary era of globalization from the 1970s on. O'Rourke and Williamson maintain that the process was halted after World War I, and that the interwar decades represented a backlash against globalization.

26. The sharp rivalry for colonial expansion within Western Europe, which led to the formation of two confronting military alliance systems, the Entente Cordiale and the Central Powers, in the 1880s, did not preclude a process of economic integration of nation-states.

27. The difference in the price of jute between London and Calcutta dropped from 35% to 4%, and that of rice between London and Rangoon fell from 93% to 26%, during a forty-year period before World War I. The difference in

cotton prices between Liverpool and Alexandria, Egypt decreased from 63.2% in 1837–46 to 5.3% by 1890–9.

28. The combined annual average of British, French, German, north Italian, and Austrian-Bohemian imports increased from 271.3 million tons in 1833–44 to 1,912.7 million tons in 1905–13 – a sevenfold increase. The combined coal and coke imports of France, Sweden, and Italy increased from 1.1 million tons to 31.7 million tons between 1830 and 1905–13. The combined annual petroleum imports of Britain, France, Germany, Sweden, and Italy were 184,500 tons in 1865–74, and totaled 2,777 million tons in 1905–13 – a fifteenfold increase.

29. During almost the entire nineteenth century, 20% of French imports were textile raw materials. Prior to World War I, however, coal and coke comprised an additional 7% of French imports, and grain another 7%. In the Netherlands, the largest single import item was grain (17% of the total). Roughly one-third of Dutch and Swiss imports consisted of energy and raw materials.

30. North America, Argentina, India, and Australia undoubtedly increased exports of various foodstuffs and raw materials. Britain, for example, imported 86% of the wheat it needed from Europe in 1831, but only 5% by 1913. Belgium's European imports totaled 76% of its total imports in 1880, but had fallen to 66% by 1913. Europe's role in Dutch imports declined from 78% to 38% between 1880 and 1913. The rapidly industrializing countries increased their overseas imports, which were almost entirely made up of food and raw materials. Britain's overseas imports increased by nineteen times between 1796 and 1913, France's by seventeen times, Germany's by five times between 1880 and 1913, and Sweden's by six times between 1870 and 1913.

31. Several of these nations were banned from using their native languages in offices and schools, and they mostly lacked political and cultural autonomy.

32. "France concentrated on weaving and finishing... because the technical gap against Britain was least." Germany also focused on weaving and stocking-knitting for export (Pollard, 1981a, 175–8).

33. According to both authors, it was not the comparative advantage, but the scarcity factor that determined trade patterns. Countries purchase goods that are not (or less) available in their economies.

34. In the decade after 1815, Britain's capital outflow totaled $500 million, and Holland's and France's foreign investments amounted to $300 million and $100 million, respectively. By 1850, the amount of European capital exports totaled $2,000 million. This amount trebled by 1870, and then increased by nearly eight times to $46,000 million by 1913.

35. The United States did so as well, and cut a 7 percent chunk from its world capital exports.

36. Before World War I, 24%, 20%, 16%, and 9% of exported capital went to North America, Latin America, Asia, and Africa, respectively.

37. William Herschel discovered the climatic and economic consequences of sunspots in 1801. Sunspots had been known for some time, but Herschel found correlations between the number of sunspots and the price of wheat in London markets. A large number of sunspots strongly impacted the world's climate, for it increased the sun's energy output and raised the temperature of the atmosphere, while few sunspots had the opposite effect. This fluctuation caused a series of good and bad harvests, and consequent high and low wheat prices. In 1843, Heinrich Schwabe demonstrated an eleven-year-long cycle between the periods of a high and low manifestation of sunspots.

38. In Britain in 1816, 1829, 1831, 1837–8, 1848; in France in 1818, 1820, 1822, 1825, 1833, 1842, 1845–6, and several more in the 1850s and 1860s (Craig and García-Iglesias, 2010, 136).

39. The British Jevons, based on British experience, and the Dutch van Gelderen have described the existence of prolonged cycles before World War I.

Part III

The peripheries: semi-success or failure of modern transformation

CHAPTER 9

The "sleeping" peripheries, traditional institutions, and values

Time stands still

This was the impression of British travelers who sought to "discover" the exotic world of the European peripheries, a couple of thousand kilometers away from London. In the middle of the British Industrial Revolution, Edward Daniel Clark traveled to Russia and described it as a country frozen in "Asiatic barbarity" (Dolan, 2000). John Paget went to Hungary roughly forty years later and published a thorough and thoughtful description of the country in 1839. He was startled by the "laziness" he experienced: "A Magyar never moves when he can sit still." "Among many of the nobles," he also noted, "there is so great ignorance and so strong prejudice ... against losing what they consider their rights, and ... against raising the peasantry to think and feel like men" (Paget, 1839, 19, 21).[1]

"Laziness" was an impression received by visitors in the Balkans even thirty years later. "Foreign visitors called it laziness ... intellectuals sidestepped the issue by referring to the 'pre-capitalistic' attitudes of the Balkan peasantry" (Palairet, 1997, 311). Two British women traveled throughout the Balkans in the 1860s and 1870s and reported on Bosnia-Herzegovina's

fragment of [a] modern railway, lying detached and unconnected ... [which] run[s] once a day each way, conveying a ludicrously small average of goods and passengers ... Plums remained the province's most valuable product, and only one man in a hundred could read ... [In Pristina they asked a girl in a school] what is it that you learn? ... [Her answer was] to say our prayers ... Can you understand these prayers? No ... That is all that we can teach them [explained the teacher], for it is all we know ourselves. (Mackenzie and Irby, 1877, 1, 3, 91, 279, 404)

In the dynamic nineteenth century, Westerners were struck by how time stood still in Spain, where three decades went by without any major changes during the second half of the century. In an introduction to James Russell Lowell's 1899 work *Impressions on Spain*, A. A. Adee quipped: "To read Washington Irving's dispatches of fifty years ago and Mr. Lowell's of thirty years later, is to be struck by the similarity of the conditions in 1845 and 1878" (Gilder, 1899, iv).

Indeed, the *ancien régime* that was swept away in the West remained virtually intact in the peripheries until the 1860s and 1870s. Revolutions struggling to create radical social-political change were soundly defeated. In Hungary, the 1848 revolution succeeded in liberating the serfs and abolishing noble privileges and feudal institutions, but it completely failed to achieve independence from Austria. The retribution that followed created severe impediments to the country's development. Modern social-legal and institutional systems were not established before the Austro-Hungarian Compromise of 1867. In Spain, five revolutions in six decades attacked the *ancien régime*, but all were crushed. Modern institutions were sorely lacking. Liberal constitutions were rescinded, feudal fees and noble privileges, along with internal tariffs, were reimposed. An all-powerful church and entailed big estate in the south prevailed for a long time. A medieval mining law impeded the extraction of Spain's highly abundant natural resources. Moreover, the mining law of 1825 deemed that all of the country's natural resources belonged to the crown – thus assuring that landowners would have no interest in exploring for natural resources on their properties. However, the Vicálvaro Revolution of 1854 and the La Gloriosa Revolution of 1868 at last abolished the *ancien régime* in Spain. A new, liberal constitution in 1869 and a return to reforms stabilized the political situation and made modernization possible.

Portugal was on a similar trajectory. Political instability and a permanent conflict between liberal forces and the *ancien régime*, together with wars, insurrections, and civil strife, paralyzed the country throughout the nineteenth century.[2] Finally, the assassination of King Carlos (1908) assured the victory of a military-backed republican revolution in 1910.

Revolutions did not occur in most parts of the peripheral regions. Nation-building and reform from above led to a gradual and partial abolition of feudal institutions, and a half-hearted introduction of modern ones, mostly from the 1860s on. The Italian Risorgimento, the unification of the country, established modern institutions between 1860 and 1870. But Antonio Gramsci dismissed the process as *rivoluzione mancata* (a failed revolution) – a missed opportunity for social and political renewal as it was based on a compromise between the Piedmontese monarchy, the military elite, and the southern landowning nobility. The new reforms were enacted by force by the old *classe dirigente*. The Italian political dictionary created the term *gattopardismo*[3] for the mentality of the reforming old nobility: the beliefs and practices of those preferring pseudo-reforms and spurious changes of society, so as to preserve their own ingrained privileges.

Russia remained frozen in tsarist autocracy, with no semblance of parliamentarism to speak of. Serfs were tied to the land and sold as appendages of private property. This archaic state of affairs remained unchanged for a long time. Three waves of reform over an entire century were needed for gradual change to develop. The first reform in 1832, the brainchild of Pavel D. Kiselyov, Minister of State Properties under Tsar Nicholas I, improved the conditions of "state peasants," some 40 percent of the Russian peasantry, who became "free rural dwellers" living on state land. This stratum of serfs was granted personal property rights and freedom of movement as well.

After a humiliating defeat in the Crimean War in the 1850s, the regime implemented a second reform that officially abolished serfdom in 1861. The emancipation, however, effectively undermined the peasant economy, for the peasants had to pay large sums to compensate the landlords, and they lost the personal parcels they had previously cultivated. Above all, both reforms left the ancient structure of the village community intact. The peasants' land was not privately owned but belonged to the entire community, the *obshchina* (*mir*), which was responsible for paying taxes and remuneration collectively. Leaving the community required the *obshchina*'s express permission, and obtaining a passport for domestic travel was impossible without the community's agreement. The peasants thus remained bound to the land, and their mobility was strictly limited.

The process of emancipating the peasants and abolishing ancient village communities was not completed until a third reform in 1906. Pyotr A. Stolypin, the Minister of the Interior and later Prime Minister, abolished the *obshchina* and privatized more than 14 million desyatin[4] of communal lands, nearly one-third of total private peasant land, and consolidated private farmsteads. The completion of his reform, however, was not acheived until the Bolshevik Revolution.

In Poland, three failed uprisings against Russia paralyzed the partitioned country between the late eighteenth century and the early 1860s. The Polish nobility neglected burning social issues and did not liberate the serfs.[5] Paradoxically, it was the Russian tsar who emancipated the Polish serfs in 1863 against the rebellious resistance of the Polish nobility.

It took several decades to abolish serfdom and carry out agrarian reforms in the peripheral regions. Although some differences could be discerned in various sub-regions, the process was strikingly similar throughout the peripheries. First, the former feudal aristocracy took charge of the reforms and "became their chief beneficiary... The peasantry emerged weakened... they lost as a rule one-third or one-half of their land" (Conze, 1969, 55, 65–6). In the Balkans, under half a millennium of Ottoman bureaucratic-military rule, the land belonged to the sultan, and the peasants paid taxes to the sultan's military governors. The burden was especially onerous when local military rulers and unruly Janissary units disobeyed the central power and ruthlessly robbed the local populace. The peasantry was emancipated, and the Ottoman military-feudal elite eliminated, only in the 1870s, when the peninsula was freed from Ottoman rule. The peasants became landowners in large parts of the Balkans, but their parcels were insufficiently large to produce goods for the market, and they were bound to the village community, the *zadruga*. Consequently, Balkan agriculture was largely one of subsistence farming.

Hence, feudal institutions, serfdom, and noble privileges persisted in the peripheral regions for another seventy to eighty years after the French Revolution. And hence, modernization was consequently delayed. The surviving elements of the *ancien régime* continued to infiltrate the new institutions. The legacy of the past posed a heavy burden on the present. Arno Mayer's over-generalized and thus somewhat controversial theory for *all of* prewar Europe was absolutely true regarding its peripheries:

Premodern elements were not the decaying and fragile remnants of an all but vanished past but the very essence of Europe's incumbent civil and political societies... The entire regime was suffused with the legacy of feudalism... the nobles retained their wealth and status... [although the region] became post-feudal in economic terms. (Mayer, 1981, 5–9)

As Goethe's Mephisto declared, "The laws and statutes of a nation/Are an inherited disease,/From generation unto generation/And place to place they drag on by degrees" (Goethe, 1961, 203). The remnants of the past blocked the way towards a modern transformation. The noble landowning elite monopolized large swaths of land even after the abolition of their feudal privileges, and thus continued to hold most of the wealth of the peripheral countries and to determine the scope and direction of those countries' investments. Alexander Gerschenkron emphasized the fact that, in addition to the rate of accumulated capital, it is equally important that the wealthy strata "are willing and able to transfer the wealth to industrialization" (Gerschenkron, 1957, 363). In the best case scenario, the landowning aristocracy in the peripheral regions invested in their own estates, but, as Vilfredo Pareto concluded from the south Italian experience, they usually evolved from being *classes dirigantes* to becoming *classes digerantes* (the digesting class). The mostly absentee landed aristocracy squandered a large part of their wealth.

Small wonder that starvation and a Malthusian trap remained a genuine reality in the less developed peripheral countries. The last two major food crises of the nineteenth century affected Europe's peripheral regions. The best-known and most tragic nineteenth-century famine was the Irish potato famine in 1846–8. The potato became the most important staple food for 3 million Irish citizens in the early or mid-nineteenth century. A series of disasters destroyed a large part of the crop in consecutive years in the late 1840s, and no less than two-thirds of it in 1846.[6] Mass starvation and devastating diseases, particularly typhus, killed more than a million people between 1846 and 1851.[7] Another million emigrated. The 1851 census found 6.6 million people in Ireland, down from 8 million in 1841. Emigration continued unabated for the rest of the century; by 1911, Ireland had a population of only 4.4 million, as many as it had in 1800.

The last major famine in Europe nearly decimated Finland's population in the "years of the great hunger" of 1866–8. Floods, frost, consecutive crop failures, and finally a devastating freeze in August 1866 led to mass starvation. The death toll totaled 137,000 Finns, nearly 8 percent of the country's population.[8] Spain suffered famine in 1857, 1868, 1879, and 1898. Russia's situation is well expressed by the regular outbreaks of starvation and cholera, and the eruption of thousands of local peasant uprisings, throughout the nineteenth century.

Modern society failed to materialize in the peripheries, and the nobility retained its predominance and assured the survival of archaic, authoritarian regimes. In Spain, south Italy, Hungary, Poland, and Russia, a modern Western *burgher* society with an entrepreneurial business elite, a rising middle class, and an urban, industrial proletariat remained in an embryonic state. Instead, a "dual society" emerged, with a dominant feudal (though somewhat modernized) elite and an emancipated peasantry on the one hand, and a small modern, urban society on the other. The noble landowner elite and the gentry-based bureaucratic-military middle class monopolized political power in these societies. The emancipated but still socially excluded mass of landless peasantry, and the peasants struggling in small subsistence plots, represented most of those at the bottom of the social hierarchy. Feudal paternalism persisted between landlords and agrarian contractual or even wage laborers.

Nevertheless, the modern, urban elements of the slowly transforming peripheries gradually formed a parallel society comprising an entrepreneurial-business elite that lacked political power and, in several countries, were considered non-indigenous foreigners – be they Greeks, Germans, or Jews. This emerging modern middle class was extremely weak both in numbers and in social standing. Moreover, the new industrial working class represented only 7–17 percent of the population before World War I. The modern elements of these dual societies were subordinated to the traditional noble elite.

A similar phenomenon of "parallel elites" characterized Spanish society. The political class was formed from the traditional provincial elite, "untitled professional and rentier hidalgos that became bureaucratic nobility... The Spanish government and bureaucracy were still being recruited via clientage and patronage" (Ringrose, 1996, 362–3, 367). Probably the only major difference was the connection between the bureaucratic and business elites. Unlike in Central and Eastern Europe, the sharp ethnic-religious division did not exist between the two elites in Spain, and they "had a great deal in common. The traits that they shared include a tendency toward 'aristocratic' values, similar provincial origins, similar family trajectories... similarities in behavior" (Ringrose, 1996, 364).

The peripheral countries' incomplete modernization enabled them to retain their old political systems in somewhat modernized form. Autocratic power was replaced, mildened by authoritarian regimes that introduced a veneer of formal parliamentarism which concealed large remnants of the *ancien régime*, brutal oppression, and entrenched corruption. As Barrington Moore argues in *Social Origins of Dictatorship and Democracy*,

The... weakness of towns and town dwellers, the reintroduction of serfdom, and the "manorial reaction" to the advance of commerce blocked the road to attaining the prerequisites of modern democracy... The socioeconomic and political development of these countries thus created the social origins of dictatorship. (Moore, 1966, 417)

Incomplete nation-building in much of the peripheral regions actually strengthened and legitimized the unquestioned rule of an authoritarian monarch and oligarchy. They were now embraced as the embodiment of the "national interest" and the "saviors of the nation" in the fight against the "enemies of the nation," foreign oppressors, hostile minorities, and rival neighbors. The old, aristocratic elite's predominance in the army and state bureaucracy seemed "natural" to the region's populace. "Deformed, interrupted national development led both to chauvinism and autocratic, authoritarian regimes and policies" (Bibó, 1986, 343). In the Balkans, "[a]ll power was concentrated in the hands of those who managed the government... Centralized autocracies dominated by narrowly recruited bureaucracy" (Sugar, 1999, 13–14).

Russia did not even go this "far" and remained autocratic without even a semblance of formal democracy. The tsarist regime remained strictly centralized, and the "service nobility," subordinated to the tsar, comprised the government bureaucracy. A parliament did not even exist in Russia until the twentieth century. At the turn of the century, the Russian nobility totaled 1.4 million people. Autocratic power and paternalistic practices predominated throughout the nineteenth century (Pearson, 1989, 257). In the most backward peripheral regions, the state turned against its own population – in sharp contrast to the entrepreneurial state in the West. The aristocratic military-bureaucratic elite ran corrupt, "kleptocratic" regimes. William McNeill (1963, 1964) speaks of the *predatory* Balkan and Russian ruling elites, who turned inward against their own peasant populations.[9] This comes close to the view of the prominent Romanian historian Nicolae Iorga, who characterized the Romanian state as a *stat de pradă*, or predatory state. The remnants of feudal society and the authoritarian state created, to use Stephen Kotkin's (2009) term,[10] an *uncivil society*.[11] In these countries, closed social networks, patronage, and subordination were the rule, as was a culture in which people did not take their destiny into their own hands and did not organize to improve their social standing.

In the late eighteenth century, Adam Ferguson contrasted civil society with "barbarous" ones, where no law governs and "corruption... tends to political slavery." The uncivil society was a highly disadvantageous social and institutional environment for modern transformation. History, indeed, had not treated the peripheries kindly. They suffered from foreign invasions and prolonged occupations by non-European powers. The Reformation and the Enlightenment did not reach them. Painful historical circumstances created a pervasive negativism and insouciance in the face of major challenges. From time to time, desperate helplessness would be suddenly replaced by quixotic heroism and the waging of ultimately hopeless battles, which inevitably led to even greater desperation and self-pity. Some would celebrate these fiascos with national holidays. They embraced values that placed the fighters of futile battles on pedestals, while scornfully rejecting anyone willing to compromise, no matter how successful. They nurtured the bitter feeling of being heroically isolated, of being the victims of history, and of being the pawns of stronger, luckier, and evil enemies. This demoralizing negativism eradicated any determination to win peaceful, day-to-day battles for a better future. This was 180 degrees different from the response of the Swedes and Danes to their historical defeats and loss of empire and/or national territory. For them, external setbacks had to be met with internal fortitude. Difficult circumstances created positive responses, and consequently led to recovery and progress.

With the survival of traditional society in the guise of partially reformed political systems, old ways of thinking, tired value systems, and obsolete attitudes remained dominant. The Polish elite were preoccupied with national ideals. As Cyprian Norwid, the mid-century poet-philosopher, suggested, an "unjustified national religion" destroyed all secular ideas in Poland, which was guided by "mystical heroic deeds." Beginning in the 1870s, the so-called Warsaw Positivists advocated *praca organiczna* (organic work) in the place of heroic national struggles, and called for the pursuit of happiness through education, commerce, industry, and agriculture (Berend, 2003, 100–2).

Oppressive authoritarian regimes prevailed in the Balkans. The new ruling elite, which emerged during the military campaigns against the Ottomans, inherited that empire's culture of corruption,[12] which oiled the rusty machine of the central and local bureaucracy and became a natural, everyday phenomenon in the independent Balkans. Two British travelers in the 1860s reported that "In former days... the Christians had only to bribe [the Ottoman governor] in order to secure a certain amount of protection. Now-a-days, the governor must still be bribed, but... all the medjilis [local town councils] must be bribed too" (Mackenzie and Irby, 1877, 257).

The long survival of the *ancien régime* was accompanied by a lack of education, and mass illiteracy. In the mid- to late nineteenth century, 75% of Spaniards and 75–80% of Italians were illiterate, and 70% of Spaniards remained so as late as 1890. Illiteracy dropped to 25% in Italy by 1914, but it was much higher in the south of the country, where more than half the children did not attend school or did so on an irregular basis.[13] Until the late decades of the century, roughly 80% of Russians and no less than 90% of the Balkan populace were illiterate – and it did not drop to 70–75% until World War I. In Portugal, only one-quarter of the population was literate as late as 1911.

In addition, the people of the backward, uneducated peripheries held on to *traditional values and social behaviors*. An aristocratic mentality, known as the *hidalgo* attitude, survived and fused with a suppression of secular and scientific thinking in Spain – an oppressive legacy of the Inquisition since the sixteenth century. This mindset did not disappear when Spain discarded its feudal institutions, and it remained a strong obstacle to the country's modernization during the eighteenth and nineteenth centuries.

Practicing industry or commerce still seems incompatible with the status of nobility... the ideal of aristocratic life impregnated the mentality of all strata of Spanish society in the Old Regime and was solidly rooted in the lower layers, so much so that work on some trades was socially rejected. (quoted in Tortella, 1994a, 190)

Even in 1906, S. P. Cockerell, the British economic attaché in Madrid, reported that "Spaniards are not enterprising in business, and few care to venture on a new industry or undertaking" (Parliamentary Papers, 1908, 55). Those who entered business eschewed competition, and "the ease with which they could obtain rents from the state... made it more attractive to expend their resources and energy in search of [monopoly] rent" (Fraile, 1991, 202). "The heavy hand of the Inquisition, the interference of the Church with learning was at its worst in Spain" (Hamilton, 1938, quoted in Tortella, 2000, 223). The social traits that were "responsible for backwardness," Tortella concluded, were the "old aristocratic prejudice against work... the traditional Catholic distrust of capitalism... intellectual passivity and respect for orthodoxy... [and a] long mercantilist tradition supporting state intervention" (Tortella, 2000, 224).

A similar aristocratic value system predominated throughout the peripheries. An entrepreneurial outlook was mostly lacking. The elite, emulated by a large part of the population, looked down on business as not being "gentlemanly" and as an alien undertaking for a Pole, Hungarian, or Russian.[14] Portugal lacked an exclusively industrial-entrepreneurial class, for its merchants, industrialists, and entrepreneurs preferred to engage in the lucrative colonial trade, tax farming, and other monopolistic endeavors (Pedreira, 1991, 362–3). An indigenous entrepreneurial class was barely present in these regions, and most of the early entrepreneurs were native-born minorities who were largely considered foreigners, or who had recently arrived from abroad. Foreign entrepreneurs, mostly from France and Britain, established the entire banking and mining industry in Spain. "A society that was frozen in orthodoxy," Gabriel Tortella observed, "found itself three centuries later without a competitive and inventive entrepreneurial class" (Tortella, 1994a, 192).

Forty percent of the entrepreneurs in Moscow, and 30 percent in St. Petersburg, were "German-speaking foreigners" in 1869–70 (Dahlmann, 2006, 169).[15] In Łódź, the "Polish Manchester," the most advanced textile center of the country, 67 percent of the inhabitants were German, and nearly 20 percent Jewish, in 1864 (Kossert, 2006, 150). William Blackwell notes that "[r]eligious outcasts, such as the Old believers and Jews, were among the earliest of industrial capitalists and bankers in the tsarist empire" (Blackwell, 1982, 21, 40–1). The majority of the Hungarian and Romanian business elite were also Jewish and German. The capital cities of these countries, in which the bulk of modern economic sectors were concentrated, were strongly Jewish. While Jews comprised 5 percent of the total population in both countries, they made up one-quarter of Budapest's, and one-third of Bucharest's, inhabitants; no less than half of Romania's urban population was Jewish (Berend, 2003).

Box 9.1   Manfred Weiss: the rise of a Jewish industrialist in Hungary

Hungary was an agricultural country, the breadbasket of the Habsburg Empire in the European periphery. It preserved its feudal system, serfdom, and noble privileges until 1848, but did not truly begin a modern capitalist transformation before 1867, when the Austro-Hungarian Compromise restored autonomy and created the requisite legal and economic conditions. The partly absentee landowning aristocracy continued to control Hungary's economy and political institutions. They looked down on business as an activity not worthy of a gentleman. The lower nobility, the gentry, lost their free serf labor and noble tax exemptions, and gradually lost their land as well. They, however, did not turn to trade or industry, but established themselves in the civil service and the army, thereby remaining part of the bureaucratic-military elite. Although formally free, the peasantry was not integrated into Hungarian society, but remained excluded and uneducated. Consequently, both upward and downward social mobility was extremely limited.

In this situation, modern trades and occupations were out of reach for the peasants and unattractive to the former noble elite. The only mobile layer that filled these intermediary positions consisted of minority peoples, Greeks, Germans, and particularly Jews. Though some of these communities had lived in Hungary for centuries, they were considered non-indigenous. The number of Jews increased tenfold in nineteenth-century Hungary, due to the westward migration of Jews from Russia and the former Polish Galicia, which had become part of the Habsburg Empire in the late eighteenth century. Jews made up 5 percent of Hungary's population, but in Budapest, the capital city and the cultural, trade, and industrial center of the country, they comprised 20–25 percent. One-third of then were peddlers and workers until 1848, and more than 30 percent were lumberjacks, even at the turn of the century. Legally excluded from landownership and several occupations, a majority of them became innkeepers, shopkeepers, and artisans.

The economic floodgates opened up to the Jews after their emancipation in 1867. Their economic mobility only made this process easier. More than a third of them were self-employed, totaling 54 percent of the country's self-employed population. Twenty percent of banking personnel, half of the medical doctors, nearly half the lawyers, and 38 percent of engineers were Jewish.

The story of the Weiss family begins at this point. The first record of Adolf Weiss originates from the 1850s, when he was a pipe-maker in a village. However, he would soon move to the capital to avail himself of its abundant opportunities, and there enter the grain trade. This was Hungary's most booming business from the 1860s on, as the modernization of Hungarian agriculture assured that the country would be exporting more and more produce, mostly grain, for the empire's industrializing Austrian-Bohemian provinces. Adolf Weiss accumulated some capital from this lucrative business. In the late 1860s, he built flour mills with several other grain traders so that he could export more valuable and expensive processed grain, and he became a shareholder of three major flour mills.

Adolf had two sons, Berthold and Manfred. The latter was sent abroad to be educated. In the 1880s, the two brothers established their own business. Based on their family wealth, they opened a canned food factory. People did not eat canned food in the late nineteenth century. The only stable market was the Austrian-Hungarian army. After years of selling their products to the army, these innovative entrepreneurs increased their profitability by making their own cans. With this step, their food processing firm began to produce light metal products as well.

Their next idea was an extension of their move to produce cans: having installed the can-making machinery, and having the army as a regular buyer, why not use the machinery to manufacture cartridge cases for the army? The initiative worked. The next step followed in 1893: why not produce the whole cartridge, including the explosives? This time, because of the danger of explosions, they had to move their factory from the inhabited area of the city to the Danube island of Csepel, where gardeners grew fresh vegetables. Although the company remained somewhat small-scale, it was the only private factory in the country making munitions for the army. In 1900, Manfred Weiss asked the Ministry of Commerce to intervene with the Austro-Hungarian Ministry of Defense to assure that Hungarian companies got a fair share of military orders, equal to Hungary's contribution to the joint budget. This meant that 40 percent of the army's business would go to Hungarian factories, and markedly less to Austrian and Czech ones. With machines totaling 5,000 horsepower capacity, Manfred Weiss began producing various kinds of cartridges, including shells for artillery and the navy.

Production and supply for the Hungarian military was carried out by both the Manfred Weiss factory and the state-owned Diósgyőr engineering firm. Manfred Weiss continually fought to increase his company's share of this lucrative market. In 1906, the factory won the assistance of the Association of Industrialists, which petitioned that state-owned companies be allowed to produce only those products that private industry could not provide. The Manfred Weiss Company gradually emerged as the country's largest military manufacturer.

Prior to World War I, Austria-Hungary upped its war preparations. A new law in 1911 increased the size of the joint army in peacetime to half a million, and raised the wartime force from 877,000 to 1.52 million. The military build-up switched to fifth gear. Manfred Weiss expanded his munitions factory, installed new iron and steel furnaces, and opened metallurgical, copper, nickel, and aluminum producing sections. By 1913, the company employed 5,000 workers, and its machinery had a 20,000 horsepower capacity. Before the war, the factory supplied munitions to Russia, Serbia, Bulgaria, Portugal, Spain, and Mexico. Its workforce rose to 30,000 during the war, and Manfred Weiss, the "Hungarian Krupp," was ennobled and became Baron Manfred Weiss von Csepel – joined in that honor by several Jewish bankers and industrialists.

Based on Berend and Ránki (1955) and Berend (2003).

An anti-Western, anti-capitalist mindset, similar to that in Spain, abounded among a large majority of the Central and Eastern European elite. Bolesław Prus, the Polish Nobel Laureate writer, describes the aristocratic ethic in his novel *Lalka* (The Doll) of 1890: "He who makes a fortune is called a miser, a skinflint, a parvenu, he who wastes money is called generous, disinterested, open-handed... Simplicity is eccentric, economy is shameful" (quoted in Holmgreen, 1998, 70–7). These characteristics were extremely traditional and widespread in Poland. *Glos szlachcica polskiego* (The Voice of a Polish Gentleman), an anonymous pamphlet published in 1880, rejected the notion of nation-building through commerce and industry.[16] "Engaging in urban occupations," Maria Bogucka asserted, "was shameful and dishonest by their very nature" (Bogucka, 1993, 110).

When discussing the history of Hungary during the nineteenth century, Gyula Szekfű, the leading Hungarian historian of the interwar period, spoke of the "anti-commercial and anti-capitalist talents of the Hungarian race."

The principle of trading and producing for profit disagreed with the Hungarian nature... Bourgeois characteristics were quite far from the mental habit of Hungarians, nobility and peasantry alike... Undoubtedly, the Hungarians may be listed among those peoples who have the least inclination to develop in a capitalist direction. (Szekfű, 1920, 291; 1922, 81–2)[17]

Frozen in rigid autocratic traditionalism, an immobile and uneducated Russian society did not even long for the country's modernization. Religious fatalism, fear of innovation, and resistance to monetized market relations were deeply embedded in Russia's peasant society. Alexandr Nikolaevich Engelgardt's *Letters from the Country*, published in the 1870s and 1880s, illuminated these attitudes most authentically (Engelgardt,1993; see Box 9.2). While dreaming of the peasantry's liberation from tsarist oppression, the Russian populist movement Narodnaya volya (People's Will), which emerged in the 1870s, idealized the "uncorrupted peasant virtue" and rejected industrialization because it destroys the natural egalitarian values of peasant life.[18]

Box 9.2   The *muzhiks'* non-capitalist attitudes in Russia

Alexandr Nikolaevich Engelgardt became the most authentic reporter of Russian peasant life in the 1870s and 1880s. A nobleman, he was educated at the Mihailovskii Artillery School in St. Petersburg and earned a degree in chemistry in 1853. He became a professor at the St. Petersburg Agricultural Institute in 1866, and was appointed rector of the institution by 1870. However, the security police held him responsible for radical student "disturbances" at the institute, arrested him, and banished him from all university cities. He was forced to withdraw to his old family estate in Batishchevo in the Smolensk Province. He began to manage his estate, and, beginning in 1872, published "Letters from the Country" in the progressive journal *Notes of the Fatherland*, edited by the famous satirist and critic M. E. Saltykov-Shchedrin. In his third letter, Engelgardt describes peasant fatalism, their attitude towards innovation, and their communal, non-capitalistic attitudes.

"Having taken up farming two years ago, I quickly calculated that to farm in the old way... was not worthwhile." He wanted, therefore, to introduce new grains, and decided to plant flax. "The peasants, of course, were against this innovation, they said that flax would not grow here...would ruin the soil..." Engelgardt went ahead and planted the flax on a piece of land, but, when the new shoots appeared, an "incalculable quantity of earth fleas" attacked the field and began eating the young leaves. "The flax was perishing before my eyes." He called his steward to discuss what could be done to save the crop. At first the steward would not believe that the earth fleas were destroying the plants because "there are few insects this summer." When, over the next several days, he became convinced that the insects were indeed doing so, he rejoined, "It is God's will." Engelgardt persisted: "What are we going to do?" he demanded. "Ivan [the steward] does not say anything...and [is] trying to turn my thoughts away from the flax... [He points to] how well the cattle are eating!" Engelgardt perused German books to find a solution, but the steward resisted: these are not simple insects, he declared, "but some kind of curse laid on by evil people out of envy...It would be best of all to call the priest to say prayers. God is not without mercy...you've noticed yourself that the fleas fear God's dew." The priest himself explained to Engelgardt: "After you live in the country a bit...you'll get to know...that you can't protect yourself against an evil man."

Weeks passed. Engelgardt sought in vain to replant the flax, but the steward would hear none of it. Suddenly a heavy rain washed away the insects, and, in the end, Engelgardt had a good harvest. The old peasant thresher, Pakhomych, scolded Engelgardt: "Everything is God's will...But you wanted to plant again, you thought about going against God, you wanted to correct him. No, lord, everything is God's will; if God produces, then fine; if He does not produce, then you can't do anything."

Alexandr Engelgardt described another telling experience. "Two years ago, when I arrived in the village...my dam washed away [when the river overflowed] and the road was ruined." He wanted to rebuild them and asked the peasants to do the work. However, "the peasants demanded an unimaginable price for the job." A childhood friend explained to him: "'Just do everything the way the folks in the country do, and not the way you do it in St. Petersburg...You want to do everything with money...that is not the way we do things here.'"

But how else?

"'Why do you have to hire them? Just call them to help you, everyone'll come out of respect for you, and they will repair both the road and the bridge. Of course, give them a glass of vodka each...As neighbors, we shouldn't take your money, but everyone'll come out of respect...Your dam's been ruined – you immediately hire for money; that means you don't want to live as a neighbor, it means you're going to do everything the German's way, with money...It's better to live as neighbors – we help you, and you don't turn us down ... ' I [indeed] sent my steward to ask in the two neighboring villages for help repairing the dam and clearing the road. The next day, twenty-five men showed up ... even the rich peasants sent their children, with twenty-five horses, and they did everything in one day. Since then, we have begun to live as neighbors ... "

Based on Engelgardt (1993, 57–9, 64–71).

The conservative and nationalist Slavophils celebrated the unspoiled Russian values of common ownership and "real and concrete equality." In his milestone *Russia and Europe* of 1869, Nikolai Danilevsky differentiated between two distinct types of peoples, the "Germano-Romans"[19] and the Slavs. The latter, in his mind, possess the superior traits of a communal society and follow the only true religion, Greek Orthodoxy. In 1895, the German ambassador summarized the anti-Western views in Russia: "Western Europe is rotten ... it is a moral danger to Russia, and therefore she must prevent close contact with the West as much as possible" (Laue, 1969, 120–1).

Giorgio Mori speaks about the "radical anti-industrialism, latent or explicit, of a large part of economic thought and of the culture of the ruling classes of the Italian states." Representative was Lorenzo Fabbroni, who argued against the enormous concentration of "restless and turbulent" workers in big industry and in 1861 advocated for small-scale production (Mori, 1991, 328–9).

The illiterate peasant masses of Russia, the Balkans, southern Italy, and Spain preserved pre-industrial behavioral patterns. The renowned Russian economist A. V. Chayanov suggested that peasant families did not conform to standard neo-classical notions on the marginal productivity of labor, but worked on different principles, understandable only on their own terms. If their income was sufficient to meet their usual consumption needs, they opted to spend more time engaging in leisure rather than working harder to earn more in order to rise up the social ladder (Chayanov, 1966). Several contemporary observers in the 1880s had similar impressions. An entrepreneur in the Russian cottage-industrial textile center of Pavlovo described his experience in the following way: the *kustar* (cottage-industrial) peasant families are not concerned about economic opportunities nor do they care about the market laws of supply and demand. "[The] majority work less when demand is big and their income is high, and vice versa, they work more when [demand is low] and the piece-payments are declining" (Moskovskie Vedomosti (1858), Semevskij (1882), and Bezovrazov (1884) quoted in Gestwa, 1999, 152).[20]

What was, in the modern sense, irrational behavior was also connected to a culture of excessive alcohol consumption. This affected Russia's entire rural society, including women and adolescents from the age of ten or twelve. More than 10 percent of the income of a typical Russian family was spent on alcohol. In one of his famous letters from the Russian countryside, A. N. Engelgardt reported in January 1879 that "[a]ll of the diggers are happy to drink vodka, love to drink, and when they are idle at home, they drink a lot, in the Russian manner, several days without a break" (Engelgardt, 1993, 161).[21]

Mass illiteracy, deep poverty, superstition, and extremely traditional ways of thinking rendered the peripheral societies "uncreative," for tolerance of non-conformism and deviations from the norm are important and characteristic qualities of innovation (Mokyr, 1990, 11, 76). In other words, the human element in modernization was mostly absent or extremely weak in the peripheries. The human ability to adopt new technology was a very high threshold to meet, especially during the latter decades of the nineteenth century. "The new technologies," notes David Landes, "are so esoteric and difficult as to be almost unlearnable, except for those who leave to study in advanced countries" (Landes, 1991, 18). The consequences of these lapses went beyond blocking the transfer of technology or the spread of innovation. They obstructed the capitalist transformation, economic modernization, and basic institution-building in the region.

The demonstration effect: the West as model

Time stands still: this was the feeling of the young progressive elite of the peripheries as well. Count István Széchenyi, a Hungarian aristocrat and leading reformer, noted in his diary when traveling to England in 1822, "I feel profound pain and downheartedness at the situation . . . of our country . . . *Our country is sleeping*" (Széchenyi and Wesselényi, 1985, 212). Nearly eighty years later, Sergei Witte, Russia's dynamic Minister of Finance, used the same metaphor in a lecture in 1900: "On the shoulders of the present generation has fallen the task of making up what the empire has missed in two hundred years of economic sleep" (Laue, 1969, 190).

When the western half of the continent embarked on a spectacular modern transformation, the peripheries did not budge. However, in what is a relatively small continent, the various regions and countries have been quite well connected since the early modern period, if not earlier. The transformation in the West had a tremendous impact on the sleeping peripheries.

One aspect of this influence was the demonstration effect. The landowning and urban elite, if not the entire population, learned of the transformations taking place in the West. Many were frightened by the revolution in France, but many more longed for the profound changes, the new technology, and the rapid economic growth. Foreign entrepreneurs began arriving from the West and established mines, modern factories, and banks. Railroads became a symbol of modernity and an exciting novelty to possess. In any case, they physically connected the various parts of the continent. As Alexander Gerschenkron maintained, "however backward Russia's political structure was... the impact of the *Zeitgeist* upon it was irresistible" (Gerschenkron, 1968, 161).

The irresistible *Zeitgeist* permeated the peripheries. A specter was haunting Europe, the specter of modernization and industrialization.[22] The old landowning elite realized that there were enormous markets for their products, but they could do nothing about it because they used ineffective serf labor and did not share the dividends of the Western agricultural revolution. In an age of fervent nationalism throughout the peripheries, the feelings of shame and frustration at lagging behind prevailed among much of the elite. Nationalism became a primary engine of modernization.

Until the 1860s–1880s, when West European industrialization took off, none of the Mediterranean, Central, or Eastern European peripheries was able to embark on industrialization. Still, there was no Chinese wall within Europe. Western prosperity and the beginnings of rapid economic growth had multiple effects on the peripheral regions. First, the West was elevated as a model to emulate. Enlightened members of the aristocratic and intellectual elite followed developments, read reports, and sometimes gained personal experience of the ongoing transformation. After all, a new world was in the making only a few hundred or thousand kilometers away. The elites were well aware that their countries were excluded from the most auspicious advances. The ideas of the Enlightenment, that humans are not subject to an immutable destiny but can change their prospects through action, at last took root in the peripheries. Leading intellectuals and statesmen sought to raise their nations to a higher plane.

Stanisław Konarski argued in favor of following the British pattern: "Let us govern ourselves like sensible people... the God of nature did not search for different clay when he made Poles from what he used for Englishmen" (Brock, 1972, 12).[23] The Polish landowning aristocrat Dezydery Chłapowski traveled to Britain between 1811 and 1819, and then established a model farm on his estate. After three heroic but futile

Polish uprisings, the "Warsaw Positivists" insisted on another course in the 1860s and 1870s: "In order to take their place among the modern nations of Europe," they declared, "the Poles must first improve trade and industry . . . build towns and railways, and raise the rate of literacy" (quoted by Davies, 1986, 170).

Two young Hungarian aristocrats, István Széchenyi and Miklós Wesselényi, traveled to the Netherlands, France, and Britain in 1822. Wesselényi described the modern crop rotation system in France in his diary, and marveled at the advances in Britain: "One glass factory, coal mine, and iron works next to the other . . . The steam engines are used everywhere and they are exquisite." In his 1830 book, characteristically entitled *Hitel* (Credit), Széchenyi asks rhetorically: "Hungary has no commerce . . . Did we do enough to increase our output . . . and promote marketing? Many look down on commerce" (Széchenyi, 1830, 155–6).[24]

England became the model to study and emulate. Several leaders of the 1848 Hungarian revolution, and other leading liberal reformers, visited Britain during the first decades of the century. Lajos Kossuth, the future leader of the revolution, learned English in prison in 1839. The Romanian Junimea (youth) movement, established in 1863, emphasized "the need for Rumania to evolve toward a modern civilization on the Western model" (Hitchin, 1994, 62–3). Even Tsar Alexander II, in his January 1857 *ukaz*, suggested that the West was "the example of all other countries . . . [as well as] private industry, and . . . [that Russia must] utilize the considerable experience which has been gained in the construction of thousands of miles of railways in Western Europe" (Laue, 1969, 7). Nearly half a century later, Sergei Witte, the Russian Minister of Finance, urged the tsar to invite Western investors and implement reforms "[i]n order to . . . remove the unfavorable conditions which hamper the economic development" (Laue, 1969, 85).

Box 9.3   Sergei Witte: the railroads and industrialization of Russia

I was born in Tiflis in 1849 . . . my father . . . a member of the nobility . . . was born a Lutheran, in the Baltic provinces. His ancestors were Dutch who settled in the Baltic provinces when they still belonged to Sweden. (Witte, 1990, 3)

These are the first sentences of Count Sergei Witte's nearly 800-page memoir. He was born in autocratic and deeply backward Russia and was four years old when Russia, the "Sleeping Giant," was attacked by, and suffered a humiliating defeat at the hands of, the allied Turkish, British, French, and Sardinian expedition armies landing in Crimea. The war underscored Russia's technical and economic inferiority, for it possessed only 630 kilometers of railroad in the entire country and proved unable to mobilize its army. This wakeup call led to the emancipation of the serfs and the beginning of railroad construction.

In this environment, young Sergei studied physics and mathematics, graduated from the Novorossiisk University in Odessa, and then, in 1871, began working in the office of the governor of Odessa and Bessarabia. This talented man was soon appointed chief of operations and, in 1886, manager of the Southwestern Railroad. At the same time, he became a member of the E. T. Baranov Committee investigating the fitness of the badly built Russian railroads. When, in 1888, the imperial train derailed with the tsar and his family on board, killing twenty-two people, Witte was assigned to investigate the case; this was a turning point of his career. In 1889, he was appointed director of the newly established Department of Railroad Affairs within the Ministry of Finance.

The most spectacular project of the country's modernization, the Trans-Siberian Railroad, is linked to Witte. In his memoirs, he describes Tsar Alexander III's complaining to him that building the railroad "had been delayed by individual ministers, by the Committee of Ministers, and by the State Council" (Witte, 1990, 125). Witte became the main advocate for its construction. In 1892, at the age of forty-two, he became acting Minister of Communication and, as such, a member of the State Council. His main task was the Trans-Siberian Railroad, which he personally oversaw. A few months later, he was appointed Minister of Finance, thus becoming the chief "economic tsar" of the country. The tsar called a special conference regarding the Trans-Siberian Railroad. Witte suggested financing the project by issuing 90 million rubles of inconvertible paper money, although his predecessors, who were present at the meeting, opposed the plan. The tsar accepted Witte's recommendation to build the railroad from both ends in three stages. Witte also proposed other actions, such as assisting peasant emigration from the European parts of the empire to Siberia, a move bitterly opposed by what he dismissively called "serfdom Russia." Among his plans was the development of mining and industry in the regions the railroad traversed (Laue, 1969, 84). Witte succeeded. Between 1890 and 1900, government expenditures, foreign loans, and government-guaranteed private investments in railroads totaled 3.5 billion rubles.

The 9,441 kilometer Trans-Siberian Railroad, the longest in the world, connected Moscow and the Pacific Ocean at Nakhodka port, beyond

Vladivostok. More than 80% of the line cut across the Asian part of the empire, linking the center with Siberia, spanning seven time zones, and crossing sixteen major rivers. This heroic, entirely Russian construction project was carried out mostly by soldiers and convicts. The construction required great technical bravura, particularly for the 2.6 kilometer Amur Bridge and 7 kilometer Amur tunnel, as well as bridges over the Ural and Ob rivers. The Trans-Siberian Railroad effected a major turn in Russia's economic conditions by assisting mass migration to Siberia and facilitating a freer and growing agriculture there as well as a booming export market. A modern region was developing. The railway connected St. Petersburg and Moscow with Nizhniy-Novgorod, Perm, Yekaterinburg, Omsk, Irkutsk, Lake Baikal, Ulan-Ude, Khabarovsk, and Vladivostok. Some of the cities had been only recently established, such as Vladivostok, the first buildings of which (military barracks) were built in 1860, and (Nikolaevsk) Novosibirsk, founded in 1893. The new railroad created a main artery of circulating economic activity.

For Witte, as with Friedrich List, whose major work he translated, the railroad was the agent of industrialization and modernization. He was convinced that

extensive railroad construction would stimulate the growth of the metal-lurgical and fuel industries supplying rails and other equipment. In turn, the expansion of the heavy industries would create favorable conditions for the growth of light industries . . . [As Witte stated in his second budget report, railroad construction is] a powerful weapon . . . for the direction of the economic development of the country. (Laue, 1969, 77–8)

Witte was the primary advocate of industrialization by imposing pro-tective tariffs and attracting Western investment. He was restless, hard-working, and full of initiative. He bombarded the tsar with proposals to change the law to allow the creation of joint-stock companies. Corpora-tion laws, he argued, are "in effect in the majority of civilized countries." Witte also argued for a free inflow of foreign capital, since this was the "chief means for Russia in her present economic condition to speed up the accumulation of native capital . . . human energies which accompany foreign capital are . . . creative ferment . . . imported cultural forces thus become an inseparable part of the country itself" (Laue, 1969, 180–2).

He more than deserved the witty French moniker, "Monsieur Vite" (Mr. Speedy), as well as those of the "Russian Cobden" and "Russia's evil genius." Witte was highly ambitious, not averse to plotting against rivals when necessary, and, as his biographer put it, "very intelligent, possibly a genius" (Harcave, 2004, 3, 41). Under his stewardship until

1903, when he was promoted to the post of prime minister, Russia's belated modernization did in fact gain momentum. Industrial output doubled during the 1890s, and the number of miners and factory workers nearly doubled. The economy was modernized in Siberia and the Donets region. "Russia was undergoing in the 1890s the fundamental economic change . . . associated with the industrial revolution" (Blackwell, 1982, 42). As Witte himself summed up in his memoirs, "a Russian national industrial system had been established . . . This was made possible by the system of protectionism and by attracting foreign capital" (Witte, 1990, 321).

Although Witte's achievements were all connected with railroad construction and industrialization, his last major act was political. After Russia had lost its war with Japan, Witte drafted the tsar's October Manifesto of 1905 introducing a modicum of civil liberties and a kind of parliamentary system. At the same time, Witte was appointed as Russia's first constitutional Prime Minister. He left this post in 1906, and died in 1915.

Based on Laue (1969), Harcave (2004), and Witte (1990).

Following the British example, however, was not simply a question of will. To take full advantage of the immense markets for their commodities, countries in the periphery needed to build railroads to reach the West, increase their output to create export surpluses, and produce machinery to modernize their economies. Sergei Witte soberly recognized that, given his country's low rate of capital accumulation, it desperately needed foreign capital investment and credit. At the same time, the peripheral countries had to join the emerging free trade system and integrate into the European market. All this became possible from the 1860s–1870s on, when capital exports from the advanced West abounded, when the framework of Europe's free trade system and the gold standard were established, and when international railroad construction became rampant.[25]

Ready-made solutions were at hand. In creating a modern education system and a proper legal framework for the transformation, a pattern emerged of discarding the old, obsolete institutions and replacing them with Western ones. Allowing banks to open, joint-stock companies to function, and foreign investment to flourish became characteristic throughout the peripheries. Establishing the building blocks of a modern transformation, cementing economic connections with the advanced countries, and increasing exports to Western markets became important parts of the peripheral countries' arsenal.

Still, it became increasingly clear that social, political, and cultural factors were impeding the modern economic transformation. Revolutions, reform movements, reforms from above by the liberal wing of the aristocratic elite, and struggles for independence had all led to a gradual change. In the latter decades of the nineteenth century, the *anciens régimes* throughout the peripheries were reformed according to the Western model. But these reforms were not only late, but, to varying degrees, incomplete, for they retained a number of obsolete institutional elements and continued to adhere to the region's social and cultural legacy. The same institutions that worked efficiently in the West had far less effect in the peripheries, where corruption, clientalism, and authoritarianism continually undermined them. The partial reforms, however, led the way to stronger links with the West.

International relations, the relatively peaceful half-century before World War I, and the breakthrough of globalizing tendencies with predominant free trade and gold standard policies, all contributed to the growing economic ties between the European core and the peripheries. The timing of the peripheries' transformation coincided with the expansion of the railroad age and industrialization in the West. During the last third of the century, the increasing demand for food and raw materials in the industrializing half of the continent created a genuine trade boom. This was strongly expedited by a rapidly increasing capital flow from the rich countries to the less developed ones. Territorial proximity and the simultaneous transportation and banking revolutions in the West induced some adjustment to the European economic system in the southern and eastern peripheries.

Emulating the West a century later, however, did not mean doing the exact same thing. The entire world environment had changed. Technology was no longer of the simple and cheap variety of the first Industrial Revolution. Modern technology of the second Industrial Revolution was science-based, expensive, and complicated, and it required the use of highly trained experts. The size and scale of the economy became incomparably larger and thus required more massive investments and more sophisticated management at a time when the peripheries were much less affluent and educated. They were not equipped to engage in the necessary capital formation and had a limited social ability to adopt foreign technology. The most mobile layers of their societies emigrated and sought opportunities abroad.

Belated development potentially offered the "advantage of backwardness," as A. Gerschenkron described the prospect of adopting advanced technology and management techniques from the core countries and attaining a faster growth rate (Gerschenkron, 1962). Meanwhile, the time-lag and backwardness created much larger obstacles to transformation. The steps taken in the West in an earlier period were now no longer applicable. Rather different challenges faced the peripheries. Establishing textile factories was not the same as it was a century earlier, because Europe already had a strong export-oriented textile industry. Building railroads almost concurrently with the West (and sponsored by the West) took place too early to create industrial linkages, because of the lack of existing industries. Consequently, the railroads were only partially used in the peripheries before industrialization. The adoption of free trade, which began in the West after a long period of preparation and increasing economic strength, played out quite differently in the peripheries, separated as they were by the huge development gap between themselves and the West. In reality, there were many more disadvantages of backwardness than there were advantages.

Is it possible to assess whether advantages or disadvantages were more prevalent? David Landes succinctly asks and answers this question in the following way: "Does it pay to be late? Sometimes yes and sometimes no" (Landes, 1991, 20). One may dismiss this as glib or facetious, but it's actually the only realistic answer. The experience of the peripheries in the nineteenth century clearly shows that "the integration of a more backward country did not necessarily and in all cases lead to its 'peripherization'; nor, however, was it necessarily an opportunity for catching up" (Berend and Ránki, 1982, 160). A general pattern did not exist. Whether advantages or disadvantages prevailed was dependent on domestic circumstances. Some countries and regions were better prepared to follow the Western transformation than were others, but all of the peripheries tried to do so – some beginning in the 1860s, others only at the turn of the century. Some reacted more quickly, some more slowly, some were more successful, others less so. Some began modernizing and industrializing, and developing agricultural-industrial structures, with higher income levels. Others, while taking steps towards a modern transformation, remained in an agricultural state and had the lowest income levels of the continent. Even in the latter cases, there emerged within them some scattered, often isolated, industrialized enclaves during the two decades before World War I. The domestic factors that influenced the outcome of these modernization attempts were mostly social, political, institutional, and cultural – in a word, "non-economic." While Western Europe and Scandinavia went through a significant social, political, and cultural transformation in the early modern centuries, the peripheral regions were unable to do so.

Debate proliferated in the peripheries, but little action. Was the path to modernization blocked forever? A Chinese wall hardly separated the rapidly advancing regions of Europe from the stagnating, less developed ones. The repercussions of Western progress trickled down, and economic, trade, and financial ties became the principal yeast of peripheral transformation.

The "Europeanization" of the continent moved rapidly forward, driven by international agreements, free trade and gold standard systems, and a dramatic rise of intra-European trade. The value of world trade increased by thirty-three-times between 1820 and 1913, and this surprisingly remained intra-European trade: both in 1870 and 1913, some two-thirds of world trade was composed of European trade. Consequently, the role of the peripheries increased tremendously: in 1860, their share of European trade was 16–17 percent; by 1913, it had reached 26 percent.

The central question remains: were the peripheries able to jump at the opportunity and satisfy the Western demand for food and raw materials? To do so, they would have had to increase their agricultural and mining output significantly; and to do that, they would have needed capital to invest in their economies, and modern transportation systems to link them to the Western markets. The governments of the peripheral countries, however, suffered from permanent financial crises and were plagued by continual indebtedness, which proved difficult to pay back, and, in the worst cases, led to insolvency.

Population explosion and emigration

In a most paradoxical way, despite their retention of the *ancien régime* and their lack of a modern economic transformation, the peripheries experienced virtually the same demographic revolution throughout the nineteenth century, and exhibited more or less the same population growth, as did the West. The dramatic demographic changes in Western Europe beginning in the mid-eighteenth century were closely connected to fundamental agricultural, economic, and educational modernization, and to the emergence of a modern civilization. The peripheral regions lagged a century behind. Still, several Western achievements trickled down to the south and east. The causes of demographic changes in the West are a hotly debated issue: did economic modernization generate the demographic revolution or vice versa? Were population changes and economic transformations mutually determinative?

There is no such debate, however, regarding the peripheries. Economic modernization, let alone industrialization, took place much later than did the radical turn of demographic trends. There was not a close interrelationship between the domestic economy and demography. Instead, the connection might be found between *Western* modern transformations and *peripheral* demographic changes.

The intriguing question, therefore, is how these two processes, demographic change and economic modernization, which had occurred simultaneously and jointly in the West, became chronologically decoupled in the peripheries. Based on the Spanish case, Jorge Nadal draws the following conclusion: "The reasons for a phenomenon . . . must be individual for each country . . . The lack of agricultural revolution reveals in the end the true nature of the demographic pseudo-revolution . . . There was neither industrial not demographic revolution . . . population grew unaccompanied by any fundamental economic changes" (Nadal, 1973, 533, 537–8). In other words, the similarity of the peripheries' population growth to that of the West is accidental, and it was caused by rather different factors in each peripheral country. Nadal explains Spanish population growth as the positive outcome of the loss of Spain's European possessions.[26] The only economic factor that Nadal considers as being at work in the peripheries' demographic growth was their adoption of maize and potatoes, which had saved their populations from starvation. But how was it possible that the vast stretches of peripheral territories, from Russia, Central and Eastern Europe to the Mediterranean region, all had similar demographic surges? Was it simply a historic coincidence, a series of "demographic pseudo-revolutions" stemming from accidental, domestic circumstances?

A clue to the answer might be found in the end results of population growth. According to widely accepted estimates, the population of the peripheries roughly trebled between 1800 and 1910, while it grew by three and a half times in the Western core during this same period. Hence, peripheral population growth was only slightly slower. Using the more credible figures of 1820 and 1913, and comparing three regions (the combined Western and Scandinavian regions,[27] the regions of semi-successful modernization,[28] and the regions of retarded, partial, or failed modernization),[29] the numbers are even more surprising. (See Table 9.1.)

Part of the explanation of faster peripheral growth is that population increases started accelerating earlier, already in the eighteenth century, in the West (particularly in the Northwest), and became even faster during the first decades of the nineteenth century. In contrast, population growth in the peripheries sped up only from the mid-nineteenth century onwards.[30] On the other hand, nineteenth-century population growth reflected a chaotic diversity within the various regions. In the advanced world, an

Table 9.1 Population growth in Europe 1820–1913, by regions

Regions	Population increase by 1913 (1820=100)
Successful regions	216
Semi-successful regions	218
Strongly belated, partly modernized, and failed regions	267

Sources: Based on Maddison (2001), Mitchell (1975), and Palairet (1997).

Figure 9.1
Population growth
by European
region,
1820–1913
(percent)
(Maddison,
1995)

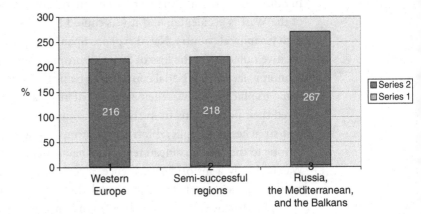

extreme disparity characterized the population growth in France, which rose one and a half times, the Netherlands, which rose threefold, and Britain, which rose fourfold. Among the peripheries, the Mediterranean countries less than doubled, the Balkans more than doubled, Poland more than trebled, Finland nearly quadrupled, and Russia more than quadrupled their populations. In other words, similar disparities – very rapid and relatively moderate increases – differentiated countries in the core and the peripheries alike. Although this underscores the importance of local cultural-social characteristics, it does not mean that population growth randomly differed country by country. As mentioned earlier, the regions exhibited basic similarities and, at the end of the day, a pan-European population growth. (See Figure 9.1.)

Beyond general demographic similarities, however, the detailed parameters reflect a major and typical core–periphery difference. Population growth in Europe was a result of steeply declining death rates and more moderately declining birth rates.[31] In the peripheries, the dynamics of demographic change were rather different. As a whole, both death and birth rates also declined. Here, however, the sharp decline of death rates (from 37–38 per 1,000 to 22–30 per 1,000), though much less significant than in the West, nevertheless generated a massive population explosion.[32] An important factor in the decline of death rates in the West was the decrease of child and infant mortality. Between the first quarter of the nineteenth century and the first decade of the twentieth, infant mortality (the death of newborns in the first year of life) dropped from 144 to 127 per thousand. Sweden achieved the most significant progress, dropping from 178.5 to 84.5. In contrast, infant mortality in the Southern and Eastern peripheries lingered at 160–200 per 1,000 births before the war.[33]

On the other hand, birth rates in the peripheries only slightly followed the Western pattern: compared with 14–20 per 1,000 in the West, they stayed at 35–40 births per 1,000. Birth rates were 33–37 per 1,000 in the Mediterranean and Central European regions, and remained almost unchanged, at 40–46 per 1,000, in the Balkans and Russia. In other words, surprisingly high and stable birth rates and more moderately, but still significantly, declining death rates produced the same population growth in the peripheries as in the core countries.

At the same time, the average life expectancy at birth differed markedly in the core and the peripheries. Traditional life expectancy was 25–30 years for all of Europe, and it hardly changed for a millennium. By 1820, however, it increased to 30–40 years in Britain, France, the Netherlands, and Sweden. By the early twentieth century, it reached 47–56 years in the Western and Scandinavian regions. The peripheries exhibited much more traditional conditions: in 1900, life expectancy was 39, 35, and 32 years in Hungary, Spain, and Russia respectively. The average 30- to 40-year life expectancy in less developed regions was 10 to 20 years shorter than in the West.

Based on these more detailed demographic data, it is quite clear that, random country-by-country differences notwithstanding, there are quite easily recognizable similarities in the peripheral regions. Their general characteristics can be summarized as rapid population growth based on traditional high birth rates and declining death rates, a significantly lower population density, and a somewhat increased, but still low, life expectancy that lagged far behind the West. What were the main causes of the peripheries' demographic peculiarities? First, the peripheral regions remained overwhelmingly or entirely agricultural and rural. The population's educational levels were low and illiteracy rates high. Furthermore, marriage habits differed widely between the core and the peripheries. In the West, women began working outside the household, the stem family was dissolved, and young people married later than they did before. John Hajnal's celebrated work, "European Marriage Patterns in Perspective" (1965), unveiled the growing disparity of marriage customs on the continent. Marriage patterns of nineteenth-century Europe, he noted, gradually separated along a dividing line between Trieste and St. Petersburg (often called the "Hajnal line"). Fewer people married west of that line, and those who married did so much later. By 1910, only 15–16 per 1,000 people married in Western Europe per year, while 18 per 1,000 did so in Hungary, and 20 per 1,000 in Serbia. The percentage of unmarried women between the ages of twenty-five and thirty in the West increased to 35 percent and even 50 percent, while it remained only 10 percent in Hungary. On the eastern side of the dividing line, people married five to six years earlier than on the western side.[34] A postponement or absence of marriage, Hajnal observed, decreased the number of children in the advanced countries. A lack of change in marriage patterns kept birth rates high in the less developed zones (Hajnal, 1965).

Although birth rates in the peripheries did not follow the Western trend, death rates most certainly did (though they remained higher than in the core). What was the reason for this difference? Most importantly, the advance of healthcare in the West, vaccinations, modern sanitation measures, and basic education gradually spread to the peripheral regions. This took place before economic modernization and industrialization had begun. In a typical example, the enlightened absolutist empress of the Habsburg Empire, Maria Theresa, introduced her *Normativum sanitatis* in 1770, inspired and directly influenced by Western progress, with the explicit goal of emulating the West and establishing a modern sanitation system. Health reforms and institutions were introduced as "a peculiarity of the rather small, economically backward Habsburg provinces . . . [such as] Galicia, Bukovina, and Transylvania" (Sechel, 2008, 97).

How did it happen that the empire's easternmost provinces and the Balkans, the continent's least developed regions, followed the West? Teodora D. Sechel argues that Maria Theresa was in permanent competition with the emperor of Prussia, and closely followed Western development. She invited a Dutch scholar, Van Swieten, to be the director of the Court Library and the dean of the University of Vienna. Van Swieten was a disciple of the Dutch scientist-physician Herman Boerhaave, and he played a central role in implementing health reforms across the Habsburg Monarchy, including establishing medical schools and creating a health administration (Sechel, 2008, 99). Sanitary inspections, standardized medical service, and a well-organized pyramidal institutional system quickly followed, headed by the Sanitas Hof-Deputation in Vienna with territorial branches. A state health organization was established in the mining regions, offering doctors and qualified midwives. The doctors of the state institutions also served as "medical police" who inspected the health conditions in the cities. A *cordon sanitaire* was created along the borders to prevent epidemics; quarantine areas were established at the borders, both inland and coastal.

Public health was further modernized in the nineteenth century. In the relatively backward agrarian half of Austria-Hungary, the Public Health Act of 1876 introduced an advanced Western sanitation system in Hungary. The government made registration of all deaths and inquiries into their causes mandatory. Prevention became the duty of public authorities. Sanitary norms were set for housing, schools, shops, and institutions. Vaccinations of people and animals became compulsory; the building of hospitals in a single decade raised the number of hospital beds by a third. State-run food inspection and ambulance and first-aid service were also introduced. Despite these developments, the quality of health services lagged behind that in the less developed regions. Based on the number of medical doctors and hospital beds, health services in Southern and Eastern Europe were only one-quarter to one-half the Western levels.[35]

To be sure, the decline of the death rate gradually shifted from the Northwest to the East and South. Sweden's death rate was 205 per 1,000 in the 1750s, and it had dropped in all of Scandinavia to less than 20 per 1,000 by 1860. England matched this level in 1880, the Netherlands in 1890, Italy and Austria in 1910, and Spain and most of Eastern Europe only after World War I (Glass and Grebenik, 1965, 70).

Although both death and birth rates in the peripheries loosely followed the Western pattern, though remaining much higher than in the West, the widening gap between the two created rapid population growths. In the first half of the nineteenth century, population growth throughout the agrarian peripheries of Europe was still slower than in the advanced regions. In contrast to a 223% increase in the West, the population grew by 143% in Mediterranean Europe and 153% in Central and Eastern Europe. Between 1850 and 1910, however, Western advances spread to the peripheries, and the dynamic markedly changed. Because of increasing urbanization and modernization, population growth slowed to 62% in Western Europe, while in the peripheries it more than doubled (216%).[36] Population density in the peripheries, however, remained much lower than in the West. Before World War I, there were 223 inhabitants per square kilometer in Northwestern Europe, roughly 95 in the mid-continental regions,[37] 55 in Hungary, Romania, and Bulgaria,

39 in the Iberian peninsula, and only 26 in Russia. These figures reflect a nearly ninefold discrepancy between regions.

Europe could not cope with the population explosion. Large numbers emigrated from the British Isles and Germany in the first half of the nineteenth century, but they stopped doing so in the last third. Replacing them were masses of emigrants from rapidly growing populations in the peripheries. Latecomer Scandinavia also saw a large part of its rising population emigrate. In 1880, 45% of all European emigrants had left Scandinavia, Italy, and Central and Eastern Europe. By 1890, this increased to 72%, and by the early twentieth century, to 80%. Between 1880 and 1914, Italians comprised 24% of European emigrants, Spaniards 13%, and Scandinavians 6% – and roughly a quarter came from Central and Eastern Europe and Russia. This massive emigration made up 20–25% of the population increase of those regions.

Irish emigration represents a special chapter in the history of nineteenth-century European migration.[38] Some 1 million people left Ireland between 1845 and 1848, and no fewer than 4.2 million people emigrated between 1851 and 1911 – a number that exceeded the natural increase of the population. The crisis that befell Ireland was unique, but severe food shortages were hardly rare occurrences in the peripheries. They were seen in Spain in 1857, 1868, 1879, and 1898. Famine struck the eastern half of Galicia, a province of the Habsburg Empire, in 1847, 1849, 1855, 1865, 1876, and 1889. The last famine in Finland in 1868 killed 8 percent of the country's population. Landlessness and hunger pushed millions to emigrate from the backward regions of Europe.

The very backward Balkans, however, remained largely immobile. Poverty, very high rates of illiteracy, a paucity of information, and the surviving village communities strongly restricted social mobility. The only significant population change was caused by mass Muslim emigration to Turkey, with more than a million fleeing the newly independent Balkan states for Anatolia. Similar conditions limited Russian emigration as well. Russian peasants either stayed or moved within the country, usually to obtain free land in sparsely populated Siberia, which attracted significant numbers from the European half of the country. Emigrants to the United States or elsewhere were overwhelmingly made up of minorities: 90 percent of emigrants from Russia were oppressed Jews, Poles, Latvians, Estonians, and Lithuanians. The low emigration rate from Spain reflected a major and certainly common obstacle to mass emigration from some of the poverty-stricken regions. Spanish emigration, Blanca Sánchez-Alonso points out, "was income constrained," since the cost of the trip consumed 153 days of wages in 1880, and 195 days in 1892–1905. Along with the agricultural crisis in the late nineteenth century, a particular Spanish currency depreciation increased travel prices significantly (Sánchez-Alonso, 2000a, 319, 327).[39]

However, the peripheries were not merely areas of emigration beginning in the last third of the century; in some areas mass immigration was already characteristic. After Greece became independent, tens of thousands of Greeks returned home from Asia Minor, Romania, and the Habsburg Empire; Russia invited western peasants to settle in its sparsely populated areas such as Siberia between 1860 and 1880; and from the 1890s on, Chinese, Persian, and Turkish immigrants settled in Russia's newly occupied territories. Between 1825 and 1915, a total of 4.2 million people, two-thirds of them from Europe, moved to Russia. In addition, 7 million Russians migrated from the European half of the empire to the newly annexed territories of Siberia and Central Asia. Some 1–2 million Jews left Russia, the Polish territories, and Habsburg-occupied Galicia for Romania and Hungary.

Moreover, demographic changes were accompanied by changes in the traditional family structure. As discussed earlier, the nuclear family predominated in the West. In the peripheries, large joint households continued to prevail for much longer, although with increasing regional differences. In many places, the traditional village family still contained some twelve to forty people or more, constituting the family commune. In 1814, nuclear families represented only one-third of the total number in Russia, while three-generation families comprised 60 percent, and four-generation families 7 percent. Likewise, the south-Slavic *zadruga* comprised twenty to thirty, and in some cases even eighty, family members until the mid-nineteenth century. In 1863, only 2 percent of the population of Orasać, Serbia lived in single-couple families.

In the 1860s, a contemporary demographer reported on Hungary: "Patriarchal life is dominant... the villagers usually live together still; in some villages, there are families with thirty to forty members under one roof" (Pap, 1865, 58). While hardly more than a fifth of the families were nuclear in some regions, close to 40–50 percent were in other regions of the same country. The traditionally large families virtually disappeared from most parts of Europe by World War I.

As Western demographic trends trickled down to the peripheral regions, so did *educational* development. Compulsory, free basic education and the elimination of illiteracy, the main educational achievement of the West, were also seen in the backward peripheries. Educational reform was implemented at the same time as health regulations, at times surprisingly early. In 1868, József Eötvös, Hungary's Minister of Education, made primary education compulsory and free for ages six to twelve, limited the number of students in each classroom, and fixed the ratio of students and teachers. Teacher training schools were established, and extensive school construction began. The German-type gymnasium also spread steadily in Hungary: 150 gymnasiums offered elite education for some 5 percent of the high school generation in the 1860s, and 350 did so by World War I. Hungary offered compulsory and free primary education decades before Britain and France did.

Similar reforms spread throughout the peripheries, but mostly in later decades and almost always without strict enforcement. A large percentage of children were not enrolled, and some who were did not attend school for a part of the year. In the overwhelmingly agricultural, non-urbanized regions, children often had to work in the fields or with animals and had to walk several kilometers to school, and poor families were unable to buy them shoes. Traditional ways of thinking opposed the education of girls, and illiteracy remained much higher among them. In mostly illiterate Romania, where only 27% of primary school-age children in the countryside were enrolled in schools, the proportion of girls among them was only 13%. Only 7% of the female population could read and write. In Poland, 70% of female service workers were illiterate in 1900. Illiteracy remained a mass phenomenon throughout the peripheries, comprising 40–80% of the population until World War I.

Along with the enticing spectacle of Western industrial transformation, the population explosion provided a major challenge for the peripheries. How can a region that had hardly changed for centuries possibly feed a population three times as large? Additional land was not available, and increased revenues and employment could only come from a modernized economy, higher productivity, and industrialization. But internal sources were not sufficient to initiate it. The point of departure towards the peripheries' modern transformation was a massive capital inflow from the West.

Notes

1. When a reformer proposed introducing steam navigation on the Danube, "even his best friends shook their heads. Steam in Hungary! Yes, indeed, in another century!" He visited Debrecen, a town of 50,000 inhabitants, and noted that it had no resemblance to a European town: "In rainy weather the [unpaved] street becomes one liquid mass of mud" (Paget, 1839, 137, 324).

2. The liberal revolution in Porto, and a modern constitution in 1821, did not last long. A military-led liberal uprising and civil war in 1832–4 was followed

by permanent insurgencies between 1834 and 1853, including a new civil war in 1846–7. A republican revolution was defeated in 1891.

3. This was based on the title of the renowned novel of Giuseppe Tomasi di Lampedusa, *Il Gattopardo* (The Leopard), which described the southern social-political conditions of the Risorgimento.

4. A Russian land measurement: 1 desyatin = 2.7 acres.

5. Their unique feeling of superiority was expressed by the myth of their "Sarmatian origin," which supposedly distinguished them ethnically from the Slav Polish peasantry.

6. Various fungi and other potato diseases often destroyed large parts of the crop in many regions, as occurred in 1807, 1821–2, and 1835.

7. The exact figures are uncertain. Some estimates place the death toll between 1.3 and 1.5 million people. In the regions of Munster and Connaught, the population decreased by 22 percent and 29 percent respectively.

8. In the region of Vörå, 16 percent of the population died.

9. In his two celebrated works, *The Rise of the West* (1963) and *Europe's Steppe Frontiers 1500–1800* (1964), William McNeill speaks of a fundamentally Asian culture of steppe nomads in the Balkans, modified by the geographical (mountainous) environment (McNeill, 1963, 1964). Samuel Huntington, in his renowned *The Clash of Civilizations*, repeats the theme of a distinct "Euro-Asiatic" civilization of the 70–90 percent Greek Orthodox East European societies (Huntington, 1996).

10. Kotkin introduced this term in connection with post-communist, transforming societies in East-Central Europe, which, he claims, are not creating a civil society. He, however, does not contextualize this phenomenon with the historical development of the region (Kotkin, 2009).

11. The Scot Adam Ferguson was probably the first to use the term "civil society" in his *Essay on the History of Civil Society* in 1767. Ferguson spoke of "considerable parties, or collective bodies [who] chose to act for themselves." His civil society can exist only in "liberty, [which] results, we say, from the government of laws" (Ferguson, 1768, 193–4, 404). Civil society did not exist in nineteenth-century Europe, except possibly in Britain, where self-organized bodies and institutions played important roles in the Industrial Revolution. The existence of civil society in America deeply impressed the Frenchman Alexis de Tocqueville more than half a century later. As he described his experiences there in *Democracy in America*, he differentiated between political and civil society and spoke of intermediary organizations between the individual and the state. De Tocqueville clearly recognized that this kind of society, the active association of people, might emerge only in countries with strong social mobility, traditional local autonomy, and long-standing self-government (de Tocqueville, [1835, 1840] 2000).

12. Balkan historiography either overestimates the Ottoman impact, explains the region's historical "deformation" as its mere consequence, or it underestimates and even denies that legacy. Maria Todorova (1997) maintains that the "Ottoman legacy was insignificant" as far as political institutions were concerned, since the new Balkan states broke with the past after their liberation.

13. In Hungary in 1868, when compulsory and free elementary education was introduced, 68% of the population was still illiterate – a number that decreased to 35% by World War I. Conditions in the easternmost and southern provinces of Austria-Hungary, Poland, Russia, and the Balkans were much worse. In Dalmatia, only 1% of the conscripts could sign their names in 1870. In Galicia, 59% of the population remained illiterate by 1910.

14. As one of the heroes of Anton Chekhov's *The Cherry Orchard* (1904) declared, "The human race [is] progressing... Meanwhile in Russia a very few of us work. The vast majority... [of the elite] seek for nothing, do nothing, and... [are] incapable of hard work... they treat the peasants like animals... Only dirt, vulgarity, and Asiatic plagues really exist" (Chekhov, [1904] 1917). A Russian contemporary of Chekhov, Baron Nicholas E. Wrangel, made a similar observation: "You want to work? How odd! Don't you know that a civil servant who works is a lost man?... There are gentlemen, who don't do anything... and in a few years become State Councilors, and who can get anything they want" (quoted by Harcave, 2004, 35).

15. In Belarus 90% of the merchants were Jewish in 1897. Jews comprised 85% of the merchants of Vitebsk and 98% of those of Wilna (Kištymau, 2006, 222).

16. "[The Polish noblemen] lived according to the customs of their forebears and not the customs of shopkeepers... [The nobility rejects] the worship of the golden calf and utilitarianism... [They are] the exclusive heir to the entire historic national past... Religion, Motherland, Family and Tradition" (quoted in Jedlicki, 1999, 218–19).

17. Similar views were expressed about the Romanian aristocratic elite: "Educated Romanians have shown a tendency to avoid following a commercial career, leaving this field of activity to alien elements... The country... is thus deprived of the opportunity of building up an independent middle class" (Logio, 1932, 115, 118).

18. In this view, Western capitalism is degrading and destructive. Populist intellectuals prophesied an independent "Russian road" based on cooperation and an avoidance of capitalism.

19. "Germano-Romans" are power loving and aggressive, under either the despotic Catholic Church or the "religious anarchy" of Protestantism. They are materialistic and have embraced the "anarchy of democracy."

20. Another *Verlag* merchant spoke of the peasants' "love to do nothing." Yet another entrepreneur referred to their "low motivation to work." The peasant-industrial workers do not take advantage of the labor market to earn higher wages. Klaus Gestwa, who quoted these contemporary statements, called this pre-capitalist behavioral pattern "subsistence economic reproduction logic."

21. K. Zamorski speaks of an anti-modern peasant mentality, in which "in the common value system money was never of utmost importance." He cites an analysis of will and testaments and official inventories in a peasant proto-industrial region, which proved that "peasant merchants as well as producers directed their fortune towards the institutions which were not connected with production... They remitted to the church all their capital for religious reasons." In some cases, 20 percent of a decedent's wealth was spent on a lavish funeral (Zamorski, 1998, 44).

22. This paraphrased opening of the Communist Manifesto of 1848 presents a more realistic picture of the continent.

23. Konarski personally witnessed the Industrial Revolution during the years he spent in Britain. When he returned to Poland at the end of the eighteenth century, he established the *Monitor*, the country's first modern magazine.

24. The enlightened Hungarian statesman József Eötvös spent nine months in Paris and London in 1836–7. He became a member of the revolutionary government in 1848, and served as the Minister of Education in the Hungarian government after the 1867 Austro-Hungarian Compromise. He noted in his diary, "Since the time of the French Revolution, the development of most of the European countries demonstrates that the model for new institutions was taken from England; ideas and concepts were copied from France" (Eötvös, 1902, 39).

25. Even the Ottoman Empire realized the need for reforms based on the Western pattern. Halil Pasha, the son-in-law of Mahmud II and commander-in-chief of the army, argued in 1830: "If we do not adopt European ways, we shall have no choice but to return to Asia." Seven years later, Mustafa Reshid Pasha repeated this warning: "Only through reform that will bring Turkey closer to the norms of European life can we get over the enduring political and economic crisis" (quoted in Petrosian, 1977, 63–5). Nearly a quarter of the top military and political leaders of the Ottoman Empire between the 1820s and 1870s were educated in the West or spent time in Western countries. Among them, Hayrettin Pasha, who was educated and had lived in Paris, was invited back by Sultan Abdulhamit to be his financial advisor and then Grand Vizier in the 1870s. As Orhan Pamuk observed, the Pasha "was one in the long line of foreign educated financial experts who... went beyond dreaming... of national reform along Western lines... [P]eople expected a

great deal from this pasha, simply because he was more a Westerner than an Ottoman" (Pamuk, 2005, 25).

26. Permanent imperial warfare left more than a thousand villages deserted and halted all population growth. Quoting a statement from 1768, Nadal notes that imperial wars led to "the depopulation of the Realm . . . in order to retain distant provinces" (Nadal, 1973, 536).

27. Western Europe, including the western half of Germany, north Italy, and the western provinces of the Habsburg Empire.

28. The central part of the Habsburg Empire, particularly the Hungarian kingdom (with Transylvania and present-day Slovakia), Ireland, the eastern parts of Germany, and the western provinces of the Russian Empire, including Finland, the Baltic region, and Russian Poland.

29. The Mediterranean countries (including southern Italy), Russia, the Balkans, and the easternmost and southern provinces of the Habsburg Empire.

30. Between 1750 and 1800, Britain's and the Netherlands' populations increased by 42% and 31% respectively, while Spain's and Portugal's grew by only 26% and 28% respectively. Between 1797 and 1860, peripheral Spain had an annual 0.63% population growth compared with the 1.25% English rate.

31. The number of deaths per 1,000 inhabitants was about 37–38 in Western Europe during the last decades of the eighteenth century, while birth rates were 30–36 per 1,000. Before World War I, birth rates declined to 25–30 per 1000, but death rates dropped to 14–20 per 1,000.

32. Regional differences within the peripheries were not significant: in 1901–10, the death rate was 25.2 per 1,000 in Spain, 23.2 in Bulgaria, 26.0 in Romania, 25.7 in Hungary, and 30.0 in Russia.

33. Typical for the Balkans, 232 of 1,000 newborns died in the first year of life in Serbia at the turn of the century.

34. A majority of Serbian women and men still married between the ages of sixteen and twenty-seven at the turn of the twentieth century. The average age for marriage in late nineteenth-century Hungary was eighteen for women and twenty-three for men.

35. There were 34 medical doctors per 100,000 inhabitants in Germany and 38 per 100,000 in France. In contrast, there were only 23 per 100,000 in Hungary, 15 in Transylvania, 12 in Galicia, and 9 in Croatia and Russia.

36. Between 1830 and 1910, Britain's annual rate of population growth was 0.80%, but Bulgaria's was 1.87% and Russia's 1.13%.

37. Scandinavia was an exception and remained scarcely populated before the war: there were 71 people per square kilometer of land in Denmark, 12 in Sweden, and 7 in Norway.

38. The population of Ireland increased markedly between the mid-eighteenth century and 1841, rising from 3 million to 8.2 million, i.e. by 2.7 times.

However, the population then dramatically declined to 5.8 million by 1861 and 4.4 million by 1911, nearly half the the number in 1841. This unparalleled situation was a consequence of agricultural backwardness and economic decline. During the decades of population growth, Ireland never escaped from the Malthusian trap. Repeated failures of the potato crop in 1740–1, 1799–1800, 1816–17, 1819, 1822, 1836, and most tragically in 1845–8, 1851, and 1879, were followed by starvation and famine, especially in the poorest regions of the west.

39. Without the currency depreciation, Sánchez-Alonso adds, Spanish emigration would have increased by 25 percent and equaled the Italian emigration rate (Sánchez-Alonso, 2000a, 309, 327).

CHAPTER 10

The Western sparks that ignite modernization

Capital inflow to the peripheries

Reforms from above introduced some basic elements of the West's modern legal and institutional systems into the peripheral regions during the 1860s and 1870s. The enactment of a modern property law, and the possible estrangement of the noble land, the abolition of medieval monopolies (such as the archaic Spanish mining law), and several other reforms cleared the way for foreign investment in the peripheries. Guaranteeing interest for investors in railroads, issuing government and municipal bonds, and other important steps made investment attractive. These factors led to a major acceleration of capital inflow into the backward European regions. Capital exports became one of the prime movers of European economic integration and the mainspring of modernization in the Mediterranean region and Central and Eastern Europe beginning in the last third of the nineteenth century. (See Figures 10.1 and 10.2.)

Investments in the colonies and semi-colonies on other continents embodied naked economic expropriation and a monopolization of resources, but it was not exactly so in the European peripheries. The recipients' governments and leading financial players performed an important mediatory role that prevented the capital exporters from holding absolute sway over the recipients' economy or brutally subordinating it to their own interests. While the smaller and weaker countries (especially in the Balkans) had less power to intercede, the politically and militarily more important ones (especially Russia) were in a much better position to do so.

Geographic proximity and the availability of raw materials attracted investors to the Mediterranean region quite early. The London and Paris stock exchanges issued a series of state loans. The French stock market took over Spanish government bonds, which constituted nearly a third of

Figure 10.1
Gross nominal
value of invested
capital in Europe,
1914 (percent)
(Maddison,
2001, 99)

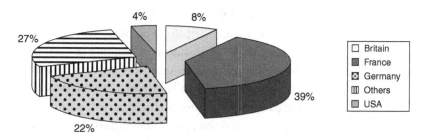

Figure 10.2
Gross nominal
value of invested
capital abroad,
1914 (percent)
(Maddison,
2001, 99)

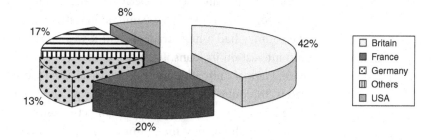

France's foreign capital investments between 1816 and 1851. The London stock exchange appropriated Spanish government securities, comprising a quarter of the credits made available to Europe. Construction took off with the passage of the Spanish Railway Law (1855), with French financial groups providing 60 percent of railroad investment in Spain after 1866.

Between 1856 and 1868, foreign investors turned to the Spanish banking sector and established the first major banks in the country. The French Péreira Bank opened the Sociedad Generale de Credito Mobiliare Español (with 465 million pesetas capital), the French Rothschilds founded the Sociedad Español Mercantil e Industrial (304 million pesetas), and French financial groups were behind the creation of the Compañia General de España (399 million pesetas). Local banks paled in significance compared with these institutions: the largest among them, the Credito Mobiliaro de Barcelona, had capital of only 12 million pesetas.

The extraction of Spain's abundant mineral resources had already attracted foreign investors in the first half of the nineteenth century. New mines, especially in the Sierra de Gádor and Sierra de Almenara, led to a sevenfold increase of lead output between the 1830s and 1910. Spanish lead mining led the world from the 1860s on. The Rothschilds modernized Spanish copper mining in 1873. The most important Rio Tinto copper mines produced 58 million tons of copper ore between 1875 and 1914, extracting 2.5 million tons per annum in the latter years. Spain produced nearly half of the world's copper output at the beginning of the twentieth century. Massive British investment was channeled into Spanish iron ore mining after 1868, when a new mining law was passed. By 1875, twenty-two British companies were mining the abundant iron reserves of Vizcaya and transporting 4 million tons per year to Britain.[1] Only 9 percent of the country's most important mineral resource, iron ore, was processed in Spain. Around the turn of the century, however, the mining of minerals, most of all iron ore, became the basis of a late, but spectacular, start of industrialization in the Vizcaya region. Foreign investment in raw material extraction ultimately led to a belated industrialization drive.

Portugal accumulated $700 million in outstanding debt by 1890. Since the country had a huge trade deficit, it was unable to pay the principal and interest on its loans. It was also unable to pay for the roughly 1,000 kilometers of railroad lines under construction before World War I. As a result, the railroads were put under foreign supervision, and additional state loans were not provided. Only direct investments were made in the country by the turn of the century, though the amount invested was not significant. Neither Spain nor Portugal obtained significant foreign capital in the early twentieth century. The total amount of foreign investment in the Iberian peninsula, $1.5 billion, represented 3–4 percent of total foreign investment worldwide.

Austria-Hungary received a large amount of foreign capital in the decisive early period of its modern transformation, but the peripheral eastern part of the empire remained a major capital importer until the war.[2] Only 12% of French capital exports were earmarked for the Danube monarchy by 1902, and only 5% in 1914. However, Germany's political and economic interests centered on Austria-Hungary. Before the war, Germany invested nearly 23% of its capital exports there, which was the largest amount it gave to any European region.

In the western, Austrian-Bohemian half of the empire, 35% of invested capital was foreign by the end of the nineteenth century. Until the 1880s, foreign capital predominated in the finance of railroad construction, through both direct investment and state loans. After that period, however, the importance of foreign financial resources dwindled. Austria-Bohemia itself became an "exporter" of capital before the turn of the century. Austrian-Czech investment mostly targeted the less developed parts of the Monarchy, as well as the Balkans. It equaled 80% of German and other foreign capital in the Monarchy.

Foreign banks, 23% of which were Austrian, provided more than half (55%) of the state loans in Hungary. Of municipal bonds, 55% were financed abroad and 27% in Austria; 70% of railway shares were held by foreigners, mostly Austrians and Germans. The leading Hungarian banks, established after 1867, were mostly subsidiaries of Austrian banks, and 45% of their shares were owned by Austrians. Foreign financial groups also controlled about a third of Hungary's industrial firms at around the turn of the century. During the first Hungarian *Grüderzeit* between 1867 and 1873, 60% of the investments in Hungary were financed from abroad, mostly from Austria and Germany. Increasing domestic capital accumulation decreased this to 25% between 1900 and 1914.[3]

Moreover, foreign companies took the first steps in extracting newly discovered resources in the eastern provinces of the empire, such as Galicia. When oil deposits were discovered, small, rudimentary, mostly wax-producing local companies were established. Extraction began in primitive ways. Several foreign-owned companies were founded following the law of 1881, which allowed foreign joint-stock companies to run mining operations.[4] Galicia produced 1.2 percent of the world's oil in 1900, but this rose to 5 percent by 1909, making Galicia the third largest oil producer in Europe.

At the other end of the empire, in Bosnia-Herzegovina, which was incorporated into Austria-Hungary in the 1880s, the *Landesregierung* of Count Benjamin Kállay carried out a colonial type of "civilizing mission." The government founded and owned a majority share of Gewerkschaft Bosnia, which began extracting the region's large mineral deposits.[5] In addition, a German industrialist, Otto Steinbeis, established giant saw mills and a pulp factory, employing 10,000 workers. Aside from these Austrian and German investments, most of the local industrial firms were small-scale.[6]

The Austrian and foreign-owned large companies in Bosnia-Herzegovina concentrated on raw material extraction and the production of semi-finished products for export to processing firms in Austria-Hungary. Bosnian industry achieved an annual growth of 12.4 percent between 1881 and 1913, much faster than in neighboring Serbia and Bulgaria. Bosnia attained somewhat higher levels of economic development as well: although representing only 21 percent of the combined population of Bosnia, Serbia, and Bulgaria, Bosnia produced 54 percent of the area's combined industrial output. Still, Bosnia-Herzegovina was part of the least developed province of the Monarchy.

The picture in Romania was somewhat similar, though the amount of productive foreign investment was greater. Half of foreign loans to the country went to railroad construction, and one-fifth to the military. Large oil deposits were discovered at around the turn of the century, and Western companies immediately invested in oil extraction.[7] Investments in oil were almost entirely from abroad: domestic sources comprised only 4.5% of the total, while 27.5%, 23.7%, 20.0%, and 10.0% came from German, British, Dutch, and French financial groups, respectively, and the remaining 14% from American, Belgian, and other foreign investors. The oil sector remained a foreign enclave that procured 60% of total industrial and mining investment in Romania. Oil extraction increased by 15% per annum, from 300,000 tons in 1901 to 1.8 million tons by 1914. Romania became the world's fifth largest oil producer. Crude oil increased from 0.8% to 12% of the country's exports between the turn of the century and the war. In the latter year, this represented one-quarter of Romanian mining and industrial production. Nearly the entire crude output was exported to Western refineries in the investing countries. In return, Romania imported processed oil products. As in Galicia, the oil industry remained a foreign enclave without any significant spin-off effect.

The same scenario played out with other Romanian industrial sectors. In 1900, foreigners owned the country's few existing industrial firms and 80 percent of the shares of its joint-stock companies.[8] This was also true of the banking industry. More than 60 percent of the capital of Romania's eight largest banks was in foreign hands in 1914 and foreign investment comprised 75 percent of the total capital of Romanian banks.[9] The leading German D-banks and the French Crédit Mobilier were big players in the country.

Foreign capital inflow to all other Balkan countries was even more detrimental. Greece's experience was typical. In politically unique circumstances, Greece became an important player in the anti-Ottoman wars and was the first Balkan country to receive foreign capital already in the first half of the century. British credits were used to pay its newly formed army and to buy ships. In 1830, when Greece gained independence, the Rothschilds loaned the country 60 million francs, of which 14 million was spent on the Bavarian army stationed in Greece, and 11 million was paid out as compensation to the Ottoman Empire. The rest was used mostly to pay old debts. At the end of the day, the new government received only 0.5 million francs. Consequently, it came as no surprise that the country became insolvent in 1843. However, in later decades new credits and income from issuing state bonds generated new capital inflow. Military expenditures and railroad construction were financed by foreign loans. Up till 1893, foreign capital inflow had totaled 750 million francs; however, because most of this went to the military and other non-productive spending – only 6 percent were productive investments – Greece again became insolvent that year. As in Romania, foreign investment established the embryonic modern industry in Greece. By 1909, foreign industrial investment was one and a half times greater than domestic investment, and it comprised 64 percent of the total.[10]

Later all the other Balkan countries became capital importers. Serbia acquired Russian loans in 1867 and 1876 to finance the military struggle against the Ottoman army. French, German, and Austrian capital inflow became significant there from the 1870s on. The Länderbank and the Union Générale financed the construction of the Serbian parts of the Berlin–Constantinople railroad line, and additional railroad investment came from abroad in 1885 and 1886. During the 1880s, a number of loans went toward procuring armaments, compensating Ottoman landed estates, and providing deficit financing. By 1895, Serbia had accumulated 350 million francs of debt; the new Serbian state could not pay the annual 17 million francs in principal and interest and declared insolvency that year. A massive consolidation loan and the imposition of foreign control on state finances solved the problem. Altogether, Serbia received twenty-six major loans: ten of them (316.5 million dinars) were used for repaying debt, eight (443.5 million dinars) for military expenses, and another eight (304 million dinars) for economic investments.

The first major iron works was founded in Smederovo with British financing. French mining companies, particularly the Mines de Cuivre Saint Georges, extracted copper from the abundant resources in Majdanpek and Bor, and coal mining began with Belgian investment. Altogether, roughly half of the 62 million dinars in industrial capital (invested in 470 firms) came from abroad. Direct foreign industrial investment, however, represented only 3 percent of foreign capital inflow to Serbia.

Bulgaria received 850 million francs in state loans from France, Britain, Russia, and Austria. As with other Balkan countries, 40 percent of these loans were used for state deficit financing and armaments, and roughly 40 percent went into railroad construction, financed mostly by the Deutsche Bank. At the turn of the century, nearly a third of Bulgaria's state income was used for repayment. Small wonder that Bulgaria also became insolvent in 1901. A French–British financial group provided a consolidation loan, garnering all state revenues and controlling Bulgarian finances for repayment. In contrast, direct economic investment was insignificant: there was none at all before 1895, although 15 million francs were invested into thirteen industrial firms, and 42 million francs into other parts of the economy, between 1896 and 1911. Direct investments thus represented only 5 percent of state loans. The newly established banks, the Banque Générale de Bulgarie, Crédit Foncier Franco-Bulgar, and Banque des Balkans, were all French establishments. France provided 60 percent of foreign direct investment.[11] Direct industrial investment remained much more limited – as it had in Serbia. It made up only 3–5 percent of the massive loans to the Serbian government, and was used for raw material extraction, mostly copper and iron ore mining and logging ($5–6 million). Limited as it was, foreign direct investment in mining made up 40 percent of total industrial and mining investment in Serbia.

The situation was much the same in Bulgaria, except for a lack of mining possibilities; thus the limited direct investment targeted power station construction. All the Balkan countries became heavily indebted. On a per capita basis, each citizen of a Balkan country was 150–330 French francs ($50) in debt. But even this relatively moderate sum could not be paid back, as the loans to the region were not profitably invested and thus did not produce income for repayment. Only some 5 percent of imported capital served productive investment, while the bulk of the money was used for building up state bureaucracy, investing in "symbolic modernization," that is, erecting impressive government and public buildings, and financing the deficit and armaments. As an unavoidable consequence, Greece, Serbia, and Bulgaria fell into insolvency around the turn of the century.[12]

Russia was more fortunate. The country became the largest capital importer in Europe. Initially Britain was the primary lender, but from the 1870s on was replaced by France, the main buyer of Russian bonds and securities. For a while, Germany, out of political interest, tried to compete with France and invested heavily in Russian railroads and natural resources.[13]

According to various estimates, foreign capital inflow to Russia increased from 537 million rubles in 1861 to 7,634 million by 1914. Nearly half (46%) of the latter amount went to railroad construction, 21% to state loans (and was primarily used for railroads as well), 19% to industry, 4% to banking, and 3% for mortgage credits, mostly for agriculture. The rest was channeled to communal investments. By 1914, 47% of Russian government bonds, 74% of all municipal bonds, and 40% of other types of bonds were sold abroad. France alone lent $2.4 billion by World War I to strengthen Russia's military potential. In all, Russia absorbed 25–30% of the total West European capital exports to Europe.

Until 1881, 94% of Russian railroad investment came from abroad. Although this would decrease in later years, it remained high (74%) before World War I. Industrial investment continued to be less important, amounting to only 17% of total investment in Russia. Unlike Spain and the Balkans, Russia attracted huge amounts of foreign capital for its industrial sector from 1890 on: 88% of the shares of the smelting and mining sectors, and 50% of the entire industrial sector, were in foreign hands. After the discovery of abundant iron deposits in the Donets Basin, 40–45% of foreign investment went to that region to build up a large and modern iron and steel center. Another significant part of foreign investment targeted the oil fields discovered in the Caucasus. Foreign investment increased more than fifteenfold between 1861 and 1914 and tenfold between 1890 and 1913, and it was indispensable for initiating industrialization in the country. By 1914, foreign investors provided 63% of the financing in key sectors such as mining and the iron industry, 63% in engineering, 41% in the chemical industry, and 21% in textiles.

Moreover, foreign direct investment played a central role in establishing the modern Russian banking sector. Mostly French financial groups supplied 60% of the capital of the country's four biggest banks, and German capital provided 35–40% of the financing of the four next largest banks. Altogether, 40% of the capital of the ten largest banks in Russia was in foreign hands.[14] Domestic capital accumulation and investment increased, however, after the turn of the century. Before 1881, invested domestic capital comprised only 18% of foreign investments; by 1881–1900, it was 89%; and by 1900–14, it had surpassed foreign investment by 24%.

The peripheral countries of Europe attracted massive investment from the western half of the continent, which was mostly channeled into railroad construction, banking, and raw material extraction, and occasionally combined with the production of semi-finished goods. Investment in processing industries was the exception. Significant investment created isolated enclaves without influencing the countries' domestic economies as a whole. The amount of exported capital from the West European core totaled $46,000 million by 1913, and 26 percent of it went to the peripheral countries of Europe. Foreign investment played a decisive role at the beginning of economic modernization, although to different degrees in various peripheral regions. The most important outcome was the creation of modern banking and transportation systems.

The rise of strong, modern banking systems

Modern banking was a Western creation in the peripheries. It had not existed in those regions before the mid-nineteenth century. In the best case, an embryonic banking system had emerged consisting of small, locally important savings and a few issuing banks. The first wave of the Western banking revolution was of no consequence in the peripheries.

The breakthrough occurred when France's Crédit Mobilier banks appeared on the scene and initiated international activity in the mid-century. The Crédit Mobilier established banks in Milan and contributed to the foundation of the Wiener Bankverein in 1869, and (via the Viennese bank) to the reorganization of the Pesti Magyar Kereskedelmi Bank in Budapest after the crisis of 1873. It played a similar role in Italy, Russia, Hungary, and Romania.

The rise of the German investment banks had an even greater impact, since they expanded their market-share throughout the continent. Although, as Richard Tilly noted, "the leading characteristic of the German banking system . . . in the second half of the nineteenth century was certainly not its international orientation," the German type of investment banks operated in a broad European context (Tilly, 1991b, 90). They were crucial to the development of the Swedish, Austro-Hungarian, Spanish, Romanian, and Russian banking systems. The foundation of major banking institutions throughout Europe was a pan-European affair, with various large Western banks acting in consortiums.

When the peripheral regions began modern banking in the second half or the last third of the nineteenth century, they enjoyed the "advantage of backwardness" and adopted the most modern banking practice. Investment banks were established on the model of Crédit Mobilier and the large German banks, and they subordinated the local savings banks and built up large banking monopolies.

In Austria-Hungary, the Austrian-Bohemian provinces were the prime movers in creating modern banking in Hungary. Before 1867, Hungary had an embryonic banking system that mostly comprised thirty-six small local savings banks. After the Austro-Hungarian Compromise in 1867, however, the large Vienna banks founded filial institutions in Hungary.[15] The banks' primary activity in agricultural Hungary was providing mortgage credits for the big estates, which absorbed 50–60% of the banks' assets. But these Hungarian banks provided only 40% of the agricultural mortgage credits; a larger share came dirctly from Austrian banks. Based on German banking practice, 36% of Hungarian industrial shares were in the hands of big banks. A majority (55%) of the shares of the modern Hungarian banks were in foreign hands.

In most of the peripheral regions, the big banks of the West were the initiators of modern banking. Ireland is an outstanding example. An 1821 statute modified the banking industry by allowing the foundation of private joint-stock banks, but it limited this right to residents of Ireland. When this restriction was abolished three years later, English capital inflow began playing a central role in Irish banking. Based on English investment, the Provincial Bank, Hibernian Bank, National Bank, and Royal Bank were established between 1825 and 1836. On the other hand, the Northern Bank Company and the Belfast Banking Company, established in the second half of the 1820s, were mostly financed from local sources. Extensive network building followed, with more than 170 branches operating in 89 towns by the mid-century. When the independent Irish currency was abolished in 1826, the role of the Bank of Ireland[16] declined and was replaced by English banking and crediting endeavors.

Spanish banking was limited to a few issuing banks, and their activities were restricted by traditional laws and small financial resources. Modern banking was the consequence of political changes in 1854, which took place at the same time as French banking was being revolutionized. Modern Spanish banking was born between 1856 and 1868.[17]

A similar pattern characterized the Russian situation. Before 1860, one can hardly speak of Russian banking. The first commercial bank, the State Bank, was founded in 1860, and the first joint-stock bank, the Moscow Merchant Bank, in 1865. Only fifty joint-stock banks were in operation in the entire country in 1913, and they had very limited assets. Before the twentieth century, the modern, influential role of banking did not exist in Russia, and direct foreign investment was key to financing the economy. The French Crédit Mobilier opened its first Russian branch (called the Northern Bank) in 1901. After its merger with the Russo-Chinese Bank, the Russo-Asiatic bank became the largest banking institution in Russia, dominated by the Crédit Mobilier and Paribas.[18]

Modern domestic banking hardly existed in the Balkans. In Greece, 65% of total investment in the economy was foreign, mostly French, before World War I, and 57% of the assets of the Greek private banks were in Western hands. In Romania, 92% of industrial investment came directly from abroad by 1900. Foreign capital established five of the eight leading Romanian banks.[19]

It is evident that peripheral banking emerged as part of a Europe-wide system and as subsidiaries of multinational banking companies. Western investment had created modern banking throughout the peripheral regions long before industrialization began. Because of its strong Western connections, banking made up the most advanced sector of the peripheral economy. Using a great amount of Western money, banks played leading roles in issuing agricultural credits, building railroads, financing trade, and investing in industry. Banks owned entire industrial sectors, organized cartels, and became the real captains of industry.

Building the modern transportation systems

The latecomer peripheral regions looked upon the railroads as the symbol of modernity and the primary vehicle of industrial progress. Camillo Cavour, the architect of the Italian Risorgimento, declared in 1846: "The railroad... [is] a powerful weapon... [against] industrial and political infancy... The locomotive has a mission to diminish, if not obliterate completely, the humiliating inferiority to which several branches of the great Christian family are now reduced" (Laue, 1969, 12). Five years after the opening of the world's first railroad line in Britain, the king of Naples and the tsar of Russia, rulers of two of Europe's most backward countries, built family railroads between their winter and summer palaces. The industrializing West, in need of food and raw materials from the peripheries, began investing in these regions' railroads – a very lucrative business in itself, as most of the regions' governments paid a guaranteed 5 percent interest rate. The Balkan railroads, for instance, were an entirely German enterprise, serving German imperial ambitions connecting Berlin to Bagdad via Constantinople and throughout the Balkans. The German government signed agreements with its Balkan counterparts, and German finances led to the construction of the first trunk railroad lines throughout the peninsula.[20]

Railroad construction in the Mediterranean and Central and Eastern European peripheral regions consequently *preceded industrialization and general economic modernization*. This took place even before the late and partial agricultural semi-revolution. The latter was made possible by the new transportation outlets to Western markets. The beginning of industrial development decades later was even more directly a consequence of railroad construction, which generated the need for coal extraction, and iron, steel, and some engineering production for railroads.

Road and water transportation

Roads hardly existed or were in terrible shape in several peripheral regions. Complaints were regularly heard in early nineteenth-century Hungary that local authorities were damaging the existing roads to protect local markets. The transport of bulky, heavy goods was extremely difficult, and the dirt roads were unusable during rainy periods or wintertime. Spain constructed 37 kilometers of roads per year in the second half of the eighteenth century. A few improved roads, the Guadarrama, Reinosa, and Peña de Orduña highways, royal highways connecting Madrid with the main seaports, could be used only in dry weather. Spain went on to build

85 kilometers of roads each year during the first third of the nineteenth century.

[P]oorly built, and even more poorly maintained... roads were impassable except by foot or on horseback... Overland transportation in Spain was expensive, slow, and risky. [In 1884] transportation costs represented about 40% of the average price of wine... The cost of a 190-kilometer haul would quadruple the price of a cartload of English coal. (Gómez-Mendoza, 1987, 92–3)

A late eighteenth-century writer, Jovellanos, observed that the price of grain increased by nearly 270% over a distance of just 200 kilometers (Gómez-Mendoza, 1995, 133).

Likewise, "Russian road transportation was almost impossible, because of the virtual absence of paved roads... Road maintenance did not exist... Delivering freight and passengers was virtually impossible during spring and autumn" (Kahan, 1989, 28). It took two years for heavy iron ore from the Ural Mountains to reach the St. Petersburg ironworks. Waterways offered a better solution for cheap, mass transportation. Following the West, Russian water transportation and canal building began rather early.

Several of the peripheral regions, such as Ireland and Hungary, were parts of large, developed empires. In these cases, regulating rivers and building canals were part of the imperial modernization process. Canals were built in Ireland in the mid- to late eighteenth century. The construction of a network of canals began as early as 1715, and duties were levied for financing it from 1730 on. Navigation works began on the Shannon, Boyne, and Barrow rivers, and two companies were established to conduct two major projects in the 1770s.[21] In Central Europe, the Bega canal connected Temesvár (Timişoara) to the Danube River at Ujvidék (Novisad) already in the early eighteenth century. Canals were built on the Great Plain in Hungary (the Ferenc canal in 1803, and the Ferenc József canal in 1875), but a kilometer of waterway an average served a territory of more than 100 square kilometers in the country.[22]

Baron von Haxthausen's two-volume, mid-nineteenth-century work on Russia painted a dark picture on transportation.

[Russian] interiors are at great distance from the sea... navigable rivers are shut up three-fourths of the year... high-roads are impassable during the rain... Without [improved means of communication, Russia] is a colossal, unwieldy giant, whose hands and feet are tied... The greatest requirement of

Russia is improved and suitable means of communication. (von Haxthausen, 1856, quoted in Crisp, 1976, 390)

Canals provided cheap mass transportation only for relatively small countries or regions next to international waterways, seas, or oceans, and for areas with mild weather. Even navigation was impossible in Russia during its long winter season. Canals could not provide the means for necessary transportation in the large, mostly landlocked peripheral regions. Sea transport was viable for only a few peripheral regions such as the Mediterranean countries and the Baltics, and could be used in only a very limited way in the others.[23] Antonio Gómez-Mendoza notes that contemporary observers in Spain had widely recognized that the primary barrier to modern transformation was the lack of transportation. Several canal projects were planned, including one connecting the Atlantic and Mediterranean seaboards, but hardly any were actually built. "With the exception of the Canal of Castile and the Imperial of Aragon, the remaining canals were much closer to an irrigation channel than to a real waterway fit for navigation" (Gómez-Mendoza, 1995, 136). Spain's hilly terrain made construction prohibitively expensive, and the country's intermittent rainfall led to regular water shortages. Despite a huge investment, construction of a canal to cross the Sierras in the Murcia region was halted because of a lack of water. The building of a few hundred kilometers of canals did not change the situation, and even coastal shipping remained inadequate because of a lack of suitable port facilities.

The mountainous Balkans, expansive Russia, and most of Central Europe were genuinely land-locked regions. Practically none of them was able to build a large commercial fleet and navy. In a unique way, backward Greece emerged as a great shipping power. Between 1875 and World War I, the carrying capacity of its fleet quadrupled; it was ten times its 1850 level, and totaled 1 million tons before the war, compared with the 32 million-ton total capacity of all the world's merchant fleets.[24] Two-thirds of the small Russian merchant fleet was composed of sail boats as late as 1914, and only 10 percent of the merchant ships entering Russian ports were Russian owned (Blackwell, 1982, 50). The Portuguese and Spanish fleets, dominant in the early modern centuries, became relatively insignificant.

Backward countries with developed railroads

Compared with the 38,600 kilometers of railroad lines in Western Europe and Scandinavia, only 7,800 kilometers were opened in the peripheries by 1860. Extensive construction work began during the 1860s and 1870s. A

51,000 kilometer network of railroad lines served the peripheral regions by 1880, and one of 140,600 kilometers did by 1914 – representing roughly 40 percent of Europe's total railroad lines.

The first Hungarian railroad was opened in 1847, but the real railway boom began after the 1867 Austro-Hungarian Compromise. By 1913, 22,000 kilometers of railroads created a dense network; each kilometer of line served an area of 15.7 square kilometers, and every 100,000 inhabitants were served by 110 kilometers of railway. Hungary's railroad density was the sixth largest in Europe, ahead of some of the more advanced Western countries. The "secret" of its exceptional railroad construction – half of the railroad lines of Austria-Hungary were built in non-industrialized Hungary – was the extensive Austrian investment serving the military and economic interest of the Habsburg Empire. The level of railroadization was much higher than the general economic level of the country. The easternmost and southern provinces of the empire, however, remained far behind. While 1 kilometer of railroad served an area of 10 square kilometers on average in the Czech lands, it served 28 square kilometers in Galicia and 100 square kilometers in Dalmatia.

One of the most instructive, but also one of the most extreme, examples was the construction of the Balkan railroads. A British syndicate reached an agreement with the Ottoman authorities to build a railroad line connecting the western half of the continent with Turkey.[25] But since the Balkan countries had become independent, new arrangements had to be made with the new countries' governments. Germany took over the entire project in 1883. United Germany's expansionist dreams led to the construction of the Berlin–Bagdad railroad. The newly established Betriebsgesellschaft der Orientalischen Eisenbahnen, financed by the Deutsche Bank, signed a contract with Turkey and three Balkan countries. By 1888 the Vienna–Constantinople line was completed.[26] Western expansionist designs had created the Balkan railroads. In Serbia, for example, a 460 kilometer stretch of the Vienna–Constantinople line became the backbone of the Serbian railroads. By World War I, only an additional 400 kilometers were built connecting other parts of the country to the trunk line. Similarly, the core of the Bulgarian railroads was the 697 kilometer Bulgarian section of the Vienna–Constantinople line. Several sidelines were added by 1914, enlarging the line to 1,948 kilometers. The Balkan railroads did not create national or regional networks, but were rather parts of international lines.[27] (See Map 10.1.)

Romania exhibited a somewhat better development. The first railroad line in the Balkans was built in Romania between Cernavodă and Constanța. Although construction began in 1857, the first 200 kilometers

Map 10.1 The Balkan railroads: not a complex network. The most important transportation road is the River Danube (Kunz and Armstrong, 1995, 107)

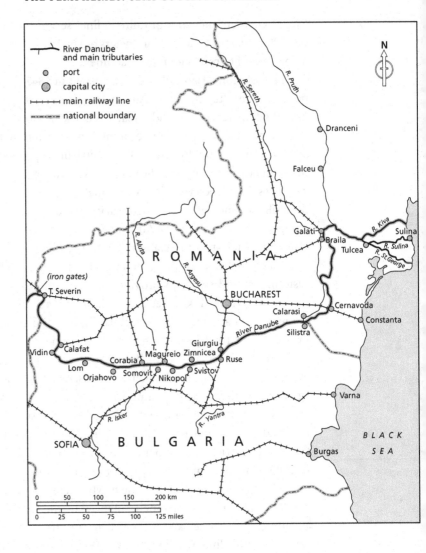

were opened only in 1869. By 1914, a 3,500 kilometer network connected all the agricultural centers with the capital city and main ports, as well as to the Austro-Hungarian Empire.

In Russia, the largest land-locked country, the first line was built in the 1830s, but only 1,600 kilometers of railroad lines were in operation by 1860, including the important Moscow–St. Petersburg line (opened in 1852). However, Russia drew on the bitter lessons of the Crimean War, when it was unable to mobilize and transport its army to the Crimean peninsula.[28] Feverish construction finally created a network during the last third of the century, radiating from Moscow to Kursk, Voronezh, and Nizhniy-Novgorod. From the 1880s on, railroads connected the newly built mining and industrial centers of the Donets Basin, Krivoj Rog, and the Urals.[29] By 1913, a 70,000 kilometer network crisscrossed the entire country, nearly half as long as the West European railroads put together. Motivated by economic and particularly political and military interests, France financed a great part of the extensive construction to create a strong ally behind its German archenemy.

Spain's railway construction offers another telling example of peripheral railroad history. The Barcelona–Mataro line, the first in the country, opened in 1848. The Madrid–Paris line connected Spain to France in 1864, and the Santander lines linked the country to Portugal two years later. A total of 5,000 kilometers of railroad lines were in operation in Spain by 1868, and 14,700 kilometers by 1910, with each kilometer serving an area of 34.1 square kilometers, and 74 kilometers serving every 100,000 inhabitants. Spain's nineteenth-century economic development was strongly tied to the railroads. During the first construction boom of the 1860s, investment in railroads exceeded industrial investment by sixteen times. The enormous capacity of the railroads, however, was only partially used. The Spanish railroads transported only 146,000 tons of goods per inhabitant annually, compared with 1.2 million tons in Britain.

British investment initiated the early start of the Irish railroads: the first, 10 kilometer line between Dublin and Kingstown was opened in 1834, but extensive construction commenced in the mid-1840s. The length of the railroads increased from 1,500 to 3,000 kilometers between 1854 and 1866, but only another 1,789 kilometers were added by 1913. Half of the investments in Irish railroads originated from England.

The peripheral railroads clearly demonstrate that modern railway transportation was not a national but a European agenda. A total of 40% of British foreign investment was channeled into railway construction. French banks invested 15% of their capital exports in railroads, and 50% in state, municipal, and public loans that partly also financed railroad construction. Of the investments in Russian railroads, 94% were foreign in 1881, and three-quarters of them were as late as 1914. Thanks to Western investment, the railroad density in the European peripheries was two-thirds the Western level in terms of the length of railroads per 100,000 inhabitants, but only 37% in terms of the area served by each kilometer of line.[30] (See Figure 10.3.)

Railroad capacity in the peripheries was only partially used. The weight of transported goods per inhabitant was only 20 percent of the Western level, and the number of rail journeys per inhabitant hardly surpassed 10 percent of the that in the West. The peripheries' railroad density before World War I was 50 percent that of Western Europe, while the use of the relatively dense network was only about 14 percent of the Western level. As

Table 10.1   Level of European railroad development in 1911

Region	Average area served by 1 km of railroad (km²)	Length of railroad per 100,000 inhabitants (km)	Weight of goods transported per inhabitant per year (100,000 tons)	Number of railroad journeys per inhabitant per year
Western Europe	10.14	90.2	8.18	21.9
Scandinavia	48.55	180.9	4.09	8.8
Mediterranean	25.14	61.0	1.37	3.3
Central and Eastern Europe	20.49	50.4	1.59	1.7
Russia	324.17	42.3	1.47	1.3
Periphery total	123.27	51.23	1.48	2.1
(Periphery excluding Russia)	(22.81)	(55.7)	(1.48)	(2.5)
Periphery as % of West Europe[a]	44.5	56.8	18.1	10.4

Source: Based on Berend and Ránki (1982, 100).

Note: [a] Excluding Russia.

Figure 10.3
Level of railroad development in the European peripheries, 1911 (Berend and Ránki, 1982, 100)

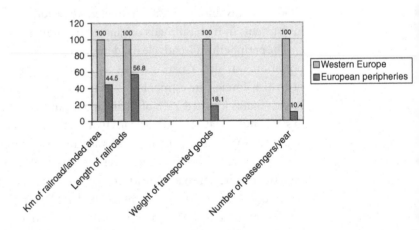

has been said about Ireland, one can generally state that the peripheries had an underdeveloped economy with a highly developed transport system. (See Table 10.1.)

Railroads were built "ahead of time, out of harmony with the economic stage" of the region, partly emulating the West, and partly out of military, strategic considerations (Pollard, 1981a, 207–10). In an earlier work that

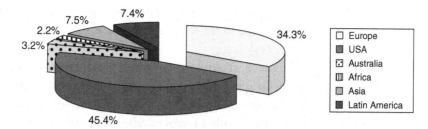

Figure 10.4 The world's railroad network, 1900 (Woodruff, 1982, 253)

he later corrected, Gabriel Tortella went further regarding the Spanish railroads. The failure of Spanish industrialization, he concluded, was partly caused by an overinvestment in railroads, which "absorbed those resources that otherwise would have been used by other sectors." According to his estimates, investment in railroads in the 1860s was 6.6 times higher than investment in industry (Tortella, 1973, 170, 335).

It is true that the appeal of modernity and the symbolic importance of railroads prompted the governments of backward countries to open railway lines. It is also true that the railroads had more than just an economic function, and that strategic considerations had also been an important factor in their construction. From a narrow national point of view, too early railroadization had indeed occurred in the peripheries and was clearly not economical. But the fact of the matter was that the railroads were the classic prerequisite for modernization, for they contributed to the development of export sectors and to the beginning of industrialization. A dearth of transportation was the main obstacle to development. Reflecting the views of other governments, the Spanish leadership was "convinced that investment in the transport sector was a necessary prerequisite to ... the development of the Spanish economy" (Gómez-Mendoza, 1987, 95–6).

Furthermore, since most of the investment in the peripheries had originated from the developed countries precisely to improve their food supply, facilitate the transport of mineral resources to their factories, and create markets for their own industrial products, one cannot say that railroad construction had "hijacked" investment from industrialization. Foreign investors had no interest at that time in investing in processing industries in the peripheries.

Most of all, one should not evaluate the importance of railroads by comparing the capacities created with the real use of them. Railroads were extremely important in generating modernization in the backward peripheries. (See Figure 10.4.) Sergei Witte, the main architect of Russian modernization, spoke about railways in a poetic way when he lectured to the young grand duke in 1900: "The railroad is like a leaven, which creates a cultural fermentation among the population. Even if it passed through an absolutely wild people along its way, it would raise them in a short time to the level prerequisite for its operation" (quoted in Laue, 1969, 191).

In practical terms, modern, cheap, mass transportation was the prerequisite for agricultural modernization for exports. Markets could not have been integrated, and the leading export sectors could not have emerged, without railroads. Moreover, railroads created the need for domestic coal, iron, and engineering production. Their construction enabled peasants to leave the countryside, and, at a somewhat later stage, to gravitate towards industrial work. In 1863, 56,000 peasant workers were employed in Spanish railroad construction. Social savings of the GDP, which was relatively moderate in the West, totaled 10–20 percent in the mostly land-locked peripheral countries – a huge proportion for further development. In the case of Spain, the railroads contributed to economic growth by 5 percent of per capita GDP between 1858 and 1890, and more than 6 percent by 1914 (Herranz-Loncán, 2006, 873). Paul Gregory insists that railroadization was as important as the emancipation of serfs in Russia (Gregory, 1994, 16). Railroads led to industrialization in some of the peripheral countries. I still argue that it is "hardly possible to overestimate the importance of ... railways, for the economic transformation of the European peripheries" (Berend and Ránki, 1982, 101).

Notes

1. Sixty-four British mining companies were established between 1871 and 1919. Iron ore extraction increased fiftyfold, from 0.2 million tons in 1865 to 9.9 million tons in 1913. At that latter date, 8.3 million tons, 84 percent of production, was exported. By 1913, more than 150 foreign mining companies invested half of the total invested capital in Spanish mining. One-quarter of the capital of the mining companies was British, 12% was French, and a little over 10% was German, Belgian, and Swiss. Of the 9–10 million tons of iron, lead, zinc, mercury, and other non-ferrous metals extracted, 90% was exported to the investor countries.

2. French capital had initially expressed great interest: 10 percent of exported French capital went to Austria-Hungary in 1850, and 14 percent by 1880. Because of political considerations, French involvement sharply decreased afterwards.

3. Austria-Bohemia, the western provinces of the Monarchy, "exported" capital mostly to the eastern provinces of the empire. At the beginning of the twentieth century, of the 5.5–6.0 billion crowns of capital outflow from Austria-Bohemia, 4.7 billion crowns were invested in Hungary.

Austrian investment was decisive in the construction of Hungarian railroads. Two leading Austrian companies, the Austrian State Railway Co. and the Danube Steam Shipping Co., both in the hands of the Vienna branch of the Rothschild family, initiated coal extraction in Hungary, and 75–80 percent of Hungarian coal mining was in Austrian hands. As early as 1863, 17 percent of the steam engines operating in the country were in the factories of the Austrian State Railway Co. During the 1850s, the Austrian sugar companies established fourteen factories in Hungary.

4. The French Société Générale pour l'Exploitation de Cir Minérale et Pétrole, the Canadian William MacGarvey, and the British John S. Bergheim began operating in Galicia. Output surged ahead during the 1890s. German, British, French, Belgian, and American companies arrived on the scene when one of Europe's richest oil fields was discovered in Borysław. Before the war, the most important company controlling Galician oil extraction was the British Premier Oil and Pipeline Co., which produced one-quarter of the output. Deutsche Erdöl and Standard Oil were also involved. As was the case in other backward peripheral regions, Western companies made every important investment in mineral resources in Galicia.

5. In 1885, the company's iron mines were taken over by another state-dominated company, the Varešer Eisenindustrie AG. In 1892, a third state company began iron production.

6. The 1907 business census listed 29,243 industrial establishments in Bosnia, mostly in clothing and food processing. The overwhelming majority (29,056 firms) were proto-industrial. Moreover, 25,385 establishments had no employees at all except their owners, and the rest employed an average of two to three workers.

7. German investors founded the Steaua Română, the British-Dutch multinational Royal Dutch Shell established the Astra Română, Belgian entrepreneurs founded the Telega Oil Co., a French group established the Aquila Franco Română, and Standard Oil created the Româno-Americană.

8. Foreigners owned 95.5% of the shares of the gas and electric power generation industry, 94% in the sugar industry, and between 70% and 74% in the iron, chemical, and timber industries.

9. The Banca Natională, Banca Generală Română, and the Banca de Credit Romană were entirely foreign establishments, and the Banca Marmorosch Blank partly so.

10. Private foreign investment totaled another 1 million francs before the war: 45% of municipal and transportation investments, 25% of shipping investments, 64% of industrial investments, and 57% of banking investments originated from foreign sources. Altogether, nearly two-thirds of total economic investment came from abroad – mostly from France, which provided 64% of foreign

capital inflow. Having played an important role during the first years, Britain ultimately supplied only 27% of the total foreign capital inflow.

11. British capital investment targeted the Balkans between 1820 and 1830, and mostly French and German capital investment did so after 1870. Britain invested about $100 million, France $540 million, and Germany $400 million. Combined Swiss, Dutch, Belgian, and Austrian investments amounted to about $200 million. Altogether, 6 billion francs ($1,250 million) in foreign capital inflow reached the Balkans, an amount significant enough to stimulate some economic modernization.

12. These countries and their entire budgets became financially supervised by foreign countries. As H. Feis commented about the series of Balkan bankruptcies: "Any independent state can buy enough rope to hang itself, if it will pay enough" (Feis, 1965a, 263).

13. Between 1861 and 1893, some 2.5 billion rubles of foreign capital financed the Russian state, 90 percent of it used for railroad construction and only 5 percent for industrial investments. Between 1893 and 1900, one-third of the capital inflow was already invested in industry. During the prewar years, foreign capital inflow totaled 1,707 million rubles, and nearly half of it (800 million) was channeled into industry.

14. French capital dominated, comprising 31% of total foreign investment, and focusing mostly on financing the banking, coal, iron, and engineering industries. British investment represented 25% of foreign capital, and it played a decisive role in oil extraction. Germany followed with 21%, and Belgium with 12%. Both Germany and Belgium invested heavily in the engineering and electric industries.

15. The most significant first step was made by the Vienna Credit-Anstalt, which founded the Magyar Általános Hitelbank in 1867. The Wiener Bankverein transformed the existing small Pesti Magyar Kereskedelmi Bank into a modern big bank after the bank crisis of 1873. This was also the case with the first Hungarian banking institution, the Pesti Hazai Első Takarékpénztár. By 1873, 637 banks, created mostly with Austrian or German capital, existed in Hungary. The amount of Hungarian banking capital increased significantly from 172 million krowns in 1867 to 6.7 billion krowns in 1913.

16. Founded in 1797, the Bank of Ireland monopolized joint-stock banking and financed the Irish economy.

17. The Sociedad General de Credito Mobiliare Español was established by the French Péreira brothers; the Sociedad Española Mercantil e Industrial by the French Rothschilds. The third largest bank, the Compañia General de España, was also founded by French investment. Although some other big banks were established at around the turn of the century, and some of the genuinely

Spanish banks (such as the Credito Mobiliaro de Barcelona) were added to the leading financial group, their role nonetheless remained secondary compared with the 4 billion peseta direct foreign investment in railroads, mining, banking, and industry.

18. French banks reorganized and enlarged the St. Petersburg Private Bank and the Moscow United Bank in the 1910s. A consortium led by the German Disconto-Gesellschaft financed the St. Petersburg Discount Bank; and Bethmann and Erlanger, with some Hamburg bankers, stood behind the St. Petersburg International Trading Bank. The Russian Bank for Industry and Trade was the creation of the London-based Anglo-Russian Bank in 1911 (Bovikin and Ananich, 1991, 154).

19. Behind the Banca Naţională, the Banca Generală Română, and the Banca de Credit Român stood the German Disconto-Gesellschaft, the Bleichröder Bank, Länder Bank, Darmstädter Bank, Deutsche Bank, and the French Crédit Mobilier.

20. French banks initiated and financed the Spanish rail system. French and German investors heavily financed the Russian railroads. The Hungarian, Galician, and Croatian networks were parts of the Austro-Hungarian system and were financed mostly by Austrian and German banks.

21. One of them, the Grand Canal, was completed by 1804, and three additional branches were opened by 1836. The second project, the Royal Canal, began operating in 1817, while the Ulster canal, the Ballinamore canal, and the Ballyconnell canal were completed by 1842 and 1860, respectively.

22. Canal construction also took place in the east German, Polish, and Russian regions. The Plauen canal (1745) and the Finow canal (1746) created a waterway connecting the River Elbe, via the Havek River, to the Oder River near Stettin. The Bydgoszcz canal (1774) connected the Noteć, Warta, and Oder rivers. The Vistula and Oberland canals were completed in 1850 and 1860 respectively. The Augustów canal (1830) and the Dnieper–Bug canal connected the Neman and Vistula water systems and the Dnieper and Vistula systems in 1841. A 1,450 kilometer canal connected the Volga and the Baltic Sea, and also the White Sea and the Dnieper. The Baltic Sea was also connected to the Black Sea. In the vast territory of European Russia, these extensive canal systems created 1 kilometer of waterway for, on average, an area of 88 square kilometers – nearly three times more land than for 1 kilometer of canal than in Britain.

23. Even Spain, bordered by the Mediterranean Sea and the Atlantic Ocean, was basically land-locked. Rivers were only partially navigable. The heartland plateau of the Iberian peninsula is not flat, and is surrounded by large belts of mountains more than 2,000 meters high that create a natural barrier to the coastal regions.

24. At the same time, steamers began to predominate: while only 1.2 percent of the fleet's capacity in 1875, steamers made up 94 percent of the Greek merchant fleet on the eve of the war.

25. Construction began in the 1860s on a line running from Varna to the west. According to the plan, a line 2,500 kilometers long would connect the Ottoman Balkans to Vienna. An Austrian-French company, led by Baron Hirsch, built three separate parts during the 1870s.

26. The Deutsche Bank continued construction in Macedonia from Salonika to Monastir. In addition, the French Banque Impériale Ottoman built a 660 kilometer line along the sea from Salonika to the east.

27. Since the country was not located in the core of international commercial routes, the Greek railroads remained even more backward, with only 1,500 kilometers of lines built between 1869 and 1912.

28. Minister of Finance Mikhail Reutern called for a vigorous railroad construction program in 1862. "Without railroads and mechanical industries Russia cannot be considered secure in her boundaries" (Douglas and Frazier, 1992).

29. An average of 1,500 kilometers of lines were completed annually between 1865 and 1875, and 2,500 kilometers during the 1890s.

30. Including Russia, this level was only 16 percent.

CHAPTER 11

Advantage from dependence: Central Europe, the Baltic area, Finland, and Ireland

The massive inflow of foreign capital and its role in creating modern banking and transportation systems spearheaded the modern transformation in the peripheries. The prospect of unlimited Western markets enabled the peripheral countries to sell huge quantities of agricultural products and food. The need to increase agricultural output to meet Western demand stimulated their modernization. Parts of the peripheries, from Russian-occupied Finland, the Baltic region, and Poland, to the Hungarian half of the Habsburg Empire, the eastern provinces of Prussia (later United Germany), and British-ruled Ireland, underwent a relatively successful agricultural revolution. Although half a century late, modernization in these areas was quite impressive. Their agricultural modernization took off from the middle of the nineteenth century.

These areas enjoyed the geopolitical advantage of being located next to the rapidly industrializing West and being part of huge imperial markets. At the same time, they had relatively higher cultural-educational standards than had other peripheral regions. Finland and some of the Baltic region had at one point belonged to Sweden and had thus preserved some elements of the Scandinavian social-legal institutional systems. In some of these regions, large minority populations, such as German landowners and businessmen and Jewish intermediaries, represented a strong business orientation that compensated somewhat for the traditional anti-business prejudices of the local nobility and peasantry. The minorities were highly concentrated in the urban centers, and they facilitated the region's urbanization to a certain extent. Protestantism also gained ground in relatively large parts of these areas, unlike in most of the peripheries. Protestantism influenced business culture and popular behavior in Finland, parts of the Baltic region, and a part of Hungary. Educational levels rose significantly, generally in between the Western and Eastern or Southern standards. For historical reasons, a number of modern institutions had emerged in these areas in early modern times, in contrast to other peripheries.

These regions profited economically from being parts of large multinational empires, which was quite paradoxical, considering their national myths and the nationalist historiography that painted dark pictures of the consequences of a lack of independence. National historiography, most noticeably in Poland and Hungary, had from the outset portrayed the lack of national independence as a kind of "semi-colonial" state that halted or deformed local development.[1] The Poles and Lithuanians repeatedly rebelled against Russian rule, the Hungarians launched one of the century's most dramatic revolutions against Austria, and the Irish never accepted British rule. The imperial division of labor and the vast imperial markets, however, offered significant economic advantages for them – though in a controversial way.

Despite the political disadvantages to belonging to Europe's most despotic, oppressive, and backward empire, the economic backwardness of Russia actually offered lucrative business prospects for the Finnish, Baltic, and Polish regions. They were given the opportunity of supplying an immense, protected Russian market without having to compete with the imports (including industrial imports) of the more advanced Western countries. In contrast, Hungary, Ireland, and Prussia belonged to the much more advanced Habsburg, British, and German empires. The fact that their products did not enjoy the same protection definitely impacted negatively on certain sectors of their economies, and it contributed to their remaining primarily agricultural regions. On the other hand, they were compensated by the advanced empires' introduction of several modern institutions and modern legal and education systems. Imperial transportation policy strongly contributed to the construction of a relatively highly developed railroad system and to a better capital supply. Most of all, they could take advantage of the advanced and safe food markets of the developed parts of the empires. Nevertheless, economic, social, and cultural obstacles in the peripheries created massive roadblocks that delayed and slowed down progress.

Imperial markets and agricultural modernization

Though it exhibited trends of transformation similar to those in the Baltic and Central European regions, Finland still represents a special case. Finland was taken from Sweden and became part of the Russian Empire in 1809, but it attained considerable autonomy as a grand duchy in 1816. In an attempt to weaken Swedish influence, a new capital city, Helsinki, was founded in 1812 – becoming one of the most beautiful "Russian" cities. At the same time, however, Finland was able to retain the judicial, religious, and local institutions from the period when it was part of Sweden. Swedish laws, including property rights, remained in force; even Swedish currency was used for decades. The social structure of the country was similar to that of Scandinavia. Serfdom was never introduced, big estates hardly existed, and Finnish farms were owned and cultivated by free peasants.[2] The mercantile elite, the Estate of Burghers, enjoyed political power in late eighteenth-century Sweden and Finland. "The political and economic system that had been in force in the time of Swedish rule remained intact" (Kaukiainen, 2006, 38).

Thanks to its autonomy in internal affairs, Finland adopted modern liberal and democratic institutions from 1860 on. Unlike autocratic Russia, Finland introduced the parliamentary system in the 1870s. Uniquely in Europe, the grand duchy became the pioneer of general suffrage for both men and women in 1906. The country attained a high level of education and successfully eliminated illiteracy by World War I. While not Scandinavian but geopolitically a Nordic country par excellence, Finland was strongly influenced by Scandinavia during the entire nineteenth century, and it adopted several elements of Scandinavian economic modernization. Based on its domestic social-political and cultural advantages, Finland was able to take advantage of the opportunities offered by the huge and undeveloped Russian market.

At the periphery of the Russian Empire, Finland remained agricultural. The absolute number of Finns in the primary sector (including agriculture, forestry, and fishing) consistently increased to comprise three-quarters of the population by 1880. The grain economy was predominant in the country during the first half of the nineteenth century, but, because of the climate, it could meet no more than half the domestic consumption needs. The agrarian proportion of the population began to decrease in the late nineteenth century, and had declined to two-thirds by World War I. The Russian grain economy rendered Finnish grain production superfluous, and Finland began importing cheap Russian grain. The modernization of agriculture progressed slowly from the southwest towards the northeast of the country, but the latter remained traditional until well into the twentieth century. On the eastern edge of the country, peasants practiced slash-and-burn land cultivation (Ojala and Nummela, 2006, 70–1).[3]

Although the Finns introduced a modern rotation (*koppeli*) system and successfully increased their potato output by one and a half times, their real progress was seen in specialized areas such as animal husbandry and the milk economy (Ojala and Nummela, 2006, 87).[4] Finland produced only 44 percent of the grain consumed in the country, but no less than 90 percent of the animal products. Agriculture became commercialized in the late nineteenth century.

Agricultural products continued to represent one-third of Finnish exports to the Russian market until the 1890s, but their importance declined afterwards. Following the Swedish model, forestry and wood exports became much more important. The saw mill industry produced timber for exports in the 1860s and 1870s (two decades later than in Sweden), and it trebled its volume of production and exports in a single decade, making Finland the third largest timber producer in Europe (Kaukiainen, 2006, 143).

Still, Finland remained an agricultural and primary production country. In 1860, the primary sector comprised 60% of its GDP and employed 80% of its population. By 1910, 70% of Finns worked in the primary sector, compared with only 46% of the Western population.

The Baltic area exhibited certain similarities. Estland, Courland, and Livland were incorporated into the Russian Empire in the eighteenth century, but, like Finland, they had a background that was rather different from that of the Russian mainland. The region belonged to the Hanseatic League in earlier centuries, and then became a base for the Dutch trade network in the seventeenth century. Estland and Livland belonged to the Swedish kingdom for some seven decades in the sixteenth and seventeenth centuries. Since medieval times, the landowner elite had been German in both these provinces, and they followed the Prussian pattern. Historical legacy and outside influences were important factors in the Baltic region during the tsarist regime. The Peasant Law for Livland in 1804, for example, was based on the principles laid down by the Swedish administration in 1688. Following the Prussian model, the peasants of Estland, Courland, and Livland became free in 1816, 1817, and 1819 respectively. The Prussian type of *Gutsherrschaft* and noble landownership, however, did not change until the mid-nineteenth century, when new laws stipulated that the peasants owned the land that they worked on if they had bought it from the landlord. By 1912, 95 percent and 85 percent of the peasant land were purchased for perpetual ownership in Courland and Livland respectively. Baltic peasants enjoyed the right of free movement beginning in the 1860s, quite unlike their Russian counterparts.[5]

Following in the footsteps of Prussia, German landlords in the Baltic region modernized their large holdings and created capitalist estates. Modern rotation systems prevailed, and fallow land drastically decreased from

28 percent in 1860 to 9 percent by 1880. The potato became a field crop in the 1830s and 1840s, followed by clover in the mid-century – occupying one-quarter of the landed area, compared with 2 percent in Russia. Innovations appeared from the late eighteenth century on, when the Livländische Gemeinnützige Ökonomische Sozietät was founded and propagated new agricultural methods.[6]

Most importantly, animal husbandry gained ground during the last third of the nineteenth century. The region imported merino sheep and pedigree cattle from the Netherlands and Britain, established breeding control, and, in 1891, set up a General Society of Dairy Producers for all three Baltic provinces.

Part of the Habsburg Empire since the sixteenth century, Hungary became economically integrated in the Monarchy's more advanced Austrian-Bohemian provinces and emerged as its breadbasket. The main achievements of the agricultural revolution could be seen in Hungary during the second half of the century, although they were only partial compared with the West. The abolition of serfdom and noble privileges in 1848, and the creation of a customs union with the western provinces of the empire after 1851, triggered rapid transformation.[7]

Although a great part of the peasantry continued to practice traditional subsistence farming, modern rotation systems proliferated and fallow land rapidly decreased. Wheat yields doubled between 1870 and 1910. With the capitalization of the big estates, the proportion of fallow land dropped from 30–40 percent to 5–10 percent before the war. The use of manure, on average every ninth year instead of the required every fourth year, was accompanied by the use of artificial fertilizer at the turn of the century. From the 1870s on, the number of horse-driven sowing/harvesting machines and cutting machines increased by seven and three times respectively. The number of steam threshers increased by three and a half times to 8,900, with each machine serving 945 hectares. These were modest figures compared with Germany and France, and threshing was the only fully mechanized agricultural activity in Hungary.

Hungarian agriculture remained strongly monocultural, with 60 percent of the arable land used for grain before the war. Grain output increased more than two and a half times, and the combined wheat and corn output increased by four and a half times. Animal husbandry also profited from the agricultural revolution. The number of cattle increased by more than 30 percent, from 5.1 million to 7.2 million head, between 1850 and 1910, representing 44 percent of the Monarchy's total. Pigs comprised 46 percent of Austria-Hungary's supply. The quantitative increase of the animal stock, however, does not reflect the real progress. The cattle and pigs that

Hungary possessed were much higher quality animals. Imported high milk- and meat-producing Swiss cattle represented 70 percent of the cattle stock. Altogether, the value of Hungarian agricultural production had increased by nearly two and a half times, that is, by 2 percent per annum between 1867 and 1913.

Hungary exhibited typical Central and East European characteristics, but it profited from the Habsburg Empire's enormous market and food requirements and made better progress in agriculture than did its neighbors. The existence of Austria-Hungary, and its turn to agricultural protectionism from the 1870s on and especially in 1906, protected the large, 50 million strong domestic market from the severe European grain crisis and price decline of the last third of the century. Like their counterparts in most of the peripheries, the Hungarian peasants reacted to the grain crisis in a conservative way: by increasing grain output, instead of changing the structure of production. This did not prove to be counterproductive, however, because, in the Monarchy's well-protected market, grain prices increased by 30 percent between the 1870s and the war while declining by 30 percent on the world market. Hungary's five leading export items were grain and wheat flour and unprocessed animal products. Agricultural products made up 80 percent of Hungary's exports to Austria-Bohemia. Hungarian exports jumped from '$30 million in 1850 to $368 million by 1913. Half of the exports comprised wheat and wheat flour.

The eastern provinces of Prussia and later unified Germany (the areas east of the River Elbe) followed a somewhat similar road. As noted earlier, Germany was not an economically homogeneous country even after unification, and its eastern and northeastern provinces embodied typical Central-Eastern European characteristics. While Germany's western provinces achieved the highest levels of industrialization, the eastern provinces remained agricultural and rural: 44% of Prussia's population worked in agriculture in 1882, but 56–60% did so in the three East Prussian provinces. By 1907, 32% of western Germans worked in agriculture and 37% in industry, compared with 47% of East Prussians in agriculture and 24% in industry. In the northeastern part of Prussia, the agricultural population still hovered near the 60% mark.[8]

East Prussia emerged from the typical East European type of *leibeigenschaft*, or second serfdom, after the Prussian reform in the early nineteenth century. The nobility preserved their landed estates. Noble estates represented 43 percent of the big estates after unification, and nearly 40 percent as late as 1910. The Emancipation Act of 1807 and the decree of 1811 granted the serfs personal freedom and the right to own the land they cultivated, but required redemption payments that, in addition to money, led to the loss of large parts of peasant-cultivated land to the landlords.[9] As G. F. Knapp noted, the liberation of serfs in Germany resulted in *Landsmann ohne Dienst* and *Dienstmann ohne Land*, a landowning peasantry without work possibilities and peasant agricultural workers without land. Half of the peasants were still landless in the eastern half of Germany in the 1860s. The reform also enclosed the communal land by dividing it among the proprietors.

On the other hand, the big Junker estates were gradually transformed into modern capitalist ones. Two-thirds of all investment during the first half of the nineteenth century was channeled into the land, and only 2–4 percent into industry. The grain crisis of the 1870s–1880s was the driving force behind the modern transformation of the big noble estates (Buchsteiner, 1994, 46). Noble landowners sold parts of their estates to finance modernization. Between 1725 and 1755 74 percent of the Prussian nobility owned landed estates, but only 30 percent did so in 1876–1905. The majority of the big landowners (57 percent in 1910) were bourgeois entrepreneurs, and most of the landowners farmed out their land.[10]

Absentee landowners, predominant in Romania and ubiquitous in Russia, were virtually non-existent in eastern Germany. The Junkers hired wage laborers, among them a large number of migrant seasonal workers from Poland and Austria-Hungary. They also contracted families as permanent field workers (*dinstleute*), or, in the framework of the *deputat* system,[11] used peasants who were bound to the big estate but who worked only in the high seasons. The latter forms of employment might be considered remnants of feudal relations, but the Junker estate became a capitalist enterprise. Since unification put the Junker elite into the political driver's seat, they enjoyed various privileges from the state, including protective tariffs, tax privileges, the ability to entail estates, and preferential rates on state railways. Prussia's draconian master-and-servant law subordinated the peasants and excluded them from the newly introduced welfare institutions. Railroads connected the region with the industrialized western provinces and cities. The industrializing west offered unlimited markets for the agricultural east.

The vast differences in land tenure were preserved until World War I. In East Prussia, Mecklenburg, Silesia, Brandenburg, and Pomerania, peasant land up to 100 hectares represented nearly 60 percent of the arable land, while the big estates comprised more than 40 percent. The reform made the land marketable, thereby increasing the concentration of peasant land in the hands of the more well-to-do peasantry, as it did in many other places. A significant number, however, were emancipated without land or with mini-parcels insufficient to sustain families.[12] In other words, emancipation created an immense free labor force.

It is no wonder that migration, which reached its peak in the 1850s in the western half of Germany, began only in the 1860s in the eastern half of the country. A massive *landflucht* (flight from the land) from the east to the west characterized the second half of the century. Some 20 percent of East Prussian migrants moved to Berlin, and another 25 percent to the industrialized Rhineland and Westphalia.

Productivity trebled during the long nineteenth century; grain production increased by 64 percent, potato output nearly doubled, and sugar beet production more than trebled between 1875–84 and 1905–14. Cattle stock increased by 60 percent, pig stock by five times. Meat and milk production, along with agricultural output, doubled in the first half of the nineteenth century, and the value of output nearly trebled by World War I.[13]

This latter development was connected to the innovations of modern cultivation that took off during the second half of the century. The rapidly growing chemical industry produced, and the big estates and large peasant farms utilized, increasing quantities of artificial fertilizer.[14]

The eastern German lands primarily specialized in rye and beet crops, which also made it possible to combine agricultural activities with food processing, especially sugar refining and alcohol distillation. Production was often combined with processing on the big estates. East German agriculture flourished. Agricultural output per land unit increased by 4.4 percent per decade between 1800 and 1840, and by 7.9 percent per decade between 1840 and 1907. Cultivated land increased by one-third, and productivity increased by 50 percent. In rapidly industrializing Germany, the eastern provinces remained basically agricultural, though the industrial transformation also advanced towards an agrarian-industrial structure (Padhi, 1997; Tebarth, 1991; Blackbourn, 1998, Caumanns, 1994; Baranowski, 2001; Buchsteiner, 1994).

In the period under discussion, all of the peripheries of Europe became strongly involved in international trade. Responding to the challenge of Western industrialization, they became the main producers and exporters of agricultural products and certain raw materials. These mostly self-sufficient regions became export-oriented. Except for special products and tropical goods, the colonies did not play a decisive role in supplying the West. The import demands of the West coincided with the export possibilities of the European peripheries. Eventually, the peripheries developed those sectors of their economies that could easily gain access to Western markets.

Exports from the peripheral regions, therefore, increased significantly faster than the European average. Between 1860 and 1880, export growth was 3.7% per annum in the peripheries, compared with a 3.2% European average. The two rates were 3.2% and 1.3% between 1880 and 1890, and 3.4% and 3.2% between 1890 and 1910 (based on Bairoch, 1973b). Finnish export growth was quite exceptional: 5.1% per annum between 1860 and 1910. In terms of value, the peripheries' contribution to European exports was 14% in 1860 and grew to 22% between the 1890s and the war.

The rapidly growing peripheral exports were overwhelmingly made up of unprocessed agricultural products. Regions that went halfway down the path of transformation, however, were relatively successful in starting to process some of their export items. Following the Danish model, export-oriented milk processing and butter production, as well as wood processing, became more important in Finland.[15] Paper exported to the Russian market made up only 2% of total exports in 1860, but 39% by 1913. Finnish industry also profited from Russia's backwardness. Finnish exports to Russia were rather different from its exports to the West. The share of pulp and paper exported to the West was only 9%, but wood exports increased from 54% to 60% between 1880 and 1913. As Riita Hjerppe suggests: "In the early phase of industrialization the Russian markets offered better development opportunities than the domestic markets" (Hjerppe, 1982, 122).

The Baltic region exhibited similar trends. Based on the Danish pattern, they also organized agricultural cooperatives in dairy production (the first one in 1904), followed by trade and credit cooperatives. At the beginning of the twentieth century, the Baltic provinces moved from grain production to the export of dairy products (Kahk and Tarvel, 1997, 91).

One of the most important developments for Hungarian agricultural exports was the rise of food processing, especially the flourmill industry. Besides Finland and the Baltic region, Hungary was a rare example of a peripheral country in which elements of Dutch–Danish modernization became an important factor in economic development. Budapest emerged as the world's second largest flour mill center, behind Minneapolis in the USA. Two-thirds of Hungary's exported wheat was processed, and it supplied roughly 24 percent of the world's wheat-flour exports.

At this point, I am reminded of the debates on the benefits of peripheral trade. Liberal and neo-liberal economics repeat David Ricardo's concept of comparative advantage, which maintains that both parties, advanced and backward, gain from trade. However, rising dependency theories expressed an opposite view after World War II, and especially from the 1970s onward. The exchange of agricultural (or in general primary) products of low value-added for manufactured goods of high value-added, these theories suggest, represents uneven trade and leads to the exploitation of the dependent agricultural and raw material producers (Amin, 1970; Frank, 1976; Emmanuel, 1969).

None of these theories stands up to the test of reality. The trade between industrialized and agricultural countries often led to losses for the backward countries and the preservation of backwardness.[16] But the exploitation theory in its generalized form is also wrong, because trade between advanced and backward regions often paved the way for the modern transformation and development of the weaker party. The primary argument used to prove the thesis of exploitation of the agricultural regions is the declining terms of trade. At first glance, the relationship between import and export prices indeed reflects the advantage of the industrial countries. The world market price of machine products increased by 16% between 1872 and 1900, and then by another 31% by 1913. At the same time, grain prices, which had been rising during the third quarter of the century, dramatically declined: wheat by 33%, rye by nearly 25%, and oats by 10%. On average, raw material prices fell 33% during the last third of the century.

This general trend of price movement, however, is misleading. The terms of trade for a country or region depend on the exact structure of exports and imports. For instance, while Britain's terms of trade improved by 20 percent in the half-century before World War I, Germany's deteriorated by 20 percent between 1880 and 1913. The terms of trade of Sweden and Denmark – at that time both food and raw material exporters – improved in those decades, but Norway's declined. The prices of high-tech chemical products and shipping services, for example, declined; because of technological progress, the prices of meat and meat products went up. Hence, selling products of decreasing prices might be counterbalanced by changing the production structure and the type of exports according to the market's requirements.[17] Russia and the Balkans are extreme examples of the opposite scenario, while Finland, the Baltic area, and Hungary stood somewhere in between. Furthermore, the terms of trade are not the appropriate factors for evaluating the advantages or disadvantages of trade.[18] Trade, even in the case of declining terms of trade, may positively influence economic activities and investments, and may provide important incentives for growth.

Economic history clearly shows that countries that are sellers of food and raw materials may derive tremendous incentives and advantages from

the process and grow economically.[19] If domestic social-political and educational prerequisites are favorable, producing and exporting food and raw
materials may pave the way to processing those same goods, and then pro-
ceeding in the direction of industrialization and modernization. Scandinavia offers a convincing example. In a more limited way, this development
trend became quite important for Finland, the Baltic region, Hungary, and
Ireland. They were semi-successful on this path to modernization. Finnish
milk and wood processing, Hungarian grain processing, Irish brewing and
distilling, and the combined agricultural and food processing of the east
Prussian Junker estates clearly signaled progress. Incentives and opportunities for modernization developed because of trade connections with
large or more advanced markets. However, foreign trade could not provide
the inspiration and impetus if social capability was lacking, if the educational system and infrastructure were backward, and/or if the society was
suspicious about innovation and change. The key to understanding the
possible advantages or disadvantages of peripheral trade is the domestic
cultural, political, and social factors, the social capability and value system
in any given society. Trade itself is thus neither good nor bad, for its impact
depends on the domestic environment. Still, trade definitely played a positive role in the regions under discussion, which ventured onto the road
of modern transformation at the edge of huge empires.

The beginning of industrialization

Agricultural modernization, as well as the development of food and primary product processing, clearly served as the basis for the beginning of
industrialization in this region. On the peripheries, cottage and small-scale
handicraft industry continued to predominate for another hundred years
after the British Industrial Revolution, virtually until the last third of the
nineteenth century.

In the Hungarian half of Austria-Hungary, industrialization did not
make real progress until the 1860s, but non-mechanized proto-industry
did. One of the most peculiar elements of industrial progress was the
importance of manorial proto-factories until the mid-nineteenth century.
This development was not solely a Hungarian phenomenon, but characterized those Central and Eastern European countries where noble big estates
remained dominant. We have already seen this phenomenon in Bohemia,
but it was equally important in the eastern provinces of Prussia, Hungary,
and in Russia. One of Hungary's largest textile proto-factories was established in the second half of the eighteenth century by Count Antal Forgách
on his estate in Gács. Landowners used the wood of their forests to produce

glass in newly established factories on their estates; altogether thirteen of Hungary's twenty-three glass factories were opened by noble landowners on their estates.[20] Between 1830 and 1848, sixty-two industrial firms were established in Hungary, 75 percent of which were on the nobles' big estates. Using serf labor, the aristocratic big estates processed products in non-mechanized industrial factories, producing sugar and alcohol, using their forests or coal fields as sources of energy, and processing wool, iron, and other raw materials that they extracted. Merchant-owned proto-factories were much less important in Hungary.[21] The 1841 census listed only nine steam engines in the country, and mechanized factories employed only 23,000 workers in total.

Within the Habsburg Empire, industrial development was determined by a marked division of labor between the Austrian-Bohemian hereditary provinces and the Hungarian hinterland. Having manifested a uniquely strong, especially textile proto-industrial development, Austria-Bohemia served as the industrial supplier of Hungary, which did not develop its own textile industry. Until World War I, Austrian-Bohemian products supplied 70 percent of the domestic textile consumption in Hungary. On the other hand, the demand for food in the industrializing western provinces led to agricultural modernization in Hungary, and this became the springboard of its industrial progress.

Grain deliveries to Austria-Bohemia led to the accumulation of wealth in the hands of an affluent Hungarian merchant class. Beginning in the 1860s, one of the most profitable investments attracting those merchants was food processing. The first large mechanized wheat mill, the Pesti Hengermalom Társaság, was established in 1838, and the country's first steam engine was installed there.[22] The beginning of Hungarian industrialization was concentrated in food processing.[23] In several industrial branches, including textiles, leather, paper, and building materials, mechanization had not yet started. The steam engine capacity of flour mills, however, increased by thirteen times, and the capacity of the leading Budapest flour mill industry increased by more than eight times, between 1866 and 1879.

Besides the large quantities and outstanding quality of Hungary's wheat production, a major technological innovation strongly contributed to the success of its flour mill industry. In the 1870s, András Mechwart, a German engineer who immigrated to Hungary to become the managing director of the Ganz Co. (established by Abraham Ganz, a Swiss immigrant), invented and patented the cast iron roller frame. Replacing the usual stone or china rolling mills reduced the cost of production, improved the quality of flour, and made the production of various kinds of wheat flours possible. This patent guaranteed decades of technological primacy for the Hungarian flour mill industry. By 1913, 300 commercial mills processed 24 million quintals of wheat. The ten largest flour mills in Budapest represented nearly a third of the industry's capacity in the country. Unlike all other peripheral grain-exporting countries, Hungary exported 67 percent of its grain in processed form. The milling industry continued to predominate until the war.[24] Food processing represented roughly half of Hungary's total industrial output until the 1880s, when the iron, steel, engineering, and electrical industries began to develop. By the turn of the century, mechanized factories produced 65–70 percent of Hungary's industrial output. By the outbreak of the war, ten engineering factories were already employing more than a thousand workers.[25] The Engineering Company of the Hungarian State Railroad, established in 1873, produced a thousand locomotives by the end of the century, and its product won the gold medal at the Paris Exhibition in 1900. Hungary became self-sufficient in supplying its dense railroad network, with two-thirds of its engineering industry's output going to the railroads. Agricultural machinery production, however, met only half the domestic consumption needs.

The iron, steel, and coal industries also made significant progress. Iron production increased by six times in Hungary between 1867 and 1913, but this was only half of the Austrian-Bohemian, and less than 10 percent of the German, output, and it supplied only 58 percent of domestic consumption. Five big mining companies, partly Austrian–German establishments, had increased coal output by fourteen times between 1867 and 1913, but the per capita coal output was less than a third of the Austrian and 13 percent of the German. Coal imports consequently doubled by the end of the century. The first steps were also taken in the new electric and chemical industries. Electricity generation increased by six times between 1898 and 1913. Two large firms became noteworthy in the European electric industry.[26]

Industrial growth reached 5 percent per annum between 1867 and 1913, but the real breakthrough occurred from the 1890s on. The number of industrial workers almost doubled between 1898 and 1913, and the total horsepower capacity of industrial machines trebled. (See Table 11.1.)

Hungary exhibited one of the most auspicious beginnings of modern economic transformation in the peripheries, but it was still only partially successful. The combination of specialized agriculture with food processing, and the initial promising steps in establishing modern electrical industries, were unique achievements in the peripheral regions. But the one-sided grain economy and incomplete, intermittent industrialization

Table 11.1 The industrial development of Poland and Hungary, 1860–1913

Year	Number of Polish industrial workers 1860 = 100	Value of industrial output in Poland 1860 = 100	Capacity of Hungarian industry 1860 = 100	Value of industrial output in Hungary 1860 = 100
1860	100	100	100	100
1900	227	269	3,840	800
1913	442	816	11,080	1,450

Sources: Kula (1947, 42); Berend and Ránki (1972, 63).

still precluded its joining the club of industrialized nations. Prior to World War I, Hungary remained an agrarian country, albeit one that was making impressive strides towards an agrarian-industrial structure. Agriculture still produced more than 60 percent of its GDP and employed 64 percent of its labor force, while industrial employment was only 24 percent.

In east Prussia, agriculture also served as the basis for beginning industrial development. In 1801, Franz Kurt Achard, a professor at the Berlin Academy, established the first sugar refinery in Silesia. Sugar beet production increased by twenty-four times between 1835–44 and 1905–14, with refineries opening up throughout the big estates (Wagner, 1982, 128). Germany emerged as a leading sugar producer. Output soared from 9,000 tons in 1835–44 to nearly 2 million tons by 1905–14. Railroad construction was also a major factor in the industrial transformation of East Prussia. Important steam engine and locomotive production industries appeared on the scene.[27]

Horst Dumke (1979) has called attention to the role of East Prussian grain, wood, and wool exports in the early industrialization of Germany. He speaks of a *Dreieckshandels*, a triangle trade that hastened industrialization.[28]

Finland had a somewhat more promising transformation. The country also remained agricultural-industrial. In 1880 75%, of the labor force still worked in the primary sector, and 66% did so in 1910. The country remained fundamentally rural with only a 15 percent urban population before the war. At that time, per capita income in Finland reached the Hungarian level. The Finnish transformation exhibited some noteworthy developments. The population quadrupled between 1800 and 1913, and agricultural specialization advanced to a greater degree than it did in any other peripheral country. Grain imports comprised 12% of total imports in the mid-century, and doubled to 24% by 1900. Butter exports made up 14% of Finland's exports to the Russian market and 9% of its butter exports went to Western markets in 1860.

The most progressive development in Finland appeared in the late nineteenth century. Agricultural and processed food exports, one-third of which went to Russia and one-quarter to the West in 1860, declined to one-fifth to Russia and one-sixth to the West by 1913. This change was the consequence of a new development trend, the adoption of the Swedish–Norwegian model of wood and timber exports. The quantity of wood and timber exports increased by fourteen times between 1860 and 1913.

From woodcutting and timber producing, Finland turned to pulp and paper production. The industry's output more than quadrupled in value. Only 2 percent of Finnish exports to the Russian market were paper in 1860, but this increased to 39 percent by 1913. The export structure represented a lower standard to the Western markets,[29] but wood, pulp, and paper exports rose to 70 percent of total exports before the war. Finland was thus able to conquer the Russian market for wood and paper even though Russia had immense forests and unlimited quantities of wood, because the latter lacked processing potential.

Despite adopting the Scandinavian industrialization paradigm, Finland's performance lagged far behind that of Scandinavia. Its butter exports comprised only half of the Swedish and 10 percent of the Danish prior to the war, and its pulp exports were only one-fifth of the Norwegian and one-eighth of the Swedish.

In 1885, Russia abolished duty-free trade with Finland. Consequently, Finnish exports to Russia dropped from 47 percent of the total in 1860 to 28 percent in 1913. Again like Scandinavia, Finland adjusted to the vicissitudes of the market in a flexible way. Exports to Russia, which had comprised half of Finnish trade in 1860, fell to less than 30 percent by 1905. Instead, Western exports increased to 70 percent of Finland's total exports, and Britain became the primary market for Finnish goods in the 1890s.[30]

Finish carriers transported most of the country's export products until the 1880s. Water transport connections were established between Helsinki and St. Petersburg, Tallinn, and Stockholm. Finnish seaborne exports increased sevenfold between 1810 and 1870, and then doubled again in

Table 11.2 Structure of employment in Finland and Hungary, 1870–1910 (percent)

Sector	1870 Hungary	1880 Finland	1910 Hungary	1910 Finland
Agriculture	80	75	65	66
Industry	9	7	17	12
Others	11	18	18	22

Sources: Jörberg (1973, 392); Berend and Ránki (1972, 79).

the 1870s. Though relatively small in size, its merchant fleet was fifth in the world on a per capita basis (number of population/tonnage of shipping capacity). It was large enough to generate service income from international cross-trade. Thereafter, however, the merchant fleet's capacity declined by 10 percent by 1913. Foreign ships delivered 70 percent of Finnish goods and 90 percent of its timber exports.

Finland emerged as a semi-successful modernizer. Once an agricultural and raw material producer and exporter, it became an agrarian-industrial country with medium-level income. An export-oriented industrialization was well on its way (Hjerppe and Pihkala, 1977; Hjerppe *et al.*, 1984, 42–59; Jörberg, 1973; Ojala *et al.*, 2006). (See Table 11.2.)

The Baltic region, incorporated into the Russian Empire in the eighteenth century, saw similar developments. Latvia and the Livonian and Kurland provinces rose to become important industrial centers of the Russian Empire. Here too, exports to Russia were the primary factor in industrialization: 70% of the output of the region's timber, chemical, leather, and textile industries, 60% of the glass, china, and paper industries, 30% of the butter industry, and 90% of the metal, engineering, and rubber industries went to the Russian market. This small region produced one-third of the empire's cable and nail production; three rubber factories produced 28% of the empire's total rubber output. (See Figure 11.1.)

Enjoying a higher cultural level and a large German entrepreneurial class, the Baltic region surpassed Russia in industrial development.[31] The division of labor between the small Baltic provinces and the huge Russian Empire led to an unusual structure in the Baltic economy. While the modern export branches of the engineering, chemical, and electrical industries produced 65% of Latvia's industrial output, the consumer good

Figure 11.1
Employment
structure in
Finland, Hungary,
and the
borderlands of
the Habsburg
Empire, 1910
(percentage
employed in
industry,
agriculture, and
other) (Hjerpe,
1982;
Berend-Ránki,
1982)

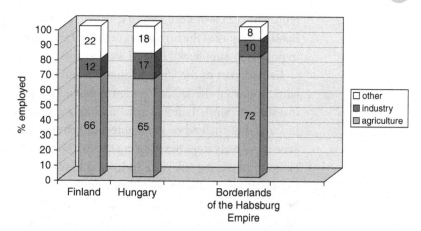

industries producing for local markets represented only 35% of its total industrial production. In the Livonian and Kurland provinces, 31% of the active population worked in industries that produced 53% of their GDP. The share of agriculture and services was only 47% (Nietyesin, 1980, 54–60; Eiduks and Grosvalds, 1962, 153–6; Ivanovskis, 1970, 209).

A somewhat similar situation characterized Russian Poland, the two-thirds of the partitioned country (with 45 percent of its population) that was incorporated into the Russian Empire at the end of the eighteenth century. Huge and economically backward Russia provided an enormous market for Poland, which was home to some 15 million of the empire's 124 million inhabitants in the 1910s. Poland emerged as the empire's third industrial center once tariff barriers were eliminated after 1851, and once canals (the Vistula–Niemen canal) and railroad lines connected Poland with the Russian centers from the 1860s on. Industrial output increased twentyfold between 1864 and 1910, and growth was especially rapid between 1890 and 1910 – with output increasing by nearly four times during these two decades. Three industrial branches particularly took off. The Polish coal industry rose to European importance and produced 40% of the empire's coal output. The mining, iron, and engineering industries employed 27% of the Polish workforce and produced 20% of the indus-trial output, with 40% their products going to Russia. The Polish textile industry in Łódź (the "Polish Manchester") and Sosnowiec emerged as the export industry par excellence, employing 44% of the industrial workforce and producing 45% of total industrial output. Russian markets absorbed 80% of the products of this industry. The engine of Polish industrial development, therefore, was exports to Russia. The value of foreign trade increased by twenty-seven times between 1864 and 1910. Polish industry represented 23% of steel, 15% of iron, and 20% of textile production in the Russian Empire at the turn of the century. Per capita industrial production in politically suppressed Poland was twice as high as in Russia.

Ireland, part of the United Kingdom and next door to industrial England, imported the factory system rather early, in part thanks to British investment. More than 290 non-mechanized factories were in operation in Ireland at the end of the eighteenth century. For quite a while, however, these early steps in following the British example remained more the exception than the rule. The Industrial Revolution dramatically changed the situation. Textile imports from England doubled in a single decade between 1825 and 1835, and cloth output in the Dublin area halved by 1838. The previously flourishing Irish cottage industry mostly collapsed.[32] Money began to flow out of Ireland into England, and half of the Munster and Kilkenny banks collapsed. English industry increased its exports to the Irish market by 233 percent by 1835, and Irish proto-industry was basically eliminated by the 1880s. What remained was mostly distilling and brewing, and these sectors delivered half of their output of whiskey and beer to Britain. In 1841, Ireland was home to 31% of the United Kingdom's population but generated less than 15% of its GDP. By 1871, the Irish population dropped to 21% of the UK's and its share of its GDP was 11%. Real wages increased in Britain by 50% between 1785–9 and 1866–70, compared with an increase of only 15% in Ireland (Geary and Stark, 2004, 362–3). "Ireland was becoming more rural, more agricultural, than it had been . . . A forthcoming annihilation of industrial activity in much of Ireland seemed imminent" in the 1880s (Cullen, 1987, 121, 129, 148).

Nevertheless, the country was able to develop certain industrial branches that played a supplementary role in the English economy. This was even more so after 1826, when the independent Irish currency was abolished. From the mid-1840s on, extensive railroad construction connected the country economically to Great Britain. Half of the private railroad investments came from England. While modern transportation played an important role in the collapse of local industries, export industries began to develop. Some agricultural products, such as live and processed animals and butter, were delivered to the English market. One of the beneficiaries of producing for the English market was the mechanized linen industry; another was the brewing and distilling industry.[33] The Dublin-based Guinness factory produced three-quarters of total beer production and 96% of Ireland's beer exports at the turn of the century. Half of whiskey and one-third of beer production were sold on the English market. The food and beverage industry employed fewer than 6% of the British labor force, but more than 12% of the Irish. Ireland's share of Britain's industrial output was only 3.2% in 1907, but nearly 9% of its food and beverage production. The net output per head reached three-quarters of the British level, and 110% in brewing and malting.

In addition to linen and drinks, Belfast shipbuilding emerged as one of the most important export industries. The tonnage of Irish ship production, especially the giant Harland and Wolff Company, increased by two and a half times between 1891 and 1914, and Irish shipbuilding on a per capita level reached more than 81% of the British total. Half of Ireland's agricultural and industrial output was sold in England. Irish deliveries to England doubled in the single decade between 1904 and 1914.

Irish "exports" to England, therefore, ignited industrialization in the country and enabled it to reach the agricultural-industrial level. Industry produced one-third of the combined output of agriculture and industry. Within the industrial sector, export-oriented linen, brewing, distilling, and shipbuilding industries produced 80 percent of output. Prior to the war, 23 percent of the Irish labor force worked in industry and construction, and industry's share of GDP surpassed 20 percent – placing Ireland "much in the middle rank of European industrial countries" (Bielenberg, 2008, 822–3, 833). Ireland thus suffered somewhat but also profited economically from British rule, as did Hungary, Poland, the Baltic region, and Finland under the Austrians and the Russians. The enormous imperial markets provided an opportunity for launching industrialization and led to the rise of an agricultural-industrial structure.

Going halfway towards modern transformation, Ireland, Finland, and countries from Central Europe and the Baltic region began to emerge from peripheral backwardness. Their one-sided agricultural character receded: employment in their agricultural sectors dropped to 64–65% while industrial employment rose to 15–24%. Agriculture continued to be a primary contributor to GDP (between 50% and 62%), but industry's share increased to 25–26%. Demographic trends began to mirror those of the West. The population grew by 338%, and the literacy rate, with some exceptions, reached 70–90%. The combined per capita GDP of Finland, Ireland, and Hungary increased by 268% between 1820 and 1913, nearly as much as Western Europe's 287%. (See Table 11.3.)

The region as a whole reached nearly two-thirds of the West European per capita income level in 1820, and moderately declined to 57% in 1913. Unlike Scandinavia, this region was unable to catch up with the West. But it didn't lose much ground, either.

Table 11.3 The development of GDP in the half-modernized economies of Finland, Ireland, and Hungary, as compared with Western Europe, 1820–1913

	1820	1870	1900	1913
Finland	759	1,107	1,620	2,050
Ireland	954	1,773	2,495	2,733
Hungary	820[a]	1,269	1,682	2,098
Average (unweighted)	**844**	**1,383**	**1,932**	**2,294**
Western Europe (seven countries)	1,372	2,337	3,456	4,013
The region as % of Western Europe	**62**	**59**	**56**	**57**

Source: Maddison (1995, 194, 198, 200).
Note: [a] Estimated figure.

Notes

1. In my first book, written with György Ránki before we received our BA degrees, we embraced this traditional concept of Hungarian historiography (Berend and Ránki, 1955). However, in our 1966 study on the national income between 1867 and 1914 (Berend and Ránki, 1970), we were the first to challenge this concept.

2. The so-called "Old Finland," the eastern part of the country, was an exception, since this region belonged to Russia and adopted the Russian system in the eighteenth century; it became part of the Finnish Grand Duchy only later.

3. In a labor-intensive way, forests were burned to create good soil – often leading to 40:1 yield-to-seed ratio. However, the land could be sown only once or twice after burning, and another eighty to a hundred years would have to pass before it could be burnt again.

4. The cattle stock increased two and a half-times from 600,000 to 1.5 million between 1824 and 1907. Type improvement further increased production. At the end of the eighteenth century, one cow produced an average of 300–400 kilograms of milk in a year. Production increased to 500–600 kilograms by the mid-century and to 1,000 kilograms by the beginning of the twentieth century.

5. In Lithuania, after the nobles' anti-Russian uprising of the early 1860s, the tsarist government allowed the peasants to buy noble land. Peasant land increased by 30–50% in the Vilnius and Kaunas regions by 1870. However, 34% and 40% of the land remained in the hands of nobility in these two areas.

6. By the 1860s, the manor landlords practiced crop rotation on 65 percent and 80 percent of the arable land in Livland and Courland, respectively. Drainage systems were laid down in several estates. The Society invited Danish engineers, and a Bureau of Land Melioration was established in 1897. Plows were imported from Western Europe in the 1830s–1850s, the scythe replaced the sickle, and threshing machines were imported from Scotland. Their number topped 3,750 in Estland by 1910, and thousands of seed drills, reapers, and hay movers were also in operation.

7. The acreage of arable (and tree crop) land significantly increased from 5 million hectares to 16.1 million between 1800 and 1910, especially in the second half of the century. Some 100 drainage societies turned 4.8 million hectares of marshland and landed areas around regulated rivers into cultivated land. As 60 percent of the peasantry was emancipated without land or with tiny parcels, 39 percent of the agrarian population became wage laborers on the surviving former noble big estates.

8. At the turn of the century 43% of Prussia's population lived in urban settlements, but only 28–30% did so in eastern Prussia, with some provinces claiming less than a 20% urban population.

9. One-third to one-half of the land, roughly 1 million hectares, became part of the Junkers' big estates. The peasants had to pay compensation for the abolition of feudal fees, which cost them one-third to three-quarters of their monetary income.

10. Leasing took place in only 30 percent of the estates of more than 200 hectares in Mecklenburg, where the phenomenon was relatively more widespread. The East Prussian average, however, declined from 32 percent to 22 percent.

11. This type of worker received a fixed payment in kind, a small cash wage, a rent-free cottage, and a small plot of land, and in return was available to work on the big estate when needed.

12. In 1849 45 percent of the agricultural population was landless, but 60 percent of the male agricultural labor force was landless by 1871, the time of Germany's unification.

13. A large part of the estates' income was invested into the land to increase output and productivity and replace hand workers. Drainage systems, mechanization, the use of artificial fertilizers, increased animal stock, and significant type improvement through the import of east Frisian (Dutch) and Holstein oxen significantly contributed to production. Mechanization was also markedly upgraded. The big estates were able to use steam technology-based agricultural machinery; the number of threshing machines almost quadrupled between 1882 and 1907, and sowing and harvesting machines proliferated as well. By 1900, 1,696 steam plows were in use in Germany, each one with a capacity to sow 17,000 hectares. Nearly 26,000 steam threshers were in operation,

i.e. one thresher for each 111 hectares. Steam sowing also developed, with each machine covering 170 hectares. Incentive for investing in agricultural production rose significantly after the introduction of protectionism.

14. Thomasphosphate production jumped from 130,000 tons in 1866 to more than 2.4 million tons by 1913. German scholars discovered the impact of potassium chloride and produced 8.2 million tons before the war. At that time, Germans used 54 kilograms of phosphorous fertilizer per acre of land, notably less than the 98 and 83 kilograms used in Belgium and Britain, but enough to significantly increase yields.

15. Exported butter increased from 1.8 million to 12.6 million tons between 1860 and 1913 and played an important role in exports. The pulp and paper industry increased its output by more than four times between 1885 and 1905.

16. David Ricardo used the example of the Methuen agreement, one of the first free trade agreements between industrializing Britain and wine-producing Portugal, to prove the mutual benevolence of trade. Ricardo was "fortunate" not to live long enough to see Portugal's decline from among the wealthiest three to four to the poorest three to four countries of Europe.

17. The classic food-exporting Holland and Denmark are the best examples of flexibility.

18. Britain's terms of trade declined in the first half of the nineteenth century, and it had to export 50 percent more for the same value of imports by 1860. The German decline of terms of trade took place during the period of the country's most successful industrial and economic growth.

19. The United States and Canada, for example, had classical "backward" export structures during the last third of the nineteenth century. Between 1868–70 and 1896–1900, more than 90 percent of their exports were agricultural products and raw materials, and 87 percent remained so as late as 1914 (Kindleberger, 1962, 41, 43).

20. Seventeen proto-factories produced paper between 1790 and 1815, twelve of them on noble big estates. Until the end of the 1830s, sixteen of the twenty-two sugar refineries in operation were manorial factories. Coal mining was initiated in Tokod and Dorog on the Esterházys' Tata-Gesztes estate, and a large distillery was also established. One of the leading sectors of the manorial industry was iron production. Count György Andrássy established iron works on his estates in Betlér and Dernő in 1845 and 1847, and sent some of his serfs to Baden for training. In the 1830s, about a hundred manorial iron works represented the overwhelming majority of Hungary's iron industry.

21. Johan Puthon, a Viennese merchant, founded the largest textile manufactur in Sasvár. Based on cottage industry, Sasvár contracted with 20,000 households to supply thread in 1800. The Valero silk factory was established in Pest in 1776,

and 500 workshops and proto-factories operated by 1848. Eleven percent of the population worked in the handicraft industry at that time.

22. Affluent, mostly Jewish grain merchant families opened a number of mills during the 1860s: the Weiss, Deutsch, and Brüll families were among the shareholders of several mills, including fourteen large ones in Budapest.

23. Until the 1840s, only nine steam engines, with just 100 horsepower capacity, operated mostly outside the industry. By the early 1860s, the availability of machines in the country was still sporadic: 480 steam engines were in operation with more than 8,000 horsepower capacity. Of those engines, 308 worked in food processing, 100 in iron, metal, and engineering, and 29 in timber industries.

24. By 1913, food processing employed nearly 19 percent of the entire industrial workforce, owned 30 percent of industrial machine capacity, and produced 41 percent of the total gross value of industrial output. The flour mill industry emerged as the most important export sector in the country. After protectionist measures curbed exports to Western Europe, the flour mill industry sold its products in the protected markets of the Monarchy's Austrian-Bohemian provinces.

25. The Ganz factory patented its chill-casting railroad freight car's wheel, and, with four other engineering companies, produced 28,000 freight cars in the 1890s.

26. The Egyesült Izzólámpagyár took over a significant part of the European bulb market, and the Ganz Villamossági Gyár electrified the Italian Valtellina railroad.

27. Altogether 69,000 workers were employed in these industries in Germany in 1900, with more than 14,000 (21 percent of the total) in the East Prussian provinces. Based on abundant natural resources, mining (with 175,000 work-ers) and an iron industry (75,000 workers) were developed in East Prussian Silesia, the most industrialized province of the region, with the number of workers totaling 280,000 (Tebarth, 1991; Voth, 2001). Of the 401,210 cotton spindles in Prussia, 234,903 operated in the eastern provinces of Prussia in 1840. The capacity of the cotton industry not only met the regional demand, but supplied export products as well.

28. The triangle trade signified East Prussian exports to England, English exports of industrial products (mostly half-products) to West Prussia, and West Prussian deliveries of agricultural equipment and machinery to East Prussia (Dumke, 1979).

29. The share of paper remained low, 9% in 1913, while unprocessed wood exports increased from 54% to 60% between 1860 and 1913.

30. In addition to the leading industrial export sectors, the textile and iron indus-tries made considerable progress, based on the Russian market. The first

mechanized factories in these sectors were mostly foreign establishments. A Scotsman established the first textile factory. Before World War I, the Finlayson (Tampere) and Barker (Turku) textile works employed 2,200 and 1,100 workers, respectively. Russian investors established iron works in the eastern provinces. Among the ten largest factories, two paper mills and four saw mills were also in operation (Ojala and Karonen, 2006, 107).

31. Members of the Technical University of Riga contributed to the creation of the empire's largest cement factory at the end of the 1860s. E. Arnold, the head of the electrotechnical laboratory at the University of Riga, began production of generators and elevated the Detman factory to imperial importance.

32. In 1836, the Poor Law Commission reported that the number of weavers dropped to one-third or one-quarter of their previous numbers. Sugar refineries that had supported 4,000 families in 1769 employed only 19 people by 1861. The relative boom, based on a 40 percent increase in the volume of exports and a 120 percent price increase between 1793 and 1815, suddenly came to a halt at the end of the Napoleonic wars. Beef exports decreased by two-thirds, and pork exports by one-half. Grain prices declined by 50 percent, meat prices by one-third, and export prices in general dropped by the year 1820 compared with the 1770s.

33. By 1852, twenty-eight linen factories operated in Belfast for the English market. The export deliveries of distilleries doubled between the 1860s and 1870s, and doubled again by the early twentieth century. In 1907, 8.5 million gallons of whiskey were exported, mostly from four large distilleries located in Belfast.

CHAPTER 12

Profiting from foreign interests: the Mediterranean and Russia

In certain regions of the continent, the modern economic transformation could not start as early as in the core countries. This was the case in a number of independent countries, some of them former great powers that had enormous colonial empires and had enjoyed world dominance in the early modern centuries, such as Spain and Portugal. Others were like the expansionist military giant Russia, which had incorporated vast European and Asian territories into its empire in the eighteenth and nineteenth centuries, but had became frozen under its *ancien régime*. The Kingdom of Naples, the southern, Mezzogiorno part of united Italy during the last third of the century, shared several similar features and remained the backward part of a modernizing Italy.

The decline of the Mediterranean area, the European economic power-house of the late medieval and early modern centuries, is one of the most challenging historical problems. "From the fourteenth to the sixteenth centuries the Mediterranean was the world unto itself, a world economy" (Tabak, 2008, 1). Spain, Portugal, and the north Italian city-states were then the strongest and most flourishing part of Europe. By the nineteenth century, however, they were part of the backward peripheries. What happened? Civilizations have continually risen and fallen throughout history, but this doesn't explain the Mediterranean decline. North Italy was the birthplace of the Renaissance and modern capitalism; long-distance trade and banking had been established there. Spain and Portugal had been major world powers with enormous colonial empires enriched by vast amounts of silver and gold. Modern capitalism, however, did not mature there, but shifted to Northwestern Europe. A series of military calamities certainly explain part of the story. But the question might immediately be asked, why were those areas militarily defeated and occupied in the first place?

Faruk Tabak has provided a geo-historical answer. The decline, he suggests, was gradual and began in agriculture, and then accelerated between the fourteenth and sixteenth centuries. This was during the early period of the so-called Little Ice Age, a climatic disaster from the turn of the thirteenth to the mid-fifteenth century, in which the Black Sea froze over, incessant rains and continual flooding destroyed the arable land, and a large part of the Mediterranean plains was turned into marshland. Flooding shifted more than 5 million cubic meters of soil from the Arno Valley to the sea each year. Swamps abounded at river deltas, and malaria decimated the population. Earlier deforestation made the situation much worse. Extreme weather conditions, soil erosion, and landslides reverted "sizable stretches of the Mediterranean plains . . . back to the wild." Arable land decreased by more than a third in southern France, Maremma of Siena, and the basin of lower Guadalquivir in Spain. The eradication of commercial cultivation pushed the population from the plains to the hillsides and mountainous areas during the seventeenth and eighteenth centuries. Famine, migration, and the devastation of villages became the rule in the Mediterranean countryside. The region "rapidly fades into obscurity" in the seventeenth century. The lowlands were reclaimed only during the nineteenth century, resettled and cultivated mostly by landlords who introduced the sharecropping system that became the norm in southern France, Italy, and the Balkans (Tabak, 2008, 18, 189, 194–6, 201, 217, 241, 307).

The decline fortified the old regime. The unchallenged authority of the feudal nobility, with its strong anti-capitalist, anti-business attitudes on the one hand, and the survival of collectivist-egalitarian village communities on the other, created an institutional and cultural heritage that hindered modernization. Modern institutions and legal systems were sorely lacking, and mass illiteracy remained the norm. These characteristics excluded these regions from modern transformation during most of the nineteenth century.

Modernization and industrialization commenced quite late here. When it finally did so from the 1890s on, it created only isolated industrial islands and modernized agricultural pockets in a vast ocean of traditionalism. The achievements of the agricultural revolution were not adopted in most of these regions for most of the period under discussion. If it did occur, it began very late and only in certain areas such as Siberia in Russia, Catalonia in Spain, and certain parts of the Mezzogiorno. Proto-industry remained dominant for practically the entire century and mostly failed to lead to modern industrialization.

However, all of these areas benefited from the transforming European environment and the market integration of the continent. All experienced the impact of European population growth, capital flow, and the construction of modern transportation and financial systems with Western investment. All became gradually involved in rapidly developing European trade. Their economic prospectiveness, vast unexploited markets, agricultural export potential, and valuable raw material resources attracted the market-seeking and import-craving West in search of lucrative investment opportunities. The allure of the West's industrial transformation and its inevitable military challenge prompted some reform. The response of the peripheral elite was slow and belated: we now see an attempt to adjust to the new realities and profit from the export opportunities. A series of failed endeavors and half-hearted reforms ultimately led to small cracks in the massive edifice of the *ancien régime*. Consequently, some of the achievements of the agricultural revolution were extremely late to arrive. Although the land and peasant question remained unsolved, and the modernization of agriculture remained unfinished, a partial adoption of new methods began.

Foreign interest and agriculture

On the Iberian peninsula, the only significant undertaking that affected agriculture during the first half of the century was the selling of nationalized church estates in the south. This was accomplished in three major waves by the 1850s. The state auctioned off former church estates and municipal and state estates, totaling some 10 million hectares – 50 percent of the country's arable land – to increase revenues and pay public debts. The amount of cultivated land increased by 65 percent between 1800 and 1910, but the ownership structure did not change, as the aristocrats, high-ranking officers and bureaucrats, landowners, and businessmen purchased the land (Tortella, 2000, 57). The traditional big estates had prevailed in the south and the middle of the country since the Reconquista. The contrast was extreme: seventy-four big estates, each with more than 5,000 hectares of land on the one hand, and nearly 10 million peasant landholdings, each of an average of only 0.6 hectares, on the other. At the turn of the century, more than 96 percent of the estates comprised only 30 percent of the landed area. Two million peasants lived in such poverty that they were exempt from taxation. Viable peasant farms existed only in Catalonia, the Basque lands, and some other coastal provinces.

The structure of cultivation did not change much throughout the century. A monoculture, subsistence grain economy prevailed in the Spanish interior. While the proportion of the agricultural population increased within the active population, the gross agricultural product decreased from 732 million pesetas to 722 million in constant prices between 1860 and 1910. Sánchez-Albornoz compared the economic situation of Castile to that of the contemporary Third World (Sánchez-Albornoz, 1987, 248–9). By 1900, grain production characterized more than three-fourths of agricultural land in Spain and produced more than half its agricultural output. Although maize production grew threefold and rice more than sevenfold, cereal output altogether increased by only 90 percent between 1800 and 1910. Yields remained far behind those of Western Europe. Germany's yields in wheat and rye were twice those of Spain, Portugal, and southern Italy.[1] As Gabriel Tortella noted, "Spanish agriculture (and Southern Europe as a whole) remained tied to the two-field rotation of cereal cultivation, with the 'light plow' scratching the sandy soils" (Tortella, 1987, 51). He also maintained that if an agricultural revolution ever happened in Spain, it happened in the later twentieth century.

Although the area of cultivated land increased, the primitive methods of cultivation led to a decline of yields prior to 1880. Even a population growth that was the slowest in Europe exceeded the increase of output. Per capita grain production decreased, and land and labor productivity stagnated even during the last two decades before World War I. One male laborer produced 1,188 pesetas in 1893, but only 1,127 pesetas in 1910 (Tortella, 1987, 53). Recurrences of severe grain shortages and starvation hit Spain several times during the nineteenth century.

Small wonder that agriculture did not emancipate the labor force in Spain, for it was practically the only country in Europe to see a rise in agricultural employment. The percentage of the active population working in agriculture was 65.3% in 1797, 64.1% in 1877, and 66.0% by 1910 (Pérez Moreda, 1987, 35).[2] At the turn of the century, only Catalonia exhibited a semi-modernized employment structure, with 52.6% agricultural and 27.6% industrial employment (Domínguez Martín, 2002, 370).

Thanks to the Western markets, however, agricultural specialization did gain some ground on the Iberian peninsula: the grape and wine economy developed to an impressive degree and became the only sector that produced a significant export surplus.[3] Spain temporarily took advantage of the outbreak of phylloxera that destroyed a great part of the French vineyards, but the plague quickly spread to Spain and halted further development. Wine exports dropped by 40 percent in the single decade of the

1890s. By 1913, wine comprised the second largest Spanish export, with less than 12 percent of the total.

The unlimited demand of Western, mostly British and French, markets provided enormous incentive to expand citrus production in the mid-nineteenth century.[4] The quantity of exported oranges rose three and a half times in the last two decades of the century. Valencia, devoid of industrialization, became one of the most important export regions of Spain. Before the war, more than 60 percent of Spanish exports left Valencia's ports.

As in the Mediterranean region generally, olive trees occupied roughly the same landed area as grapes, mostly in Valencia, Andalusia, and Aragón. In the late 1860s, olive oil exports totaled 7.5 million tons, and increased to 21.4 million tons by the early twentieth century. In other words, specialized agriculture in coastal areas (grapes, olives, and citrus cultures) expanded to become an important export sector in the quarter-century before the war. The more advanced coastal regions, however, represented only a small portion of the Spanish population. Catalonia and Valencia made up 19 percent of the country's population, and their small territories were the most densely populated (Domínguez Martín, 2002, 367).[5]

However, traditional agriculture was preserved even in Valencia. Cereals were grown on nearly 60 percent of irrigated land, and "the economy still devoted a large part of the most productive land to growing subsistence crops to feed the region's population" (Palafox, 1987, 269, 272, 282). Orchard cultivation produced only 12 percent of agricultural output, and fruit became the fourth largest export item (8.4 percent).[6] Exports of wine increased nearly twentyfold between 1865 and 1890, and it was the country's leading export item until the 1890s; olive exports increased by three times. By 1913, ores and textile products ranked among Spain's ten leading export items, while wine and fresh fruit represented one-fifth of total exports.

Spain's agricultural production stagnated at 0.3–0.4 percent annual growth during the first half of the century. Still, it became somewhat more dynamic with an annual 1.0 percent growth, while the traditional, backward grain economy in the middle of the country hardly changed at all.[7]

In central and particularly southern Italy, agriculture remained stuck in nearly medieval conditions for a long time. Unlike in most of the peripheral regions, especially Russia, serfdom had been abolished early on by Joseph Bonaparte in the continental Mezzogiorno (1806).[8] Although the peasants became legally free, the feudal structures were preserved. First, the traditional big estates survived and remained dominant in most of the overpopulated south. Noble *latifondi* were large, between 1,000 and 6,000 hectares. The free peasants became contracted tenant workers in a traditionally patriarchal society. Long-term contracts, at times for twenty years, were highly exploitative. Enrico Dal Lago describes the persistent survival of feudal relations. In the case of citrus groves that required intensive cultivation, regular irrigation, and supervision, "landowners fixed the tenants' share at a maximum of one-eighth of the total crop . . . The specific form of subordination which psychologically and morally tied the peasants to the landowners in nineteenth century Mezzogiorno . . . [was] a much more subtle kind of slavery" (Dal Lago, 2005, 75, 76).

Social conditions remained unchanged within the family and all of society. Traditional family structures and extended families were preserved in the south, in contrast to the predominant nuclear family in the north. Marriage practices requiring women to marry at the age of twenty were more stringent than Western norms in the north (Foreman-Peck, 2006, 19). A paramount, rigid hierarchy survived, including a feudal type of paternalistic relations between masters and servants. In the Kingdom of Naples, petrified medieval conditions remained dominant before unification.[9] In Tuscany and Umbria, most of the peasants worked in the *mezzadria* (metayage) system as tenant sharecroppers, paying one-third to one-half of their output to the landowners, who supplied the land and tools and paid the taxes. The church and seventy families owned some 60 percent of the land in 1880.

Contemporary observers painted a dark picture of the Mezzogiorno. When Francesco Ferrara published his *Nuova antologia* in 1866, his dismal description of Italy reflected the situation in the south. "The nation is tied to its past . . . it does not feel the need for great undertakings . . . The world around us moves in feverish strides . . . but Italy just looks on and admires" (quoted in Luzzatto, 1968, 203). Cohen and Federico (2001, 26) quote two harsh depictions of southern conditions: the oft-quoted Florentine aristocrat Leopoldo Franchetti wrote that the south in the 1880s was characterized by "a very unequal distribution of wealth; by the absolute lack of the concept of equal rights under law; by the predominance of individual power; by the exclusively personal character of social relations" (Bevilacqua, 1993, 28). Giustino Fortunato noted that the north was linked to Europe, and the south to Africa, by tradition, geography, climate, and customs (Cafagna, 1994, 28). As the Italian Labor Party declared in 1893, Italy is a country in which a divide of almost a century separates one region from another (quoted in Pollard, 1965, 229).

Cultivation did not change for centuries. In the interior, extensive grain cultivation rotated with pastureland in a two- or three-rotation system.

Tools did not change either: wooden plows, sickles, and threshing with oxen reflected medieval technology.[10] Aggregate agricultural output increased by 0.7% per year, but, as Paul Bairoch (1976a) has shown, Italian per capita agricultural output grew by a minimal 0.4% annually during the quarter-century after unification – a virtual stagnation. Agricultural productivity per hectare in the Two Sicilies was a third of that in Lombardy and 40% less than in Veneto, and agricultural output per head in 1857 was only 43% of Parma-Modena's and 34% lower than Liguria's (Zamagni, 1993).[11] Landlessness and a lack of jobs and even food pushed southerners to the more developed and industrializing north and then overseas. Small wonder that 14 million people emigrated at least once, and nearly 6 million people (20% of the population) left permanently between 1881 and 1910.

Recent research, however, has modified the picture somewhat. An important new element was growing bourgeois landownership. Many new owners destructively copied the behavior and attitudes of aristocratic absentee landowners, but some began to manage the land and modernize. In the coastal regions, *latifondi* turned to cash crop cultivation; around Naples and coastal Apulia, Calabria, and Sicily, citrus groves, vineyards, and olive cultivation were expanded to produce for exports. Italy exported olive oil to Britain for the lubrication of machinery and to France for soap production. Commercialized agriculture had already begun to develop before unification. The *latifondi* exhibited a mixed agriculture, a somewhat specialized production and a crop partly produced for exports.[12] The big estate was not entirely frozen in the Middle Ages, but began adjusting to nineteenth-century requirements. Sicilian landowners invested in planting lemon and orange groves, and southern peasants began exporting wine in the 1880s. An enormous amount of capital accumulated in the hands of capitalist landowners, and what was not squandered on luxuries was mostly reinvested in agriculture. Pockets of modernized agriculture and higher growth were connected with export-oriented agriculture (Dal Lago, 2005: Dal Lago and Halpern, 2002; Bevilacqua, 1989; Petrusewicz, 2002).

In southern Italy, 64% of the population still worked in partly premodern agriculture in 1911, and the per capita value of output was 16% lower than in Lombardy and only 43% of that of Britain. Southern backwardness was exhibited in various areas. The north held 46%, and the south only 19% of the country's cattle stock. The road network was 5,600 kilometers per thousand inhabitants in Piedmont and Lombardy, but only 1,500 kilometers in the south, including Sicily and Sardinia (Eckaus, 1961, 291–2). The south's illiteracy rate was 84% in 1871, and it declined to

64 percent by 1911, but this paled in comparison with the north's rate of 19 percent. Per capita income level in the south was only 62% of that in the north.

The so-called physical quality of life index, developed by Giovanni Federico and Gianni Toniolo, combines three characteristic social-cultural phenomena: literacy rate,[13] infant mortality, and life expectancy at age one. This index on a scale of 0 to 100 (the worst to the best performance) pegs northwest Italy at 40.5 in 1870, and southern Italy (including the islands) at only 17.6. The south's index was only 43% of that of the north and 28% of those of Britain and France. The situation improved, however, between 1880 and 1910; in the latter year, the south's index was 70% of that of the north and 59% of France's (Federico and Toniolo, 1991, 200–1).

Genuine integrating links, actual or potential, between north and south were lacking both before and after unification. Trade of the Kingdom of Naples (both island and mainland) with France and Britain represented 51.4% of the total, while trade with the rest of Italy comprised only 12.9% before unification. Similarly, Lombardy sold only 30% of its exports in other Italian states, but 70% in Switzerland (Foreman-Peck, 2006, 11).

The north widened its advantage by improving nearly 329,000 hectares of land by 1914, compared with only 2,400 hectares in the south. Nevertheless, the south did make some progress. Railroad links to the industrializing north stimulated southern agriculture. During the half-century after unification, gross agricultural production increased nearly threefold in the north but also more than twofold in the south. Specialization enhanced southern performance in corn, wine, citrus, and olive oil production. Italy remained an agricultural country, but, in a rather unique way, without significant agricultural exports. From the 1880s on, 10–20 percent of its grain had to be imported, and only its wine, citrus, and olive products became major exports – partly the result of modernizing southern agriculture. Fruit exports were the second largest after olives.[14]

Growth of the traditional grain economy in Russia

At the eastern end of the continent, the rapidly expanding Russian Empire embodied the most typical East European agricultural model. Serfdom survived in Russia for a protracted period: according to certain, albeit contradictory figures, half of the peasant population were serfs at the end of the 1850s. An additional 40 percent were crown serfs who had won their personal freedom in the 1830s but worked on state land. The entire country remained frozen in a traditional pre-modern institutional and legal framework. Serfs cultivated the predominant big estates, and their burden of labor service had quadrupled since the time of Catherine the Great. According to certain estimates, the productivity of serf labor was only half that of wage laborers.

The Crimean War in 1853–6 led to a humiliating Russian defeat at the hands of 60,000 Western expeditionary troops. Even the 349 day long siege of Sebastopol did not suffice to mobilize the million-strong Russian army, for the country was frozen in pre-modern conditions and lacked modern transportation. The defeat signified a wakeup call to the need for modernization. In an age when European markets had opened up and were in dire need of agricultural products, reform became crucially important.

Russia was not integrated into the international economic system until the nineteenth century,[15] when it became one of the world's primary grain exporters. Its agricultural exports increased 5.5 fold, and its grain exports, comprising two-thirds of its total exports in 1861 (decreasing to one-half by 1900 and one-fifth by 1913), represented one-quarter of the world's grain exports at the turn of the century.

This was the direct result of reform and the gradual, partial dismantling of the feudal regime. After four years of preparation, the tsar signed a decree to emancipate the serfs on March 3, 1861. The nobles' big estates, however, remained intact and comprised one-third of the country's arable land. The reform instead truncated the peasants' land.[16] The big estates could not turn to wage labor for some time after the serfs' emancipation. Former serfs continued cultivating the manorial land, doing the harvesting, hoeing, and providing other labor services with their own tools, in exchange for an allotment of sharecropping plots.[17] The remnants of the old system (called *otrabotochnaia sistema*), including labor service, characterized Russian agriculture for decades to come. Unlike in Prussia or Hungary, the big aristocratic estates were not transformed into capitalist agricultural enterprises. As a contemporary Russian economist A. I. Chuprov noted in 1906, "Civilized gentry estates, well-endowed with capital and know-how, are isolated outposts, concealed among a mass of mediocre and neglected properties, based simply upon the leasing of land to the peasantry and the extortion of rent" (quoted in Gatrell, 1986, 119).

Russia did not develop its cultivation technology and preserved the two- and three-rotation systems, with more than one-third of its arable land remaining fallow – decreasing to 28 percent by 1875. Agricultural production hardly changed since the Middle Ages. Extreme monocultural structures perpetually endured, and 97 percent of the arable land was used to cultivate grain by 1870. This medieval performance led to a sharp decrease of per capita grain production, as the population had increased by 50 percent in that period alone.[18] Peasant uprisings were common occurrences from the 1770s until 1861.[19]

Mention should be made of the peasant cottage industry (*kustar*), which will be discussed later in this chapter, for it had a symbiotic relationship with Russian agriculture. The cottage industry was a general phenomenon in early modern and nineteenth-century Europe, but it was much more prevalent and protracted in Russia than anywhere else on the continent. The number of Russian industrial factory workers increased by 60 percent between 1865 and 1890, but the size of the small-scale industrial and *kustar* workforce rose by 150 percent.[20] M. I. Tugan-Baranovsky, one of the best contemporary Russian economists, considered rural small-scale, *kustar* industry as a dead-end road for economic development (Barnett, 2004, 43). Recent research has revisited Tugan-Baranovsky's thesis and has introduced the concept of a "dual industrial economy" in early twentieth-century Russia, in which the traditional rural peasant industry and modern industrial factories were in symbiosis, partly competing and partly complementing each other. Russia's rural proto-industry did not signify an introductory stage toward modern industry. "The proto-industry . . . [was] integrated into the traditional social and economic system," and into a rural-centered pre-modern economy (Gestwa, 1999, 21, 27, 582, 589)

A number of scholarly interpretations paint highly different portraits of Russia's peasant economy. The traditional view, which has prevailed in economic history literature since the 1950s, is Alexander Gerschenkron's concept of a primitive peasant economy that was overburdened by taxation, compelling the peasants to sell parts of their production by reducing family consumption. In this way, the tsarist regime forcibly increased grain exports (Gerschenkron, 1962). Sergei Witte, the Minister of Finance, spoke of the "prolonged agony of Russian agriculture" at the turn of the century (Laue, 1969, 183). Carol Leonard suggests that "pre-capitalist practices were the main feature of agriculture" in Russia (Leonard, 1989, 509). Olga Crisp generally concluded that "Large areas of the economic landscape [were] unaffected by modern development . . . Poverty was too long seated and endemic . . . Islands of modern growth were surrounded by a sea of traditional or semi-traditional economies" (Crisp, 1976, 217).

These views have been thoroughly challenged by Paul R. Gregory, who denies the existence of a pre-capitalist state of agriculture in Russia. His main argument is based on his calculation of an impressively increasing labor productivity of 1.35 percent per annum in the country between the

1880s and 1910s. Agricultural output increased by 2.55 percent per annum, twice as much as population growth, during the last two decades of the nineteenth century. Grain consumption grew three times faster than did the rural population. Gregory presents a picture of a growing market economy and a significantly modernized agriculture (Gregory, 1994, 29, 44, 47). Anthropometric research also paints a more positive picture: the average height of recruits from the Saratov Province grew from 163.2 centimeters in 1853 to 167.8 centimeters by 1889 – similar to the West European norm (Mironov and A'Hearn, 2008, 912, 915).[21] Echoing Vladimir Lenin's thesis, several Soviet historians spoke of the spread of market capitalism in the Russian countryside and the polarization of the peasantry. I. D. Kovalchenko maintains that "The household economy was connected with the market . . . It was most significant in crop cultivation (26.3%), livestock raising (71.6%) . . . for the more prosperous peasants . . . the overall level of market ties for the peasant economy was extremely high" (Kovalchenko, 1989, 459–60). However, he also notes that the poor peasants had a more limited connection to the market (only 15–17 percent), and the proportion of poor peasants was high. In contrast, Daniel Field's modern Gini index calculations demonstrate a lack of peasant polarization, and "[p]rovide some ammunition for those historians who emphasize the weight of the dead hand of the past on prerevolutionary Russian villages and give little encouragement to those who emphasize the burgeoning of capitalism" (Field, 1989, 502).

This polarization of viewpoints is perhaps surprising, but the various interpretations are linked to particular political agendas.[22] Gregory (1994) also questions the broadly accepted view of the negative role of the traditional village community. Unlike in other parts of Europe (with the exception of the Balkans), the Russian medieval village community, the *obshchina*, survived and preserved the medieval form of community life, including communal work and egalitarian distribution. Moreover, fourfifths of peasant land in European Russia belonged to the community, and the *obshchina* regularly redistributed the land in equal parcels among its members. The paucity or the very limited nature of peasant ownership and private property hindered agricultural investment to improve and mechanize. The egalitarian policies of the Russian village community even hindered the development of the *kustar* industry in the 1840s, for it prohibited the introduction of machines in cottage industry. When its proscriptions were ignored, the *obshchina* levied a special tax on machines (500–1,000 rubles per machine), which undermined the competitiveness of mechanized cottage industry (Gestwa, 1999, 384–5).

The community also limited the free movement of the peasantry, because taxes and other fees had to be paid collectively. Fewer members would increase the per capita burden. Free movement was not allowed in despotic Russia, and peasants had to pay a fee to obtain a passport to travel within the country. The community controlled the issuing of passports and allowed people to leave only if they paid their part of the common debt. Only some 10 percent of peasant households had created independent farms by 1915, but just 25 percent of those farms had fully departed from the village (Barnett, 2004, 37).

Redistribution of land was re-regulated only in 1893, when the government limited redistribution to every twelve years. This change took place only a few years before Stolypin abolished the *obshchina* in 1906. According to Gregory, however, the "internal migration of the Russian population after 1861 prove[s] that the commune's hold on departing family members was weak ... and did not prevent the settlement of a vast frontier ... The Russian commune was probably much more flexible in its actual working arrangements then its formal rules suggest" (Gregory, 1994, 51–2). This is certainly an exaggeration. The reality was much more complex and nuanced. In 1882, N. K. Bunge established the Peasant Land Bank to assist the purchasing of land. Gentry (*dvoryanstvo*) landholding sharply declined from 85.1 million to 39.0 million desyatins between 1863 and 1905. Half of the gentry lost their land. "The main land buyers were the peasantry" (Munting, 1992, 26). In reality, peasants became more mobile because entire families could not sustain themselves on the land, and some family members had to work outside the village to help pay taxes and other fees. Young males were compelled to work on the big estates, at construction sites, or even in industry to help make ends meet. Jeffrey Burds (1998) substantiates that more passports were issued close to the central industrial region than in more remote areas.[23] More importantly, the "overwhelming majority of passports were short-term." Between 1890 and 1896, nearly half the passports in European Russia were issued for three months, 27 percent for six months, and only 24 percent for a whole year (Burds, 1998, 21, 59). The village community thus issued millions of passports for temporary workers.[24]

However, the argument that the issuing of large numbers of passports to peasants is proof of a more flexible community policy and a greater freedom of movement is not convincing. Likewise, the settling of frontiers with millions of peasants does not diminish the fact that the *obshchina's* role was indeed negative. State peasants, comprising 40 percent of Russia's peasantry, had the right to move freely, and this may partly explain the possibility of internal migration. The extremely rapid fourfold population growth in the nineteenth century, and the population's uniquely limited emigration to other continents (minorities excluded), may easily explain why those who could not find work at home were allowed to settle on the frontiers. The regime tended to allow migration to Siberia from certain parts of the empire, for instance, from western provinces with high concentrations of national minorities. In addition, some 5 percent of the settlers were deported criminals and political convicts.

The traditional view that overtaxation of the peasantry forced it to sell grain for exports and accumulate money on behalf of the government for industrialization – Gerschenkron's main argument – is also vigorously challenged by the new literature.

Several authors doubt that there was overtaxation. The tax reform of 1885–6 drastically decreased taxes and increased indirect taxation, which became the main source of state revenues; this eased the peasants' onerous tax burdens during the first two decades after the reform. However, direct and indirect taxes increased significantly between 1861 and 1913 – growing by nearly five times and more than eight times, respectively. The per capita tax burden in constant prices more than doubled (Kahan, 1989, 62). Were the peasants overtaxed? Paul Gregory suggests not. "Peasants could not be forced by direct taxes to market output against their wishes," he assures us (Gregory, 1994, 46).

Nevertheless, contemporary documents quite convincingly suggest the opposite. As Minister of Finance Vyshnegradsky declared in the late nineteenth century, "We may go hungry, but we will export!" (Blackwell, 1982, 26). When Sergei Witte addressed the issue at a March 17, 1899 ministerial conference presided over by Tsar Nicholas II, he pointed out that "per capita consumption in Russia stood at only one-fourth to one-fifth of what was considered the minimum of Western Europe" (Laue, 1969, 185, 220–1).[25]

In a March 1901 article, The Economist predated Gerschenkron's argument: the fact that the Russian "government [is] eager to be up with the West has forced on an industrial development which has done much to break up Russian life and sow the seed of discontent" (quoted in Laue, 1969, 231).[26]

Russian agriculture, however, was not stagnant. Land reform, which had begun in the 1830s and had received a major impetus in 1861, was at last completed by 1906 with the Stolypin reform that abolished (though not entirely and immediately) the obshchina. By 1916, 2.5 million peasant farms, one-quarter of the total, legally became private property. The nobility remained in a commanding position, since the feudal institutions were abolished only in 1918. Paul Gregory and others agree that informal

Figure 12.1
Increase in
Russian grain
output and
exports,
1860–1900
(1860 = 100%)
(Khromov, 1950,
163, 408)

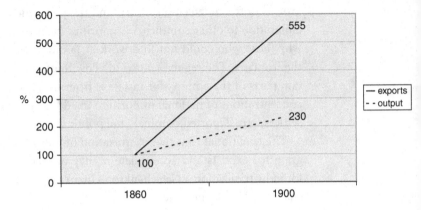

or quasi-private property rights consistently expanded, and this created a relatively fluid land market. The village commune was probably not an absolutely rigid institution, for, as new calculations show, productivity and output slowly but steadily increased in communes and private farms. One should emphasize, however, that no other country on the continent abolished its feudal institutions so late, so gradually, and so incompletely as did Russia.

Such deficiencies, however, did not hinder better cultivation. Three-quarters of European Russia's increased production was the result of higher yields, and only one-quarter came from the expansion of cultivated land. The domestic market gradually expanded and absorbed 60 percent of marketed grain, one and a half times more than exported grain. (See Figure 12.1.)

As was the case throughout Europe, various developments took place simultaneously in this enormous country, and some led to the rise of a capitalist economy and market-oriented agriculture. This was definitely true in the newly colonized Siberian region and in parts of the black-soil area. New settlers in Siberia obtained 100 desyatin (or 270 acres) of land, did not have to pay taxes for twenty years, and were exempt from military conscription for ten years. These attractive conditions led to a marked increase of cultivated land area, mostly by new settlements in previously uncultivated regions of the empire's newly expanded peripheries, such as Siberia, northern Caucasus, Transcaucasia, Central Asia, and Kazakhstan. Some 3.3 million settlers migrated eastward between 1861 and 1914, and around 4 million German peasants moved to Siberia to acquire free land and tax holidays. The population growth was also significantly more rapid in these new territories than in European Russia, at 1.8 percent instead of 1.4 percent per annum. One-third of population growth in the non-European areas was due to immigration between 1861 and 1896, and two-thirds between 1897 and 1913. The population of Siberia grew from 2.7 million in 1858 to 10.3 million by 1913.

Originally, all land in Siberia belonged to the state and 82 percent of peasants settling on crown lands rented their plots. Cultivated land increased by 75 percent between 1890 and 1914, compared with only 14 percent in European Russia.[27] A strong affluent peasant (*kulak*) layer emerged that accumulated 56 percent of the total value of peasant property (Goriushkin, 1989, 442–4). The average peasant farm comprised 3–4 hectares in the black-soil area, and 3–7 hectares in other regions. Agriculture in these peripheries was relatively free from feudal and communal restrictions.

Siberian agriculture was more advanced and dynamic than that in European Russia. Specialization reached significantly higher levels, and settlers had a more developed milk economy. The ratio of cattle to population was 42 per 100 in Siberia, compared with 17–18 per 100 in European Russia. Siberia provided 30 percent of Russia's butter exports, and 16 percent of the world's total butter exports, before World War I. Siberian farmers produced cash crops, long-fibered flax, sugar beets, fruit, and melons. The peasant economy was much more highly mechanized. The Migration Administration established a fund to assist mechanization.[28]

Modernization began slowly and gradually. Nevertheless, impoverished semi-subsistence, pre-modern peasant plots continued to exist in most parts of European Russia. Similarly, some of the big estates began to gradually transform into market-oriented, capitalist enterprises, but many more were rented out and continued to use the traditional sharecropping system without modernization. When the nobles' lands were sold, 50–60 percent of them were purchased by well-to-do, market-oriented peasants. After 1870, peasants in the black-soil area gradually replaced the three-rotation system with modern rotation. Agricultural production increased by 60 percent during the first twenty years after the reform, and grain output more than doubled between the 1860s and the war. Several scholars have concluded that Russia's per capita agricultural growth was no slower than that of the West between 1885 and 1913. Still, it continued to lag behind Russia's rapid population growth: the country's population grew by 90 percent, but per capita grain production increased by only 20 percent.[29] A sign of agricultural backwardness was the fact that, unlike most parts of Europe, Russia did not rid itself of famine prior to the war, and it suffered a severe food crisis in 1911–12.[30]

Agricultural technology changed very little in most of the big estates, and the majority of the work was carried out in a traditional way.[31] Manure and especially artificial fertilizer were rarely used. Russia used

Table 12.1 Grain output and exports in Russia between the
1860s and 1910s

	Output 1860s=100	Exports 1860s=100
1860s[a]	100	100
1890s	205	505
1900[b]	230	555

Sources: Khromov (1950, 163, 408); Pokrovskij (1947, 317–22).
Notes:
[a] For output: 1864–6; for exports 1861–5.
[b] For output: 1906–10; for exports 1896–1900.

1.3 kilograms of phosphorous fertilizer per acre of farmland, which was only one-quarter of the limited quantity employed in Hungary, 10 percent of that used in France, and a trifle compared with Germany's usage of 54 kilograms during the same period. Russian yields were only one-quarter to one-third of those in the West. Russia remained an overwhelmingly agricultural country: while the proportion of those working in agriculture declined from 89 percent in 1860 to 75 percent before the war, no less than 85 percent of the population made their living from agriculture (combined with some industrial activities). Russian agriculture remained backward at the beginning of the twentieth century, and it was made up of large swaths of semi-subsistence farms that in many ways hindered modern industrialization. Still, this limited modernization and relatively slow agricultural growth notwithstanding, Russian grain exports increased much faster than did output and consumption (rising 5 percent per annum between 1860 and 1900), and did so because of increased marketization and the expansion of cultivation in Siberia. (See Table 12.1.)

Russia exported nearly one-third of its wheat output at around the turn of the century, but only one-fifth before the war. Grain comprised one-third of Russia's exports in the early 1860s, and half at the turn of the century. The country became the largest grain exporter in the world, furnishing one-quarter of the world's grain exports that were almost entirely (98 percent) unprocessed. This surprisingly high export "surplus" was partly the result of the overtaxation of the peasantry, and partly the development of a market orientation and increased output. Contrary to previous estimates, peasant consumption did not decline, but rather increased together with expanded cultivation and slowly increasing productivity. Industrialization probably did not begin at the expense of agriculture.

The impact of the grain crisis from the 1870s

A part of the economic history literature speaks of a "Great Depression" between 1873 and 1896. Several scholars, however, have questioned the existence of such a depression. Still, there is no doubt that a severe *grain crisis* shook the grain-producing countries of the continent. The sharp rise in cheap grain imports to Europe from overseas, combined with an immense increase in Russian exports, led to the collapse of European grain prices. In time, prices plummeted by 30 percent. The decline of prices affected countries differently depending on their level of development. Some countries enhanced their agriculture with labor-saving machinery and an increased use of fertilizer, while others undertook a major structural adjustment by shifting from grain production to animal husbandry, cash crops, and other areas.[32]

The grain-producing peripheries, mostly in Central and Eastern Europe, were unable to adjust to the new market situation because the economic and cultural conditions in their societies paralyzed them. All the grain-producing countries in Southern and Eastern Europe were hit hard by the grain crisis, and all reacted in the most counterproductive way possible: they increased grain output and export for less money to counterbalance declining prices. In sharp contrast to north Italy, which reacted to the crisis by implementing structural changes, planting mulberry trees, and cultivating silkworms, southern Italy expanded its cereal cultivation, with limited specialized agricultural activity in the coastal regions (Mori, 1991, 322). Three main grain producers, Russia, Romania, and Hungary, increased their combined grain output by 225 percent between 1870 and 1913. Romania increased its output by more than three times. But expanded production only depressed prices further. Instituting structural change, partly by turning to animal husbandry and food processing, was simply not characteristic for the grain-producing peripheral countries. The combined cattle stock of Russia, Romania, Bulgaria, and Serbia increased by only some 40 percent after the 1870s.

Those countries with severe grain deficits, such as Italy and Greece, were not adversely affected. They imported cheap grain and developed new agricultural sectors. The countries of the Iberian peninsula, the least developed eastern and southern provinces of Austria-Hungary, the Balkans, and Russia fell victim to the vagaries of the world market and their own inflexibility. The grain crisis significantly weakened a great part of the European peripheries and impeded their efforts to follow the West.

Advanced industrial pockets and predominant proto-industry

Backward agricultural systems and depressed domestic markets blocked the road toward modern industrial development in Russia, Spain, Portugal, and southern Italy. Some scholars speak of an early and significant capital accumulation based on booming silk exports and abundant foreign sources. But O'Brien and Toniolo counter that Italy's "primary sector could not supply investible funds or provide rural markets required to support more rapid industrialization and urbanization" (O'Brien and Toniolo, 1994, 347).[33] Gabriel Tortella reaches the same conclusion with regard to Spain and Portugal: "Those countries that were able to import the agricultural revolution during the nineteenth century could thereby become successful ... whereas those ... unable to 'revolutionize' their agriculture remained backward. Such was the case in our Latin countries" (Tortella, 1994b, 5, 8).

One of the most important obstacles to industrialization was the limited domestic market. Income distribution was extremely unequal. In Italy, 1 percent of the population owned 40–50 percent of the wealth at around the turn of the twentieth century. Poverty was ubiquitous in the south, and the only thing that markedly increased the standard of living (by about 20 percent) was mass emigration. "Historians still largely accept Sereni's argument that insufficient domestic demand was a major obstacle to development" (Cohen and Federico, 2001, 52). Low living standards were generally characteristic of the Mediterranean world and Russia, and they curbed domestic demand, depressed domestic markets, and assured that the regions' growth would be highly dependent on exports.

The survival of large sectors of pre-modern agriculture also meant the preservation of self-sufficient peasant households and proto-industry. Cottage industry became an important supplemental source of income during the early modern period, and peasant families began producing for the market. Proto-industry was an important factor in the western half of the continent, and in some cases led to the development of the factory system and modern industrialization. In the peripheries, cottage industry was a decisive producer for domestic markets and a substitute for mechanized factory industry throughout most of the nineteenth century.

In the case of Spain, Sánchez-Albornoz speaks of "irregular, inadequate, yet preparatory changes" toward industrialization between 1830 and 1900 (Sánchez-Albornoz, 1987, 5). Proto-industry was substantial in the late eighteenth century, when 50,000 families worked in the home linen industry in rural Galicia. Castile produced wool but did not process it. All of these home industries had by the 1830s collapsed in the face of competition from the Catalan textile industry. Spain exported saltwort and produced iron sulfate in Catalonia, and one Spanish factory produced sulfuric acid. All these enterprises collapsed, however, in the 1830s. "The Spanish chemical industry started out well [but] it could not keep up with foreign competition and suffered forty-year stagnation" (Nadal, 1987, 64–5). Insignificant iron production developed in Andalusia in the 1830s–1860s, and in Asturia in the 1860s–1870s.[34] Modern, mechanized industry appeared in some isolated regions, but industrialization had not begun.

The only promising development was the Catalan cotton textile industry. Here, specialized and export-oriented agriculture strengthened domestic markets and stimulated industrial endeavors. The first Spanish Bourbon king, Philip V, embraced mercantilist policies and established royal manufactures in the woolen, glass, silk, and tapestry industries. A market-oriented cotton proto-industry emerged from the 1770s onward. The monarchy prohibited the import of textile products in the eighteenth century, and abolished duties for raw cotton imports in 1760. It also licensed cotton textile production outside the guilds, which had been restricted to Catalonia. Annual cotton imports skyrocketed from 14,245 lb in the mid-eighteenth century to 767,209 lb by the 1780s–1790s. The Royal Manufacture Spinning Company was established in Barcelona in 1773. An advanced proto-industry, based on family work and embedded in agriculture, served as the springboard for mechanization that started very early: the spinning jenny arrived in the 1780s, Arkwright machines began to be manufactured in Barcelona in 1793, and Crompton's mule was introduced in 1806–7. The Barcelona Chamber of Commerce reported in 1792 that "The progress... which has been made in the machinery for cotton during the last four years is notorious" (Thomson, 2005, 703, 717, 728). More than two decades later, the Chamber of Commerce continued to laud the flourishing proto-industry: "Even in the most remote corners of Catalonia, whole families were busily occupied with the spinning wheel, the loom and the hoe... The rise in the number of children, ordinarily viewed as a burden... was now considered a blessing" (quoted in Maluquer de Motes, 1987, 175).

A modern, mechanized textile industry grew out of the cottage cotton industry as early as the 1830s, and it became the leading industrial sector in Catalonia. Still, only 4 percent of its spindles were mechanized in 1838, and half of its weaving was carried out by hand as late as 1860. Other Spanish industries were not yet mechanized. The cotton textile industry produced for the domestic market, and most of the Catalan products were sold in Madrid and the Basque region. The Catalan wool industry also prospered, employing nearly half of the Spanish wool industry's spindles and three-quarters of its power-driven looms. In addition, furniture, paper, and publishing industries also emerged. But since its domestic market was limited, Spain's textile industry declined, and industry overall slowed down, from the early 1870s on. Between 1890 and 1913, the Spanish growth rate was the lowest in Europe. From the 1870s on, no cycles of expansion occurred comparable to that of the mid-nineteenth century (Carmona *et al.*, 1990).

As a result of a groundbreaking mining law in December 1868 that introduced modern subsoil property rights, Spain witnessed an enormous mining boom beginning in the 1870s. This development was also closely connected to the railroad boom and the inflow of foreign capital – mostly British and French investment in iron ore, lead, and copper mining. "Foreign companies exploited Spanish mining interests on a massive scale," noted Jordi Nadal (1987, 70). In 1913, 564 mining companies operated in the country, half of them in British and French hands.[35] Iron ore turned out to be the country's most important resource. Output soared from 69,000 tons in 1856 to 9.9 million tons by 1913. Spanish iron ore production comprised more than 13 percent of Europe's output between 1881 and 1913. Half of foreign investment in the Spanish mining industry came from Britain in the period 1870–1913. Spain's abundant mineral resources were mostly exported and processed in Britain and other Western countries. This was the case with almost its entire lead and copper production. Between 1861 and 1913, only some 10 percent of the country's extracted iron ore was processed at home (Anez Alvarez, 1970; Voltes Bou, 1974, 179).

Thanks to the mining boom and the export of almost all extracted raw materials, minerals became Spain's second largest export item. At the same time, however, the minerals industry evinced classic peripheral characteristics. Prados de la Escosura concludes that the core's "demand for raw materials did not foster modern economic growth in Mediterranean Europe during the nineteenth century" (Prados de la Escosura, 1987, 146). He approvingly quotes Sánchez-Albornoz's and Joseph Harrison's depiction of Spanish mining as a typical peripheral phenomenon: "the mines were converted into foreign enclaves, linked only territorially to Spain, and lacked articulation with the rest of the Spanish economy"

(Sánchez-Albornoz, 1977, 21) Indeed, Joseph Harrison equated Spain with Latin America, since both were "converted into satellites of the industrial metropolis of north-west Europe, which extracted often irreplaceable supplies of raw materials for its own use" (Harrison, 1978, 54). Spanish economic history literature has attributed Spain's slow industrial and economic growth to the foreign capital inflow and the country's massive current account deficit between 1850 and 1890.[36] However, blaming the current account deficit (i.e. the massive capital inflow) for the sluggishness or lack of modernization is baseless. As Leandro Prados de la Escosura's recent analysis aptly demonstrates,

The sustained deficit on current account over 1850–90 highlights the fact that net inflows of foreign capital made [it] possible to meet the demand for domestic investment and, thus, boosted Spanish economic performance... [There are] serious doubts on the widespread view of an external restriction to Spain's growth during the nineteenth century... Without an inflow of foreign capital – Spain would have grown [at] a slower speed. (Prados de la Escosura, 2009, 2, 27)

Although Spain's extraordinarily rich and strategically important raw material resources did not generate successful industrialization in the country, its mining and relatively well-developed transportation system created a solid base for a very late and limited industrialization process. Modern pockets of development began to emerge in two small provinces of the country a decade and a half before the war.

Accumulating income from iron ore mining and exports led to the advent of processing in Spain's Basque region.[37] Iron production rose from 46,000 tons in the early 1870s to more than 412,200 tons in the 1910s. The rise of the iron and steel industry spurred the development of coal mining in Asturia. Output dramatically increased from 300,000 tons a year in 1861 to 3.5 million tons in 1913. Spanish mines covered 60 percent of the country's consumption before the war, and imports supplied the rest.[38] Basque shipbuilding and engineering companies became the primary consumers of iron and steel, and its engineering industry began producing for the railroads. The Basque region emerged as Spain's center for heavy industry. But the country's limited success is clearly demonstrated by the fact that its iron industry produced only half of Hungary's paltry iron output.

On the other side of the country, the Catalonian textile industry began expanding again in the 1890s to supply the strongly protected domestic market;[39] no fewer than 2 million spindles were in operation in 1907.

However, the only Spanish export-oriented industry supplying the French market was cork production, with 3 million corks exported before the war. Industrial production nearly doubled in the country between the turn of the century and the war, and was concentrated in two regions: Catalonia and the Basque region, which employed 17% of the manufacturing workers in 1797, 22% in 1860, and 33% by 1910. Metallurgy, engineering, and textiles employed about 60% of the country's labor force (Rosés, 2003, 997).

Both industrial centers at the northwestern and northeastern edges of the country produced for the domestic market, and they emerged partly because of high protective tariffs introduced in 1891 and 1906. The entire central and southern parts of the country, however, remained pre-industrial and backward. "Economic historians are generally in agreement that the nineteenth century witnessed the failure of the Industrial Revolution in Spain" (Tortella, 2000, 73). Spanish industry was less developed at the beginning of the twentieth century than British or French industry was at the beginning of the nineteenth. This stark reality "justif[ies] the most drastic interpretation of the word failure, in relative terms" (Prados de la Escosura, 1988, 175). Most Spanish economic historians agree that, in the best-case scenario, a dual economy arose as the result of partial modernization. Income levels[40] roughly doubled during the nineteenth century, but they were still about a third of the European average prior to the war. In 1910, 71% of the active population worked in agriculture, which produced 53% of Spain's GDP. The industrial sector employed only 17% of the country's workforce and generated 18% of GDP. With economic growth slower than in the West, Spain's relative backwardness intensified. Its belated and very partial industrial development was not enough to elevate the Iberian peninsula to the group of semi-successful industrializers, but it did establish a few developed enclaves. Spanish industrialization per capita was only 27% of the British, 31% of the German, 62% of the Swedish, and 78% of the Hungarian (based on Prados de la Escosura, 1988, 169).

Portugal lagged even further behind Spain. The only partial progress could be seen in the textile industry, which produced for the domestic market.[41] Paul Bairoch pegs Portuguese economic growth at 0.19% per annum between 1830 and 1913 – only one-fifth the European average. What's more, annual growth actually decreased to 0.11% between 1860 and 1913, one-tenth of the European growth rate. Per capita income rose by an astonishingly slow 17% (Bairoch, 1976b, 154). The failure of industrialization was unmistakable. A former great power, Portugal had been a resplendently rich country in the early modern centuries. But it declined to the average European income level by 1830, mustered 51% of the average West European per capita income in 1870, and plummeted to an alarming 37% by 1913.[42]

The situation was not much better in south Italy. The region's most important export sector was its people. Landlessness – afflicting half of the agrarian population – and a lack of jobs generated a spectacular migration to the north and to the United States. One of the south's most important contributions to Italian economic growth was precisely its unlimited cheap labor force. Italy's average per capita GDP was 68 percent of that of Western Europe in 1913, and Calabria's and Sicily's was roughly 40 percent of those of Piedmont and Lombardy. Calabria's and Sicily's GDP was $1,000–1,100 (in 1990 value), somewhat lower than Russia's $1,488. Mining became significant: sulfur in Sicily, iron ore in Elba, and boric acid in Larderello, Tuscany (the last enjoying a worldwide monopoly). Although mining did little to establish local industry, it provided important export items for south and central Italy.

State policy for regional development was conspicuously lacking. The government embraced the concept of state support for the south only in the early twentieth century, "but the actual measures such as the special law of 1904 for Naples, were little more than token gestures" (Cohen and Federico, 2001, 28). The state-financed iron works in Pietrarsa (near Naples), the Gregorio Macry iron works at Capodimonte, and the shipbuilding industry worked mostly for local markets. The same was true for the wool industry in the Liri Valley.[43] By 1911, 64% of the active population in the north worked in industry, but only 21% did so in the south. However, agricultural employment declined to 57% by the time of unification. At the same time, 61% of the country's horsepower capacity was employed in the north, and only 17% in the south. South Italy integrated into the national economy of the united country and helped advance northern industry by providing markets for its industrial products and supplying cheap labor and agricultural produce. But partial modernization of agriculture and limited industrial activity created a number of developed pockets in south Italy's economy.

The economic history literature is divided over the origins of southern backwardness. Richard Eckaus (1961) and Luciano Cafagna ([1989] 1994a, 1994b) maintain that the south was far behind the north well before unification. But Stefano Fenoaltea argues that, while the north produced 50 percent of aggregate industrial production at the time of unification, the south produced 31 percent; hence, "in 1871 the interregional differences are less marked than in 1911." He suggests that a west–east rather than north–south differential existed in industrialization at that time. The so-called northwestern industrial triangle was not strong in 1871, but became dominant by 1911. By then, mostly just the food industry had survived in the south (Fenoaltea, 2003b, 1069–70, 1073). In Vera Zamagni's view, the north and the south of Italy followed separate paths to economic development even after unification (Zamagni, 1990, 30). Economic connections and policies serving the interests of the industrializing north led to an increasing gap between north and south (Cafagna, 1994b, 635).[44] Calculations are highly diverse. Recent figures definitely point to a broadening gap between the two parts of Italy: the south's per capita GDP was 81 percent of that of the north in 1871, but only 55 percent in 1911 (Cohen and Federico, 2001, 15). In the best case, the gap remained constant between 1861 and 1914 (Zamagni, 1978; Federico and Toniolo, 1991). Indeed, Italian tariff policy after unification hurt southern agriculture while stimulating northern industry. Monetary policy was also disadvantageous for the south and significantly increased emigration.

As in most pre-industrial societies, industrial goods were produced in peasant households in Russia. Peasant proto-industry was more pervasive there than in several Western countries, because an urban economy was virtually non-existent. Two other types of proto-industrial enterprises developed in Russia, especially in the eighteenth century. Similar to other regions with predominant big estates, the landed nobility established industrial works to process raw materials from their estates, mostly iron ore, wool, and lumber. In time, the regime would require industrial products for its army and navy, and, as in Prussia, the state compensated for the lack of private industry by establishing iron works and shipyards.

Regarding peasant home industry, contemporary and historical literature uses the term *kustar industry* in a rather broad way. It is not the same as the cottage industry or the Verlag system, but rather comprises any kind of home industrial activity. A great many endeavors were market-oriented, producing for local markets to supplement the family's income. There were hardly any families in Russia without some kind of supplemental income, for non-modernized agriculture failed to produce enough to sustain them.

In an unusual way, *kustar* proto-industry was not only an early modern phenomenon in Russia. The period when it truly flourished was the middle of the nineteenth century, especially between 1830 and 1880. Although the *kustar* industry's prosperity crested in the 1860s, it continued to predominate until the end of the century. At the time of the serfs' emancipation, 500,000 to 1 million people worked in the *kustar* textile industry. The exact number of *kustar* peasant-industrial workers, however, is unknown, and estimates vary between 1.5 million and 15 million. According to some studies, the *kustar* industry employed 63 percent of Russia's industrial workers and produced 34 percent of its output.

Between 1865 and 1890, the number of various kinds of *kustar* industrialists increased by 150 percent, compared with only a 60 percent rise in factory workers. The most important proto-industrial centers emerged in Ivanovo, the "Russian Manchester," and Pavlovo, "the Russian Sheffield," in the central industrial region. The first major industrial center was the Moscow region, an area of 160,000 square kilometers incorporating Tula (in the south), Nizhniy Novgorod (in the east), Rybinsk (in the north), and Tver (in the west). In the Ivanovo textile industry, some 8,000 affluent peasants created a pervasive putting-out system. In Pavlovo, more than two-thirds of the households produced small iron products in 1912. The share of industrial home workers in this area remained 75 percent, compared with 25 percent factory workers at the turn of the century.[45] Uniquely, the *kustar* industry became the main path to industrialization in some regions, especially Ivanovo. When debating the Russian Populists (*narodniks*), Vladimir Lenin used *zemstvo* (local council) statistics to argue that Russia was developing a capitalist economy because the *kustar* industry had served as the cradle of capitalism. Indeed, a serf-peasant industrialist, Ivan Morozov, became the greatest industrialist, and his family's Nikolskaya Company the second largest factory, of turn-of-the-century Russia. The big Orekhovo-Zuevo and Ivanovo-Voznesensk textile centers emerged from peasant industry. In both cases, mechanization began in the 1860s.[46] In the small iron industry of Pavlovo, the *Verlag* and *Kauf* systems continued to predominate until World War I. Gestwa (1999) speaks of the "mono-structural" nature of these rising industrial regions, because the growing textile industry did not initiate the development of supplier industries. Tools and machines (often used) were imported from the West. By 1890, much of the machinery park was already forty years old. Animal- and water-generated power remained competitive with steam as late as the turn of the century. In 1908, steam engines were often heated with wood and charcoal. Factory workers continued to work as agricultural laborers, with a third of them never appearing in the factories during the summer months. Skilled workers had to be "imported" from the West with salaries ten times higher than what local workers earned. Various industrial forms coexisted in Russia, and the success of the village-centered pre-modern peasant industry was the result of a dearth of urban-burgher development (Gestwa, 1999; Gatrell, 1986; Crisp, 1976; Lenin, [1899] 1956).

Most *kustar* industry, however, was not a stepping stone to modern industrialization but was integrated into the traditional social-economic environment. Gatrell speaks of the "parallel trends in industrial activity"

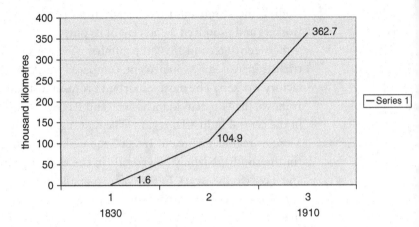

Figure 12.2 The growth of the European railroad network, 1830–1910 (in thousand kilometers) (Wojtinsky, 1927, 34–5)

when *kustar* and factory industries remained complementary, and small-scale industry played a prominent role until the war (Gatrell, 1986, 155). In contrast to Lenin, Tugan-Baranovsky, the leading Russian economist of the time, considered the *kustar* industry a dead-end road, a remnant of the pre-industrial age. Gestwa suggests that the peasant-bourgeoisie was an "ersatz" (artificial substitute) middle class (Gestwa, 1999, 591). The leading branch of textiles in manorial enterprises was the woolen industry. Landowners used their own raw materials and free serf labor in such industry[47] – as did state industry, for serfs were employed in state-owned factories.[48]

The turning point in Russian industrialization was connected to the railroads. Between 1860 and 1913, this enormous country built 70,000 kilometers of lines, the second largest network in the world. (See Figure 12.2 and Table 12.2.) From the 1860s on, railroads generated an insatiable demand for iron, which was initially covered by imports that had increased by thirty times between the 1850s and the late 1870s. The value of imported machinery grew by seven times: 80% of locomotives, 94% of freight cars, and 82% of railway carriages had to be imported, as did rails and even screws. Altogether, only 40% of railroad construction and operation was covered by domestic production even in the late 1870s.

In the late nineteenth century, however, protective tariffs and a ban on imports of railroad equipment created an enormous market for the domestic iron, steel, and engineering industries. The government began promoting industrialization, including attracting foreign investment, as a result of military considerations and great power ambitions. British, French, and German investors competed with one other for lucrative investment contracts and credits on the Russian markets. A massive amount of foreign

Table 12.2 Railroads in the Iberian region and Russia, 1911

	Area per 1 km of railroad (km²)	Length of railroads per 100,000 inhabitants (km)	Weight of freight per inhabitant (thousand km)	Number of journeys per inhabitant per year
Spain	34.14	74.2	1.46	2.5
Portugal	31.16	48.1	0.81	2.5
Russia	324.16	42.3	1.47	1.3
Average (unweighted)	**129.82**	**54.9**	**1.24**	**2.1**
Western Europe	**10.14**	**90.2**	**8.18**	**21.9**

Source: Berend and Ránki (1982, 100).

capital flooded the country from the 1890s on.[49] One-quarter of imported capital was invested in joint-stock companies. Forty-four percent of total investments were channeled into the mining and iron industries in 1890, rising to 54% in 1900; 12% had been earmarked for engineering in 1890, only to double to 24% ten years later. Half of industrial investment originated abroad between 1904 and 1908. In 1900, 45% of Russian industry's capital was in foreign hands – including 71–72% of the mining, metallurgy, and engineering industries, 31% of the chemical industry, and 20% of the textile industry. Foreign control of Russian industry decreased somewhat to 41% by 1914, and it dropped in the key sectors of heavy industry to 63%. Although domestic investors supplied 60% of new industrial investment in the early twentieth century, the 40% foreign share was still significant. During the industrialization era of 1885–1913, concludes Paul Gregory, "Russian growth was high by international standards... During the last thirty years of the Russian empire... economic growth was more rapid than western Europe's, but the rapid population growth held per capita growth to the west European averages" (Gregory, 1994, 26, 36). Western industrial output increased by 2.7% per year between 1870 and 1913, while Russian output, beginning from a much lower base, rose by 3.25%. Industrialization took off from the 1880s on. Between 1900 and 1913, Russian coal production increased from 1,003 million to 2,214 million puds,[50] pig iron from 177 million to 283 million, and steel output from 163 to 247 million.

As in the Basque and Catalan regions of Spain, certain parts of European Russia saw belated but important progress in industrialization. Enclaves of advanced industry emerged in the Donets Basin, around St. Petersburg, and Moscow. Foreign investment financed the impressive development of the iron and steel industries in the Donets region, where abundant coal and iron ore reserves were discovered. The traditional and obsolete iron industry in the Urals lost its importance, and its share of iron production decreased from 66% to 28% between 1870 and 1900. The new Donets industrial center, which had produced only 1.4% of pig iron in 1870, predominated with 52% of output by 1890. The 1891 protective tariffs and the regime's banning of imports for railroads increased both iron ore and pig iron production by leaps and bounds. Iron ore extraction increased eightfold, and iron output rose by more than eightfold over a thirty-year period, most dramatically during the 1890s. Massive foreign investment targeted the coal and iron industries. The Donets region became the center of interest, attracting 40–45% of foreign investors (Bovikin, 1967, 35–6; 1973, 99–135).

The cotton industry had long been connected to the peasant *kustar* industry. A home-based modern textile industry developed in the Moscow region. In contrast to the coal and iron industries, which were highly dependent on foreign investment, the cotton industry had strong local roots, as even its most prominent magnates (such as Ivan Morozov) had peasant backgrounds. Still, prior to World War I, one-fifth of the textile industry's capital originated abroad. Textiles employed nearly 400,000 workers around the turn of the century, and reached an annual 8 percent growth rate in the 1890s.[51]

Oil extraction began in the 1870s in the Baku region. By the end of the century, Russia produced half of the world's oil output. Foreign investors including the Swedish Nobel Company, the Deutsche Bank, the Rothschilds, and the Royal Dutch Shell Company played crucial roles in extraction and transportation. The transcaucasian railroad linked the oil fields to the sea in 1883. The oil industry's relative importance, however, would prove to be transitory: producing nearly 7 percent of Russian exports in 1900, it dropped to hardly more than 2 percent by 1912.

Between 1900 and 1913, a genuine industrialization boom exploded in Russia. In that short period of time, iron and steel production increased by 50–60 percent, and coal output, the number of cotton spindles, sugar production, and, indeed, industrial output in general all doubled. Prior to the war, food processing and textiles both comprised more than 28 percent of Russia's industrial production, and iron, engineering, and oil industries made up over 32 percent. The chemical industry remained insignificant

(1.9 percent of total industrial production), as did other consumer goods industries such as leather, paper, and lumber.

The "sleeping Russian giant," frozen in an *ancien régime* for a century after Britain's Industrial Revolution and a half-century after that in Western Europe, finally woke up. Industrialization took off and created a number of advanced industrial centers. Paul Gregory, for one, has overemphasized this progress. He speaks of Russia as a "major economic power," fourth or fifth in the world economy, and roughly equal to Britain, bigger than France, and twice the size of Austria-Hungary in gross GDP. "Given Russia's large population," he argues, "exceptionally low per capita levels would be required to prevent Russia from being one of the world's major economic powers" (Gregory, 1994, 17). Comparing gross GDP rather than per capita GDP, however, makes little sense.

Except for the Donets region, St. Petersburg, and Moscow, Russia did not enter the age of modern industry. This was also indicated by the crucially important roles the Polish, Finnish, and Baltic industries played in supplying this vast, backward empire (discussed in Chapter 11). Its above-mentioned achievements notwithstanding, the Russian industrial sector remained highly backward. Mechanization was still in its infancy, averaging 1.6 horsepower per 100 inhabitants, hardly more than a tenth of the German and 6 percent of the British rate. Steel output was 63 tons per 100 inhabitant, less than north Italy's. The value of industrial production lagged at less than $9 per head, only a third of the Italian and Austro-Hungarian levels. In 1913, as much as 72% of the Russian labor force continued to work in agriculture, and only 18% in industry. Although the country's per capita GDP increased by 45% between 1870 and 1913, it remained significantly behind West European development and, indeed, was even more so as time went on: Russia's per capita GDP was 48% of the Western level in 1870, but only 40% in 1913. Russia remained an unindustrialized, overwhelmingly agricultural country with low levels of productivity and a mostly illiterate population – one of the most backward countries of Europe. Modernization and industrialization unquestionably failed, though isolated pockets of advanced modern industry and efficient agriculture emerged. The per capita industrialization level index of the region was only one-third that of the West. (See Tables 12.3 and 12.4.)

Based on Angus Maddison's calculations, the Mediterranean region (including south Italy) and Russia made only modest progress in the nineteenth century. Their combined per capita GDP increased by 88 percent from $905 to $1,699 between 1820 and 1913. In this respect, it is important to note that the rate of population growth exceeded the rate of

Table 12.3 Per capita levels of industrialization in the Iberian region and Russia, 1800–1913, compared with the West and the European average

	1800	1860	1913	% of West in 1913
Portugal	7	8	14	25
Spain	7	11	22	40
Russia	6	8	20	36
Regional average	6.7	9	18.7	34
Advanced West	8	16	55	–
European average	8	17	45	82

Source: Bairoch (1991, 3).

Table 12.4 The index of the development of the leading iron and textile industries, 1830–1910 (iron production per capita and cotton consumption per capita in kilograms)

	Iron			Cotton		
	1830	1860	1910	1830	1860	1910
Portugal	–	–	–	0.1	0.5	2.8
Spain	1.5	3.2	20.1	0.3	1.3	4.2
Russia	2.9	3.5	20.5	0.1	0.5	2.1
Regional average	2.0	3.4	20.3	0.2	0.8	3.0
Western average	6.0	19.9	100.4	0.7	2.5	6.3
Region as % of West	33	17	20	29	32	48

Source: Bairoch (1991, 8).

income growth. In 1820, the number of inhabitants of the Russian and Mediterranean regions was 75.9 million; by 1913, it had increased by 265 percent to 201.0 million. These regions' per capita income was 70 percent that of Western Europe in 1820, but only 46 percent in 1913. The gap had dramatically widened (Maddison, 1995). (See Figure 12.3 and Table 12.5.)

Table 12.5 The development of GDP per capita in the Iberian region and Russia, 1820–1913

	1820	1870	1900	1913
Spain	1,063	1,376	2,040	2,255
Portugal	–	1,085	1,408	1,354
Russia	751	1,023	1,218	1,488
Average (unweighted)	**907**	**1,161**	**1,555**	**1,699**
Western Europe (seven countries)	1,372	2,337	3,456	4,013
The region as % of Western Europe	**66**	**50**	**45**	**42**

Source: Maddison (1995, 198, 200).

Figure 12.3
Russian and
Mediterranean
GDP per capita
combined,
compared with
the West,
1820–1910
(Maddison,
1995, 200)

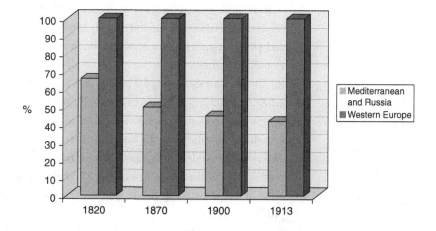

The comparison between the Mediterranean and Scandinavian regions is very telling. Based on real wages, the Mediterranean region had a per capita GDP that was 60% that of Scandinavia in 1850, but it achieved only 0.9% annual growth between 1850 and 1913, compared with Scandinavia's 1.29%. In the crucial period between 1870 and 1913, the West European growth rate was 1.14% per year, but Scandinavia's reached 1.36% – enabling this previously backward region to join the "convergence club." Scandinavia substantially increased its per capita GDP from 74% of the West European income level to 82%. In the same period, the Mediterranean annual growth rate was only 0.85%, less than Western Europe's and Scandinavia's, and it declined from 50% of the Western European level to 42% (Reis, 2000, 28, 32, 34; Foreman-Peck and Lains, 2000, 76, 78). Even though they had managed a late start in agricultural and industrial development, Russia and the Mediterranean region lagged even further behind in 1913 than they had a half-century before.

Notes

1. In 1901–10, wheat yields were 9 quintals per hectare in Spain, 5.9 in Portugal, and 9.5 in Italy – in contrast to 13.6 in France, 19.7 in Germany, and 22.1 quintals in Britain (Tortella, 2000, 66).

2. Regional differences were startling. Central, western, and northwestern Spain significantly increased their share of the agricultural population during the century. Galicia, Asturias, Castile y León, and Extremadura increased, in an unprecedented way, their agricultural employment from 72.3 percent to 82.2 percent between 1800 and 1900.

3. Vineyards, mostly in Andalusia, Valencia, and Catalonia, covered 0.4 million hectares in 1800, and this rose to 1.7 million by 1890. Wine production jumped from 3.9 million hectoliters in 1800 to 10.8 and 21.6 million by 1860 and 1900, respectively. Having stagnated at roughly 1 million hectoliters during the 1860s and 1870s, exports grew to nearly 6 million by 1880, and then to more than 11 million by 1890.

4. In Valencia and Castellon, the landed area for citrus groves increased from 4,700 to 24,200 hectares between 1878 and 1904, by 6.5 percent per year. Local landowners and foreign merchants controlled the Valencia citrus industry and introduced irrigation and the use of fertilizer.

5. The areas' 60 and 70 inhabitants per square kilometer, respectively, were markedly above the Spanish average of 37 inhabitants per square kilometer.

6. Nine of the ten leading export goods in Spain in 1850 were agricultural products.

7. Primitive grain cultivation characterized Portugal as well. Three-quarters of the land was used for grain. Seventy percent of the peasants cultivated small parcels and were unable to market their crops. They earned only 10 percent of the agricultural revenues. Cereal output per capita reached the highest level in the mid-nineteenth century. "The last thirty years of the century may then be aptly described as an age of crisis for Portuguese agriculture . . . [that] failed to modernize in the eighteenth and again in the nineteenth centuries" (Pedreira, 1991, 353). The only exception in Portugal's stagnating agriculture was the traditional grape and wine economy. The landed area and the wine production rapidly increased, particularly from the middle of the century onward. Wine exports quadrupled between 1870 and 1886. Prior to 1870, the special port wine comprised 70% of wine exports, but this declined to 25% by 1885. While wine exports were 80% greater in the mid-1890s than they were in 1870, their value increased only by 10%.

8. In Sicily, a British protectorate at the time, the noble parliament abolished feudal institutions in 1812. Ferdinand I retained the abolition after the Bourbon restoration in the Kingdom of Naples in 1815.

9. In 1860, 94 percent of landed peasants possessed mini-parcels with an average size of 1.5 hectares on nearly 40 percent of the landed area.

10. A parliamentary investigation of 500 estates between 1908 and 1910 determined that only 33 had modern machinery, mostly steam threshers. Yields from the intensive northern cultivation, including rice production, were twice as high as in the south.

11. Evidence of continued subsistence agriculture is provided by the fact that the value of trade per inhabitant in the Two Sicilies was less than half that in Piedmont, Lombardy, and Parma-Modena at the time of unification.

12. "Revisionist" views have reevaluated the *latifondi* as "a rational response to a hostile environment, highly variable yields and poor communication" (Cohen and Federico, 2001, 38).

13. The literacy gap between the north and south was 46:26.

14. Fruit totaled 454 quintals in 1862 and 4.3 million quintals in 1913.

15. As Immanuel Wallerstein noted (1974, 68), Russia was not part of the emerging international economic system before the nineteenth century. "In the course of the renewed economic expansion . . . of the period 1733–1817 . . . the European world-economy broke the bounds . . . and began to incorporate vast new zones into the effective division of labor . . . most importantly . . . the Ottoman Empire [and] the Russian Empire" (Wallerstein, 1989, 129).

16. Twenty-five percent of peasant land was cut off and incorporated into the big estates in twenty-one provinces of the best black-soil area, and 10 percent in fifteen other provinces. Roughly 15–20 percent of the peasantry was emancipated without land.

17. Emancipated peasants temporarily had to work for forty days a year and pay high compensation – a total of 2 billion rubles – to take possession of their land.

18. In the early nineteenth century, grain yields exceeded the quantity of sown seeds by three times, and the ratio was still 3.4:1 between 1840 and 1860.

19. Between 1771 and 1773, a great part of the huge country was rocked by the formidable Pugachev uprising. Between 1826 and 1861, 1,185 local or provincial uprisings broke out, with peasants refusing to work, occupying land, killing landlords, and burning mansions.

20. V. I. Lenin heralded the spread of peasant *kustar* industry as proof of the capitalist transformation of Russia. In reality, it led to the rise of modern industry only sporadically, mostly in the Ivanovo and Pavlovo regions. In most parts of the country, the *kustar* was not a stepping stone towards modern

industry, but was rather an inseparable part of peasant household economy. The home industry was crucial to the peasants' survival in several regions, where only 50 percent of peasant income came from agriculture (Kovalchenko, 1989, 459).

21. These data described 20,000 recruits from a more developed region. Any generalization for Russia as a whole is impossible because of the major regional differences.

22. Peter Gatrell differentiates three political approaches to evaluating the tsarist economy since the turn of the twentieth century: liberal, populist (*narodnik*), and Marxist (Gatrell, 1986, xiv–xvi). Since nationwide statistics are missing or scattered, each camp was able to pinpoint regional facts and documents to prove their theories by generalizing from provincial statistical data. This is possible because of the major differences among various regions. Although Paul Gregory's recent challenge is based on modern quantitative methods (cliometrics), he also has a political agenda that is clearly expressed in the introductory chapter of his 1994 book.

23. In 1896, 30–40 percent of adult males living near Moscow and in six surrounding provinces obtained passports and worked outside their villages, while only three passports were issued for every hundred villagers in certain peripheral provinces of European Russia.

24. In his study, *Russkoe bogatsvo* (1898), A. V. Peshekhonov speaks of peasants as "disguised workers," or combined peasant-workers when, in a usual peasant family, some members became workers outside the family (Perrie, 1992, 69, 77).

25. Taxation, he declared in his annual report in 1901, "rests undoubtedly upon the agricultural masses, seriously impairing their purchasing power." He describes an agricultural crisis that exhausted "the paying powers of the population."

26. To illustrate how controversial the "overburden" issue is, allow me to borrow the conclusion of Evsey Domar's sarcastic short article on a similar debate: "Were the peasants overcharged for their land? They most probably were. Perhaps they were overcharged much more than anyone has ever suggested. And perhaps much less, or not at all" (Domar, 1989, 437).

27. Consequently, the acreage of arable land, which had hardly changed during the first half of the century and had totaled 82.5 million hectares in the 1850s, rapidly increased to 113.4 million hectares by 1913.

28. Around the turn of the century, eighteen agricultural machinery firms had marketing offices in Siberia, and a quarter of the machines marketed in Russia were sold in that region (Wood, 1991, 143–9).

29. The animal stock exhibited very moderate growth: cattle, horse, and pig stocks increased by 38, 45, and 21 percent, respectively.

30. During this crisis, four-fifths of the farms in Tobolsk Province were auctioned off, and one-third to one-half of the cattle and horses were slaughtered (Goriushkin, 1989, 447).

31. A third of the plows continued to consist of primitive wooden tools, and another third were wooden tools with iron parts. A total of 27,000 steam threshers were in operation in Russia's 12 million estates.

32. Countries with advanced Western agriculture responded immediately and in manifold ways. First, agricultural growth significantly slowed down, dropping in Germany from an annual 2.3 percent between 1850 and 1864 to 1.1 percent between 1864 and 1881. Farmers in the west and south, and Junkers in the east demanded protective tariffs that Bismarck introduced in 1878–9. Meat imports were drastically restricted in 1900, and radical tariff increases followed in 1906: grain tariffs jumped from 28–35 to 50 marks per ton, oxen tariffs from 25 to 40 marks per head, and cattle tariffs from 9 to 32 marks per head.

    The most advanced West European agriculture was able to adjust to the situation by increased productivity and the replacement of grain production with intensive cultures, specialized production, and processing. Some countries (besides the ones that had already done so) began to import grain and even profited from the low prices. Britain, the Netherlands, and Denmark all followed this pattern. Dutch farmers expanded their horticultural activity, used twice as much fertilizer as they did before, and increased their animal stock. Denmark radically restructured its agriculture, abolished the grain economy, and turned to animal husbandry and food processing. Germany expanded sugar beet and root crop cultivation. Arable yields rapidly increased, the use of fertilizers nearly doubled, and grain yields increased by 20–25 percent in the brief period between the turn of the century and the war. Pig and cattle stock rose by 71 percent and 11 percent, respectively, during the two decades after 1873.

33. "Many scholars argue that the lack of capital . . . acted as a serious constraint on industrialization. The argument is at best debatable" (Cohen and Federico, 2001, 56).

34. The first charcoal furnace was built in 1832, and the first coke-heated furnace only in 1865. During the first half of the 1880s, Spain produced 8 kilograms of cast iron per capita, which was only 80 percent of Hungary's production, 6.4 percent of that of France, and 0.1 percent of Belgium's.

35. Lead production increased by 40 percent, and copper output by more than thirteen times, between the 1860s and 1913. Spanish mines produced 20 percent of the world's lead bar output and 38% of the European. Pure copper extraction reached 3.2 million tons in 1913, and comprised 10% of the world output, and 51% of the European.

36. According to J. Vicens Vives, the persistent deficit was a heavy burden that contributed to the Restoration regime's economic failure from the mid-1870s on (Vicens Vives, 1953). A. P. Thirlwall spoke of an "external constraint on growth" (Thirlwall, 1979).

37. In 1882, the Sociedad de Altos Hornos y Fábricas de Hierro y Acero de Bilbao opened its modern Siemens–Martin works. At nearly the same time, the Metalurgia y Construcción La Vizcaya and a third metallurgical company began producing iron and steel. Within a few years, the three companies merged. Three new mills were opened in 1890, 1891, and 1892.

38. In the early twentieth century, however, two hydroelectric power stations were also built in the Basque region. By 1913, with 300,000 horsepower capacity, the country produced 62 million kWh of electric energy.

39. Cotton imports increased from 17,000 tons in the 1860s to 90,000 tons in the 1910s, and were processed mostly in Barcelona.

40. The former colonial empire was one of the wealthiest in Europe a few centuries earlier, and its income was close to the European average as late as 1860.

41. By 1910, mostly small-scale industry employed 100,000 workers, and altogether twenty-five industrial firms operated with more than 500 employees. The demand for industrial goods was met with increased imports, financed from wine exports. Because of decreasing exports and increasing import prices, the terms of trade declined by 30 percent, and the country racked up a huge trade deficit.

42. According to Jorge Pedreira, the country was more backward than Spain and "displayed a pattern that could more rightly be compared to Italy's Mezzogiorno... Dualism between North and South, as well as between litoral and hinterland, was marked" (Pedreira, 1991, 355–6).

43. The silk industry in Sicily and Calabria, and the cotton industry that had been established by Swiss entrepreneurs, had already emerged before unification, but they did not change the agricultural character of south Italy. Before the unification of the country, strong protectionism led to the emergence of more advanced industrial pockets (in mechanical engineering and other fields) around Naples.

44. Southern literature has often interpreted unification as a northern invasion and seen the unified state as northern exploitation of the south. Consequently, it blamed the north for the development gap in unified Italy, maintaining that the southern level had been roughly the same as the north's in 1860, but plunged after unification thanks to deliberate northern policies (Davis, 2000).

45. The center of the shoe proto-industry was concentrated in the Tver region, the silk industry in Bogorodsk and Bronnicy, toy production in Dmitrov, linen in the Jaroslav region, leatherwear in Bogorodsk, the pin industry around

Nizhniy-Novgorod, and icon painting in the Vladimir region. In Russian Bessarabia, where the average peasant plot was 4.5 acres, *kustar* carpet making was prevalent among large families between later October and early April and was their most important source of income (Wright, 1991).

46. One of the entrepreneurs, Jakov Garelin, reported the spread of the power loom in the Ivanovo textile industry in 1884. In 1860 48 percent of calico production in Ivanovo was already made in mechanized works. The mechanization of various procedures was gradual, and, in most cases, was completed only in the 1890s.

47. The traditional feudal landlord-owned iron industry that used serf labor in the Urals, and the similar sugar and distillery industries in the big estates, remained important in Russia until the 1860s. Their modernization and mechanization was a slow and partial process. The sugar industry was also located on the big estates and used serf labor. Half of the country's 95,000 industrial workers were serfs in 1804, but only 15 percent of its 565,000 workers by 1860.

48. Peter the Great began industrialization to supply his army in the war against Sweden. He founded two industrial centers, one in the newly built capital, St. Petersburg, and one in the Urals, where he established twelve iron mills. By the end of the eighteenth century, 165 iron mills were in operation in the Urals.

49. Totaling 2,662 million rubles in 1881, and 7,634 million rubles by 1914.

50. Traditional Russian measure. 1 pud = 16.38 kilograms, or 36.11 pounds.

51. Cotton consumption increased by more than twenty times between 1870 and 1910, the number of spindles more than quadrupled from 2 million to 8.3 million, and the number of looms rose from 87,000 to 213,000.

CHAPTER 13

The predator Leviathan in peasant societies: the Balkans and the borderlands of Austria-Hungary

As discussed in Chapter 11, a part of the peripheral regions, such as Finland, Ireland, the Baltic countries, Poland, and Hungary, began to undergo a Western-type transformation from the 1860s and 1870s on. The Mediterranean region and Russia began to do so in the 1890s (see Chapter 12). In the relatively homogeneous geographical region of the Balkan peninsula, and the connected easternmost and southernmost provinces of Austria-Hungary (such as Galicia, Bukovina, Bosnia-Herzegovina, and Dalmatia), the first tentative steps of modernization were taken, if at all, in the early twentieth century, but were stopped by the Balkan wars. This region failed to industrialize.

Pre-modern agriculture – return to a grain economy

The Balkan region became part of the Ottoman Empire in the late fourteenth and early fifteenth century. The empire preserved an unchanging non-European land tenure system, without private property. The Balkan population became serfs of the autocratic, militarily organized Ottoman state.[1] This perpetuated an entirely peasant society that was almost totally illiterate, lacked a local elite, and was bounded by the ancient village communities, the *zadruga*, or three-generation families. At times sixty to eighty members of these extended families lived under one roof and worked together. During its "golden age," the Ottoman Empire made certain positive contributions to Balkan agricultural development. But during the long period of Ottoman decline, and especially during the eighteenth and nineteenth centuries, the central government disintegrated and was replaced by local Ottoman warlords and unruly Janissary hordes, which tyrannized and looted the peninsula. The decentralized Ottoman state became a predatory Leviathan that provided nothing to, but systematically ravaged, its subjugated populace. People escaped from the lowlands,

Box 13.1   Backwardness and illiteracy: the Balkans and the borderlands of Austria-Hungary

Among the causes of the failure of industrialization and modern economic transformation in the Balkans and the borderlands of Austria-Hungary, one cannot ignore the dearth of human capital thanks to, among other things, the continued pervasiveness of illiteracy until World War I. Education virtually did not exist in the region before the 1850s or 1860s. Prior to an 1864 Romanian law mandating compulsory four-year elementary education in the country, roughly 90–95 percent of the Romanian population was illiterate. At that time there was not a single elementary school in all of Moldavia. In Bulgaria, the first girls' school was opened in 1857. Two British travelers visited schools in Serbia in the 1860s and observed students learning to

read Serbian and Old-Slavonic, and write a little. "That is all that we can teach them," explains the teacher, "for it is all we know ourselves . . . " [In another school, none of the students could read or write. The British visitors asked,] "then what is it that you learn there?" "To say our prayers" . . . "Can you understand these prayers?" "No." (Mackenzie and Irby 1877, 277, 279, 404)

Introduction of compulsory elementary education did not radically improve educational levels. Parents refrained from sending their children to school in the backward countryside. In early twentieth-century Habsburg Dalmatia, Bukovina, and Bosnia-Herzegovina, 67%, 36%, and 15% of school-age children attended school, respectively. In Galicia, nearly 70% of school-age children failed to attend school, and almost 60% of the population was still illiterate in 1910. In 1900 60% of Romania's school-age generation were not enrolled in school, though the number dropped to 40% in 1909. At the turn of the twentieth century, only 11% of Romania's rural and 40% of its urban population was literate.

Elementary school education was rare in Bulgaria, where half the children did not attend schools and illiteracy remained at 72% before World War I. Elementary education was thus considered to be a high level of training. Luben Karavelov, one of the very first Bulgarian writers, depicts his protagonist, Hadji Gencho, delaying a decision by saying, "I must ask Naiden, you know, [he] is a learned and clever man – seven years he has studied" (Colombo and Roussanoff, 1976, 69).

Mass illiteracy was not evenly divided between the male and female population. The female half remained almost entirely illiterate. Of the

27% of Romanian school-age children enrolled in schools in the late nineteenth century, only 13% were girls, that is, only 3% of all Romanian girls. Female illiteracy at the turn of the century remained nearly absolute: only 3% of the rural and 7% of the total female population could read and write (Ronnas, 1984, 227–32).

Social traditions rejected the concept of female education. In her pamphlet "The Need for Women's Education" in 1898, Elena Maróthy Soltésova, a Slovak feminist writer, describes the mentality of the male population in Slovakia (at that time the northern part of the Hungarian kingdom):

The majority [of middle-class men] only want their wife to be beautiful... They require her to have only social skill... [The lower class] group of men believe that a woman exists... for her material use... Any sort of education... is a disadvantage, not a benefit... a husband is the ready-made enemy of his wife's education through his conviction that it leads her away from her duty. (Soltésova, [1898] 1991, 134–6)

Still, the Slovak minority in northern Hungary was in a somewhat better situation than were their Galician or Bosnian counterparts.

Within the extremely narrow base of Balkan elementary education, secondary and tertiary levels hardly existed. For the most part, the region only began training highly qualified experts, such as engineers, chemists, and medical doctors, just a few years before the war. The so-called Belgrade Higher School was reorganized as Belgrade University only in 1905, with philosophy, law, and technical schools. The Sofia higher pedagogical school, founded in 1888, became the University of Sofia in 1904, with 1,379 students.

The only Balkan country to establish a university during the nineteenth century was Romania. The Princely Academia, a mid-seventeenth-century institution, was reorganized as the University of Iasi in 1860. Nevertheless, the intellectual and political elite of the country were mostly trained abroad. Vienna University, the second largest in Europe, served as the Balkans' most popular higher education destination. Nearly 3 percent of its students, and more than 4 percent of its medical students, were Romanians between 1880 and 1900. Universities in Paris, Prague, and Budapest were also popular with students from the Balkans, and especially for the very small intellectual layers from the Austro-Hungarian borderlands.

Based on Berend (2003, 226–7).

renounced cultivation, and migrated to more hidden and safer mountain areas, where they primarily turned to primitive animal husbandry. This migration had probably started earlier during the Little Ice Age that hit the Mediterranean and destroyed the Balkan lowlands with torrential rains and massive flooding. The Balkans were isolated from Europe and devastated by continual warfare, local and nationwide revolts, and foreign military interventions up till the 1870s. Even closely located communities were isolated from one another. Roads did not exist at all in Bosnia until 1851, and they were not maintained after Osman Pasha's road construction initiative had finally built them. The fewer than 90 kilometers between Naoussa and Thessaloniki in Macedonia took fourteen hours to traverse. The railroad finally arrived in 1892, but a rail trip, including the cart rides to and from the stations, still took four hours. Isolation was the order of the day. According to Michael Palairet,

The period of warlordism and banditry, whose intensity peaked early in the nineteenth century... was associated with population shifts... the peasants' population tended to withdraw to remote areas... Most of these were uplands... The hills provided an adequate environment for stock raising and subsistence agriculture... Contemporary writers considered the peasants to be highly resistant or inadaptable to anything other than a pastoral existence. (Palairet, 1997, 37–8, 147)

In Bulgaria in the mid-nineteenth century, two- and three-rotation systems continued to predominate. The average holding in the more developed Plovdiv area was 3.4 hectares, with half the arable land remaining fallow and used for grazing. Both animal husbandry and grain production stagnated between the mid-1860s and 1870s. Roughly half of Serbia's agricultural output was produced by pre-modern animal husbandry until the mid-1870s, together with more than 62 percent of Bosnia's. Harsh winters often reduced the animal stock by one-fifth or more.

During the first half of the nineteenth century, the Ottoman military and administrative elite, the *spahijas* and *kapetans*, gradually converted the imperial tithes into their own *čitluks* (or chiftlik). In Bosnia and Macedonia, relatively large estates, sometimes 400–1,400 hectares in size, were privately owned. Sharecropping became the primary form of an extremely exploitative agricultural system, which allowed the native peasants, the *kmets*, to keep less than one-fifth of the harvest. The market-oriented chiftlik agriculture took root only in areas adjacent to ports, for local transportation and urban markets did not exist.

After their liberation from Ottoman rule during the last third of the nineteenth century, the Balkan countries broke out from their isolation

Table 13.1 Birth and death rates in the Balkans, 1901–10

	Birth rate per 1,000 inhabitants	Death rate per 1,000 inhabitants
Greece	28.9	21.5
Romania	40.2	26.0
Serbia	39.5	24.0
Bulgaria	41.4	23.2
Average (unweighted)	**37.5**	**23.7**
Western Europe	**26.7**	**15.1**

Source: Glass and Grebenik (1965, 68–9).

and seized the initiative to provide Western Europe's rapidly increasing food imports. Demographic trends only partially followed the Western pattern; death rates moderately declined, but birth rates remained high, understandably near pre-industrial levels. (See Table 13.1.) Consequently, the population growth was as explosive here as in other parts of Europe. Greece's population increased by two and a half times, and Serbia's nearly trebled between 1860 and 1910, and the Balkan population more than trebled between 1800 and 1910, growing by more than 70 percent during the half-century after 1860. Despite this relatively rapid population growth, the population density remained low compared with Central and Western Europe. (See Table 13.2.)

The land that had belonged to the Ottoman occupiers now became peasant land in Greece, Bulgaria, and Serbia. Local peasants in Greece could gain title to the former Ottoman land if they continually cultivated it for a certain period (between one and fifteen years, depending on the province). Land redistribution created peasant plots of an average of 13–25 acres. In Bulgaria, the government redistributed the Ottoman land fairly equally among peasants: 41% of the peasants possessed more than 42% of the land, while estates larger than 75 acres were in the hands of 1.8% of the farmers, who owned 14% of the land. Similarly, only some 10–13% of Serbian families remained landless in 1896, and only 784 farms consisted of more than 50 hectares. Three-quarters of the arable land in these two countries was made up of peasant farms of fewer than

Table 13.2 Balkan population and population density, 1800–1910

Year	Serbia	Greece	Bosnia	Bulgaria	Turkey	Balkans	Population density (per km²)
1800	183,000	634,000	720,000[a]	–	5,294,000	5,738,000	12.9
1860	1,102,000	1,090,000	1,220,000	2,769,000[b]	7,520,000	10,428,000	23.4
1910	2,922,000	2,689,000	1,898,000	4,338,000	5,176,000	17,872,000	40.1

Source: Palairet (1997, 20).

Notes:

[a] 1820.

[b] In 1870, with east Rumelia.

20 hectares (Stavrianos, 1963). This was the antithesis of the situation in Prussia, Central Europe, and Russia.

The historiography of agriculture often maintains that agrarian prosperity is strongly contingent on the existence of big estates or their transformation into peasant farms, and that modernization requires land reform that breaks up the big estates.[2] In reality, however, any value judgment regarding the role of land tenure is questionable. Any big estate or peasant farm could be modern and highly productive or stuck in extensive, low-productivity cultivation. In some cases, the big estates benefited from their large sizes, which enabled them to achieve optimal efficiency through mechanization and management. Their unit cost of production was lower and their marketing position better. The British, east German, and Austro-Hungarian big estates became efficient capitalist enterprises, while small peasant farms in Poland and the Balkans were frozen in primitive subsistence farming. Only one-third of Bulgaria's farm products were marketed and Serbian farms of less than 10 hectares consumed about 80 percent of their output.

Modern social-property relations and property rights are important to assure freedom, establish security, and generate long-term interest in investment and development. Long-term commitments positively impact on intensive agricultural performance. The small farms in less developed regions, however, preserved the medieval village community system (called *obshchina* in Russia and *zadruga* in the southern Slav regions) for most of the nineteenth century. The communal system organized joint communal work and distribution. The *zadruga* gradually dissolved during the later decades of the nineteenth century, but mutual assistance continued.

Moba (the collective cultivation of land), *pozajmica* (mutual harvesting and labor exchange), and *sprega* (reciprocal loans of livestock, equipment, and even cash) were signs of continued communal collectivism (Halpern and Halpern, 1972, 52–3). An egalitarian distribution of income was preserved in several places until the early twentieth century, and worked decisively against a modern capitalist transformation.

Persistent warfare, spontaneous peasant uprisings, and harsh Ottoman retribution shook Serbia from 1804 to the 1870s. Armed conflict, Russian–Ottoman clashes, great power interventions, the incorporation of Bosnia-Herzegovina into the Habsburg Empire in the 1880s, and two Balkan wars prior to World War I made peaceful economic activity virtually impossible. There emerged in the independent Balkan states a military-bureaucratic elite that was as corrupt and predatory as the previous Ottoman rulers. Peasants owning small impoverished parcels continued to engage in subsistence farming, and their marketing of goods was marginal.

Land tenure in Romania, Macedonia, and Bosnia was rather different from that in Serbia and Bulgaria. Despite land reforms that had parceled out state and church land (with peasant farms receiving one-third of the land in Bosnia in 1871), 60% of the land in Bosnia still belonged to the big estates in 1910, together with 50% in Romania and 75% in Macedonia. The Romanian agricultural system was unique in Europe and represented an odd mixture of feudal and capitalist agriculture, containing the worst elements of both. The absentee landed aristocracy rented out their estates – 75% of those larger than 3,000 hectares, and 60% of those larger than 100 hectares – to merchants (often Austrians) who sub-let small parcels to peasants for sharecropping (mostly on a yearly basis) and took 50% of the output. The intermediaries were farming speculators, renting for short periods at excessive rents and seeking to get rich in a few years. Seton-Watson notes that in "the Golden Age of irresponsible landlordism . . . the peasant found himself as much exploited, as fatally tied to the soil, as in the vanished days of serfdom" (Seton-Watson, 1963, 369). This uniquely exploitative agricultural system led to the outbreak of Europe's last major peasant uprising in Romania in 1906.[3]

Balkan agriculture was unable to apply the innovations of the agricultural revolution, and made only tentative steps toward introducing them in the early twentieth century. Modern technology and rotation systems did not affect agricultural performance. Four-fifths of Bulgaria's plows were still wooden before World War I. Costas Lapavitsas describes how 46 percent of the arable land remained fallow, at times rented to transhumant shepherds for grazing. Fallow land clearly points to the survival of the medieval two- or three-rotation systems. The first signs of capitalist transformation appeared in the chiftlik sector, which introduced wage labor and an improved rotation system (Lapavitsas, 2006, 689). Instead of agricultural modernization, the *chorbaji* private landowner elite in Bulgaria turned to textile proto-industry and established one of the most flourishing proto-industrial textile centers in the Ottoman Empire.

Relatively speaking, Romania achieved the best results in agricultural mechanization. Steam threshers and horse-driven sowing machines appeared in the fields in the early twentieth century, but they served an area three times larger than in Hungary, and ten times larger than in Germany. The first steam threshing machines appeared in Bulgaria before the war, but they served an area fifteen times larger than in backward Romania. Horse-driven sowing machines in Bulgaria served areas twenty times larger than in Romania. The modern rotation system was a rarity in Serbia, where harvesting was carried out with sickles, and stall-feeding was unknown in animal husbandry. Consequently, yields were rather stagnant.[4] Because of the population growth, per capita agricultural output actually declined by 14 percent in Bulgaria and 28 percent in Serbia between the 1870s and early 1910s. Per capita production of livestock products halved in Serbia and stagnated in Bulgaria and Bosnia. All farm production decreased by one-third in Serbia and one-sixth in Bulgaria, and stagnated in Bosnia and Montenegro, between 1859 and 1913.

The lack of modernization was partly the consequence of a lack of investment in Balkan agriculture. Modern mortgage credit was limited or did not exist at all, and the peasants continued to be victimized by medieval-like usury. A report on 1,200 Bulgarian villages at the beginning of the twentieth century revealed that many poor farmers had to pay 200 percent interest. Peasants needed loans simply to survive and took out usurious loans in advance for their crops. Another report, based on a quarter of Bulgaria's villages, disclosed that peasant families were in debt for the whole, or at least more than one-quarter or one-half, of the expected value of their crops.

Nonetheless, one can still speak of a breakthrough at least in land cultivation. The increasing population gradually inhabited the previously deserted lowlands and returned to cultivate the arable land. Between the 1860s and World War I, grain cultivation increased to an impressive degree. The landed area given to grain grew from 2.1 million hectares to 5 million hectares in Romania, and grain production increased by three times by the turn of the century, and another 50 percent by World War I. Serbia and Bulgaria had a very limited grain economy before their liberation, but their landed area for grain cultivation increased from 2.8 million to 3.6 million hectares between the 1890s and 1910s. Wheat output doubled after the late 1890s. A monocultural grain economy gained ground throughout the Balkans, except for Greece, which imported a large amount of grain. In Romania and Bulgaria, 86–87 percent of the arable land was given to grain; in Serbia, more than half of it. Grain became one of the region's leading export items. The Romanian, Serbian, and Bulgarian wheat and corn production nearly doubled from 39.4 million to 72.2 million quintals between the 1880s and 1910s. Bulgaria exported 30 percent of its grain output, Romania 50 percent.

Those Balkan countries that had not become part of the international division of labor and European trade network before the 1860s did so during the last third of the nineteenth century. Serbia's exports increased more than sevenfold and Greek exports by five and a half times, between the early 1860s and 1910. Romanian exports grew by four and a half times between the 1870s and 1910, and Bulgarian exports grew by almost five times between the 1880s and 1910. These countries' main export items were all agricultural products and the five leading items comprised three-quarters to four-fifths of their total exports (Mitchell, 1975, 489–97).

Grain comprised 40% of Romania's total exports in 1866, and 80% by 1911 – representing more than 8% of the world's wheat exports, and signifying Romania's international stature in grain production. Similarly to Russia, 92% of Romania's grain was also exported unprocessed.[5] Serbian grain exports remained limited, with 12% of its output sold abroad, but its sheep and pig exports became the first, and cattle exports the third largest in the world, relative to its population (2,516 sheep per 1,000 inhabitants, 988 pigs per 1,000, and 623 cattle per 1,000). Live and slaughtered animal exports began to predominate in Serbia.

Specialization in agricultural production was marginal. The most striking results were seen in the Greek raisin, olive, and tobacco economy.[6] Serbia developed a prune economy from the mid-century on. Plum trees blanketed much of the country, and the women of peasant families dried the fruit in the sun or in primitive ovens (*pušnica*). Merchants collected the prunes and exported them. In the late 1880s, prunes made up one-quarter of Serbian exports.

Agricultural products represented 75% and 78% of Greek exports in 1887 and 1912, respectively. Romania's dominant export item was grain, comprising 77% of its total exports in the late 1880s and 80% in 1910. Grain made up two-thirds of Bulgaria's exports before the war, and grain and unprocessed animal products represented nearly 60% of Serbia's. In some peripheral regions, agricultural and raw material exports consisted of one or two items that represented half or two-thirds of total exports.

Table 13.3 The most important export item's share of total exports, 1886–1911

Years	Greek raisins	Romanian grain	Serbian grain	Serbian animal products	Bulgarian grain
1886–90	54.7	76.8	17.8	38.0	72.2
1896–1900	42.0	74.2	27.7	29.9	72.7
1906–10	30.8	79.7	43.5	11.8	64.4

Source: Lampe and Jackson (1982, 64).

Table 13.4 Pig raising in Serbia, 1859–1912, annual average in constant price, million dinars

Year	Output	Exports
1859–60	79.2	10.1
1891–5	48.2	14.6
1911–12	42.7	8.5

Source: Palairet (1997, 307).

During the 1880s, raisins alone comprised 55% of Greek exports. (See Table 13.3.)

This situation weakened the Balkan countries' market position because they were dependent on a single export item and at times on a single market. Romania and Serbia, for instance, sold a large part of their few export goods on the markets of the Habsburg Empire in the late nineteenth century. Tariff wars, such as the Austro-Hungarian and Serbian "pig war" at around the turn of the century, might halt their exports to that market. This had devastating consequences for the exporter countries. (See Table 13.4.)

The Balkan countries had a fragile market position. If their single export item had high price elasticity (i.e. its ability to be sold is highly subject to price variations), the exporter's standing was endangered. In these cases, price increases led to shrinking markets. Importers turned to substitute goods. To increase exports, it was necessary to decrease prices. Having only one or two export items and/or a high price elasticity is definitely a serious obstacle to a country availing itself of trade opportunities. Most countries in the region experienced all these difficulties.

The easternmost and southern provinces of Austria-Hungary, such as Bukovina, Galicia, Dalmatia, and Bosnia-Herzegovina, were more or less in a similar situation. Galicia, which had been incorporated into the Habsburg Empire after the partition of Poland at the end of the eighteenth century and gained autonomy in 1867, exemplified the agricultural backwardness typical of the eastern and southernmost provinces of the empire. Feudal labor service was abandoned in 1848, and small subsistence farming characterized some 80 percent of peasant agriculture – with the average landholding composed of 2.3 hectares at the end of the nineteenth century. The populace remained overwhelmingly agrarian, the proportion of the overall population declining by only 16 percent between 1850 and 1910. Seventy-three percent of Galicia's and Bukovina's inhabitants, and no less than 97 percent of the populace in the eastern Ruthenian half of Galicia, worked in agriculture. Monocultural potato plantations and a low quality beef cattle economy predominated. Modernization barely affected this region, and famines recurred on a regular basis. Unlike in Hungary, the market of the Habsburg Empire did not stimulate the borderlands' agriculture (Lampe and Jackson, 1982, 278–9).

Agricultural output and livestock production could not keep pace with the population growth in the Balkans and the Habsburg borderlands. Per capita agricultural output and livestock production significantly declined in Serbia and Montenegro. Bulgarian farm production declined by 17 percent and animal production stagnated. Bosnia exhibited a modest 22 percent increase in farm output and a 40 percent growth in animal production. (See Tables 13.5 and 13.6.)

Lack of industrialization

The Balkans remained non-industrialized, with very few small foreign industrial enterprises, as late as the turn of the century. Industrial activity continued to be almost entirely peasant cottage industry. In Ottoman-ruled Bulgaria, for example, the wool proto-industry in Koprivshtitsa, a settlement at 1,060 meters above sea level with scant, infertile land and 150 inhabitants in 1810, became an industrial center of the empire with a population of 8,000 by 1860. The village inhabitants produced tailored and embroidered woolen clothing, hosiery, and slippers for markets in Constantinople and Plovdiv. Some 73,000 people were engaged in woolen

Table 13.5 Per capita output of Balkan farm population in 1910 francs

Year	Serbia	Bulgaria	Bosnia	Montenegro
1865	170.3	223.4	95.2	140.8[a]
1879	178.2	163.0	75.6	143.1[b]
1901	112.1	167.2	114.5	129.6[c]
1912	120.3	185.5	115.7	130.4

Source: Palairet (1997, 366–7).
Notes:
[a] 1863.
[b] 1880.
[c] 1900.

Table 13.6 Per capita livestock production of Balkan farm population in 1910 francs

Year	Serbia	Bulgaria	Bosnia	Montenegro
1865	78.9	43.1	48.0	86.4[a]
1879	75.1	37.5	52.4	64.6
1901	47.8	45.3	63.3	79.1[b]
1912	46.7	45.7	67.1	70.3

Source: Palairet (1997, 366–7).
Notes:
[a] 1863.
[b] 1900.

manufacturing in the Bulgarian provinces before independence (Palairet, 1997, 67, 69–70). Bulgarian proto-industry, mostly in flourishing hillside settlements, reached its peak in the 1860s and then began to decline because of textile imports. Mechanized factories appeared during the last years of Ottoman rule in the 1870s. In Greece, the Ambelakia dyed cotton thread proto-industry flourished until British cotton imports strangled it. In Serbia and Bosnia, even this proto-industrial phase was lacking until the 1850s–1860s.

The declining Ottoman power, in permanent warfare with the Western powers and Russia, was forced by Britain to open its market for imports. Already the Treaty of Kücük Kaynarci and Jossi in the late eighteenth century, but especially the Treaty of Balta Liman in 1838, curbed Ottoman exports to the West and rendered the empire defenseless against British exports. In 1820, the empire had been self-sufficient in cotton and woolen textiles, but, after the treaty, domestic spinning fell by almost a third by 1870. Imported goods supplied only 3 percent of the domestic textile market in 1820, but nearly 80 percent by 1910. "De-industrialization forces were powerful up to the 1860s" (Pamuk and Williamson, 2011, 166–7).

In the Balkans, urban settlements barely existed. Only 90,000 people resided in Belgrade, 103,000 in Sofia, 167,000 in Athens, and 341,000 in Bucharest prior to World War I. Only about 7 percent of the population was concentrated in urban settlements before the 1860s, and some 14–20 percent before the war. Urban markets were rather limited.

Home industry and small-scale handicraft production supplied the population. After Bulgaria's liberation from Ottoman rule, the previously prosperous proto-industry declined, and woolen and cloth output decreased by 61 percent and 73 percent, respectively. Mechanized industry appeared from the 1870s on, though big industry did not begin to develop in Bulgaria until the 1910s. In the region between Thessaloniki and Karaferye (Veroia), Ağostos (Naoussa), and Voden (Edhessa), a region of almost perpetual primitive agriculture, the local Christian *chorbaji* landowning and merchant elite turned to the textile industry in the 1870s. Labor, consisting of young peasant girls from the neighboring villages, was extremely cheap, even in Thessaloniki. Proto-industry produced processed wool, linen towels, and even weaponry. Twenty to thirty percent of Naoussa's inhabitants were wage laborers by 1912. Naoussa was considered an industrial city with six cotton-spinning mills with 43,400 spindles; 80 percent of the horsepower and 90 percent of the employees of the mechanized woolen cloth industry were located there. When Ottoman rule ended in Macedonia, families from the Naoussa region and the surrounding area controlled nearly one-third of the empire's total mechanized cotton-spinning capacity. Otherwise, very limited industrialization developed.

In addition to small foreign industrial investment, the independent Balkan states began offering limited subsidies to encourage industrialization. In 1893 and 1898, Serbia granted tariff-free imports of machinery and materials, and instituted tax holidays and lower rates on state railroads for industrial firms that employed more than fifty workers. Bulgarian state subsidies comprised 4.3 percent of total industrial investments. These state contributions, however, were too moderate to make a difference.

As noted earlier, foreign investors targeted railroads, raw material extraction, and banking, but showed little interest in manufacturing industry. Greece offers a typical example. During the half-century between 1867 and 1917, the number of industrial workers increased by five times, the invested industrial capital by eight times, and industrial output by seventeen times. Only 282 industrial firms employed more than 26 workers, totaling 23,000, before the war, while small handicraft firms employed another 13,000. In those years, a single Hungarian company, the Manfred Weiss engineering firm, employed 30,000 workers. Moreover, the food processing industry, mostly local mills and distilleries, produced 60 percent, and textiles another 10 percent, of the industrial output. In other words, modern market-oriented big industry was practically non-existent in Greece until the war.

Romania was not much better. By 1902, 625 "factories" were in operation, half of them still in food processing. In 1914, a minimal 1.5 percent of GDP was invested in industry. Except for oil extraction, mostly local mills and small-scale handicraft shops made up the industrial sector. Romania's entire industry employed fewer workers than a single German big factory.[7] Domestic production covered only a small segment of consumption: the "most developed" branch of textiles, cotton spinning, covered 12 percent, and engineering companies about 10 percent, of domestic consumption.

One of the most negative peripheral features of the Balkan economy was manifested after the discovery of Romania's abundant oil fields. Massive foreign investment rushed in.[8] The world's leading oil companies monopolized Romania's extraction, which increased from 298,000 tons in 1901 to 1.8 million tons in 1914. Oil output increased by 15 percent per year in that period, and crude oil became the second most important export item (comprising 12 percent of total exports) in 1912. Oil refining, however, hardly developed, and most of the refined oil products were imported. A similar situation characterized Serbia's copper extraction: 40 percent of industrial investment was channeled into mining, and the extracted copper went straight to the West.

Bulgaria's industry was mostly made up of handicraft shops and a few firms in the woolen, flour mill, and distillery industries. Before the war, large-scale firms existed only in two sectors, food processing and textiles, which concentrated 60 percent of total industrial investment. By 1911, food processing produced half of the value of industrial output. Here too, the country's entire industry did not employ as many workers as a major Central European company. Domestic industry covered only a third of the country's modest consumption of industrial goods. The iron and engineering industries were virtually non-existent. Modern manufacturing industry represented only one-fourth of total industrial production, which generally did not emerge from its small-scale, handicraft stage. Serbia exhibited a similar lack of modern big industry. Only 7 percent of the active population was employed in industry, and more than one-third of them were in mining and local food processing. The mining, iron, and food industries produced 60 percent of industrial output. Several industrial branches did not exist, including engineering, paper, and metallurgical industries.

Modern industrial development took its first steps in the Balkans mostly in the early twentieth century. Romania's industrial workforce increased by 43 percent, and production trebled, between 1902 and 1915; Bulgaria's industrial workforce more than trebled, and the value of output more than quadrupled, between 1900 and 1911. But the Balkans as a whole remained overwhelmingly steeped in agriculture, which employed roughly 75 percent of the active population. Agriculture accounted for 70–80 percent of the Balkans' GDP before the war, while industry continued to generate between one-seventh and one-fifth of GDP. Small-scale handicraft industry made up two-thirds of industrial production. Michael Palairet speaks of the "post-liberation economic collapse" in the case of Bulgaria. "[L]arge-scale industry," he observed, "began to grow rapidly in the last pre-war decade, but as an aggregate it remained insignificant" (Palairet, 1997, 341, 361). New calculations strengthen this evaluation: around the turn of the century, when the first steps toward modernization were taken, Bulgaria virtually stagnated. Its gross national product increased by 28 percent between 1892 and 1911, but the population increased by nearly a third. Consequently, "per capita incomes neither declined nor increased substantially" (Ivaros and Tooze, 2007, 684, 699). The per capita level of industrialization remained far behind the average European level, and hardly reached more than a quarter of it. (See Tables 13.7 and 13.8.)

Regarding the leading industrial sectors of the nineteenth century, the region's backwardness is equally striking. In 1910, when per capita cotton consumption in the advanced West was 6.3 kilograms, and the European average was 5.4 kilograms, the Balkans' average totaled only 0.3 (Bairoch, 1991, 8).

Neither the 20 million strong Ottoman market nor the 50 million strong Habsburg market stimulated Balkan production during and after Ottoman rule. This was in sharp contrast to the previously discussed Finnish, Baltic, Hungarian, and Polish cases. The Balkans simply lacked the capacity to take advantage of the opportunity. Before the war, the value-added industrial

Table 13.7 Large-scale industry indicators in the Balkans, 1910

Country/ province	Population (millions)	Establishments	Employees per establishment	Employees per 1,000 inhabitants
Bulgaria	4.34	333	45.2	3.5
Serbia	2.92	465	34.6	5.5
Bosnia	1.81	187	166.9	11.3

Source: Palairet (1997, 222).

Table 13.8 Per capita industrialization level in the Balkans compared with Europe (Britain in 1900 = 100)

Countries	1800	1860	1913
Advanced countries	8	16	55
European average	8	17	45
Bulgaria	5	5	10
Greece	5	6	10
Romania	5	6	13
Serbia	5	6	12

Source: Bairoch (1991, 3).

output did not reach 10 percent of the total gross output of the three Balkan countries.

Compared with the most advanced Western level, the Balkans achieved only 13 percent of per capita industrial production. In relative terms, the economy of the southern and eastern peripheral regions of Europe sharply declined between 1820 and 1913. The very late and sluggish turn towards industrialization failed.

The easternmost and southern provinces of the Habsburg Empire hardly attained more progress than had the Balkans. After the Compromise of 1867, Austria-Hungary emerged as the most diverse political unit. Its western Austrian-Bohemian provinces became virtually part of the successfully industrializing West; its central section, particularly

Hungary, represented a semi-successful pattern of transformation; but Galicia, Bukovina, Dalmatia, and Bosnia-Herzegovina embodied the failure of modern transformation. Before World War I, agriculture employed only 35% of the active population in Austria-Bohemia and 64% in Hungary, but the figure was 73% in Galicia and Bukovina and 82% in Dalmatia. This remained almost constant: between 1880 and 1910, Galicia's agrarian population decreased only by 2%.

The Habsburg Empire's northeast province, Galicia, enjoyed a special status and broad political autonomy after 1867, following the Austrian-Hungarian *Ausgleich* (Compromise). The situation is best illustrated by the beginning of oil extraction in the 1880s. After the discovery of oil fields in Galicia, an oil-rush began.[9] Shafts were manually dug rather than drilled, and if they were drilled at all, they were done so with hand drilling. As one of the first entrepreneurs stated in 1888, "We in Galicia... have a miraculous and rich nature. We lacked until now the people who were able to make use of it" (Frank, 2005, 88).

At the later stage, the leading Western oil companies took over. When production significantly increased, processing was conducted mostly outside Galicia (Topolski, 1982). Otherwise, large-scale industry did not exist at all in the province. The same was true for the non-Austrian-Bohemian parts of the so-called "hereditary provinces". Galicia, Bukovina, and Dalmatia represented 40 percent of the population of the hereditary provinces (11 million people), but together they produced only 15 percent of the total industrial output, while Austria-Bohemia produced 85 percent.

Bosnia-Herzegovina, liberated from Ottoman rule but occupied by (1878) and annexed into (1908) Austria-Hungary, exhibited interesting semi-colonial characteristics. The province had abundant wood, coal, rock salt, and metal resources. The Vienna government established the *Landesregierung*, headed by Count Benjamin Kállay, who launched a "civilizing mission" and an industrialization policy in the province. State-owned companies[10] were established and began raw material extraction. By 1907, state-owned companies employed a third of the mining and industrial labor force. In addition to extraction, they produced only semi-finished products. Long-term concessions invited foreign investors, especially in the forestry and timber industry.[11] The Bosnian raw material and semi-finished product industries worked for exports. Before the war, 87% of the province's industrial labor force was employed in export sectors. By 1910, 17% of the population worked in large-scale industry.[12] Wage levels were higher than in Serbia (by 20%) and Bulgaria (by 33%). Habsburg Bosnia achieved higher levels of industrialization than did the Balkans.

The province's population was 21% of the inhabitants of Bosnia, Serbia, and Bulgaria combined, but it represented 54% of the large-scale industry in those three countries (Palairet, 1997, 237).[13]

The export sectors, however, remained isolated enclaves in the Bosnian economy. Croatia reflected similar backwardness in industrialization.[14] As in most of the Balkan cases, mechanization and industrial employment in the entire country did not exceed the size of a single large European company.

Backwardness in these regions was a complex phenomenon, and it was exhibited in various areas. Those eastern and southern provinces of Austria-Hungary displayed similar backwardness in agriculture, transportation, literacy, and health services. While the ratio between length of railroads and landed area was 1:8 in Austria and 1:10 in Bohemia and Hungary, it was 1:28 in Galicia and 1:100 in Dalmatia, illustrating an acute lack of railroad networks. Illiteracy endured – as high as 59 percent in Galicia in 1910. And unlike other parts of the Monarchy, it was continually reproduced there, as 70 percent of the school-age population did not attend schools. Reproduction of illiteracy was similarly high in Bukovina, where only 36 percent of school-age children attended schools, and in Bosnia-Herzegovina, where only 15 percent did so. In contrast to Austria-Bohemia's thirty-five medical doctors per 100,000 inhabitants (the German and French level), there were only twelve doctors in Bukovina, and nine in Croatia, per 100,000 people.

Alexander Gerschenkron has suggested that, in cases of extreme backwardness, the state substitutes the lacking prerequisites of industrialization to facilitate economic development. This was not the case, however, in the most backward parts of Europe. State intervention was insignificant and did not foster industrial investment. As one of the preeminent experts on the Balkans, Michael Palairet, noted, "Neither in Serbia nor in Bulgaria, nor even in Bosnia, was the state a central actor in the industrialization process" (Palairet, 1997, 330).

Local capital was insufficient in these peasant societies where, in most cases, subsistence farming characterized the peasants' meager plots. Foreign capital investment played the central role in initiating modern transformation in the peripheral regions, but this was not the case in the Balkans and the least developed provinces of Austria-Hungary.

Corruption and reluctant foreign investors

What was the reason that Western entrepreneurs and banks were so unforthcoming with Balkan investments? Lampe and Jackson speak about a "reluctant imperialism" and a "relatively weak penetration of European financial institutions into the Balkan countries" (Lampe and Jackson, 1982, 225). Some extremely valuable natural resources, such as Romanian and Galician oil, Serbian copper, and important mineral resources in Bosnia, attracted foreign investors. Direct investment in the banking and processing industries, however, remained extremely limited before World War I. Why? Infrastructural and educational backwardness and the lack of agricultural modernization were significant factors. The permanent financial crisis of the independent Balkan states also strongly contributed. A huge debt burden, an inability to repay, and frequent state bankruptcies made creditors extremely jittery. The states' plight had very negatively impacted interest rates and credit to the private sector. According to Palairet,

these countries failed to attract inward industrial investment, less because of a lack of interest by foreign promoters, more through the creation of an environment which deterred foreign participation . . . [i.e.] the combination of xenophobia, official corruption and undeveloped local business ethics which trans-national firms encountered. (Palairet, 1997, 331)

Xenophobia is probably too strong a term in this case. It would be more correct to say that all the countries that were liberated from half a millennium of Ottoman rule suffered from an instinctive suspicion of any foreign power, especially foreign economic or military power, in their newly independent countries. At the same time, these countries' governments strongly preferred local investors and companies, and they confused political with economic independence. When the Austrian Länderbank acquired Serbian railway stocks and its tobacco monopoly in 1886, the government rushed to nationalize them in 1889 and 1890. In 1909, the Serbian cabinet opposed any large banking venture that was dominated by foreigners. When the concession for the Prince Boris coal mine in Trajvna, Bulgaria was granted in 1897 with a major contribution from the French Paribas, production was blocked by a missing railway link to existing trucking routes. When the French investor sought permission to build the link, the government refused, because it would not tolerate private railroads. In 1905, the Paribas gave the Bulgarian government an ultimatum that they would freeze all loans if the concession was not granted. The Société d'exploitations minières du Serbie planned a major mining project in 1906, but it hit a wall of resistance among local authorities and, in the end, cancelled the project.

The region's oriental business culture was probably an even bigger obstacle to overcome. The new independent states built up huge state and local bureaucracies. This was an "ersatz class," for the state bureaucracy and army took the place of a modern bourgeoisie as the leading elite in these countries. The central government of Bulgaria employed 47,000 functionaries in 1910, almost three times as many people as the country's industrial labor force. The Greek and Romanian state apparatus employed 50,000 and 87,000, respectively. These numbers exceeded 5 percent of the active population, which was equal to the prewar French state bureaucracy, considered the largest in Europe (Lampe and Jackson, 1982, 235; Cameron, 1957, 438).

The vast state apparatus consumed one-quarter to one-half of the state budget, and its bureaucrats used their offices to enrich themselves as quickly as possible. Formerly a province of the Ottoman Empire, Bessarabia became part of the Russian Empire in 1812. Count Kiselev told the tsar: "Everything is for sale, and the prefects are obliged to steal more than the rest" (Seton-Watson, 1963, 561). In a speech to the Romanian parliament upon becoming Prime Minister in 1881, Dumitru Brătianu attacked the "hungry wolves" among the professional panamist politicians of his own Liberal Party. "His parliamentary career," Robert Seton-Watson observed, "was thus finished before it had really begun." His brother, Ion, took over the government, and "found it convenient to encourage the 'spoil system' and to build up his party organization on the basis of *enrichissez-vous*" (Seton-Watson, 1963, 354–5).

The deeply rooted tradition of Ottoman corruption was a destructive legacy for these independent countries. Stories abound of foreign businesses that failed because of the ubiquitous corruption. A British meatpacking company lost its concession because "in spite of strong advice to conform to the customs of the country, Marshall [the promoter] persistently refused to bribe in any way . . . Demands by officials for bribes were coupled with threats that in the event of non-compliance the business of the company would not be allowed to proceed smoothly" (Palairet, 1997, 336, 338). Western embassies continually warned potential compatriot investors against doing business in the Balkans. The French consul reported in 1875 that bankruptcy was the usual way to avoid repayment. The various parliaments regularly expunged debts to foreign investors. The Hungarian and German consuls advised against doing business in Serbia. The British consul complained about the

unfortunate absence of public morality in Serbia . . . The slightest hitch or interruption to the works might be made to serve as a plausible excuse for

Table 13.9   National product per capita in the Habsburg
borderlands and the Balkans, 1910

Country	Per capita national product (1970 US $)	As % of Austria-Bohemia
Austria	810	–
Czech lands	819	–
Hungary	684	84
Bosnia	546	67
Croatia	542	66
Serbia	462	57
Greece	455	56

Source: Palairet (1997, 233).

cancelling the contract, and confiscating the security... When a tender was issued by the Serbian State Railways for rolling stock, the British consul advised not to bid, fearing that they would not be paid. (Palairet, 1997, 333, 334)

Because of a lack of solid statistics, one cannot know the income level of this region in 1820, and even the figures on 1913 are incomplete. According to the calculations of Paul Bairoch (1976b), the average gross per capita income level of the four Balkan countries in 1860 was $499. This doubled by 1900 and increased two and a half times to $1,231 by 1910. Based on Angus Maddison's (1995) figures, we can estimate that the average per capita GDP in 1913 was roughly $1,383. This was only 37 percent of the West European average, and was 8 percent behind the Russian and 39 percent behind the Spanish per capita income level. Modernization and industrialization failed in the Balkans.[15] Compared with the Austrian-Bohemian level, the Balkans and the Habsburg borderlands achieved only one-half to two-thirds of the imperial core's per capita national product. (See Table 13.9.) The structure of the Balkans' economy also remained on a pre-Industrial Revolution level, with an overwhelmingly agricultural workforce (nearly three-quarters of the total). (See Table 13.10.) The region's GDP was basically produced by agriculture, and industry remained in an embryonic phase.

Table 13.10 The economic structure of the Balkans

	Agriculture				Industry			
	Employed in (%)		Contribution of total to GDP (%)		Employed in (%)		Contribution of total to GDP (%)	
	1860	1910	1860	1910	1860	1910	1860	1910
Greece	88	64	75	55	9	13	17	18
Romania	–	75	–	70	–	10	–	20
Serbia	84	75	–	79	–	7	–	14
Bulgaria	82	75	–	80	7	10	–	15
Balkans average	85	72	75	71	8	10	17	17

Source: Berend and Ránki (1987, 641).

Notes

1. "Instead of private landownership, the state's (i.e. the Sultan's) land and income were managed by an appointed bureaucratic-military elite... [that] was joined by domestic Serbian, Bulgarian, Bosnian, and Albanian pseudo-elites. The subordinated native elite consisted... of the village and *knezina* chiefs who served as middlemen between the Ottoman authorities and the local population" (Berend, 2003, 204).

2. Niek Koning notes the advantages of family farms: "from the late nineteenth century a higher efficiency of family farms began to be proclaimed... Large farms declined because the squeeze on profits and rents reduced their technical lead, while the rise of wages allowed an increase in the labor price advantage of small farmers" (Koning, 1994, 172). Comparing Andalusia's big estates with small peasant farms in Flanders, J. P. Cooper demonstrated that the big estates in Andalusia did not boost productivity, while the small peasant farms in Flanders did (Cooper, 1985).

3. This began in the Botoşani region on the estate of the Austrian Fischer Company, and spread throughout the country – with a peasant army marching against Bucharest. The royal army ruthlessly put down the uprising, killing 10,000 peasants.

4. In Romania, yields increased from 5.0 to 6.7 quintals per acre between the first half of the 1880s and the 1910s. In Bulgaria and Serbia, they reached 6.2 and 5.2 quintals before the war, respectively. The Bulgarian and Romanian wheat yields totaled hardly more than half of the British, and roughly one-third of the Danish, yields.

5. The Balkans and Russia combined (together with Hungary) produced nearly half of the European wheat output.

6. Tobacco production increased from 1,200 to 8,800 tons, and raisin exports increased from 1,200 to 141,000 tons, between 1860 and the turn of the century.

7. In 1915, industry employed a total of 53,000 workers, 7,000 of whom were engaged in local food processing.

8. German investors established the Steaua Română and the Creditul Petrolifer, Royal Dutch Shell founded the Astra Română, and British and Belgian investors created the Telega Oil Co. French capital stood behind the Aquila Franco Română, and Standard Oil established the Româno-Americană oil company.

9. Nearly 50 refineries and 205 oil and wax-producing companies operated in 1881. The oil resources were abundant: Galician-extracted oil made up 1.2 percent of the world's oil output in 1900, and this rose to 5 percent by 1909. However, only seven 38-horsepower steam engines were installed in the entire Galician oil industry and only a single 16-horsepower steam engine was used in oil extraction.

10. The Gewerkschaft Bosnia and the Varaser Eisenindustrie A. G.

11. The Bavarian Otto Steinbeis opened large saw mills and employed 10,000 workers. In 1907, he added a pulp factory.

12. Compared with 14 percent in Russia, 5.5 percent in Serbia, and 3.5 percent in Bulgaria.

13. Nevertheless, of 29,000 industrial establishments in Bosnia, 25,000 did not employ workers, and another 4,000 had only two employees. The 187 large firms operated mostly in the extracting and lumbering industries and worked for export.

14. In 1913, industry employed only 31,100 workers, and the total capacity of all machinery was 43,700 horsepower.

15. Although they tried to present a balanced conclusion, Lampe and Jackson end their narrative with a surprisingly positive tone that is inconsistent with their findings on the failure of the Balkan economy: "The Habsburg borderlands, like the Balkan states, thus found themselves on the war's eve *with a set of modern financial and industrial sectors. They approached European best practice* and had recorded rapid rates of growth since 1900 . . . but had failed to

effect structural change within their ... economies ... These essentially native enclaves awaited some positive connection with the rural sector and the governments ... before broadly based development could occur" (Lampe and Jackson, 1982, 322; emphasis added).

CHAPTER 14

Epilogue: economic disparity and alternative postwar economic regimes

Europe was enormously prosperous, and continued to constitute a huge part of the world economy at the end of the long nineteenth century.[1] (See Figure 14.1.) The affluence of the West led to the advance of Western ideas. Admirers of the West in the luckless peripheries eagerly called for the emulation of the British paradigm. This was precisely what István Széchenyi urged Hungary to do in his book *Hitel* in 1830. "England has reached a level higher than ever before achieved by any people . . . [and has become] practically the core of the world . . . copying others presents no danger, we can adopt their century-long experiences" (Széchenyi, 1830, 139–40, 258). Having stagnated in their *anciens régimes* until the mid- to late nineteenth century, the peripheries gradually adopted Western institutions through reform. They joined the Western club of laissez-faire countries, introduced the gold standard, and pursued an export-based industrialization policy. They took the first steps toward modernization in the 1860s and 1870s, but most areas did not get around to it until the turn of the century. Facilitating these policies were Western investment, the construction of railroads, and the opening of markets for agricultural and other primary products. Some peripheral regions made significant progress, but even the best cases only partially succeeded and did not become industrialized. Other regions managed to create only isolated enclaves of economic modernity in a vast sea of self-sufficient agriculture and traditional proto-industry. The least successful regions of Europe failed to industrialize and modernize. Their attempt to follow the West did not lead to their catching up. According to Angus Maddison's calculations, Southern Europe's per capita GDP was 62% of Western Europe's in 1820, but only 53% in 1870 and 47% in 1913. The same was true for Eastern Europe: its per capita GDP fell from 60% of that of the West in 1820 to 51% in 1870 and 46% in 1913. The gap thus kept widening (Maddison, 1995).

Table 14.1 Regional differences in the development of GDP per capita, 1820–1913 (1990 Geary Khamis dollars)

Regions	1820	%	1870	%	1913	%
Successful development	1,372	100	2,337	100	4,013	100
Semi-successful development	844	62	1,154	49	2,294	57
Pre-industrial region with modern pockets	907	66	1,161	50	1,699	42
Failure of industrialization	–	–	–		1,037	26

Source: Maddison (1995, 23).

Figure 14.1
Europe's share of world GDP, 1700–1913 (percent of total) (Maddison, 2001, 263)

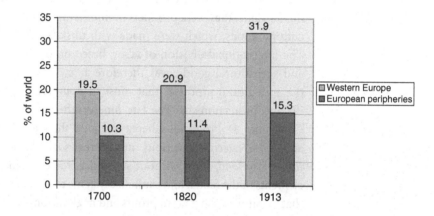

Some regions were partially successful in their modernization drive. The eastern provinces of Germany, the western provinces of the Russian Empire (Finland, Poland, and the Baltic region), the central part of the Habsburg Empire (the Hungarian kingdom), and Ireland achieved 62% of Western per capita GDP in 1820 and 57% in 1913. Most of the peripheries, however, were unable to break through. Russia, the Iberian peninsula, and southern Italy saw their GDP decline from 66% of that of the West in 1820 to 50% in 1870 and 42% in 1913. Their export-led development plan did not help them catch up. (See Table 14.1.)

The overly sanguine and near-religious embrace of the Western paradigm was gradually replaced by bitter disappointment and even rebellion against the West. Backward regions had seen, to use Karl Marx's expression in his preface of *Das Kapital*, "the image of [their] own future" in the British present. But that would soon evaporate. The peripheries suffered from "the incompleteness of development" and languished in a straitjacket of "modern evils [and] a whole series of inherited evils . . . [of] antiquated modes of production" (Marx, [1867] 1932, 13). They refused to chase after the mirage any longer. They began to question the first wave of globalization, reject the previously accepted free trade policies, and turn to protective tariffs between the 1870s and World War I.

"To understand the role of ideas . . . in mobilizing effort and in generating commitment," David Landes reminds us, "the most powerful [idea] was nationalism" (Landes, 1991, 7, 8). Nationalism, indeed, was one of the driving forces of peripheral economics. In Romania, Alexandru D. Xenopol, who had studied in Germany and became a professor of history at the University of Iași, argued in 1879 that non-industrialized countries are exploited by the unequal exchange of industrial and agricultural products. Based on Ricardo's labor value theory, Xenopol maintained that manufactured goods were the result of greater labor input and thus had higher value; they were products of *munca inteligenta*, as opposed to agricultural goods, which were made with unskilled labor or *munca bruta*. The international division of labor, based on the exchange of industrial and agricultural goods, was therefore a "swindle" – an exploitation of the agricultural producer that must be counterbalanced with high tariffs and protectionism. The late nineteenth-century Romanian Marxist Constantin Dobrogeanu-Gherea analyzed the clash between Romania's adopted Western institutions and its real social structure. He spoke of *forma fara fond*, form without substance, the combination of the worst elements of the feudal and capitalist systems to form a predatory economy that maximizes short-term profits and neglects long-term concerns (Love, 2002, 108, 119–20).

Oliveira Marreca expressed similar views in mid-nineteenth-century Portugal. Like List, he rejected Smithian cosmopolitanism in favor of national interest, and distinguished between "retarded countries" and "rich manufacturing countries." Challenging Ricardo's famous example of the mutual benefits of the 1703 British–Portuguese Methuen Agreement on free trade (and the 1810 commercial treaty between the two countries), Marreca insisted that Portugal's economic backwardness was a direct result of its misguided specialization stemming from its asymmetric relations with Britain. He called for strengthening and defending the domestic market and renouncing the division of labor imposed by the more advanced countries. Protectionism and state economic intervention, he asserted, are the only viable weapons for the "retarded" countries. His vision of the state's active role in the national economy is a comprehensive one. The state is to replace non-existent investment banks, lend money with zero interest, and carry out irrigation, canal, and road-building projects. Marreca heralded "Government as a great consumer of manufactures, as a great distributor of incomes, as a great borrower, as a great tax collector, as a great capitalist, as a great protector of production, as a great entrepreneur, as a great road builder, and as a great promoter of technological training" (quoted in Bastien, 2002, 242).

The belief in protectionism and state interventionism, which had been rendered obsolete in the 1860s, made a remarkable comeback in the European peripheries during the last quarter of the century. Several countries washed their hands of the free trade system and turned to protectionism beginning in the 1870s.

Disappointed intellectuals and radical political groups yearned for change. "We want proper democracy and are crying for universal suffrage," declared the Hungarian poet Endre Ady in 1910, "yet the achievements of far more cultured societies that had been ahead of us for centuries have destroyed our appetite for such things" (Ady, 1973, 138). Right-wing populism and proto-fascist ideologies emerged in Russia, Romania, and Italy. Left-wing radicalism was also on the rise in Eastern and parts of Southern Europe. Bolshevik ideology provided a revolutionary solution. The seeds of relentless conflict and revolt had been sown.

Acute competition and rising hostility held sway in the West as well. Latecomer Germany advanced to surpass the industrial strength of Britain and France. The latter two countries increased their GDP by 214 percent between 1870 and 1913, but Germany's rose by 329 percent (Maddison, 1995). Based on its highly developed science and technology, Germany emerged as the leader of the second Industrial Revolution. Germany created the world's preeminent engineering, chemical, and electric industries. Small wonder that the country demanded a bigger piece from the colonial pie. Military alliances and war preparations portended the end of four peaceful decades in Europe.

Uneven development and intensifying conflict culminated in World War I, history's first mechanized "Great War." The five-year life and death struggle spawned new economic innovations to assure a stronger economic foundation for the military effort. Britain's and particularly Germany's war economy provided an alternative economic model. The production and supply of raw materials were centrally directed in Germany by the Kriegsrohstoffabteilung. Market prices were abolished and replaced by state-regulated price formation. State programs oversaw the production of import-substituting goods, and the free labor market was superseded by compulsory labor service for the war economy. A supreme war office, Oberstes Kriegsamt, militarized the entire German economy and had the power to close factories, reorganize industrial branches, and prop up the economy with hidden inflationary financing. The government also introduced the term *Planwirtschaft* (planned economy), and its Hindenburg Plan set production protocols and organized the economy to meet state objectives. The state now owned key sectors of the economy, which worked astonishingly well for military production. The rising star economist John Maynard Keynes noted in 1924 that "War experience in the organization of socialized production has left some near observers optimistically anxious to repeat it in peace conditions. War socialism unquestionably achieved a production of wealth on a scale far greater than we ever knew in Peace . . . [The] change is in the air" (Keynes, 1927, 5, 52–3). As the title of Keynes' lecture prophesied, "The End of Laissez-faire" did in fact transpire. During the interwar decades, more a twenty-year armistice than a real peace, economic warfare continued. The "backlash" of the first globalization, as Ronald Findlay and Kevin O'Rourke called it, led to the victory of economic nationalism. "World War I brought the liberal economic order of the late nineteenth century to an abrupt halt. It thus marked the end of an era" (Findlay and O'Rourke, 2007, 429). During the troubled interwar period, postwar inflation, reconstruction, and (after a brief intermezzo of promising development in the second half of the 1920s) the Great Depression combined with war preparations to abolish laissez-faire. Protectionism replaced free trade, and the gold standard collapsed. The state became a dominant factor in the economy.

Desperate peripheries rose up in rebellion. After the war, left- and right-wing revolutions rocked these regions. New political regimes emerged – all of them *modernization dictatorships* embracing economic self-sufficiency. They introduced import substitution in the place of the now discredited export-led development policies, and they turned to alternative economic models. The new models, Keynesian regulated market systems, and Bolshevik and Fascist dirigiste and planned economies, although politically diametrically opposed to each other, had common roots in the German war economy.

The Bolshevik economic system started out with a war-dirigiste model. In his *The Immediate Tasks of the Soviet Government* written in April 1918, Vladimir I. Lenin called for adopting the "last word of capitalism" and employing the "best system of accounting and control." A month later, he outlined his idea in more detailed form in his *Left-Wing Childishness and the Petty-Bourgeois Mentality*.

Take the most concrete example of state capitalism . . . It is Germany. Here we have "the last word" in modern large-scale capitalist engineering and planned organization, subordinated to *Junker-bourgeois imperialism*. Cross out the words in italics, and in place of the militarist Junker, bourgeois, imperialist state put also a state, but different social type . . . a Soviet state . . . and you will have the sum total of the conditions necessary for socialism. (Lenin, 1971, 417, 443)

The non-market, centrally planned Soviet economic system gradually emerged with an accelerated dirigiste, isolationist war-economy character.

Almost simultaneously, an extreme right-wing system, Fascism, emerged in postwar Italy. Its point of departure was the proposition of Enrico Corradini's Italian Nationalist Party that Italy is a "proletarian nation" that has to revolt against the "bourgeois nations" to realize its interests. Self-sufficiency and state-run, forced modernization stood at the center of a gradually developed Fascist economic doctrine. Benito Mussolini declared, "If the nineteenth century was the century of individualism . . . [the twentieth century] is a collective century, and therefore the century of the State. [The totalitarian state is also] an economic organization of the nation" (Mussolini, 1935, 31). The Fascist state directed the entire economy and owned a large part of it. Mussolini nationalized most of the big banks, and established the Istituto per la Riconstruzione Industriale, a giant holding company, and several other state companies by nationalizing key sectors. In January 1944, his Fascist Republic in north Italy declared the "abolition of capitalism" and the nationalization of all companies that employed more than a hundred employees (Gregor, 1969).

The Bolshevik system or its variants spread over the Central and Eastern European peripheries, arising in Hungary, Bulgaria, and even in Bavaria in 1919, but being quickly overthrown militarily. The Italian Fascist economic model or its variants were soon introduced in Primo de Rivera's and Francisco Franco's Spain, António Salazar's Portugal, and General Metaxas' Greece. Important elements were later adopted in Austria and Hungary. During the Great Depression, in chaotic conflict-ridden, revenge-seeking and war-preparing Germany, an even stricter type of state-run and planned fascist economic model was introduced. In the German *Grossraumwirtschaft*, Hitler, with bilateral agreements, created a large economic backyard in subordinated Central and Eastern Europe and introduced trade in kind. Countries of the region paid one another with goods and used currency in an extremely limited way.

Various new economic regimes emerged after World War I in the place of a *laissez-faire* system and a globalizing Europe, which had marked the last third of the nineteenth century. These included the Keynesian regulated market system, the autarchic, state-run and partly state-owned Fascist model, and the non-market, entirely state-owned Soviet model. The weaknesses and conflicts of nineteenth-century European economic development, and the failure or semi-success of the peripheries, thus generated strong state interventionism, nationalization, and centralized planning in the non-industrialized European peripheries and the regulated market economies in the advanced West. Most of these new economic systems served self-sufficiency and war preparation. The transformation culminated in World War II, history's most forbidding and destructive war.

Note

1. This epilogue is based on Berend (2006a).

References

Acworth, William, 1925. *Financial Reconstruction in England, 1815–1822*, London: P. S. King and Son.

Ady, Endre, 1973. *Összes prózai művei*, Vol. X, Budapest: Akadémiai Kiadó.

A'Hearn, Brian, 2003. "Anthropometric Evidence on Living Standards in North Italy, 1730–1860," *Journal of Economic History*, Vol. 63, No. 2.

A'Hearn, Brian and U. Woitek, 2001. "More International Evidence of the Historical Properties of Business Cycles," *Journal of Monetary Economics*, Vol. 47.

A'Hearn, Brian, Jörg Baten, and Dorothee Crayen, 2009. "Quantifying Quantitative Literacy: Age Heaping and the History of Human Capital," *Journal of Economic History*, Vol. 69, No. 3.

Aldcroft, Derek H., 1964. "The Entrepreneur and the British Economy, 1870–1914," *Economic History Review*, 2nd series, Vol. 8.

Aldcroft, Derek H. and Harry W. Richardson, 1969. *The British Economy 1870–1939*, London: Macmillan.

Alford, B. W. E., 1977. "Entrepreneurship, Business Performance and Industrial Development," *Business History*, Vol. 19.

— 1999. "Flagging or Failing? British Economic Performance, 1880–1914," in Jean-Pierre Dormois and Michael Dintenfass (eds.), *The British Industrial Decline*. London: Routledge.

Allen, Arthur, 2007. *Vaccine. The Controversial Story of Medicine's Greatest Lifesaver*, New York: W. W. Norton.

Allen, Robert C., 1994. "Agriculture during the Industrial Revolution," in Frederick Floud and Donald McCloskey (eds.), *The Economic History of Britain since 1700*, Vol. 1: 1700–1860, 2nd edn, Cambridge University Press.

— 1998. "Tracking the Agricultural Revolution," Discussion Paper no. 98–18. Department of Economics, University of British Columbia, available at http://web.arts.ubc.ca/econ/.

___ 2004. "Britain's Economic Ascendency in a European Context," in Leandro Prados de la Escosura (ed.), *Exceptionalism and Industrialization. Britain and its European Rivals, 1688–1815*, Cambridge University Press.

___ 2009a. *The British Industrial Revolution in Global Perspective*. Cambridge University Press.

___ 2009b. "The Industrial Revolution in Miniature: The Spinning Jenny in Britain, France, and India," *Journal of Economic History*, Vol. 69, No. 4.

Amin, Samir, 1970. *L'accumulation à l'échelle mondiale*, Paris: Anthropos.

Anez Alvarez, R., 1970. "Los inversions estranjeros en España de 1855 a 1881," in Pedro Schwartz (ed.), *Enayos sobre la economia española a mediados del siglo XX*, Madrid: Banco de España.

Appleby, Joyce, 2010. *The Relentless Revolution. A History of Capitalism*, New York: W. W. Norton.

Arendt, Hannah, 1966. *The Origins of Totalitarianism*, Cleveland, Ohio: Meridien.

Armengaud, André, 1973. "Population in Europe, 1700–1914," in Carlo Cipolla (ed.), *The Fontana Economic History of Europe*, Vol. III. *The Industrial Revolution*, London: Collins.

Armengaud, André and Marcel R. Reinhard, 1961. *Histoire générale de la population mondiale*, Paris: Éditions Montchrestien.

Armstrong, John, 1995. "Inland Navigation and the Local Economy," in Andreas Kunz and John Armstrong (eds.), *Inland Navigation and Economic Development in Nineteenth-Century Europe*, Mainz: Verlag Philipp von Zabern.

Ashton, Thomas S., 1948. *The Industrial Revolution, 1760–1830*, Oxford University Press.

Aslanian, Sebouh David, 2011. *From the Indian Ocean to the Mediterranean. The Global Trade Networks of Armenian Merchants from New Julfa*, Berkeley: University of California Press.

Baasch, E., 1927. *Holländische Wirtschaftsgeschichte*, Jena: G. Fischer.

Baghdiantz McCabe, Ina, Gelina Harlaftis, and Joanna Pepelasis Minoglou (eds.), 2005. *Diaspora Entrepreneurial Networks. Four Centuries of History*, Oxford: Berg.

Bairoch, Paul, 1973a. "Agriculture and the Industrial Revolution, 1700–1870," in Carlo Cipolla (ed.), *The Fontana Economic History of Europe*, Vol. III: *The Industrial Revolution*, London: Collins/Fontana.

___ 1973b. "European Foreign Trade in the 19th Century: The Development of the Value and Volume of Exports," *Journal of European Economic History*, Vol. 2, No. 1.

___ 1976a. *Commerce extérieur et développement économique de l'Europe au XIXe siècle*, Paris: Mouton.

___ 1976b. "Europe's Gross National Product: 1800–1975," *Journal of European Economic History*, Vol. 5, No. 2.

— 1982. "International Industrialization Levels from 1750 to 1980," *Journal of European Economic History*, No. 11.

— 1989. "European Trade Policy 1815–1914," in Peter Mathias and Sidney Pollard (eds.), *The Cambridge Economic History of Europe*, Vol. VIII, Cambridge University Press.

— 1991. "How and not Why? Economic Inequalities between 1800 and 1913: Some Background Figures," in Jean Batou (ed.), *Between Development and Underdevelopment. The Precocious Attempts at Industrialization of the Periphery, 1800–1870*, Genève: Librairie Droz.

Baldwin, Peter, 1990. *The Politics of Social Solidarity. Class Bases of the European Welfare States, 1875–1975*. Cambridge University Press.

Baltzarek, Franz, 2005. "Finanzrevolutionen, Industrializierung und Crédit Mobilier Banken in der Habsburgmonarchie," in Oliver Rathkolb, Theodor Venus, and Ulrike Zimmerl (eds.), *Bank Austria Creditanstalt*, Vienna: Paul Zsolnay Verlag.

Baranowski, Shelley, 2001. "Agrarian Transformation and Right Radicalism: Economics and Politics in Rural Prussia, 1830–1947," in Philip G. Dwyer (ed.), *Modern Prussian History, 1830–1947*, Harlow: Pearson Education, 146–165.

Barnett, Vincent,1998. *Kondratiev and the Dynamics of Economic Development: Long Cycles and Industrial Growth in Historical Context*, London: Macmillan.

— 2004. *The Revolutionary Russian Economy, 1890–1940. Ideas, Debates and Alternatives*, London: Routledge.

Barsby, Steven L., 1969. "Economic Backwardness and Characteristics of Development," *Journal of Economic History*, Vol. 29, No. 31.

Bastien, Carlos, 2002. "Friedrich List and Oliveira Marreca: Some Odd Coincidences," in Michalis Psalidopoulos and Maria Eugénia Mata (eds.), *Economic Thought and Policy in Less Developed Europe. The Nineteenth Century*, London: Routledge.

Baugh, Daniel A., 2004. "Naval Power: What Gave the British Navy Superiority?" in Leandro Prados de la Escosura (ed.), *Exceptionalism and Industrialization. Britain and its European Rivals, 1688–1815*, Cambridge University Press.

Baxa, Jacob and Guntwin Bruhns, 1967. *Zucker in Leben der Völker. Eine Kultur- und Wirtschaftsgeschichte*, Berlin: Bartens.

Belich, James, 2009. *Replenishing the Earth. The Settler Revolution and the Rise of the Anglo-World, 1783–1939*, Oxford University Press.

Berend, Ivan T., 2003. *History Derailed. Central and Eastern Europe in the Long Nineteenth Century*, Berkeley: University of California Press.

— 2006a. *An Economic History of Twentieth-Century Europe. Economic Regimes from Laissez-faire to Globalization*, Cambridge University Press.

— 2006b. "Organization and Management as Growth Factors in the 20th Century European Economy," in Vassilis Angelis and Leonidas Maroudas (eds.),

Economic Systems, Development Policies and the Enterprise Strategies in the Age of Globalization, Athens: Papazissis.

Berend, Ivan T. and Tamás Csató, 2001. *Evolution of the Hungarian Economy, 1848–1998*, Boulder, Colo.: Social Science Monographs.

Berend, Ivan T. and György Ránki, 1955. *Magyarország gyáripara 1900–1914*, Budapest: Szikra Kiadó.

— 1970. "Nationaleincommen und Kapitalakkumulation in Ungarn, 1867–1914," *Studia Historica*, No. 62.

— 1972. *A magyar gazdaság száz éve*, Budapest: Közgazdasági Kiadó.

— 1973. "Méthodologie et concept de l'Allgemeine Wirtschaftsgeschichte. Une approche pour la période moderne relative à l'Europe de l'Est," in Branislava Tenenti (ed.), *Méthodologie de l'histoire et des sciences humaines, Mélanges en l'honneur de Fernand Braudel*, Paris: Privat.

— 1974. *Economic Development in East-Central Europe in the 19th and 20th Centuries*. New York: Columbia University Press.

— 1982. *The European Periphery and Industrialization 1780–1914*, Cambridge University Press.

— 1987. *Európa gazdasága a 19. században, 1780–1914*, Budapest: Gondolat.

Berg, Maxine, 1994. "Factories, Workshops and Industrial Organization," in Roderick Floud and Donald McCloskey (eds.), *The Economic History of Britain since 1700*, Vol. I: *1700–1860*, 2nd edn, Cambridge University Press.

Berg, Maxine, Pat Hudson, and Michael Sonenscher (eds.), 1983. *Manufacture in Town and Country before the Factory*, Cambridge University Press.

Berlin, Isaiah, 1999. *The Roots of Romanticism*, edited by Henry Hardy, The A. W. Mellon Lectures, Bollingen series 45, Princeton University Press.

— 2000. *The Power of Ideas*, edited by Henry Hardy, Princeton University Press.

Besomi, Daniele, 2009. "Clément Juglar and his Contemporaries on the Causes of Commercial Crises," *Revue européenne des sciences sociales*, Vol. 47, No. 143.

Bettin Lattes, Gianfranco and Ettore Recchi (eds.), 2005. *Comparing European Societies. Towards a Sociology of the European Union*, Bologna: Monduzzi.

Bevilacqua, Piero, 1989. *Storia dell' agricultura italiana in età contemporanea*, Venice: Spazi e Paesaggi.

— 1993. *Breve storia dell'Italia meridionale all'ottocento a oggi*, Rome.

Bibó, István, 1986. *Válogatott Tanulmányok*, Vol. II. Budapest: Magvető Könyvkiadó.

Bielenberg, A., 2008. "What Happened to Irish Industry after the British Industrial Revolution? Some Evidence from the First UK Census of Production in 1907," *Economic History Review*, Vol. 61, No. 4.

Bjerke, K. and N. Ussing, 1958. *Studier over Danmarks Nationalprodukt 1870–1950*. Copenhagen: Gads Forlag.

Blackbourn, David, 1998. *The Long Nineteenth Century. A History of Germany, 1780–1918*. Oxford University Press.

Blackwell, William L., 1982. *The Industrialization of Russia. An Historical Perspective.* 2nd edn, Arlington Heights, Ill.: Harlan Davidson.

Blanc, Alan, Michael McEvoy, and Roger Plank (eds.), 1993. *Architecture and Construction in Steel,* London: E. and F. N. Spon.

Bloch, Marc, [1941] 1992. *The Historian's Craft,* Manchester University Press.

Bogart, Dan, Mauricio Drelichman, Oscar Gelderblom, and Jean-Laurent Rosenthal, 2010. "State and Private Institutions," in Stephen Broadberry and Kevin H. O'Rourke (eds.), *The Cambridge Economic History of Modern Europe,* Vol. I: *1700 to 1870,* Cambridge University Press.

Bogucka, Maria, 1993. "Social Structures and Customs in Early Modern Poland," *Acta Poloniae Historica,* Vol. 68.

Bohac, Rodney, 1989. "Agricultural Structure and the Origins of Migration in Central Russia, 1810–1850," in George Grantham and Carol S. Leonard (eds.), *Agrarian Organization in the Century of Industrialization: Europe, Russia, and North America,* Greenwich, Conn.: Jai Press.

Bonin, Herbert, 1991. "The Case of the French Banks," in Rondo Cameron and V. I. Bovikin (eds.), *International Banking 1870–1914.* Oxford University Press.

— 2007. "French Investment Banking at Belle Époque: The Heritage of the 19th Century Haute Banque," paper presented at the Congress of the European Business History Association in Geneva, www.unige.ch/ses/instec/EBHA2007/papers/Bonin.pdf.

Borchardt, Knut, 1973. "Germany 1700–1914," in Carlo Cipolla (ed.), *The Fontana Economic History of Europe,* Vol. IV: *The Emergence of Industrial Societies,* Part I, Glasgow: Collins/Fontana.

Boserup, Ester, 1990. *Economic and Demographic Relationships in Development,* Baltimore: Johns Hopkins University Press.

Bouvier, Jean and R. Girault, 1976. *L'impérialisme français d'avant 1914,* Paris: Mouton.

Bovikin, Valerij I., 1967. *Zarozhdienie finansovo kapitala v Rossii,* Moscow University.

— 1973. "Oroszország ipari fejlődésének társadalmi-gazdasági problémái," *Történelmi Szemle,* Nos. 1–2.

Bovikin, Valerij I. and B. V. Ananich, 1991. "The Role of International Factors in the Formation of the Banking System in Russia," in Rondo Cameron and V. I. Bovikin (eds.), *International Banking 1870–1914.* Oxford University Press.

Braudel, Fernand, 1979. *Civilisation matérielle, économie et capitalisme, XVe–XVIIIe siècle,* Vol. I: *Les structures du quotidian: le possible et l'impossible,* Paris: Colin.

Brenner, Robert, 2001. "The Low Countries in the Transition to Capitalism," in Peter Hoppenbrouwers and Jan Luiten van Zanden (eds.), *Peasants into*

Farmers? The Transformation of Rural Economy and Society in the Low Countries (Middle Ages to 19th Century) in Light of the Brenner Debate, Turnhout: Brepols.

Brenner, Robert, and Christopher Isett, 2002. "England's Divergence from China's Yangzi Delta: Property Relations, Microeconomics, and Patterns of Development," *Journal of Asian Studies,* Vol. 61, No. 2.

Broad, John (ed.), 2009. *A Common Agricultural Heritage? Revising French and British Rural Divergence,* Exeter: British Agricultural History Society.

Broadberry, Stephen, 2006. *Market Services and the Productivity Race, 1850–2000. British Performance in International Perspective,* Cambridge University Press.

Broadberry, Stephen and Carsten Burhop, 2008. "Resolving the Anglo-German Industrial Productivity Puzzle, 1895–1935. A Response to Professor Ritschl," *Journal of Economic History,* Vol. 68, No. 3.

Broadberry, Stephen and Bishuprya Gupta, 2006. "The Early Modern Great Divergence: Wages, Prices and Economic Development in Europe and Asia, 1500–1800," *Economic History Review,* Vol. 59, No. 1.

Broadberry, Stephen and Kevin H. O'Rourke (eds.), 2010. *The Cambridge Economic History of Modern Europe,* Vol. I: *1700 to 1870;* Vol. II: *1870 to the Present,* Cambridge University Press.

Broadberry, Stephen, Giovanni Federico, and Alexander Klein, 2010. "Sectoral Development, 1870–1914," in Stephen Broadberry and Kevin H. O'Rourke (eds.), *The Cambridge Economic History of Modern Europe: 1700 to the Present,* Vol. II: *1870 to the Present,* Cambridge University Press.

Brock, Peter, 1972. *Nationalism and Populism in Partitioned Poland,* London: Orbis Books.

Brock, Thomas D., 1999. *Robert Koch: A Life in Medicine and Bacteriology,* Washington, D.C.: ASM Press.

Broder, Albert, 1991. "Banking and the Electrotechnical Industry in Western Europe," in Rondo Cameron and V. I. Bovikin (eds.), *International Banking 1870–1914.* Oxford University Press.

Brunt, Liam, 2004. "Nature or Nurture? Explaining English Wheat Yields in the Industrial Revolution, *c.* 1770," *Journal of Economic History,* Vol. 64, No. 1.

— 2006. "Rediscovering Risk. Country Banks as Venture Capital Firms in the First Industrial Revolution," *Journal of Economic History,* Vol. 66, No. 1.

Buchsteiner, Ilona, 1994. "Besitzkontinutät, Besitzwechsel und Besitsverlust in den Gutswirtschaften Pommerns 1879–1910," in Heinz Reif (ed.), *Ostelbische Agrargesellschaft im Keiserreich und in der Weimarer Republic,* Berlin: Akademie Verlag, 125–140.

Buganov, Viktor I., 1989. "The Russian Peasant Movement in the Eighteenth and Nineteenth Century," in George Grantham and Carol S. Leonard (eds.), *Agrarian Organization in the Century of Industrialization: Europe, Russia, and North America,* Greenwich, Conn.: Jai Press.

Bukharin, Nikolai, [1915] 1966. *Imperialism and World Economy*, New York: Howard Fertig.

Burds, Jeffrey, 1998. *Peasant Dreams and Market Politics. Labor Migration and the Russian Village, 1861–1905*, University of Pittsburgh Press.

Butterfield, Herbert, [1950] 1962. *The Origins of Modern Science*, New York: Collier.

Cafagna, Luciano, [1989] 1994a. "Discussion of the Origins of Italian Economic Dualism," in Gianni Federico (ed.), *The Economic Development of Italy since 1870*, Aldershot: Elgar.

— 1994b. *Nord e sud: non fare a pezzi l'unità d'Italia*, Venice: Marsilio.

Cain, P. J. and A. G. Hopkins, 2001. *British Imperialism, 1688–2000*, 2nd edn, London: Longman.

Calvo, Angel, 2006. "The Shaping of Urban Telephone Networks in Europe, 1877–1926," *Urban History*, Vol. 33, No. 3.

Cameron, Rondo, 1957. "Profit, croissance et stagnation en France au XIXe siècle," *Économie appliqué*, Vol. 10, Nos. 2–3.

— 1966. *France and the Economic Development of Europe 1800–1914*, 2nd edn, Chicago: Rand McNally.

— 1967. *Banking in the Early Stages of Industrialization. A Study in Comparative Economic History*, Oxford University Press.

Cameron, Rondo and V. I. Bovikin (eds.), 1991. *International Banking 1870–1914*, Oxford University Press.

Cameron, William Bruce, 1963. *Informal Sociology. A Casual Introduction to Sociological Thinking*, New York: Random House.

Capie, Forrest, 2001. "The Origins and Development of Stable Fiscal and Monetary Institutions in England," in Michael D. Bordo and Roberto Cortés-Conde (eds.), *Transferring Wealth and Power from the Old to the New World. Monetary and Fiscal Institutions in the 17th through the 19th Centuries*, Cambridge University Press.

Carmona, Badia, Albert Carreras, and Jorge Nadal (eds.), 1990. *Pautas regionales de la industrialización española, siglos XIX y XX*, Barcelona: Editorial Ariel.

Carnegie, Andrew, 1905. *James Watt*, New York: Doubleday.

Caron, François, 1979. *An Economic History of Modern France*, New York: Columbia University Press.

Caumanns, Ute, 1994. *Technischer Fortschritt und sozialer Wandel in deutschen Ostprovinzen*, Bonn: Kulturstiftung der deutschen Vertriebenen.

Chadwick, Owen, 1975. *The Secularization of the European Mind in the Nineteenth Century*, Cambridge University Press.

Chandler, Alfred D. Jr., 1977. *The Visible Hand. The Managerial Revolution in American Business*, Cambridge, Mass.: The Belknap Press of Harvard University Press.

— 1990. *Scale and Scope: The Dynamics of Industrial Capitalism*, Cambridge, Mass.: Harvard University Press.

Chapman, Stanley D., 1972. *The Cotton Industry in the Industrial Revolution*, London: Macmillan.

— 2006. *The Rise of Merchant Banking*, London: Routledge.

Chayanov, Alexander V., 1966. *The Theory of Peasant Economy*, New York: R. D. Irwin.

Chekhov, Anton P., [1904] 1917. *The Cherry Orchard*, trans. Julius West, New York: Scribner's.

Chirot, Daniel, 1997. "Conflicting Identities and the Danger of Communalism," in Daniel Chirot and Anthony Reid, *Essential Outsider: Chinese and Jews in the Modern Transformation of Southeast Asia and Central Europe*, Seattle: University of Washington Press.

Cipolla, Carlo M. (ed.), 1973. *The Fontana Economic History of Europe*, Vol. IV: *The Emergence of Industrial Societies*, Part 2, London: Fontana.

— 1994a. *Before the Industrial Revolution. European Society and Economy 1000–1700*, 3rd edn, New York: W. W. Norton.

— 1994b. "The Industrial Revolution," in Frederick Floud and Donald McCloskey (eds.), *The Economic History of Britain since 1700*, Vol. I: *1700–1860*, 2nd edn, Cambridge University Press.

Cipolla, Carlo and Knut Borchardt (eds.), 1985. *Europäische Wirtschaftsgeschichte*, Vol. IV, Stuttgart: Gustav Fischer Verlag.

Clancy-Smith, Julia A., 2011. *Mediterraneans, North Africa and Europe in an Age of Migration, c.1800–1900*, Berkeley: University of California Press.

Clapham, John H., 1930. *An Economic History of Modern Britain*, Vol. I, Cambridge University Press.

Clark, Christopher and Wolfram Kaiser (eds.), 2003. *Culture Wars. Secular–Catholic Conflict in Nineteenth-Century Europe*. Cambridge University Press.

Clark, Gregory, 1993. "Agriculture and the Industrial Revolution, 1700–1850," in J. Mokyr (ed.), *The British Industrial Revolution*, Boulder, Colo.: Westview.

— 2007. *A Farewell to Alms. A Brief Economic History of the World*, Princeton University Press.

Clark, Gregory and Gillian Hamilton, 2006. "Survival of the Richest. The Malthusian Mechanism in Pre-Industrial England," *Journal of Economic History*, Vol. 66. No. 3.

Coale, A. J. and E. M. Hoover, 1958. *Population Growth and Economic Development in Low-income Countries*, Princeton University Press.

Cobden, Richard, 1994. *The European Diaries of Richard Cobden, 1846–1849*, edited by Miles Taylor, Aldershot: Scholar Press.

Cohen, H. Floris, 2007. "Reconceptualizing the Scientific Revolution," *European Review*, Vol. 15, No. 4.

Cohen, John and Giovanni Federico, 2001. *The Growth of the Italian Economy, 1820–1960,* Cambridge University Press.

Cohen, Jon S. and Francesco L. Galassi, 1990. "Sharecropping and Productivity: 'Feudal Residuel' in Italian Agriculture, 1911," *Economic History Review,* Vol. 43, No. 4.

Colombo, John Robert and Nikola Roussanoff (eds.), 1976. *(The) Balkan Range: A Bulgarian Reader,* Toronto: Hounslow Press.

Conze, Werner, 1969. "The Effect of Nineteenth-Century Liberal Agrarian Reforms on Social Structure in Central Europe," in F. Crouzet, W. H. Chaloner, and W. M. Stern (eds.), *Essays in European Economic History 1789–1914,* New York: St. Martin's Press.

Cooper, J. P., 1985. "In Search of Agrarian Capitalism," in T. H. Aston and C. H. E. Philpin (eds.), *The Brenner Debate. Agrarian Class Structure and Economic Development in Pre-Industrial Europe,* Cambridge University Press.

Cotrell, P. L., 1991. "Great Britain," in Rondo Cameron and V. I. Bovikin (eds.), *International Banking 1870–1914,* Oxford University Press.

Crafts, Nicholas, 1985. *British Economic Growth during the Industrial Revolution,* Oxford: Clarendon Press.

— 1994. "The Industrial Revolution," in Roderick Floud and Donald McCloskey (eds.), *The Economic History of Britain since 1700,* Vol. I: *1700–1860,* 2nd edn, Cambridge University Press.

— 1995. "Exogenous or Endogenous Growth? The Industrial Revolution Reconsidered," *Journal of Economic History,* Vol. 55, No. 4.

— 1997. *Britain's Relative Economic Decline, 1870–1995,* London: Social Market Foundation.

Crafts, Nicholas and C. Knick Harley, 2004. "Precocious British Industrialization: A General Equilibrium Perspective," in Leandro Prados de la Escosura (ed.), *Exceptionalism and Industrialization. Britain and its European Rivals, 1688–1815,* Cambridge University Press.

Crafts, Nicholas, S. J. Leybourne, and T. C. Mills, 1988. *Economic Growth in Nineteenth-Century Britain. Comparisons with Europe in the Context of Gerschenkron's Hypotheses,* Coventry: University of Warwick.

Crafts, N. F. R., S. J. Leybourne, and T. C. Mills, 1991. "Britain," in Rychard Sylla and Gianni Toniolo (eds.), *Patterns of European Industrialization. The Nineteenth Century,* London: Routledge.

Craig, Lee A. and Douglas Fisher, 1997. *The Integration of the European Economy, 1850–1913,* Houndmills: Macmillan.

Craig, Lee and Concepción García-Iglesias, 2010. "Business Cycles," in Stephen Broadberry and Kevin H. O'Rourke (eds.), *The Cambridge Economic History of Modern Europe,* Vol. I: *1700 to 1870,* Cambridge University Press, 122–144.

Crisp, Olga, 1976. *Studies in the Russian Economy before 1914*, London: Macmillan.

Croce, Benedetto, [1921] 1960. *History – Its Theory and Practice*, New York: Russel and Russel.

Crossick, Geoffrey and Serge Jaumain (eds.), 1999. *Cathedrals of Consumption. The European Department Store, 1850–1939*, Aldershot: Ashgate.

Crouzet, François (ed.), 1972. *Capital Formation in the Industrial Revolution*, London: Methuen.

—— 1985. *The First Industrialists: The Problem of Origins*, Cambridge University Press.

—— 1991. "France," in Mikuláš Teich and Roy Porter (eds.), *The Industrial Revolution in National Context. Europe and the USA*, Cambridge University Press.

—— 1996. *Britain, France, and International Commerce from Louis XIV to Victoria*, Aldershot: Ashgate.

—— 2001. *A History of the European Economy, 1000–2000*, Charlottesville: University Press of Virginia.

—— 2003. "The Historiography of French Economic Growth in the Nineteenth Century," *Economic History Review*, Vol. 56, No. 2.

Cullen, Louis M., 1987. *An Economic History of Ireland since 1660*, London: B. T. Batsford.

Dahlmann, Dittmar, 2006. "Religion und Geschäft. Deutsche Unternehmer in Moskau und St. Petersburg von der Mitte des 19. Jahrhunderts bis 1914," in Jörg Gebhard, Rainer Lindner, and Bianka Pietrow-Ennker (eds.), *Unternehmer im Russischen Reich. Sozialprofil, Symbolwelten, Integrationsstrategien im 19. und frühen 20. Jahrhundert*, Osnabrück: Fibre Verlag.

Dal Lago, Enrico, 2005. *Agrarian Elites. American Slaveholders and Southern Italian Landowners, 1815–1861*, Baton Rouge: Louisiana State University Press.

Dal Lago, Enrico and Rick Halpern (eds.), 2002. *The American South and the Italian Mezzogiorno: Essays in Comparative History*, New York: Palgrave Macmillan.

Datta, N. C., 2005. *The Story of Chemistry*, New Delhi: Universities Press India.

Davies, Norman, 1986. *Heart of Europe. A Short History of Poland*, Oxford University Press.

Davis, John A. (ed.), 2000. *Italy in the Nineteenth and Twentieth Century, 1796–1900*, Oxford University Press.

Dean, Phyllis and W. A. Cole, 1962. *British Economic Growth, 1688–1959*, Cambridge University Press.

Debré, Patrice, 2000. *Louis Pasteur*, Baltimore: Johns Hopkins University Press.

Delaisi, Francis, 1929. *Les deux Europes*, Paris: Payot.

Dhondt, J., [1955] 1969. "The Cotton Industry at Ghent during the French Régime," in F. Crouzet, W. H. Chaloner, and W. M. Stern (eds.), *Essays in European Economic History, 1789–1914*, New York: St. Martin's Press.

Dincecco, Marc, 2009. "Fiscal Centralization, Limited Government, and Public Revenues in Europe, 1650–1913," *Journal of Economic History*, Vol. 69, No. 1.

Dobbs, Betty Jo Teeter and Margaret C. Jacob, 1995. *Newton and the Culture of Newtonianism*, Atlantic Highlands: Humanities Press.

Dolan, Brian, 2000. *Exploring European Frontiers. British Travellers in the Age of the Enlightenment*, Houndmills: Palgrave Macmillan.

Domar, Evsey D., 1989. "Were Russian Serfs Overcharged for their Land by the 1861 Emancipation? The History of One Historical Table," in George Grantham and Carol S. Leonard (eds.), *Agrarian Organization in the Century of Industrialization: Europe, Russia, and North America*, Greenwich, Conn.: Jai Press.

Domínguez Martín, Rafael, 2002. *La riqueza de las regions. Las desigualdades económicas regionales en España, 1700–2000*, Madrid: Alianza Editorial.

Dormois, Jean-Pierre and Michael Dintenfass (eds.), 1999. *The British Industrial Decline*, London: Routledge.

Douglas, Rachel and Barbara Frazier, 1992. "Mendeleyev and Witte – The Fight to Bring the 'American System' to 19th Century Russia," and "Introduction" to the English edn of Sergei Witte, The Fight for Russian Industry, *Executive Intelligence Review*, January, available at http://members tripod.com/~american_almanac.

Dumke, Horts R., 1979. "Anglo-deutscher Handel und Frühindustrialisierung in Deutschland 1882–1865," in Richard Tilly (ed.), *Deutsche Frühindustrialisierung, Geschichte und Gesellschaft*, Vol. 5, No. 2.

Dyos, Harold J. and Derek H. Aldcroft, 1974. *British Transport: An Economic Survey from the Seventeenth Century to the Twentieth*, Leicester University Press.

Eckaus, Richard S., 1961. "The North–South Differential in Italian Economic Development," *Journal of Economic History*, No. 3 (September).

Eckermann, Johann Peter, [1835] 2006. *Gespreche mit Goethe in letzten Jahren seines Lebens*, Frankfurt: Insel Verlag.

Eckstein, Alexander, 1958. "Individualism and the Role of the State in Economic Growth," *Economic Development and Cultural Change*, Vol. 6, No. 2.

Eden, Lorraine, 2000. "Bringing the Firm Back In: Multinationals in International Political Economy," in Richard Higgott and Anthony Payne (eds.), *The New Political Economy of Globalizations*, Vol. I, Cheltenham: Edward Elgar.

Eiduks, G. and J. Grosvalds, 1962. "Cementa rūpniecības iesākums un attīstība Latvijas PSR teritoriā līdz 1941.g," in *Par technikas vēsturi Latvijas PSR*, Riga: Ziņatne Akadēmijas Izdeuniecība.

Eisenman, Stephan, 1994. *Nineteenth Century Art. A Critical History*, London: Thames and Hudson.

Emilsson, Erik Örjan, 2005. *Before the European Miracle: Four Essays on Swedish Preconditions for Conquest, Growth and Voice*, University of Gothenburg Press.

Emmanuel, Arghiri, 1969. *L'Échange inégal. Essai sur les antagonismes dans les rapports économiques internationaux*, Paris: Maspero.

Engelgardt, A. N., 1993. *Aleksandr Nikolaevich Engelgardt's Letters from the Country, 1872–1887*, trans. Cathy A. Frierson, Oxford University Press.

Engels, Friedrich, [1844] 1975. "The Condition of the Working Class in England in 1844," in *Collected Works of Marx and Engels*, Vol. IV, New York: International Publisher.

Engerman, Stanley L., 2004. "Institutional Change and British Supremacy, 1650–1850. Some Reflections," in Leandro Prados de la Escosura (ed.), *Exceptionalism and Industrialization. Britain and its European Rivals, 1688–1815*. Cambridge University Press.

Eötvös, József, 1902. *Tanulmányok*, Budapest: Révai Testvérek.

Epstein, S. R., 2008. "Craft Guilds in the Pre-Modern Economy. A Discussion," *Economic History Review*, Vol. 61, No. 1.

Erle, Lord, 1925. "The Land and its People," in Eric L. Jones (ed.), *Agriculture and Economic Growth in England, 1650–1815*, London: Methuen.

___ [1912] 1961. *English Farming: Past and Present*, London: Heinemann.

Essemyr, Mats, 1992. "Nutritional Needs and Social Esteem: Two Aspects of Diet in Sweden during the 18th and 19th Centuries," in Hans J. Teuteberg (ed.), *European Food History. A Research Review*, Leicester University Press.

Esteban, Javier C., 2004. "Comparative Patterns of Colonial Trade: Britain and its Rivals," in Leandro Prados de la Escosura (ed.), *Exceptionalism and Industrialization. Britain and its European Rivals, 1688–1815*. Cambridge University Press.

Federico, Giovanni, 2005. *Feeding the World. An Economic History of Agriculture, 1800–2000*. Princeton University Press.

Federico, Giovanni and Gianni Toniolo, 1991. "Italy," in Richard Sylla and Gianni Toniolo (eds.), *Patterns of European Industrialization: The Nineteenth Century*, London: Routledge.

Feinstein, C. H., 1972. *National Income, Expenditure and Output of the United Kingdom 1855–1965*, Cambridge University Press.

Feis, Herbert, 1965. *Europe, the World's Banker, 1870–1914*, New York: Norton.

Fenoaltea, Stefano, 1983. "Italy," in Patrick O'Brien (ed.), *Railways and the Economic Development of Western Europe*, London: Macmillan.

___ 2003a. "Notes on the Rate of Industrial Growth in Italy, 1861–1913," *Journal of Economic History*, Vol. 63, No. 3.

___ 2003b. "Peeking Backward. Regional Aspects of Industrial Growth in Post-Unification Italy," *Journal of Economic History*, Vol. 63, No. 4.

Ferguson, Adam, 1768. *Essay on the History of Civil Society*, London: A. Millar and T. Cadell.

Fichte, Johann Gottlieb, [1800] 1920. *Der geschlossene Handelsstaat*, Jena: Gustav Fischer.

Field, Daniel, 1989. "The Polarization of Peasant Households in Prerevolutionary Russia: Zemstvo Censuses and Problems of Measurement," in George Grantham and Carol S. Leonard (eds.), *Agrarian Organization in the Century of Industrialization: Europe, Russia, and North America*, Greenwich, Conn.: Jai Press.

Findlay, Ronald and Kevin H. O'Rourke, 2007. *Power and Plenty. Trade, War, and the World Economy in the Second Millennium*, Princeton University Press.

Flandreau, Marc, Juan Flores, Clemens Jobst, and David Khoudour-Casteras, 2010. "Business Cycles, 1870–1914," in Stephen Broadberry and Kevin H. O'Rourke (eds.), *The Cambridge Economic History of Modern Europe*, Vol. II: *1870 to the Present*, Cambridge University Press.

Flinn, Michael, 1966. *The Origins of the Industrial Revolution*, London: Longmans.

Floud, Roderick, 1994. "Britain, 1860–1914: A Survey," in Roderick Floud and Donald McCloskey (eds.), *The Economic History of Britain since 1700*. Vol. II: *1860–1939*, 2nd edn, Cambridge University Press.

Fogel, Robert, 1964. *Railroads and American Economic Growth. Essays in Econometric History*, Baltimore: Johns Hopkins University Press.

Fontaine, André, 2001. "Farewell to the United States of Europe, Long Live the European Union," www.opendemocracy.net/content/articles/PDT/344.pdf.

Foreman-Peck, James, 1983. *A History of the World Economy. International Economic Relations since 1850*, Brighton: Wheatsheaf.

— 1999. "The Balance of Technological Transfers 1870–1914," in Jean-Pierre Dormois and Michael Dintenfass (eds.), *The British Industrial Decline*, London: Routledge.

— 2006. "Lessons from Italian Monetary Unification," Working Paper, Vienna: Oesterreichische Nationalbank.

Foreman-Peck, James and Pedro Lains, 2000. "European Economic Development. The Core and the Southern Periphery, 1870–1910," in Şevket Pamuk and Jeffrey G. Williamson (eds.), *The Mediterranean Response to Globalization before 1950*, London: Routledge, 76–106.

Foreman-Peck, James and R. Millward, 1994. *Public and Private Ownership of British Industry, 1820–1990*, Oxford: Clarendon Press.

Fraile, Pedro, 1987. "The Basque Provinces and the World Market," in Nicolás Sánchez-Albornoz (ed.), *The Economic Modernization of Spain, 1830–1930*, New York University Press.

— 1991. *Industrialización y grupos de presión: la economía política de la proteción en España, 1900–1950*, Madrid: Alianza.

Frank, Alison Fleig, 2005. *Oil Empire. Visions of Prosperity in Austrian Galicia*, Boston: Harvard University Press.

Frank, Andre Gunder, 1976. "Multilateral Merchandise Trade Imbalances and Uneven Economic Development," *Journal of European Economic History*, Vol. 5, No. 2.

___ 1998. *ReOrient: Global Economy in the Asian Age*, Berkeley: University of California Press.

Frank, Andre Gunder and Barry Gills (eds.), 1993. *The World System: Five Hundred Years or Five Thousand?* London: Routledge.

Freudenberger, Herman, 2003. *Lost Momentum. Austrian Economic Development 1750–1830*, Vienna: Böhlau.

Fridenson, Patrick, 1997. "France: The Relatively Slow Development of Big Business in the Twentieth Century," in Alfred D. Chandler, Franco Amatori, and Takashi Hikino (eds.), *Big Business and the Wealth of Nations*, Cambridge University Press.

Fridlizius, G., 1963. "Sweden's Exports 1850–1960," *Economy and History*, Vol. 4.

Frieden, Jeffrey, 1994. "International Investment and Colonial Control: A New Interpretation," *International Organization*, Vol. 48, No. 4.

Fritzsche, Bruno, 1991. "Switzerland," in Mikuláš Teich and Roy Porter (eds.), *The Industrial Revolution in National Context. Europe and the USA.* Cambridge University Press.

Galbraith, John Kenneth, 1961. *The Great Crash, 1929*, Boston: Houghton Mifflin.

Gall, Lothar, 2000. *Der Aufstieg eines Industrieimperiums*, Berlin: Siedler.

Gallagher, Jack and Ronald Robinson, 1953. "The Imperialism of Free Trade," *Economic History Review*. 2nd series, Vol. 6, No. 1.

Gardiner, Patrick, 1959. *Theories of History*, Glencoe, Ill.: The Free Press.

Gatrell, Peter, 1986. *The Tsarist Economy, 1850–1914*, London: Batsford.

Geary, Frank and Tom Stark, 2004. "Trends in Real Wages during the Industrial Revolution. A View from across the Irish Sea," *Economic History Review*, Vol. 57, No. 2.

Gelderblom, Oscar and Joost Jonker, 2004. "Completing a Financial Revolution: The Finance of the Dutch East Indian Trade and the Rise of the Amsterdam Capital Market, 1595–1612," *Journal of Economic History*, Vol. 64, No. 3.

___ 2011. "Public Finance and Economic Growth: The Case of Holland in the Seventeenth Century," *Journal of Economic History*, Vol. 71, No. 1.

Gerschenkron, Alexander, 1957. "Reflection on the Concept of 'Prerequisites' of Modern Industrialization," *L'industria*, Vol. 42.

___ 1962. *Economic Backwardness in Historical Perspective*, Cambridge, Mass.: Belknap Press.

___ 1968. *Continuity in History and Other Essays*, Cambridge, Mass.: Belknap Press.

___ 1970. *Europe in the Russian Mirror: Four Lectures in Economic History*, Cambridge University Press.

Gestwa, Klaus, 1999. *Proto-Industrialisierung in Russland. Wirtschaft, Herrschaft und Kulture in Ivanovo und Pavlovo, 1741–1932*, Göttingen: Vandenhoek and Ruprecht.

Gilder, Joseph B. (comp.), 1899. *Impressions of Spain. James Russell Lowell*, introduction by A. A. Adee, Boston: Houghton, Mifflin.

Girard, L., 1965. "Transport," in H. J. Habakkuk and M. Postan (eds.), *The Cambridge Economic History of Europe*, Vol. VI, Cambridge University Press.

Glass, D. V. and E. Grebenik, 1965. "World Population, 1800–1950," in H. J. Habakkuk and M. Postan (eds.), *The Cambridge Economic History of Europe*, Vol. VI, Cambridge University Press.

Goethe, J. W. von, 1961. *Faust*, trans. and with an introduction by Walter Kaufman, New York: Doubleday.

Gold, John R. and Margaret M. Gold, 2005. *Cities of Culture. Staging International Festivals and the Urban Agenda, 1851–2000*. Aldershot: Ashgate.

Gómez-Mendoza, Antonio, 1987. "Transportation and Economic Growth, 1830–1930," in Nicolás Sánchez-Albornoz (ed.), *The Economic Modernization of Spain, 1830–1930*, New York University Press.

___ 1995. "Europe's Cinderella: Inland Navigation in Nineteenth-Century Spain," in Andreas Kunz and John Armstrong (eds.), *Inland Navigation and Economic Development in Nineteenth-Century Europe*, Mainz: Verlag Philipp von Zabern.

Goose, Nigel and Lien Lun (eds.), 2005. *Immigrants in Tudor and Early Stuart England*, Brighton: Sussex Academic Press.

Goriushkin, Leonid, M., 1989. "The General and the Specific in Siberian Agrarian Development in the Second Half of the Nineteenth and the Beginning of the Twentieth Century," in George Grantham and Carol S. Leonard (eds.), *Agrarian Organization in the Century of Industrialization: Europe, Russia, and North America*, Greenwich, Conn.: Jai Press.

Gracia Delgado, José Luis, 1987. "Economic Nationalism and State Intervention, 1900–1930," in Nicolás Sánchez-Albornoz (ed.), *The Economic Modernization of Spain, 1830–1930*, New York University Press.

Grafe, Regina, Larry Neal, and Richard W. Unger, 2010. "The Service Sector," in Stephen Broadberry and Kevin H. O'Rourke (eds.), *The Cambridge Economic History of Modern Europe*, Vol. I: *1700 to 1870*, Cambridge University Press.

Grantham, George and Carol S. Leonard (eds.), 1989. *Agrarian Organization in the Century of Industrialization: Europe, Russia, and North America*, Greenwich, Conn.: Jai Press.

Greenfield, Kent Roberts, 1965. *Economics and Liberalism in the Risorgimento. A Study of Nationalism in Lombardy, 1814–1848*, Baltimore: Johns Hopkins University Press.

Gregor, James A., 1969. *The Ideology of Fascism. The Rationale of Totalitarianism*, New York: The Free Press.

Gregory, Paul R., 1992. "Rents, Land Prices and Economic Theory: The Russian Agrarian Crisis," in Linda Edmondson and Peter Waldron (eds.), *Economy and Society in Russia and the Soviet Union, 1860–1930*, New York: St. Martin's Press.

— 1994. *Before Command. An Economic History of Russia from Emancipation to the First Five-Year Plan*, Princeton University Press.

Greif, Avner, 2006. *Institutions and the Path to the Modern Economy. Lessons from Medieval Trade.* Cambridge University Press.

Grigg, David, B., 1980. *Population Growth and Agrarian Change: An Historical Perspective*, Cambridge University Press.

Gross, Nachum, 1966. "Industralization in Austria in the Nineteenth Century," Ph.D. dissertation, University of California, Berkeley.

Guinnane, Timothy W., William A. Sundstrom, and Warren Whatley (eds.), 2004. *History Matters. Essays on Economic Growth, Technology, and Demographic Change*, Stanford University Press.

Gunn, Geoffrey C., 2003. *First Globalization. The Eurasian Exchange, 1500–1800*, Lanham, Md.: Rowman and Littlefield.

Gustafsson, Bo, 1991. "The Industrial Revolution in Sweden," in Mikuláš Teich and Roy Porter (eds.), *The Industrial Revolution in National Context. Europe and the USA*, Cambridge University Press.

Hajnal, John, 1965. "European Marriage Patterns in Perspective," in V. D. Glass and D. E. C. Eversley (eds.), *Population in History*, London: E. Arnold.

Halpern, Joel M. and Barbara Krewsky Halpern, 1972. *A Serbian Village in Historical Perspective*, New York: Holt, Rinehart and Winston.

Hamilton, Alexander, [1791] 1961–79. "Report on Manufactures," December 5, 1791, in *The Papers of Alexander Hamilton*, Vol. II, edited by Harold C. Syrett *et al.*, 27 vols., New York: Columbia University Press.

Hamilton, E. J., 1938. "The Decline of Spain," *Economic History Review*, Vol. 8, No. 2.

Hannah, Leslie, 1991. "Scale and Scope: Towards a European Visible Hand," *Business History*, Vol. 33.

Harcave, Sidney, 2004. *Count Sergei Witte and the Twilight of Imperial Russia. A Biography*, Armonk, N.Y.: M. E. Sharpe.

Harley, C. K. and D. N. McCloskey, 1981. "Foreign Trade: Competition and the Expanding Economy," in R. C. Floud and D. N. McCloskey (eds.), *The Economic History of Britain since 1700*, Vol. II, Cambridge University Press.

Harris, R. John, 1998. *Industrial Espionage and Technology Transfer. Britain and France in the Eighteenth Century*, Aldershot: Ashgate.

Harris, Ron, 2000. *Industrializing English Law: Entrepreneurship and Business Organization, 1720–1844*, Cambridge University Press.

Harrison, Joseph, 1978. *An Economic History of Modern Spain*, Manchester University Press.

Harrison, Peter, 2007. "Was there a Scientific Revolution?" *European Review*, Vol. 15. No. 4.

Hartel, Hans and Harald Faber, 1918. *Co-operative Danish Agriculture*, London: Longmans.

Hartog, Adel P. den, 1992. "Modern Nutritional Problems and Historical Nutrition Research, with Special Reference to the Netherlands," in Hans J. Teuteberg (ed.), *European Food History. A Research Review*, Leicester University Press.

Hartwell, R. Max, 1971. *The Industrial Revolution and Economic Growth*, London: Methuen.

— 1973. "The Service Revolution: The Growth of Services in the Modern Economy, 1700–1914," in Carlo Cipolla (ed.), *The Fontana Economic History of Europe*, Vol. III: *The Industrial Revolution*, London: Collins/Fontana.

Hatton, Timothy J., Kevin H. O'Rourke, and Alan M. Taylor (eds.), 2007. *The New Comparative Economic History. Essays in Honor of Jeffrey G. Williamson*, Cambridge, Mass.: MIT Press.

Haudrère, Philippe, 2006. *Les Compagnies des Indes orientales. Trois siècles de rencontre entre Orientaux et Occidentaux, 1600–1858*, Paris: Desjonquères.

Haupt, Heinz-Gerhard and Jürgen Kocka, 2009. "Comparison and Beyond. Traditions, Scope, and Perspectives of Comparative History," in H.-G. Haupt and J. Kocka (eds.), *Comparative and Transnational History. Central European Approaches and New Perspectives*, New York: Berghahn Books.

Heckscher, Eli, [1919] 1949. "The Effect of Foreign Trade on the Distribution of Income," in Howard S. Ellis and Lloyd A. Metzler (eds.), *Readings in the Theory of International Trade*, Philadelphia: Blakiston.

— 1954. *An Economic History of Sweden*, Cambridge, Mass.: Harvard University Press.

Hegel, G. W. F., [1806] 2005. *The Letters*, trans. Clark Butler and Christine Seiler, Bloomington: Indiana University Press.

Heilbron, John L., 2007. "Coming to Terms with the Scientific Revolution," *European Review*, Vol. 15. No. 4.

Heimann, Eduard, 1964. *History of Economic Doctrines*, Oxford University Press.

Heller, Klaus, 2006. "Auf dem Weg zum Bourgeois? Das 'Moskau der Kaufleute' vor 1917. Gesellschaftliche Vorurteile gegenüber dem 'Kaufmann' im alten und neuen Russland," in Jörg Gebhard, Rainer Lindner, and Bianka Pietrow-Ennker (eds.), *Unternehmer im Russischen Reich. Sozialprofil, Symbolwelten, Integrationsstrategien im 19. und frühen 20. Jahrhundert*, Osnabrück: Fibre Verlag.

Herranz-Loncán, Alfonso, 2006. "Railroad Impact in Backward Economies. Spain, 1850–1913," *Journal of Economic History*, Vol. 66, No. 4.

Hertner, Peter, 1981, "Il capitale staniero in Italia, 1883–1914," *Studi storici*, Vol. 22, 767–795.

Heyn, Ugo, 1981. *Private Banking and Industrialization*, New York: Arno Press.

Hicks, John, 1969. *A Theory of Economic History*, Oxford: Clarendon Press.

Hildebrand, Karl-Gustaf, 1992. *Swedish Iron in the Seventeenth and Eighteenth Centuries. Export Industry before Industrialization*, Skriftserie 29, Södertälje: Jernkontorets Berghistorika.

Hilferding, Rudolf, [1910] 1981. *Finance Capital*, London: Routledge.

Hills, Richard L., 1993. *Power from Steam. A History of the Stationary Steam Engine*, Cambridge University Press.

Hitchin, Keith, 1994. *Rumania: 1866–1947*, Oxford University Press.

Hjerppe, Riita, 1982. "Finland in the European Economy 1860–1980," in *Festskrift til Kristof Glamann*, Odense.

Hjerppe, Riita and E. Pihkala, 1977. "The Gross Domestic Product of Finland in 1860–1913," *Economy and History*, Vol. 20, No. 2.

Hjerppe, R., M. Peltonen and E. Pihkala, 1984. "Investment in Finland, 1860–1979," *Scandinavian Economic History Review*, Vol. 32, No. 1.

Hobbes, Thomas, [1651] 1956. *Leviathan*, Chicago: Gateway.

Hobsbawm, Eric, 1964. *Labouring Men. Studies in the History of Labour*, London: Weidenfeld and Nicolson.

___ 1969. *Industry and Empire*, Harmondsworth: Penguin Books.

___ [1975] 1996. *The Age of Capital, 1848–1875*, New York: Vintage Books.

___ 1989. *The Age of Empire, 1875–1914*, New York: Vintage Books.

Hobson, John A., 1902. *Imperialism. A Study*, London: James Nisbet.

Hodgson, Marshall G. S., 1977. *The Venture of Islam. Conscience and History in World Civilization. The Gunpowder Empires and Modern Times*, Vol. III, University of Chicago Press.

___ 1993. *Rethinking World History: Essays on Europe, Islam and World History*, Cambridge University Press.

Hoffman, Philip T., David Jacks, Patricia A. Levin and Peter H. Lindert, 2002. "Real Inequality in Europe since 1500," *Journal of Economic History*, Vol. 62, No. 2.

Hoffman, W. G., 1955. *British Industry 1700–1950*, Oxford: Blackwell.

Hohenberg, Paul M., 2008. "Toward a More Useful Economic History," *Journal of Economic History*, Vol. 68, No. 2.

Holm, Edvard, 1888. *Festskrift i Anledning af den Nordiske Industri-, Landbrugs- og Kunstudstilling*, Copenhagen: G. E. C. Gad.

Holmgreen, Beth, 1998. *Rewriting Capitalism: Literature and the Market in Late Tsarist Russia and the Kingdom of Poland*, University of Pittsburgh Press.

Hoppenbrouwers, Peter and Jan Luiten van Zanden (eds.), 2001. *Peasants into Farmers. The Transformation of Rural Economy and Society in the Low*

Countries (Middle Ages to 19th Century) in Light of the Brenner Debate, Turnhout: Brepols.

Huang, Philip, 1991. "The Peasant Family and Rural Development in the Jangtzi Delta, 1350–1988," *Journal of Asian Studies*, Vol. 50, No. 3.

— 2002. "Development or Involution in Eighteenth Century Britain and China. A Review of Kenneth Pomeranz's *Great Divergence*," *Journal of Asian Studies*, Vol. 61, No. 2.

Hudson, Pat, 1983. "From Manor to Mill: The West Riding in Transition," in Maxine Berg, Pat Hudson, and Michael Sonenscher (eds.), *Manufacture in Town and Country before the Factory*, Cambridge University Press.

Hunt, Lynn, Margaret Jacob, and Wijnand Mijnhardt, 2010. *The Book that Changed Europe: Picart and Bernard's 'Religious Ceremonies of the World'*, Cambridge, Mass.: Harvard University Press.

Huntington, Samuel, P., 1996. *The Clash of Civilizations. The Remaking of the World Order*, New York: Simon and Schuster.

Israel, Jonathan, 1995. *The Dutch Republic. Its Rise, Greatness, and Fall, 1477–1806*, Oxford: Clarendon Press.

Ivanovskis, V., 1970. "Rīgas Politehnikais Institūts," in *Latvijas PSR Mazā enciklopēdija*, Riga: Ziņatne Akadēmijas Izdevniecība.

Ivaros, Martin and Adam Tooze, 2007. "Convergence or Divergence on Europe's Southeastern Periphery? Agriculture, Population, and GNP in Bulgaria, 1892–1945," *Journal of Economic History*, Vol. 67, No. 3.

Jacob, Margaret and Larry Stewart, 2004. *Practical Matter. The Impact of Newton's Science from 1687 to 1851*, Cambridge, Mass.: Harvard University Press.

Jeannin, Pierre, 1980. "La proto-industrialisation: développement ou impasse?" *Annales*, Vol. 35.

Jedlicki, Jerzy, 1999. *A Suburb of Europe: Nineteenth-Century Polish Approaches to Western Civilization*, Budapest: Central European Press.

Jensen, Einar E., 1982. *Bonde og Landbrug: Traek af Dansk Landbrugs Historie*, Odense: Landhusholdningsselskabets Forlag.

Jensen, Hans, 1945. "Danks Jordpolitik 1757–1919," in Anden Del, *Faestevaesenets Afvikling og Jordlovgivningen i Perioden 1910–1919*, Copenhagen: Nordisk Forlag.

Johansen, Hans-Christian, 1991. "Banking and Finance in the Danish Economy," in Rondo Cameron and V. I. Bovikin (eds.), *International Banking 1870–1914*, Oxford University Press.

John, Michael, 2000. "The Napoleonic Legacy and Problems of Restoration in Central Europe: The German Confederation," in David Laven and Lucy Riall (eds.), *Napoleon's Legacy. Problems of Government in Restoration Europe*, Oxford: Berg.

Jones, Eric Lionel (ed.), 1967. *Agriculture and Economic Growth in England, 1650–1815*, London: Methuen.

—— 1981. *The European Miracle: Environments, Economies, and Geopolitics in the History of Europe and Asia*, Cambridge University Press.

Jones, Geoffrey and Harm G. Schröter (eds.), 1993. *The Rise of Multinationals in Continental Europe*, Aldershot: Edward Elgar.

Jonge, Jan Aart de, 1969. *De industrialisatie in Nederland tussen 1850 en 1914*, Nijmegen: Socialistische Uitgeverij.

Jörberg, Lennart, 1973. "The Nordic Countries 1850–1914," in Carlo Cipolla (ed.), *The Fontana Economic History of Europe*, Vol. 4: *The Emergence of Industrial Societies*, Part 2, London: Collins/Fontana.

Juglar, Clément, 1862. *Des crises commerciales et de leur retour périodique en France, en Angleterre et aux Etats-Unis*, Paris: Guillaumin.

Kaelble, Hartmut, 2009. "Between Comparison and Transfer – and What Now? A French–German Debate," in Heinz-Gerhard Haupt and Jürgen Kocka (eds.), *Comparative and Transnational History. Central European Approaches and New Perspectives*, New York: Berghahn Books.

Kahan, Arcadius, 1989. *Russian Economic History. The Nineteenth Century*, University of Chicago Press.

Kahk, Juhan and Enn Tarvel, 1997. *An Economic History of the Baltic Countries*, Stockholm: Studia Baltica Stockholmiensia no. 20.

Kardasis, Vassilis, 2001. *Diaspora Merchants in the Black Sea. The Greeks in Southern Russia, 1775–1861*, Lanham, Md.: Lexington Books.

Katus, László, 1970. "Economic Growth in Hungary during the Age of Dualism (1867–1913)," *Studia Historica*, No. 62.

Kaukiainen, Yrjö, 2006. "Foreign Trade and Transport," in Jari Ojala, Jari Eloranta, and Jukka Jalava (eds.), *The Road to Prosperity. An Economic History of Finland*, Helsinki: Suomalaisen Kirjallisuuden Seura.

Kautsky, Karl, 1914. "Der Imperialismus," *Neue Zeit*, Vol. 2.

Kemp, Tom, 1969. *Industrialization in Nineteenth-Century Europe*, London: Longman.

Kenwood, A. G. and Alen L. Lougheed, 1971. *The Growth of the International Economy, 1820–1960*, London: Allen and Unwin.

Keynes, John Maynard, 1927. *The End of Laissez Faire*, London: Leonard and Virginia Woolf.

Khromov, P. A., 1950. *Ekonomicheskaia razvitie Rossii v 19–20 vekah (1800–1917)*, Moscow: Gozizdvo Polit.

Kindleberger, Charles, 1962. *Foreign Trade and National Economy*, New Haven: Yale University Press.

—— 1975. "The Rise of Free Trade in West Europe," *Journal of Economic History*, Vol. 35, No. 1.

Kisbán, Eszter, 1992. "Food and Foodways as the Subject of Historical Analyses in Hungary," in Hans J. Teuteberg (ed.), *European Food History. A Research Review*, Leicester University Press.

Kištimau, Andrej, 2006. "Jüdische Unternehmer in Weissrussland. Zeitgenössische Wahrnehmung, Sozialprofil und Wirtschaftsformen," in Jörg Gebhard, Rainer Lindner, and Bianka Pietrow-Ennker (eds.), *Unternehmer im Russischen Reich. Sozialprofil, Symbolwelten, Integrationsstrategien im 19. und frühen 20. Jahrhundert*. Osnabrück: Fibre Verlag.

Klíma, Arnošt, 1991. *Economy, Industry and Society in Bohemia in the 17th–19th Centuries*, Prague: Univerzita Karlova.

Kocka, Jürgen, 1980. "The Rise of the Modern Industrial Enterprise in Germany," in Alfred D. Chandler and Herman Daems (eds.), *Managerial Hierarchies: Comparative Perspectives on the Rise of the Modern Industrial Enterprise*, Cambridge, Mass.: Harvard University Press.

___ 2010. "History and the Social Sciences Today," in Hans Joas and Barbro Klein (eds.), *The Benefit of Broad Horizon. Intellectual Preconditions for a Global Social Science*, Leiden: Brill.

Kocka, Jürgen and John Breuilly (eds.), 1988. "Bürger und Bürgerlichkeit im 19. Jahrhundert," *Bulletin of the German Historical Institute*, Vol. 10, No. 3.

Kołodziejczyk, R. and R. Gradowski, 1974. *Zarys dziejów kapitalizmu w Polsce*, Warsaw: Państwowe Wydawnicestwo Naukowe.

Komlos, John, 1983. *Economic Development in the Habsburg Monarchy in the Nineteenth Century*, Boulder: East European Monographs.

___ 1998. "Shrinking in a Growing Economy? The Mystery of Physical Stature during the Industrial Revolution," *Journal of Economic History*, Vol. 58, No. 4.

Kondratiev, Nikolai, [1922] 1984. *The Long Wave Cycle*, New York: Richardson and Snyder.

Koning, Niek, 1994. *The Failure of Agrarian Capitalism. Agrarian Policies in the United Kingdom, Germany, the Netherlands and the USA, 1846–1919*, London: Routledge.

Kossert, Andreas, 2006. "Gelobte Land? Religiosität und unternehmer in der Industriegesellschaft Lodz und Manchester in langen 19. Jahrhundert," in Jörg Gebhard, Rainer Lindner, and Bianka Pietrow-Ennker (eds.), *Unternehmer im Russischen Reich. Sozialprofil, Symbolwelten, Integrationsstrategien im 19. und frühen 20. Jahrhundert*, Osnabrück: Fibre Verlag.

___ and Jerzy Tomaszewski, 1966. *Historia gospodarcza Polski XIX i XX wieku*, Warsaw: Wiedza Powszechna.

Kotkin, Stephen, 2009. *Uncivil Society: 1989 and the Implosion of the Communist Establishment*, New York: The Modern Library.

Kovalchenko, I. D., 1989. "The Peasant Economy in Central Russia in the Late Nineteenth and Early Twentieth Century," in George Grantham and Carol

S. Leonard (eds.), *Agrarian Organization in the Century of Industrialization: Europe, Russia, and North America*, Greenwich, Conn.: Jai Press.

Kriedte, P. H., H. Medick, and J. Schlumbohm, 1981. *Industrialization before Industrialization: Rural Industry in the Genesis of Capitalism*, Cambridge University Press.

Kudrle, Robert T. and Theodor R. Marmor, 1981. "Social Security: The Importance of Socioeconomic and Political Variables," in Peter Flora and Arnold J. Heidenheimer (eds.), 1981. *The Development of the Welfare States in Europe and America*, New Brunswick: Transaction.

Kuhn, Thomas S., 1962. *The Structure of Scientific Revolutions*, University of Chicago Press.

Kula, W., 1947. *Historia gospodarcza Polski 1864–1918*, Warsaw: Spółdzielnia Wydawnicza "Wiedza".

Kunz, Andreas and John Armstrong, 1995. *Inland Navigation and Economic Development in Nineteenth-Century Europe*, Mainz: Verlag Philipp von Zaben.

Kussmaul, Ann, 1994. "The Pattern of Work as the Eighteenth Century Began," in Roderick Floud and Donald McCloskey (eds.), *The Economic History of Britain since 1700*, Vol. I: *1700–1860*, 2nd edn, Cambridge University Press.

Kuznets, Simon, 1963. "Economic Growth and the Contribution of Agriculture: Notes on Measurements," in *The Role of Agriculture in Economic Development*, Oxford University Press. (Reprinted from the *International Journal of Agrarian Affairs*, Vol. 3, April 1961.)

— 1966. *Modern Economic Growth. Rate, Structure, and Spread*, New Haven: Yale University Press.

Lafferty, W., 1971. *Economic Development and the Response of Labour in Scandinavia*, Oslo: Universitetsforlaget.

Lains, Pedro, 1999. *L'économie portugaise au XIXe siècle. Croissance économique et commerce extérieur 1851–1913*, Paris: L'Harmattan.

Lamartine Yates, P., 1959. *Forty Years of Foreign Trade. A Statistical Handbook with Special References to Primary Products and Under-Developed Countries*, London: Allen and Unwin.

Lamoreaux, Naomi R., 2009. "Scylla or Charybdis? Historical Reflections on Two Basic Problems of Corporate Governance," *Business History Review*, Vol. 83.

Lamoreaux, Naomi, Daniel Ratt, and Peter Temin, 2003. "Beyond Markets and Hierarchies: Toward a New Synthesis of American Business History," *American Historical Review*, Vol. 108, No. 4.

Lampe, John R. and Melvin R. Jackson, 1982. *Balkan Economic History, 1550–1950. From Imperial Borderlands to Developing Nations*, Bloomington: Indiana University Press.

Lampe, Marcus, 2009. "Effects of Bilateralism and the MFN Clause on International Trade. Evidence for the Cobden-Chevalier Network, 1860–1875," *Journal of Economic History*, Vol. 69, No. 4.

Landes, David S., [1969] 1995. *The Unbound Prometheus. Technological Change and Industrial Development in Western Europe from 1750 to the Present*, Cambridge University Press.

— 1991. "Does it Pay to be Late?" in Colin Holmes and Alan Booth (eds.), *Economy and Society. European Industrialization and its Social Consequences. Essays Presented to Sidney Pollard*, Leicester University Press.

— 1998. *The Wealth and Poverty of Nations. Why Some Are So Rich and Some So Poor*, New York: W. W. Norton.

— 1999. "The Fable of the Dead Horse; or the Industrial Revolution Revisited," in Joel Mokyr (ed.), *The British Industrial Revolution. An Economic Perspective*, 2nd edn, Boulder, Colo.: Westview Press.

Landry, Adolphe, 1934. *La révolution démographique*, Paris: Sirey.

Lapavitsas, Costas, 2006. "Industrial Development and Social Transformation in Ottoman Macedonia," *Journal of European Economic History*, Vol. 35, No. 3.

Laue, Theodor H. von, 1969. *Sergei Witte and the Industrialization of Russia*, New York: Atheneum.

Laven, David and Lucy Riall (eds.), 2000. *Napoleon's Legacy. Problems of Government in Restoration Europe*, Oxford: Berg.

Lee, Clive, 1994. "The Service Industries," in Roderick Floud and Donald McCloskey (eds.), *The Economic History of Britain since 1700*, Vol. II: *1860–1939*, 2nd edn, Cambridge University Press.

Lenin, Vladimir I., [1899] 1956. *The Development of Capitalism in Russia*, Moscow: Foreign Language Publisher.

— 1971. *Selected Works*, One-Volume Edn, New York: International Publisher.

— [1917] 1974. *Imperialism, the Highest Stage of Capitalism. A Popular Outline*, Moscow: Foreign Language Publisher.

Leonard, Carol S., 1989. "Postscript," in George Grantham and Carol S. Leonard (eds.), *Agrarian Organization in the Century of Industrialization: Europe, Russia, and North America*, Greenwich, Conn.: Jai Press.

Leonard, Carol and Jonas Ljungberg, 2010. "Population and Living Standards," in Stephen Broadberry and Kevin H. O'Rourke (eds.), *The Cambridge Economic History of Modern Europe*, Vol. II: *1870 to the Present*, Cambridge University Press.

Le Play, Frédéric, 1871. *L'organisation de la famille*, Paris: Téqui.

Lévy-Leboyer, Maurice, 1968. "La croissance économique en France au XIXe siècle," *Annales*, No. 4.

Lewis, Arthur, 1978. *Growth and Fluctuations 1870–1913*, London: Allen and Unwin.

Liedtke, Rainer and Stephan Wendehorst (eds.), 1999. *Emancipation of Catholics, Jews, and Protestants. Minorities and the Nation State in Nineteenth-Century Europe*, Manchester University Press.

Lindert, Peter H. and Jeffrey G. Williamson, 1983. "English Workers' Living Standard during the Industrial Revolution. A New Look," *Economic History Review*, Vol. 36, No. 1.

List, Friedrich, [1841] 1947. *Das nationale System der politischen Ökonomie*, Stuttgart: J. G. Cotta'scher Verlag. Parts reprinted in the 1885 translation of Sampson S. Lloyd in *Introduction to Contemporary Civilization in the West*, prepared by the Contemporary Civilization Staff of Columbia College, New York: Columbia University Press, 1947.

Livi-Bacci, Massimo, 1991. *Population and Nutrition: An Essay on European Demographic History*, Cambridge University Press.

Locke, John, [1690] 1947. *Two Treatises on Government*, New York: Hafner.

Logio, George Clenton, 1932. *Rumania: Its History, Politics and Economics*, Manchester: Sherratt and Hughes.

Long, Jason, 2006. "The Socio-economic Return to Primary Schooling in Victorian England," *Journal of Economic History*, Vol. 66, No. 4.

Love, Joseph L., 1996. *Crafting the Third World. Theorizing Underdevelopment in Rumania and Brazil*, Stanford University Press.

___ 2002. "Resisting Liberalism: Theorizing Backwardness and Development in Rumania before 1914," in Michalis Psalidopulos and Maria Eugénia Mata (eds.), *Economic Thought and Policy in Less Developed Europe*, London: Routledge.

Lundström, Ragnhild, 1991. "Sweden," in Rondo Cameron and V. I. Bovikin (eds.), *International Banking, 1870–1914*, Oxford University Press.

Luxemburg, Rosa, [1973] 1975. *Gesammelte Werke*, Vol. V, Berlin: Institut für Marxismus-Leninismus.

Luzzatto, G., 1968. *L'economia italiana dal 1861 al 1894*, Turin: Einaudi.

Lyons, John S., Louis P. Cain, and Samuel H. Williamson (eds.), 2007. *Reflections on the Cliometrics Revolution: Conversation with Economic Historians*, Abingdon: Routledge.

McCloskey, Deirdre, 2006. *The Bourgeois Virtues. Ethics for an Age of Commerce*, University of Chicago Press.

McCloskey, Donald (ed.), 1972. *Essays on a Mature Economy: Britain after 1840*, London: Macmillan.

___ 1994. "1780–1860: A Survey," in Roderick Floud and Donald McCloskey (eds.), *The Economic History of Britain since 1700*, Vol. I: *1700–1860*, 2nd edn, Cambridge University Press.

McEvedy, Colin, 2002. *The New Penguin Atlas of Recent History*, London: Penguin.

Mackenzie, Georgina M. M. and A. P. Irby, 1877. *Travels in the Slavonic Provinces of Turkey-in-Europe*, 3rd rev. edn, London: Bell and Daldy. Daldy, Isbister.

MacLeod, Christine, 2004. "The European Origins of British Technological Predominance," in Leandro Prados de la Escosura (ed.), *Exceptionalism and Industrialization. Britain and its European Rivals, 1688–1815*, Cambridge University Press.

McLeod, Hugh, 2000. *Secularisation in Western Europe, 1848–1914*, New York: St. Martin's Press.

McNeill, William H., 1963. *The Rise of the West: A History of the Human Community*, University of Chicago Press.

— 1964. *Europe's Steppe Frontier 1500–1800: A Study of the Eastward Movement of Europe*. University of Chicago Press.

Maczak, Antoni, 1967. *U zrodel nowoczesnej gospodarki europejskij*, Warsaw: PWN.

Maddison, Angus, 1995. *Monitoring the World Economy 1820–1992*, Paris: OECD.

— 2001. *The World Economy. A Millennial Perspective*, Paris: OECD.

— 2007. *Contours of the World Economy 1–2030 AD: Essays in Macro-Economic History*, Oxford University Press.

Magnusson, Lars, 2000. *An Economic History of Sweden*, London: Routledge.

— 2005. Review Wittold Kula, *The Problems and Methods of Economic History*, Aldershot: Ashgate, 2001, in *Journal of Economic History*, Vol. 63, No. 3.

Maizels, Alfred, 1969. *Industrial Growth and World Trade*, Cambridge University Press.

Malthus, Thomas, R., 1798. *An Essay on the Principles of Population*, London: J. Johnson.

— 1830. *A Summary View of the Principles of Population*, London: John Murray.

Maluquer de Motes, Jordi, 1987. "The Industrial Revolution in Catalonia," in Nicolás Sánchez-Albornoz (ed.), *The Economic Modernization of Spain, 1830–1930*, New York University Press.

Manchester, William, 1968. *The Arms of Krupp 1587–1968*, Boston: Little, Brown.

Mann, Charles C. and Mark L. Plummer, 1991. *The Aspirin Wars. Money, Medicine, and 100 Years of Rampant Competition*, New York: Alfred A. Knopf.

Mann, Thomas, 2005. *Joseph and his Brothers*, trans. John Woods, New York: Knopf.

Mantoux, Pierre, 1928. *The Industrial Revolution in the Eighteenth Century*, London: Methuen.

Marcovits, Claude, 2000. *The Global World of Indian Merchants, 1750–1947. Traders of Sind from Bukhara to Panama*, Cambridge University Press.

Marfany, Julie, 2010. "Is it Still Helpful to Talk about Proto-Industrialization? Some Suggestions from a Catalan Case Study," *Economic History Review*, Vol. 63, No. 4.

Marsden, Ben, 2004. *Watt's Perfect Engine. Steam and the Age of Invention*, New York: Columbia University Press.

Marsella, Mauro, 2004. "Enrico Corradini's Italian Nationalism: The 'Right Wing' of the Fascist Synthesis," *Journal of Political Ideologies*, Vol. 9, No. 2.

Martin, Ged, 2004. *The Impossible Necessity of History*, University of Toronto Press.

Martín Aceña, Pablo, 1987. "Development of Modernization of the Financial System, 1844–1935," in Nicolás Sánchez-Albornoz (ed.), *The Economic Modernization of Spain, 1830–1930*, New York University Press.

Marx, Karl, [1867] 1932. *Capital: A Critique of Political Economy*, Vol. I. Chicago: Charles H. Kerr.

Marx, Karl and Friedrich Engels, [1847] 1970. *The German Ideology*, London: Lawrence and Wishart.

März, Edward, 1968. *Österreichische Industrien und Bankpolitik in der Zeit Franz Joseph I*, Vienna: Europa Verlag.

Mason, Peter, 1984. *Blood and Iron*, Ringwood, Victoria: Penguin.

Mathias, Peter, 1969. *The First Industrial Nation. An Economic History of Britain, 1700–1914*, London: Methuen.

Matis, Herbert, 1972. *Österreich Wirtschaft, 1848–1914*, Berlin: Duncker und Humblot.

Mayer, Arno J., 1981. *The Persistence of the Old Regime. Europe to the Great War*, New York: Pantheon.

Medick, Hans, 1976. "The Proto-Industrial Family Economy: The Structural Function of Household and Family during the Transition from Peasant Society to Industrial Capitalism," *Social History*, No. 3.

Meinecke, Friedrich, 1908. *Weltbürgertum und Nationalstaat: Studien zur Genesis des deutschen Nationalstaates*, Munich: R. Oldenbourg.

Mendels, Franklin F., 1972. "Proto-industrialization: The First Phase of the Industrialization Process," *Journal of Economic History*, No. 32.

Mérei, Gyula, 1983. *Magyarország törtéente, 1790–1849*, Budapest: Akadémiai Kiadó.

Mill, John Stuart, [1859] 1946. *On Liberty*, in *Introduction to Contemporary Civilization in the West*, New York: Columbia University Press.

— [1861] 1946. *Consideration on Representative Government*, in *Introduction to Contemporary Civilization in the West*, New York: Columbia University Press.

Miller, Michael B., 1981. *Bon Marché. Bourgeois Culture and the Department Store, 1969–1920*, Princeton University Press.

Milward, Alan and S. B. Saul, 1973. *The Economic Development of Continental Europe, 1780–1870*, London: Allen and Unwin.

____ 1977. *The Development of the Economies of Continental Europe, 1850–1914*, London: Allen and Unwin.

Minardi, Tomasso, [1834] 1987. "On the Essential Quality of Italian Painting from its Renaissance to the Period of its Perfection," in Joshua C. Taylor (ed.), *Nineteenth-Century Theories of Art*, Berkeley: University of California Press.

Mironov, Boris and Brian A'Hearn, 2008. "Russian Living Standard under the Tsars: Anthropometric Evidence from the Volga," *Journal of Economic History*, Vol. 68, No. 3.

Mitchell, R. C., 1973. "Statistical Appendix," in Carlo Cipolla (ed.), *The Fontana Economic History of Europe*, Vol. IV: *The Emergence of Industrial Societies*, Part 2, London: Fontana.

____ 1975. *European Historical Statistics 1750–1970*, New York: Columbia University Press.

Mitterauer, Michael and Reinhard Sieder, 1982. *The European Family. Patriarchy to Partnership from the Middle Ages to the Present*, University of Chicago Press.

Moe, Nelson, 2002. *The View from Vesuvius. Italian Culture and the Southern Question*, Berkeley: University of California Press.

Mokyr, Joel, 1990. *The Lever of Riches. Technological Creativity and Economic Progress*, Oxford University Press.

____ 1994. "Technological Change, 1700–1830," in Roderick Floud and Donald McCloskey (eds.), *The Economic History of Britain since 1700*, Vol. I: *1700–1860*, 2nd edn, Cambridge University Press.

____ (ed.), 1999. *The British Industrial Revolution. An Economic Perspective*, Boulder, Colo.: Westview Press.

____ 2000. "The Rise and Fall of the Factory System: Technology, Firms, and Households since the Industrial Revolution," paper presented at the Carnegie-Rochester Conference, Pittsburg in November, available at www.faculty.econ.northwestern.edu/faculty/mokyr/pittsburg.PDF, accessed October 2, 2007.

____ 2002. *The Gift of Athena. Historical Origins of the Knowledge Economy*, Princeton University Press.

____ 2005. "The Intellectual Origins of Modern Economic Growth," *Journal of Economic History*, Vol. 65, No. 2.

____ 2006. "Preface: Successful Small Open Economies and the Importance of Good Institutions," in Jari Ojala, Jari Eloranta, and Jukka Jalava (eds.), *The Road to Prosperity. An Economic History of Finland*, Helsinki: Suomalaisen Kirjallisuuden Seura.

Mokyr, Joel and Hans-Joachim Voth, 2010. "Understanding Growth in Europe, 1700–1870: Theory and Evidence," in Stephen Broadberry and Kevin H. O'Rourke (eds.), *The Cambridge Economic History of Modern Europe*, Vol. I: *1700 to 1870*, Cambridge University Press.

Molinas, César and Leandro Prados de la Escosura, 1989. "Was Spain Different? Spanish Historical Backwardness Revisited," *Explorations in Economic History*, Vol. 26, No. 4.

Mols, Roger S. J., 1974. "Population of Europe, 1500–1700," in Carlo Cipolla (ed.), *The Fontana Economic History of Europe*, Vol. II: *The Sixteenth and Seventeenth Centuries*, London: Collins.

Montesquieu, Charles-Luis, [1748] 1946. "The Spirit of the Law," in *Introduction to Contemporary Civilization in the West. A Source Book*, Vol. I, New York: Columbia University Press.

Moore, Barrington Jr., 1966. *Social Origins of Dictatorship and Democracy: Lord and Peasant in the Making of the Modern World*, Boston: Beacon Press.

Morgan, Kenneth, 2002. "Mercantilism and the British Empire 1688–1815," in Patrick K. O'Brien and Donald Winch (eds.), *The Political Economy of British Historical Experience, 1688–1914*, Oxford University Press.

Mori, Giorgio, 1975. "The Genesis of Italian Industrialization," *Journal of Economic History*, No. 4.

— 1991. "Industry without Industrialization. The Italian Peninsula from the End of French Domination to National Unification, 1815–1861," in Jean Batou (ed.), *Between Development and Underdevelopment. The Precocious Attempts at Industrialization of the Periphery 1800–1870*, Geneva: Librairie Droz.

Morris, Cynthia Taft and Irma Adelman, 1988. *Comparative Patterns of Economic Development, 1850–1914*, Baltimore: Johns Hopkins University Press.

Mosse, George L., 1988. *The Culture of Western Europe. The Nineteenth and Twentieth Centuries*, 3rd edn, Boulder, Colo.: Westview Press.

Munting, Roger, 1992. "Economic Change and the Russian Gentry, 1861–1914," in Linda Edmondson and Peter Waldron (eds.), *Economy and Society in Russia and the Soviet Union, 1860–1930*, New York: St. Martin's Press.

Mussolini, Benito, 1935. *Fascism. Doctrine and Institutions*, Rome: Ardita.

Musson, Albert E., 1978. *The Growth of British Industry*, London: Batsford.

— 1982. "The British Industrial Revolution," *History*, No. 67.

Musson, Albert Eduard and Eric Robinson, 1969. *Science and Technology in the Industrial Revolution*, Manchester University Press.

Nadal, Jorge, 1973. "Spain 1830–1914," in Carlo Cipolla (ed.), *The Fontana Economic History of Europe*, Vol. IV: *The Emergence of Industrial Societies*, Part 2, London: Fontana.

— 1987. "A Century of Industrialization in Spain, 1833–1935," in Nicolás Sánchez-Albornoz (ed.), *The Economic Modernization of Spain, 1830–1930*, New York University Press.

Neal, Larry, 1990. *The Rise of Financial Capitalism. International Capital Markets in the Age of Reason*, Cambridge University Press.

Neugebauer, Wolfgang and Ralf Pröve (eds.), 1998. *Agrarische Verfassung und politische Struktur*, Berlin: Arno Spitz.

Nietyesin, J. N., 1980. *Promislennij capital Latvii 1860–1917*, Riga: Ziņatne Akadēmijas Izdevniecība.

North, Douglas C., 1958. "Ocean Freight Rates and Economic Development 1750–1913," *Journal of Economic History*, No. 18.

___ 1990. *Institutions, Institutional Change, and Economic Performance*, Cambridge: Cambridge University Press.

___ 2005. *Understanding the Process of Economic Change*, Princeton University Press.

North, Douglas C. and Robert P. Thomas, 1973. *The Rise of the Western World. A New Economic History*, Cambridge University Press.

North, Douglas C. and Barry Weingast, 1989. "Constitutions and Commitment: The Evolution of Institutions Governing Public Choice in Seventeenth-Century Britain," *Journal of Economic History*, Vol. 49, No. 4.

North, Michael (ed.), 2000. *Deutsche Wirtschaftsgeschichte*, Munich: Verlag C. H. Beck.

O'Brien, Patrick K., 1983. "Transport and Economic Development in Europe, 1789–1914," in Patrick K. O'Brien (ed.), *Railways and the Economic Development of Western Europe, 1830–1914*, Basingstoke: Macmillan.

___ 2000. "War and Economic Development," in C. Holmes (ed.), *The Oxford Companion to Military History*, Oxford University Press.

___ 2002. "Fiscal Exceptionalism: Great Britain and its European Rivals – From Civil War to Triumph at Trafalgar and Waterloo," in Patrick K. O'Brien and Donald Winch (eds.), *The Political Economy of British Historical Experience, 1688–1914*, Oxford University Press.

___ 2004a. "The British Economy from Dominance to Decline," mimeo, Tokyo.

___ 2004b. "The Cost and Benefits of British Imperialism,1846–1914," *Past and Present*, Vol. 120, No. 1, 163–200.

O'Brien, Patrick K. and Leandro Prados de la Escosura, 1998. "Balance Sheet for the Acquisition, Retention and Loss of European Empires Overseas," Working Paper 98–99, Economic History and Institution Series, 08, London.

O'Brien, Patrick K. and Gianni Toniolo, 1994. "The Poverty of Italy and the Backwardness of its Agriculture before 1914," in Giovanni Federico (ed.), *The Economic Development of Italy since 1870*, Aldershot: Edward Elgar.

Ogilvie, Sheilagh, 2007. "Whatever is, is Right? Economic Institutions in Pre-Industrial Europe," *Economic History Review*, Vol. 60, No. 4.

Ó Gráda, Cormac, 1988. *Ireland Before and After the Famine. Exploration in Economic History, 1800–1925*, Manchester University Press.

Ohlin, Bertil, 1966. *Interregional and International Trade*, Cambridge, Mass.: Harvard University Press.

Ojala, Jari and Petri Karonen, 2006. "Business: Rooted in Social Capital over the Centuries," in Jari Ojala, Jari Eloranta, and Jukka Jalava (eds.), *The Road to Prosperity. An Economic History of Finland*, Helsinki: Suomalaisen Kirjallisuuden Seura.

Ojala, Jari and Ilkka Nummela, 2006. "Feeding Economic Growth: Agriculture," in Jari Ojala, Jari Eloranta, and Jukka Jalava (eds.), *The Road to Prosperity. An Economic History of Finland*, Helsinki: Suomalaisen Kirjallisuuden Seura.

Ojala, Jari, Jari Eloranta, and Jukka Jalava (eds.), 2006. *The Road to Prosperity. An Economic History of Finland*, Helsinki: Suomalaisen Kirjallisuuden Seura.

Olson, Mancur, 1982. *The Rise and Decline of Nations. Economic Growth, Stagflation and Social Rigidities*, New Haven: Yale University Press.

Ormrod, David, 2003. *The Rise of Commercial Empires. England and the Netherlands in the Age of Mercantilism, 1650–1770*, Cambridge University Press.

O'Rourke, Kevin H., 2000. "Tariffs and Growth in the Late Nineteenth Century," *Economic Journal*, Vol. 110, No. 463.

O'Rourke, Kevin H. and J.G. Williamson, 2000 "When did Globalization Begin?" Working Paper, April, www.nber.org/papers/w7632, amend May 15, 2012.

__ 2001. *Globalization and History. The Revaluation of a Nineteenth-Century Atlantic Economy*, Cambridge, Mass.: MIT Press.

Orwin, Cristobel S. and Edith Whetham, 1964. *History of British Agriculture, 1846–1914*, London: Longmans.

Pach, Zsigmond Pál, 1994. *Hungary and the European Economy in Early Modern Times*, Aldershot: Variorum.

Padhi, Sakti, 1997. "Historical Paths of Capitalist Development in Agriculture," *Economic and Political Weekly*, Vol. 32, No. 4.

Paget, John, 1839. *Hungary and Transylvania. With Remarks on their Condition, Social, Political, and Economic*, Vol. I. London: John Murray.

Palafox, Jordi, 1987. "Exports, Internal Demand, and Economic Growth in Valencia," in Nicolás Sánchez-Albornoz (ed.), *The Economic Modernization of Spain, 1830–1930*, New York University Press.

Palairet, Michael, 1997. *The Balkan Economies c. 1800–1914. Evolution without Development*, Cambridge University Press.

Pamuk, Orhan, 2005. *Istambul. Memories of a City*, London: Faber and Faber.

Pamuk, Şevket and Jan Luiten van Zanden, 2010. "Standard of Living," in Stephen Broadberry and Kevin H. O'Rourke (eds.), *The Cambridge Economic History of Modern Europe*, Vol. I: *1700 to 1870*, Cambridge University Press.

Pamuk, Şevket and Jeffrey G. Williamson, 2011. "Ottoman De-Industrialization, 1800–1913. Assessing the Magnitude, Impact, and Response," *Economic History Review*, Vol. 64, No. 1.

Pap, Gy, 1865. *Palócz népköltemények*, Sárospatak: Forster.

Parker, William N., 1984. *Europe, America and the Wider World. Essays on the Economic History of Western Capitalism*, Vol. I: *Europe and the World Economy*, Cambridge University Press.

— 1991. "Europe in an American Mirror: Reflections on Industrialization and Ideology," in Richard Sylla and Gianni Toniolo (eds.), *Patterns of European Industrialization. The Nineteenth Century*, London: Routledge.

Parliamentary Papers, 1908. House of Commons. Vol. 126. London.

Pearson, Robin, 2001. "The Birth Pain of a Global Reinsurer: Swiss Re of Zurich, 1864–79," *Financial History Review*, Vol. 8, No. 1.

Pearson, Thomas S., 1989. *Russian Officialdom in Crisis: Autocracy and Local Self-Government, 1861–1900*, Cambridge University Press.

Pedreira, Jorge Miguel, 1991. "The Obstacles of Early Industrialization in Portugal, 1800–1870. A Comparative Perspective," in Jean Batou (ed.), *Between Development and Underdevelopment, 1800–1870*, Genève: Droz.

Pepelasis Minoglou, Joanna, 2002. "Ethnic Minority Groups in International Banking: Greek Diaspora Bankers of Constantinople and Ottoman State Finance, c. 1840–81," *Financial History Review*, Vol. 9, No. 2.

Pérez Moreda, Vicente, 1987. "Spain's Demographic Modernization, 1800–1930," in Nicolás Sánchez-Albornoz (ed.), *The Economic Modernization of Spain, 1830–1930*, New York University Press.

Perrie, Maureen, 1992. "'A Worker in Disguise': A. V. Peshekhonov's Contribution to the Debate on the Peasants at the Turn of the Century," in Linda Edmondson and Peter Waldron (eds.), *Economy and Society in Russia and the Soviet Union, 1860–1930*, New York: St. Martin's Press.

Persson, Karl Gunnar, 2010. *An Economic History of Europe. Knowledge, Institution, and Growth, 600 to the Present*, Cambridge University Press.

Petőfi, Sándor, 1985. *Költeményei*, Budapest: Helikon.

Petrosian, J., 1977. "Die Idee 'der Europäisierung' in dem sozialpolitischen Leben des osmanischen Reiches in der Neuzeit (End des 18., Anfang des 20. Jahrhunderts)," in Maria N. Todorova (ed.), *La révolution industrielle dans le sud-est européen – XIX s*, Sofia: Institut d'Etudes Balkaniques.

Petrusewicz, Marta, 2002. "Land-based Modernization and the Culture of Landed Elites in the Nineteenth-Century Mezzogiorno," in Enrico Del Lago and Rick Halpern (eds.), *American South and Italian Mezzogior no. Essays in Comparative History*, New York: Palgrave.

Pfiffner, Albert, 1991. "Henri Nestlé and the Pioneers of the Swiss Food Industry," in Gerard Geiger (ed.), *The Swiss Economy, 1291–1991*, St-Sulpice: SQP.

Pichler, Rupert, 2001. "Economic Policy and Development in Austrian Lombardy, 1815–1859," *Modern Italy*, Vol. 6, No. 1.

Pierenkemper, Toni, 1979. *Die Westphalischen Schwerindustriellen 1852–1913. Soziale Struktur und unternehmerischer Erfolg,* Göttingen: Vandenhoek and Ruprecht.

___ (ed.), 2002. *Die Industrialisierung Europäischer Montanregionen im 19. Jahrhundert,* Stuttgart: Franz Steiner Verlag.

Pierenkemper, Toni and Richard Tilly, 2004. *The German Economy during the Nineteenth Century,* New York: Berghan Books.

Platt, D. C. M., 1980. "Overseas Investment," *Economic History Review,* February.

Pokrovskij, S., 1947. *Vnyesnaia torgovlja i vnyesnaia torgovaja politika Rossii,* Moscow: Mezhdunarodnaia Kniga.

Polanyi, Karl, 1964. *The Great Transformation: The Political and Economic Origins of our Time,* Boston: Beacon.

Pollard, Sidney, 1965. *The Genesis of Modern Management. A Study of the Industrial Revolution in Great Britain,* London: Edward Arnold.

___ 1981a. *The Integration of the European Economy since 1815,* London: Allen and Unwin.

___ 1981b. *Peaceful Conquest. The Industrialization of Europe 1760–1970,* Oxford University Press.

___ 1989. *Britain's Prime and Britain's Decline. The British Economy 1870–1914,* London: Edward Arnold.

___ 1990. *Typology of Industrialization Process in the Nineteenth Century,* Chur: Harwood Academic.

___ 1994. "Entrepreneurship, 1870–1914," in Roderick Floud and Donald McCloskey (eds.), *The Economic History of Britain since 1700,* Vol. II: *1860–1939,* 2nd edn, Cambridge University Press.

___ 1996. "The Industrial Revolution – An Overview," in Mikuláš Teich and Roy Porter (eds.), *The Industrial Revolution in National Context. Europe and the USA,* Cambridge University Press.

Pomeranz, Kenneth, 2000. *The Great Divergence: China, Europe, and the Making of the Modern World Economy,* Princeton University Press.

Poni, Carlo and Giorgio Mori, 1996. "Italy in the *Longue Durée:* The Return of an Old First-Comer," in Mikuláš Teich and Roy Porter (eds.), *The Industrial Revolution in National Context. Europe and the USA,* Cambridge University Press.

Postan, Michael M., 1967. *An Economic History of Western Europe, 1945–1964,* London: Methuen.

Prados de la Escosura, Leandro, 1987. "Foreign Trade and the Spanish Economy during the Nineteenth Century," in Nicolás Sánchez-Albornoz (ed.), *The Economic Modernization of Spain, 1830–1930,* New York University Press.

___ 1988. *De imperio a nación. Crecimiento atraso económico en España, 1780–1930,* Madrid: Alianza.

___ (ed.), 2004. *Exceptionalism and Industrialization. Britain and its European Rivals, 1688–1815*, Cambridge University Press.

___ 2007. Review of J. W. Drukker, *The Revolution that Bit its own Tail, Economic History Review*, Vol. 60, No. 4.

___ "Spain's International Position, 1850–1913," Working Papers in Economic History, http://d.repec.org/n?u=RePEc:cte:whrepe:wp09-09&r=his, accessed October 2009.

Prebisch, R., 1981. *Capitalismo periférico: crisis y transformación*, Mexico City: Fondo de Cultura Económica.

Purš, J., 1960. *The Industrial Revolution in the Czech Lands*, Prague: Historica II.

Rabb, Theodore K., 2007. "The Scientific Revolution and the Problem of Periodization," *European Review*, Vol. 15, No. 4.

Ragon, Michel, 1988. "Az ipari forradalom és az építészet," in Nóra Aradi (ed.), *Művészet Történet. A Századvég és a Századelő*, Budapest: Corvina.

Rappaport, Erika D., 1999. "Acts of Consumption: Musical Comedy and the Desire of Exchange," in Geoffrey Crossick and Serge Jaumain (eds.), *Cathedrals of Consumption. The European Department Store, 1850–1939*, Aldershot: Ashgate.

Ravnholt, Henning H., 1945. *Andelsbevaegelsen. Den Folkestyrede Økonomi*, Copenhagen: Det Danske Forlag.

Reis, Jaime, 2000. "How Poor was the European Periphery before 1850?" in Şevket Pamuk and Jeffrey G. Williamson (eds.), *The Mediterranean Response to Globalization before 1950*, London: Routledge.

Rémond, René, 1999. *Religion and Society in Modern Europe*, Oxford: Blackwell.

Rerum Novarum, 1891. Available at (www.vatican.va/.../hf_I-XIII_enc_15051891rerum_novarum_en.html).

Reynolds, Joshua, [1777] 1987. "Discourses on Art," in Joshua C. Taylor (ed.), *Nineteenth-Century Theories of Art*, Berkeley: University of California Press.

Ringrose, David R., 1996. *Spain, Europe, and the "Spanish Miracle," 1700–1900*, Cambridge University Press.

Romer, Christian, 1994. "The End of Economic History?" *Journal of Economic History*, Vol. 25, No. 1, 49–66.

Ronnas, Per, 1984. *Urbanization in Romania*, Stockholm: Stockholm School of Economics.

Rosenthal, Jean-Laurent, 1992. *The Fruits of Revolution. Property Rights, Litigation, and French Agriculture, 1700–1860*, Cambridge University Press.

Rosenthal, Jean-Laurent and R. Bing Wong, 2011. *Before and Beyond Divergence. Politics and Economic Change in China and Europe*, Cambridge, Mass.: Harvard University Press.

Rosés, Joan R., 2003. "Why isn't the Whole of Spain Industrialized? New Economic Geography and Early Industrialization 1797–1910," *Journal of Economic History*, Vol. 63, No. 4.

Rossi, Nicola, Gianni Toniolo, and Giovanni Vecchi, 2001. "Is the Kuznetz Curve Still Alive? Evidence from Italian Household Budgets, 1881–1961," *Journal of Economic History*, Vol. 61, No. 4.

Rostow, Walt W., 1960. *The Stages of Economic Growth: A Non-Communist Manifesto*, Cambridge University Press.

Rothschild, Emma, 1992. "Commerce and the State: Turgot, Condorcet and Smith," *Economic Journal*, Vol. 102.

___ 2001. *Economic Sentiments: Adam Smith, Condorcet, and the Enlightenment*, Boston: Harvard University Press.

___ 2002. "The English Kopf," in Patrick K. O'Brien and Donald Winch (eds.), *The Political Economy of British Historical Experience, 1688–1914*, Oxford University Press.

Rousseau, Jean-Jacques, [1755] 1983. *Discourse on the Origin of Inequality*, Indianapolis: Hackett.

___ [1762] 1946. "The Social Contract," in *Introduction to Contemporary Civilization in the West*, New York: Columbia University Press.

Rudolph, Richard, 1976. *Banking and Industralization in Austria Hungary*, Cambridge University Press.

Samuelson, Kurt, 1958. "The Banks and the Financing of Industry in Sweden, c. 1900–1927," *Scandinavian Economic History Review*, Vol. 6, No. 2.

___ 1968. *From Great Power to Welfare State. 300 Years of Swedish Social Development*, London: Allen and Unwin.

Sánchez-Albornoz, Nicolás 1977. *España hace un siglo: una economía dual*, Madrid: Alianza.

___ (ed.), 1987. *The Economic Modernization of Spain, 1830–1930*, New York University Press.

Sánchez-Alonso, Blanca, 2000a. "European Emigration in the Late Nineteenth Century: The Paradoxical Case of Spain," *Economic History Review*, Vol. 53, No. 2.

___ 2000b. "What Slowed Down the Mass Emigration from Spain before the First World War? A Comparison with Italy," in Sevket Pamuk and Jeffrey G. Williamson (eds.), *The Mediterranean Response to Globalization Before 1950*, London: Routledge.

Sandberg, L. G., 1979. "The Case of the Impoverished Sophisticate: Human Capital and Swedish Economic Growth before World War I," *Journal of Economic History*, March.

Sandgruber, Roman, 1994. "The Electric Century: The Beginnings of Electricity Supply in Austria," in Herbert Matis (ed.), *The Economic Development of Austria since 1870*, Aldershot: Edward Elgar.

Sassoon, Donald, 1996. *One Hundred Years of Socialism*. New York: The New Press.

___ 2006. *The Culture of the Europeans. From 1800 to the Present*, London: HarperCollins.

Saul, S. B., 1969. *The Myth of the Great Depression, 1873–1896*, Basingstoke: Macmillan.

Schabas, Margaret, 2005. *The Natural Origins of Economics*, University of Chicago Press.

Schama, Simon, 1988. *The Embarrassment of Riches: An Interpretation of Dutch Culture in the Golden Age*, Berkeley: University of California Press.

Schiemenz, Günter P., 1993. "A Heretical Look at the Benzolfest," *British Journal for the History of Science*, Vol. 26, No. 2.

Schlote, Werner, 1952. *British Overseas Trade from 1700 to the 1930s*, Oxford: Blackwell.

Schlumbohm, Jürgen, 1983. "Seasonal Fluctuations and Social Division of Labour: Rural Linen Production in the Osnabrück and Bielefeld Regions and the Urban Woollen Industry in the Niederlausitz, *c.* 1770–1850," in Maxine Berg, Pat Hudson, and Michael Sonenscher (eds.), *Manufacture in Town and Country before the Factory*, Cambridge University Press.

Schmoller, Gustav, 1884. "Das Merkantilsystem in seiner historischen Bedeutung," *Jahrbuch für Gesetzgebung, Verwaltung und Volkswirtschaft*, vol. 8.

Schofield, Roger, 1994. "British Population Change, 1700–1830," in Frederick Floud and Donald McCloskey (eds.), *The Economic History of Britain since 1700*, Vol. I: *1700–1860*, 2nd edn, Cambridge University Press.

Scholliers, Peter, 1992. "Historical Food Research in Belgium: Development, Problems and Results in the 19th and 20th Centuries," in Hans J. Teuteberg (ed.), *European Food History. A Research Review*, Leicester University Press.

Schön, Lennart, 1988. *Industri och hantverk 1800–1980*, Historiska Nationalräkenskaper för Sverige 65, Lund.

Schram, Albert, 1997. *Railways and the Formation of the Italian State in the Nineteenth Century*, Cambridge University Press.

Schröter, Harm G., 1997. "Small European Nations: Cooperative Capitalism in the Twentieth Century," in Alfred D. Chandler, Franco Amatori, and Takashi Hikino (eds.), *Big Business and the Wealth of Nations*, Cambridge University Press.

Schulze, Max-Stephan, 1996. *Engineering and Economic Growth. The Development of Austria-Hungary's Machine-Building Industry in the Late Nineteenth Century*, Frankfurt am Main: Peter Lang.

Schumpeter, Joseph, 1939. *Business Cycles: A Theoretical, Historical and Statistical Analysis of the Capitalist Process*, New York: McGraw-Hill.

Scranton, Philip, 1991. "A Review of Scale and Scope," *Technology and Culture*, Vol. 32, No. 4.

Seccombe, Wally, 1992. *A Millennium of Family Change: Feudalism to Capitalism in Northwestern Europe*, London: Verso.

Sechel, Teodora Daniela, 2008. "The Emergence of the Medical Profession in Transylvania 1770–1848," in Victor Karády and Borbála Zsuzsanna Török (eds.), *Cultural Dimensions of Elite Formation in Transylvania (1770–1950)*, Cluj-Napoca: EDRC Foundation.

Seton-Watson, Robert W., 1963. *The History of the Roumanians*, London: Archon.

Shapin, Steven, 1996. *The Scientific Revolution*, Chicago University Press.

Shea, William R., 2007. "The Scientific Revolution Really Occurred," *European Review*, Vol. 15. No. 4.

Sievers, Kai Detlev (ed.), 1998. *Hunger und Elend in Ländern des Mare Balticum. Zum Pauperismus im Ostseeraum zwischen 1600 und 1900*, Neumünster: Wachholtz Verlag.

Simson, James, 2004. "European Farmers and the British Agricultural Revolution," in Leandro Prados de la Escosura (ed.), *Exceptionalism and Industrialization. Britain and its European Rivals, 1688–1815*, Cambridge University Press.

Singer, Edward N., 1998. *Twentieth Century Revolutions in Technology*, Commack, N.Y.: Nova.

Skinner, A. S., 2001. "Adam Smith (1723–90)," in Neil J. Smelser and Paul B. Baltes (ed.), *International Encyclopedia of Social and Behavioral Sciences*, Amsterdam: Elsevier.

Smelser, Neil J. and Paul B. Baltes (eds.), 2001. *International Encyclopedia of Social and Behavioral Sciences*, Vol. XX, Amsterdam: Elsevier.

Smil, Vaclav, 2005. *Creating the Twentieth Century: Technical Innovations of 1867–1914 and their Lasting Impact*, Oxford University Press.

Smith, Adam, [1776] 1976. *An Inquiry into the Nature and Causes of the Wealth of Nations*, University of Chicago Press.

Snyder, Wayne, 2006. "Occupational Evolution in XVIIIth and XIXth-Century France," *Journal of European Economic History*, Vol. 35, No. 3.

Solow, Robert, [1985] 2006. "Economic History and Economics," in John A. Hall and Joseph M. Bryant (eds.), *Historical Methods in the Social Sciences*, Vol. I, London: Sage.

Soltésova, Elena Maróthy, [1898] 1991. "The Need for Women's Education," in Norma Rudinsky (ed.), *Incipient Feminists: Women Writers in Slovak National Revival*, Columbus, OH: Slavica.

Stahl, Henri H., 1980. *Traditional Romanian Village Communities: The Transition from the Communal to the Capitalist Mode of Production in the Danube Region*, Cambridge University Press.

Stasavage, David, 2003. *Public Debt and the Birth of the Democratic State: France and Great Britain, 1688–1789*, Cambridge University Press.

Stavrianos, Leften S., 1963. *The Balkans since 1453*, New York: Holt.

Stern, Fritz, 1977. *Gold and Iron. Bismarck, Bleichröder, and the Building of the German Empire*, New York: Alfred Knopf.

Stromberg, Roland N., 1990. *European Intellectual History since 1789*, 5th edn, Englewood Cliffs, N.J.: Prentice Hall.

Stuivenberg, J. H. van, 1977. *De economische geschiedenis van Nederland*, Groningen: Wolters-Noordhof.

Suchit, Arora, 2001. "Health, Human Productivity, and Long-Term Economic Growth," *Journal of Economic History*, Vol. 61, No. 3.

Sugar, Peter F., 1999. "Continuity and Change in Eastern European Authoritarianism: Autocracy, Fascism and Communism," in Peter F. Sugar, *East European Nationalism, Politics and Religion*, Aldershot: Ashgate, Variorum.

Supple, Barry, 1973. "The State and the Industrial Revolution," in Carlo Cipolla (ed.), *Fontana Economic History of Europe*, Vol. III: *The Industrial Revolution*, London: Fontana.

— 2007. "Institution and Economic Development: Economic History and Human Arrangement," in W. R. Garside (ed.), *Institutions and Market Economies: The Political Economy of Growth and Development*, Houndmills: Palgrave Macmillan.

Sylla, Richard, 2002. "Financial Systems and Economic Modernization," *Journal of Economic History*, Vol. 62, No. 2.

Sylla, Richard and Gianni Toniolo (eds.), 1991. *Patterns of European Industrialization. The Nineteenth Century*, London: Routledge.

Széchenyi, István, 1830. *Hitel*, Pest: Petrózai Trattner.

Széchenyi, István and Miklós Wesselényi, 1985. *Feleselő naplók. Egy barátság kezdetei*, Budapest: Helikon.

Szekfű, Gyula, 1920. *Három nemzedék. Egy hanyatló kor története*, Budapest: Kiralyi Magyar Egyetemi Nyomda.

— 1922. *A magyar bortermelő lelki alkata. Gazadságtörténeti tanulmány*, Budapest: Minerva Társaság.

Tabak, Faruk, 2008. *The Waning of the Mediterranean, 1550–1870. A Geohistorical Approach*, Baltimore: Johns Hopkins University Press.

Taine, Hippolyte, [1865] 1987. "The Philosophy of Art," in Joshua C. Taylor (ed.), *Nineteenth-Century Theories of Art*, Berkeley: University of California Press.

Talmon, Jacob L., 1967. *Romanticism and Revolt. Europe 1815–1848*, San Diego, Calif.: Harcourt, Brace and World.

Tawney, R. H., 1954. *Religion and the Rise of Capitalism. A Historical Study. Holland Memorial Lecture, 1922*, New York: Mentor.

Taylor, James, 2006. *Creating Capitalism: Joint Stock Enterprise in British Politics and Culture, 1800–1870*, Woodbridge: Boydell Press.

REFERENCES

Tebarth, Hans-Jakob, 1991. *Technischer Fortschritt und sozialer Wandel in deutschen Ostprovinzen. Ostpreussen, Westpreussen und Schlesien im Zeitalter der Industrialisierung*, Berlin: Mann Verlag.

Temin, Peter, 1966. "The Relative Decline of the British Steel Industry, 1880–1913," in Henry Rosovsky (ed.), *Industrialization in Two Systems: Essays in Honor of Alexander Gerschenkron*, New York: John Wiley.

Teuteberg, Hans J. (ed.), 1992. *European Food History. A Research Review*, Leicester University Press.

Thirlwall, A. P., 1979. "The Balance of Payment Constraint as an Explanation of International Growth Rate Differences," *Banca Nazionale del Lavoro Quarterly Review*, Vol. 128.

Thomson, J. K. J., 1983. "Variations in Industrial Structure in Pre-industrial Languedoc," in Maxine Berg, Pat Hudson, and Michael Sonenscher (eds.), *Manufacture in Town and Country before the Factory*, Cambridge University Press.

— 2005. "Explaining the 'Take-off' of the Catalan Cotton Industry," *Economic History Review*, Vol. 58, No. 4.

Thorbecke, Erik, 1969. "Introduction," in Erik Thorbecke (ed.), *The Role of Agriculture in Economic Development*, New York: National Bureau of Economic Research.

Thoré, Théophile, [1857] 1987. "New Tendencies in Art," in Joshua C. Taylor (ed.), *Nineteenth-Century Theories of Art*, Berkeley: University of California Press.

Tilly, Richard, 1967. "Germany, 1815–1870," in Rondo Cameron (ed.), *Banking in the Early Stages of Industrialization. A Study in Comparative Economic History*, Oxford University Press.

— 1991a. "German Industrialization," in Mikuláš Teich and Roy Porter (eds.), *The Industrial Revolution in National Context. Europe and the USA*, Cambridge University Press.

— 1991b. "International Aspects of the Development of German Banking," in Rondo Cameron and V. I. Bovikin (eds.), *International Banking, 1870–1914*, Oxford University Press.

Tímár, Lajos, 1992. "Regional Economic and Social History or Historical Geography?" *Journal of European Economic History*, Vol. 21.

Tipton, Frank B., 1995. "The Regional Dimension in the Historical Analysis of Transport Flows," in Andreas Kunz and John Armstrong (eds.), *Inland Navigation and Economic Development in Nineteenth-Century Europe*, Mainz: Verlag Philipp von Zabern.

Tipton, Frank B. and Robert Aldrich, 1987. *An Economic and Social History of Europe, 1890–1939*, Houndmills: Macmillan.

Tocqueville, Alexis de, [1835, 1840] 2000. *Democracy in America*, University of Chicago Press.

Todorova, Maria, 1997. *Imagining the Balkans*, Oxford University Press.

Toniolo, Gianni, 1990. *An Economic History of Liberal Italy, 1850–1914*, London: Routledge.

— 2004. "Laudatio Patritii: Patrick O'Brien and European Economic History," in Leandro Prados de la Escosura (ed.), *Exceptionalism and Industrialization. Britain and its European Rivals, 1688–1815*, Cambridge University Press.

Topolski, Jerzy, 1982. *Zarys dziejów Polski*, Warsaw: Wydawnictwo Interpress.

Tortella, Gabriel, 1972. "Spain 1829–1874," in Rondo Cameron (ed.), *Banking and Economic Development*, Oxford University Press.

— 1973. *Los orígenes del capitalismo en España. Banca, industria y ferrocarriles en el sieglo XIX*, Madrid: Tecnos.

— 1987. "Agriculture: A Slow-Moving Sector, 1830–1935," in Nicolás Sánchez-Albornoz (ed.), *The Economic Modernization of Spain, 1830–1930*, New York University Press.

— 1994a. "Economic Entrepreneurship: A Scarce Factor in Spain: The Banking Sector, 1782–1914," in Paul Klep and Eddy Van Cauwenberghe (eds.), *Entrepreneurship and the Transformation of the Economy*, Leuven University Press.

— 1994b. "Patterns of Economic Retardation and Recovery in South-western Europe in the Nineteenth and Twentieth Centuries," *Economic History Review*, Vol. 47, No. 1.

— 2000. *The Development of Modern Spain. An Economic History of the Nineteenth and Twentieth Centuries*, Cambridge, Mass.: Harvard University Press.

Toutain, Jean-Claude, 1961. *Le produit de l'agriculture française de 1700 à 1958*, Vol. II, Paris: ISEA.

Tracy, James D., 1985. *A Financial Revolution in the Habsburg Netherlands: Renten and Rentiers in the County of Holland, 1515–1565*, Berkeley: University of California Press.

Trebilcock, Clive, 1981. *The Industrialization of the Continental Powers 1780–1914*, London: Longman.

Treitschke, Heinrich von, [1898] 1916. *Politics*, Vol. I, London.

Turgot, Anne-Robert-Jacques, [1766] 1921. *Reflections on the Formation and Distribution of Riches*, New York: Augustus M. Kelley.

Turnbull, Gerard L., 1987. "Canals, Coal and Regional Growth during the Industrial Revolution," *Economic History Review*, Vol. 40.

Van Bavel, Bas J. P. and Jan Luiten van Zanden, 2004. "The Jump-Start of the Holland Economy during the Late Medieval Crisis, c. 1350–1500," *Economic History Review*, Vol. 57, No. 3.

Van der Wee, Herman, 1977. "Monetary, Credit and Banking Systems," in E. E. Rich and Charles Wilson (eds.), *The Cambridge Economic History of Europe*,

Vol. V: *The Economic Organization of Early Modern Europe*, Cambridge University Press.

—— 1996. "The Industrial Revolution in Belgium," in Mikuláš Teich and Roy Porter (eds.), *The Industrial Revolution in National Context. Europe and the USA*, Cambridge University Press.

—— 1999. "Was the Dutch Economy during the Golden Age Really Modern?" *European Review*, Vol. 7, No. 4.

Van der Wee, Herman and Monique Verbreyt, 1997. *The General Bank 1822–1997*, Tielt: Lannoo.

Van Poppel, Frans W. A., Hendrick P. van Dalen, and Evelien Walhout, 2009. "Diffusion of a Social Norm: Tracing the Emergence of the Housewife in the Netherlands, 1812–1922," *Economic History Review*, Vol. 62, No. 1.

Van Zanden, Jan Luiten, 2001. "A Third Road to Capitalism? Proto-industrialization and the Moderate Nature of the Late Medieval Crisis in Flanders and Holland, 1350–1550," in Peter Hoppenbrouwers and Jan Luiten van Zanden (eds.), *Peasants into Farmers? The Transformation of Rural Economy and Society in the Low Countries (Middle Ages to 19th Century) in Light of the Brenner Debate*, Turnhout: Brepols.

—— 1993. *The Rise and Decline of Holland's Economy*, Manchester University Press.

—— 2002. "The Revolt of the 'Early Modernists' and the 'First Modern Economy': An Assessment," *Economic History Review*, Vol. 55, No. 4.

Vicens Vives, Jaime, 1953. *Manual de historia económica de España*, Barcelona: Teide.

Voltaire [François-Marie Arouet], 1946. "Philosophical Dictionary" and "Essay on Toleration," in *Introduction to Contemporary Civilization in the West*, New York: Columbia University Press.

Voltes Bou, Pedro, 1974. *Historia de la economía española en los siglos XIX y XX*, Madrid: Editoria Nacional.

Voth, Hans-Joachim, 2001. "The Prussian Zollverein and the Bid for Economic Superiority," in Philip G. Dwyer (ed.), *Modern Prussian History, 1830–1947*, Harlow: Pearson, 109–125.

Vries, Jan de, 2001. "The Netherlands in the New World: The Legacy of European Fiscal, Monetary, and Trading Institutions for New World Development from the 17th to the 19th Centuries," in Michael D. Bordo and Roberto Cortés-Conde (eds.), *Transferring Wealth and Power from the Old to the New World. Monetary and Fiscal Institutions in the 17th through the 19th Centuries*, Cambridge University Press.

—— 2008. *The Industrious Revolution. Consumer Behavior and the Household Economy, 1650 to the Present*, Cambridge University Press.

Vries, Jan de and Ad Van der Woude, 1997. *The First Modern Economy. Success, Failure, and Perseverance of the Dutch Economy, 1500–1815*, Cambridge University Press.

— 2001. "The Transition to Capitalism in a Land without Feudalism," in Peter Hoppenbrouwers and Jan Luiten van Zanden (eds.), *Peasants into Farmers? The Transformation of Rural Economy and Society in the Low Countries (Middle Ages to 19th Century) in Light of the Brenner Debate*, Turnhout: Brepols.

Vries, P. H. H., 2001. "Are Coal and Colonies Really Crucial? Kenneth Pomeranz and the Great Divergence," *Journal of World History*, Vol. 12, No. 2.

Wadsworth, Alfred P. and Julia De Lacy Mann, 1931. *The Cotton Trade and Industrial Lancashire*, Manchester University Press.

Wagner, Ursula H., 1982. *Die preussische Verwaltung des Regirungsbezirks Marianwerder 1871–1920*, Cologne: Grote.

Wallerstein, Immanuel, 1974. *The Modern World-System*, Vol. I: *Capitalist Agriculture and the Origins of the European World Economy in the Sixteenth Century*, New York: Academic Press.

— 1989. *The Modern World System*, Vol. III: *The Second Era of Great Expansion of the Capitalist World-Economy, 1730–1840*, San Diego: Academic Press.

Wallsten, Scott, 2008. "Returning to Victorian Competition, Ownership, and Regulation. An Empirical Study of European Telecommunication at the Turn of the Twentieth Century," *Journal of Economic History*, Vol. 65, No. 2.

Walter, François, 1991. "From a Land of Shepherds to the Protected Peasant: One and a Half Centuries of Changes in Agriculture (1860–1914)," in Gerard Geiger (ed.), *The Swiss Economy, 1291–1991*, St.-Sulpice: SQP.

Ward, Mariane and John Devereux, 2003. "Measuring British Decline. Direct versus Long-Span Income Measure," *Journal of Economic History*, Vol. 63, No. 3.

Weber, Eugen, 1960. *Paths to the Present: Aspects of European Thought from Romanticism to Existentialism*, New York: Dodd, Mead.

Wehler, Hans-Ulrich, 1995–2005. *Deutsche Gesellschaftsgeschichte*. Vol. II: *1815–1845–49*; Vol. III: *1849–1914*, Munich: C. H. Beck.

Wengenroth, Ulrich, 1997. "Germany: Competition Abroad – Cooperation at Home, 1870–1900," in Alfred D. Chandler, Franco Amatori, and Takashi Hikino (eds.), *Big Business and the Wealth of Nations*, Cambridge University Press.

Wheatcroft, S. G., 1992. "The 1891–92 Famine in Russia: Towards a More Detailed Analysis of its Scale and Demographic Significance," in Linda Edmondson and Peter Waldron (eds.), *Economy and Society in Russia and the Soviet Union, 1860–1930*, New York: St. Martin's Press.

White, N. Eugene, 2001. "France and the Failure to Modernize Macroeconomic Institutions," in Michael D. Bordo and Roberto Cortés-Conde (eds.), *Transferring Wealth and Power from the Old to the New World. Monetary and Fiscal Institutions in the 17th through the 19th Centuries*, Cambridge University Press.

Wieland, Thomas, 2006. "Scientific Theory and Agricultural Practice. Plant Breeding in Germany from the Late Nineteenth to the Early Twentieth Century," *Journal of the History of Biology*, Vol. 39, No. 2.

Wilkins, Mira, 1970. *The Emergence of Multinational Enterprise*, Cambridge, Mass.: Harvard University Press.

— 1988. "An Important Type of British Foreign Direct Investment," *Economic History Review*, Vol. 41.

Wilkins, Mira and Harm Schröter (eds.), 1998. *The Free-Standing Company in the World Economy 1830–1996*, Oxford University Press.

Wilson, Jeffrey K., 2008. "Environmental Chauvinism in the Prussian East. Forestry and Civilizing Mission on the Ethnic Frontier," *Central European History*, Vol. 41.

Wilson, John, 1995. *British Business History, 1720–1994*, Manchester University Press.

Wilson, R. G. and Terence R. Gourvish (eds.), 1998. *The Dynamics of the International Brewing Industry since 1800*, London: Routledge.

Winch, Donald, 1973. "The Emergence of Economics as Science 1750–1870," in Carlo Cipolla (ed.), *The Fontana Economic History of Europe*, Vol. III: *The Industrial Revolution*. London: Fontana.

Winks, Robin W. and Thomas E. Kaiser, 2004. *Europe from the Old Regime to the Age of Revolution*, Oxford University Press.

Witte, Sergei, 1990. *The Memoirs of Count Witte*, trans. and ed. by Sidney Harcave, Armonk, N.Y.: M. E. Sharpe.

Wojtinsky, W. S., 1927. *Die Welt in Zahlen*, Berlin: Rudolf Mosse.

Wolf, Nikolas, 2009. "Was Germany Ever United? Evidence from Intra- and International Trade, 1885–1933," *Journal of Economic History*, Vol. 69, No. 3.

Wong, Bin R., 1998. *China Transformed: Historical Change and the Limits of European Experience*, Ithaca: Cornell University Press.

Wood, Alan (ed.), 1991. *The History of Siberia from Russian Conquest to Revolution*. London: Routledge.

Wood, J. C., 1984. *Adam Smith: Critical Assessments*, Beckenham: Croom Helm.

Woodruff, William, 1973. "The Emergence of an International Economy, 1700–1914," in Carlo Cipolla (ed.), *The Fontana Economic History of Europe*, Vol. IV: *The Emergence of Industrial Societies*, Part 2, London: Fontana.

— 1982. *The Impact of Western Man. A Study of Europe's Role in the World Economy 1750–1960*, Washington D.C.: University Press of America.

Wright, Richard E., 1991. "Weaving in Bessarabia," Research Report, Vol. 9, No. 3, available at www.richardwright.com/9105˙bessarabia.html-24k.

— 2001. "The Transition to Capitalism in a Land without Feudalism," in Peter Hoppenbrouwers and Jan Luiten van Zanden (eds.), *Peasants into Farmers? The Transformation of Rural Economy and Society in the Low Countries (Middle Ages to 19th Century) in Light of the Brenner Debate*, Turnhout: Brepols.

Wrigley, Edward Anthony, 1962. *Industrial Growth and Population Change*, Cambridge University Press.

— 1988. *Continuity, Chance and Change. The Character of the Industrial Revolution in England*, Cambridge University Press.

Yerxa, Donald A., 2007. "Introduction: Historical Coherence, Complexity and the Scientific Revolution," *European Review*, Vol. 15, No. 4.

Zamagni, Vera, 1978. *Industrializzazione e squilibri regionali in Italia. Bilancio del'età giolittiana*, Bologna: Il Mulino.

— 1980. "The Rich in a Late Industrializer: The Case of Italy 1800–1945," in W. D. Rubinstein (ed.), *Wealth and the Wealthy in the Modern World*, London: Croom Helm.

— 1990. *Della periferia al centro. La seconda rinascita economica dell'Italia, 1861–1981*, Bologna: Il Mulino.

— 1993. *The Economic History of Italy, 1860–1990*, Oxford: Clarendon Press.

Zamorski, Krzysztof, 1998. "Necessity of Freedom. Economic, Social, and Political Consequences of Late Industrialization in Poland in the 19th Century," in Pasquate Fornaro (ed.), *Transizione e sviluppo. Le peripherie d'Europa (secc. XVIII–XIX)*, Catanzaro: Rubbettino.

Index

Printed in the United States
by Baker & Taylor Publisher Services